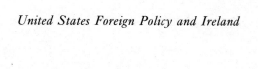

United States Foreign Policy and Ireland

United States Foreign Policy and Ireland

From Empire to Independence, 1913–29

BERNADETTE WHELAN

FOUR COURTS PRESS

Set in 10.5 on 12.5 point Ehrhardt for
FOUR COURTS PRESS LTD
7 Malpas Street, Dublin 8, Ireland
e-mail: info@four-courts-press.ie
http://www.four-courts-press.ie
and in North America by
FOUR COURTS PRESS
c/o ISBS, 920 N.E. 58th Avenue, Suite 300, Portland, OR 97213.

ISBN (10 digit) 1–84682–010–3
ISBN (13 digit) 978–1–84682–010–6

A catalogue record for this title
is available from the British Library.

Printed in England
by MPG Books, Bodmin, Cornwall

Contents

Tables

Abbreviations

AANC	All American National Council
AARIR	American Association for the Recognition of the Irish Republic
ARCS	American Red Cross Society
AFSC	American [Society of] Friends Service Committee
ABA	Archdiocese of Boston Archive
ACRI	American Committee for Relief in Ireland
AEF	American Expeditionary Force
AFL	American Federation of Labour
AIHS	American Irish Historical Society
AOH	Ancient Order of Hibernians
BL	British Library
CCPL	Calvin Coolidge Presidential Library and Museum
CG	Clan na Gael
CPI	Committee on Public Information
FDRPL	Franklin D. Roosevelt President Library
FOIF	Friends of Irish Freedom
GOP	Grand old party (Republican Party)
HHPL	Herbert Hoover Presidential Library
IMP	Imperial War Museum
IPL	Irish Progressive League
IWCS	Irish White Cross Society
IRA	Irish Republican Army
IRB	Irish Republican Brotherhood
LC	Library of Congress
NAI	National Archives of Ireland
NARA	National Archives and Records Administration of the United States
NLI	National Library of Ireland
NYPL	New York Public Library
PPM	Presidential Papers Microfilm
RIC	Royal Irish Constabulary
TNA	The National Archives
UCDAD	University College Dublin, Archives Department
UILA	United Irish League of America
UVF	Ulster Volunteer Force
YULMC	Yale University Library Manuscript and Archives Collection

Acknowledgments

This work has been a long time in gestation and I am grateful to many people for assistance and support. The staff in the following libraries and archives were always helpful and courteous and I acknowledge their assistance: the American Irish Historical Society, Archdiocese of Boston Archive, British Library, Calvin Coolidge Presidential Library and Museum, Dwight E. Eisenhower Presidential Library, Herbert Hoover Presidential Library, Imperial War Museum, London, Library of Congress, Mary Immaculate College, Limerick, National Archives and Records Administration, Washington, National Archives of Ireland, National Library of Ireland, New York Public Library, The National Archives, London, The Queen's University of Belfast, Trinity College Dublin, Franklin D. Roosevelt Presidential Library, University College Dublin, Yale University Manuscripts and Archives Department, New York. Permission to use material was granted by the Yale University Manuscripts and Archives Department and the American Irish Historical Society. A special mention must go to Anne Butler and Carmel Ryan in the inter-library loan section of the Glucksman Library, University of Limerick for their efficiency and courtesy in dealing with requests. The assistance of David Fleming, Maureen Foley, Brid Ingoldsby, Aideen MacMahon, Jean Murray, Cian O'Driscoll was much appreciated. More recently, the editorial guidance and work of Kathryn Marsh has been invaluable and encouraging.

The research for this work could not have been completed without financial assistance received from the Office of the Vice-President Research, the College of Humanities, the Department of History and the University of Limerick Foundation in the University of Limerick, the Dwight E. Eisenhower Presidential Library travel grant and the John Fitzgerald Kennedy Library travel grant. In 2005, the award of a Government of Ireland Senior Research Fellowship from the Irish Research Council for the Humanities and Social Sciences allowed for an earlier than expected conclusion to this research project.

Others whose advice and help has been much appreciated along the way are Brendan Bolger, Ciara Breathnach, Maurice Bric, Liam Chambers, William Colbert, Lisa Collins, Jean Conacher, Catriona Crowe, Maura Cronin, Vincent Cunnane, Eoin Devereux, Mary Daly, Seamus Helferty, Teresa Hereward-Ryan, Liam Irwin, Declan Jackson, Robert Johnson-Lally, John Lancaster, Tereasa Landers, Catherine Lawless, Pádraig Lenihan, David Lilburn, Deirdre MacMahon, Fionnuala MacMahon, Alistair Malcolm, Mary McCarthy, Anthony McElligott, Gerardine Meaney, Jennifer Moore, Susan Mulcahy, Una Ní Bhroiméil, John O'Brennan, Catherine O'Connor, Pat O'Connor, Annemarie O'Donnell, Ruán O'Donnell, Brendan O'Donoghue, Mary O'Donoghue, Gráinne O'Donovan, Mary O'Dowd, Eunan O'Halpin, Connor Reidy, Susannah Riordan, Ann Ryan, Romanie Van Son, Oonagh Walshe.

In particular I want to record my thanks to Joe Lee, Professor of History and Glucksman Professor of Irish Studies, Director, Glucksman Ireland House, New York University and John Logan, Senior Lecturer, Department of History, University of Limerick for their constant encouragement and belief in my research ideas over many years. Their support and friendship is much valued.

I am grateful to Michael Kennedy, Executive Editor, Documents on Irish Foreign Policy Series, Royal Irish Academy, who has always been willing to discuss this project and to share research documents. Thanks to Michael Adams, Aoife Walsh and Martin Fanning in Four Courts Press for their guidance and advice.

I would also like to thank Catherine Bird, Sally Fossitt, Hugh Lilburn, John Logan, Nuala MacDermott for their on-going friendship. The support of family is much appreciated. In recent months Markree House became my technological support unit as well as a centre of generous hospitality.

CHAPTER ONE

Introduction

This book is concerned with the formulation and implementation of United States foreign policy towards Ireland between 1913 and 1929. The topic is an ambitious one, even over-ambitious. It is hugely complex, drawing on a myriad of sources. It is important, therefore, from the beginning to define the research criteria which underpin this study. Firstly, the focus is on the three presidents who served during the period: Woodrow Wilson, Warren Harding and Calvin Coolidge, and the role each played directly in the formulation of US foreign policy and specific policy in relation to Ireland. Secondly, the study is concerned with their personal, pre-presidential and presidential links and ties to the Irish-American community and to Ireland. Thirdly, it examines the factors which influenced their attitudes to and formulation of policy on Ireland. It also deals with how that policy was implemented, specifically from the point at which a decision was made in the White House or in the State Department to its implementation and effect. Thus, while the site of the study is Washington, examining the impact of US policy also requires a focus on Ireland and Britain. The work of US representatives in Ireland and Britain is a significant part of this study. In addition to implementing policy these men faced many challenges when conducting their routine work. Their views on the upheavals in Ireland between 1914 and 1923 and into the period of state building offer another perspective on events. Consequently, a further research criterion is that the focus of the work is more the US-Irish relationship than its Irish-American counterpart. Another aim was to contextualize US-Irish relations against the wider background of US foreign relations in order to identify the status accorded by three US presidents and their administrations to Irish issues over time.[1]

In many ways this book is a map of the main themes and factors which influenced the formulation and implementation of US policy towards Ireland and how

---

1 The term United States is used as much as possible rather than America, for example, when possible US citizens are referred to instead of Americans. In order to distinguish between republicans of an Irish and US variety, the word in its lower case version is used for Irish republicans whereas the upper case is used for members of the Republican Party. The term Irish-America is a broad church and where possible an attempt is made to differentiate between its religious, political, geographical and social components. For a discussion on the term American-Irish see K. Kenny, *The American Irish: a history* (2000), p. 46; M. Doorley, *Irish-American diaspora nationalism: the friends of Irish freedom, 1916–35* (2005), p. 12.

that policy unfolded in Ireland. It revisits existing controversies and debates surrounding the Irish revolutionary period (1916–23) but only in order to highlight and elucidate the US dimension. Undoubtedly, some of the conclusions reached here will be elaborated by future historical research. At the same time the study attempts to reveal and unravel new themes in the US–Irish relationship, particularly through focusing on three presidents' contacts with Ireland and the Irish, as Ireland moved from subordinate to dominion status within the British empire. The work crosses the historiographical areas of foreign relations, diplomacy and diaspora, particularly Irish immigration to the US.

The historiography of the Irish diaspora in the US in the nineteenth century is immense and Kenny has divided it into 'new' and 'old' with the former representing a 'from the top down' approach and the latter 'from the bottom up.'[2] In other words, while themes relating to 'high politics, diplomacy and business' are being examined, other areas, such as the 'formation of identities', are being increasingly explored through the lens of 'class, race, ethnicity and gender'. However, he warns of the dangers of generalizing and over emphasizing a break, a trend also evident in the historiography of the Irish nation-state.[3] In 1999, Doyle cautioned about the return to famine themes in diaspora studies because it was 'conceptually regressive' and again allows for generalization. He extrapolates from the literature the 'positive achievements' of the Irish in the US, namely the 'political rise, charitable work and institutional consolidation of the Irish middle class.'[4] One consequence of the emergence by 1900 of the Irish-American politician at local, state and congressional level and the 'Irish vote' in general was that the concerns of this immigrant community entered the political arena. Studies by O'Grady and Gerson on immigrant influence on US foreign relations and diplomacy illustrate the comparative successes and failures of Irish-American leaders in realizing their respective agendas.[5] But in terms of making foreign policy and maintaining diplomatic relations, according to McKercher, the key factor lies in understanding why foreign policy-makers make certain decisions.[6] While the Irish in the US had become a political force at many political levels by 1912, that alone was not sufficient to sway policy-makers. Consequently, it becomes important to learn how the creators of US policy on Ireland viewed the world around them, how those views turned into policy and how that policy was implemented on the ground. A glance at the literature on US foreign relations and diplomacy suggests that Ireland featured little therein, particularly in the early twentieth century.

2 For a synopsis of the current state of the historiography of the Irish diaspora in the US see J.J. Lee, 'The Irish diaspora in the nineteenth century' in L.M. Geary & M. Kelleher (eds), *Nineteenth century Ireland: a guide to recent research* (2005), pp. 165–82.   3 K. Kenny, 'General introduction: new directions in Irish-American history' in K. Kenny, *New directions in Irish-American history* (2003), pp. 1–11.   4 D. Doyle, 'Cohesion and diversity in the Irish diaspora', 433, 432.   5 J.P. O'Grady (ed.), *The immigrants' influence on Wilson's peace policies* (1967); L.L. Gerson, *The hyphenate in recent American politics and diplomacy* (1964).   6 B.J.C. McKercher, *The second Baldwin government and the United States, 1924–29: attitudes and diplomacy* (1984), p. 1.

Walter LaFeber's masterly survey *The American age: United States foreign policy at home and abroad since 1750* does not include Ireland in the index.[7] There are twenty-four references to Ireland in the authoritative two-volume, *American foreign relations since 1600: a guide to the literature* published by the Society for Historians of American Foreign Relations in 2003. Clearly Ireland has not been a prominent theme in the study of US foreign relations. Perhaps it is more useful to examine the contributions made to our understanding of the US–Irish official relationship. Gerson reveals that by 1914, immigrant communities had become very interested in the affairs of their indigenous countries.[8] According to Brown in *Irish-American nationalism, 1870–1890*, Irish independence was a central demand of Irish-Americans, particularly Catholic ones, from US governments. Cronin's survey of US-Irish relations between 1916 and 1986 indicates that successive US governments had an Irish policy but that it was set aside when larger interests dictated while Ward's *Ireland and Anglo-American relations, 1899–1921* and Carroll's *American opinion and the Irish question, 1910–23* illustrate how domestic politics influenced foreign policy and particularly how they influenced the 'Irish question' in the US-British relationship between 1899 and 1923. Both works unravel the respective roles of the US political system, press and public in influencing government policy on Ireland, particularly during world war one. For the leaders of Irish-America, some of whom were just as radicalized by the events after the 1916 rising as their Irish counterparts, the end of world war one brought hope that President Woodrow Wilson would bring the cause of Irish independence to the Paris peace conference. Fitzpatrick and Mooney Eichacker's work have helped unravel the galvanizining effect of the arrival in the US of 1916 Irish republican activists on nationalist Irish-Americans, while Carroll, Duff, Hopkinson, Noer and O'Grady emphasize Wilson's failure to deliver Irish self-determination and the deterioration in the relationship between republican Irish-America, particularly its leadership, and Wilson. Each also reveals the dangers of treating the Irish in the US as a homogenous grouping, as does the work of McKillen on the Chicago Federation of Labor, Buckley on the New York Irish and more recently Doorley's study of the Friends of Irish Freedom.[9] Except for McCarthy's work on the English-Speaking Union and the Society for American

7 W. LaFeber, *The American age: United States foreign policy at home and abroad since 1750* (1989). 8 Gerson, *The hyphenate*, p. 5. 9 D. Fitzpatrick, *Harry Boland's Irish revolution* (2003); J. Mooney Eichacker, *Irish republican women in America: lecture tours, 1916 to 1925* (2003); T. Brown, *Irish-American nationalism, 1870–1890* (1966); S. Cronin, *Washington's Irish policy, 1916–1986: independence, partition neutrality* (1987); F.M. Carroll, 'The American commission on Irish independence and the Paris Peace conference of 1919', 103–18; F.M. Carroll (ed.), *The American commission on Irish independence, 1919. The diary, correspondence and report* (1985); J.B. Duff, 'The Versailles Treaty and the Irish-Americans', 528–98; M. Hopkinson, 'President Woodrow Wilson and the Irish question', 89–111; T.H. Noer, 'The American government and the Irish question during World War 1', 95–114; B. McKillen, *Chicago labor and the quest for a democratic diplomacy, 1914–24* (1995); J.P. Buckley, *The New York Irish: their view of American foreign policy, 1914–1921* (1976); Doorley, *Irish-American*; O'Grady, *The immigrants' influence*; Gerson, *The hyphenate*. For a guide to other regional

and British Friendship based in New York, there is no significant study of the political influence of the Irish in the US who favoured Anglo-American friendship above all else.[10] Yet, such differences could be overcome, at least temporarily, when the humanitarian dimension of the Anglo-Irish war of independence united Irish-Americans and other Americans.[11] For the post 1922 period, two final works should be mentioned: Carroll's study of the Dáil Éireann loans, particularly the State Department's role, and his study of the visit of US secretary of State Frank B. Kellogg to Dublin in 1928.[12] Carroll's corpus of work has led the way towards a fuller understanding of the influence of the Irish-American factor and the place of Irish issues in US foreign policy, both before and after the foundation of the Irish Free State, while many gaps have been filled in on individual politicians and events by the Funchion edited *Irish-American voluntary organisations* and Glazier's *The encyclopedia of the Irish in America*.[13]

Beyond Carroll's work, the field of US-Irish official relations, particularly before 1939, is largely untouched. Part of the reason for this is the dispersed location of archives. The topic requires investigating official and private sources in two continents and three countries. This leads to a second reason: the relationship was not simply a bilateral one between the US and the Irish. Throughout the period of this study, it was a triangular relationship. The US government did not have a bilateral diplomatic relationship with Ireland because until the Government of Ireland Act in 1920 and the Anglo-Irish treaty in 1921 Ireland was part of the British empire; it did not have an autonomous government or foreign policy. Instead, the turn of the nineteenth century found US governments, preoccupied with continental expansion and the aftermath of the 1861–5 civil war, remaining largely aloof from European affairs save for the expanding Anglo-American relationship. It was in this context that issues relating to the Panama Canal, Mexican, Irish and Canadian affairs were dealt with. Consequently, in 1913 there was a well-established relationship between State Department and Foreign Office officials within which Irish problems were dealt with. Hartley emphasizes the dichotomous nature of the Irish issue in Anglo–American relations between 1914 and 1918.[14] The emergence of an Irish republican provisional government after 1916 forced a change therein. With the establishment of the Irish Free State, a new diplomatic relationship had to be developed by US, British and Irish Free State officials and political leaders, although Ireland's

studies see M. Glazier (ed.), *The encyclopedia of the Irish in America* (1999).   10 D.J. McCarthy, 'The British' in O'Grady (ed.), *The immigrants' influence*, pp. 90, 97.   11 For example see Carroll, 'The American committee for relief in Ireland, 1920–22', 30–49.   12 F.M. Carroll, *Money for Ireland: finance, diplomacy, politics and the First Dáil Éireann loans, 1919–1936* (2002); Ibid., 'Protocol and international politics, 1928: The secretary of State goes to Ireland', 45–57. Carroll's most recent work *The American presence in Ulster: a diplomatic history, 1796–1996* (2005) is a survey of the links between the US and Ulster and vice versa from colonial to contemporary times and, therefore, is wider than the title suggests.   13 M.F. Funchion (ed.), *Irish American voluntary organizations* (1983); Glazier, *The encyclopedia*.   14 S. Hartley, *The Irish question as a problem in British foreign policy, 1914–18* (1987).

dominion status remained a complicating issue for State Department officials.

Among the questions that this work attempts to answer are: who made US foreign policy in the period 1913 to 1929? What was the attitude of foreign policy makers grappling with isolationism, internationalism, world order, imperialism, national sovereignty and self-determination towards Irish issues? In particular, to what extent did domestic factors including the ethnic issue, influence foreign policy making? What priority, if any, was the 'Irish question' given and why? How did foreign policy decisions made in Washington transfer to Ireland? The role of US foreign service representatives in the field in Ireland provided the vital link between the decision makers in the centre of power in Washington, and the location of effect. The work of US consuls and, later, diplomats based in Ireland, did not just provide important information but their reports personalized events on the ground and sometimes revealed a unionist, nationalist or British bias along with the expected neutral, dispassionate one. Consequently, they provided their political masters with very personal explanations and insights into local conditions that also contributed to foreign policy decision-making. This evidence is a vital element when identifying and interpreting the course of the US–Irish official relationship following the end of the Irish civil war in 1923 and during the Harding and Coolidge presidencies.

What follows is both chronological and thematic. From the beginning it seeks to provide a context to the Irish policies of three presidents; the Democrat Wilson and Republicans Harding and Coolidge. In order to get a sense of the personality and attitude of each man, an attempt is made to examine his path to the presidency, his interest in foreign policy generally and, specifically, his role in policy formation. Then it moves to identifying their pre-presidential contacts with the Irish in the US and in Ireland and the avenues through which representatives of Irish-American and Irish groups inside and outside the US Congress could access the president and influence the foreign policy process. Set in this context of three US administrations, it examines the Irish issues of self-determination, legitimacy, recovery, state-building, immigration and commerce as well as the Irish dimension to US foreign policy aims: waging war, making peace, debt recovery, rearmament and economic growth. This study offers the views and decisions of key policy-makers in Washington and the policy-enforcers in far off Dublin, Belfast, Cork and London. By focusing on both parts of the foreign policy process, the work will clarify the extent to which Irish issues actually figured in US foreign policy in the period 1913 to 1929.[15]

15 An attempt has been make to preserve the original wording of quotations, however, where irregular spelling, punctuation, grammar and capitalization affects the flow of the piece, the publishers' conventions have been applied. Full citations are provided in the first reference in each chapter. Subsequent footnotes are in shortened version but the relevant reference numbers for primary source material is provided. A complete bibliography is provided.

CHAPTER TWO

The Wilson presidency, foreign policy and Ireland, November 1913–June 1914

'Oh, the foolish Irish ... would to God they might all have gone back home.'[1]

Woodrow Wilson, the twenty-eighth president of the United States of America, uttered these words in 1921 when it was clear that the cornerstone of his plan for a post-world war one international order, the League of Nations, had failed to win US congressional support. He believed that the opposition of nationalist Irish-America inside and outside Congress had contributed to that failure. The extent of his disappointment at the turn of events comes through in his desire to find a scapegoat and put the blame on his opponents. There were many reasons why he wanted to assign the blame to the Irish-American community. However, nine years earlier, when Wilson's election in November 1912 had broken the Republican Party's sixteen-year stranglehold over the post of president, his victory was welcomed by all supporters of the Democratic Party, including its Irish-American base. Hopes were high among these traditional party supporters that their concerns would be addressed and dealt with by Wilson.

Path to the presidency

In November 1912 Wilson's 42 per cent share of the popular vote was less than that achieved by William Bryan, the previous Democratic candidate, in any of the three presidential elections he contested in 1896, 1900 and 1908. Despite this Wilson won the 1912 electoral college vote by a landslide, with 435 votes. His victory resulted from a number of factors: his personality, his policies, the support of a well-organized Democratic Party and a split in the Republican ranks.[2]

---

1 A.S. Link (ed.), *The papers of Woodrow Wilson* (hereafter *PWW*), 69 vols (1966–94), 67, Wilson quoted in William Edward Dodd to Alexander Frederick Whyte, 9 January 1921, p. 44.   2 P. Thompson, *Cassell's dictionary of modern American history* (2000), pp. 449, 5–7. Voting in the US

Wilson's background was solidly establishment. Born on 28 December 1856 in Staunton, Virginia, he was raised in a staunch Presbyterian middle class household in Georgia and in the Carolinas during the Reconstruction era which moulded him into a lifelong opponent of economic oppression. Furthermore, he became a moral and idealistic adult, unyielding when he believed he was right. None of his grandparents was American-born. His mother's family had moved from Scotland to Carlisle, England, before straitened circumstances forced them to emigrate to the United States in 1835. His father's parents were also Scottish emigrants although his grandfather, James Wilson, was born in Ulster, at Dergalt, near Strabane in county Tyrone and married Annie Adams from Sion Mills in the same county. They emigrated to the US in 1807 and, as will be seen, this old world part of his background provided him with a certain understanding of the immigrant experience.[3]

Further dichotomies emerged in Wilson's later life. Although the Wilson household expected their eldest son to become a minister in their church, in 1879 he graduated from the Ivy League Princeton University with a law degree and in 1902, he became the first lay president of Princeton.[4] While he was moderately successful as an academic and administrator at Princeton, he was interested in putting political theory into practice and soon became a target for 'political kingmakers.'[5]

Wilson's public profile and reformist ideas drew the attention of conservative businessmen and party political bosses within the Democratic Party. These hoped that he would take control of the party from the progressive William Bryan and would ultimately win back the White House for them. Wilson played these groups to his own advantage until he won the Democratic nomination for governor of New Jersey in 1910. He put aside his distaste for the party machinery to accept the support of Senator James Smith, the Democratic boss of New Jersey, and subsequently won the election. The latter had picked Wilson to give a cloak of respectability to a political machine that was based on the corruption, clientelism and patronage which existed in New Jersey as well as in other states. Smith also hoped that Wilson's appointment would thwart the growing progressive movement in the state but his hopes of controlling Wilson·and his views soon faded. Once elected, the next step in Wilson's strategy unfolded when his moral and

presidential elections consists of the popular vote and the electoral vote. A majority in the popular vote does not always translate into a majority in the electoral vote. The latter is determined by a state's population and a presidential candidate could by winning enough populous states gain election despite winning a minority of the total number of votes cast by the electorate nationwide. Ibid., pp. 135, 317.   3 His parents were Jessie Woodrow Wilson and the Reverend Joseph Ruggles Wilson, a scholar and clergyman of the Presbyterian Church of the South. See L. Ultan, *The presidents of the United States* (1989), pp. 56–7.   4 Ibid.   5 In 1883 he abandoned a legal career to study for a doctorate in political science at Johns Hopkins University. In 1890, he became professor of Jurisprudence and Political Science at Princeton University where his disciplined and orderly approach led him upwards in the university's hierarchy. See J. Milton Cooper, Jr., 'Thomas Woodrow Wilson' in M.L. Urofsky (ed.), *The American presidents* (2000), pp. 292–3.

political beliefs led him to break with Smith and his machine, to block Smith's re-election and to embark on a programme of progressive legislation. Destroying the boss system, combined with Wilson's record as governor, not only established his personal credentials as a leader but helped bring him the nomination as Democratic candidate for the 1912 presidential election. Another factor that assisted him was the calibre of the men he gathered around himself, such as William McCombs, a young lawyer whom he disliked but whose organizational abilities he recognized, and Edward House, who controlled Texan politics and hoped to control the presidency.[6] Wilson courted the elderly Democratic leader, Bryan, even though he was a 'dangerous demagogue.'[7] He secured financial support from Wall street financiers including Cleveland Dodge, Bernard Baruch and Henry Morgenthau, with Baruch praising Wilson's 'practical idealism.'[8]

Despite having all these factors in his favour, and that he was a good public speaker, Wilson had few political friends and limited support in the country at large. His victory in 1912 owed much to former President Theodore Roosevelt's decision to contest the election and thus split the Republican vote. Wilson obtained 6,296,547 votes (42 per cent of the popular vote), Roosevelt 4,118,571 (27.4 per cent) and William H. Taft 3,436,720 votes (23 per cent), giving the two Republican candidates a combined vote of 1,258,744 more than Wilson. However, in the electoral college Wilson easily won a majority, gaining 435 votes compared to Roosevelt's 88 and Taft's 8.[9] Inwardly, he believed that his elevation was providential and ordained by God.[10] Wilson was elected president on 5 November 1912 and began his presidency on 4 March 1913 with a programme characterized by his reforming, Christian-based beliefs.

Wilson and foreign policy

In 1913, prior to leaving Princeton for Washington, Woodrow Wilson noted to a friend that 'it would be the irony of fate if my administration had to deal chiefly with foreign affairs.'[11] This statement was prophetic. His presidency was dominated by world war one, the Paris peace settlement and the League of Nations. Link notes that, while few men who became president were better trained in the theory and techniques of domestic leadership and governance than Wilson, he did not have the same strengths in foreign relations. In *Congressional government*, Wilson's study of federal government published in 1885, and *The State*, pub-

6 P. Lee Levin, *Edith and Woodrow: the Wilson White House* (2001), p. 75.   7 Anonymous, 'William J. Bryan' in S.F. Bemis (ed.), *The American secretaries of state and their diplomacy* (1929), pp. 6–7. 8 Dodge and Baruch were Jewish as were other wealthy subscribers to Wilson's 1912 campaign such as Hy Goldman, Jacob Schiff, Samuel Untermeyer, Nathan Strausss, Charles S. Guggenheimer. See J.A. Schwarz, *The speculator: Bernard M. Baruch in Washington, 1917–1965* (1981), pp. 35–7. 9 Thompson, *Cassell's dictionary*, p. 507.   10 *PWW*, 25, Wilson to Harvey, 5 November 1912, p. 515.   11 A.S. Link, *Wilson the diplomatist: a look at his major foreign policies* (1965), p. 5.

lished four years later on comparative government, foreign relations are only casually mentioned. However, while he revealed an understanding of US foreign relations and an ability to place it in historical context, Wilson had not thought systematically and seriously about the complexity of foreign policy, at least up to 1913. Instead he assumed that his beliefs and philosophy about domestic governance could be transferred to the foreign stage. Indeed, during the Democratic nomination and presidential campaigns, he mentioned foreign issues only in the context of domestic ones – something not unique in US presidential campaigns.[12]

Wilson's political thinking reflected religious and ethical beliefs and values imbibed from the Christian tradition and from his own version of Presbyterian theology. These spiritual views informed the main themes of his political thinking and, consequently, of his foreign policy. He wrote that foreign policy must be more concerned about human rights, democracy and that the United States had a role to play in international affairs.[13] Link has offered an insight into the weaknesses of his vision, specifically that Wilson had a tendency to oversimplify the complexity of international politics, his blind faith in democracy brought an unreal quality to his thinking and policies and that he had the 'appearance of the Pharisee who thanked God that he was better than other men.'[14] Essentially Wilson searched for control and order at home and abroad.[15]

Wilson's conduct of foreign policy and his style of leadership would also be influenced by his personality. The matter of his disposition remains a controversial one. He worked hard but his health failed at times. In September 1919, Wilson suffered the first of three strokes, which interfered with his work. Outside of these troubled times, he was a man driven to achieve his goals and was totally committed to his vision. He was also egotistical, believing in his own superiority and wishing to dominate those around him. His reading and knowledge of the workings of the US government and powers of the president made him want to control areas of government that he considered important. Foreign affairs was one of these areas – specifically US relations with Mexico, relations with the European powers and settling the peace agreement.[16] William Castle, who entered the State Department in 1919 and rose to the position of under secretary of State in 1931, concluded that Wilson used his secretary of State as an 'agent for the transmission of [his] own ideas' and there was never 'any legal doubt as to where final authority resided.'[17]

After the election in November 1912, Wilson was obliged to appoint Bryan as secretary of State as a reward for his service to the Democratic Party and for his imprimatur to Wilson's candidacy, which had guaranteed Wilson the Democratic nomination. Furthermore, Wilson needed him for the political advan-

12 Ibid., pp. 4–12.   13 Ibid., pp. 12–19.   14 Ibid., pp. 19–21.   15 For further see L.E. Ambrosius, *Wilsonianisn: Woodrow Wilson and his legacy in American foreign relations* (2002), pp. 31–47.   16 Link, *Wilson the diplomatist*, pp. 21–3.   17 Herbert Hoover Presidential Library (hereafter HHPL), West Branch, Iowa, US, William R. Castle Papers (hereafter WRCP), Box 33, 'The tools of American diplomacy (1) The Department of State', p. 4.

tage that would be gained by having him at the cabinet table. Bryan was a vital link between Wilson and the Democrats in both the Congress and the wider party.[18] He had a definite foreign policy agenda as a life-long pacifist, supporter of free trade and opponent of imperialism, and for many Democrats he represented the conscience of the party.[19] He also shared Wilson's idealism and a desire to promote the cause of world peace.

However, Bryan had a simple view of international problems and a narrow range of official experience and Wilson distrusted his advice on sensitive matters.[20] The shape of US involvement in the world war would eventually present insurmountable problems between the two, as will be seen. Castle, who was a life-long Republican, said that Bryan 'found little time for the real work of the Department' including the much-needed reform of the foreign service.[21] By summer 1914, British Ambassador Cecil Spring Rice confirmed that Bryan's 'ignorance on some points, especially those connected with the business of his office is astonishing ... the diplomatic corps refuse to take him seriously, and those who do, suffer from a degree of exasperation which I should think, was unequalled in diplomatic annals.'[22] Spring Rice could speak from a position of authority as he had been attaché to Lord Sackville, British minister to the US, in 1886 and from then onwards had been in constant communication with Theodore Roosevelt and other prominent Americans.[23] Following Bryan's resignation on 9 June 1915, due to a disagreement with Wilson over equal treatment of Germany and Britain, Robert Lansing, a counsellor in the State Department, took over as secretary. Castle described him as a 'student and in some ways a dreamer. He saw few people because he shut himself up.'[24] Not only was Lansing, unlike Bryan, inaccessible to many people, but Wilson regarded him as nothing more than a dignified clerk whose legal and bureaucratic experience was needed, while Wilson was the real secretary of State. When the pro-British Lansing

18 W.G. McAdoo, *Crowded Years: the reminiscences of William G. McAdoo* (1931), p. 180. The first Wilson cabinet comprised Thomas Marshall (vice-president) and the following secretaries; William Bryan (State), William McAdoo (Treasury), Lindley Garrison (War), James McReynolds (Justice), Josephus Daniels (Navy), Franklin Lane (Interior), David Houston (Agriculture), William Redfield (Commerce), William Wilson (Labour) and Albert Burleson (Postmaster General). McAdoo had some contact with Irish-American activists in 1911. As chief magistrate in New York, he promised George Freeman, one of John Devoy's assistants, to provide him with an introduction to an influential newspaper editor in order to raise the profile of the Irish question in the US. National Library of Ireland (hereafter NLI), Joseph McGarrity Papers (hereafter JMcGP), MS17636, George Freeman to McGarrity, 24 February 1911.   19 G.H. Stuart, *The Department of State: a history of its organizations, procedure and personnel* (1949), pp. 224–5; Thompson, *Cassell's dictionary*, pp. 58–9.   20 Link, *Wilson the diplomatist*, p. 25; J.F. Findling, *Dictionary of American diplomatic history* (1990), pp. 80–1.   21 HHPL, WRCP, Box 33, 'The tools of American diplomacy (1) the Department of State', p. 12.   22 K. Bourne & D.C. Watt (general eds), *British documents on foreign affair* (hereafter *BDFA*), part 1, series C, North America, xv, Annual Report for the United States (hereafter Annual Report) for 1913, p. 291.   23 B. Willson, *Friendly relations: a narrative of Britain's ministers and ambassadors to America (1790–1930)* (1934), p. 313.   24 HHPL, WRCP, Box 33, 'The tools of American diplomacy (1) The Department of State', p. 12.

attempted to exert his authority during Wilson's illness in the autumn and winter of 1919–20, and appeared to encourage opposition to the Paris peace settlement, he was forced to accept presidential authority and resigned on 7 February 1920 (as will be outlined in chapter five). Bainbridge Colby, his replacement, was another political appointment but he was a man of liberal political views and an enthusiastic supporter of Wilson's post-war settlement. When Wilson was incapacitated, Colby was willing to go on the road to promote the settlement to the public. Colby survived until 4 March 1921, when the Harding administration took over, but on this final major foreign policy issue he was largely Wilson's mouthpiece.[25]

Wilson had little choice in Bryan's appointment and indeed in some others. Having been out of power for sixteen years, the demand from Democratic Party officials, activists and supporters for political positions in cabinet and federal government was great. The State Department offered many opportunities for the office-hungry Democrats, from ambassadorial, ministerial and consular positions to first secretaries and vice consuls. By 1913 most chiefs of missions, consuls and first secretaries within the State Department, who had no tenure, expected to be replaced when a new party took over government and generally handed in their resignations.[26] The president reserved for himself the appointment of ambassadors to the most important posts, much to Bryan's annoyance. Wilson's choices were made on the basis of personal knowledge as well as pressure from the party, with the result that he appointed party supporters to head the embassies in Berlin, St Petersburg, Rome and Madrid.[27] The London appointment is of particular interest to this study.

Wilson wanted to appoint former President Eliot of Harvard University to replace Whitelaw Reid at the Court of St James, but Eliot refused the invitation, as did the former secretary of State, Richard Olney. Instead this plum ambassadorial job went to Wilson's third choice and university friend, Walter Page, editor of the *World's Work* and a partner in the publishing company, Doubleday Page. Page accepted and was appointed on 21 April 1913.[28] The *New York Times* noted that Page, who had no experience of foreign policy, 'was a capable man but could not be expected to represent his country in London, in the broad sense as Choate, Hay, Bayard and Lowell had done.'[29] Before the outbreak of war Page had promoted Anglo–American relations in the belief that this would guarantee world peace. When he arrived in London he confided to British Foreign Secretary

25 McAdoo, *Crowded years*, pp. 413–14; Link, *Wilson the diplomatist*, pp. 26–7; Stuart, *The Department of State*, pp. 226–57;. W. LaFeber, *The American age: United States foreign policy at home and abroad since 1750* (1989), p. 310; F.M. Carroll, *American opinion and the Irish question, 1910–23: a study in opinion and policy* (1978), p. 196; N.A. Graebner (ed.), *An uncertain tradition: American secretaries of state in the twentieth century* (1961), p. 103.   26 Stuart, *The Department of State*, p. 226–7; Graebner, *An uncertain tradition*, p. 102.   27 Link, *Wilson the diplomatist*, p. 25.   28 Stuart, *The Department of State*, p. 227.   29 Quoted in B. Willson, *America's ambassadors to England (1785–1928): a narrative of Anglo–American diplomatic relations* (1928), p. 441.

Edward Grey that, although he had not been given permission to talk to him, he was worried about the growing anti-British feeling in the US. Page felt such feeling was founded on 'misapprehensions and misstatements' because 'there was certainly nothing in the attitude of the British government to cause it.'[30] Like Bryan, Page had an idealistic view of international relations, but on the outbreak of the war, his pro-British bias led him into difficulties with the State Department, and also with House and Wilson.[31] Page opposed US neutrality, favoured US intervention on the Allied side and, as will be seen later, was not as effective in carrying out his instructions as he could have been. As early as February 1914, Page complained about 'the dispiriting experience of writing and telegraphing' the State Department about 'important things' and 'never hearing a word concerning them.'[32] By this time Bryan was bypassing Page and dealing with Consul General Robert Skinner.[33]

A second, and more important, consequence of Wilson's appointment of unsuitable party men to the posts of ambassador and secretaries of state was to consolidate the highly personalized nature of US foreign policy during the Wilson tenure. Even before he became president Wilson believed in Theodore Roosevelt's 'stewardship theory', which stated that it was 'not only [the president's] right but his duty to do anything that the needs of the Nation demanded, unless such action was forbidden by the Constitution or by the laws.' Wilson added that 'the president's … office is anything he has the sagacity and force to make it … His capacity will set the limit.'[34] Coupled with this belief was the fact that Wilson, and indeed Bryan, distrusted the State Department and regarded it as 'being too slow-moving and conservative.'[35] Consequently, Wilson personally oversaw the conduct of America's more important relationships with Mexico and Europe. He was the first president to participate in an international conference abroad and, in 1918–19, was the first US president to be officially received in four major European capitals on a single trip (Paris, London, Rome and Brussels). Although presidents are empowered to make treaties, few have exercised the right personally: Wilson was the rare exception who participated in the negotiation of the peace settlement in Paris at the end of world war·one, much to the surprise of Lansing, Congress and the country.[36]

As a president who assumed a personal mediation role in diplomacy and active leadership in foreign affairs, particularly during a time of crisis, Wilson also resorted to appointing personal emissaries. It was these un-elected 'executive agents', instead of diplomatic representatives' who carried out Wilson's foreign

30 The National Archives (hereafter TNA), London, Foreign Office (hereafter FO), The papers of Edward Grey, 800/241, Grey to Spring Rice, 28 October 1913.   31 Findling, *Dictionary*, pp. 368–9.   32 B.J. Hendrick, *The life and letters of Walter H. Page*, 2 vols (1930), i, p. 238.   33 Library of Congress (hereafter LC), Manuscript Division (hereafter MD), Wilbur Carr Papers (hereafter WCP), Box 17, Biography material, Diary, 13 October 1916.   34 E. Plischke, *Diplomat in chief: the president at the summit* (1986), pp. 6–8.   35 Stuart, *The Department of State*, p. 231.   36 Plischke, *Diplomat in chief*, pp. 6–8, 227.

policies.[37] By the summer of 1914, the representatives of foreign countries based in Washington were perplexed about their relations with the Wilson government because Wilson 'would not talk business with them while he is the sole directing force in the government.'[38] In 1918 and 1919, journalists Ray Stannard Baker and George Creel were respectively asked by Wilson to go to Ireland and report on conditions (see chapter five). But it was Edward House who played a most distinctive role in US foreign policy. Although he was not a government minister, beginning in 1911 House was at the heart of the creation and implementation of US foreign policy and became more important in the creation of policy than State Department officials.[39]

Wilson may have had little interest in foreign affairs before 1913 but his administration was soon immersed in affairs in China, Mexico, the Caribbean and Europe.[40] He was, however, well-prepared to deal with one country; Britain. He shared with the US public a belief in the existence of common ground – language, traditions, growing economic links – between the US and Britain. Furthermore, diplomatic relations had improved since 1895, after the British recognized US dominance in the western hemisphere and shared with the US a commitment to the open door policy in Asia.[41] Yet, strong cultural and economic ties combined with good diplomatic relations existed alongside an anglophobic strain throughout US society.[42] In 1908 British Ambassador James Bryce had identified the causes of US resentment towards England, 'school histories ... class feeling ... popular works ... Civil War.' Not surprisingly, he indicated that anti-British sentiment was strongest amongst the Irish- and German-Americans and the people of the 'western states – the most American part of America.'[43] His successor, Spring Rice, agreed with him on the over arching influence of the Irish and German 'vote' in questions affecting Britain.[44] Yet, both ambassadors felt that the grounds for friendship and a sense of unity between Britain and the US were stronger than those for their absence.[45] Nevertheless, Wilson also inherited a situation where the balance of power between the two countries was shifting with the emergence of US superiority in economic, financial and technological resources, although Britain still controlled the largest battle fleet. In 1913 the effect of this transformation on the US–British political and diplomatic relationship was still unclear.[46] Wilson accommodated all these contradictions in US–British relations alongside his own progressive views.

37 Ibid., p. 78.   38 BDFA, xv, Annual Report for 1913, p. 290.   39 Stuart, The Department of State, pp. 231–2.   40 LaFeber, The American age, pp. 258–68. By 1914, Bryan's China policy had failed and Latin Americans began to describe US capitalists as 'State Department troops'. In other words, Wilson's progressive idealism proved to be unworkable.   41 LaFeber, The American age, p. 269.   42 J.D. Startt, 'American propaganda in Britain during world war one', 16–17.   43 BDFA, xiii, North American affairs 1908–09, Bryce to Edward Gray, 4 January 1908.   44 Ibid., xv, Bryce to Grey, Annual Report for 1913, p. 257.   45 Ibid., xiii, Bryce to Edward Gray, 4 January 1908.   46 H.C. Allen, Great Britain and the United States: a history of Anglo-American relations (1783–1952) (1994), pp. 26–7; H. Temperley, Britain and America since Independence (2002), p. 83.

Wilson's views on the rest of the European powers were shaped by his read-ing of history and his moral and religious beliefs. He was cautious of imperial Russia's motives and actions, not merely because the autocratic regime and the anti-Jewish pogroms of the late nineteenth century offered evidence of its repres-sive nature but because Russian expansionism was a constant worry for Americans and he detested change through revolution. He wanted a sense of order in inter-national relations but only if the means of achieving it could be controlled by the US. Democratic France was a potential ally as was imperial Germany. Moreover, the latter's rapid economic development made it an increasingly lucrative mar-ket for US goods. By 1913, however, Germany's expansionist colonial policies, combined with its militaristic Prussian culture, made it a potential challenger to British leadership of Europe and a threat to order in Europe. The smaller coun-tries featured little in Wilson's world view and in 1913 his concern with them was only in relation to the activism and potential voting power of their immi-grant communities within the US. It is in this context that we come to Wilson's view of Ireland.

Wilson, Ireland and foreign policy

Scholars of ethnicity often point to Wilson's Scots-Ulster lineage as the first evi-dence of his connection to Ireland. Indeed, his lineage reveals an important link to the old world. In a speech to the Friendly Sons of St Patrick on 18 March 1912, Wilson said, 'All the Irish that is in me arises to greet you. My father's parents were born in Ireland; born farther north, perhaps, than most of you would approve of. But there was no one with more Irish in him than my father.'[47] Having clearly played the Irish card on that occasion, among his first remarks to Bryce, whom he met for the first time in February 1913, was that 'he had a personal tie with England in the fact that his mother was born a British subject.'[48] Both sets of remarks reveal his sensitivity to the religious and political divide present within Irish, British and US societies. While campaigning in October 1912, he had revealed another view of his own ethnicity when stating, 'I have in me a very inter-esting and troublesome mixture of bloods. I get all my stubbornness from the Scotch, and there is something else that gives me a great deal of trouble, which I attrib-ute to the Irish. At any rate, it makes me love a scrap.'[49] Despite this stereotyp-ing, he was familiar with the complexities of Irish and British politics. As a young man he had written knowledgeably in 1880 about William Gladstone's Irish pol-icy and about the impact that the disestablishment of the Church of Ireland, land and educational reform had on Ireland. However, there appears to have been no formal contact between Wilson's family and the local Irish-American community.

47 *PWW*, 24, A news report of an after-dinner address in Elizabeth, New Jersey, p. 251. 48 *BDFA*, xv, Bryce to Edward Gray, 21 February 1913. 49 *PWW*, 25, A campaign address in Chicago, p. 400.

There is no evidence of Scots-American or Irish-American activism in Staunton, Virginia, before 1892, but by that time the Scots-Irish community was strong enough in the state to establish a chapter of the Scotch-Irish Society of America. There is no record that Wilson's parents were members of this society (nor was he). In 1901 he delivered the address at the annual dinner of the Pennsylvania chapter of the society, in which he spoke about the Scots-Irish in Ulster and the United States. On the other hand, while his Scots-Irish lineage may have been important to him and his Presbyterian-inspired religious fervour infused his political thinking, Wilson was not anti-Catholic. His admiration of Gladstone's attempts to solve the Irish question placed him in opposition to others of his background.

In addition to admiring Gladstone's political ideas and ability to alter his views as well as his leadership skills, Wilson praised his policies, including that of home rule for Ireland. In a letter written from the University of Virginia in Baltimore to his first wife, Ellen Wilson, on 27 February 1889, he wrote about the 'good news' from London, where the journalist, Richard Pigott, had just admitted to forging a series of letters that had incriminated Charles Stewart Parnell in criminal activity. Wilson wrote with glee that '*The Times* is thoroughly discredited in the whole matter. Parnell is virtually cleared, and, what is more, it now looks as if the Nationalist cause has received an important impulse forward.' He concluded that the next elections promised 'to give the Gladstonians a signal triumph. The news has positively excited me.'[50] Clearly he was well informed about the Irish situation and supported the constitutional path adopted by Parnell and promoted by Gladstone. Unfortunately, when he visited Ireland in August 1899 he was not impressed due to an uncomfortable steamer voyage, not being able to stay in Dublin because of the annual horse show and the 'singularly unattractive, plebeian' city streets. He lamented to Ellen that he had not gone to Antwerp instead.[51]

Although he was disappointed with Ireland, it is clear that as an aspiring presidential candidate, Wilson had an interest, albeit a limited one, in Irish politics for four reasons. Firstly, he was obsessed with Gladstone's beliefs and policies, so much of which focused on Ireland. Secondly, there was the influence of Irish-America within his party and US politics generally. Thirdly, Irish politics offered Wilson a prime test case for analysis of his evolving ideas on democracy, sovereignty, anti-imperialism and human rights. Finally, and perhaps most significantly, Ireland featured in Wilson's pre-presidential agenda because of the new world situation he was facing with regard to US isolationism versus involvement in international affairs.

With regard to the Irish-American political influence. During the nineteenth century the Irish in America acquired 'numbers, leaders and organization' to cre-

50 *PWW*, 8, Two letters to Ellen Axson Wilson, 27, 28 February 1889, pp. 116–17.   51 Ibid., 11, Two letters to Ellen Axson Wilson, 20, 22 August 1899, pp. 234–5.

ate political pressure, particularly within the Democratic Party. Central to wielding this power within the US political establishment was the threat of the Irish vote, and the strained relations between the US and Britain.[52] After 1858, when Fenian-organized efforts proved that the ballot box, together with a deterioration in Anglo–Irish relations, could force the US government to respond, the Irish-American nationalist community began to speak with one voice at times. Not all Irish-Americans agreed with the Fenians or their tactics but the potential strength and power of Irish-America at the ballot box became evident to all.[53] During the Republican tenure, from 1897 to 1913, organized nationalist Irish-America had become frustrated by its failure to disrupt the US–British relationship. The British disliked Irish-America's anglophobia and anti-imperialism. In turn Irish- and German-America heavily criticized the administration for its sympathy with the British government in relation to the second Boer war (1899–1902). John Hay, secretary of State between 1898 and 1905 and formerly US ambassador to Britain, complained in 1899, 'What ever we do, Bryan will attack us as slaves of England. All their [Democratic] state conventions put an anti-English plank in their platforms to curry favour with the Irish (whom they want to keep) and the Germans whom they want to seduce.' In the following year, Hay felt that Irish-American and German-American criticism of the administration had affected its efforts to negotiate friendly settlements of long-standing disputes with Britain. He wrote:

> ... every senator I see says, 'For God's sake, don't let it appear we have any understanding with England.' ... that we should be compelled to refuse the assistance of the greatest power in the world, *in carrying out our own policy* [in China], because all Irishmen are Democrats and some Germans are fools—is enough to drive a man mad.[54]

By 1903, Hay's exasperation with ethnic opposition to his policies had reached a crucial juncture. On 23 April, he commented to President Roosevelt:

> It is a singular and ethnological and political paradox that the prime motive of every British subject in America is hostility to England and the prime motive of every German-American is hostility to every country in the world, including America, which is not friendly to Germany ... The Irish of New York are thirsting for my gore. Give it to them if you think they need it.[55]

---

52 J.P. O'Grady, 'The Irish' in J.P. O'Grady (ed.), *The immigrants' influence on Wilson's peace policies* (1967), pp. 56–7; D. Burner, *The politics of provincialism: the Democratic party in transition, 1918–1932* (1970), p. 15.   53 J.P. O'Grady, *How the Irish became Americans* (1978), pp. 50–6.   54 W.R.Thayer (ed.), *The life and letters of John Hay*, 2 vols (1915), ii, pp. 220, 231, 235.   55 Thayer (ed.), *The life and letters of John Hay*, ii, p. 291.

Roosevelt did not look for Hay's resignation but in the following years, when Hay was negotiating the arbitration treaties to reduce the likelihood of war, the administration encountered vociferous opposition in the Senate. Hay saw the hand of Clan na Gael at work behind the Senate opposition. But it was not sufficiently strong to thwart the passage through the Senate of the arbitration treaty with Britain in 1908.[56] Irish-America was unable to influence US policy alone, particularly when there was a Republican administration. However, in 1911 and 1912 the same forces combined to dilute further arbitration treaties with Britain and France leading the Senate to heavily amend the legislation, with the result that Republican President Taft refused to sign them.[57] The Irish-American vote had not featured during the 1908 presidential election when Taft came into office. However, the Democrats had gained 45 per cent of the vote in that election which encouraged the Republicans, in Bryan's words, 'to reach [out to] our Catholic Democrats' in 1910 and again in 1911–12.[58] Taft attended the St Patrick's Day celebrations of the Irish Fellowship Club while Roosevelt met with Irish members of parliament in London. Both events accorded a respectability to the Irish cause and placed it centre-stage in US national politics once again. In 1912, Taft went further when he supported the release of the Fenian, Luke Dillon, who had been imprisoned in Canada for attempting to dynamite the Welland Canal in 1900.[59]

Wilson launched his campaign for the presidency in May 1911 and, like Taft, could ignore neither the Irish vote nor any other ethnic voting group. Although Irish bosses ran the Democratic Party in New Jersey and in most of the larger cities, Wilson did not have to fight them on the question of US official support for Irish home rule because few of the Irish bosses in the Democratic Party promoted the cause of Irish nationalism or were active in voluntary ethnic organizations.[60] Other Democratic politicians, however, had furthered the Irish question inside and outside Congress such as senators James D. Phelan from California, James O'Gorman from New York state (described by Page as the 'leader of the anti-British crusade in American politics'), David I. Walsh from Massachusetts and Thomas J. Walsh from Montana and in the House of Representatives were William Bourke Cockran from New York, Oscar Underwood of Alabama, who was House majority leader, Champ Clark, speaker of the House, from Missouri and William E. Mason from Illinois. Edward F. Dunne the reformist governor of Illinois was another nationalist.[61] On the other side of the ethnic political divide was John Sharp Williams, the Democratic senator from

---

56 Ibid., p. 392. Clan na Gael led by the Fenian John Devoy, was the small revolutionary Irish-American political organization that opposed home rule and supported the Irish Republican Brotherhood's preparations for the 1916 rising. See J. Devoy, *Recollections of an Irish rebel* (1969). 57 Findling, *Dictionary*, pp. 20–1; LaFeber, *The American age*, p. 264. 58 L.W. Koenig, *Bryan: a political biography of William Jennings Bryan* (1971), p. 448. 59 Carroll, *American opinion*, pp. 17–18; A.J. Ward, *Ireland and Anglo-American relations, 1899–1921* (1969), pp. 49, 55, 59, 60. 60 S.P. Erie, *Rainbow's end: Irish-Americans and the dilemmas of urban machine politics, 1840–1985* (1988), pp. 27–8. 61 J. McGurrin, *Bourke Cockran: a free lance in American politics* (1948), pp. 219–40;

Mississippi, who favoured the achievement of US–British understanding above all else; he was hated for this by the Irish-American nationalists.[62] By 1912 any differences between Democratic politicians on Irish nationalist issues were subsumed and they were more interested in ousting the Republicans from office first and in resolving local issues second, while in Ireland home rule appeared to be just around the corner. Wilson seemed to offer the best chance to achieve all three aims.

Outside the Democratic Party the presidential nominee saw himself as representing an 'enlightened public opinion' which suggested that the voice of organized Irish-America, like that of other immigrant groups, would be heard by the new president.[63] During these pre-war years the predominant Irish-American political organization was the United Irish League of America. The *Irish World*, the League's New York-based mouthpiece publication, had a circulation of 60,000 in 1912 and supported home rule. The smaller extremist Clan na Gael expressed its support for an independent republic in Ireland through the pages of John Devoy's *Gaelic American*, which had a circulation of 30,000 in 1914.[64] Given the size of the Irish-American portion of the US population in 1910 as indicated in table 2.1, none of these organizations and newspapers seemed to have an extensive membership or active support within Irish-America. The William Randolph Hearst-owned newspapers also acted as mouthpieces for immigrant grievances at various times. A British embassy report on the US press concluded that the status of the press was lower than ten years previously but that the collective influence of the Heart newspapers remained 'profound', particularly in New York where 'the majority of residents are of foreign extraction.'[65] Securing Irish readers was as important to Hearst as securing Irish votes was to Wilson. While the Irish-American organizations and press, with the exception of Clan na Gael, were largely partisan towards home rule, as was Wilson, their support could not be taken for granted. As will be seen, Wilson felt the heat of criticism from the Hearst press early on in the presidential campaign for apparently derogatory comments about immigrant communities.

With regard to the labour movement, by 1900, Irish immigrants or their descendants were to be found across the spectrum of the US labour movement and they held presidential posts in over fifty of the 110 unions in the 'thoroughly respectable' American Federation of Labour (AFL), the umbrella body of US trade unions. In 1906, it had over 1,676,000 members. The natural affiliation of the AFL voter was to the Democratic Party and its president, Samuel Gompers, was a firm Wilson supporter and would continue to be up until 1920. This posi-

Hendrick, *The life and letters of Walter H. Page*, i, p. 243. Spring Rice believed that O'Gorman 'hates England.' Gwynn, *The letters and friendships*, ii, p. 195.   **62** Carroll, *American opinion*, pp. 194–207.   **63** Link, *Wilson the diplomatist*, p. 18; J.P. O'Grady, 'Introduction' in O'Grady (ed.), *The immigrants' influence*, pp. 4–5.   **64** J.P. Buckley, *The New York Irish: their view of American foreign policy, 1914–1921* (1976), pp. 9, 10.   **65** *BDFA*, vii, The American press, 1920–22, The press, January 1922, pp. 57, 59.

tion, however, masked the opposition of many Irish-American union members at local level to Wilson's foreign policies as McKillen illustrated in relation to the Chicago Federation of Labour. But in 1912 most union voters awaited the chance to vote Democratic again.[66]

What was the attitude of the religious leaders of Irish-America on party politics? In 1920 Catholics comprised over nineteen per cent of the entire population of the US; the principle composition of the Catholic body, by national origin, was Irish, German and, to a lesser extent, Italian. A British embassy survey in 1920 of the Catholic community said that the influence of Catholics in civic and social life was 'considerable.' However, the Catholic Church as a whole was not deemed to be biased towards any one political party, not least because it would be 'repugnant to the American mind' and because there was a 'very genuine dislike of Catholics on the part of non-Catholics through fear of their uniting to attain some political end.'[67] Wilson himself had often entered this debate during his career; in the University of Virginia in 1880, he had pronounced that the Catholic Church was not a threat to US society because of the existence of self-government, democracy and the constitution. However, two years later, Wilson criticized the editor of the Wilmington *Morning Star* because of his praise of speeches by Archbishop James Gibbons of Baltimore on the installation of a new bishop in the city. Wilson admonished the editor for encouraging 'the aggressive tendencies of an organization whose cardinal tenets are openly antagonistic to the principles of free government.' Wilmington Catholics responded angrily but Wilson dismissed their concerns in a light-hearted manner.[68]

Before the first world war, managing this anti-Catholic sentiment was a central objective for the Catholic hierarchy. County Kilkenny-born Archbishop John Richard Ireland, of St Paul, Minnesota, dedicated himself to the integration of ethnic communities into mainstream US life. Ireland, however, identified himself with the Republican party and met with President William McKinley in an attempt to prevent the Spanish–American war in April 1898. The leading Catholic churchman during the period was Cardinal James Gibbons of Baltimore. Born in Baltimore to natives of Tourmakedy, county Mayo, Gibbons embraced ecumenism and was deeply patriotic and dedicated to Americanism. He was called on repeatedly to say the opening prayers at both the Democratic and Republican national conventions, which he did in 1912 for the former party and in 1920 for the latter. Gibbons was forever conscious of the importance of demonstrating his loyalty to the state and its representatives. Both Ireland and Gibbons had even

66 Gompers negotiated a commitment from the Democratic Party leadership to exempt unions from anti-trust legislation and Wilson rewarded AFL support in the 1912 election with the Clayton Anti-Trust Act in 1914. P.J. Blessing, 'Irish' in S. Thernstrom (ed.), *The Harvard encyclopedia of American ethnic history* (1980), p. 538; P. Thompson, *Cassell's dictionary of modern American history* (2000), p. 26; B. McKillen, *Chicago labor and the quest for a democratic diplomacy, 1914–1924* (1995), p. 21. 67 *BDFA,*, vii, Catholic papers in America, January 1920, pp. 1, 2. 68 J.M. Mulder, *Woodrow Wilson: the years of preparedness* (1978), p. 70.

defended their version of Americanism against Pope Leo XIII's attack on and Pope Pius X's crusade against modernism.[69] Gibbons was conspicuously silent on the Irish question and deplored the hyphenated 'Irish' in the titles of national societies and organizations, preferring them to be 'more American in name and spirit.' Both he and Ireland were supporters of Irish home rule.[70] Before the Irish rising of April 1916, Ireland and Gibbons told Shane Leslie, a Catholic home ruler and landowner, that they held John Redmond, leader of the Irish Parliamentary Party, in 'high esteem' and approved his 'difficult but honourable course' of supporting recruitment for the British army in Ireland.[71] Another national figure in the Catholic hierarchy was county Armagh-born Cardinal John Farley of New York, who generally maintained a neutral position on foreign policy issues.[72]

With the exception of Archbishop Ireland's Republican connections, in general these Catholic prelates displayed a non-aligned political position during the pre-war period. Despite this, the British embassy acknowledged that most Catholics voted Democrat at this time. But when it came to elections few party strategists could afford to take for granted any specific support base, particularly the multi-layered structure – hierarchy, clergy, press, ordinary voter – that comprised Catholic America and that made it potentially so powerful. The Catholic press comprised two hundred periodicals, quarterlies, monthlies, weeklies and a daily paper, which were printed in English and many other European languages, and it reached the remotest parts of the country. In theory at least, the Catholic press was non-political, but if Catholic interests were detrimentally affected, it would go on the offensive.[73]

The third reason for Wilson's interest in Irish politics was that it afforded him scope to evolve his ideas on democracy, sovereignty, anti-imperialism and human rights in the context of self-determination. As governor of New Jersey,

69 L.J. McCaffrey, 'Catholicism, Irish-American' in M. Glazier (ed.), *The encyclopedia of the Irish in America* (1999), p. 132.   70 Buckley, *The New York Irish*, p. 13; M.E. Brown, 'Farley, John Murphy Cardinal' in Glazier (ed.), *The encyclopedia*, p. 311; C.F. Crews, 'Ireland, John Richard', in Glazier, *The encyclopedia*, p. 417; A.E. Smith & V. de P. Fitzpatrick, *Cardinal Gibbons: churchman and citizen* (undated), pp. 164–5; A. Sinclair Will, *Life of Cardinal Gibbons, Archbishop of Baltimore*, 2 vols (1922), i, p. 791; T.W. Spalding, 'Gibbons, James Cardinal' in Glazier (ed.), *The encyclopedia*, p. 361.   71 NLI, John Redmond Papers, MS15236(14), Leslie to Redmond, 2 March 1916. Leslie who came from an Anglo-Irish family, was a first cousin to Winston Churchill and related to William Bourke Cockran. Leslie converted to Catholicism and was a supporter of home rule. He was in the US in 1916 and 1917 to get support for home rule and edited *Ireland* for a short period. He was friendly with Joseph Tumulty, Cardinal Gibbons, Archbishop Ireland, among other influential Americans. Ibid. As a home ruler he found common ground with British figures in the US also for example, Arthur Willert, *The Times* correspondent in Washington and Colonel Arthur Murray, assistant British military attaché in New York. See Yale University Manuscript and Archive Collection (hereafter YULMC) William Wiseman papers (hereafter WWP), box 5, file 141, Willert to Phillips, 10 January 1918.   72 Buckley, *The New York Irish*, p. 13; Brown, 'Farley', p. 311; Crews, 'Ireland', p. 417; McCaffrey, 'Catholicism', p. 132.   73 BDFA, vii, Catholic papers in America, January 1920, p. 2.

Wilson made one of his first public references to Ireland when he delivered a speech in New Brunswick, New Jersey, on 26 October 1910, in which he said:

> Have you read the papers recently attentively enough to notice the rumours that are coming across the water? Some very unusual and interesting things are happening in England ... the liberal and conservative factions are holding a joint conference in order to effect concerted action with regard to a common programme. And what are the rumours? The rumours are that the programme probably includes self-government for Ireland ... no little group of men like the English people have the right to govern men in all parts of the world without drawing them into real substantial partnership.

He continued 'this voice that has been crying in Ireland, this voice for home rule is a voice which is now supported by the opinion of the world.'[74] Such an understanding of, and support for, Irish home rule revealed a belief on Wilson's part that it was the responsibility of the British government to realize it. Even though he was not in office at the time, Wilson, with an eye to the presidential elections, did not identify any role for the US government in relation to home rule. Even in 1910, he did not promote US interference in what he characterized as a structural, constitutional and human rights problem facing the British political leadership. Despite this endorsement of the key issue that unified nationalist Irish-America, his views on the subsuming of the immigrants' home identity into that of their newly chosen home revealed the complexity of his thinking. On 19 January 1912, during the nomination campaign, he spoke in Ann Arbor, Michigan, about the ties that bound Americans together; 'we speak the same language, discuss the same things from the same point of view, and everywhere we find the independence and freedom of expression.' He continued:

> I am looking forward to an era of unprecedented national action. We are now coming to an era where there will be but one single expression and but one single thought. I protest against speaking of German-Americans, or Irish-Americans or Jewish-Americans, for these nationalities are becoming indistinguishable in the general body of Americans. Drop out the first words, cut out the hyphens and call them all Americans.[75]

He returned to the theme again during speeches in 1912 to the Periodical Publishers' Association of America in Philadelphia (2 February), to the Friendly Sons of St Patrick in New Jersey (18 March) and at Democratic Party rallies in Milwaukee (24 March).[76] Wilson's views on the hyphen issue did not waver and,

---

74 *PWW*, 21, Speech in New Brunswick, 26 October 1910, p. 441.   75 Ibid., 24, A news report of two speeches in Ann Arbor, Michigan, 19 January 1912, pp. 57–8.   76 Ibid., A news report of an

after the outbreak of war, would increasingly colour his attitudes towards the Irish-American community and their domestic and foreign issues.

Gerson notes that Wilson was the first US president to feel the heat of 'concentrated hyphenate pressures' on US foreign policy.[77] Consequently the altered international situation, the isolationism versus involvement issue in US foreign policy and the impact of these factors on US citizens of foreign origins, provide the final and perhaps more significant reasons why Ireland featured in his pre-presidential agenda.

Table 2.1 outlines the size of the foreign-born and first generation communities in the US in 1910.

Table 2.1

Main foreign elements in the United States population, 1910

(Total population in United States: 91,972,266)

Country of origin	Fb	Natives with 2 Fb parents	Natives with 1 Fb parent	Total
Germany	2,501,181	3,911,847	1,869,590	8,282,618
Austria–Hungary	1,670,524	900,129	131,133	2,701,786
United Kingdom (ex. Ireland)	1,212,968	852,610	1,158,474	3,231,052
Ireland	1,352,155	2,141,577	1,010,628	4,504,360
Russia and Finland	1,732,421	949,316	70,938	2,752,675
Italy	1,343,070	695,187	60,103	2,098,360
Total for all countries (incl. those not listed)	13,345,545	12,916,311	5,981,526	32,243,282

Fb foreign born
Source: Ward, *Ireland and Anglo-American relations*, p. 84.

Almost one-third of the total population of the US in 1910 was either foreign-born or first generation. An immigration commission chaired by William P. Dillingham published its report in 1911 and this supported further restrictions, particularly on 'new' arrivals from the south of Europe.[78] Immigration became an important issue for Wilson during the 1912 presidential campaign. However, he did not share widespread fears about the impact of immigration on US society and believed that 'the vast majority who come to our shores come on their own initiative and have some understanding as to what they want and a definite object in view.' He abhorred prejudice. His support for immigration led him into

after-dinner address in Elizabeth, New Jersey, 18 March 1912, pp. 252; ibid., A news report of three addresses in Milwaukee, 24, 25 March 1912, 259–60; ibid., 25, Three news reports, 17 May 1912, pp. 404–7.   **77** L. Gerson, *The hyphenate in recent American politics and diplomacy* (1964), p. 63.   **78** H. Brogan, *The Penguin history of the United States of America* (1985), pp. 404, 416.

controversy with ethnic groups during the 1913 election campaign and in 1914, he vetoed the introduction of literacy tests in immigration legislation.[79]

While, in 1910, Wilson the politician may have sympathized with the cause of oppressed foreign peoples and supported the principle of immigration, in 1902 Wilson the academic had published his views on the qualities of different immigrant communities. In *A history of the American people*, he wrote:

> [T]here came multitudes of men of the lowest class from the south of Italy and men of the meaner sort out of Hungary and Poland, men out of the ranks where there was neither skill nor energy nor any initiative of quick intelligence; and they came in numbers which increased from year to year, as if the countries of the south of Europe were disburdening themselves of the more sordid and hapless elements of their population, the men whose standards of life and of work were such as American workmen had never dreamed of hitherto ... yet the Chinese were more to be desired, as workmen if not as citizens, than most of the coarse crew that came crowding in every year at the eastern ports.[80]

In late June 1912, prior to Wilson's nomination as the Democratic Party's presidential candidate, this passage was uncovered by Wilson's Republican opponents with assistance from the Hearst press.[81] In the eastern states the Hearst newspapers reprinted the passage quoted above and ran editorials condemning Wilson's contempt for Italians, Poles and Hungarians, along with the unemployed, trade unionists and pensioners.[82] In the western states, particularly California, where the question of Chinese and Japanese immigration was a controversial issue, Wilson's alleged support for Asian immigration was widely publicized by the *San Francisco Examiner*.[83] The Republicans seized on his words and played on the fears and prejudices of European-born immigrant communities. Although the Irish were not specifically named, immigrant communities' newspapers and propaganda leaflets urged voters of European origin not to vote for Wilson.[84] Link suggests that there was some concern within the Irish-American community that Wilson was '"narrow and bigoted" in religious matters.'[85] He had certainly upset the Irish-American Democratic politician James Phelan, who had served three terms as mayor of San Francisco and aspired to represent his state in Congress. He asked McCombs to get Wilson to publicly retract his apparent

79 *PWW*, 24, A news report of an after-dinner address in Elizabeth, New Jersey, 18 March 1912, p. 252; Ward, *Ireland and Anglo-American relations*, p. 85.   80 Quoted in Gerson, *The hyphenate*, p. 62.   81 H. Eaton, *Presidential timber: a history of nominating conventions, 1868–1960* (1964), p. 227–31; for further on the anti-Wilson campaign see also, A.S. Link, *Wilson: the road to the White House* (1947), pp. 348–80.   82 J. Beatty, *The rascal king: the life and times of James Michael Curley (1874–1958)* (1992), p. 124.   83 *PWW*, 24, Wilson to James Duval Phelan, 3 May 1912, pp. 382–3. 84 Ibid., Wilson to Francis Ignatius Drobinski, 7 February 1912, to Agostino De Biasi, 7 February 1912, to Marcus Braun, 7 February 1912, pp. 134–6; Gerson, *The hyphenate*, p. 63.   85 Link, *Wilson: the road to the White House*, p. 389.

support for Chinese and Japanese immigration.[86] Archbishop Ireland also reacted to Wilson's remarks. He believed that *A history of the American people* expressed Wilson's real feelings about Catholics.[87] This combination of Catholic, immigrant and Hearst-driven opposition unnerved Wilson at this crucial time, when the Democratic nomination for the presidency was not yet decided and his main opponent, Speaker Champ Clark was performing strongly, with victories in the primaries in Kansas and Oklahoma.[88]

In the face of this criticism from inside and outside his party, Wilson went on the offensive. He permitted a telegram, drafted by Phelan, to be issued in his name on 3 May; it declared that 'in the matter of Chinese and Japanese coolie immigration I stand for the national policy of exclusion (or restricted immigration).' Phelan gave the telegram to the local newspapers but only one published it on the front page. Link concludes that the telegram came too late to alter the outcome of the California presidential primary on 14 May, which Clark won with 43,163 votes to Wilson's 17, 214. However, the telegram was widely used by the Wilson camp during the presidential campaign.[89] Wilson also permitted the publication of a letter he wrote to Francis Ignatius Drobinski on 7 February, in which he apologized for his 'clumsiness in expressing himself.'[90] He also informed his publishers that he wanted to rewrite certain passages of the reprinted book 'in order to remove the false impressions which they seemed to have made.'[91] This strategy of dealing directly with the issue appeared to comfort the immigrant communities. The Italian-American Alliance announced, after meeting Wilson in Philadelphia on 5 May, that it endorsed Wilson's understanding of the position and importance of the Italian-American in US society.[92] Despite his offensive on this issue, Wilson entered the Democratic convention, in Baltimore in late June 1912, with fewer primary victories and, therefore, with fewer delegates than Champ Clark. British Ambassador Bryce noted that Clark was 'personally popular', but felt that he did not have the 'requisite balance of judgement and staying qualities' to make him a successful presidential candidate for the Democratic Party and thought that some 'dark horse' would come to the front.[93] Clark had powerful backers however, including Tammany Hall and the Hearst press, who pushed his candidacy as far as they could in the nominating convention.

Wilson emerged victorious on the forty-sixth ballot due to firstly, the Democratic Party's rule that candidates required two-thirds of the delegates' votes

86 Phelan served a single term in the US senate from 1914 to 1920. J.A. Barnes, 'Phelan, James', in Glazier, *The encyclopedia*, p. 768; *PWW*, 24, Wilson to James Duval Phelan, 3 May 1912, p. 383, fn. 1.   87 J.H. Moynihan, *The life of Archbishop John Ireland* (1976), pp. 258, 260.   88 The other challenger for the Democratic presidential nomination was Oscar W. Underwood of Alabama who was House majority leader.   89 *PWW*, 24, Wilson to James Duval Phelan, 3 May 1912, p. 383, fn. 1.   90 Ibid., Wilson to Francis Ignatius Drobinski, 7 February 1912, Wilson to Agostino De Biasi, 7 February 1912, pp. 134–6; Gerson, *The hyphenate*, p. 63.   91 Quoted in Gerson, *The hyphenate*, p. 63.   92 *PWW*, 24, Three news reports, 17 May 1912, pp. 404–7.   93 *BDFA*, xv, Bryce to Grey, 21 January 1912; Ibid., Bryce to Grey, 1 April 1912.

rather than a simple majority, secondly, the predominance of factional interests, thirdly, the haggling between candidates' managers and finally, Bryan's support for him as the anti-corruption candidate. His debt to Bryan was immense and was repaid, as was previously mentioned, with the post of secretary of State, but he never forgave those who opposed him, particularly New York city judge Daniel Cohalan, New York lawyer John Quinn and Boss Murphy, who had organized the opposition to block his nomination. The consequences of this would become obvious later when Cohalan vociferously opposed US entry into the war on Britain's side and, as leader of the Friends of Irish Freedom, led the fight against the League of Nations.[94]

Despite these great struggles between the progressives and the machine bosses, Mitchell Innes in the British embassy maintained, on 8 July, that the 'prospects of the Democratic party are brighter than they have been ever since their last victory in 1892.' He reported to Grey that Wilson was 'a sincere progressive, and bears an untarnished reputation, which gives no hold to his enemies, and he has not embarrassed himself with pledges.'[95] The Democratic platform focused on domestic concerns and declared support for import duties, income tax, popular election of senators and opposition to insider dealing, trusts and monopolies. Foreign policy did not feature and there were no statements of support for the political agendas of specific ethnic communities. Bryce noted that Wilson abstained as far as possible from the details of constructive proposals in order 'to give few openings for hostile criticism.'[96] Despite the controversy at the Baltimore convention and the Democratic focus on domestic issues in the platform, Wilson did not back away from ethnic issues. The Wilson campaign included special bureaus located in New York and Chicago that were dedicated to wooing for-eign-born voters to the Democratic side. While Henry Green, director of the American Immigration and Distribution League, worked to reassure foreign-born voters that Wilson was 'sound' on the question of immigration, Wilson used the hustings to further articulate his views on the place of immigrant communities within US society.[97] In August 1912, Roosevelt, in correspondence with Horace Plunkett, the Anglo-Irish rural reformer and politician, wrote:

[F]or your private information I will say again that I think it probable at present that Wilson will win ... he will take the majority of the progres-

---

94 Buckley, *The New York Irish*, pp. 7, 8; *BDFA*, xv, Bryce to Grey, Annual Report for 1912, p. 152.   95 *BDFA*, xv, Innes to Grey, 8 July 1912. The Republican presidential convention was held in Chicago on 18 June 1912. Elihu Root became chairman and there were only two candidates President Taft and former President Roosevelt. Following bitter exchanges, Taft's candidacy won out with the convention. But Roosevelt accused Taft of 'stealing' his delegates and he chose to run for the presidency upon the nomination of the Progressive Party which also met in Chicago. Ibid., Bryce to Grey, Annual Report for 1912, p. 151.   96 TNA, FO371/1550, Bryce to Grey, 14 November 1912.   97 Link, *Wilson. The road to the White House*, pp. 483, 499.

sive Democrats and he will not only keep all the reactionary Democrats, but he will take some reactionary Republicans.[98]

A few weeks later Bryce predicted that Wilson would win the presidential election.[99] Wilson swept the country with a larger number of states than any candidate had won for many years. Neither his derogatory comments on immigrants nor his rumoured 'bigoted and narrow' attitudes towards Roman Catholics affected his vote.[1] Bryce maintained that 'the forces at work ... were too large to admit of the denominational factor playing any considerable part in the result', although he did take Ohio with its large Roman Catholic vote.[2] In October a poll of 2,313 Catholic priests and brothers in the following states and cities: New York, Massachusetts, Connecticut, Ohio, Indiana, St Louis, Louisville, Chicago, Milwaukee, Detroit, Oklahoma revealed that 60 per cent of Irish-American priests supported Wilson while 90 per cent of the Italian-American priests and 70 per cent of Polish-American priests supported Roosevelt.[3] Wilson's gains were in the immigrant strongholds in the northern cities of Massachusetts, New York, Connecticut and Rhode Island. The division of the Republican vote between Taft and Roosevelt and the combination of the southern liberal vote with this northern urban support gave Wilson victory. He was elected on domestic issues and on his reputation as a progressive governor, and he regarded himself 'as being fully prepared only in regard' to internal problems.[4] His foreign policy, such as it was, was not tied to fulfilling specific election promises but was underpinned by the principles of controlling vested interests, of obeying the popular will and of promoting the welfare of society in the US and elsewhere.[5]

Therefore, no promises were made to Irish-Americans or any ethnic groups and, for most Democratic supporters, after sixteen years of Republican domination it was enough to have a candidate who was capable of competing for the presidency. Bryce commented that after the Baltimore convention Wilson enjoyed the support of a 'practically undivided Democratic Party.'[6] Despite Wilson's views on hyphenism and despite the assumption by Spring Rice that by 'birth and education he is probably inclined to sympathize with the English or Scotch point of view', expectations were high among all interest groups that their agendas would be fulfilled when their Democratic candidate assumed the presidency and Democrats controlled Congress.[7] Immediately after the election it was the com-

98 NLI, Horace Plunkett Papers (hereafter HPP), P6584, reel 1 of 2, The American letters of Sir Horace Plunkett, 1883–1932, Theodore Roosevelt to Horace Plunkett, 3 August 1912.   99 TNA, FO371/1548, Bryce to Grey, 27 September 1912; BDFA, xv, Bryce to Grey, Annual Report for 1912, p. 152.   1 Link, Wilson: the road to the White House, p. 500.   2 BDFA, xv, Bryce to Grey, Annual Report for 1912, p. 153; TNA, FO371/1550, Bryce to Grey, 14 November 1912.   3 Link, Wilson: the road to the White House, p. 500.   4 Gerson, The hyphenate, p. 62.   5 Carroll, American opinion, p. 19, fn. 9 pp. 212–13; Link notes that Wilson tried to control public opinion also. Link, The Diplomatist, p. 27.   6 BDFA, xv, Bryce to Grey, 14 November 1912.   7 Ibid., Annual Report for 1913.

position of Wilson's administration that was closely watched by ethnic communities for evidence of his commitment to their cause.

As indicated previously, Wilson compiled his cabinet and administration, with House as his primary adviser, between November 1912 and March 1913. Although for the most part he ignored representations from Tammany Hall, Irish-Americans and Catholics were among his appointments. He retained Maurice Frances Egan, Thomas St John Gaffney and Nelson O'Shaughnessy in the State Department.[8] Gaffney was born in Ireland in 1864 and President Roosevelt appointed him to the US consular service in 1905 for his services to the Republican Party. His eventual resignation from his post as consul general in Munich in 1915 because of alleged anti-British actions was controversial, as will be seen.[9] Egan had held a higher position as ambassador to Denmark from 1907 and, therefore, was more vulnerable but remained in the post until 1918. His retention by Wilson revealed the latter's attempt to be neutral between the conflicting interest groups. Following a meeting with Wilson in the spring of 1914, Egan wrote that the president 'who had been most kind to me' thanked him for staying in the post and said 'I never make merely political appointments, if I find a man "in", who is not of my party and is better than the man who is "out" and who wants to get "in", I retain the better man.' Not surprisingly, Egan was disappointed to hear from the Protestant Bryan that 'he was glad there was a Catholic in the diplomatic service', to which Egan replied that neither Roosevelt nor Taft nor Wilson 'had appointed me because I was a Catholic.' According to Carroll, Egan tended to act on the Irish question in a low-key fashion through the Catholic Church.[10] However, any welcome by Irish-America of these men must have been tempered by two appointments; that of John Bassett Moore, a professor of international law and State Department researcher, who had extensive contact with the Foreign Office and whose appointment as counsellor to Bryan was welcomed by British embassy staff and that of Walter Page, the anglophile ambassador to the Court of St James. Critics of such appointments were not to know that Wilson was not enamoured in general with the quality of personnel or service provided by the State Department, nor did they know that he intended conducting his own foreign policy. But there were other potentially important Irish-connected appointees such as the Catholic Irish-American Joseph Tumulty, who Wilson appointed as his private secretary.[11]

8 Wilson also appointed Catholic Irish American and Clan na Gaeler James Sullivan as US minister to San Domingo. Later Wilson appointed the Kansas city labour lawyer, Frank P. Walsh as joint president of the War Labour Conference Board and the National War Labour Board.   9 Gaffney received the cross of Knight of the Legion of Honour of France and was nominated an Officer of the Order of Leopold II by the late king of Belgium in 1905. T. St. John Gaffney, *Breaking the silence: England, Ireland, Wilson and the war* (1930), p. 143.   10 M.F. Egan, *Recollections of a happy life*, (1924), p. 295; Carroll, *American opinion*, p. 198.   11 Bryan denied any Irish connection but was well informed about his family's English connections. He was nominally sympathetic to home rule. W.J. Bryan & M. Baird Bryan, *The memoirs of William Jennings Bryan* (1925), pp. 20, 21. Bryan

Wilson first met Tumulty during his campaign for governor of New Jersey in 1910. Tumulty was born in Jersey City in 1879 and was the grandson of an emigrant from county Cavan in Ireland. He was reared in the Democratic machine politics of Jersey City but was admitted to the Bar in 1902, becoming a police court lawyer. He continued to immerse himself in local politics and served four terms as an assemblyman. He was about to leave politics when he offered to help out in Wilson's campaign for the governorship.[12] Tumulty had opposed Wilson's nomination for the post but when the latter opposed Boss Smith, he became devoted to him. Wilson trusted and valued Tumulty's political acumen, influenced to some extent by the respect that Ellen Wilson, William McAdoo and House had for him.[13] While Wilson did not appoint 'conspicuous Irish-American nationalists' as confidants, he certainly faced strong criticism for making the Jesuit-educated Tumulty his private secretary. Anti-Catholics alleged that Wilson favoured Catholics over Protestants in the patronage stakes, while southern bigots raged about the Jesuitical menace and warned that Tumulty would reveal state secrets to the papacy in the Vatican. However, House did not see any difficulty with having a Catholic secretary and Wilson ignored the anti-Catholic and anti-Irish mail he received when he appointed his 'dear friend.'[14] This behaviour was also in line with Wilson's policy at Princeton, when he appointed the first Catholic and first Jew to the faculty, thereby breaking the Presbyterian grip.[15] Nevertheless, tensions over appointments of Catholics to the administration simmered throughout the period.[16] Tumulty endured this sort of prejudice throughout his political life but his usefulness to Wilson lay in his political acumen.

Tumulty was steeped in Democratic Party politics and, although he did not consider himself a 'professional Irish-American', his elevation to the White House in 1913 was regarded by the Irish-American nationalist community as significant.

visited Ireland in 1903 and a dinner was given in his honour by the mayor of Dublin. He denied that he had dropped the 'O' before his surname. Carroll, *American opinion*, p. 195. 12 Lee Levin, *Edith and Woodrow*, p. 170. 13 J.M. Blum, *Joe Tumulty and the Wilson era* (1951), pp. 51–2. Wilson's second wife, Edith Bolling Galt complained about Tumulty's lack of breeding but Wilson trusted him for over ten years. Lee Levin, *Edith and Woodrow*, p. 170. Tumulty was well-versed in playing the Irish card when he needed, for example during the Democratic nomination process for the New Jersey senate seat when he used former Senator James Smith's comments promoting the much-despised 'Anglo-Saxon alliance' as a way to bring the Irish vote to the Wilson-backed candidate, James Martine. J. Tumulty, *Woodrow Wilson as I know him* (1922), pp. 65–71. 14 Carroll, *American opinion*, pp. 19, fn. 9 pp. 212–3; Blum, *Joe Tumulty*, pp. 51–2. 15 Cooper, 'Thomas Woodrow Wilson', p. 292. Later Wilson appointed his friend Bernard Baruch as chairman of the War Shipping Board. 16 Spring Rice believed it emanated from Protestants and social reformers. TNA, FO371/2153, Spring Rice to Grey, 16 February 1914. These forces were to emerge again when Warren Harding wanted to appoint William J. Burns, a Catholic, as chief of the Bureau of Investigation and were most evident during the 1929 presidential election when the Catholic Democrat Al Smith opposed Protestant Republican Herbert Hoover. In 1932, Harry Daugherty, attorney general in Harding's administration, wrote 'there are people who foolishly believe that Catholics should not be appointed to public office.' H.M Daugherty, *The inside story of the Harding tragedy* (1932), p. 105.

Through him organized nationalist Irish-America expected to have another route to the president.[17] Tumulty recalled that, long before 1914, he had discussed 'the Irish cause' with Wilson who felt that the British government's policy of force and reprisal in Ireland had strengthened 'the tenacious purpose of the Irish people' and had served to maintain 'under the surface the seething dissatisfaction of that indomitable race.' Wilson and Tumulty talked of how to make Wilson's influence felt in a way that would bring results without him becoming involved in diplomatic 'snarls' with Britain.[18] Tumulty may not have deliberately furthered the nationalist cause with Wilson but he certainly brought Irish affairs to Wilson's attention.[19]

Another avenue through which Irish affairs came to Wilson's attention was his contact with Horace Plunkett.[20] Plunkett was described by his biographer as an 'Anglo-American Irishman', a description which accurately reflected his Irish, English and American backgrounds.[21] Plunkett was a home ruler and supporter of constitutional nationalism but found himself drawn to the extremist nationalists because he believed 'one gets a far better love of Ireland from the non-parliamentary section.'[22] Between 1900 and 1907, he was vice-president of the department of Agriculture and Technical Instruction and was mainly interested in publicizing agricultural reform, particularly through the co-operative movement. Among his circle of American friends was President Roosevelt which did not go unnoticed in the British embassy in Washington.[23]

During a trip to the US in 1913, Plunkett met Wilson on 21 January to discuss agricultural reform. Following the meeting, Wilson asked Plunkett to remain in contact with him.[24] At this time, Plunkett also met Edward House who knew of 'his love for America' and he described him as 'among the most eminent of living British statesmen.' In 1925 Plunkett recalled, 'thus began this precious friendship of my later years.'[25] Both men saw a great deal of each other during

17 LC, MD, Joseph Tumulty Papers (hereafter JTP). The collection contains one file on Ireland dated from March 1921 to October 1927. LC, MD, JTP, Box 98, file Ireland, March 1921 to October 1921; Blum, *Joe Tumulty*, p. 98.   18 Tumulty, *Woodrow Wilson*, p. 393.   19 Carroll, *American opinion*, p. 18.   20 See NLI, HPP, P6584, reel 1 and 2 of 2, The American letters of Sir Horace Plunkett, 1883–1932. Between 1900 and 1914 Plunkett corresponded also with Walter Page in the latter's capacity as a publisher but it did not continue into the war-time period. Ibid.   21 The young Plunkett had farmed in Wyoming from 1879 to 1889, and maintained business interests in the US after his return to Ireland. He was also interested in politics and had been elected as a Liberal Unionist Member of Parliament for south Dublin in 1892. T. West, *Horace Plunkett: co-operation and politics, and Irish biography* (1986), p. 137; NLI, HPP, P6584, reel 1 of 2, The American letters of Sir Horace Plunkett, 1883–1932, 'Introduction'.   22 Quoted in West, *Horace Plunkett*, p. 137.   23 Plunkett shared with Roosevelt common interests in land conservation, agricultural development and improving standards of living in rural areas. Moreover, Plunkett was instrumental in persuading Roosevelt to establish the Commission on Country Life. Walter Page was a member of the commission also. *BDFA*, xiii, Bryce to Edward Grey, 28 May 1908, p. 133; Quoted in West, *Horace Plunkett*, p. 134.   24 *PWW*, 27, Wilson to Crane, 17 January 1913, p. 60 and fn.2; NLI, HPP, P6584, reel 1 of 2, The American letters of Sir Horace Plunkett, 1883–1932, Plunkett to Byrne, 21 January 1913; ibid., Plunkett to Wilson, 29 January 1913; ibid., Wilson to Plunkett, 30 January 1913.   25 C. Seymour (ed.), *The intimate papers of Colonel House*, 4 vols (1927–8), i, p.

House's visit to London between February and June 1913. Plunkett arranged interviews for House with British government ministers and officials and was impressed by House's grasp of the European political situation; 'He is a remarkable man, capable of taking a wonderful, philosophic and detached view of things. He is one of the coolest hands I have ever known and his political intuitions are really remarkable.' He was disappointed when House returned to the US in June 1915.[26] However, before he left London, House asked Plunkett to correspond with him 'upon matters which were not ripe for official communication' but which had an important bearing upon questions he would be discussing with Wilson, the press and British officials. He wanted someone who was familiar with both the US and English ways of life and was known to figures in authority in both countries. Plunkett filled both roles and agreed 'to serve in this capacity.'[27] Wilson endorsed House's approach and wrote to Plunkett that there would never be 'the slightest hesitation on my part about resorting to you in any possible contingency.'[28] During the war, therefore, Plunkett was used by House and Wilson as a go-between for themselves and members of the British cabinet, particularly Grey and his successor Arthur Balfour in the Foreign Office.

In June 1915, arrangements were made by Balfour, who was then first lord of the Admiralty, to facilitate the transmission of cables between House and Plunkett through the British Admiralty, the British embassy in Washington and the Irish Office. Balfour also authorized the exclusive use of a secret code.[29] The Plunkett–House correspondence continued until 1932 and the more sporadic Plunkett–Wilson correspondence until 1923. House's replies to Plunkett were longer than those written by Wilson which were 'warm but brief and formal.' Plunkett never viewed his role as anything but advisory to House and Wilson. Nonetheless, the access he had to the heart of the British cabinet, combined with his moderate nationalist views on the Irish question, provided the two Americans with an important window into British and Irish politics, particularly at a time when Page's position was compromised.[30] Ultimately, however, no single individual influenced Wilson's decision-making.

It was not long after his installation as president that Wilson directly encountered the Irish-American lobby and its attempts to interlink US, British and Irish issues. Between November 1912 and March 1913, Wilson worked with party leaders to decide a legislative programme for Congress. Then he recalled the newly elected Democratic-dominated Congress into session in April 1913. He broke a further tradition by addressing Congress and keeping it in session for

149.   26 NLI, HPP, P6584, reel 2 of 2, Plunkett to House, 8 June 1915; ibid., reel 1 of 2, Plunkett to Byrne, 11 June 1915.   27 Ibid., reel 2 of 2, Plunkett to House, 8 June 1915.   28 Ibid., Wilson to Plunkett, 17 June 1915.   29 Ibid., Plunkett to House, 8 June 1915.   30 Ibid., 'Introduction'; Ibid., 'Private code between E.M. House New York and 'Organize Dublin' [Plunkett] or Juverna Audley London' [principal secretary, Admiralty]. Plunkett also sent long reports to Karl Walter about the importance of interpreting British opinion for the mid-western US press and vice versa and he supported the work of the Reciprocal News service. Ibid., 'Introduction'.

eighteen months without break.[31] The major legislative highlights of this session were the repeal of the Panama Canal Tolls Act combined with the introduction of the first permanent and graduated income tax, the reform of the banking and currency system and finally, the reform of big business.[32] Controversy centred on the canal legislation because of the exemption enjoyed by US ship owners from the tolls charged to ships using the Panama Canal. The British government objected on the grounds that it violated the 1901 Hay–Pauncefote treaty which stipulated that the canal should be open to the vessels of all nations 'on terms of entire equality.' Most Democratic senators and congressmen had voted for the 1912 exemption bill and the Democratic presidential platform in the 1912 campaign, drafted by Senator James O'Gorman of New York with Clan na Gael backing, had endorsed the act. During the presidential campaign Wilson had supported free tolls and, once elected, he decided to move on the issue. In February 1913 he told Bryce that 'the friendship of the United Kingdom and the United States could not but be of the greatest service to the maintenance of the peace of the whole world', and added that he deplored the attempt made with the Panama tolls question, 'to sow discord between the two countries.'[33] Once the Wilson government took office, Bryce wrote to Bryan expressing the hope that the act would be referred to arbitration.[34] Immediately, Wilson fulfilled the highest of British hopes by accepting their argument that US shipping should not be exempted from paying canal tolls. The Republicans supported continued exemption although Senator Henry Cabot Lodge recognized in 1900 that 'we made a promise there which ought not to [have been made].'[35] Not surprisingly, the issue that had united Irish-Americans, German-Americans, anglophobes and shipping lobbyists since 1911, provoked the same reaction.

In October 1913, Wilson formally announced that he intended repealing the legislation and on 5 March 1914 he sent his request to Congress. Ellen Wilson had advised her husband against the move because she felt that it would split the Democratic Party. Similarly, Tumulty laid out the full political implications for Wilson; he indicated that it would 'irritate large blocks of Irish, Germans and other anti-British elements' and that 'we might expect that the leaders in our own party ... would be found in solid opposition.' He was also worried that the move might open up divisions within the party. Wilson was very aware of the disunity within his own party even though the Democrats dominated Congress. Indeed, Wilson had directed Tumulty, Bryan, McAdoo and the postmaster general, Albert Burleson, to liaise directly with the Democratic leaders in Congress

31 *BDFA*, xv, memorandum by Lord Percy, 28 November 1913.   32 Cooper, 'Thomas Woodrow Wilson', pp. 295–6. For further on Wilson's domestic programme see amongst other works K.A Clements, *The presidency of Woodrow Wilson* (1992); A.S. Link, *Woodrow Wilson*, 5 vols. (1947–65). 33 *BDFA*, xv, Bryce to Grey, 21 February 1913.   34 Willson, *Friendly relations*, p. 308.   35 Hendrick, *The life and letters of Walter H. Page*, i, p. 243; British Library, Manuscripts Division (hereafter BLMD), Balfour Papers (hereafter BP), Add. 49742, Lodge to Henry White, US embassy, London, 18 December 1900.

to keep the southern Democrats, northern urban Democrats and Bryan's supporters united behind his congressional programme.[36] Wilson knew 'that the Irish, through the Hearst newspapers, will cry out that I have surrendered to England, that I am attempting to hand over to Europe a quasi-control over the Panama Canal.' But he told Tumulty:

> I have calculated every element in the situation and ... concluded where the path of duty lies. If we begin to consider the effect upon our own political fortunes of every step we take in these delicate matters of our foreign relations, America will be set adrift and her word questioned in every court in Europe. It is important that every agreement that America subscribes her name to shall be carried out in the spirit of those who negotiated it.[37]

Wilson was willing to risk losing party support in order 'to right a great wrong.'[38] In November 1913, during a conversation with William Tyrell, private secretary to Foreign Secretary Grey, he confirmed his determination 'to overcome the opposition.'[39] Not surprisingly Grey was impressed by Wilson's decision to repeal.[40] Immediately the opposition lined up against the president. Spring Rice wrote to Tyrell on 30 March:

> I am very sorry to say that it seems to be believed that the President's action with regard to Panama has broken up his party, as it has brought to a head all the various animosities which have existed against him since his sudden nomination and election. The elections for the House take place in the summer, and it is freely threatened that those who have voted with the President will lose their seats, partly owing to the Irish and Germans, and floating mass of ultra-American voters. His act was one of great courage, and I fear that in American politics, honesty and courage are not always rewarded with success.[41]

Not all viewed Wilson's actions in such a virtuous way.

The Democratic Party leaders visited Wilson and told him of their opposition to repeal. Some made it clear that they attributed the party's success in 1913 to the continued loyalty of Irish-Americans and worried about the loss of that vote with primary elections pending in many states. Senators O'Gorman (New York state), Martine (New Jersey) and Reed (Missouri) were concerned about the effect on their Irish and German constituents and they led the Democratic

---

36 Tumulty, *Woodrow Wilson as I know him*, p. 162; Blum, *Wilson*, pp. 68–9; Cooper, 'Thomas Woodrow Wilson', p. 295.   37 Tumulty, *Woodrow Wilson as I know him*, p. 167.   38 Ibid., p. 167. 39 TNA, Edward Grey Papers, F800/241, Tyrell to Grey, 14 November 1913.   40 Quoted in Hendrick, *The life and letters of Walter H. Page*, i, p. 254.   41 Gwynn, *The life and friendships*, ii, pp. 196, 205.

opposition on the measure. The *Congressional Record* was soon filled with dis-senting congressmen reading petitions and objections into the record to publi-cize their credentials on the matter.[42] Other prominent Irish-Americans, such as Democratic Congressman William Bourke Cockran, represented the Committee for the Preservation of American Rights in the Panama Canal at a hearing of the Committee on Inter-Oceanic canals.[43] A further potential source of congressional opposition to the legislation was identified by Spring Rice in March 1914. He was concerned the support of the chairman of the Senate Foreign Relations Committee, Senator William J. Stone from Missouri, a state with a large German-American population, could not be counted on and even less in cases where domestic politics cut across foreign relations. Spring Rice stated that Stone was supporting Wilson's position on the tolls question but that he might shift depend-ing on the 'exigencies of domestic popularity hunting.'[44] During summer 1914 Wilson's emissaries to Congress worked to prevent Stone and others from desert-ing the president's side.

Outside Congress, Irish-American organizations and societies showered Congress and Wilson with petitions. Clan na Gael organized mass meetings in New York. Among those who attended were Colby, Wilson's last secretary of State, a former law partner of nationalist John Quinn and a friend of Cohalan. After one meeting, Colby wrote to Cohalan, 'it was a great meeting – such fer-vour and such earnestness, I never saw before.'[45] Other public demonstrations took place in Philadelphia, the home city of Clan na Gael leader, Joseph McGarrity and in Boston.[46] Tumulty recalled that Wilson's decision on the tolls issue brought the 'bitterest criticism ... a shower of personal abuse and vituper-ation from Irish organs and from a group of newspapers which presently were to appear as the chief supporters of Germany.'[47] Within these anglophobic groups, the pro-British element in Wilson's background was now confirmed as a sign of political weakness. He was accused of seeking an alliance with Britain and sacri-ficing US shipping interests to the well-being of British trade.

With the debate raging inside and outside Congress, Wilson's new ambassa-dor in London, Walter Page, entered the fray also. Page's arrival at the US chancery in Victoria street, London on 25 May 1913, was the first time he had been inside an US embassy. Until then the only embassy he had been familiar

42 Blum, *Wilson*, p. 70.   43 Ward, *Ireland and Anglo–American relations*, p. 83.   44 TNA, FO371/2153, Spring Rice to Grey, 30 March 1914.   45 American Irish Historical Society (here-after AIHS), New York, Daniel F. Cohalan Papers (hereafter DFCP), box 3, folder 6, Colby to Cohalan, 24 March 1914.   46 NLI, McGP, MS. 17636, Matthew Harford to McGilligan, 26 March 1914; TNA, FO 371 2154, Consul General to Foreign Office, 9 March 1914.   47 Tumulty, *Woodrow Wilson as I know him*, p. 167; Blum, *Wilson*, p. 69. Colby was a former law partner of the promi-nent Irish-American, John Quinn. The latter was a lawyer for Standard Oil company and supporter of the Irish cause. Quinn considered himself to be a 'sympathiser with Irish ideas ... [but] ... always opposed to the irreconcilable Irish both in this country and in Ireland.' NLI, John Quinn Papers (hereafter JQP), MS18436, 'In the matter of Sir Roger Casement and the Irish situation in America', 2 June 1916.

with the inside of was the British embassy in Washington. Despite this inexperience he had made up his mind about some matters prior to his arrival. He believed that:

> Blood carries with it that particular trick of thought which makes us all English in the last report ... And thus, despite the fusion of races and of the great contribution of other nations to her hundred millions of people and her incalculable wealth, the United States is yet English-led and English-ruled.[48]

On hearing these sentiments in August 1913, Americans of Irish and German descent petitioned Wilson for Page's removal from London but Wilson refused to act. Page's views on the Panama Canal tolls issue were set also.[49] He believed that the British interpretation of the Hay–Pauncefote treaty was correct. The US government could not charge ships owned by its own citizens different toll rates to those charged to ships belonging to other nationals but he recognized that Wilson was in a difficult position.[50]

Page started to press Wilson towards repeal as soon as he arrived in London and in early March 1914 made his own views public, delivering an impromptu speech to the American Chambers of Commerce that was half-serious and half-humorous in intent. He stated, 'I would not say that we constructed the Panama Canal even for you ... we built it for reasons of our own. But I will say that it adds to the pleasure of that great work that you will profit by it. You will profit most by it, for you have the greatest carrying trade.' He then repeated Wilson's policy on the Monroe Doctrine and used the expression, 'we prefer that European powers shall acquire no more territory on this continent.' According to himself, the speech was incorrectly reported in the 'England-baiting press', but once a report of it hit the US, there was immediate criticism inside and outside Congress. On 18 March, Page admitted to Wilson that the speech had been a mistake, but only because of the timing and the embarrassment it might cause the president. It seemed to Page that 'the Irish and the Confederates ... have gone clean daft.' Wilson was inundated with petitions for Page's removal. Irish-American groups in the US 'resolved' against Page as an ambassador who 'looks on English claims as superior to American rights' and they demanded his recall. The furore had little impact on Wilson who reassured Page 'I want you to feel constantly how I value the intelligent and effective work you are doing in London. I do not know what I should do without you.' Page remained *in situ* until 1918

48 Ibid., p. 258.   49 En route to his London posting in early spring 1913, Page's boat stopped at Queenstown in Ireland and he recalled that he was confronted by a number of reporters who wanted to know what he thought of Ireland. He recorded in his memoirs 'Some of them printed the important announcement that I was quite friendly to Ireland!' When he arrived in London he was disappointed because 'all the Cabinet are all the time going about making speeches on Ireland.' Hendrick, *The life and letters of Walter H. Page*, i, p. 108, 137, 158–9.   50 Ibid., p. 243.

but he admitted to being hounded by 'anglophobics – Irish and Panama.'[51] Even after Congress passed the Panama Canal bill, Page constantly lamented the overarching influence of immigrant groups on US foreign policy:

> We've no foreign policy, no continuity of plan, no matured scheme, no settled way of doing things and we seem afraid of Irishmen or Germans or some "element" when a chance for real action comes … We're in the game. There's no point in letting a few wild Irish or cocky Germans scare us.[52]

Page regarded the criticism of him as a badge of honour and a sign that he was doing his job well. As will be seen, during the war years the British government had in effect two ambassadors to the US; one in Washington on their own payroll and one in London paid by the US government. But Page's pro-British views, which were inspired by admiration for all things English and had an anti-Irish tinge, became more pronounced as he became embedded in English society.

On 1 June 1914, Wilson acknowledged to Spring Rice that the 'Irish societies had been mobilized against the [Panama] bill with some success.' But he felt by then that it was beginning to be understood by the US public that the only people who would benefit from the exemption were the ship owners who already enjoyed a complete monopoly.[53] Tumulty, McAdoo, Bryan and Burleson managed to hold sufficient Democrats behind Wilson, while Republicans were convinced by the brilliant and effective speech delivered by Elihu Root, Roosevelt's secretary of War and secretary of State, in favour of the legislation. The Democratic-controlled House of Representatives passed the bill by 216 to 71 votes and the Republican-dominated but divided Senate by 50 to 35 votes. Wilson's control of the Congress held and he signed the bill into law. He had seen off the immigrants' attempt to influence his foreign policy but Ward suggests that this attack may have influenced one of his most trenchant attacks on hyphenate communities.[54]

On 16 May 1914, during a ceremony to honour John Barry, pioneer of the US navy, he stated:

> John Barry was an Irishman, but his heart crossed the Atlantic with him. He did not leave it in Ireland … Some Americans need hyphens in their names because only part of them has come over; but when the whole man has come over, heart and thought and all, the hyphen drops of its own

---

51 Ibid., pp. 259–60, 262, 257, 262, 108, 133, 137, 152.   52 Ibid., p. 261.   53 *PWW*, 27, Spring Rice to Edward Grey, 3 June 1914, pp. 141.   54 Ward, *Ireland and Anglo-American relations*, pp. 82–3. The Wilson administration inherited one other Irish issue which centred on the claim by Solomon Jacob, a US citizen against the British government 'on account of the alleged illegal detention of a schooner on the Irish coast in 1899.' The matter came to Grey's attention in November 1912 who concluded that it could only be resolved by an arbitration tribunal under the pecuniary claims agreement, or the US government would have to abandon it altogether. TNA, FO371/1544, Walter Langley, November 1912.

weight out of his name. This man was not an Irish-American; he was an Irishman who became an American. I venture to say if he voted he voted with regard to the questions as they looked on this side of the water, and not on the other side, and that is my infallible test of a genuine American that when he votes or when he acts or when he fights, his heart and his thoughts are nowhere but centred in the emotions and the purposes and the policies of the United States.[55]

Tumulty did not link the Barry speech and the Panama tolls legislation.[56] Nevertheless, the themes in the Barry speech on hyphenated Americans were not new and accorded with Wilson's beliefs in the principles of equality and democracy and in the greatness of the US. Either way since March 1913, Wilson had quickly taken hold of US foreign policy, followed his own path, emerged victorious and maintained the Democrats' hold on Congress, but he had experienced the heat of hyphenate opposition, and specifically of 'hibernianism', to use Wilson's word.[57] Within a few short months, it would re-emerge to challenge his neutrality policy, but on the Panama canal issue he had illustrated his toughness as a maker and enforcer of policy.

As previously indicated, Wilson dedicated himself during the months leading up to August 1914 to the problems of revolutions in China, Mexico and the Caribbean region. He favoured non-military solutions to achieve legitimate, democratic government although he became a military interventionist later on. Meanwhile he was receiving bulletins from Edward House, who was touring the European capital cities to gather support for his and Wilson's plan for US–British–German co-operation. Little attention was paid by Wilson, House, Bryan or State Department officials to the collapsing Austro–Hungarian and Ottoman empires or to events in the Balkans. This neglect would change soon.[58] On a personal level, Ellen Wilson died on 7 August and Wilson admitted 'the days sap me – sap me easily and quickly.'[59] It was a combination of these momentous events and their consequences that formed the context for Wilson's response to gathering events in Ireland in summer 1914.

In March 1913, when Wilson entered the White House, the Ulster Volunteer Force (UVF) had been created to defend Ulster Protestants against direct rule from a Dublin-based Catholic government and Edward Carson had planned a provisional government for Ulster. The third Irish Home Rule bill had been introduced into the British parliament in April 1912 and was expected to become law in 1914. Home rule appeared inevitable to many, including William Bryan, whose earliest comments as US secretary of State brought him public attention and led Bryce to believe that Bryan did not have a full grasp of the Irish question.[60]

55 *PWW*, 30, An address to Commodore John Barry, pp. 35–6.   56 Tumulty, *Woodrow Wilson*, pp. 392–7.   57 TNA, FO800/241, Tyrell to Grey, 14 November 1913.   58 LaFeber, *The American age*, pp. 277, 280, 282, 284.   59 Quoted in Lee Levin, *Edith and Woodrow*, p. 133.   60 *BDFA*, xv,

Bryan had in fact visited Ireland in late 1903 and proclaimed his support for home rule.[61] But on 24 March 1913 Bryan gave a public statement to the *New York Evening Post* that was critical of the House of Lords and indicated that the Irish question had been solved since home rule would automatically come into force. Bryce commented, 'Mr Bryan, I incline to think, culls his history from the morning papers, cursorily read.' This lapse of propriety did not become a subject for diplomatic dispute between the US and British governments even though two English papers carried the comments. However, it revealed Bryan's assumption that Irish home rule was an issue of 'historic interest rather than actual controversy.'[62] Bryan's simplistic reading of the Irish situation was shared by others in the home rule movement in both Ireland and the US. But it was a complex matter. Radical nationalists in Ireland and the US wanted an independent republic and adopted a militant posture much to the unease of British diplomats in Washington.[63] November 1913 saw the formation of the Irish Volunteers. Its executive committee included individuals such as Eoin MacNeill, who regarded it as a defensive force to secure the implementation of home rule, while others, such as Patrick Pearse saw it as an army to be used to win independence.

In 1914, Ulster unionism was strengthened. In March sixty British cavalry officers, based in the Curragh camp in county Kildare, had resigned their commissions rather than obey orders to coerce Ulster unionists into accepting Dublin-based home rule. The UVF could call on 50,000 men to resist home rule while the Irish Volunteers had a membership of 70,000. In June home rule leader John Redmond, now fearful of losing control of nationalist Ireland, insisted that twenty-five of his nominees sit on the provisional committee of the Irish Volunteers to equal the existing membership. The committee accepted and membership rose to about 160,000. But Redmond's commitment that the Volunteers would support the British war effort in August split the force. Redmond led the bulk of the Irish Volunteers membership into the newly-established National Volunteers while the 2–3,000 remaining Irish Republican Brotherhood-dominated Irish Volunteers, along with the Irish Citizen Army, would effect the rising two years later.[64] Both Irish and Ulster Volunteers were arming themselves. On 24–25 April, the UVF landed arms and ammunition from Germany at Larne, Donaghdee and Bangor in county Down.[65] The escalating situation dominated British cabinet meetings where there was a good deal of personal sympathy with Carson for having successfully defied the law, while Prime Minister Asquith decided to take no action except to send a squadron of destroyers to patrol the Irish coast.[66]

Bryce to Grey, 24 March 1913.   **61** L.W. Koenig, *Bryan: a political biography of William Jennings Bryan* (1971), pp. 363–4.   **62** *BDFA*, xv, Bryce to Grey, 24 March 1913.   **63** Ibid., Spring Rice to Grey, 27 May 1913.   **64** K. Jeffrey, 'Curragh Mutiny' in S.J. Connolly, *The Oxford companion to Irish history* (1998), p. 131; P. Connolly, 'Irish Citizens Army' in ibid., p. 265; J. Augusteijn, 'Irish (National) Volunteers' in ibid., p. 270; J. Loughlin, 'Irish Republican Brotherhood' in ibid., pp. 272–3; A. Jackson, 'Ulster Volunteer Force' in ibid., pp. 563–4.   **65** J.J. Lee, *Ireland 1912–1985: politics and society* (1989), p. 18.   **66** E. David (ed.), *Inside Asquith's cabinet: from the diaries of Charles*

But what type of information on the Irish situation would have been available in the State Department at this time, if Wilson had requested it? Officials could obtain information about Ireland from a number of sources located inside and outside the department. First, there was the British embassy. Contact between the State Department and the embassy operated at a formal and a routine level. Both Bryan and Lansing had a difficult relationship with Spring Rice because of his oversensitive defence of British interests; nevertheless they shared his views on Ireland and, specifically, shared his hopes for Irish home rule.[67] Moreover, even when Wilson began to rely more on House and William Wiseman, as foreign policy intermediaries and emissaries in his dealings with the British government and less on Bryan, Lansing and Spring Rice, there was little or no difference between their views on the Irish question. As will be seen, these men shared a desire for a solution to the Irish question because, as Wiseman and House agreed in early 1917, 'The Irish question is a perpetual obstacle to really satisfactory relations' between the US and Britain.[68]

The State Department–British embassy relationship also operated between officials and at an informal level centred on the position of the counsellor in the State Department. In July 1913, when British diplomats were encountering obstacles in the State Department that hampered their work, Spring Rice described the extraordinary state of affairs whereby

> the Secretary of State was absent to open an hotel for one of his friends. He will shortly leave for a six weeks lecturing tour in the west. The assistant secretary of state was on a tour in the West Indies; the second assistant on leave in Europe; the third assistant attending the Brazilian foreign minister on his visit to America. There is no solicitor to the Department and there is only one assistant solicitor, though two are provided by law ... The business of the Department, even when Mr Bryan is present, has to give way to the numerous claims of politicians and office seekers ... The bulk of the actual work rests on the shoulders of the Counsellor of the Department ... The department which, unlike other departments in Washington, used to contain a certain number of men with long and technical trainings, is according to public repute, becoming a political machine the integral parts of which are being selected on purely political grounds.[69]

Edward Grey commented that this was 'a scandalous state of things.'[70] It was Frank Polk who worked most closely with Washington's diplomatic corps and whose relationship with British diplomats in many ways informed the State Department's position on Ireland.

Hobhouse (1977), pp. 168–71.   **67** Findling, *Dictionary*, pp. 270–1; Quoted in Hartley, *The Irish question*, p. 13.   **68** YULMC, WWP, World war one and peace conference, select correspondence, box 7, file 109, Relations between the United States and Great Britain, 1917.   **69** TNA, FO371/1859, Spring Rice to Grey, 21 July 1913.   **70** Ibid., Grey, July 1913.

Polk was a Yale law graduate who had joined the State Department as a counsellor in 1915. He was a Democrat, but on the reforming wing of the party, and
a political appointee. From 1915 to 1921 he developed close relations with British
diplomats, official and journalists. His relationship with Colville Barclay, his counterpart in the embassy, was strong and friendly.[71] Along with Lansing, he was a
personal friend of Arthur Willert, *The Times* correspondent in Washington and
unofficial press attaché for Spring Rice.[72] Polk also came to admire Arthur Balfour
and his private secretary, Eric Drummond, and by the end of the war, he
described 'our British friends' as being 'fine people', and he found 'extraordinary' the 'unreasonable feeling that a number of men' in Washington had on the
subject of Britain.[73] He was even personally disposed 'to beat up some of these
Irish gentlemen if they get gay' and threatened Ambassador Alexander Geddes'
safety, having already provided him with secret service agents for protection.[74]
Consequently, at this lower level of official contact, where positions were still
filled by 'men of Anglo-Saxon ancestry', both Polk and embassy officials fully
agreed about the primacy of having a smooth US–British diplomatic relationship
and of the British government solving the 'irritant' that was the Irish question
along home rule lines.[75]

Newspapers, however, offered foreign-policy makers conflicting viewpoints.
By 1914 one of the barometers used by British embassy officials when assessing
the bias of a US newspaper was its editorial position on the Irish question; this
gives us an indication of the extent of the newspaper coverage of Irish affairs.
The *Washington Post* was 'bellicose and ... rather Anglophobe' in its tone, while
the *New York Sun*, with an 'unwavering friendship for Great Britain', enjoyed
the confidence of State Department officials, as did the pro-Wilson *New York
Times*. The Hearst-owned press and the *Gaelic American* and the *Irish World* were
considered to be anti-British and pro-Irish.[76]

State Department chiefs and their masters also received information through
the Department's formal channels. Each diplomat or consul in the field was
expected to report to the State Department at least every two weeks. Although
each dispatch from the man in the field was addressed to the secretary of State
or to an assistant secretary it actually went to the relevant division, where its
content was recorded and depending on the information, the divisional chief
would discuss it with the officer dealing with the matter. It was then passed on
to the appropriate assistant secretary and possibly the under secretary or secretary for a decision. The decision-making could take a day or a week.[77] In the

71 YULMC, FLPP, box 2, file 029, Barclay to Polk, 15 June 1919.   72 A. Willert, *Washington and
other memories* (1972), p. 79.   73 YULMC, FLPP, diary, 1917; ibid., box 1, file 016, Auchincloss
to Polk, 9 November 1917; ibid., file 019, Polk to Auchincloss, 20 December 1918.   74 Ibid., Polk
to Auchincloss, 21 April 1919; ibid., box 2, file 128, Polk to Davis, 26 May 1920.   75 Koenig,
Bryan, p. 536.   76 *BDFA*, xiii, 'Report by Mr Grant Watson on the Press of the United States
and its methods', 3 April 1908, pp. 120–8; ibid., Bryce to Grey, 3 April 1908, p. 120; ibid., vii, The
press, January 1922, p. 63.   77 HHPL, WRCP, 'The tools of American diplomacy (1) The

context of Ireland in 1914, US interests were the responsibility of consular officers in Ireland and of the embassy in London. The US ambassador in London
was expected to report on political matters in Ireland, but this often depended
on the personal interests of the incumbent and on the extent to which Irish affairs
dominated British politics at any given time. Page wrote directly to Wilson from
the time of his appointment in 1913, until the war began and was Wilson's 'best
source of opinion abroad.'[78] He reported on the enmity which characterized
British party politics and it was in that context and not Irish politics, that he
explained the Irish situation to Wilson on 1 May. He wrote that 'The Conservatives had used Ulster and its army as a club to drive the Liberals out of power
and they have gone to the very brink of civil war. They don't really care about
Ulster. I doubt whether they care much about Home Rule.' He believed that
Conservative/Unionist opposition to the Liberal/Irish Parliamentary Party coalition was based on the formers' antipathy towards liberalism. He also offered
Wilson his personal opinion; 'If I were an Ulsterman, I fear I, too, should object
to being bound to the body of Dublin.'[79]

Page was not alone in the embassy in his views on Ireland. Irwin Laughlin,
first secretary and counsellor in the London embassy, knew 'perfectly well' that
the 'embassy and everyone in it' was believed to be 'excessively pro-British'. He
admitted to Polk that 'this has always been so' and to being pro-British himself.
But he justified his position on the grounds that 'I find the greater interests of
my country march with theirs.' Polk did not disagree with Laughlin's reasoning
but the admission simply confirmed existing views in the State Department and
White House about bias in embassy reports.[80] By summer 1916, the situation was
so bad that House advised Polk to withdrawn Page from London so that he might
be 'sent West to get a complete bath of American opinion.'[81] Another consequence of the pro-British stance within the London embassy was Wilson's decision to despatch Ray Stannard Baker to Europe in 1918 to report on events in
England, Ireland and later Italy. Polk accorded him the title 'special assistant',
with a salary and diplomatic passport.[82] In that capacity he visited Ireland and
reported directly to Polk and Wilson as will be seen. It is clear that the upper
echelons of the State Department and the White House recognized that the views
of US diplomats based in London were of limited value on many matters, including Ireland. However, when it came to getting information and views on the Irish
situation, the US administration also had representatives based in Ireland.

The structure and resources of the US consular service in Ireland will be
examined in chapter three, but on the eve of the war there was no US diplomatic representative stationed in Ireland as it was part of the empire and the US

Department of State', pp. 15–18. 78 Link, *The Diplomatist*, p. 27. 79 Hendrick, *The life and letters of Walter H. Page*, i, pp. 158–9; Quoted in Carroll, *American opinion*, p. 25. 80 Ibid., box 9,
file 320, Laughlin to Polk, 22 October 1916. 81 YULMC, FLPP, box 8, file 266, House to Polk,
25 July 1916. 82 Ibid., box 1, file 030, Polk to Baker, 8 July 1918; ibid., Baker to Polk, 8 July
1918.

ambassador was based in London. Instead the consular branch of the foreign service, dedicated to handling US economic and commercial matters abroad, handled US interests in Ireland. Nor was there a senior consular officer, a consul general, *in situ* and the quality of the nine US consular representatives in Ireland and their work varied. For example, Consul Wesley Frost, who was based in Queenstown, county Cork, did not think it was necessary to respond until 31 July 1914 to a Central Instruction from the State Department issued on 27 April, which requested information on shipping activity in southern Ireland. The reason he gave was that the State Department had 'undoubtedly' obtained 'the essential facts' from press despatches to America, and 'no American vessels call here ordinarily (except such steamers as will be notified by their companies).' Furthermore, he admitted that the report titled 'Military and Naval Activity in the South of Ireland' which he sent to Bryan on 31 July, could have been 'a more thorough report' but he wanted to send it off in the next available transatlantic mail service.[83] The report was received in the Consular bureau and in this case was then forwarded to the secretary of State's office.

In late July 1914, Frost informed Bryan, that since the royal proclamation in December 1913 prohibiting 'gun-running', naval activity had been 'pronounced' in the region with the aim of preventing 'the landing of arms for the nationalist Volunteers and other irregular armed forces.' The Irish coast was patrolled incessantly by naval vessels. Queenstown, where he was stationed, was the centre of the British Admiralty in Ireland and ordinarily had eight cruisers stationed there, while four torpedo boats, scout cruisers or mine sweepers appeared frequently. But, because of policing duties elsewhere, the harbour had been virtually empty for several weeks in late July. However, Frost commented that, in spite of the 'officious zeal of the naval vessels, daily gun-running coups are credibly reported.' He said that in the previous two days, the newspapers reported at least eight separate landings of artillery or ammunition.[84] In the following days, consignments intended for the nationalists were landed on the Wicklow coast and the rest brought ashore on 26 August at Howth, county Dublin, when British soldiers seized some of the guns. During the soldiers' return to the barracks some shot at a hostile crowd, killing three people and wounding thirty-eight.[85] Frost believed that the successful landings should be interpreted 'not as an impeachment of the efficiency of the naval vessels, but as evidence that the British ministry are not really anxious to enforce the proclamation.' The situation was, he reported, suddenly 'rendered inconspicuous' by the worsening continental crisis. The British Admiralty took over control of the Queenstown port, with all its approaches and numerous ramifications, from the civil authorities. British troops were re-organ-

83 *Papers relating to the foreign relations of the United States* (hereafter *FRUS*), 1914 supplement the world war (1928), Frost to the Secretary of State, 31 July 1914, p. 58.   84 *FRUS*, 1914 supplement the world war, Frost to the Secretary of State, 31 July 1914, p. 58.   85 S.J. Connolly, 'Howth gun-running' in Connolly, *The Oxford companion*, p. 251.

ized in Ireland, newspapers were asked not to report military movements and all shipping traffic into the harbour, including transatlantic liners, was subject to rigorous supervision.[86] Despite his apparent inefficiency, Frost had placed Irish events in a wider context and given vital information on British preparations, although he made no reference to the imminent conference on Ireland that opened in Buckingham Palace on 21 July.[87]

However, when Congressman James Gallivan from Massachusetts and member of the House Committee on Foreign Affairs, asked Bryan on 29 July, whether or not any American citizens 'were either killed or wounded in the trouble at Dublin on Sunday last', Bryan replied two days later that no report had been received by the State Department from the US consul at Dublin with reference to the trouble. He felt sure that if any Americans had been killed or wounded the consul would have cabled the department immediately.[88] In this case, the Wilson administration relied on the efficiency of the US consul in Dublin, Edward Adams. Adams, a former newspaper editor, had entered the service aged fifty-one years of age, and had been consul in Dublin since 1909. Unfortunately, by 1914 he was suffering from a nervous condition that led Consul General at Large Ralph Totten to note:

> This officer is a courteous gentleman but knows nothing at all of the routine or clerical work of a consulate. He cannot supervise the work nor does he know whether it is properly done or not ... The Consul was in such a physical condition at the time of inspection that the Inspector can only say he is interested in the office but is not prompt, active nor alert ... This officer should be given a long rest and then he might be able to take charge of a small office.

By late July 1914, the date of Totten's fourth inspection visit, Adams had apparently left every aspect of consular business in the hands of two subordinates and had 'lost all touch' with the work. During 1913 he had submitted to the State Department just seven reports instead of the thirty expected for a district of the size of Dublin.[89] It was not surprising, therefore, that he did not report on the Howth gun-running and subsequent deaths, but it was notable that neither Bryan

86 *FRUS*, 1914 supplement the world war, Frost to the Secretary of State, 31 July 1914, p. 58.
87 The conference broke down on 21 July and the British government decided on 23 July to permit any Ulster county to vote itself out of a Dublin-ruled political entity.   88 National Archives and Records Administration, Maryland (hereafter NARA), Records of the Department of State relating to internal affairs of Great Britain, 1910–29, Record Group 59 (hereafter RG59), M580/6, 841.00/01, Gallivan to Bryan, 29 July 1914; ibid., Bryan to Gallivan, 31 July 1914. On 17 July 1914, Richard Westacott, vice and deputy consul general had forwarded a copy of the London *Times* of 16 July 1914 containing a political map of Ireland which showed the 'position and relative political strength of the opposing parties.' Ibid., 841.00/9, Westacott to Bryan, 17 July 1914.   89 NARA, RG59, Inspector's report foreign service personnel (hereafter IRFSP), Dublin, Ireland, 28 February, 5 November 1914.

nor Wilson pursued the matter. When Wilson did react to events in Ireland, it was in late August and his views on the impending crisis in Irish affairs were shaped more by his belief in democracy than by the information available to him from State Department officials, newspapers or Irish-American politicians thereby setting a pattern of personalized policy-making on Ireland.

Edward Carson's statement, after the passage of the home rule bill in the House of Lords in summer 1914, when he said, 'we solemnly and mutually pledge ourselves not to recognise its authority. I do not care two pence whether this is treason or not' gained nation-wide attention in newspapers. When Wilson heard about it, Tumulty recalled his 'passionate resentment' and his words:

> I would like to be in Mr Asquith's place. I would show this rebel [Carson] whether he would recognise the authority of the government or flaunt it. He ought to be hanged for treason. If Asquith does not call this gentle-man's bluff, the contagion of unrest and rebellion in Ireland will spread until only a major operation will save the Empire ... If those in authority in England will only act firmly now, their difficulties will be lessened.

Wilson was certain that a little of Andrew Jackson's 'firmness' and 'courage' in handling the Ulster unionists would settle the Irish question immediately.[90] This response would have been welcomed by many nationalist Irish-Americans as would his privately expressed view to Tumulty that 'there never can be real comradeship between America and England until this [Irish] issue is definitely settled and out of the way.'[91] His criticism of the Ulster unionists and hopes for a settlement of the Irish question would soon be tested. In the short term Wilson had to respond to the outbreak of war in Europe and his foreign service had to implement that policy throughout Europe.

*

Wilson's path to the presidency was not trouble-free, but he did have certain advantages and came along at a propitious time. Sixteen years of Republican gov-ernment combined with a divided Republican camp ensured that this scholarly, serious man of probity offered the perfect option for Democratic voters and also for some disaffected Republicans, as suggested by the electoral college vote. For most Irish-American voters who were aligned to the Democratic side his candi-dacy was attractive because of his support for Irish home rule which seemed imminent. However, just as his innate beliefs made him sympathetic to the unjustness of the Irish position within the British empire, his views on 'American-ism' made him critical of the 'hyphenate' element in US society and he admired

90 Tumulty, *Woodrow Wilson as I knew him*, p. 397.   91 Ibid., pp. 392–7; Carroll, *American opin-ion*, p. 19.

the British parliamentary system. The repeal of the Panama Canal tolls had illustrated this paradoxical position and pointed up future tensions. Despite Wilson's annoyance towards the Irish-American agitators on that issue, he was critical of the Ulster unionists and his support for a constitutional solution to the Irish question remained intact.

The president, who did not expect to have to deal with foreign affairs during his tenure, had to formulate a response to the British declaration of war on Germany on 4 August 1914. But it would fall to the US foreign service representatives on the ground in Ireland and elsewhere, to deal with the every day consequences of the war in which they found themselves. A complicating factor for the Irish-based consuls was the radicalization of Irish nationalism.

CHAPTER THREE

Wilson, neutrality and Ireland, 1914–1917

There were many levels and layers to Wilson's Irish policy during the war. At the highest level within the White House diplomacy involved Woodrow Wilson, Edward House, Joseph Tumulty and the State Department, where William Bryan and subsequently, Robert Lansing presided. Another layer in Wilson's approach to Ireland was made up of their contacts with representatives of all shades of Irish political opinions in the guise of the Irish-American organizations, other US opinion, and individuals and groups based in Ireland. Then there were the United States diplomatic and consular representatives in Ireland, and indeed Britain, who implemented policy and dealt with the routine business of the protecting and promoting US interests in Ireland. There was also the Washington/London axis mentioned previously.

While the causes of world war one are not of direct concern to this study, their implications were of significance for America's formal and informal relationship with Ireland.[1] Wilson was guided by two influences. Firstly, he believed in American 'exceptionalism' and secondly, there was his concept of US national security. As the war unfolded, the president identified two external threats to this latter idea; balance of power politics in general and, specifically Germany's power. To him the situation looked like a 'a natural raking out of the pent-up jealousies and rivalries of the complicated politics of Europe.'[2] However, over time he felt that 'nothing in particular started it but everything in general.'[3]

---

1 These questions still loom large in historiography, not least because of the publication of *The papers of Woodrow Wilson* edited by A.S. Link during the past thirty years. The following have also contributed to the debate A.S. Link, *Woodrow Wilson: revolution, war and peace* (1979); L.E. Ambrosius, *Wilsonian statecraft: theory and practice of liberal internationalism during world war I* (1991); Ibid., *Woodrow Wilson and the American diplomatic tradition: the treaty fight in perspective* (1987); F.S. Calhoun, *Power and principle: armed intervention in Wilsonian foreign policy* (1986); J.M. Cooper, Jr., *The warrior and the priest: Woodrow Wilson and Theodore Roosevelt* (1983); D.M. Esposito, *The legacy of Woodrow Wilson: American war aims in world war I* (1996); R.A. Kennedy, 'Woodrow Wilson, World War I, and an American conception of national security', 1–31; T. Knock, *To end all wars: Woodrow Wilson and the quest for a new world order* (1992); N.G. Levin, Jr., *Woodrow Wilson and the world politics: America's response to war and revolution* (1968); C. Schwabe, *Woodrow Wilson, revolutionary Germany and peacemaking, 1918–19* (1985); T. Smith, *America's mission: the United States and the worldwide struggle for democracy in the twentieth century* (1994). 2 Kennedy, 'Woodrow Wilson', p. 1. 3 A.S. Link (ed.), *The papers of Woodrow Wilson* (hereafter *PWW*), 69 vols (1966–94), 30, p. 462.

Wilson's response to the outbreak of world war one

On 3 August 1924, German troops crossed the Belgian border and the British government issued an ultimatum to the German government demanding the maintenance of Belgian neutrality. The ultimatum expired at eleven o'clock that night and on the following day Britain declared war on Germany.[4] Soon the central powers, consisting of Germany, Austria–Hungary and Turkey, faced the allied powers of Britain, France, Russia and, from 1915, Italy.

None of the State Department foreign representatives located in Europe transmitted any specific warning about the imminence of war to Washington. US Consul Frank Mallet, based in Budapest, sent a report on 13 July stating that the view prevailed in Hungary that war between Austria–Hungary and Serbia was unavoidable. But consuls do not send high priority political reports and, therefore, his warnings were not heeded.[5] Consequently, it was not until 28 July, when Bryan read a despatch from US Ambassador Myron Timothy Herrick in Paris urging Wilson to offer to negotiate, that the seriousness of the situation in Europe was appreciated. Once Wilson heard of Herrick's warning, he asked Bryan to instruct Ambassador Page in London to inquire of the British government whether US intervention was acceptable. Page answered in the negative; nonetheless Wilson did send a message on 4 August to US representatives in all the European capital cities offering to mediate.[6] But it was too late for US good offices to make a difference and on the same day as the British war announcement, Wilson announced that the US would observe neutrality in the conflict. Two weeks later Wilson urged Americans to be 'neutral in fact as well as in name ... impartial in thought as well as in action.'[7] Wilson's declaration reflected public opinion.[8] Tumulty believed that Wilson 'as a profound student of history ... saw with a clear vision the necessity of neutrality and of America remaining disentangled in every way from the embroilments of Europe.'[9] There were other factors also: the geographical and psychological isolation already integral to the American tradition, competitive commercial forces and Wilson and his advisers' wish to negotiate. But in addition he was mindful of the immigrant support base that, as indicated previously, had rowed in behind him during the presidential election. In a country where one in three persons was either foreign born or first generation and presumably still had strong ties with the old country, the issue of allegiance remained a destabilising influence. Small calculates that as much as twenty per cent of the US population was strongly pro-German because of their links to the old world. The depth of this bias could be questioned but the real-

4 M. Gilbert, *Churchill: a life* (1991), pp. 264–75.   5 G.H. Stuart, *The Department of State: a history of its organizations, procedure and personnel* (1949), pp. 233–4.   6 Stuart, *The Department of State*, pp. 233–4.   7 Quoted in W. LaFeber, *The American age: United States foreign policy at home and abroad since 1750* (1989), p. 285.   8 A.S. Link, *Wilson the diplomatist: a look at his major foreign policies* (1965), p. 33: A.J. Ward, *Ireland and Anglo-American relations, 1899–1921* (1969), p. 85.   9 J. Tumulty, *Woodrow Wilson as I know him* (1922), p. 225.

ity of an immigrant vote, compared to the ambivalent attitude towards Britain, whereby anglophobia existed beside anglophilism, left Wilson with little room for manoeuvre.[10] On the day of his neutrality declaration in August 1914, he told Tumulty that the 'various racial groups in America will seek to lead us now one way and then another. We must sit steady in the boat and bow our heads to meet the storm.'[11] Any other stance might have undermined his presidential and party position, particularly with congressional elections due in November, and might have emphasized the many fault-lines in US society.

How did Irish-America react to Wilson's decision? Many factors influenced the response. Firstly, there was the Democratic Party, secondly, the Catholic Church and thirdly, the community's political organizations. The majority of nationalist Irish-Americans were not members of Irish-American political organizations but their loyalty to the Democratic Party kept them behind Wilson's policy of neutrality at least until the sinking of the *Lusitania* in early May 1915 and the British government's ordering of the executions of the leaders of the Easter rising in 1916 forced them to rethink their position. The war seemed remote to most Americans until early 1915 and it impinged little on their day-to-day lives but both events shook Irish-American Democrats' faith in neutrality, and indeed their tenuous support for Wilson, in different ways, as will be seen. However, in 1914, Irish-America's support for Wilson was not surprising because, as Patrick Ford, editor of the popular *Irish World* for over forty years, commented, the typical Irish-Americans were 'notably patriotic, democratic and intensely loyal to American institutions.'[12] Moreover, as Thomas B. Fitzpatrick, secretary of the pro-Redmond United Irish League of America (UILA), noted in late 1914, 'it is ... generally assumed that this great cause, called the 'Irish Question' is virtually settled', a view shared by Wilson.[13] Mainstream newspapers reflected the widespread support for neutrality and the public were soon fed propaganda about events in Europe from British, French and German undercover organizations.[14] William McAdoo, secretary of the Treasury, recalled that by the end of 1914 British publicity efforts in the US were most successful, as their agents operating out of New York, 'managed to create an impression that the Germans were barbarians ... and managed to make a large part of the American people believe that German soldiers had cut off the hands of Belgian children ... [and were] boiling the bodies of their own dead soldiers to produce fats.'[15] The campaign was greatly assisted by the release in December 1914 of

---

10 M. Small, *Democracy and diplomacy: the impact of domestic politics on US foreign policy, 1789–1994* (1996), p. 42.   11 Tumulty, *Wilson as I know him*, pp. 225–8; Ward, *Ireland and Anglo–American relations*, p. 85.   12 Quoted in T.J. Rowland, 'Strained neutrality: Irish-American Catholics, Woodrow Wilson, and the *Lusitania*', 59–60.   13 National Library of Ireland (NLI), John Redmond Papers (hereafter JRP), MS15524, Thomas B. Fitzpatrick to Redmond, 23 November 1914.   14 See H.C. Peterson, *Propaganda for war: the campaign against American neutrality, 1914–17* (1939).   15 W.G. McAdoo, *Crowded years: the reminiscences of William G. McAdoo* (1931), p. 322.   16 Peterson, *Propaganda for war*, p. 53.

the report compiled by James Bryce's committee which dealt with the atrocities in Belgium.[16]

Such propaganda may have been effective during the early days of the war but the response of the majority of Irish-Americans was influenced by another factor: religion. Most Catholics faced a dilemma because, as British Ambassador Spring Rice identified, the attitude of the Catholic Church was 'problematical'. On the one hand, the papacy evinced a position of strict neutrality.[17] Moreover, the Catholic hierarchy in the US, particularly cardinals Gibbons and O'Connell and Archbishop Ireland, promoted the message of loyalty and steadfastness to the state among all American Catholics above all else, including the cause of Irish freedom.[18] These pro-allies messages were revealed in their Catholic newspapers, the power of which could not be underestimated. Although British officials believed that an anti-British sentiment was integral to Catholic America, the Catholic press was not considered party political. Among the more important Catholic press outlets existing in 1914 was the weekly review, *America*. It was edited by the New York based Jesuit Richard H. Tierney and had a circulation of 25,000. After the outbreak of the war, it adopted an anti-German position in support of Catholic Belgium although it changed this to one of 'intense anti-British' over time, as it came to support the establishment of an 'Irish republic.' British officials considered that *America* editorials carried 'an amount of finality in most matters among Catholics' and during the early stage of the war, Tierney refused to admit any German propaganda whatever into the office, ordering the destruction of copies of *The king, the kaiser and Irish freedom*, a book written by James K. McGuire in support of Irish freedom. The *New World*, the official organ of the archbishop of Chicago, Monsignor Mundelein, was also considered 'quite friendly' to the allies; it had a circulation of 25,000 in February 1920. The *Baltimore Catholic Review*, the official organ of Cardinal Gibbons, which had a circulation of 50,000, was fully behind Wilson's neutrality and 'at no time carried an attack on England.' These influential outlets and others supported Wilson's war policy. Yet, while American Catholics as 'good Americans' were united behind Wilson in 1914, British officials acknowledged:

> It can hardly be hoped that they will forget at once how they have been taught to regard England as the oppressor of Ireland; France as the country which expelled the religious orders and banished Christian teaching from the schools; Italy as the usurper of the patrimony of the Holy See; Portugal as the oppressor of the Catholic Church, and Russia as the hereditary enemy of Catholicism.[19]

---

17 S. Gwynn (ed.), *The letters and friendships of Sir Cecil Spring Rice: a record*, 2 vols (1929), i, p. 260.   18 K. Bourne & D.C. Watt (general eds), *British documents on foreign affairs* (hereafter *BDFA*), part ii, series c, North America, 25 vols (1986–95), vii, The American press, 1920–22, Catholic papers in America, February 1920.   19 *BDFA*, vii, Catholic papers in America, February 1920.

In addition there were pro-German voices within the US hierarchy at the outset of the war; for example, Dr Messmer, archbishop of Milwaukee, who believed that German actions against Belgium were deserved, was in the forefront of opposition to Wilson and neutrality and the bishops of Wheeling and Oklahoma, had little sympathy for the allied cause.[20] Thus, while the moderate, Irish-American, Catholic majority followed the leadership of Wilson, Gibbons and Ireland, a minority of republican Irish-American Catholics did not. They provide a third strand to Irish-America's response to neutrality.

In 1914, most ethnic communities in the US were not organized and did not have structures through which to influence politicians, but most quickly learnt how to do so. The opportunity to influence Wilson's post-war peace plans and resolve their respective national problems, led them, in late 1914 and into 1915, to meet, select leaders, set out their post-war aims, publicize their programmes and establish contact with the US administration. The Zionists, the Slovaks, the Czechs and the south Slavs came into this category but the Irish and Germans were in a different category and were well-organized and experienced in the lobbying and propaganda game, whether or not they had been successful.[21] The chief Irish-American political organizations in summer 1914 were Clan na Gael and the United Irish League of America. Until the outbreak of the war, the two groups had been declining in size but in August 1914 Clan na Gael with Joseph McGarrity as a member of its executive committee, shared the Irish Republican Brotherhood's (IRB) view that 'England's difficulty is Ireland's opportunity.' It had been subsidizing the IRB with £350 annually since 1905, and on the outbreak of war the Clan leadership in the US, John Devoy and Daniel Cohalan, acted to realize the Brotherhood's plans for a rising in Ireland against British rule. Immediately they reverted to their traditional strategy of internationalizing the Irish question and hoping to reap the benefits from strategic alliances with the German-American community and representatives of the German government. Count Johann von Bernstorff, German ambassador in the US, wrote that during the first few months of the war, Dr Dernberg, a German agent's 'connection with Irish leaders' laid the foundation for co-operation which in 1915 was of 'great' importance to Germany's position in the US. He felt that if his government had given more 'intelligent backing' to the tie, it might have been 'more fruitful still.'[22] Such co-operation between the two communities was not unknown before 1914. Despite differences, both sides effectively opposed the Hay–Pauncefote arbitration treaties and Wilson's Panama Canal repeal bill. John

20 Ibid., Catholic papers in America, January 1920; ibid., Catholic papers in America, February 1920. 21 J.P. O'Grady, 'Introduction' in J.P. O'Grady, The immigrant's influence on Wilson's peace policies (1967), pp. 3–6. 22 Count J. Bernstorff, My three years in America (1920), p. 47; T.J. Noer, 'The American government and the Irish question during world war 1', 97. Joseph McGarrity emigrated from county Tyrone in 1892 and a 'hatred of the landlord, of the police and of the soldiers', imbibed his views and work in Clan na Gael in the US. K. Miller, Emigrants and exiles: Ireland and the Irish exodus to north America (1985), p. 469.

Quinn, the moderate Irish-American, regarded war time co-operation as a continuation of the previous relationship.[23]

The shelving of Irish home rule on the outbreak of war in August 1914 and John Redmond's call to arms in September reinvigorated Clan na nGael. Buoyed by the belief that Redmond was selling out to the Liberal government in London, it aligned itself with the National German-American Alliance, which had two million members and was the largest ethnic minority organization in the US, to show common cause. From August 1914 until April 1917, meetings were held every week in Irish and German centres to express sympathy for the Germans, protest against British imperialism and militarism and insist that America be neutral 'in fact as well as in principle.'[24] These messages and hostility towards Wilson were reinforced using the machinery of propaganda and agitation in Congress. By October 1914, therefore, Clan na Gael's activities were bearing fruit and newspapers such as *Irish Voice*, *Irish Review*, *Irish Press* and *Irish World* collectively reported that Germany was only fighting a defensive war against Britain for freedom of the seas. Wilson and the mainstream US press were criticized for misrepresenting the war to the US public and every government decision was interrogated for evidence of unneutral views.[25] The campaign intensified during the winter months of 1914.

One indicator of the increased significance of Clan na Gael's activities was the attempt in early August 1914 by Gloster Armstrong, a British agent based in New York and later British consul general there, to recruit as paid informers, Liam Pedlar and James McGuinness, both members of Clan na Gael and associates of McGarrity. Armstrong expanded on the work in a letter to Pedlar on 9 February 1915: 'I want you to send me a complete list of the clubs ... names, the numbers and as far as possible the officers of each, the places and dates of the meeting and indicate what ones besides your own you are in a habit of visiting. Making this list as complete as possible.' Pedlar and McGuiness' replies were dictated by McGarrity and Pedlar was eventually recruited by Armstrong who sent him $60 as a first payment on 15 February.[26] Pedlar worked for both sides but there were other British-paid spies, both detected and undetected, within the Clan ranks. This evidence of illegal allied activities in the US provided McGarrity with evidence of US government co-operation with the British government.

Clan na Gael's response to the war took a further form which became of direct concern to the Wilson administration. A few weeks after the war began a com-

23 NLI, John Quinn Papers (hereafter JQP), MS18436, Quinn, 'In the matter of Sir Roger Casement and the Irish situation in America', 2 June 1916, p. 2; F.M. Carroll, *American opinion and the Irish question, 1910–23: a study in opinion and policy* (1978), p. 48; NLI, JQP, MS18436, Quinn, 'In the matter of Sir Roger Casement and the Irish situation in America', 2 June 1916, p. 2.   24 Ward, *Ireland and Anglo-American relations, 1899–1921*, p. 89; Carroll, *American opinion*, p. 47.   25 The *Gaelic American* was another vigilant newspaper. M. MacLoughlin, 'Nationalism and world war one' in M. Glazier (ed.), *The encyclopedia of the Irish in America* (1999), pp. 652–3.   26 NLI, Joseph McGarrity Papers (hereafter JMcGP), MS17482, Armstrong to McGuinness, 10 August 1914, Armstrong to Pedlar, 3, 9, 15, 19 February 1915, McGarrity to Pedlar, 3 February 1915.

mittee of the Clan met with von Bernstorff and his military attaché, Franz von Papen, in the German Club in New York, to ask for arms and technical advice in support of a rising in Ireland. They explained that this would divert British troops from the continental war-theatre and it would be in Germany's interests. John Devoy recalled that von Bernstorff listened with 'evident sympathy' and requested time to consider the proposal but the former was pessimistic. Devoy decided to enlist the help of Roger Casement, a founder of the Irish Volunteers and distinguished British diplomat, who was in the US fund-raising to buy arms for the Volunteers and to persuade the 'temperamentally Anglophile' German diplomat of their plan. Casement wrote a number of memoranda on the subject and visited the German embassy in Washington in late September, where he suggested that Irish troops in the British army who had been captured by German soldiers might be persuaded to change their allegiance. The idea appealed to von Bernstorff who recommended to the German Foreign Office, 'falling in with Irish wishes, provided that there are really Irishmen prepared to help us. The formation of an Irish legion from Irish prisoners would be a grand idea, if it could only be carried out.' Buoyed by this success, the Clan also funded Casement's mission to Germany in October 1914 to persuade the German government to issue a declaration supporting Irish self-determination and the establishment of an Irish brigade in German prisoner of war camps.[27]

While the outbreak of war and the opportunity to achieve an Irish republic through a rising reinvigorated Clan na Gael's leadership, the United Irish League of America was thrown into confusion. It had been fully behind John Redmond's home rule campaign but on 17 September 1914, Redmond wrote to the Philadelphia lawyer, Michael J. Ryan who was national president of the League:

> events have developed so rapidly here that it is very difficult to keep up with them ... The Home Rule bill will receive Royal assent tomorrow ... we have been able ourselves to supply several thousands of rifles; but we want tons of thousands more ... the general sentiment of our people is unquestionable on the side of England in this war ... I feel certain that in a short time there will be a large recruiting all over the country ... The truth is, the only way in which we can make sure of arming and drilling properly a sufficient force to make sure that that at the end of the war we will have a real Irish army is though the War Office and the British army.[28]

But the simultaneous suspension of the home rule bill for the duration of the war and Redmond's call to arms combined to split the Irish Volunteers, damaged the UILA's confidence in Redmond and lost him the support of the *Irish*

27 B. Inglis, *Roger Casement* (1973), pp. 266–9. M.F. Funchion (ed.), *Irish American voluntary organizations* (1983), p. 86; S. Cronin, *The McGarrity papers: revelations of the Irish revolutionary movement in Ireland and America 1900–1940* (1972), pp. 50–1. 28 NLI, JRP, MS15254, Redmond to Ryan, 17 September 1914.

World. As early as 28 September Thomas B. Fitzpatrick, UILA secretary, informed Redmond that it would be difficult to collect money for arms for the Irish Volunteers who were defending the British government 'against its foes now in the field.'[29] A few weeks later, Redmond lost the support of individuals within the UILA leadership. For example, Ryan was a candidate for the governorship of a state with many German voters. Edward Gallagher felt that it would be too much to ask him 'after all he has done, to sacrifice his political future by a plain statement in favour of sending Irish recruits to war.'[30] Fearing a permanent split in the UILA, the remaining leadership agreed to defer the upcoming convention. Redmond's decision left it vulnerable to constant attack from the *Irish World* and the *Gaelic American*, from Clan na Gael and from more militant organizations such as the Friends of Irish Freedom (FOIF) and the Irish Progressive League (IPL). Not only had Clan na Gael made contact with German diplomats but it had allied with the German-American societies' to demand the strict enforcement of neutrality.[31] Wilson's fears, and those of British officials, that the war would emphasize divisions in US society came true.

Nonetheless, in the immediate aftermath of the announcement of neutrality Spring Rice was impressed by the 'very friendly feeling' in the US towards Britain and its 'strong' anti-German sentiment.[32] While the majority of Irish-Americans may not have felt such extreme sentiments, many would have agreed with House's opinion in September 1914 that 'for the present American sympathy was strongly with the Allies.'[33] For many Irish-American home rulers, such as John Quinn, the onset of the war 'changed everything. Thoughtful Irishmen in this country who believed that Ireland's destiny was linked with England's felt that Irishmen should be loyal to England in the war.'[34] Moderate Irish-Americans had faced a dilemma but most supported the allied cause because of their Americanism and their belief that such support would bring rewards for Ireland.

The State Department and formulation of neutrality

Between August 1914 and April 1917, the Wilson administration pursued, in theory at least, a policy of neutrality and it fell to State Department officials located in Washington and in the field to implement that policy. According to Lansing, the State Department was 'amply equipped' for its work in times of peace but when the war broke out it was forced to reorganize immediately to meet the

---

29 Ibid., Thomas B. Fitzpatrick to Redmond, 28 September 1914.   **30** Ibid., Edward J. Gallagher to Redmond, 5 November 1914.   **31** Ibid., P.T. Barry to Jordan, 29 October 1914; ibid., Edward J. Gallagher to Redmond, 5 November 1914; ibid., Ryan to Redmond, 13 November 1914; ibid., John G. Coyle to Redmond, 11 November 1914.   **32** Gwynn, *The letters and friendships of Sir Cecil Spring Rice*, ii, Spring Rice to Grey, 25 August 1914.   **33** Ibid., Spring Rice to Grey, ii, 22 September 1914.   **34** NLI, JQP, MS18436, Quinn, 'In the matter of Sir Roger Casement and the Irish situation in America', 2 June 1916, pp. 6–7.

changed conditions and the enormous increase of its business. For the officials in Washington the war immediately increased the burden of every-day work and added new demands. At the outbreak of war, the State Department received some sixty thousand inquiries regarding the location and welfare of Americans in Europe which had to be answered and arrangements had to be made for their protection and/or repatriation. Moreover, banking credits had disappeared and telegraphic communication was uncertain. To assist stranded Americans in Europe, Congress passed a joint resolution appropriating $2.75 million for the relief, protection and transportation of American citizens in war zones. Lines of credit were established in the various European countries and the funds were administered by the State Department through its foreign representatives abroad who could draw on them. The Department became 'the diplomatic clearing-house of the world, as well as the banker, transportation agent, and medium of communication for Americans abroad.'[35] Dealing with this increased workload led to the hasty establishment of new bureaus and additional, often inexperienced, recruits were taken on. The staff in Washington, which had numbered 210 in 1909, grew to 714 by 1921. During the war years officials worked days, nights and Sundays. Lansing continued 'things have to be *done*, not studied these days. The motto, "*do it now*" is not a piece of advice in the department of State. It is a *command*.' Consequently, the customary slow and dignified ways of diplomacy were replaced by this 'touch and go' method which was decidedly innovatory and compelled change in the diplomatic machine.[36]

In late summer and autumn 1914, while organizing itself to cope with the increased demands, the State Department worked out the technical details of preserving US neutrality and the Joint State and Navy Neutrality Board was established by Wilson to advise departments on 'the correct interpretation of international law.'[37] During 1914 and early 1915, it fell to Lansing to oversee the legal aspects of neutrality, but he often had a wider remit because Bryan was not only still obsessed with finalizing his arbitration treaties but was also absent from Washington on speaking tours during the congressional election campaigns.[38] Lansing was well aware of the limitations of his situation and in 1925 recalled to Wilbur Carr that Wilson 'hated lawyers, did not think like a lawyer, cared nothing for facts, easily laid down principles ... and when his mind was made up nothing would move him.' Neither did Lansing have much time for Tumulty who 'never told them anything.'[39] Wilson treated Lansing as a clerk but valued

35 Stuart, *The Department of State*, p. 244; 'Editorial comment, Robert Lansing, the Department of State and the war–admission to the diplomatic service', 479–80.   36 'Editorial comment, Robert Lansing, the Department of State and the war–admission to the diplomatic service', 479; H. De Santis & W. Heinrichs, 'United States of America: the Department of State and American foreign policy' in Z. Steiner (ed.), *Foreign ministries of the world* (1982), p. 579.   37 Link, *Wilson the diplomatist*, p. 37.   38 L.W. Koenig, *Bryan: a political biography of William Jennings Bryan* (1971), p. 538.   39 Library of Congress (hereafter LC), Wilbur Carr Papers (hereafter WCP), Box 3, diary 1925, 20 January 1925.

his legal training very highly, particularly when it came to defining and maintaining neutrality. In February 1915, he outlined the implications of the decision to remain neutral:

> neutral nations have had to meet a series of problems ... The liability of error, the danger of unintentional impartiality, and the constant complaint of one or another of the belligerents make the path of neutrality rough and uncertain.[40]

In the absence of a recognized rule of law, he had to create a rule based not only on using the fundamental principles of law but also from his own knowledge and having due regards to the facts of the situation. In this context, therefore, from August 1914 onwards, Lansing recognized that British naval superiority, particularly the blockade of the German ports in the North Sea, would shape US neutrality.[41]

The State Department was immediately given first-hand notice of the preparedness of the British navy in the Atlantic region from Wesley Frost, US consul at Queenstown, county Cork. On 31 July 1914, he wrote that on the previous day the British Admiralty had taken over control of Queenstown harbour and its approaches with the support of the military. Other major centres of British naval and military strength in Ireland, Lough Swilly in county Donegal and Berehaven in Bantry Bay further along the Cork coastline, were being fortified 'to control and protect the transatlantic shipping in the event of a general European war.'[42] By February 1915 the British navy had mined the North sea (thus removing any possibility of a German invasion of Ireland) and had blockaded the sea routes between Germany and neutral Sweden and the Dutch and Danish coastlines. All possible routes by which supplies could reach Germany were closed off. London had also extended the number of articles described as contraband and liable to seizure and confiscation from 12 in August 1914, to 26 in late October, 29 in December and 37 in March 1915. Not only was trade with Germany and Austria effectively ended but US ships engaged in commerce with neutral countries were intercepted and taken into British ports where cargoes were confiscated, sometimes on only the presumption that the goods were intended for Germany.[43]

While the British maritime system probably contravened international law, the reality of British power, Wilson's unwillingness to force matters and the need to appease US business interests by replacing lost axis markets with allied ones, led to America becoming an 'Allied warehouse', from which munitions, food,

---

40 'Editorial comment, Robert Lansing, the Department of State and the war–admission to the diplomatic service', 478–8.   41 R. Lansing, *War memoirs of Robert Lansing: secretary of State* (1935), p. 120.   42 *Papers relating to the foreign relations of the United States* (hereafter *FRUS*), 1914 supplement the world war (1928), Frost to Washington, 31 July 1914, pp. 59–60. See A. McIvor, *A history of the Irish naval service* (1994), p. 37.   43 Lansing, *War memoirs*, p. 121; A.S. Link et al., *American epoch: a history of the United States since 1900 volume 1: 1900–1945*, 2 vols (1987), i, p. 118.

and other vital war supplies flowed. Throughout the period, US trade with Germany and Austria declined while US trade with the allies increased.[44] The pro-British Lansing had drafted the US response to the British blockade, asserting US neutral rights but also recognizing the right of British ships to stop and search neutral ships suspected of carrying contraband to the central powers. Obviously the policy worked to Britain's advantage.[45]

Yet, whatever their personal feelings, Lansing, House and Wilson had to balance the reality of British naval supremacy without appearing to stray from the path of neutrality. As early as 25 August, Spring Rice reassured Grey:

> All the State Department are on our side except Bryan who is incapable of forming a settled judgement on anything outside party politics. The President will be with us by birth and upbringing, but he is very much in the hands of some of our worst enemies, and his name is rather compromised by the Panama affair. He will have to be rather conspicuously neutral, and that he is trying to be.[46]

Among the enemies that Spring Rice was referring to were the vocal Irish-American elements who were still incensed with the president over the Panama Canal tolls issue. Spring Rice accurately gauged the extent of Wilson's dilemma and saw how important it was for him to appear to be meticulously pursuing neutrality, particularly during autumn 1914. Pressure on the White House from the Irish-American and German-American radical political organizations and from every other Wilson critic intensified during this period. Indeed, with the congressional elections looming in November, Tumulty broached the subject of the British blockade with Wilson. He outlined 'the use our enemies were making of his patient action toward England.' Wilson replied that 'England is fighting our fight and you may well understand that I shall not, in the present state of the world's affairs, place obstacles in her way ... Let those who clamour for radical action against England understand that.' Wilson had little time for the senators and congressmen who were 'thinking only of German votes in their districts' and were not 'thinking of the world crisis that would inevitably occur should there be an actual breach between England and France over the [British] blockade.' For Wilson, the morality of the war predominated and Britain had to be given a chance to adjust to the 'great war crisis.'[47] Also he had ignored the hyphenates' propaganda campaigns on the grounds that he did not think they represented the majority of their respective communities, but it was more difficult to ignore the results of the election and the embargo campaign which was launched in early December 1914.[48]

44 Lansing, *War memoirs*, p. 121; Link et al., *American epoch*, i, p. 119.   45 LaFeber, *The American age*, pp. 285–6; Lansing, *War memoirs*, p. 112.   46 Gwynn, *The letters and friendships of Sir Cecil Spring Rice*, ii, Spring Rice to Grey, 25 August 1914.   47 Tumulty, *Woodrow Wilson*, pp. 230–1. 48 A.S. Link, *Wilson: the struggle for neutrality. 1914–1915* (1960), pp. 161.

Following the November election, Spring Rice had reported to Grey that Bryan had returned to the State Department and seemed pleased with the results. Wilson retained a majority in the House and the Senate but the House majority was reduced to thirty-five because of the reunion of the Republicans. Wilson and House were 'pleased with the result' also. But Spring Rice felt that 'the professional Democrat is not at all pleased and looks upon Wilson as a beaten man' and he worried that the Tammany Hall control of the House might be 'unfavourable' to the British.[49] Although Spring Rice's reports on the political strength of Irish-Americans were often contradictory, Tumulty supported this analysis. He recalled that this election result 'had dispirited Democratic friends throughout the country' and he was convinced that maintaining US neutrality would be central to winning the presidential election in 1916 as well as to out-manoeuvring Tammany Hall and gaining more votes from the agrarian voters in the west and the reformers in the eastern states.[50] Nonetheless, the extent of the apparent co-operation between the US and the allies drove the peace activists, as well as Irish-American and German-American activists, to demand the introduction of an embargo on the sale of war supplies and provision of financial aid to all the belligerents. Spring Rice felt, on 29 December, that while an embargo on contraband 'would be the best way to get at us', US economic interests would prove to be too influential with Wilson and Congress equally.[51] In January 1915, the American Independence Union was established, supported by Clan na Gael and Jeremiah O'Leary's American Truth Society along with the German-Irish Central Legislative Committee. Mass meetings were held throughout the country and resolutions sent to sympathetic congressmen to persuade the president to prohibit the export of arms and ammunition from US.[52] In the following weeks, not only was there substantial agitation in Congress but there was also considerable excitement throughout the country. The *Literary Digest* poll in January 1915 reported that 167 of 440 newspapers favoured the embargo and that those in the mid-west region heavily supported it.[53]

Wilson had to tread carefully and the State Department responded to the twenty charges of impartiality towards Germany and Austria listed by Senator William J. Stone, chairman of the Senate Foreign Relations Committee, in a letter to Bryan on 8 January 1915. The various grounds of the complaints centred firstly, on allied interference with US shipping, trading, communications and citizens, secondly, on US government tolerance of the allied land and sea campaigns and thirdly, on US government intolerance of similar axis activities.[54] The task

49 Gwynn, *The letters and friendships of Sir Cecil Spring Rice*, ii, Spring Rice to Grey, 13 November 1914.   **50** Tumulty, *Woodrow Wilson*, pp. 183–5; J.M. Blum, *Joe Tumulty and the Wilson era* (1951), p. 80.   **51** Gwynn, *The letters and friendships of Sir Cecil Spring Rice*, ii, Spring Rice to Valentine Chirol, 29 December 1914.   **52** For further on this see Ward, *Ireland and Anglo-American relations*, pp. 89–90; Link, *Wilson: the struggle for neutrality*, pp. 163–4; S. Hartley, *The Irish question as a problem in British foreign policy, 1914–18* (1987), p. 30.   **53** Ward, *Ireland and Anglo-American relations*, pp. 89–90.   **54** *FRUS*, 1914 supplement the world war, Stone to Bryan, 8 January 1915.

of compiling a reply fell to Lansing who, before the end of 1914, had already enunciated America's neutral rights on the matter of the British blockade of German ports. As mentioned above, he had also gone far towards recognizing Britain's right to stop and search neutral vessels carrying contraband goods. Lansing's reply, published in late January, rebutted each of the twenty charges point by point using sound international law and provided the case against the imposition of an embargo. His overall position was that the neutral US was entitled to trade freely in all goods but he concluded that it was the responsibility of the belligerent, not the neutral, to prevent any of these from reaching the enemy. The embargo struggle continued in Congress during February but eventually the resolutions were buried in committees or failed to get sufficient votes as amendments to other bills. This indicated the limits of the hyphenates' campaign to influence Wilson's foreign policy. Spring Rice was proved correct and the matter caused little comment in the Foreign Office. But the campaign's relative popularity in late 1914 and early 1915, forced the Wilson administration to use a cautious approach in the definition and prosecution of neutrality which favoured Britain more than Germany.[55]

Throughout 1915 and 1916, Lansing drafted further notes and messages of complaint to Britain and Germany for their transgressions of US neutrality, but he later admitted:

> I saw with apprehension the tide of resentment against Britain rising higher and higher in this country … I did all I could to prolong the disputes … by preparing … long and detailed replies and introducing technical and controversial matters in the hope that before the extended interchange of arguments came to an end something would happen to change the current of American public opinion or to make the American people perceive that German absolutism was a menace to the liberties and to democratic institutions everywhere.[56]

Lansing was convinced that the US would enter the war on Britain's side and his strategy appeared vindicated when, in February 1915, the Germans reacted to the tightening British blockade and announced a submarine campaign against allied and neutral ships.[57] The neutralist Bryan interpreted the German announcement as confirmation of his fears that America's impartiality would force Germany to act against it.[58] Whether or not Bryan's interpretation was accurate, as news

55 Link, *Wilson: the struggle for neutrality*, pp. 166, 185.   56 Lansing, *War memoirs*, p. 112. During this period, House appealed to Plunkett to ensure that the British press used its influence against government action that would harm the US cotton industry. House felt that any action would result in Congress retaliating. House's cable finished with 'The matter is of extreme urgency'. Plunkett forwarded the cable to Arthur Balfour who brought it to the attention of the government. NLI, Horace Plunkett Papers (hereafter HPP), P6584, reel 2 of 2, House to Plunkett, 20 July 1915; ibid., Plunkett to House, 20 July 1915; Ibid., 23 July 1915.   57 LaFeber, *The American age*, p. 286.   58

of American losses of life, cargo and ships filtered home, the hyphenates' propaganda campaigns came to be widely regarded as disloyal and treasonous and,
therefore, became less effective in White House circles. On 14 May, Wilson
directed William McAdoo, secretary of the Treasury, to use the US Secret
Service to act against 'violations of neutrality.' Immediately, they began to target the activities of the German embassy and McAdoo soon learnt that the
embassy was not the 'only source of illegitimate operations' in the US, although
he was convinced that von Bernstorff 'knew what was going on, even if he did
not personally have the directing hand.'[59] A few months later Wilson vested overall control of US espionage in the State Department, where Frank Polk supervised the gathering of intelligence, oversaw counter-espionage conducted by other
government intelligence agencies, investigated allegations of violations of US neutrality and kept in close touch with British intelligence in the US.

Colonel H.A. Packenham, who represented Military Intelligence section five
(MI5) of the British security service in the US, was based in the US Military
Intelligence Section in the War College in Washington and MI5 also directed
the Military Control office in New York. A further arm of the British intelligence network in the US resulted in William Wiseman, who had been wounded
in the war, being sent to New York in November 1915 to organize the US branch
of foreign intelligence unit of the War Office, MI1(c). 1. In January 1916, Major
Norman Thwaites, also wounded in the war, established the office and work
focused on:

> Contra-espionage: The investigation of suspects about whom the author-
> ities at home required information.
> Irish sedition: A general watch on the Irish movement in the United
> States, and investigation of suspects.
> Investigation into Hindu sedition in America.

In addition to the above, MI1(c) also undertook propaganda work until 1917,
when the US entered the war and Geoffrey Butler in the Foreign Office News
department took over. The services of the New York office of MI1(c) were also
used by the British embassy, the consul general in New York and all British missions in the US when they required confidential information or needed to have
investigations made in any part of the US.[60]

Not only was this network of British security and secret services personnel
active in the US but US spies were used also to keep an eye on the 'internal enemies of the British empire.'[61] Thus, on the one hand, Wilson would proclaim his

Koenig, *Bryan*, p. 539.   59 McAdoo, *Crowded years*, pp. 324–5.   60 Yale University Library,
Manuscripts and Archives Collections (hereafter YULMC), William Wiseman Papers (hereafter
WWP), box 6, file 175, 'New York office, section v and other activities', undated, probably, 1918.
61 National Archives and Records Administration, Maryland (hereafter NARA), Records of the

support for the principles of self-determination but on the other hand, his administration supported the allied empires in many ways. This US and British secret
service network combined with the 'Americanization' drives soon targeted disloyal and un-American behaviour, including an Irish involvement in the German
spy network which will be discussed later in this chapter.

Between August 1914 and May 1915, the Wilson administration gradually
formulated its neutrality policy. But it was the men in the US embassies, legations and consulates who were in the front line of the war and, according to
Lansing, were taxed beyond their capacity 'not only in caring for our people but
in caring for the interests of other nationals confided to them.'[62]

The state of preparedness in US foreign service offices in Ireland in 1914

Although Wilson mainly formulated and conducted his foreign policy with the
advice of his advisers rather than that of the State Department, his policy still
had to be implemented by the State Department men in the field. Consequently,
the quality of these representatives became significant. In Berlin, the Tammany
Hall connected James Gerard presided from 1913 until 1917. From the outset,
Wilson had little regard for him or confidence in him and eventually described
his pro-German ambassador as 'gullible and unreliable.'[63] Unlike Gerard, it was
Walter Page's friendship with Wilson that brought him the ambassadorial appointment to Britain in 1913. From when he arrived he worked hard for Anglo-
American friendship. Wilson's faith in Page and his effectiveness lasted longer
than it did in Gerard's case largely because the pro-British Page offered a stronger
possibility of bringing about peace.[64] Page and Robert Skinner, consul general,
were also in charge of the US consuls located in Ireland.

The 310 consular posts abroad were divided into 56 cities of capital importance where a consul general was based and 254 commercially important cities.
The posts were classified from one to eight and only two capitals, London and
Paris were served by consul generals of the highest class one, Skinner assumed
that position in London. The other consuls were graded according to the rated
importance of the places in which the US maintained consulates.[65] In Ireland, in

Department of State relating to internal affairs of Great Britain, 1910–29, Record Group 59 (hereafter RG59), M580/1, entry '20 September 1920'; R.J. Jones, *American espionage: from secret service to CIA* (1977), pp. 42, 45, 117.   **62** 'Editorial comment, Robert Lansing, the Department of
State and the war–admission to the diplomatic service', 489.   **63** J. Findling, *Dictionary of American
diplomatic history* (1990), p. 190.   **64** R. Gregory, *Walter Hines Page: ambassador to the Court of St
James* (1970), p. 158. Also in the embassy was Irwin Laughlin (first secretary), Chandler Anderson
(legal counsel), Colonel Squier (US military attaché), Robert Skinner (consul general) and Richard
Westacott (vice consul and deputy consul general).   **65** LC, WCP, Box 17, Bio. Mss. Dr Crane,
pp. 210, 211. Liverpool was the only city in the highest consular class one at a salary of $8,000,
Manchester the only one in class two at a salary of $6,000; the rest of the cities were grouped in

August 1914, the Cork post, actually based in Queenstown, was designated class eight, with a consuls' salary of $2,500 and a deputy and vice consul also present in the office. The Dublin post was class five, with a salary of $4,000 for the consul, who had the help of a vice consul while the Belfast posting had the highest rating at class three, with a salary of $5,000, and this also had a vice and deputy consul. There were four consular agents in Limerick, Galway, Ballymena and Londonderry who were not salaried and were remunerated by keeping the fees collected for services rendered.[66] In other words, these consular agents were still paid according to the pre-1906 method. Despite the introduction of salaries for consular officials they did not receive housing or other allowances.

In many ways the work of the consular officers could be more extensive than that of their diplomat counterparts. The responsibilities of the consular officer focused on promoting US trade and commerce within the district along with protecting the interests of US citizens. The work, therefore, divided into three main areas: firstly, administration, which focused on certifying incoming and outgoing US vessels, cargoes and crew, ensuring compliance with all commercial and health regulations, secondly, the development of contacts within the local commercial community to encourage the purchase of US manufactures and general trade extension and thirdly, the provision of assistance to US citizens, particularly seamen and tourists. Table 3.1 illustrates the extent of the work undertaken in US consular offices in Ireland in the pre-war years.

The major duties of the US consular staff in Ireland in 1914 related to trade and emigration. The Belfast office was the busiest of all, due to the extensive trade in textiles to the US from the district, while the Dublin staff were in demand for notary services, particularly authenticating emigrants' birth, marriage, death and property documents which could be used in US courts and businesses, and also for certifying food exports. In Queenstown, the work focused on issuing bills of health to outgoing vessels and emigration. But there may have been an under-reporting of trading links with the US because most of it was conducted through British ports and was, therefore, indirect. This work was conducted by twelve men who represented, protected and promoted US interests in Ireland throughout the war and, in the absence of an embassy, they became more involved in political and military affairs than had been the case since the American civil war.[67] In summer 1914 each office was visited by Ralph J. Totten, consul

classes three to nine, with eight cities in class three for which the salary was $5,000 and sixty-nine in class nine for which the salary was $2,000. In 1914, the salary for a secretary of state was $12,000, counsellor, $7,500, assistant Secretary of state, $4,500, chief of division, $2,100–$3,000, ambassador, $17,500, minister, $10,000, secretary of embassies and legations, $1,200–$3,000. *Register of the Department of State, January 1 1914* (1914), pp. 22–5.   66 NARA, RG59, Inspection reports on foreign service posts (hereafter IRFSP), Dublin, July 1914; ibid., Belfast, August 1914; ibid., Cork (Queenstown), July 1914; ibid., Limerick, July 1914; ibid., Londonderry, August 1914; ibid., Galway, July 1914.   67 B. Whelan, 'The consuls who helped sink a fleet: Union consuls in Ireland, intelligence and the American Civil War' (unpublished). The impact and involvement of US consular

Table 3.1

The nature and extent of US consular work in Ireland, 1913–14

	Invoices issued	Notarial services	Landing certificates	Bills of health issued	Sanitary reports	Extradition and protection cases	Pure-food certificates issued	Chinese visas	Seamen: shipped discharged deserted deceased relieved	Letters received	Letters sent
Belfast	8,115	467	0	23	51	0	273	0	0	1,472	1,728
Dublin	1,028	763	0	14	52	0	888	0	0	1,303	1,433
Cork	112	330	0	215	52	0	0	0	0	843	1,025
Limerick (agency)	126	283	0	3	0	0	114	0	0	277	314
Londonderry (agency)	124	140	0	71	0	0	9	0	0	393	585
Galway (agency)	57	152	0	0	0	1	4	0	0	0	175

Source: NARA, RG59, IRFSP, Dublin, July 1914; ibid., Belfast, August 1914; ibid., Cork (Queenstown), July 1914; ibid., Limerick, July 1914; ibid., Londonderry, August 1914; ibid., Galway, July 1914.

general at large, who was a member of a roving inspection corps dedicated to improving the efficiency and accountability of each office and officer.[68] His reports provide a useful insight into the state and ability of the US consular service in Ireland at the time.

The US was one of seven countries that had consular representation in Dublin in summer 1914. The others were Italy, France, Argentina and Persia. The German and Austro–Hungarian consulate offices were closed. Totten was the fourth inspector to visit the US consulate since Edward Adams had taken charge in 10 June 1909. Adams represented the classic consular type who entered the service at the age of fifty-one and was socially popular but inefficient and unprofessional. His past record showed some signs of this weak performance, as he had been appointed secretary of legation and consul general at Stockholm on 2 June 1902 and was promoted to consul general in 1906 but was afterwards awarded a consular post on 1 March 1909 and moved to Dublin. In 1914, Totten described him as a 'courteous gentleman but knows nothing at all of the routine or clerical work of a consulate. He cannot supervise the work nor does he know whether it is properly done or not.' Adams' disposition appears to have directly affected the work rate and office procedures as indicated in chapter two. Totten felt that although he was 'more than usually able to observe matters of political interest', he sent only seven instead of a minimum of thirty reports to the State Department in 1913. Letters and reports were not well researched and he gave little time or thought to extending US trade and commercial activity in the district. Unfortunately for Adams, his vice consul, Arthur Piatt, died in early 1914 and the latter's successor, John Claffey, did not make up for the consul's weaknesses. Claffey, a US citizen, was thirty-two and had entered the service a month prior to Totten's visit. He was not considered a 'very efficient officer' due to his lack of experience and of proper instruction in the job. Totten felt he had potential but a 'certain uncouthness of diction' and his 'grammar in conversation' needed remedying before he would become a 'good' officer. He concluded that Adams was interested in the office but was not 'prompt, active or alert ... seems to be suffering from a bad attack of nervous indigestion ... this officer should be given a long rest and then he might be able to take charge of a small office.' In addition, Totten recommended that the office hours should be extended and the 'poor' condition of the building and offices at 9 Leinster Street, should be improved; the 'importance of Dublin as a centre and as the capital of Ireland would seem to indicate that we should have better quarters.'[69]

The difficulties with Adams were all the more serious because of the 'social and political importance of the city as well as ... the importance of American

officers during the American civil war is the subject of a future study on the origins and development of the US consular service in Ireland from 1776 to 1913. 68 De Santis & Heinrichs, 'The Department of State and American foreign policy', p. 578. 69 NARA, RG59, IRFSP, Dublin, July 1914.

trade with the district.' Exports from the Dublin region to the US in 1913 were valued at $1,460,357 and comprised stout, mineral waters, whiskey, hides, ales, biscuits, oatmeal and gin. But Totten believed that 'almost nothing' was done for some time to extend the trading or commercial work and Adams was not aware of any US citizens engaged in business in Dublin. Imports consisted of watches, shoes, cash registers, typewriters, tobacco, Ford and Jackson cars, petroleum and oils. Totten felt that a good officer would exploit the trade and commercial opportunities, particularly as there was 'no prejudice against American manufacturers and many firms stock our goods' and there were openings for direct trade between the US and Dublin. Fortunately, Adams had detailed three US firms that operated in his district and six that handled US goods, but Totten felt it would take a 'well' man to do the work. While there was no ill-feeling against Adams, his lack of knowledge of his work was 'beginning to be remarked upon.' Totten recommended a rating of 'poor' for Adams' office and suggested that additional clerical assistance be recruited locally for the office and that one of the experienced consular assistants be sent to Dublin, so that Adams could take a much needed rest. This did not happen and the task of managing US interests in Dublin during the war remained with Adams and the inexperienced Claffey.[70]

The comparison with the Belfast consul and consulate could not have been greater. Hunter Sharp, US consul in Belfast, was visited by Totten four times between 1 February 1911 and 3 August 1914. The US was one of twenty-four countries with foreign consuls, vice consuls and consular agents present in Belfast but the only one with a professional consul. The others countries employed local individual such as ship owners, merchants and solicitors and in some cases several countries were represented by the same person. But Belfast was important to the US because it was the 'first city in Ireland in respect to manufactures and trade.'[71] Exports from Belfast to the US in 1913–14 were valued at $16,104,287 and consisted primarily of linen goods. This trade accounted for the much greater number of invoices issued by the Belfast office compared to that in Dublin as indicated in table 3.1. However, US interests in the district also extended to protecting US residents, enterprises and seamen. Nineteen citizens had registered with the consulate and there were branches of two insurance companies, three mercantile houses, one mercantile agency, a shoe store, and nine locally held agencies. The Belfast consuls did not have to look after shipped, discharged or deserted American seamen during the period. In addition to the above, the day-to-day business of issuing invoices, providing notarial services, bills of health, sanitary reports and pure-food certificates, answering letters and of returning goods purchased by local people directly from the US, was extensive.[72]

Overseeing the Belfast office at the 'convenient and central' location of 2 Wellington Place, and also the consular agency in Aberdeen, was Sharp, a career

---

70 Ibid.   71 NARA, RG59, IRFSP, Belfast, August 1914, p. 34.   72 Ibid., passim.

man with twenty years in the service, who was assisted by deputy consul Hugh Watson (a US citizen) and clerks Edward Harvey and Sophia Page, both British because Americans could not be secured for the compensation available. Totten concluded that Sharp 'has the ability and does maintain a very high standard of efficiency.' Unlike Adams, Sharp wrote all reports, part of the trade letters, received visitors and generally supervised the routine work of the office. Professionally, he was 'a credit to the service' and, it seemed, personally also. He played tennis and golf, was involved in the 'ordinary diversions of society' and was popular among the local community with a 'large acquaintance among the business men.' Totten continued ' the social life at this post consists to a great extent of the better class of business men so that all social intercourse is to advantage as leading to friendly relations with those able to assist in securing trade information.' Thus, it may have been that most of his professional and personal contacts were with the Protestant and Presbyterian élites who dominated the commercial life of the city and attendant social activities. Nevertheless, he was not expected to provide political reports but only trade ones and the office was rated as 'excellent' in August 1914.[73] Events soon revealed his political leanings.

Thirty-year old Wesley Frost, the consul responsible for the Cork district, entered the service with some competence in Spanish, French, and German and an interest in law and had previously been a consul at Charlottetown. When Totten visited he had been in charge since 16 May 1914. Totten rated him as 'one of the most earnest and efficient young officers of the service' because of the amount of work he had accomplished, the number of 'acquaintances and friends in both the business and official sets' he had made and the respect felt for him by Americans and foreigners in his district. The US consular office was based in the 'satisfactory' location of 1 Scott Square in Queenstown, where most of the other nineteen consuls were based also. Frost reckoned that the twenty-eight US citizens registered with the consulate were only about ten per cent of those living locally while many of the rest had allowed their citizenship to lapse. Totten considered it an important post and justified its existence on the basis of commercial possibilities and volume of emigration work. However, Totten and Frost believed that the office would be vastly more useful if located in Cork city rather than in Queenstown where no US commerce took place. Exports to the US from the district were valued at $117, 502.12 in 1913. Thus, the sole reason for its Queenstown location was 'convenience in handling the inspection of emigrants and issuance of bills of health.' But Totten noted that this subject had been covered in previous despatches to the department and he concluded that the matter could be left in abeyance which it was until after the war.[74] Lewis Thompson, Frost's vice consul, was twenty-nine years of age; a young man who had the 'right sort of service spirit' and was studying for the consular examinations. George Dawson, a British citizen, was the deputy consul, having been was

73 Ibid.   74 NARA, RG59, IRFSP, Cork (Queenstown), July 1914, passim.

appointed in August 1911; he was seventy-one years of age. His responsibilities related to disinfections and all matters relating to emigration and inspection and he acted for the American Bureau of Shipping of New York city.

A US consul was also responsible for the business of consular agencies within his district. Edmund Ludlow, a British citizen had been the consular agent in Limerick city since November 1896, and had his office in a 'rather dingy brick building' in 24 Glentworth Street. He was forty-seven and Totten considered Ludlow 'too busy with other matters to take the proper interest in the agency which I am afraid he looks upon as an advertisement for his ticket selling agency … has no idea of consular organization and I believe it would be difficulty to get him to properly keep his records or to follow instructions.' He had submitted a 'few' reports since 1911 and, while the district was not considered 'a very broad field for commercial reports' with $161,458 worth of exports to the US in 1913, Ludlow had made 'absolutely no effort to utilize the opportunities which existed.' But he was efficient, courteous and obliging to visitors, got on well with local people and the office offered important notarial services. Totten recommended that the decision on maintaining the office be made on the basis of Frost's recommendations. But Wilbur Carr did not wait and instructed Frost to sack Ludlow because he was using the consular agency to advance his private interests.[75] The latter was the ultimate transgression for the consular agents and a prime reason for the on-going reform of the consular service.

Another British citizen, Robert Tennant, was the consular agent in Galway. He had commenced duty on 4 May 1901 and his office, located at New Docks, was 'a bit dingy and unattractive in appearance' but Tennant was seen as a man of 'considerable intelligence and ability' who maintained a high standard of efficiency for an agency. He was well liked and respected in the community, knew all of the businessmen in his district and, while there were few opportunities for trade, had made some effort to inform himself of them. In 1913 exports from the district to the US were worth $134,413. Other 'close connections' to the US from the region resulted from, in Tennant's words, the 'exodus of peasantry to America' which produced much notarial work for him. So, while Galway had little or no economic importance for the US and 'scarcely justified' its consular presence, Totten felt that as there was 'a very efficient man, that is compared to other agents, and as the notarial work of the district is of considerable importance', the office should not be closed.[76]

Totten considered Londonderry, like the other agencies, 'an unimportant post'; exports to the US were only valued at $121,858 in 1913. Its existence was justified only by the fact that 75 bills of health were issued to departing steam-

75 NARA, RG59, IRFSP, Limerick, July 1914, passim; Ibid., Carr to Frost, 25 September 1914. Carr was director of the consular bureau. Frost was asked to nominate a suitable US citizen to succeed Ludlow even though Totten had advised that it would not be possible to get an American for the position due to the low remuneration.   76 Ibid., IRFSP, Galway, July 1914, passim.

ers and 208 notarial services were attended to in 1913–14. The consular agent, Philip O'Hagan, a British citizen with an office at 1 East Wall, began duty on 18 May 1908. He double jobbed, as did the other agents. But Totten concluded that O'Hagan, as a lawyer, was an 'intelligent man … his consular duties are relatively unimportant but he has a fairly good grasp of his duties'; he was quick at interpreting instructions, in regular contact with the Belfast consul and genuine in his loyalty to the department. Totten rated him 'good' and considered his work significant enough to merit the office's continued presence.[77]

The quality of the consuls in Ireland in 1914 varied and, even though the younger men had entered the service by examination with improved salaries and fees, some consuls had an inferiority complex. They did not have diplomatic immunity and their work was viewed as less prestigious than that of their diplomatic colleagues. However, in 1914 the consul's duties were expanded greatly, at least for those based in Europe. In Ireland, which was part of the war zone, and particularly in Queenstown, US consuls took on the role of diplomat and intelligence officer along with assisting, protecting and evacuating Americans and other nationals.[78]

Implementing neutrality and protecting US citizens in Ireland and elsewhere

From the onset of the war, US foreign representatives in Europe began to receive instructions from the State Department about prosecuting US neutrality. On 17 August Bryan reminded foreign service officers that the 'care and protection of US foreign interests in both peace and war' was based upon the 'consent' of both governments concerned and that this could be withdrawn. Consequently, the officials had to exercise 'the extra duties imposed upon you with candid impartiality.' Being neutral did not mean the exercise of official function 'but only the use of unofficial good offices.' Bryan reminded the 'gentlemen' that they could not act as a diplomatic or consular representative of another country. Ultimately they were representatives of 'a neutral power whose attitude toward the parties to the conflict is one of impartial amity.' They had to 'avoid any action which compromised the US as a neutral or affect the amicable relations between it and the country to which you are accredited.'[79] Certain issues required sensitive handling, particularly the issuing of passports.

Before the war, most travellers went abroad without a passport but after its outbreak no traveller would consider a trip without one. Visas also came into being and all prospective immigrants to the US had to obtain a US visa on their passport. Not only did the work of the Bureau of Citizenship in Washington

77 Ibid., Londonderry, August 1914, passim.   78 Heinrichs, *American ambassador*, p. 99; C. Stuart Kennedy, *The American consul: a history of the United States consular service, 1776–1914* (1999), p. 223.   79 'Official documents. Supplement, Bryan to the diplomatic and consular officers of the United States of America, 17 August 1914', 118–19.

quadruple, leading to the establishment of a division of Passport Control, but, on 13 August 1918, a separate visa office had to be established.[80] However, there were many Americans in Europe with neither a US passport nor visa who clamoured for them. On 1 August 1914, Bryan authorized foreign representatives to issue emergency passports and consular registration certificates to native and naturalized US citizens and citizens of the insular possessions. All consular offices had to maintain an up-to-date passport book to record the arrival and departure of US citizens. In August 1914, the Belfast office did not have one and Totten advised Sharp to request one from the State Department.[81] US-born citizens applying for passports were not required to produce birth certificates, but were required to submit satisfactory identification, including references to persons in the US of whom the Department could make inquiries. Naturalized Americans were required to provide certificates or old passports.[82] Ambassador James Gerard later admitted that during the early days of August 1914 the embassy in Berlin gave US passports to British and other nationalities. This practice was soon stopped once the German government ruled that all Americans leaving Berlin had to have their passports stamped by the Foreign Office. Americans in other parts of Germany were requested to contact their consular representatives.[83]

More precise instructions were forwarded from Washington on 12 September because 'many persons not American citizens', mainly Europeans, were applying for US passports and consular certificates to enable them to leave their country of residence. The US officials were instructed to observe the regulations strictly. But some discretion was allowed whereby US passports could be issued to people who had resided in the US for three years, had declared their intention to become US citizens, had been abroad for less than six months and intended returning to the US.[84] In January 1915, when Wilson signed new legislation governing the granting and issuing of US passports, the application process became more complex with a photograph and more proof of identify required.[85] The tightening of the process imposed additional burdens on consular officers. Indeed, one of the few dismissals of consular officers during the war involved citizenship. Thomas St John Gaffney found himself in a difficult situation upon the outbreak of the war; not only was he US consul general in Munich but he was quite convinced that Britain was responsible for the outbreak of the war. Nonetheless, he attempted to be unbiased in his business and, on the outbreak of war, immediately he began to assist the local British relief committee to distribute aid to needy British subjects, although he forbade 'members of the English

---

80 Stuart, *The Department of State*, pp. 244, 251; 'Official documents. Enclosure 1, rules governing the granting and issuing of passports in the United States', 386–9.   81 NARA, RG59, IRFSP, Belfast, August 1914, passim.   82 'Official documents. Supplement, Lansing to the embassies and legations in Europe, 12 September 1914', 377.   83 J.W. Gerard, *My four years in Germany* (1917), pp. 96–105.   84 'Official documents: Lansing to the embassies and legations in Europe, 12 September 1914', 377–8.   85 'Official documents: enclosure 1, rules governing the granting and issuing of passports. Supplement, 12 January 1915', 386–9.

colony to wear the American flag and pose as American citizens.' This led to complaints of anti-English prejudice being sent to the State Department and to British and US newspapers. These charges formed a lethal threat to Gaffney's consular career.[86] As will be seen, his sympathy for Irish republicanism exacerbated the situation and contributed to his dismissal by Wilson in October 1915.

Because of the particular character of the US and local communities resident within their respective districts, US consular officials in Ireland did not have to deal with belligerent peoples. Nor did US citizens flood into their offices to seek help upon the outbreak of the war. The US presence in Ireland in 1914 was divided not just into native born or naturalized citizens but, more importantly, into those with or without Irish connections. Those Americans without Irish links were mostly located in urban settings and were few in number; none contacted the consular offices seeking assistance after the outbreak of the war. Regarding the US citizens with local connections, by 1914 a pattern of low return immigration had been established for the Irish-American community. Wyman has calculated that ten per cent of post-famine Irish emigrants returned between 1880 and 1930 representing the second lowest return rate of twenty-six European races analysed.[87] This leads to a further deviation by the Irish from the general trend of return migration. As world war loomed and Americans feared permanent and absolute separation from families in Europe, 200,000 departed in 1910, rising to 300,000 in 1911 and subsequent years. The Americans with Irish connections seem to have contributed little to this phenomenon.[88] This return trend suggest that a degree of foresight about the on-coming war was present within some American ethnic communities that was not present at even the higher levels of the State Department or the Wilson administration. Although the consuls in Ireland experienced little of this return migration they still had to be familiar with all new regulations and legislation regarding US citizens in residence or in transit. On 8 February 1915, the State Department issued a notice which stated that US citizens who expected to make a prolonged stay in any foreign country should apply for consular registration to the particular US consulate in that country or nearest the place where they were residing. Later in the year, Bryan advised Americans against travelling to any country in a state of war. His department officials would not issue passports to persons who contemplated visiting belligerent countries merely for 'pleasure', 'recreation', 'touring' or 'sight seeing'.[89]

86 Gaffney had a brother James St John Gaffney, a solicitor, living in Limerick in 1904. NLI, JRP, MS15236(9), Gaffney to Redmond, 3 October 1904. Gaffney was close enough to President Roosevelt to arrange a meeting between him and John Redmond, leader of the Irish Parliamentary Party, who visited the US in 1904. See T. St. John Gaffney, *Breaking the silence: England, Ireland, Wilson and the war* (1930), pp. 88, 94–5.   87 See A. Schrier, *Ireland and the American emigration 1850–1900* (1997), p. 130; J.J. Lee, 'Emigration: 1922–1998' in Glazier (ed.), *The encyclopedia*, p. 265; M. Wyman, *Round trip to America: the immigrants return to Europe, 1880–1930* (1992), pp. 10–11.   88 See A.M. Kraut, *The huddled masses: the immigrant in American society, 1880–1921: the American history series*, (1982), p. 18.   89 'Official documents, enclosure 1, notice concerning passports and

During 1914 and up to February 1915, passenger liners continued to call at Queenstown, Belfast and Londonderry but it was largely to collect immigrants. The immigration process had become increasingly regulated and bureaucratized and by 1914 consuls certified that vessels had cleared from a port free from contagious diseases or illness subject to quarantine regulations in the US and that bedding and other household goods had been properly fumigated.[90] In theory, no ship could land in the US without a bill of health and table 3.1 illustrates that Frost issued 215 of these in Queenstown in 1913–14, almost nine times more than any other consular officer based in Ireland. Steamship companies were required also to ensure that immigrants only of the admissible classes be transported.[91] Due to these war-time controls and further legislation, particularly the introduction in 1918 of the literacy test and the exclusion of persons deemed contrary to 'public safety', the initial responsibility for examining the qualifications of the intending immigrants was transferred to the consul.[92] They authenticated immigrants' documents, issued passports if needed and certified the health of all passengers and crews. In the pre-war period, emigration to the US from the thirty-two counties had averaged approximately 35,000 per annum.[93] During the war years emigration was reduced to negligible proportions; by 1918 only 136 emigrants departed for the US from the thirty-two counties.[94] This virtual collapse in emigration clearly meant a reduced workload for the consuls in Ireland but this was balanced by the increased intelligence work.[95] Wilbur Carr recorded that consuls in western Europe 'were deeply involved in the thunders of war' and particularly praised Wesley Frost's work in Queenstown.[96]

On 4 February 1915, the German Admiralty announced that the seas around Britain and Ireland were within the war zone and launched a submarine campaign against allied and neutral shipping.[97] Every enemy ship found in the war zone would be destroyed by their newest weapon, the U-boat, and neutral ships would be 'in danger' because of the 'hazards' of naval warfare. Wilson immediately summoned his cabinet (the pacifist Bryan was absent) and the US protested against the German action as an 'indefensible violation of neutral rights', declaring that if US vessels or lives were lost, Germany would be held to 'strict accountability.' Wilson regarded submarine attacks as illegal and uncivilized.[98] The network of consular officers located around the North Sea, the Irish Sea

registration in consulates. Supplement, 8 February 1915', 390; 'Official documents, enclosure 3, notice to American citizens who contemplate visiting belligerent countries. Supplement, 17 November 1914, 17 April 1915', 391, 392.   90 Kennedy, *The American consul*, p. 213.   91 *FRUS*, 'With the address of the President to Congress December 8, 1914' (1922), Bryan, 29 August 1914.   92 Kennedy, *The American consul*, p. 224; R. Daniels & O.L. Graham, *Debating American immigration, 1882–present* (2001), p. 122.   93 This interpretation of the statistical data is based on Lee, 'Emigration: 1922–98', p. 263.   94 H.P. Fairchild, *Immigration: a world movement and its American significance* (1925), p. 446.   95 Lee, 'Emigration: 1922–1998', p. 263.   96 LC, WCP, Box 17, Bio. Mss. Dr Crane, Mss. A life of Wilbur Carr, pp. 191–2.   97 'Correspondence relating to restraints on commerce'. Supplement, Gerard to Secretary of State, 6 February 1915, 83.   98 Koenig, *Bryan*, p. 539; LaFeber, *The American age*, pp. 286–7.

and the Mediterranean kept the US government informed on the progress of German submarine warfare or, as Carr put it, 'of each ship that went down and where.'[99] The first attack came on 28 March, when a British passenger liner – *Falaba* – was sunk in St George's Channel with 111 passengers lost, including Leon Chester Thrasher, a US citizen. On 28 April, the US steamer – *Cushing* – bound from Philadelphia for Rotterdam with a cargo of petroleum and oil, was bombed by a German airship. On 1 May, the US oil tank steamer *Gulfight*, heading from Texas to Rouen, was torpedoed by a German submarine; the US captain and two crew were killed. Finding the appropriate response challenged the State Department officials, the cabinet and Wilson. The issue centred on whether Americans had a right to travel on belligerent ships, a position upheld by Wilson and Lansing, while Bryan believed that Americans should be prevented from travelling. Outside the administration, Theodore Roosevelt represented the view that the only possible response was US involvement in the war.[1]

Neutrality was maintained but, from February onwards, official protests were sent to the German government. Bryan thought that these served to 'inflame the already hostile feeling against us in Germany.' At the same time Page protested to the British government against British authorities' detention of US ships and cargoes.[2] The sinking of the British vessel *Lusitania*, by a single torpedo from a German submarine off the Irish coast at 2.23 p.m. on 7 May, provided the first serious challenge to US neutrality. 1,959 persons were on board; 1,198 lost their lives, including 124 Americans. In Queenstown, Frost, Thompson and Dawson were the first US officials to have to deal with the deadly consequences of Wilson's impartial policy.[3] Frost's detailed report was sent to the State Department on 11 May; it is used extensively here to offer an eyewitness account not only of the impact of the tragedy as it unfolded but also of the breadth of a US consul's work.

Frost's office had a view of the harbour and at 3.00 p.m. on Friday, 7 May, he noticed tugs leaving the harbour. Almost immediately a 'street rumour' confirmed his 'conjecture' that the *Lusitania* had been hit. A representative from the Cunard company, which owned the vessel, admitted on the telephone that it 'appeared probable' that the vessel was sunk or sinking', while the British Admiralty representative 'stated positively that it was gone.' Frost did not have any direct news until the rescue crafts returned because they were not fitted with a wireless but he was in phone contact with land observers at the Old Head of Kinsale further along the coast. They could not report effectively on the disaster ten miles out at sea, but stated that 'about twenty boats were floating.' It was this latter statement which he telegraphed at 4.00 p.m. to his superior, Consul

99 LC, WCP, Box 17, Bio. Mss. Dr Crane, Mss. A life of Wilbur Carr, pp. 191–2.   1 Koenig, *Bryan*, pp. 539–40, 542.   2 *FRUS*, 1915 supplement the world war (1928), Page to Secretary of State, 11 May 1915, pp. 412–13.   3 The following account is based on Frost's correspondence with the State Department. *FRUS*, 1915 supplement the world war, Frost to Secretary of State, 11 May 1915, pp. 410–12.

General Skinner in London, along with the fact that the sinking occurred twenty-three minutes after the torpedoing and that he expected the survivors to arrive into Queenstown at 7.00 p.m. Page was preparing to dine with Edward House and his wife, who were in London, when the announcement came through and, the assumption being made that the ship was destroyed but that all passengers and crew were safe, the dinner went ahead. However, the seriousness of the situation was soon evident when Frost directly cabled the State Department at 6.00 p.m. At around 7.00 p.m. Page told his wife that there had been a mistake and that more than one thousand people had lost their lives, including Americans. He telegraphed a request to Frost that all information be sent directly to him and it seems that Frost did not contact other consular officials based in Ireland. Jenkins, normally consul at Guadeloupe but detailed to Dublin, was informed of the sinking by the London consulate and telephoned Frost in the evening to know if he should come to Queenstown. Frost urged him to do so at once.[4]

Meanwhile, Frost began preparations for the arrival of the survivors. He withdrew gold from his deposit account, borrowed a further £200 in gold and sent Thompson to Kinsale in a car with £100 in case some survivors were landed there. In fact all but 134 survivors were landed at the Cunard Wharf in Queenstown. From the beginning Frost endeavoured to identify Americans but he admitted that, while the officials displayed 'infinite good heart', there was almost no organization except on the part of the British naval and military authorities. At 1.00 a.m. he transmitted the total list of over 600 survivors to Ambassador Page and the State Department. At the same time the American officials told every survivor that clothing and lodging were available and assured Americans that there would be funds to help them. The following morning the consulate was busy loaning money, making transportation arrangements and taking details of individual survivors' travel plans. Most of them departed on the 3.00 p.m. train to Dublin or elsewhere.[5] As all the survivors had been in transit they faced the unenviable necessity of taking another sea voyage. Those who travelled to England arrived in Euston station a few days later and were greeted by Page, who described them as 'listless and bedraggled.'[6] The work of identifying and embalming corpses began in the University College Cork Medical School. The bodies which remained unidentified were to be buried in Queenstown and Jenkins decided that they should be photographed before burial on Monday, 10 May. Frost was careful to record and send to the US the numbers of 'identified American dead of importance.'[7]

4 *FRUS*, 1915 supplement the world war, Frost to Secretary of State, 11 May 1915, pp. 410–12; B.J. Hendrick (ed.), *The life and letters of Walter H. Page*, 2 vols (1930), ii, p. 1.   5 *FRUS*, 1915 supplement the world war, Frost to Secretary of State, 11 May 1915, pp. 410–12. Edward House was supposed to have been on the *Lusitania* but changed his plans and left earlier. See Hendrick, *The life and letters of Walter H. Page*, i, House to Page, 18 January 1915.   6 Hendrick, *The life and letters of Walter H. Page*, ii, p. 3.   7 *FRUS*, 1915 supplement the world war, Frost to Secretary of State, 11 May 1915, pp. 410–12.

The search for bodies continued and Frost felt that it was 'wretchedly managed' by both the British Admiralty and the Cunard company, whose first tugs returned with 'neither news nor bodies.' He was so appalled at these ineffective actions that he telegraphed both the State Department and the ambassador twice on the subject and told the Cunard officials that 'diplomatic intervention would result' if immediate steps were not taken to retrieve bodies. The Cunard and Admiralty officials each shifted responsibility to the other. The former claimed that only the Admiralty had the rescue craft. The latter protested that all their vessels were on regular patrol. Frost noted that 'to my mind the importance of searching for twelve hundred odd bodies would justify some modification of the patrols.' Although he was 'much dissatisfied' in this respect, his freedom of action was curtailed because of his consular status. He appealed to Page to help expedite the situation and continued 'I do not feel called upon to adopt an abrupt tone with Admiralty, as it would impair my usefulness here later, but have tried to give vigorous hints. I do not know whether fear, indifference or financial considerations are controlling.' Eventually the company chartered a Dutch tug and sent it out on Monday evening, four days after the sinking; it collected some bodies, but not many – 'perhaps a dozen.' The State Department instructed the consular officials to perform the grisly and presumably difficult work of compiling a list of the survivors and identifying the dead, missing and almost certainly dead. They also had to secure statements from survivors and to uncover explanations. Frost was candid with Washington and said that this was secondary to 'relief of need and quieting uncertainty.'[8] However, by Sunday evening he had telegraphed Washington with lists of names of the missing which included Vanderbilt, Stone, Shields, Myers, Klein, Hubbard and Frohman, who were all prominent US citizens. He also managed to secure eleven intelligent statements and he forwarded two of these, from Mrs Jessie Taft Smith and Mr Robert Rankin, who were both first class passengers, to Washington.[9]

The consuls finally received further support from the London embassy on Sunday, 9 May, when captains Castle and Miller arrived. Frost, Jenkins and the two captains met with Vice Admiral Sir Charles Coke, who was in command in southern Ireland, and he read them the warning messages sent to Captain Turner of the *Luisitania* on Friday. Frost concluded that the latter had been given the 'bare facts only. No instructions or interpretations.' He continued 'It is true that Turner should have kept farther out; but to my mind it seemed that the Admiralty had by no means done their full duty by him.' As to the sinking of the ship, Frost noted that at least one survivor's affidavit noted that 'no warning was given.'[10] He recommended to the State Department that the accounts carried in the *New York World* and *New York Tribune* respectively 'were prob-

8 Ibid., Frost to Secretary of State, 11 May 1915, pp. 410–12.   9 Ibid., Frost to Secretary of State, 9 May 1915, pp. 386–7.   10 Robert Rankin noted in his affidavit 'Torpedo fired without warning whilst most of the passengers were below at food.' Ibid., Frost to Secretary of State, 9 May 1915, pp. 386–7.

ably very good', as their correspondents were 'good men.' One of the main responsibilities of consular officials was to deal with sea-related incidents but the extent of the *Lusitania* tragedy tested the quality of the US consular staff. Frost and his officials appear to have been personally as well as professionally affected by it. He concluded his report of 11 May, with the following, 'As I said before, there has been good will in abundance, but many human mistakes have been made – some, of course, by this Consulate, so that perhaps I should not criticise.' Frost's work was accomplished with limited manpower and authority; this was customary for a consular outpost.[11] Carr wrote:

> Consular officers ... were deeply involved in the thunders of war; it was the network of American consular officers around the North Sea, the Irish Sea and the Mediterranean that kept the government informed of the progress of German submarine warfare – of each ship that went down and where. The consul at Queenstown (Cork), Wesley Frost, reported to the Department the main facts of the sinking of the *Lusitania* on 7 May 1915, was the first to supply the names of the survivors, and did everything possible to succour the victims of the disaster and to protect American interests.[12]

Frost, as will be seen later, was recruited by the Committee on Public Information (CPI), and joined its speakers' bureau. He embarked on a sensational lecture tour, speaking about the *Lusitania* and other sinkings to promote the cause of America's 'propaganda ministry.'[13] It was subsequently discovered that the *Lusitania* was carrying a cargo of ammunition to Britain and that before it left New York for Liverpool, the German embassy had arranged for a newspaper advertizement which warned that it would be 'fair game.'[14] Wilson faced a difficult decision. The US public was outraged. House, who was in London, believed that the US could not stand by any longer and Page urged that the US join the allies and enter the war The pacifist Bryan favoured banning Americans' from travelling while Lansing wished to uphold Americans' freedom to travel. The cabinet discussions, which led to a series of three increasingly severe diplomatic notes being sent to the German government, have been detailed elsewhere. Suffice to say that the US did not go to war, but the notes insisted on Americans' right to travel and trade and on an end to the sinking of unarmed passenger liners. Also they contributed to Bryan's resignation.[15] None of the notes resulted in war and

11 Ibid., Frost to Secretary of State, 11 May 1915, p. 412. 12 LC, WCP, Box 16, 'Uncle Sam's diplomatic agents', 1 August 1923, pp. 191–2. 13 J.R Mock & C. Larson, *Words that won the war: the story of the committee on public information, 1917–1919* (1939), p. 4. 14 LaFeber, *The American age*, p. 287. 15 Bryan resigned for several reasons: the harsh language used in the first two notes, the absence of an equivalent protest to London over the naval blockade; Wilson's refusal to use the arbitration treaties and to ban Americans from travelling on belligerent ships through the blockade zone, House's 'unofficial connection' with Wilson, and in Bryan's words, 'his voyages abroad on affairs of state.' W. Jennings Bryan & M. Baird Bryan, *The memoirs of William Jennings Bryan*, 2

it appeared that Wilson's judgement had been vindicated. While he latter shared the US public's horror at the loss of life, Wilson also accurately reflected their disinclination to enter the war. After the sinking, Arthur Willert, *The Times* correspondent, wrote 'the President is determined to avoid trouble. Public opinion is scared by the possibility of war. You must expect nothing from the United States.'[16] Spring Rice reported to Grey on 9 June that 'the general consensus of opinion is that ... the President has chosen the line of action which the public demands.'[17] A few weeks later he wrote, 'the prevailing sentiment is undoubtedly for peace ... not perhaps at any price but peace at a very considerable price.'[18] The idealist Bryan had been sacrificed and his arbitration treaty edifice holed. The sinking of the *Lusitania* was a turning point in US neutrality as Wilson differentiated between Britain and Germany in his treatment of their respective warfare policies and brought the US a step nearer the allies.[19]

Throughout summer 1915, Wilson's strategy was tested further as the German attacks continued. The already over-burdened consuls in Queenstown were in the front line. At 11.00 a.m. on 31 July, Frost telegraphed Washington to notify the authorities that the steamer *Iberian* had been hit by a submarine and that an American muleteer, Wiley, had been killed. He sent two further telegrams on the same day as he gathered more depositions from ship's surgeon Dr Patrick S. Burns, Harry N. Healy and George Killeen, all US citizens. On the same day, he sent a fourth detailed report because it was the first attack since the sending of the *Lusitania* note and he felt it safer to overburden the department with details than to omit anything which might be of value. Frost outlined his handling of Wiley's body which he expected to have buried in Queenstown. Of greater importance to him now were the circumstances of the sinking. He believed that 'there cannot be the shadow of a doubt that the *Iberian* was seeking to escape and evade visit and search at the time she was shelled.' The shelling appears to have been resorted to by the submarine 'only in so far as was necessary to induce this conviction.' All the survivors united 'in praising the courtesy and consideration shown by the submarine in connection with the abandonment of the ship.'[20] He believed that the American notes had effected a change in German submarine policy. His report reached Washington on 16 August and three days later another passenger liner, the *Arabic*, was sunk at 9.30 a.m. sixty miles off the coast of Queenstown.

(1925), p. 404; The National Archives, London (hereafter TNA), Foreign Office (hereafter FO), 371/2500, Spring Rice to Grey, 9 June 1915, enclosure 2, extract from *Washington Star*, 9 June 1915. **16** A. Willert, *Washington and other memories* (1972), p. 81. **17** TNA, FO371/2500, Spring Rice to Grey, 9 June 1915. **18** Spring Rice to Grey, 23 June 1915 in Gwynn, *The life and friendships of Sir Cecil Spring Rice*, ii, p. 274. By January 1915 House was communicating with Page through 'the kindness of Sir Horace Plunkett'. Hendrick, *The life and letters of Walter H. Page*, i, House to Page, 18 January 1915. **19** LaFeber, *The American age*, p. 288; Link et al., *The American epoch*, i, pp. 119–21; Stuart, *Department of State*, pp. 235–6. **20** *FRUS*, 1915 supplement the world war, Frost to Secretary of State, 31 July 1915.

It went down in eleven minutes and eleven boats of survivors were brought ashore. Twenty-one American passengers were on the *Arabic* and Mr Edmund F. Woods and Mrs Josephine Brugiere were killed. Vice consul Thompson telegraphed the State Department with the first deposition from a US citizen, Zellah Covington, who stated that, he would take his oath 'that no warning of any kind was given but that the ship was sunk deliberately and in cold blood.' On receipt of this and, presumably, other intelligence information, Lansing, now secretary of State, telegraphed Frost immediately and requested him to 'report by telegraph' a brief summary of the affidavits taken, 'covering particularly questions of warning, ramming, convoy and whether [the] *Arabic* was going to [the] assistance of [the] *Dunsley*.' Frost replied the same day, 21 August; 'have failed in devoutest efforts to discover any evidence that *Arabic* was warned by submarine or convoyed by war vessel. She did not attempt to ram submarine nor go to assistance of *Dunsley*. It is barely possible, however, that other facts may yet be found.' Page confirmed this version following a meeting with Douglas Brownrig, chief censor of the British Admiralty, and after information had been received by the US consul at Liverpool, Horace Lee Washington, from the *Arabic* captain, Fincy, along with affidavits from six US citizens.[21]

Frost and his colleagues' handling of these events offers an insight into the consul's role during the war. Depending on your location, it could be difficult and demanding work, but for those in Queenstown it was even more so. Not only did they have to conduct routine business but they also had to deal with the consequences of these tragedies. The importance of their work to the evolution of Wilson's policy of neutrality was evident during the *Arabic* incident. The German government immediately apologized for the attack and Lansing warned that if the submarine attacks did not cease the US 'would certainly declare war.' On 1 September, the German government pledged that submarine commanders would not be permitted to sink passenger vessels unless they resisted or escaped when requested to surrender. The so-called '*Arabic* pledge' led to the abandonment of the intensive submarine campaign until January 1917.

Ireland and protecting neutrality in the US

In Washington, Wilson's policy of ignoring the hyphenates' propaganda campaign had been greatly boosted by the *Lusitania* sinking and by the uncovering of German subversive activities in the US. Von Bernstorff recalled that from mid-1915 onwards, the support of the US public ebbed away and turned towards the allied side, while John Devoy admitted that the Irish nationalist movement

---

21 Ibid., Thompson to Secretary of State, 19 August 1915; 20 August 1915, Secretary of State to Frost, 21 August 1915, Frost to Secretary of State, 22 August 1915, Page to Secretary of State, 23 August 1915, pp. 516–18.

'was going to have a hard time, owing to the new situation.'[22] The demonstrations, protests, letter writing and lobbying continued but the tide had turned against the hyphenates. Within the Irish-American community mainstream opinion separated further from the radicals. Throughout summer and autumn 1915, Wilson's *Lusitania* notes and his increasing bias towards the allies, with the supply of US loans and arms, were condemned in the *Gaelic American*, the *Irish World* and Jeremiah O'Leary's publications for the American Truth Society. Further evidence of the president's pro-British bias came with Gaffney's dismissal as US consul in Munich in October 1915.

Gaffney recounted that, during the first few months of the war, 'certain rumours were circulated in the English press to the effect that I was not acting in a neutral manner and that I was neglecting the interests of the English subjects committed to my protection'; the specific complaint was that he had refused to allow them to pose as US citizens. Complaints about him were sent to the State Department and to British and US newspapers and these threatened his consular career.[23] Nor was he helped by his involvement with the British diplomat and Irish patriot, Roger Casement, who was then in Germany seeking aid for an Irish rising. Indeed, Gaffney explained to the German under secretary in Foreign Affairs in August 1915 that he wanted help to get Casement to the US because he 'would bring a new factor to the campaign for honest American neutrality.'[24] On 1 October, Gaffney received a dispatch from Lansing informing him that the 'President will accept your resignation from the consular service if transmitted immediately. Your successor will be appointed without delay.' Gaffney immediately answered 'What are the reasons for such action? I will be able to disprove any charges if given opportunity. If, however, President insists on resignation without a hearing, it is tendered though unconscious of any grounds.' Gaffney never received an explanation from the State Department, nor was he given the chance to defend himself in any enquiry, even though he was entitled to this under the rules of the consular service.[25] Not surprisingly the newspapers speculated. The *Continental Times*, a US newspaper published in Berlin, outlined the charges made against him on 15 October:

> A lack of courtesy towards members of the American colony at Munich. Neglect of the interests of English subjects at Munich, as entrusted to him. A violent anti-English propaganda. Smuggling through of secret documents in the service of the German and Austrian governments. The publication of articles in which the policy of President Wilson is adversely criticised. Further Mr Gaffney is supposed to have perpetrated a still greater crime by giving a dinner to Sir Roger Casement – the Irish patriot.[26]

22 Bernstorff, *My three years*, p. 106; quoted in Rowland, 'Irish-American Catholics', 72.   23 Gaffney, *Breaking the silence*, pp. 94–5.   24 NLI, JMcGP, MS17590 (2), St John Gaffney to German Under Secretary, 6 August 1915.   25 Gaffney, *Breaking the silence*, pp. 94–5.   26 Quoted in ibid., p. 90.

Gaffney refuted every one of the 'unneutral' charges as did his British and American supporters. Gaffney did not believe that the pro-German Ambassador Gerard played a role in his dismissal which is probably true given the latter's lack of standing with Wilson. Ultimately Gaffney was convinced that it was his Irish origins and, particularly, his links to Casement, which led to his dismissal. Moreover, he was convinced that the British government ordered it firstly, to thwart Gaffney's attempts to maintain normal conditions for US citizens in Germany and secondly, to prevent Germany assisting Casement and the Irish republicans. Gaffney's case had provoked widespread comment from New York-based newspapers, particularly the revelation that a letter addressed to Gaffney from one Dennis A. Spellissy, a New York lawyer and treasurer of the American Committee of the Irish National Volunteers, had been found during a police raid on the New York offices of the Austrian consul. According to Gaffney, it was an innocent letter of support; the *New York Herald* projected it as evidence of Gaffney's guilt.[27]

The Irish-American radical press took up the case. The *Gaelic American* published full details of an interview Gaffney gave to an American journalist on board the *Oscar II* as he sailed from Copenhagen for New York on 16 November 1915. The article was headed 'Consul General Gaffney refutes all the charges on which Wilson dismissed him without a hearing' and stated that he was removed because 'he was *persona non grata* to England, the country with which Germany is at war, and because of that fact President Wilson removes him from office.'[28] Wilbur Carr denied any role in the case and told Gaffney that Wilson had made the decision and Lansing carried it out. Gaffney was sufficiently attuned to Wilson's style of governing to know that it was pointless requesting him to reverse his decision.[29] On his return to the US, he identified the opposing sides; the majority of the US population and press were biased towards the allies, while the 'supporters of strict neutrality' were to be found amongst Americans of Irish and German origin. The timing of his case was opportune for both sides who exploited it for their own respective ends. But Gaffney believed that ninety per cent of Irish and Germans wanted 'fair play for the Central Powers' which raises the question to what extent did the extremist Irish-Americans' demand for strict impartiality in government policy reflect the views of the majority of Irish-America?

From 1915 onwards, Samuel Gompers, president of the American Federation of Labour (AFL) kept organized labour behind Wilson's neutrality and tempered

---

27 Ibid., pp. 88–102. Interestingly Gaffney met with Dr Maurice Francis Egan, the US minister in Denmark on his way to the US in November 1915. Gaffney noted that Egan was on the side of the 'Anglo-Saxon', supported the allies but like Page in London, professed to be neutral. Ibid., p.132. 28 Quoted in ibid., p. 134. 29 Ibid., pp. 144–5; The editor of the *New York World* was Frank Irving Cobb who Devoy described as 'probably the most malignant enemy of the Irish cause on the American press' was one of Wilson's advisers. Hartley, *The Irish question*, pp. 48–9, 51; W.B. Fowler, *British-American relations 1917–1918:the role of Sir William Wiseman* (1969), p. 160, fn. 95.

the opposition of workers in places such as Butte, Montana and the Chicago Federation of Labour.[30] While the Catholic hierarchy's moderate, restrained viewpoint more than likely mirrored that of Catholic Irish-Americans. In October 1915, Monsignor Francis Kelley who was active throughout the country as founder of the Catholic Church Extension Society, felt that 'as the Pope is believed to be entirely and sincerely impartial and neutral ... that is a primary reason for American Catholics being the same.'[31] Indeed Kelley, who was in correspondence with J.D. Gregory a British diplomat in the Vatican, did not support any British attempts to use propaganda against US Catholics 'to prove the justice of our cause.'[32] Officials in the Foreign Office agreed.[33] But Spring Rice continued to worry about the 'pronouncedly pro-German' attitude of individual Catholic clergy of Irish extraction, even though he admitted that cardinals Farley and Gibbons preserved 'an attitude of scrupulous neutrality' with regard to the war.[34] One test of the loyalty to Wilson was the up-coming election in early November 1915.

Not surprisingly, the British side devoted close attention to the election. Colville Barclay reported from Washington that the results were disappointing to the Democratic Party. Tammany Hall had returned to power in New York but more important was the role of the German-American National Alliance in organizing the defeat of certain local Democratic candidates and the branding of Wilson as 'pro-British.' The radical Irish-American Jeremiah O'Leary wrote to Wilson ascribing the defeat of the Democratic candidate for one of the districts of New York to the public dislike of Wilson's attitude towards the war. Although few German voters were to be found within the Democratic ranks, Barclay felt that German influence might force candidates for all political offices to take the threat seriously. On the other hand, he admitted that this might lead to a reaction among those who did not relish the use of American votes for avowedly foreign purposes.[35] Barclay's superiors agreed that the vote was on the whole hostile to Wilson and his party, but, apart from O'Leary's role, the Foreign Office did not identify a specific Irish-American dimension in this German-inspired opposition to the Wilson administration.[36] Wilson seemed to hold the same view as illustrated by his address to Congress on 7 December. He stated:

30 Rowland, 'Irish-American Catholics', 62–75; E. Cuddy, 'Irish-American propagandists and American neutrality, 1914–17' in J.B. Walsh (ed.), *The Irish: America's political class* (1976), pp. 252–75; E. McKillen, *Chicago labour and the quest for a democratic diplomacy, 1914–1924* (1996), p. 52.   31 TNA, FO371/2501, Gregory to Grey, 20 October 1915. Kelley was born in Canada to Irish parents, joined the priesthood and in 1905, founded the Catholic Church Extension Society to raise funds for church building in rural areas. By 1915, the society had built 1,135 churches, he attended the Versailles peace conference and in 1924 became Bishop of Oklahoma. A.D. Andreassi, 'Francis Clement Kelley (1870–1948)' in Glazier, *The encyclopedia*, pp. 497–8. According to Gregory, Kelley was also in contact with Wilson on matters of Catholic policy. TNA, FO371/2501, Gregory to Grey, 20 October 1915.   32 Ibid., Sperling, 26 October 1915; ibid., Gregory to Grey, 20 October 1915.   33 Ibid., Perry, 7 November 1915; ibid., Nicholson, 12 November 1915.   34 Ibid., FO371/2793, Spring Rice to Grey, 12 February 1916.   35 Ibid., FO371/2501, Colville to Foreign Office, 12 November 1915.   36 Ibid., Louis Mallett, 26 November 1915.

There are citizens of the United States, I blush to admit, born under other flags but welcomed under our generous naturalization laws to the full freedom and opportunity of America, who have poured the poison of disloyalty into the very arteries of our national life: who have sought to bring the authority and good name of our government into contempt, to destroy our industries wherever they found it effective for their vindictive purposes to strike at them, and to debase our policies to the uses of foreign intrigues.[37]

Wilson's speech was directed at the disloyal actions such as those of the German-Americans and Irish-American, and without naming these groups, his message was clear. The activities of radical groups became a target for US propaganda and intelligence services.

For the small group of 'professional Irish politicians', as Spring Rice called them, particularly John Devoy and Daniel Cohalan in New York, Joseph McGarrity in Philadelphia and John T. Ryan in Buffalo, who comprised the Revolutionary Directory of Clan na Gael, their activities increasingly focused on supporting the IRB-planned rebellion in Ireland.[38] The Friends of Irish Freedom became their vehicle. It was established at the Irish Race Convention, held in New York on 4-5 March 1916, to act as a front for the fund-raising and gun-running of Clan na Gael. On the eve of the Easter rising in April 1916, radical Irish-Americans had been small in number, short of funds and hopeful that their German contacts would bring results.[39] Certainly they were vocal, unyielding and prominent in their pro-German sympathies, but they were not representative of Catholic Irish-Americans, the majority of whom may not have been pro-British but were not pro-German either. While the British and US secret services targeted the radicals' activities, events in Ireland altered the quiescent attitude of the majority of Irish-American nationalists and forced Wilson to clarify his views on the Irish question.

Roger Casement had arrived in Christiania, Norway, from the US on 20 October 1914. In a letter to Edward Grey, copied to Bryan, he explained that the purpose of the visit was 'to make sure that whatever might be the course of this war, my own country, Ireland should suffer from the minimum of harm.'[40] His subsequent efforts to get men and arms from the German government failed

---

37 Gwynn, *The letters and friendships of Sir Cecil Spring Rice*, ii, Spring Rice to Grey, 9 December 1915, p. 302, fn. 1. 38 Ibid., p. 309, fn. 2. In 1914 and 1915, the American committee of the Irish National Volunteers which comprised Joseph McGarrity (chairman), Denis Spellissy (treasurer), P.H. Griffin (Secretary), sent a total of $25,000 from the Irish National Volunteer Fund in the Irving National Bank in New York, to Eoin McNeill; American Irish Historical Society (hereafter AIHS), Daniel F. Cohalan Papers (hereafter DFCP), box 1, folder 11; ibid., box 16, folder, 7. 39 Rowland, 'Irish-American Catholics', 75; J.J. Splain, 'The Irish movement in the United States since 1911' in W.G. Fitzgerald, *The voice of Ireland: a survey of the race and nation from all angles by the foremost leaders at home and abroad* (1923), p. 227.

to meet his expectations but on 21 April 1916, he was set ashore off the coast of Tralee, in south-west Ireland, from a German submarine, U19. He hoped to rendezvous with a German ship, the *Aud*, carrying arms to the IRB leaders for the planned rising. By the end of 22 April, neither plan had been realized. Casement was arrested and the ship had been captured by the British navy and then scuttled by its captain. Nevertheless, the rising went ahead on 24 April but it was limited to a few areas, particularly the General Post Office in Dublin, due to confusion about mobilization orders. Douglas Hyde, cultural revivalist and later first president of Ireland, wrote that 'neither John [Eoin] MacNeill of the Council nor the majority of the Council or of the Executive Committee of the Irish Volunteers knew that a rebellion was being planned or that assistance of any kind was looked for from Germany. These designs were concealed from them.'[41] Within five days the leaders had been arrested, 450 people had died, 2,614 had been wounded and the rebellion had ended. Nonetheless the short and long-term consequences reverberated in different ways throughout US politics, in the press and with the public. How did the State Department respond to these challenges?

When the rising broke out in Dublin on 24 April, not one US consul informed the State Department and it was summer before the matter was investigated in the Consular bureau. Carr could not understand the failure of the consuls in Ireland to report either to the Department or to the embassy on recent 'occurrences' in their districts. He instructed the consuls to explain their 'failure to report.'[42] When Adams' report on events during the rising, dated 29 November, reached Washington in December, it indicated that when the fighting broke out on Easter Monday he had been at home with his son in Ross's Hotel, Kingstown, county Dublin. His vice consul, John Claffey, lived in Lindsay Road, Glasnevin, which was closer to the city. In the following days neither man was exempt from the travel restrictions placed on people due to the imposition of martial law. Claffey reached the consular office on 27 April 'by going from doorway to doorway', and he went there again on 2 May with permission from the military authorities, but it took Adams until 8 May to return to his city office in Leinster Street. On 25 April, he was prevented at gunpoint from going into the city to secure a pass to exempt him from the regulations. Twice in following days he was refused a pass and on 3 May he was even barred from returning to his home for a short while. Adams did not complain about his treatment

40 NARA, RG59, M580/6, 841.00/11, Casement to Bryan, 1 February 1915; ibid., enclosure, Casement to Grey, 1 February 1915.   41 NLI, JQP, MS18436, Douglas Hyde, undated.   42 NARA, RG59, M580/6, Hengstler, 21 August 1916; ibid., Carr to Hengstler, 22 August 1916. The only material received from the consuls in Ireland around the time of the rising were six political newspapers (*The Spark*, *Honesty*, *The Hibernian*, *Irish Volunteer*, *Nationality*, *The Gael*) sent by Consul Wesley Frost in March 1916. Frost did not think them to be of 'value', particularly as the British government permitted their distribution. NARA, RG59, M580/6, Frost to Secretary of State, 11 March 1916; ibid., 841.00/26a, Carr to Sharp, 22 August 1916; ibid., Carr to Frost, 22 August 1916; ibid., Carr to Adams, 22 August 1916.

to any official but instead patiently waited to get permission. When he obtained a pass on 4 May, some of the soldiers at the checkpoints refused to acknowledge it and to allow him passage into the city centre.[43]

By the time this thirty-four page, factual, day-by-day, account reached the State Department in December 1916, it was of little use. Adams attributed the delay in sending his report to the work involved in procuring accurate information, the tardiness in obtaining official statistics and the burden of 'additional, general work incidental to the Rebellion and its resultant investigations, correspondence, etc.'[44] But it was evident from his report that much of it was culled from official publications, that he had little understanding of the reasons for the rising but that he felt that the 'behaviour of the troops ... is exemplary in every respect. Even when suffering from unfair attack ... the men conduct themselves with remarkable patience and restraint.' Finally, he admitted to being frightened by the 'alarming' events, particularly the shooting, fighting, rioting, burning and looting.[45] But he insisted that when Claffey reached the office on 27 April, 'naturally, no business could be transacted' and that during his second visit on 2 May, Claffey telephoned him to say that there were 'no important matters for attention.'[46] When Adams finally reached the office on 4 May, he found that post had not been delivered and the telephone and telegraph service was under military control.[47] As will be seen, Adams did conduct some business, which could have been reported back to Washington, in the days surrounding the rising.

The report from Belfast was markedly different. Hunter Sharp told the State Department on 15 September that, 'not having any knowledge of the existence of political disturbances in my consular district, during the period mentioned', he contacted the commissioner of the Royal Irish Constabulary (RIC), who confirmed that 'there had been no political trouble in Ulster' during the previous five months and that the 'general conditions of the province had been quite normal.' But on 26 May, Sharp had replied to a query from Page in London, as to whether one Peter Fox, a US citizen arrested during the rising, was registered at the Belfast consulate.[48] Sharp replied the following day that Fox was not on his register of US citizens but that he had been arrested at Carrickmore, county Tyrone, as a 'Sinn Féiner and Irish Volunteer.'[49] Even though the rising did not

---

43 Ibid., 841.00/33, 'The Sinn Féin rebellion in Ireland, Easter Week, 1916' in Adams to Secretary of State, 29 November 1916.   44 Ibid., 841.00/33, Adams to Secretary of State, 29 November 1916. 45 By way of contrast to Adam's tardy reporting, Charles Bray, the US vice consul who replaced Claffey, did not arrive in Dublin until June 1916 but within a few weeks, he had managed to secure a copy of the 'Sinn Féin rebellion handbook' which he forwarded to the State Department on 21 August 1916. He believed that it contained 'many facts in connection with events which occurred in Dublin and other parts of Ireland during the weeks beginning April 24, 1916 and subsequently, and an account of the Casement trial and execution, which it is believed, may be of interest to the Department.' Ibid., 841.00/29, Bray to Secretary of State, 21 August 1916.   46 Ibid., 841.00/33, 'The Sinn Féin rebellion in Ireland, Easter Week, 1916', 29 November 1916.   47 Ibid.   48 Ibid., 841.00/30, Sharp to Secretary of State, 13 September 1916.   49 Ibid., Sharp to Page, 27 May 1916.

spread to Belfast and the Ulster province, Fox was in fact one of 1,500 people rounded up by the RIC in Sharp's consular district on Easter Tuesday, 25 April. Of those rounded up, 300 were arrested, 136 being sent to Dublin prisons and the rest incarcerated in other parts of the country. The fate of US citizens arrested will be examined later. When, on 22 September, Sharp did file a report titled 'Political conditions in Ireland', it began with an examination of the reasons for the failure of the 'disastrous rising' and concluded that a united Ireland was entirely unacceptable to Ulster's 'leaders.'[50]

When Wesley Frost in Queenstown got around to replying to Carr's instruction on 14 October, he explained that he had been without a vice consul, he was not obliged to submit political reports, he had no contacts with the insurrectionary movement and anyway his town was free of 'trouble.' But his eighty-four page report detailed significant rebellious activity in his consular district which he could have reported at the time of the rising; the country had been over run with British troops, a company of Scots Guards took charge of the railway station in Queenstown and a 'powerful' dreadnought had been brought to Queenstown harbour and anchored up the River Lee towards Cork city 'in readiness to shell the city if necessary.'[51] He provided personal experience of the 'oppressive' policing of the country at the time; 'from this window of this consulate can be seen two plain-clothes men of the force, and another is on duty at the railway station 200 yards away, while there are always a score of uniformed men on duty in this town of 8,000 persons.' But it was the section headed the 'Dublin insurrection – execution of leaders' that was marked in the State Department:

> There was an abundance of explosive material (figuratively, not literally) for the insurrection ... The German plan in aid of Casement furnished the detonating stroke, through the mechanism of the Irish-German agencies in America. America's responsibility while technically nil, must from a practical or moral standpoint be recognised as having some existence; but the stroke came from Germany.[52]

Here Frost had provided vital answers to questions that had been raised both inside and outside the Wilson administration. It was unfortunate that his report had arrived so long after the actual events of April/May 1916. Nonetheless, he confirmed two vital issues; firstly, it was the German and not the US government which ignited events in Ireland and diverted British attention from the European war theatres and secondly, it was the British executions of the rising leaders along with the shooting of pacifist Francis Sheehy Skeffington that provoked widespread sympathy for Sinn Féin. Frost wrote that the Skeffington

---

50 Ibid., Sharp to Page, 22 September 1916.   51 Ibid., 841.00/32, 'Political disturbances and political conditions in Ireland', 30 September 1916 in Frost to Secretary of State, 14 October 1916.   52 Ibid., Frost to Secretary of State, 14 October 1916.

killing was 'now admitted to be the act of a madman' although 'one not too mad to be retained among His Majesty's officers.'[53] William Phillips in the State Department described Frost's report as 'excellent' and the commendation was added to his efficiency record.[54]

All three reports were read in the division of Western European Affairs but, as Dudley Edwards commented, without Frost 'the revolt must have appeared purposeless ... it supplied a critical link in the chain of transformation of the Easter rebels from victims to leaders in American eyes, as other events were so transforming them in England and Ireland.' Frost's explanation also emerged subsequently in newspaper accounts and in a US context provided Sinn Féin with a legitimacy and status previously reserved for Charles Stewart Parnell's Irish Parliamentary Party.[55] Yet, in the days during and immediately after the rising in April 1916, the State Department was without a first hand account of events in Ireland and, therefore, had no background to the events. As will be seen, Adams' failure to contact the State Department meant that it was unaware at the time of his efforts to protect US interests in Dublin and of those of Sharp in Belfast and Frost in Queenstown.

Officials in the State Department would also have expected to receive a report on events in Ireland from the London embassy even though Lansing and Polk wished for nothing less than to 'get Page home for a rest, or permanently.'[56] After the rising, Page expressed the view that it was German-inspired and although the British had mishandled the rising and the executions of the leaders, he had little or no sympathy for the insurgents:

> Any man may become a martyr who is willing to rise and plot against England and to cry out "I die for my country" – if he be an Irishman. In other words, Irish martyrdom is perhaps the cheapest thing in the world to achieve. How they can look in a mirror and keep a straight face is astounding; and why people in other races humour and indulge them – proves the discipline strength of the Catholic Church.[57]

State Department officials were not surprised by this interpretation but when the rising started on 24 April and ended five days later, officials were caught unawares just as the US press and public, except for the handful of radicals who had been involved in its planning from the beginning.[58] Once news of it appeared

53 Ibid., 'Political disturbances and political conditions in Ireland', 30 September 1916 in Frost to Secretary of State, 14 October 1916.   54 Ibid., comments on Frost to Secretary of State, 14 October 1916.   55 O. Dudley Edwards, 'American aspects of the Rising' in O. Dudley Edwards & F. Pyle, *1916, The Eastern Rising* (1968), pp. 173–4.   56 Gregory, *Walter Hines Page*, p. 158.   57 Quoted in Gregory, *Walter Hines Page*, p. 164.   58 Horace Plunkett was in Dublin during the rising and newspaper reports of an attack on him caused House some anxiety. House was relieved when he heard from him on 4 May. Plunkett thought the rising to be German-inspired and he hoped this would quicken US entry into the war. House hoped that the rising would 'ultimately be for good rather than for evil.' NLI, HPP, P6584, reel 2 of 2, Plunkett to House, 4 May 1916; Diary 26 April

in the US press on 25 April, the immediate concerns for Wilson's administration and its representatives focused on avoiding any allegations of a US dimension to the Irish rising that had momentarily distracted the British authorities from prosecuting the war on the European continent and had compromised US neutrality. There were four issues for the administration: firstly, identifying whether or not Irish-American radicals had violated the neutrality laws in planning the rebellion.[59] Secondly, it had to refute allegations from John Devoy that the British interception of the *Aud,* carrying the weapons from Germany, resulted from information leaked by the US administration to the British government on Wilson's orders. Thirdly, it had to monitor the impact of the news on the US public in an election year and fourthly, it needed to ensure that US interests were protected, not just in Ireland but within the wider context of Wilson's continuing peace-making efforts.[60]

State Department officials had been informed by US consuls in Ireland about the arrival of gun shipments to insurgents in Ireland since 1914. Some were funded by US sources and others by Irish and British sources.[61] Furthermore, six days before the rising, four US Secret Service agents had entered the the New York offices of Wolf von Igel, German commercial attaché, and eight documents were seized which revealed details of a gun-running mission to Ireland organized by the Germans, rebel leaders in Dublin and Clan na Gael and evidence of subversion and espionage in the US.[62] Spring Rice was informed by the State Department that funds had been raised for revolutionary purposes but that the actual planning had taken place in Ireland and Germany. It seems that the Wilson administration decided to separate evidence of fund-raising for Ireland from plotting of the revolt in order to avoid British accusations of breaches of neutrality. In the State Department, Polk told Spring Rice in early June that there was 'no sign of Irish plotting' in the US.[63] In the Foreign Office, Rowland Sperling reflected his colleagues' annoyance at Polk's disingenuous statement:

> There may be a technical distinction between "plotting" and "raising funds" but the practical result is the same. That is to say it makes very little practical difference whether the funds raised are remitted to the revolutionaries direct, or are converted into arms and ammunition or passage money for agents. The U.S.G[overnment], needless to say, take a differ-

1916 in M. Digby, *Horace Plunkett: an Anglo-American Irishman* (1949), pp. 210–11; NLI, HPP, P6584, reel 2 of 2, House to Plunkett, 11 May 1916.   **59** Carroll, *American opinion*, p. 62.   **60** J. Devoy, *Recollections of an Irish rebel* (1969), p. 469.   **61** McGarrity later confirmed that £2,300 was sent to Ireland after 10 March 1916. Frost also indicated that US money financed both the gun-running in 1914 and Sinn Féin's organization. Cronin, *The McGarrity papers*, p. 60; NARA, RG59, M580/6, 841.00/32, 'Political disturbances and political conditions in Ireland', 30 September 1916 in Frost to Secretary of State, 14 October 1916.   **62** R.J. Jones, *American espionage: from secret service to CIA* (1977), p. 63.   **63** Carroll, *American opinion*, p. 62; TNA, FO371/2793, Spring Rice to Grey, 6 June 1916.

ent view where their own interests are concerned. I do not know, however, what evidence we have of Irish activities in the US beyond meetings, press articles and collections nominally for relief purposes.[64]

The US government did not disclose the contents of the von Igel papers until autumn 1917 when the US had joined the allied cause.[65]

The second concern for the Wilson administration revolved around the rumours that immediately began to circulate in Washington and New York of government collusion in the British interception of the *Aud* arms ship. One source of these accusations was the *New York Times* and another was Devoy who stated in the *Gaelic American* on 29 April, that it was not Irish informers or British spies who gave the details of the *Aud* to the British 'but that deficiency was supplied by the Washington government.' He believed that the 'anti-Irish and anti-Catholic bigot', Attorney General Thomas Gregory had, working on Wilson's instructions, released the seized documents to Frank Cobb, editor of the New York *World* who passed them on to Spring Rice and the British government, thereby alerting them to the gun-running.[66] Hartley's work reveals that the British government was not given copies of the von Igel documents by Spring Rice or by any one else but that the British ambassador did receive an indirect warning from an American journalist which he cabled to London on 22 April, two days before the rising started:

> I hear from a sure source that among papers seized by authorities in New York are indications of plan for gun-running in Ireland to begin not before April 23rd. Detachments of men are subsequently to be landed whilst German fleet and Zeppelins make demonstrations to engage the attention of our fleet.[67]

Hartley suggests that this warning was deliberately leaked by the US administration to thwart the gun-running. Lansing had seen the von Igel papers, which included a cable sent by Cohalan to Berlin to delay the gun-running until 23 April, and this probably formed the basis of the journalist's warning. But, as Ward notes, British authorities in Ireland already had information on 16 April that a ship with arms and two submarines had left Germany for Ireland.[68] Consequently, the capture of the *Aud* resulted from the unpreparedness of the IRB in Ireland, the presence of the British blockade along the south coast of Ireland and British intelligence and did not arise from a specific US government warning.

64 TNA, FO371/2793, Rowland Sperling, 7 June 1916.   65 Jeffreys-Jones, *American espionage*, p. 65.   66 Devoy, *Recollections*, pp. 469–70. Devoy exonerated Lansing from any blame in the release of the document on the grounds that he was 'normally a very straight man'. Ibid., p. 470. Charles Tansill's interpretation of these events is based on Devoy's claims. C. Tansill, *America and the fight, 1866–1922: an old story based upon new data* (1957), p. 196.   67 TNA, FO371/2804, Spring Rice to Grey, 22 April 1916.   68 Ward, *Ireland and Anglo-American relations*, p. 109.

Nevertheless, Foreign Office officials felt there was a sense of 'embarrassment' within the State Department arising from Devoy's allegations.[69] On 28 April, the administration announced in the *New York Herald* that the few von Igel documents relating to the Irish rising were not 'sufficiently specific to have enabled the American officials to tell the British anything tangible.'[70] But the article did not directly address Devoy's accusation about gun-running and instead went on to deliberately lead the public to link the rising and the gun-running with Casement's separate expedition from Germany. The State Department emphasized that there was no intelligence in the papers that 'could have aided the British government in locating or capturing the Casement expedition.'[71] The matter did not end there and the Committee on Public Information (CPI) investigated the von Igel documents. Finally, in September 1917, the CPI announced that by the time the von Igel documents had arrived in the State Department on 21 April 1916 'Casement had spent several hours in an Irish prison.'[72] As Hartley notes, this line of defence proved to be a 'deliberate and largely successful red herring.'[73] So, while the leaking of the information did not contribute to the British seizure of the guns or of Casement, it was intended to prevent the gun-running and the rising. The CPI deliberately attempted to obfuscate the administration's role therein but ultimately the US administration cannot be accused of betraying the rising as there was no hard intelligence available to them about those events.

The third concern of the Wilson administration in April 1916 related to the US public's response to the Irish rising and executions, particularly in an election year. The British government's propaganda office in Wellington House in London concluded that the rising inspired a hostile reception in western and middle-western newspapers, including the pro-British *Chicago Herald*.[74] Carroll's work on the mainstream press such as the influential *New York Times*, the *Washington Post*, the *New York World* and the *Chicago Tribune*, indicated that they regarded it as 'foolish and futile.' Their editorials regarded Casement as the leader; funding came from Germany and Irish-American revolutionaries. The *New York World*, which was close to the Wilson administration, described the rising as a 'German conspiracy.'[75] Yet, the German dimension did not automatically condemn the leaders of the rising in the eyes of some Americans. For example, Harvard University's President A. Lawrence Lowell, who was admittedly a peace advocate, wrote to Horace Plunkett on 13 May 1916, 'what a tragedy we have witnessed in Dublin ... one cannot help regretting here that the government thought it necessary to execute so many of the conspirators.'[76] Irish-America split along predictable lines. The near defunct Redmondite United Irish League met in New York on 28 April, condemned the rising and pledged its support to

69 TNA, FO371/2797, Sperling, 15 May 1916   70 *New York Herald*, 28 April 1916.   71 Ibid. See also Hartley, *The Irish question*, p. 53.   72 Ward, *Ireland and Anglo-American relations*, p. 108. 73 Hartley, *The Irish question*, pp. 52–3.   74 Peterson, *Propaganda for war*, p. 241.   75 Carroll, *American opinion*, pp. 56–7; Quoted in Hartley, *The Irish question*, p. 55.   76 NLI, HPP, P6584, reel 1 of 2, Lowell to Plunkett, 13 May 1916.

Wilson.[77] Shane Leslie, sub-editor of the pro-Redmond *Ireland* magazine, who was then in the US, confirmed that 'pro-Ally Irishmen ... were calm and sorrowful at the rising.'[78] On the other side, a Clan na Gael rally, also held in New York on 30 April, passed a resolution of sympathy and assistance for the rebels.[79] Spring Rice reported to Grey on 28 April:

> The attitude of public opinion as to the Irish rebellion is on the whole satisfactory. The press seems to be agreed that the movement is suicidal and in the interests of Germany alone. The attitude of the majority of the Irish is uncertain, but if the movement spreads the effect here will be very serious indeed. All are agreed that it will be dangerous to make Casement a martyr.[80]

Spring Rice's caution was wise; in the following weeks, the leaders of the rising were executed, Casement was held for trial on a charge of treason that carried a death sentence and by the end of April, all Ireland was placed under martial law. The combination of these events led to a change in Irish-American and mainstream US opinion on the Irish question, at least until Casement's death. Throughout May 1916, US opinion was shocked and outraged at the executions and the killing of innocent people in Ireland. Mass meetings were held throughout the country to protest against the British government's actions. Even the most anglophile of newspapers, the *New York World*, noted that the executions served 'no good purpose' and the *Washington Post* reported that 'a shock went around the civilised world' when it learnt that the leaders of the Irish revolt 'had been tried by drumhead court-martial, found guilty and sentenced in a trice and shot at sunrise against a wall of Dublin castle.'[81]

The executions brought the moderate and radical Irish-Americans closer than they had been since the 1880s. Both responded in an atavistic manner and drew to their side prominent American personalities. Clan na Gael was further energized, having been given a new cause and grievances and new martyrs and heroes.[82] The most significant public meeting was held on 14 May in an over-flowing Carnegie Hall in New York city. Among the speakers was the progressive future secretary of State, Bainbridge Colby, who equated Britain's policy in Ireland with Germany's in Belgium. Despite the heightened feelings, the acute sensitivities of moderate Irish-Americans to taunts of disloyalty led the pro-allied, pro-Irish and anti-German John Quinn and Judge Martin Keogh to insist that there should be no pro-Germanism evident during the demonstration.[83] Quinn subsequently wrote:

77 W.M. Leary, 'Woodrow Wilson, Irish Americans and the election of 1916', 59.   78 NLI, JRP, MS15236 (14), Leslie to Redmond, 16 May 1916.   79 Leary, 'Woodrow Wilson, Irish Americans and the election of 1916', 59.   80 Gwynn, *The letters and friendships of Sir Cecil Spring Rice*, ii, Spring Rice to Grey, 28 April 1916.   81 Quoted in Carroll, *American opinion*, p. 57.   82 NLI, JQP, MS18436, Quinn, 'In the matter of Sir Roger Casement and the Irish situation in America', 2 June 1916, p. 15.   83 Leary, 'Woodrow Wilson, Irish Americans and the election of 1916', 60; NLI,

the shooting of these men, as it seemed to us in perfectly cold blood, in threes and fours with intervals of two or three days, and in particular the horrible spectacle of nursing a wounded man to a condition where he could be stood up and shot, was simply horrible. It shocked public opinion in this country ... But a more colossal blunder than the shooting of them it is impossible to imagine. It is unthinkable now that this country should in this war go in on the side of Great Britain. And that change has been largely brought about by Great Britain's dull, stupid and unimaginative act in shooting these men.[84]

Quinn's belief that this was a fair reflection of US public opinion was not only based on the sentiments expressed at the meeting but was also due to his close connections with the politicians of both parties in the mid-west and Washington and to the hundreds of editorials published between the outbreak of the rising and the shootings, in which it was assumed 'that there would be magnanimity' shown to the men.[85] A non-American view of the general reaction came from Shane Leslie, who was staying with William Bourke Cockran, another of the speakers. Leslie attended the meeting and received letters and telegrams in his capacity as a journalist. He reported to Redmond in Ireland on 16 May, 'The Irish situation here ... is as bad as it could be ... the present wave of fury sweeping through Irish-America originated with the executions and not with the rising.'[86] Spring Rice forwarded press extracts to the Foreign Office 'illustrating great bitterness aroused by executions ... German-Irish co-operation will be formidable.'[87] Little could be done by Irish-America about the executed leaders, except to gather funds for relief in Ireland but many felt that the Wilson administration should intervene in other ways.[88]

In preparation for Casement's trial, Michael Francis Doyle, one of Casement's lawyers, wrote to his long-time friend, Tumulty on 29 April 1916, and inquired if Wilson might intervene on Casement's behalf 'on the grounds of humanity' but said that he did not want to embarrass Wilson's administration. Tumulty forwarded it for counsel to the State Department where Lester H. Woolsey, assistant solicitor, advised that the US had no legal basis for intervention and that official concern should be limited to the fate of US citizens involved in the ris-

JRP, MS15236 (14), Leslie to Redmond, 3 July 1916.   84 NLI, JQP, MS18436, Quinn, 'In the matter of Sir Roger Casement and the Irish situation in America', 2 June 1916, pp. 14–15.   85 Ibid., 2 June 1916, p. 15.   86 NLI, JRP, MS15236 (14), Leslie to Redmond, 16, 20 May 1916.   87 TNA, FO371/2793, Spring Rice, 19 May 1916.   88 The Irish Relief Fund Committee was established following the Carnegie Hall meeting. The president was Dr Thomas Addis Emmet and its three honorary presidents were cardinals Gibbons, Farley and O'Connell who John Quinn said were 'horrified' at the outbreak of the rising but their 'feelings too were turned' after the shootings. Gibbons and Farley insisted that pro-German politics should not be associated with the relief scheme before they lent their names as honorary presidents. NLI, JQP, MS18436, Quinn, 'In the matter of Sir Roger Casement and the Irish situation in America', 2 June 1916, p. 21; NLI, JRP, MS15236 (14), Leslie to Redmond, 3 July 1916.

ing. Tumulty forwarded the Casement file to Wilson with the query 'What reply shall I make to this?' Agnes Newman [Casement's sister] had also written to the president for help in view of Casement's humanitarian work in South America and Africa. Wilson replied 'We have no choice in a matter of this sort. It is absolutely necessary to say that I could take no action of any kind regarding it.'[89] Although he would not speak out on Casement's behalf the involvement of a US citizen would merit a reaction. Doyle wrote again on 30 May, a few days before he left for Britain, telling Tumulty that he was 'unable' to meet with Polk in the State Department but that he had written to him seeking 'help' from Page 'as he could properly do within the limitation of his official position.' Doyle reassured Tumulty that he 'confidently' expected to secure an 'acquittal' for Casement which would be of 'material assistance' to Wilson in the forthcoming presidential campaign. Tumulty endorsed Doyle's request for Page's help but Polk would not provide a letter to the Foreign Office from the State Department. However, he felt sure that Page would 'be glad to do all that he can for you' but he warned him 'you, of course, realise that [Page] is somewhat limited in his activities, owing to his position.' Wilson knew about both actions.[90] Casement was sent for trial on 26 June when Wilson's decision would be strongly challenged again. It was also clear in early June that while Tumulty had brought the matter to Wilson's attention he had not offered advice to the president. He acted only as a conduit. In the interim, Congress had taken up the Irish question and some politicians had appealed for Wilson to act on two further issues.

The rising, and British treatment of the prisoners were first raised in the Senate on 4 May. Between 12 and 17 May, three resolutions were introduced to the House that requested the British government to treat the Irish leaders as 'prisoners of war' and not as 'criminals.' All three were passed to the Senate Foreign Affairs Committee, which did not report any of them. Speeches critical of Britain were also heard in the Senate, beginning with that of Senator William Borah (Idaho) on 4 May. On 17 May, Senator John W. Kern (Indiana) introduced a resolution asking that the State Department investigate the 'safety and well-being' of US citizens in Ireland. It was sent to Senator Stone's Foreign Relations Committee and forwarded to the White House and the State Department for an opinion.[91] This request for official action to protect US citizens was accompanied by a request from the County Clare Association of California and the Knights of St Patrick for an official condemnation as well.

89 Doyle was a member of the Democratic Party. Leary, 'Woodrow Wilson, Irish Americans and the election of 1916', 61; Quoted in Carroll, *American opinion*, pp. 72–3.   90 NARA, RG59, M580/6, Doyle to Tumulty, 30 May 1916; ibid., Tumulty to Polk, 31 May 1916; M590/1, entry 'President 2 June 1916'; YULMC, FLPP, box 11, file 369, Doyle to Polk, 30 May 1916, ibid., Polk to Doyle, 31 May 1916; NARA, RG59, M580/6, Polk to Philips, 31 May 1916; ibid., Polk to Tumulty, 2 June 1916; ibid., Polk to Page, 2 June 1916.   91 G. Haynes, *The senate of the United States: its history and practice*, 2 vols (1938), i, p. 297; YULMC, FLPP, box 11, file 369, Polk to Stone, 27 May 1916.

Both requests came to Polk's attention and he reported to Stone that the Kern resolution seemed 'harmless.' He also spoke to Wilson who 'did not think there was any particular objection to it' but deemed it 'somewhat unnecessary to adopt it.'[92] In other words, they felt that the British could be trusted to uphold the rights of US citizens. However, Lansing announced that the administration would 'intervene diplomatically in cases where its citizens suffer … a failure or denial of justice.'[93] This intervention was not unusual and merely reflected existing US diplomatic policy and practice.

Unknown to State Department officials in Washington, Adams had assisted US citizens stranded in Kingstown by the conditions during the rising. Adams had set up a temporary office in King's Hotel where he received Americans needing advice and assistance including a US deportation officer who was escorting an 'insane' woman and her young baby back to her home place in Ireland.[94] He also secured a permit to work for the Associate Press journalist, Dewitt T. McKenzie, when he arrived by boat into Rosslare, county Wexford, on 28 April.[95] Along with Frost in Queenstown, Sharp in Belfast, Skinner and Page in London, Adams also became involved with the cases of US citizens directly involved in the rising.[96]

Among the thousands of arrests after the rising were persons who claimed US nationality. Frost reported a 'number' of such cases to the US embassy in London at the time and later said that there were a 'few minor incidents.' But he dealt with all in the course of his 'welfare and passport duties' and 'no concrete difficulty arose.'[97] In Belfast Sharp dealt, as previously mentioned, with the case of Peter Fox, a naturalized US citizen who was arrested by the RIC on 8 May. Sharp followed procedure and requested the police commissioner to provide details on the charges and the result of any trial. On 12 May, he was informed that Fox was a member of the Irish Volunteers and Sinn Féin, that he was in Armagh prison awaiting trial and that his US documents were with the governor of the prison. Sharp's response to this information was to send all details to Skinner in London, who informed him that he had taken all steps necessary and appropriate. Even though he received a letter of intercession from the local clergyman in Carrickmore, testifying to Fox's good character and innocence, Sharp did not visit Fox in prison, nor did he pursue the commissioner for information about the prisoner who was held without trial. Instead he passed the case to Adams in Dublin because Fox was moved to prison there.[98] It is not clear

---

92 YULMC, FLPP, box 11, file 369, Polk to Stone, 27 May 1916.   93 Quoted in Hartley, *The Irish question*, p. 61.   94 NARA, RG59, M580/6, 841.00/33, 'The Sinn Féin rebellion in Ireland, Easter Week, 1916' in Adams to Secretary of State, 29 November 1916.   95 Ibid. James M. Sullivan, former US minister to the Dominican Republic from 1913 to 1915, was detained by the British authorities but was not found to have participated in the rising. When the US entered the war he offered his services to the allies. Colonial Office, Dublin Castle Special Branch Files, (hereafter) Co904/215/420.   96 NARA, RG59, IRFSP, Cork (Queenstown), Dublin, Belfast, July, August 1914, passim.   97 Ibid., M580/6, 841.00/32, 'Political disturbances and political conditions in Ireland', 30 September 1916 in Frost to Secretary of State, 14 October 1916.   98 Ibid., M580/6,

whether Adams pursued this specific case (for Fox was transferred to Frongoch prison in Wales) but he became involved in deciding the fate of other US citizens.

When Adams was able to resume normal office work on 8 May, he handled 'numerous' requests for assistance from 'arrested persons claiming American citizenship.' He reported that some of them were 'difficult of decision and adjustment.' Cablegrams arrived from the US seeking news of relatives and friends and this also took up a lot of his time, but from 8 May onward, and during the following three weeks, his daily work consisted solely of numerous visits to Dublin Castle, Arbor Hill and Mountjoy prison on 'errands of assistance to men claiming American citizenship.' He supplied evidence as to the identity and citizenship of certain prisoners.[99] Among these were Jeremiah [Diarmuid] Lynch, John J. Kilgallon, Thomas Hughes Kelly, Joseph Smith and Eamon de Valera, who had been arrested for their respective roles in the rising and sentenced to death.[1]

According to the *Washington Post*, in response to appeals from Senator James O'Gorman and other senators, Wilson instructed Lansing in early May to contact Page 'to make representations on behalf of Lynch in order to save his life, pending an investigation of the facts in his case by the American government.'[2] When this appeal was sent to General Sir John Maxwell, commander in chief in Ireland, he informed the War Office that Lynch's death sentence had been commuted to ten years of penal servitude. Lynch made no claim for clemency based on his US citizenship.[3] Meanwhile the cases of Kilgallon, Kelly and Smith also elicited official US intervention. On 5 May, upon receipt of a cablegram from the State Department about Kilgallon, an American citizen arrested for 'bearing arms', Adams visited Sir Mathew Nathan, under secretary of state for Ireland, in Dublin Castle who gave him a letter to the chief commissioner of police. The latter promised to investigate the case and notify the consulate. Polk had requested that all information received on the case be sent to his office but Kilgallon had

Sharp to Page, 27 May 1916; ibid., Short to Sharp, 17 May 1916.   99 Ibid., 841.00/33, 'The Sinn Féin rebellion in Ireland, Easter Week, 1916'.   1 The cases of Kilgallon, Smith and Kelly are referred to in YULMC, Frank L Polk Papers (hereafter FLPP), box 11, file 369, Polk to Salmon, 12 May 1916; ibid., Polk to Page, 26 July 1916. De Valera was born in Brooklyn to an Irish-born mother and a Spanish-born father but he never formally acquired US citizenship. He had led a battalion during the rising, was court-martialled and condemned to death. Lynch was a naturalized US citizen and received the same sentence.   2 Quoted in Carroll, *American opinion*, p. 63.   3 NARA, RG59, M580/6, 841.00/36, 'The Irish question at the beginning of 1917', 19 January 1917 in Frost to Secretary of State, 23 February 1917. Lynch was transferred to Dartmoor prison in Britain to serve his ten year sentence. Frost heard from a friend who visited him that his 'dyspepsia' condition of 'many years standing' was regarded by the prison authorities as a 'subterfuge' and he reported to the State Department in early 1917 that Lynch was living on 'gruel issued with his ... breakfast' only. Ibid. After serving thirteen months, Lynch was released under the General Amnesty Act, he returned to Ireland where he was jailed again for conspiracy to steal pigs so as to prevent their export. Adams was informed about the case by the Dublin Metropolitan Police after it was disposed of. The State Department informed the attorney general's office and that of Representative Henry Flood. Ibid., 841.00/66, Adams to Secretary of State, 14 March 1918.

been deported already and had been sent from Richmond jail to Stafford jail in England. Adams passed all the evidence to the US embassy in London for action. He was also contacted by Sinéad de Valera who asked him to intervene in her husband's case on the grounds of his US citizenship. She gave him a copy of 'Edward' de Valera's birth certificate as proof of his claim to citizenship, although he had not taken an oath of allegiance to the United States government. De Valera's death sentence was commuted on 9 May.[4]

The extent to which US intervention was responsible for the reprieves remains unclear. After 8 May, Adams regularly visited the prisoners, had immediate access to prison and military authorities throughout the period and was on good terms with key officials. He claimed afterwards that his intervention at the request of de Valera's wife, led to the death sentence being commuted to imprisonment for life.[5] De Valera himself believed that neither the intervention nor lobbying had 'the slightest influence' on his escaping death:

> What was decisive was that Tom Ashe who also likely to be executed, and myself were court-martialled on the same day and just about the time when Asquith made the public statement that no further executions would take place except those who had signed the Proclamation.[6]

Indeed the British government had decided four days earlier, on 5 May, that only 'ring leaders and proved murderers' should be executed.[7] Also Prime Minister Asquith explained to Maxwell that the executions 'were having a very bad political effect in England and might turn the forthcoming elections against the government.'[8]

In the case of Lynch, Adams had attended the court martial and heard the death sentence. As he was about to leave the prison with a military escort back to the consulate, Adams saw Lynch and thought he was about to be executed. Later in the afternoon, he was informed of the commutation of Lynch's sentence to ten years. Subsequently, he visited Lynch in Mountjoy prison, where the prisoner 'expressed grateful acknowledgement of the services rendered him.' Adams' implication that his involvement had been central can be balanced by Maxwell's complaint to the War Office of being 'bombarded' with appeals, including Wilson's, for clemency for Lynch.[9] Not surprisingly the US newspapers were in no doubt but that Wilson's intervention had saved Lynch's life, while Adams

4 NARA, RG59, M580/6, 841.00/33, 'The Sinn Féin rebellion in Ireland, Easter Week, 1916'; YULMC, FLPP, box 11, file 369, Polk to Salmon, 12 May 1916. 5 NARA, RG59, M580/6, 841.00/33, 'The Sinn Féin rebellion in Ireland, Easter Week, 1916'; T.P. Coogan, *De Valera: long fellow, long shadow* (1993), p. 78. Catherine de Valera in New York, also campaigned on her son's behalf as did her other son Father Wheelright who initiated a letter writing campaign to the White House, the State Department and Congress. Ibid., p. 78. 6 Quoted in Coogan, *De Valera*, p. 78. 7 Hartley, *The Irish question*, pp. 61–2. 8 Quoted in Coogan, *De Valera*, p. 78. 9 NARA, RG59, M580/6, 841.00/33, 'The Sinn Féin rebellion in Ireland, Easter Week, 1916'.

staked his claim to a share of the credit for the commutation of the Lynch and de Valera sentences by recording not just the details of his visits but that he had kept in 'constant communication' with the British military leadership.[10] Nevertheless, on 22 May Grey asked Asquith to insist that the military authorities in Dublin refer to London prior to the imposition of the death sentence on any US citizen and that they fully inform the Foreign Office to enable it give 'early replies to enquiries from the United States government.'[11]

The US administration was obliged to protect the interests of its citizens abroad thus allowing Adams, Sharp and Frost to act. But it was a different matter when it came to the treatment of Irish citizens and issuing an official condemnation. Polk explained to Tumulty on 3 June that the government could not protest on behalf of non-American citizens.[12] Despite the unambiguous nature of the situation, Tumulty asked Polk to meet with him before he replied to Senator Phelan because 'There is so much dynamite in it that we ought to proceed with care.'[13] This appeal came just days before Tumulty headed to St Louis for the twenty-second Democratic national convention where Wilson expected to be renominated as the Democratic Party presidential candidate. In these pre-convention days any issue that threatened Wilson's chances of succeeding at the convention and polls had to be attended to. Undoubtedly Wilson's closest advisers, House and Tumulty, needed a quietening down of the Irish question.[14]

Wilson did not attend the convention until the last day and, instead, Tumulty and secretary of War, Newton D. Baker, chairman of the resolutions committee, worked together to decide platform speakers and speeches. Immediately upon his arrival Tumulty encountered difficulties.[15] On 13 June, he warned Wilson that the hyphenates might try to 'discredit' the president from the platform.[16] It seemed that some of the Democratic Party's leaders wanted to ignore 'this grave issue' but Tumulty decided that the party had to stop 'pussyfooting' on the hyphenism issue and condemn treasonous behaviour.[17] Clearly Tumulty's loyalty was to Wilson, the party and the country and

---

10 Ibid.   11 Quoted in Hartley, *The Irish question*, pp. 61–2. Interventions were made by Polk on behalf of the US citizens, Kelly and Smith. Polk informed Page that Kelly was 'very prominent in Catholic circles … trustee to St. Patrick's Cathedral … friend of three cardinals.' Smith was known by his 'relation to charity rather than to politics.' Polk asked Page 'to assist these persons' and also he contacted Spring Rice. The fate of these men is not known but their cases were considered by State Department officials to be still a 'matter of more than ordinary importance' in late July 1916. YULMC, FLPP, box 11, file 369, Polk to Page, 26 July 1916; Ibid., box 34, file 765, Office of the Solicitor to Crane, 31 July 1916. Kilgallon was released before Christmas 1917 and returned to Dublin. The US embassy in London delayed sending him money for his father until they were 'certain of him going' to the US. Kilgallon left for New York in April 1917. Co904/205/277   12 Quoted in Tansill, *America and the fight for Irish freedom*, pp. 218–19.   13 YULMC, FLPP, box 27, file 369, Tumulty to Polk, 9 June 1916.   14 For further on the influence of Irish-America on the convention see E. Cuddy, 'Irish-Americans and the 1916 election: an episode in immigrant adjustment' in J.B. Walsh (ed.), *The Irish: America's political class selected and interpreted* (1976), pp. 228–43.   15 Blum, *Tumulty*, p. 105.   16 Quoted in Tumulty, *Woodrow Wilson as I know him*, p. 189.   17 Tumulty, *Woodrow Wilson as I know*

he dealt with the concerns of Irish-America only in that order. Wilson agreed with Tumulty and sent a telegram to the resolutions committee condemning any alliance between an individual or group with a foreign power that was dangerous to America's welfare.[18] There was no reference to Ireland in the platform which endorsed Wilson's policies on Mexico and Europe and accepted that it was America's duty 'to assist the world in securing settled peace and justice.' 'Americanism' was the dominant theme but for the first time, the party adopted a policy of internationalism.[19] Wilson's re-nomination intensified the flow of hostility towards him from radical Irish-America. On 24 June, Devoy's *Gaelic American* accused the Democratic Party of being 'ruled by an autocrat whose every whim it obeys' and it backed Charles Evans Hughes, the Republican candidate and a 'man of honour' for the presidency.[20] Irish-American Democrats were horrified at events in Ireland and criticall of Wilson's response to the rising and executions but not sufficiently so to desert Wilson as their candidate or his foreign agenda. During the summer, the Democrats campaigned on the powerful slogan 'he kept us out of war' but encountered another threat to their Irish-American support base because of British policy on the Casement case and the administration's response.

The strength of Irish-American and broader American indignation about the death sentence handed down to Casement on 29 June, has been outlined elsewhere, as has the subsequent chronology of appeals calling for Wilson's intervention.[21] Of interest to this study are the respective roles of Tumulty, Page and other State Department representatives and Wilson's response. Tumulty acted to the extent of his influence but without appearing to champion Casement's cause. On 30 June, he wrote to Lansing and enclosed a memorandum prepared by David Lawrence, a journalist who was respected by Wilson.[22] Lawrence's piece is worth quoting as his words reflected Tumulty's own views on the matter:

---

him, pp. 189–90. **18** Quoted in Tumulty, *Woodrow Wilson as I know him*, pp. 190–1. **19** H. Eaton, *A history of nominating conventions, 1868–1960* (1964), p. 258. The 1910 revolution in Mexico was followed by internecine fighting but Wilson's policy of non-intervention was reversed in March 1916. The Mexican leader, Pancho Villa, invaded the US and General John Pershing was dispatched to arrest him. This US invasion of Mexico proved unsuccessful and skirmishes continued in the following three years. Relations between the two countries worsened in 1917 when the Zimmerman telegram was published. It outlined German aid to Mexico to recapture territory lost to the US in 1846–8. The dilemmas for Wilson were between his stated belief in democracy and upholding American interests, he also came under pressure from Catholics in the US who criticized US intervention. A.S Link, W.M. Leary, Jr, 'Election of 1916' in A.M. Schlesinger et al., *History of American presidential elections, 1789–2001, III, 1900–36*, 11 vols (1971), iii, p. 2253. **20** *Gaelic American*, 24 June 1916. **21** Carroll, *American opinion*, pp. 71–8. The lord chief justice at the trial was Lord Reading who was appointed by Lloyd George in January 1918 as British ambassador to the US in place of Cecil Spring Rice. Marquess of Reading, *Rufus Isaacs: First Marquess of Reading, 1914–35* (1945). **22** Lawrence had been an undergraduate at Princeton when Wilson was president. After Wilson was re-elected in 1916, Lawrence successfully pleaded with Wilson to retain Tumulty as his private secretary. Lee Levin, *Edith and Woodrow*, p. 171.

It is, of course, impossible for our government to intercede officially in the case of Sir Roger Casement, nor can we with propriety make a direct request for clemency. Yet, we can accomplish practically the same thing – a thing that would please a great many of our people – by transmitting to Ambassador Page a condensation of numerous requests which have been received at the White House and the State Department urging the United States to use its good offices for Sir Roger and to obtain a commutation. The Ambassador might be instructed to transmit this as a matter of information to the British government. Of course, the plain inference of such an action would be that there are thousands of Irish in the United States who would be very much gratified by a commutation. Even if Great Britain did not grant a commutation and carried out this sentence, the American government will be in the position of having at least tried to do what was possible. Even people not of Irish sympathy would regard our action as a humanitarian one, realising that enough blood has already been spilled over the Irish rebellion.

The advantage to England in apparently yielding to sentiment in America would be very great, in my opinion, whereas execution would only rekindle the flame of resentment which swept over this country when the execution took place.[23]

It is unlikely that Wilson saw this memorandum because, if he had, Tumulty would probably have noted the event. Nonetheless, Lawrence and Tumulty agreed on the political and humanitarian importance of some approach by the US government to the British government, particularly with the presidential elections looming. Lansing did not act but this did not deter Tumulty, who subsequently facilitated other attempts to get Wilson to intervene. An appeal to commute the death sentence had been lodged by Casement's legal team and was due for hearing in London on 17 July. Doyle, Casement's lawyer, was aware of the widespread sympathy for his client in the US and hoped to take advantage of it, but he was also a friend of Tumulty's and a Democrat and did not wish to embarrass Wilson. Doyle was strongly sensitive to Wilson's dilemma on the matter but clearly believed his client was worth saving. On 6 July, Doyle, using Tumulty's good offices, appealed again to Wilson to mediate with Grey or Asquith. The lawyer was convinced that Wilson's intercession would win clemency for Casement.[24]

At this time Tumulty was also worried about the possible loss of pro-allied Wilson supporters. He had already given an equivocal reply to eight congressmen who petitioned Wilson to intervene for clemency in late June, saying that Wilson would raise the matter with the State Department.[25] He arranged for

23 NARA, RG59, M580/6, 841.00/18, Tumulty to Lansing, 30 June 1916.   24 Quoted in Tansill, *America and the fight for Irish freedom*, pp. 208–9.   25 Blum, *Tumulty*, p. 107.

Franz H. Krebs, a journalist who was fully informed about the case and had met Casement, to discuss it with Wilson on 7 July. He hoped Krebs would persuade Wilson to intervene and the former's record of the meeting suggests that progress had been made:

> President Wilson gave me a most sympathetic hearing when I spoke to him about the great work Sir Roger had done in collecting the evidence on which the British parliament had acted and did away with King Leopold's rule in Congo; further I mentioned Sir Roger's work in connection with stopping the Putaymo outrages, President Wilson signified that he was fully informed regarding Sir Roger's activities in the past ... The general feeling in Washington is that the death penalty will be commuted.[26]

But the journalist was unsuccessful and Tumulty's plan failed. In London, the appeal to the Court of Criminal Appeal was dismissed on 18 July.[27] On 28 July, Page was informed that the State Department would take 'no action' regarding the protests against the sentence. Two days later, Wilson replied to Tumulty that 'it would be inexcusable for me to touch this. It would involve serious international embarrassment.'[28]

The probable reasons for his decision not to act can be synopsized in his firm belief in his party's electioneering slogans; 'Americanism' and 'he kept us out of war'. The former ensured that he would not appease any hyphenate groups who put the interests of their native country above those of their adopted country. In the case of the latter, he was worried that his intervention would worsen US–British relations which were already at a crisis point due to the British government's publication of the blacklist on July 19. British firms were forbidden from dealing with eighty-seven US firms who were suspected of trading with the central powers. Wilson penned a sharp note to the British government and when the latter failed to reply he requested Congress to amend the Shipping Act to prevent any vessel from entering US waters which refused to carry the cargo of a blacklisted US citizen.[29] In late July and throughout August, therefore, US relations with Britain were at breaking point.

But what about the role of the State Department? Lansing and Polk had been fully informed by both Spring Rice and Page about the apparent determination of the British government to impose the death sentence on Casement. On 6 July, Spring Rice told Polk who was acting secretary of State, that the London government 'had no intention of granting a reprieve.' The State Department had further evidence which showed that 'all the Irish prisoners in Germany who had refused to assist Casement, had been severely dealt with' by the German author-

---

26 Quoted in Tansill, *America and the fight for Irish freedom*, pp. 209–10.   27 Reading, *Rufus Isaacs*, p. 21.   28 NARA, RG59, M580/1, entry 'Great Britain 28 July 1916'; Quoted in Leary, ' Woodrow Wilson, Irish Americans and the election of 1916', 61, fn.21.   29 Link & Leary, 'Election of 1916', p. 2259.

ities. Polk suggested that 'it would be a wise thing for some cabinet officer to make a statement on the case very promptly if the facts were as stated' and Spring Rice agreed. Clearly Polk's suggestion was intended to reduce the pressure on Wilson although he felt that anything less than a reprieve for Casement would not 'satisfy the Irish ... rather a hopeless undertaking at present.'[30] Page, in London, counselled against Wilson's intervention.[31] On 1 July, Lansing telegraphed Page in London to ask him to transmit a message to Casement from his sister; 'Keep up dear heart, my dearest brother, am doing everything possible.' Page was to get the 'approval of the British authorities.' Immediately he responded:

> I fear that a request made to the British government in this matter will produce [a] very disagreeable impression. Not only does Casement, a British subject, stand convicted of treason but I am privately informed that much information about him of an unspeakably filthy character was withheld from publicity ... If the government will permit me to deliver his sister's telegram they will permit Doyle. Thus, the same result will be accomplished and our government will not become the channel of communication. If all the facts about Casement ever became public it will be well that our government had nothing to do with him or his case ...[32]

Page's personal and official opposition to the cause of Irish republicanism and to US intervention on the Irish question emerges clearly but so also does his facilitation of the British authorities' smear campaign against Casement. Page's reference to 'information' related to several diaries found by the British authorities among Casement's effects. While the British cabinet may not have sanctioned the campaign, officials in the Home and Foreign offices, along with the Admiralty, passed information or showed extracts from the diaries to newspaper journalists in Britain and to influential Americans, which, they claimed, revealed details of Casement's homosexual activities.[33] The authenticity of the diaries is not of concern here but Page believed they were true. Thus, the ambassador used the information as another reason to dissuade Wilson from making any plea of clemency for Casement. Page's rampant anglophilism and pro-allied views had limited his usefulness to the US administration by now.[34] Nevertheless, he had

---

30 LC, Robert Lansing Papers (hereafter RLP), volume 30, Polk to Lansing, 7 July 1916.   31 B. Willson, *America's ambassadors to England (1785–1928): a narrative of Anglo-American diplomatic relations* (1928), p. 452; R. Gregory, *Walter Hines Page: ambassador to the Court of St. James* (1970), p. 161.   32 NARA, RG59, M580/6, 841.00/17a, Lansing to Page, 1 July 1916; ibid., 841.00/18, Page to Lansing, 3 July 1916.   33 See Hartley, *The Irish question*, p. 85.   34 Gregory, *Walter Hines Page*, p. 162. Gerard in Germany had met Casement in early 1915 and forwarded 'without comment' letters Casement wrote to Bryan dated 1 February and 8 March 1915, which forcefully asserted that he was not in the pay of Germany, his work was dedicated to aiding Ireland only and he feared for his life from a British-orchestrated conspiracy against him. NARA, RG59, M589/6, 841.00/12, Gerard to Bryan, 8 February 1915; ibid., 841.00/13, Gerard to Bryan, 9 March 1915. Later on in

assisted in discrediting Casement and in undermining the US campaign for clemency. Finally, the actions of Page's staff on 3 August, the day of Casement's execution, also revealed a certain partiality for the British position.

While Wilson was unwilling to act, US politicians seeking votes from ethnic communities in the upcoming elections were more than willing to intervene. On 29 July, four days before the execution day, the US Senate passed a resolution requesting Wilson to transmit to the British government its plea for 'clemency in the treatment of Irish political prisoners.'[35] Polk complied with the instruction and had it transmitted to the London embassy on 2 August, where it reached the desk of Irwin Laughlin, chargé d'affaires.[36] By then Laughlin had received another telegram from Polk, sent at 5.00 p.m. on 2 August 1916; 'Please report immediately if Senate resolution presented to Foreign Office and also any further details on Casement case.'[37] Fortunately for Page, he was by then en route to Washington for 'a rest.' So, it fell to Laughlin to bring the resolution to Asquith's attention. He admitted to Polk that it was in response to the second telegram, with its urgent tone and focus on the Casement case, that he met with Grey at 10.00 a.m. on 3 August, and 'in a round about fashion' raised the Casement case and handed the resolution to Grey who asked if he could bring it to Asquith's attention. Laughlin replied 'this was the desire of his government' and the conversation continued on to other matters. Laughlin then cabled the secretary of State on 3 August at 4.00 p.m. that he had delivered the resolution but that Grey 'did not promise an answer but said he would communicate the Senate's resolution to the Prime Minister and probably lay it before the Cabinet.' The cable continued, 'Casement was executed early this morning.'[38] Casement had been executed in Pentonville prison in London, a few minutes after 9.00 a.m. on 3 August.

The reaction in the US was mixed. Spring Rice reported to London that influential newspapers had not over-reacted because of the 'timely warnings' which he had given about Casement's character to certain American journalists and to the Catholic Apostolic delegate.[39] Moreover, he reported to Grey that congressional agitation had been 'rather checked by the dread that some publication will be made exposing the private character of Casement.'[40] Nevertheless, mainstream newspa-

1917, Gerard wrote that Casement often visited German prisons where he persuaded thirty 'weaklings' to 'desert their flag and join the Germans'. The visits, the ambassador recalled, were discontinued because the 'remaining Irishmen chased him out of the camp.' See Gerard, *My four years in Germany*, p. 131.   35 NARA, RG59, M580/6, 841.00/20,Resolution, 29 July 1916.   36 *FRUS*, 1916 supplement (1929), Polk to Page, 2 August 1916; ibid., Laughlin to Secretary of State, 3 August, 1916; NARA, RG59, M580/6, 841.00/20, Polk to Embassy, 2 August 1916.   37 NARA, RG59, M580/6, 841.00/20a, Polk to Embassy, 2 August 1916.   38 *FRUS*, 1916 supplement, Laughlin to Secretary of State, 3 August 1916. Carroll details the private appeals that were made by individuals, including Cardinal Gibbons, John Quinn, Senator Henry Cabot Lodge, and groups to the British government to save Casement's life. See Carroll, *American opinion*, p. 77.   39 Inglis, *Casement*, pp. 375–6.   40 Hartley, *The Irish question*, pp. 93–4.

pers that had been critical of Casement now revealed sympathy for him. The *Washington Post* described the execution as a 'colossal blunder', the *Chicago Tribune* concluded 'England made him; England unmade him' and the moderate nationalist John Quinn wrote in the *New York Times* on 13 August, 'However technically his offence may be phrased, his actual offence, if any, was that he put the cause of Ireland before that of England or even the Allies.'[41] Quinn who was close to Spring Rice, refused to believe that Casement was 'abnormal or addicted to abnormal practices.' He believed that Casement's life 'was one of absolute purity.' Nor did he accept that Casement 'ever touched a penny of German money.' Other moderates had expected Casement to be imprisoned and not executed. In June 1916, prior to the execution, Quinn had received over fifty personal letters from people who had met Casement in the US and, despite his German activities, admired him and hoped that he would be merely imprisoned for the duration of the war.[42] Not surprisingly the attacks on Wilson from radical Irish-America ranged from venomous to indignant, particularly after the unionist Lord Robert Cecil, parliamentary under secretary at the Foreign Office, revealed on 3 August that the British government had not received an appeal from the State Department.[43]

US newspapers reported that, although the resolution had been passed in the Senate on Saturday, 29 July, it was not cabled to London until 3.00 p.m. (Washington time) and 9.00 p.m. (London time) on Wednesday, 2 August, and was not delivered to the Foreign Office until 10.00 a.m. on 3 August, an hour after Casement had been hanged.[44] The White House, the State Department and the British embassy in London were all suspected of deliberately withholding the message until it was too late to save Casement. Among those who believed this were Doyle (Casement's US lawyer), Senator Phelan and James J. McGuire the newspaper publisher and chairman of the executive committee of the Friends of Irish Freedom, who all demanded an explanation from the Wilson administration for the delay in the delivery of the resolution from the White House to the State Department.[45] Senator Henry P. Ashworth of Arizona, on behalf of John

41 Carroll, *American opinion*, p. 78.   42 NLI, JQP, MS18436, Quinn, 'In the matter of Sir Roger Casement and the Irish situation in America', 2 June 1916, pp. 9, 12. Indeed after Casement arrived in Germany, a report appeared in the *New York World* that he was in the pay of the German government and in early 1915 Casement instructed Quinn to sue for libel which he refused to do as he knew the case would not succeed. Ibid., p. 9. In February 1917, Frost in Queenstown reported that most nationalists believed that Casement was not part of the 'inner councils' in Berlin, that he had tried to stop the rising in Ireland and was 'mad.' Frost agreed with the latter comment, having met Agnes Newman whom he believed to be 'distinctly *non compos*.' Nonetheless he was sympathetic to Casement, particularly because of the continuation in position of Captain Bowen-Colthurst after the murder of Francis Sheehy Skeffington. Frost endorsed the Irish nationalists' explanation that 'If you are going to be mad it is safer to be a Unionist.' NARA, RG59, M580/33, 'The Irish question at the beginning of 1917', 19 January 1917 in Frost to Secretary of State, 23 February 1917.   43 Carroll, *American opinion*, p. 82; *PWW*, 38, Doyle to Tumulty, 29 September 1916.   44 NARA, RG59, M580/6, Moore to Ashurst, 8 August 1916. A headline in the *Washington Times* on 4 August ran 'Casement appeal arrives too late.'   45 YULMC, FLPP, box 11, file 369, Phelan to

D. Moore, national secretary of the Friends, asked Lansing on 9, 16 and 25 August for the 'particular time' the State Department received the resolution and 'on what day and at what hour' the resolution was cabled to Page.[46] On three occasions between 1 August and 29 September, Doyle requested a copy of the telegram which 'the President had sent to Ambassador Page' requesting clemency for Casement and a copy of Page's reply. On 29 September, he reported that Agnes Newman, had received letters from London stating that, had the Senate resolution been presented 'in time', her brother's life would have been spared. Doyle warned Tumulty that the Republicans are 'making a campaign issue' of the delay in sending the resolution and that the 'great bulk of Catholics and those of Irish descent are opposing the President.'[47] Tumulty learnt that the Casement matter played a 'prominent part' in the recent New Jersey primaries and he believed that it had 'resulted in bringing many votes' to Senator James E. Martine who had just won re-nomination as the Democratic senatorial candidate. His main opponent was John Wesley Wescott, a Wilson supporter.[48]

Tumulty set about getting the truth from the State Department. Immediately after Casement's execution he received an oral briefing from Polk on the facts of the State Department's role in the transmission of the resolution. On 6 and 17 August, Polk wrote minutes on the matter and circulated the latter to Lansing and William McAdoo, secretary of the Treasury. These reports, which were later expanded, indicated that the resolution passed in the Senate on Saturday 29 July was mailed to Wilson at 5.30 p.m. that evening. It arrived at the White House on Monday 31 July. But it was not until between 11.00 a.m. and noon on Wednesday 2 August, the day before the execution, that Forester, in the White House telephoned Polk and stated that the resolution was being sent to the State Department and 'to please have it forwarded as promptly as possible.' The resolution arrived soon after but was not accompanied by a 'letter of transmittal' directing 'the action to be taken' and Polk had to request this from the White House. In the interim, Polk sent off the telegram to the London embassy at 1.00 p.m. with the resolution only. After he received the instruction from the White House that Wilson wanted Page to transmit it to the Foreign Office, Polk sent a second telegram, later in the day, asking the ambassador to present the resolution 'at the earliest possible moment' and 'to report' back to Washington. It was clear, therefore, that the State Department's response was correct and that the delay occurred in the White House. Polk recorded that he spoke subsequently with Tumulty and 'understood from [him] that the reason for the delay was just

Tumulty, 4 August 1916; ibid., Tumulty to Polk, 5 August 1916. James K. McGuire, chairman of FOIF telegraphed Wilson on 5 August. Ibid., McGuire to Wilson, 5 August 1916.   46 NARA, M580/6, 841.00/23, Ashurst to Lansing, 9, 16 and 25 August 1916.   47 LC, RLP, vol 30, Doyle to Tumulty, 29 September 1916; NARA, M580/6, 841.00/28, Doyle to Tumulty, 28 August 1916. 48 LC, RLP, vol 30, Tumulty to Lansing, 29 September 1916; PWW, 38, O'Leary to Wilson, 29 September 1916, fn.2. US Catholics were already critical of Wilson's 'faltering' Mexican policy. Grady, 'Irish Americans', p. 233.

that there had been some hesitation about sending the resolution.'[49] On 7 August, he confirmed to Tumulty in writing that there was 'no delay' in the State Department.[50] In reply to yet another query from the private secretary, written on 28 August 1916, Lansing confirmed this version to Tumulty on 2 September.[51] But Tumulty needed further clarification of the administration's role because continuing criticism had made the matter one of 'most vital importance.' On 7 September, he asked Lansing for a letter for publication to indicate 'first, the reluctance of our government to intervene because of lack of precedent ... second, we went as far as we reasonably could in making known to the British Foreign Office the attitude of certain of our citizens regarding the matter ... third, that Ambassador Page ... informed the British Foreign Office.'[52] The pressure on the administration was relieved somewhat on 8 September, when senators Hughes and Phelan both exonerated US officials during a discussion in the Senate.[53] But on 29 September Tumulty appealed to Lansing 'Is there any thing new in the ... Sir Roger Casement matter?'[54]

Lansing was unwilling to help him or McAdoo, who on 5 September had asked the secretary if he had any objection to a memorandum on the subject being given to McGuire of the Friends of Irish Freedom for publication. The Friends was determined to discover why the delivery of the resolution had been 'bungled' by the White House and the State Department. Lansing replied on 9 September:

> I am convinced no good purpose can be served by doing so. While I have only met Mr McGuire two or three times and cannot claim any acquaintance with him ... I know him thoroughly by reputation ... He is, as you know, an extremist in Irish affairs and as a consequence is avowedly pro-German in his sympathies. For these reasons, I think to allow him to publish this memo. as an official statement of the State Department would be most unwise, and furthermore, would dignify him more than would be justifiable or expedient.[55]

When Lansing received Tumulty's request for an update on 29 September, he passed the matter back to Polk.[56] But the pressure on Tumulty for a public expla-

49 NARA, RG59, M580/6, 841.00/23, Polk, 17 August 1916; YULMC, FLPP, box 27, file 370, Polk 6 August 1916; NARA, M580/6, 841.00/28, Lansing to Tumulty, 2 September 1916. **50** *PWW*, 38, Polk to Tumulty, 7 August 1916. **51** Doyle appealed to Wilson also who requested advice from Lansing on his reply. NARA, RG59, M580/1, entry 'President 31 August 1916'; ibid., RG59, M580/6, 841.00/28, Lansing to Tumulty, 2 September 1916. **52** YULMC, PLPP, box 27, file 370, Tumulty to Lansing, 7 September 1916. **53** Ibid., Tumulty to Doyle, 11 October 1916. **54** LC, RLP, vol 30, Tumulty to Lansing, 29 September 1916; *PWW*, 38, O'Leary to Wilson, 29 September 1916, fn.2. **55** LC, RLP, vol 30, Lansing to McAdoo, 9 September 1916; F.M. Carroll, 'Friends of Irish Friends' in M.F. Funchion (ed.), *Irish American voluntary organizations*, p. 121. **56** LC, RLP, vol 30, Lansing handwritten note on Tumulty to Lansing, 29 September 1916.

nation led him to write again the following day and to urge 'action' on the Casement matter.[57] At this time Polk was in New York but Lansing expected him in the Washington office on 3 October and promised Tumulty that he would hand him Doyle's letter 'and ask him to write to you.' Lansing explained the State Department's position to Tumulty in a letter on 2 October:

> Of course, you know, at least I think that I told you, that the resolution was transmitted to this Department from your office with the request that it be forwarded to London on the morning of the day preceding the Casement execution. It was received at eleven a.m. and was on the wires at one p.m. of that day. The embarrassment is that it reached the Department so late, as one p.m. would correspond to six p.m. London time. It probably could not, with all diligence, have reached our embassy before midnight, where it has to be then deciphered.[58]

Lansing was clear that the resolution was dealt with promptly, that the State Department was blameless and that responsibility for the delay lay in the White House. On 5 October, Polk confirmed Lansing's view.[59] Eventually Lansing, Polk, Tumulty and senators Hughes and Phelan agreed on the same interpretation of events and the explanation that the delay did not matter because the British cabinet was made aware of the Senate resolution by Spring Rice long before the actual paper version arrived but decided to disregard it.[60] This view was presented in the Senate on 8 September, sent to Doyle on 14 October and was subsequently published in the *New York Times* on 17 October. Leary suggests that the delay was probably caused by 'administrative incompetence' but Tumulty admitted to Polk, immediately after the execution, that Wilson had hesitated over whether to send the resolution to London.[61]

Some aspects of the Casement affair deserve closer attention. Firstly, there is Tumulty's role. He was guided by his loyalty to the president, his fidelity to the Democratic Party and his belief in Americanism. During summer and autumn 1916, he treated Casement in the context of the anti-Catholic criticisms directed at the Wilson administration and their effects on Wilson's campaign. He received reports from contacts throughout the country that Catholics in general were disenchanted not just with Wilson's stance on Casement but with his Mexican policy, his decision to appoint a Protestant, James R. Mott, to the Mexican–American joint high commission and by rumours of Wilson's discourtesy towards visiting Catholic prelates. Getting Wilson re-elected was, for Tumulty, the central aim.[62]

57 Ibid., Lansing handwritten note, 9 October 1916.   58 Ibid., Lansing to Tumulty, 2 October 1916.   59 *PWW*, 38, Polk to Tumulty, 5 October 1916.   60 Ibid., Tumulty to Doyle, 14 October 1916; YULMC, FLPP, Polk to McGuire, 3 October 1916.   61 Blum, *Tumulty*, pp. 108–9; *PWW*, 38, Polk to Tumulty, 7 August, 5 October 1916, Tumulty to Doyle, 14 October 1916; Leary, 'Woodrow Wilson, Irish Americans and the election of 1916', 62, fn. 22; NARA, RG59, M580/6, 841.00/23, Polk, 17 August 1916.   62 Blum, *Tumulty*, pp. 108, 109.

Secondly, as will be seen, at a time of crisis in US–British relations, Polk behaved correctly by immediately transmitting the resolution to London in August. Polk had also had 'several conversations' with Spring Rice on the subject before the executions in which he pointed out to the ambassador that in his 'opinion' the execution would be a 'political mistake.' Polk correctly believed that Spring Rice agreed with him as he had cautioned the Foreign Office many times about turning Casement into a 'martyr' for republicans.[63] On 2 August, the ambassador told Polk that he had cabled a paraphrase of the resolution to his government immediately after it was passed and he showed the US official a return dispatch from the British government stating that it had considered the Casement case in cabinet and decided that he must be executed, in spite of the feeling in the US, as he was guilty of treason.[64] During another talk with Spring Rice on 3 August, he read to Polk a copy of another message received from Grey, which indicated that the cabinet had 'no intention' of granting a reprieve.[65] Moreover, Maurice Hankey, secretary to the cabinet, recalled that when the British cabinet came to consider the Casement case for the last time on 2 August, it had before it 'the urgent appeals for mercy from authoritative and friendly quarters in the United States.' Discussion continued for an hour and a half and the decision was 'taken with rare unanimity that Sir Roger Casement should be hanged.'[66]

Finally, Polk's explanation of events offers further insight into the lack of support present in the upper levels of the State Department for any greater level of official intervention. [67] In his rush to exonerate the State Department, Polk noted that the Senate resolution referred to 'Irish political prisoners' and 'it was the opinion of the British government and of our embassy in London that this did not apply to Casement as he was not a political prisoner.' Moreover, he offered another reason to excuse both the embassy staff and the British government; 'it was their belief that this resolution had to do with the Irishmen mixed up in the revolt.'[68] It is true that Page and Laughlin were embarrassed by the

63 NARA, RG59, M580/6, 841.00/23, Polk, 17 August 1916; YULMC, FLPP, box 27, file 370, Polk, 6 August 1916; TNA, FO371/2851, Spring Rice, 4 May 1916; Gwynn, *The letters and friendships of Sir Cecil Spring Rice*, ii, Spring Rice to Grey, 30 May 1916. One Foreign Office official commented that 'it would require a vast amount of "manufacturing" to turn Casement into a martyr.' TNA, FO371/2851, Lancelot Oliphant, undated.   64 YULMC, PLPP, box 27, file 370, Polk, 6 August 1916. Vansittart (Foreign Office) recalled that Spring Rice's cable was brought to Asquith in bed and he 'turned over and said that he would think about it.' Lord Vansittart, *The mist procession: the autobiography of Lord Vansittart* (1958), pp. 155–6.   65 Ibid., box 9, file 304, Polk to Lansing, 3 August 1916.   66 S. Roskill, *Hankey, man of secrets, volume 1, 1877–1918*, 3 vols (1970), i, p. 285.   67 NARA, RG59, M580/6, 841.00/23, Polk, 17 August 1916. Wilbur Carr met with Michael Francis Doyle on 1 August 1916. Doyle felt that Casement's 'mind was unsettled by his work in the Congo and in south America' but Carr recorded in his diary 'when I saw Casement after his return from south America he did not look like a man with an unsound mind.' Yet, Carr felt that meeting Casement and others such as former British ambassadors, Bryce and Spring Rice made his life 'most interesting.' LC, MD, WCP, box 2, diary 1916, 1 August 1916.   68 NARA, RG59, M580/6, 841.00/23, Polk, 17 August 1916.

whole episode. Laughlin, as chargé d'affaires, was responsible for the embassy business in Page's absence and was on good terms with Grey. The American diplomat, however, was embarrassed about presenting the appeal. He worried that Grey might refuse to receive the resolution and might regard it as an interference with matters that exclusively concerned Britain. Page himself had met with Asquith on 1 August and had re-assured the prime minister that he 'would guarantee the stability' of US–British relations during this time of difficulty. Page clearly endorsed Asquith's decision not to 'interfere with' the Casement case 'in spite of the shoals of telegrams that he was receiving from the United States.' Consequently, Laughlin adopted a casual approach to his meeting with Grey and, once the resolution was handed over, the conversation carried on to talk about other matters. Laughlin followed the lead given by Page on the matter and approached the meeting in a routine manner. But Polk's stated view that the embassy officials and British cabinet did not know that the resolution referred to Casement, seems disingenuous also, given the widespread attention devoted to the matter and Page's own report that 'Casement then loomed large in the daily press and the activities of the American Senate had likewise caused a commotion in London.'[69] Despite Polk's earnest attempt to deflect attention to the British cabinet there was never 'any real prospect of ministers changing their minds.' Home Secretary Herbert Samuel outlined the reasons immediately after the cabinet meeting on 2 August:

> ... his reprieve would let loose a tornado of condemnation, would be bitterly resented by the great mass of the people in Great Britain and by the whole of the army, and would profoundly and permanently shake public confidence in the sincerity and courage of the government ... Had Casement not been a man of atrocious moral character, the situation would have been even more difficult.[70]

In other words, the case was treated as a purely domestic matter, a view that was confirmed by Asquith to House on 28 August; 'we are not favourably impressed by the action of the Senate in having passed a resolution about the Irish prisoners though they have taken no notice of outrages in Belgium and massacres of Armenians.'[71] But the British cabinet was also secure in the knowledge that the smear campaign against Casement's personality would continue in the US and reduce criticism of it.

The final aspect of the Casement affair worthy of noting is the extent to which it, and the events surrounding the rising and executions, destabilized Wilson's Irish-American support outside extremist circles. This dissatisfaction with Wilson must not be taken out of context and, once again, should not be exaggerated.

---

69 Hendrick, *The life and letters f Walter H. Page*, ii, p. 168.   70 Inglis, *Casement*, pp. 365–6.   71 Ibid.

Simultaneously with the Casement matter, the Wilson government had intervened positively in Irish affairs. By July, the Irish Relief Fund Committee had raised $100,000 in the US to alleviate the 'unspeakable want and distress' created by the rising in Ireland and, on 8 July, John A. Murphy and John Gill sailed for Ireland to begin relief operations there. They were armed with a letter of introduction from Lansing to Page and were followed a week later by Thomas Hughes Kelly, a New York banker and treasurer of the committee, his wife and Joseph Smith, a Massachusetts journalist and labour leader. All were US citizens and Murphy and Gill were kept under surveillance by British authorities from the moment they arrived in Ireland to ensure that their activities were of a philanthropic, and not a political, nature. Spring Rice had counselled Grey on 16 June that a benevolent attitude should be adopted towards the distribution of funds for the 'sufferers of the revolt.' On 14 July, he wrote to Foreign Secretary Grey that it would be diplomatically useful if Smith and Kelly were also allowed to land. Lord Hardinge, the permanent under secretary, agreed but noted warily 'the bitterly hostile attitude of Irishmen in America and the suspicion surrounding J.W. Smith preclude the possibility of regarding such persons as messengers of peace.' The Foreign Office feared that the funds would be used to prepare for another rising in Ireland. The Home Office took the possibility more seriously. Smith was barred from entering Ireland because 'there was good reason for believing that he was engaged in business hostile to this country.' Kelly was barred by reason of association.[72]

When word of the detentions reached the US, it aroused anger within influential Irish-American circles that led to a congressional resolution calling for the suspension of diplomatic relations and a flood of appeals to Wilson and the State Department, including those from Cardinal Farley of New York and Mayor Curley of Boston. According to Tumulty, Wilson instructed Polk to try and persuade the British authorities to permit the relief operations. On 26 July, Polk instructed Laughlin, in the London embassy, to investigate the situation and to assist Kelly and Smith. Wilson's involvement and Polk's personal reference for Kelly, however, could not outweigh the British intelligence which confirmed that along with delivering the funds, the men wanted to discover if Ireland was ready for another rising. For the British, domestic considerations, such as securing Ireland, were supreme. In late September, Page explained to Wilson that protests and complaints about British treatment of US citizens had led the Foreign Office to regard the State Department as an 'easy recipient of personal grievances.' He believed requests to transmit US aid to Ireland were granted and declined according to British notions of 'the degree of harm they would do to their military cause.'[73] Once again the Wilson government had shown that it was willing to act,

72 Carroll, *American opinion*, p. 80; Hartley, *The Irish question*, p. 109; Ward, *Ireland and Anglo-American relations*, pp. 128–9; Gwynn, *The letters and friendships of Sir Cecil Spring Rice*, ii, Spring Rice to Grey, 16 June 1916.   73 *PWW*, 38, Page to Wilson, c. 23 September 1916, p. 244.

but only when US citizens were involved, and ultimately its intervention failed as Smith and Kelly returned to the US in late August.

Thus, against a background of deteriorating US–British relations and of the up-coming election, Wilson's practical inaction on the Casement matter can be contrasted with his willingness to intervene to protect US citizens' rights in foreign jurisdictions. Furthermore, while radical Irish-America remained hostile to him, Wilson's neutrality message appealed more to the majority of Irish America. Consequently, he was even able to rebut and survive Jeremiah O'Leary's accusations of pro-Britishness in September. O'Leary cabled him:

> Again we greet you with a popular disapproval of your pro-British policies … Your foreign policies, your failure to secure compliance with all American rights, your leniency with the British empire, your approval of war loans, the ammunition traffic, are issues in this campaign … Anglomaniacs and British interest may control newspapers, but they don't control votes … When, Sir, will you respond to these evidences of popular disapproval of your policies by action?[74]

Wilson responded immediately, drew up a reply, typed it on his personal machine and read it out at a press conference that he called for that same afternoon:

> Your telegram received. I would feel mortified to have you or anybody like you vote for me. Since you have access to many disloyal Americans and I have not I will ask you to convey the message to them.[75]

Tumulty heard the reply for the first time at a press conference that Wilson instructed him to call and House was in New York, so it seems that Wilson acted unilaterally and without consultation. Radical Irish-America seized on the reply as evidence of Wilson's hatred for the Irish, but Tumulty and Lansing felt it gave the Wilson campaign a boost. Other intelligence acquired by Lansing appeared to confirm this view. E.C. Sivect, in the legal department for the state of Nebraska, responded on 21 October to a request from Lansing to sound out local Irish-Americans on their voting intentions,

> Yesterday, I was talking with an old gentleman named McGuire from the Black Hills district of South Dakota … in the course of the conversation he mentioned that Jeremiah O'Leary matter and said that the President's reply to O'Leary was the means of swinging hundreds of Irish votes in his direction up in the Hills district. In fact the language which he used in connection with O'Leary was far from complimentary and will not bear repeating.[76]

74 Ibid., O'Leary to Wilson, 29 September 1916, p. 285.   75 Ibid., Wilson to O'Leary, 29 September 1916, p. 286.   76 LC, RLP, Sivect to Lansing, 21 October 1916.

When the election results were finalized Wilson had received 9,129,606 votes to Hughes' 8,538,221 and 277 electoral college votes to Hughes' 254. The president had increased his vote by almost three million since 1912.[77] Although Wilson believed that he had lost the Irish-American vote, Leary concluded that, in six of the nine states with large Irish-American populations, Irish-Americans voted for Wilson 'in as great or greater numbers than they had ever voted for a Democratic presidential candidate in the immediate past.' The reasons for Wilson's victory centred on his economic and social policies including the Child Labour Law and the Adamson Eight-Hour Law, Hughes' unspectacular campaign and, specifically, the promise of continued neutrality.[78]

*

Following the election, Spring Rice wrote to Grey, the 'United States does not want to go to war, and the elections have clearly shown that the great mass of the Americans desire nothing so much as to keep out of war. It is undoubtedly the cause of the President's re-election.'[79] Undoubtedly 'he kept us out of war' had a great influence, but Lansing noted that domestic issues dominated the last six weeks of the campaign and that, in that context, a distinction must be made between the guidance given by the different strands of the Irish-American leadership to Irish-American voters. Radical leaders seeking Irish independence sought a vote against Wilson but the more numerous and influential Irish-American politicians within the Democratic Party emphasized Wilson's domestic agenda which directly affected the electorate. The leadership of the labour movement, including a substantial Irish-American presence, came out strongly for Wilson, particularly after he signed the Adamson Act on 3 September. The AFL executive committee urged union members to vote for Wilson. Nor did the Roman Catholic vote desert Wilson, except in Oregon, where his Mexican policy was influential. In general Irish-America did not rise up against Wilson on 7 November when the opportunity came, instead most weighed in behind him and set aside their atavistic feelings.[80] Joyce Broderick, an Irish Roman Catholic in the Foreign Office concluded, 'the great mass of Irish voters declined to accept guidance in domestic politics from extremists, either because they mistrusted their prophecies or – what is much more likely – because loyalty to the Democrat Party gave them a fairer prospect of personal profit.'[81] A cynical view perhaps,

77 Leary, 'Woodrow Wilson, Irish Americans and the election of 1916', 64, fn. 29; Tumulty, *Wilson*, p. 214; Lansing, *War Memoirs*, *PWW*, 38, House to Wilson, 30 September, 1916, p. 317; Ward, *Ireland and Anglo-American relations*, p. 137.   78 Leary, 'Woodrow Wilson, Irish Americans and the election of 1916', 71; Ward, *Ireland and Anglo-American relations*, pp. 139–40.   79 Gwynn, *The letters and friendships of Sir Cecil Spring Rice*, ii, Spring Rice to Grey, 24 November 1916.   80 Lansing, *War Memoirs*, pp. 163–4; Link & Leary, 'Election of 1916', pp. 2259–60; D. Doyle, 'The Irish and American labour, 1880–1920', 52; E. Cuddy, 'Irish-Americans and the 1916 election', 236.   81 TNA, FO371/2793, Spring Rice, 27 March 1916; Ibid., FO371/3071, Broderick, 19 January 1917.

but it is clear that American issues, not Irish ones, influenced Irish-American voters to support Wilson, irrespective of their sympathy for the Irish at home.

It is ironic, therefore, that, having secured a mandate based on the peace issue, Wilson led the US into war within five months of re-election. But the decision to enter the war was forced upon him. For nationalist Irish-America, both radical and moderate, the context of Wilson's declaration of, and justification for war, combined with his world vision, once again offered them hope that a solution would be found for the Irish problem. And in the interim, Wilson surprised them with his own move.

CHAPTER FOUR

Wilson, war and Ireland, 1917–18

> If the people of the United States could feel that there was an early prospect of the establishment for Ireland of substantial self-government, a very great element of satisfaction and enthusiasm would be added to the co-operation now about to be organised between this country and Great Britain.[1]

Woodrow Wilson made this comment to Robert Lansing four days after Congress agreed to declare war. After the November 1916 election, he assumed that the Irish-America community had not voted for him and this says much about his perceptions of that ethnic group by then. But he would not have dwelled too much on the matter. The election was over and the new mandate provided him with the freedom to pursue foreign policy without the burden of electioneering. Wilson and Edward House intensified their mediation efforts in order to prevent the war from coming to America's shores. The Irish-Americans, just like all other Americans, expected nothing less.

In fact most Irish-Americans had not deserted Wilson. They had shown themselves to be 'American' first and not 'Irish' as Wilson had hoped. But this did not mean that they could not be mobilized on Irish issues or that such matters would not intrude on US–British relations, as illustrated above. This chapter will examine how the radicalization of Irish nationalism in 1916 subsequently altered the political landscape for the Irish in the US and in Ireland, the effect of US entry into the war on the various strands of the Irish-American community, specifically Wilson's initiative during the Balfour visit and official handling of evidence of treasonous behaviour, and how US consuls in Ireland implemented US policy on the ground and coped with the challenges presented to them during the war years. Consequently, the chapter seeks to unravel the Irish dimension to Wilson's decision to enter the war and his prosecution of it.

The United States theatre

Moderate Irish-Americans had helped to re-elect Wilson for domestic, not foreign, reasons but immediately after re-election he had to concern himself with

1 A.S. Link (ed.), *The papers of Woodrow Wilson* (hereafter *PWW*), 69 vols (1966–94), 42, Wilson to Lansing, 10 April 1917.

foreign affairs. Wilson, and indeed Lansing, were so irritated over the British blockade and blacklist that the president had agreed to the expansion of the navy, warned US bankers to exercise caution when trading with the allies and threatened to cut off loans to the allied governments.[2] President Lowell of Harvard University confirmed to his confidant, Horace Plunkett, in August 1916, 'preparations for war [are] going along here.'[3] On the German side, Wilson received intelligence that submarine warfare was about to recommence. Ambassador Spring Rice wrote to former British Foreign Secretary Edward Grey on 15 December 1916, 'war has gradually drawn nearer and nearer to the United States in spite of all their efforts.'[4] But Wilson recognized that he faced a dilemma:

> The position of neutral nations ... has been rendered all but intolerable. Their commerce is interrupted, their industries are checked and diverted, the lives of their people are put in constant jeopardy, they are virtually forbidden the accustomed highways of the sea ... If any other nation now neutral should be drawn in, it would know only that it was drawn in by some force it could not resist, because it had been hurt and saw no remedy but to risk still greater, it might be even irreparable, injury, in order to make the weight in the one scale or the other decisive; and even as a participant it would not know how far the scales must tip before the end would come or what was being weighed in the balance![5]

It was from this position that Wilson embarked, on 18 December 1916, on his final attempt at peace negotiations with the allies and the central powers. He offered his mediation service to the belligerent nations, requested them to state their peace terms and promised US involvement in a post-war international organization to keep the peace.[6] In London, the new coalition government, led by Lloyd George as prime minister and including Arthur Balfour as foreign secretary, viewed the message as offensive, ostensibly because Wilson implied that both sides were equally in the wrong and that victory by either side would not benefit the global community. US Ambassador Page reported the 'irritation' in Foreign Office circles and the 'unprintable' comments from the public. Not surprisingly, Page himself described Wilson's intervention to Lansing as 'insulting words.'[7] The sharpness of the British reaction was also brought home to Wilson by House through his contacts with William Wiseman and Horace Plunkett. Wiseman, chief of British military intelligence in the US and the liaison officer

2 B.J. Hendrick, *The life and letters of Walter H. Page*, 2 vols (1930), ii, p. 86.   3 National Library of Ireland (hereafter NLI), Horace Plunkett Papers (hereafter HPP), P6584, reel 1 of 2, Lowell to Plunkett, 10 August 1916.   4 S. Gwynn (ed.), *The letters and friendships of Sir Cecil Spring Rice a record*, 2 vols (1929), ii, Spring Rice to Grey, 15 December 1916, p. 360.   5 R.S. Baker, *Woodrow Wilson: life and letters*, 8 vols (1927–39), vi, p. 382.   6 J. Gerard, *My four years in Germany* (1917), pp. 249–51; Hendrick (ed.), *The life and letters of Walter H. Page*, pp. 204–5.   7 Hendrick (ed.), *The life and letters of Walter H. Page*, ii, pp. 206–7.

between the British and US governments from December 1917 onwards, told House that all allied peoples were convinced that Germany was totally responsible for the outbreak of the war and they 'resent any suggestion that they have selfish motives and are not fighting solely for a principle.' Plunkett 'confirmed' Wiseman's statement for House. Plunkett had suggested also that Wilson 'amend his language to take into account two years of British war.'[8] Both the allied and central power governments had expanded their war objectives to include territory, bases and indemnities, which could only be provided for by total victory.[9] But the arguments behind the British response were more textured than appeared. Spring Rice worried that rejection of Wilson's mediation offer would produce violence among the extreme Irish-Americans. Eyre Crowe, permanent under secretary in the Foreign Office, felt that allowing Wilson to mediate would, among other things, open the door to his demanding Irish independence.[10] A further reason for Foreign Office officials' intransigence was the US government's toleration of continuous and increased Irish-American agitation which had moved beyond the extremist circles.

Throughout the winter of 1916, radical Irish-American agitation remained a persistent tension in US–British relations even though most Irish-Americans were unsure whether their ultimate goal was home rule, separation or some in-between status. But until Wilson declared war in April 1917, the Friends of Irish Freedom (FOIF) and Clan na Gael not only agitated against US involvement in the war and negotiated with the Germans for arms and troops for a second rising but continued with their propaganda and fund-raising campaigns. With the assistance of recently arrived exiles from the Irish rising, moderate Irish-America came into the radicals' orbit again. Much of this latter agitation centred on New York where 'An Irish Bazaar' was opened by Nora Connolly in mid-October and ran for three weeks. Others who arrived at this time were Hanna Sheehy Skeffington with her son Owen, Liam Mellows, Patrick McCartan, Diarmuid Lynch and Captain Robert Monteith. The Friends organized receptions and speaking tours, extracting as much publicity as possible from these activities.[11] Sheehy Skeffington's propaganda activities between December 1916 and June 1918, were highly effective.[12] In January 1917, she spoke on the same platform as Bainbridge Colby, later

8 NLI, HPP, P6584, reel 2 of 2, Plunkett to House, December 1916; Diary, 22 December 1916 in C. Seymour (ed.), *The intimate papers of Colonel House: ii, from neutrality to war, 1915–17*, 4 vols (1926–8), ii, p. 409; Ibid., House to Wilson, 20 December 1916, p. 411. 9 W. LaFeber, *The American age: US foreign policy at home and abroad*, 2 vols (1994), ii, p. 293. 10 S. Hartley, *The Irish question as a problem in British foreign policy, 1914–18* (1987), p. 119. 11 F.M. Carroll, *American opinion and the Irish question, 1910–23* (1978), pp. 85–6; J.J. Splain, 'The Irish movement in the United States since 1911' in W.G. Fitzgerald (ed.), *The voice of Ireland: a survey of the race and nation from all angles by the foremost leaders at home and abroad* (1923), p. 230. Sir Horace Plunkett had negotiated with the British military authorities in Dublin to allow James Connolly's family to go to the United States. 12 Shortly after her arrival she met with Edward House and former President Roosevelt and informed them about conditions in Dublin, British brutality in Ireland. See J.M. Eichacker, *Irish republican women in America: lecture tours, 1916 to 1925* (2003).

secretary of State, provoking Rowland Sperling in the Foreign Office to reflect, in February, 'We could hardly have done worse than decide to keep her in Ireland and then let her escape.'[13] She remained in the US for eighteen months from December 1916 to June 1918, spoke in twenty-one states, at over 250 public meetings and met with the public, politicians, pressure groups and the president. Sheehy Skeffington was a fine propagandist and ensured that her messages did not work against her, particularly after April 1917. Two measures of the success of her tour were the constant attention from US and British secret service agents and her interview with Wilson in January 1918 which will be discussed later.[14]

The US Secret Service devoted more attention to Sheehy Skeffington's activities after the US entered the war in 1917 than prior to it. Under William McAdoo and, increasingly, Frank Polk's supervision, the US espionage structure expanded. By April 1917 Polk was working with House and assistant counsellor Gordon Auchincloss (House's son-in-law). Linked by ties of family, university and social clubs, this close-knit group based in the State Department co-ordinated all intelligence activity. They decided on intelligence policy and co-ordinated resources, although other departments had staff in the field. Before April 1917, the major focus of attention was on the threat from German espionage.[15] Working in conjunction with the British and French intelligence chiefs, the espionage activities of the central powers and so-called radicals were constantly monitored. But until April 1917, the Wilson administration tolerated this US-based support activity including the increased propaganda, fund-raising and lobbying by Irish-Americans. In the interim, there was little the British could do about it except for continuing the surveillance and infiltration operations.[16] In March 1917, Spring Rice was permitted to protest to the State Department about fund-raising in San Francisco to help arm the Irish Volunteers for a 'revolt' in Ireland but was reassured by Lansing that there was no evidence of military subversion in the US and, therefore, no crime committed. In the Foreign Office, Colum Crichton Stuart criticized 'the unwillingness on the part of the US government to act' but thought it 'better to remain content with what the US government are doing against the Indians and Germans and not to worry them over the Irish

13 The National Archives, London (hereafter TNA), Foreign Office (hereafter FO), 371/3071, Sperling, 19 February 1917.   14 B. Whelan, 'A family business? Irish women revolutionaries in the United States, 1916–21' (unpublished), p. 1; Ward, *Hanna*; pp. 192–3; Eichacker, *Irish republican women*, pp. 58–91: Mrs Sheehy Skeffington, *Impressions of Sinn Féin in America* (1919), p. 9; M. Ward, *Hanna Sheehy Skeffington: a life* (1997), pp. 9, 11, 12.   15 R. Jeffreys-Jones, *American espionage: from Secret Service to CIA* (1977), pp. 45–6, 56. In 1919, Congress created the post of under secretary for Polk and the intelligence unit in the State Department became known as 'U-1'. R. Jeffreys-Jones, *Cloak and dollar: a history of American secret intelligence* (2nd ed. 2002), p. 63.   16 The British intelligence network was also sophisticated enough to pick out false information as it did in the case of Robert Gill who claimed to be a member of the Boston branch of Clan na Gael and that he had been recruited to go to Ireland to ascertain whether there was sufficient sympathy for another rising. NLI, Joseph McGarrity Papers (hereafter JMcGP), MS17514, Report on Robert F Gill.

question. Even if they went to war and helped the Allies, they would in other ways be strongly averse to arousing feeling amongst the Irish.'[17] Clearly, British officials understood why Wilson did not move against radical Irish-America up to April 1917, but this did not make acceptance of it any easier. Others within the Lloyd George administration believed that the only way to appease the US public, political and press opinion was to settle the Irish question. Maurice Hankey, secretary to the cabinet, represented this view and believed that such a course of action also would release a large number of troops for service in the war theatres, 'keep the country quiet and stimulate military recruiting.'[18]

But meeting British needs was not a priority for Wilson in late 1916. He still faced the same dilemma; to remain neutral and continue to offer to mediate with the possibility of exclusion from the peace table or get involved and be assured of representation at the conclusion of the war. He moved towards the latter. On 22 January 1917, Wilson announced his post-war objectives to Congress and appealed for a 'peace without victory', annexations and indemnities where neither side could dictate terms to the other. He attacked the old European balance of power system but called for 'a community of power ... an organised common peace.' This peace settlement would include certain principles; self-determination for all nations, freedom of the seas, no more 'entangling alliances' which created 'competitions of power.' These were, he said, 'American principles, American policies' and his last attempt as a neutral to define the peace terms.[19] The German government responded with a resumption of total submarine warfare on 1 February and two days later, Wilson broke diplomatic relations with Germany. But it took the Zimmerman telegram and the torpedoing of US ships including the *City of Memphis*, which Frost in Queenstown reported to Lansing on 17 March, had been 'sunk by gunfire', before Wilson asked Congress to declare war on Germany on 2 April.[20] The Senate approved the resolution by 82 to 6 votes and the House of Representatives by 373 to 50 and the US declaration of war followed on 6 April.

Wilson acts on the Irish question

It was, therefore, within the wider contexts of the US move from neutrality to involvement as Britain's ally and of Wilson's enunciation of his guiding princi-

17 TNA, FO371/3071, Crichton Stuart on Spring Rice to Balfour, 8 March 1917.   18 S. Roskill, *Hankey: man of secrets, volume 1 1877–1918*, 2 vols (1970), i, p. 337.   19 LaFeber, *The American age*, p. 294.   20 German Foreign Secretary Arthur Zimmerman sent a telegram to the German minister in Mexico city which stated that in the event of the US and Germany going to war the two countries would ally and Mexico would join the war against the US and recover the lost lands in Texas, Mexico and Arizona in return. In addition, the minister was to approach Japan also to form an anti-America coalition. The telegram was intercepted by the British and passed by Page to Wilson. *Papers relating to the foreign relations of the United States* (hereafter *FRUS*), 1917 supplement 2 the world war, 2 vols (1932), i, Frost to Secretary of State, 18 March 1917.

ples that his Irish policy of non-intervention changed. Page in London had constantly urged Wilson to bring the US into the war and had forwarded memoranda, newspaper clippings and intelligence from within official circles to Washington detailing the anti-Americanism in the British press and public. Eventually, though, Wilson agreed with Page's view, expressed in February 1916, that the US needed to be in the war 'to control the conditions of permanent peace.'[21] Irrespective of this meeting of minds, by spring 1917, Wilson's desire to have Page home was obvious to all. Josephus Daniels, secretary of the Navy, reported 'Page meddles in things outside his domain. I do not mind this if he gave us his own opinions ... he is giving ... English opinion.'[22] His usefulness to Wilson as a cipher of British opinion was low and by way of contrast, in April 1917, Wilson 'deeply' appreciated Horace Plunkett's 'efforts to promote good feeling on both sides of the Atlantic.'[23] The issue of American–British mutual understanding had been a constant theme in House's work.

Once it was inevitable that the US would enter the war the promotion of mutual trust became urgent and clearly could not be left to the diplomats to resolve. Instead House worked with Wiseman to produce a memorandum, dated 8 March 1917, on US attitudes towards Britain and the war, for presentation to the imperial conference meeting in London in late March. The memorandum implied that it was highly likely that the US would go to war with Germany in order 'to uphold American rights and assert her dignity as a nation.' But it warned that although broad-minded Americans supported the allies as upholders of democracy, the majority of the US public were not pro-ally and even less pro-British because of the blockade, the blacklist, censorship and London's policies on Ireland, Mexico and Russia. Ireland was stated to be 'one of the greatest obstacles to a good understanding' between the US and Britain. The memorandum noted:

> There are, however, many reasonable and intelligent Americans of Irish extraction who feel very strongly on this subject, and who might be persuaded to lend their assistance with all honesty to the settlement of this question at the end of the war. Sensible opinion in the States would not expect the British to listen to Irishmen of the type of Devoy and O'Leary; but the movement is given its greatest strength by the fact that reasonable honest citizens of the type of John Quinn feel so strongly about it.

In other words, US participation in the war would not mean full support of Britain and its war aims because of pre-existing difficulties including the Irish

21 National Archives and Records Administrations, Maryland (hereafter NARA), Records of the Department of State relating to internal affairs of Great Britain, 1910–29, Record Group 59 (hereafter RG59), M581/1, 711.41/16, Page to State Department, 15 February 1916. 22 E.D. Cronon (ed.), *Josephus Daniels: the cabinet diaries of Josephus Daniels, 1913–1921* (1963), 28 March 1917, p. 123. 23 NARA, RG59, M581/1, Page to Lansing, 3 June 1916; ibid., 15 February 1916; ibid., 15 September 1916; NLI, HPP, P6584, reel 2 of 2, House to Plunkett, 29 April 1917.

problem. These would still have to be overcome either in the short term or in the post-war settlement. The memorandum which was dispatched to the Foreign Office on 9 March, did not have the standing of an official agreement on either side. However, House agreed to it and had shown it to Wilson who thought it a 'just statement.' Wiseman elaborated on Wilson's reaction; 'the President said that they represented his views and he believed the views of the great majority of the American people and he authorised [House] to let the Foreign Office have these notes as coming from him through my channel which was considered desirable.' Carroll notes that Wilson's 'modest endorsement' was important because it offered evidence of his understanding of a complex issue and because it came at a time when he was trying to keep his complicity with the allies at a low level.[24] This is a valid judgement. However, it may understate Wilson's support for the memorandum's sentiments given that he knew it would be communicated to the Foreign Office and circulated to King George V, the British cabinet and the imperial conference. Indeed Wilson's desire to see the Irish question resolved sooner rather than later emerged just four days after the US entered the war.

Between 1914 and April 1917, the Irish question was just one of many troubling issues in America's relationship with Britain. Home rule was Wilson's favoured solution but it was not his responsibility to bring it about. But once he had decided upon US participation in the war, it became clear that moving on the Irish question might appease the expanding Irish-American republican agitation, assist in uniting the nation and remove a long-standing irritant from the American–British relationship.

Irish-American agitation in the US had been given an added impetus and tighter focus on achieving Irish independence due to the continuous arrival of Irish republicans associated with the rising and with the growing political instability in Ireland. A further issue binding Irish-Americans together by early 1917 was Wilson's inclusion of the principle of self-determination for all nations in his post-war objectives. This had struck a chord with Irish nationalists in the US and also with those in Ireland, who began to send petitions and resolution to Wilson appealing for his support. On 3 January 1917, Frost had forwarded to the State Department Sinn Féin resolutions to Wilson whose 'noble words regarding the rights of small nations' were 'much appreciated.' Following Page's instructions Frost did not comment on them and he emphasized that he had 'nothing more than a superficial official acquaintance with any of the functionaries from which they emanate.' However, he believed they were representative of the views of the majority of nationalists in Ireland who were becoming more militant and radical in their views and that the 'situation has never been more grave that at the present time.'[25] In addition to providing further evidence of the deteriorat-

24 *PWW*, 41, Enclosure, pp. 346–7; ibid., Wiseman to Spring Rice, 6 March 1917; Carroll, *American opinion*, p. 90; W.B. Fowler, *British-American relations 1917–1918: the role of Sir William Wiseman* (1969), pp. 22–4, fn. 25.   25 NARA, RG59 M580/6, 841.00/35, Frost to Secretary of State, 3

ing Irish political situation, Frost's 'valuable' report once again merited an official commendation.[26] Frost sent more resolutions in March and ventured the
opinion that he thought that the 'present treatment of Ireland is neither just nor
politic.'[27] While Frost's reports and views reached the diplomatic section of the
State Department, unsurprisingly the Sinn Féin resolutions earned no response.

However, Irish-American pressure on the administration and Congress
increased in early 1917. Clan na Gael intensified its campaign to bring pressure
to bear upon congressional politicians, seeking US intervention with the British
government and to ensure that Wilson kept his promise to realise the rights of
small nations. On 7 April, a great mass meeting of protest against America 'fighting the battles of England or any other foreign power' was held in New York in
April. Attended by Congressman William Bourke Cockran from New York and
Senator Martine, who had pleaded for Casement's life, the meeting sent telegrams
to Wilson, Vice-President Marshall and Speaker Clark asking for US action to
achieve Irish independence.[28] British intelligence kept an eye on this activity and
reported that John Devoy, Joseph McLoughlin of Clan na Gael and Matthew
Cummings, president of the Ancient Order of Hibernians (AOH) in Washington,
joined together to spend 'days' in Washington to persuade politicians against
declaring war and to favour of Irish independence.[29] The success of this agitation was such that during the debates in Congress on the war resolution, the
Congressional Record was soon littered with speeches, petitions and memorials
condemning British failure to grant some kind of self-government for Ireland.
Wilson admitted to Lansing on 10 April, that he was struck by the 'recent debates
on the war resolution in Congress' when anti-war politicians who were not 'themselves Irishmen or representatives of constituencies in which Irish voters were
influential, notably several members from the south' argued for government by
consent for Ireland. On 10 April, Wilson instructed Page in London, to

> take an early opportunity in conversation with the Prime Minister to con-
> vey to him in the most confidential manner the information that the only
> circumstance which seems now to stand in the way of an absolutely cor-
> dial co-operation with Great Britain by practically all Americans who are
> not influenced by ties of blood directly associating them with Germany,
> is the failure so far to find a satisfactory method of self-government for
> Ireland ... If the people of the United States could feel that there was an

January 1917; ibid., 23 January 1917.   **26** Ibid., 841.00/36, Carr to Frost, 23 March 1917.   **27**
Ibid., 841.00/39, Frost to Carr, 21 March 1917. Frost forwarded resolutions from Cork County
Council, Limerick Federated Trades' Council and Limerick County Borough Council. The latter
were transmitted to him by John A. Dinan, US consular agent in Limerick on 16 March 1917. Ibid.
28 NLI, JMcGP, MS17649 (1), notice 11 March 1917; ibid., MS17649(2), Telegram, 8 April 1917.
29 Ibid., MS17502, Reports of British intelligence on Irish nationalists in United States, American
correspondence, Memo. notes by Z, private and confidential, The Chief Commissioner D[ublin]
M[etropolitan] Police, 25 April 1917.

early prospect of the establishment for Ireland of substantial self-government a very great element of satisfaction and enthusiasm would be added
to the co-operation now about to be organised between this country and
Great Britain.[30]

Wilson felt that if self-government for Ireland could be achieved, not only would
it bring more support to the allies' side but it would 'divorce our citizens of Irish
birth and sympathy from the German sympathizers here with whom many of
them have been inclined to make common cause.' Furthermore, he felt that
Ireland was an anomaly within the 'anti-Prussian world' in not having a democratic government. In other words, Wilson presented his case for British action
on Irish self-government in the context of the successful prosecution of the war
and without revealing his personal view on the injustice of the case. However,
there was an implied criticism of Britain when he concluded that Ireland 'has so
often been promised' self-government.[31]

   In London, Page believed that US leaders should conduct their nation's
'affairs by a large policy and not by the complaints of our really non-American
people.' However, he followed instructions and raised the matter with Lloyd
George on 17 April. On the following day, he reported back to Lansing that the
prime minister 'instantly understood and showed that he already knew the facts
that I presented and was glad that the President had instructed me to bring the
subject up. He had the American situation in mind during the whole discussion
of home rule and he was doing his best.'[32] Lloyd George's position on home
rule was difficult to gauge; although he wanted the problem solved his war cabinet included Liberals, Labour, Conservatives and Unionists and among the latter were the fiercest opponents of Irish home rule such as Foreign Secretary
Balfour, and Edward Carson, first lord of the Admiralty and leader of the Ulster
Unionists. Lloyd George described them to Page as 'madmen' on the Irish question.[33] According to Hankey, by April 1917 Lloyd George wished to 'get rid of'
Carson from his cabinet due to his attitude on the Irish question and handling
of the admiralty.[34]

   Yet, there was some evidence of room for manoeuvre on Ireland. Carson was
implacably dedicated to excluding Ulster from any home rule solution but he was
sensitive also to US criticisms, specifically that Unionists' intransigence on home
rule might delay the successful prosecution of an allied victory and portray them
as disloyal. But Lloyd George placed more hope that Balfour could be won over,
particularly during his forthcoming trip to the US as head of a British war mission. Indeed Lloyd George hoped Wilson would take the opportunity to 'give his
views to Mr Balfour' as the 'enlistment of his influence would be of great help
and the Prime Minister feels sure of a good result of a frank explanation to him

30 *PWW*, 42, Wilson to Lansing, 10 April 1917.   31 Ibid.   32 Hendrick, *Page*, ii, p. 254; *PWW*,
42, Page to Wilson, 18 April 1917.   33 Hendrick, *Page*, ii, p. 260.   34 Roskill, *Hankey*, i, p. 390.

by the President.'[35] So, having directly stepped into the middle of the Irish problem, Wilson was now given an opportunity to reveal the depth of his interest in it. Whatever the reasons were for Lloyd George's strategy – personal support for home rule, continuous US criticism of British policy in Ireland, removing 'the one menacing spot in the whole horizon' of Anglo-American relations – he had placed Balfour and Wilson in key roles for the achievement of progress. This strategy was confirmed by Sydney Brooks, the English journalist, who was in correspondence with Lloyd George and Lord Northcliffe on the home rule question at the time. After a meeting with Brooks, Tumulty told Wilson on 20 April that Brooks 'believes that just a little push by you in your private talk with Mr Balfour would put over home rule. He says if you could bring home to Balfour the amount of American public sentiment which favours it and that how a denial of it is working to the disadvantage of England in this country. It would make a great impression.'[36] Balfour's imminent arrival provided Wilson with a further opportunity to promote his new approach to Irish affairs.

The allies sent three delegations to the US to co-ordinate resources for the war effort. These were led by Balfour, Northcliffe and Reading respectively. While each co-operated with the British embassy, both Balfour and Northcliffe effectively sidelined the professional diplomats.[37] Spring Rice's role was to give guidance, if asked, and report on progress to the Foreign Office. The Reading visit differed slightly from the other two because Treasury Secretary MacAdoo had requested the visit and had communicated with the British government through the embassy and Foreign Office.[38] For the diplomats in the State Department, the visits confirmed the practice set by Wilson that had already marginalized them from the formulation of US foreign policy. Nonetheless, after the Balfour visit was announced in the US, Spring Rice wrote to Robert Cecil in the Foreign Office, on 13 April, outlining certain considerations that Balfour and his delegation needed to bear in mind. The ambassador believed there would not be a coalition government in the US, Wilson was entering the war at the earliest possible moment, the aim of Balfour's mission should be to offer advice not direction, the US was entering the war not as a 'colony' but as a partner and, finally, he was in

> no doubt that the President will speak of the Irish question. The Irish
> party are of very great political importance at the present moment. The

35 *PWW*, 42, Page to Wilson, 18 April 1917.   36 *PWW*, 42, Tumulty to Wilson, 20 April 1917. House sincerely hoped that Balfour would not become a target of Irish-American agitation. He told Plunkett that any embarrassment to Balfour would be a 'serious blow to the plan so carefully worked out in which he is such an important factor.' Yale University Library, Manuscript and Archives Collection (hereafter YULMC), The papers of Colonel E.M. House (hereafter EHP), box 91, file 3135, House to Plunkett, 9 March 1917.   37 R.M. Warman, *The Foreign Office, 1916–18: a study of its role and functions* (1986), pp. 39, 97. William Wiseman had become the main channel of communication between Washington and London from the end of 1916.   38 Gwynn (ed.), *The letters and friendships of Sir Cecil Spring*, ii, pp. 400, 410.

question is one which is at the root of most of our troubles with the
United States. The fact that the Irish question is still unsettled is continually quoted against us, as a proof that it is not wholly true that the fight
is one for the sanctity of engagements or the independence of small
nations. The President is by descent an Orangeman and by education a
Presbyterian. But he is the leader of the Democratic Party in which the
Irish play a prominent part, and he is bound in every way to give consideration to their demands.[39]

Balfour arrived in the US on 22 April; the war cabinet minutes for 10 April and
Lloyd George's *War memoirs* indicate that he was charged with examining Anglo-
American war-time co-operation and 'to make special enquiry' into the importance of the Irish question in the US.[40] Immediately upon arrival in New York,
he encountered the full force of the campaign for Irish home rule as detailed by
Hartley and Ward.[41] Nationalists of many hues railed against the presence of
'Bloody Balfour' in the US, an appellation he had acquired because of his policies during his tenure as chief secretary of Ireland (1887) and prime minister
(1902–5). A British secret agent warned his superiors that Balfour 'is one of the
most hated Britons' and that Clan na Gael might try and injure him during his
visit. Consequently, Balfour did not visit Boston or Chicago.[42] However, moderate nationalists led by Quinn responded to an invitation from Plunkett and a
widely publicized telegram from Northcliffe saying that Balfour had the power
to resolve the Irish question, and met with the foreign secretary on 4 May. Quinn
was accompanied by Morgan J. O'Brien, Lawrence Godkin and Robert Temple
Emmet and they argued that 'there were large and considerable bodies in the
United States who would be displeased unless something humane and statesmanlike were finally done about Ireland's ancient and valid grievances.' Quinn
also pushed the idea of 'generosity to Ireland as sound British policy.' According
to Quinn, Balfour was impressed by the arguments and hoped to find a way to
resolve the Irish problem to the satisfaction of both sides.[43] Balfour had already

39 Ibid., Spring Rice to Cecil, 13 April 1917, ii, pp. 391–2.   40 Hartley, *The Irish question*, p. 137;
Carroll, *American opinion*, p.92.   41 Hartley, *The Irish question*, pp. 137–43; Ward, *Ireland and Anglo-
American relations*, 1899–1921, pp. 148–9.   42 NLI, JMcGP, MS17502, Reports of British intelligence on Irish nationalists in United States, American Correspondence, Private and Confidential,
The Chief Commissioner, Memo. notes by Z, 25 April 1917; Ibid., JRP, MS15236 (14), Leslie to
Redmond, 4 June 1917. Maud Gonne's views on Balfour were representative of the Irish nationalist community generally. In August 1917, she wrote to John Quinn who had met Balfour, 'I wonder if the thought of thousands and thousands of Irish tenants evicted under his administration,
thrown out to starve while his police were battering down their houses, and of his colder lies and
jeers in parliament when deaths of starvation in Ireland were brought to his notice.' See J. & R.
Londraville (eds), *Too long a sacrifice: the letters of Maud Gonne and John Quinn* (1999), Maud Gonne
to John Quinn, 3 August 1917.   43 NLI, Bourke Papers (hereafter BP), Notes of recent American
opinion and action on the Irish home rule question', 2 June 1917. Shane Leslie confirmed that the
delegation 'spoke plainly'; Balfour 'answered sympathetically' and he was 'most tactful and cordial.'

agreed with Plunkett that it was 'important' to get the Irish question 'settled' as a means of enlisting 'American sympathy' with Britain.[44] Unfortunately for the Quinn delegation, Balfour also made it clear to them that he was there to deal with 'ships and shells' and he was not empowered to deal with 'Irish politics' but would report their views, including their opposition to a divided Ireland 'leaving Ulster out', back to his government.[45] Balfour had encountered the strength of moderate but perhaps majority Irish-America, and its congressional manifestation also emerged at this time.

On 28 April, Senator Medill McCormick organized 140 congressmen to cable Lloyd George to express their support 'if Britain would now settle the Irish problem in accordance with the principles announced by President Wilson.' Moreover, Balfour spoke to the US Congress with the agreement of these Irish-American politicians, although leaflets were distributed among the congressmen. These demanded them to 'Ask Mr Balfour: Why are you called "Bloody Balfour"?' After the Balfour address, Arthur Willert, *The Times* correspondent, said to McCormick 'So that is the worst your tough friends can do.' McCormick replied 'Your man has disarmed us. He is a salesman.'[46] Hartley has detailed how other members of the Balfour mission reacted to the Irish-American agitation that they encountered at the time. Some, such as Ian Malcolm, deplored it, while Cecil Dormer felt it was less forceful than expected.[47] Either way both men acknowledged that the Irish question was an active force in US politics and that it could not be easily dismissed. But the key question is whether or not Wilson used the opportunity to push Balfour for a settlement of the Irish question.

Wilson continued to receive petitions from Ireland and the US appealing to him to settle the Irish question. On 24 April, he received telegrams from prominent community leaders from Portland, Oregon, led by Archbishop Christie, who believed that a 'conciliatory word' from Wilson would go ' a long way towards a permanent settlement of the Irish question.'[48] He asked Lansing for an opinion as to the reply.[49] The secretary suggested a brief acknowledgement only.[50] But Wilson went further in a reply to John D. Crimmins, a New York Irish-American Democrat and Wilson supporter, who raised the same issue.[51] Wilson agreed with Tumulty that Crimmins, who was 'good friend' of his, should get more than a formal acknowledgement, but he continued 'I don't like to write any letters on this subject at present. I would appreciate it very much if you would assure him of my interest and of your knowledge of the fact that I am showing

Diary 24 April 1917 in M. Digby, *Horace Plunkett: an Anglo-American Irishman* (1949), p. 205. **44** Ibid. **45** *PWW*, 42, Tumulty to Wilson, 5 May 1917, fn. 1; NLI, BP, MS10741, 'Notes'. **46** *The Times*, 28 April 1917; A. Willert, *Washington and other memories* (1972), p. 98–9. Another member of Balfour's delegation noted 'you hear a terrific amount of the Irish question discussed, and we got shoals of letters about it.' See B.E.C. Dugdale, *Arthur James Balfour: first earl of Balfour*, 2 vols (1939), ii, p. 149. **47** Hartley, *The Irish question*, pp. 140–2. **48** NARA, RG59, M580/6, telegram, 24 April 1917. **49** Ibid., 841.00/41, Wilson to Lansing, 30 April 1917. **50** Ibid., Lansing to Tumulty, 5 May 1917. **51** NLI, JRP, MS15236(14), Leslie to Redmond, 18 May 1917.

in every way I properly can my sympathy with the claim of Ireland for home rule.' Unusually for Wilson he penned a second note to Tumulty on the subject on the same day, 5 May. He wrote, 'Confidentially (for I beg that you will be careful not to speak of or intimate this), I have been doing a number of things about this which I hope may bear fruit.' Tumulty proceeded to draft the reply to Crimmins which Wilson also approved on 5 May. Tumulty assured Crimmins that he would bring the matter to Wilson's attention and continued 'meanwhile let me assure you of the President's keen interest in this matter and of the fact that, in every way he properly can, he is showing sympathy with the claim of Ireland for home rule.'[52] Not surprisingly, Tumulty's reply was published in the *New York World* on 12 May with the following comment:

> Washington despatches to the *World* have already told us of the conferences between the President and British Foreign Secretary Balfour, at which the Irish question was discussed. Persons who are in a position to speak with authority say that the President has gone as far as the proprieties permit in bringing to the realisation of British Foreign Secretary the importance of the Home Rule proposition in this country.
>
> The President is said to have told Mr Balfour that Great Britain's failure to confer upon the Irish people the right to rule themselves constitutes almost the sole obstacle in the way of complete co-operation and sympathy between the British and the American people in the war against the autocracy of Germany.[53]

Similar news stories in the *New York Times* on 23 April and 15 May, reported Wilson's intervention on the Irish question.[54] There is no record of Wilson's meetings with Balfour but Link indicates that he urged Balfour, in the interest of Anglo-American co-operation, to find a solution to the Irish question.[55] In addition, on 5 May, Lansing told Balfour 'very frankly' that the sympathy of the American people was 'far greater' for France than for Britain because

> there lingered in the minds of our people the old feeling that the British empire was our hereditary foe, and that the failure of his government to respond to the intense longing of the Irish for the freedom of Ireland from British rule by conceding to them a measure of independence made thousands of Irish-Americans bitter enemies of Great Britain [and] pointing out to him that this was a situation with which our government found it difficult to cope.

52 *PWW*, 42, Wilson to Tumulty, 5 May, 5 May 1917; ibid., Tumulty to Wilson, 5 May 1917; ibid., Tumulty to Crimmins, 5 May 1917.   53 *New York World*, 12 May 1917.   54 *New York Times*, 23 April 1917 and 15 May 1917.   55 *PWW*, 42, Wilson to Tumulty, 5 May 1917, fn. 1.

Lansing urged him to do something 'to remove this hostility of persons of Irish blood and of their American sympathisers.' Balfour promised to lay the matter before his government when he returned to England.[56] Polk also met and talked with Balfour on 22 and 29 April but there is no reference to Ireland in Polk's diary.[57] Both Wilson and Lansing had gone as far as the limits of diplomacy would allow them and had accepted Balfour's promise of future action.

However, in his subsequent report to the British cabinet on the mission, Balfour downplayed any discussions about Ireland that took place by stating that he had 'fewer conversations on it than might have been supposed' and more importantly, 'the President never referred to it all; the Secretary of State never referred to it officially.'[58] Clearly, without a minute of the Balfour/Wilson meetings it is not possible to know whether or not the Irish question was discussed as a specific issue by the two men. Yet, Spring Rice believed that Balfour had been able to 'discuss matters quite freely and fully with' Wilson who normally remained 'entirely aloof especially from foreigners.'[59] Also, the Lansing/Balfour three hour meeting ranged over 'nearly every phase of the world situation' and Lansing's record of it elaborated on their frank discussion on the importance of settling the Irish problem.[60] Furthermore, Balfour's underplaying of discussions with Wilson and Lansing on the topic may be contrasted with his vivid awareness that 'the Irish question looms very large in the minds of United States politicians. From the domestic as well as the international point of view they are deeply concerned that no solution has been found for this ancient problem.'[61] Undoubtedly, Balfour had successfully extricated himself from the position as peacemaker on Ireland that Lloyd George and Northcliffe had accorded him, without damaging his mission's main aim; improving Anglo-American co-operation. Instead the Balfour mission was a success. Spring Rice felt that the impression he made 'on Congress, on the press and ... on the President has been very favourable and very deep.'[62] Wilson did Balfour the honour of travelling with him to a reception on 30 April and attending the foreign secretary's speech to Congress on 5 May.[63] House felt that both men 'got along marvellously well ... it was delightful to see how sympathetic their minds were.'[64] Radical Irish-America were less praising but more important for Wilson was that the moderate majority came to believe that his intervention with Balfour had forced Lloyd George to announce, in May, the establishment of the Irish Convention to be chaired by Plunkett. John Quinn wrote to Maud Gonne, 'A greater factor in the ... [Lloyd] George move was

56 R. Lansing, *War memoirs of Robert Lansing: secretary of State* (1935), p. 277.   57 YULMC, Frank L. Polk Papers (hereafter FLPP), diary, 22, 27 April 1917.   58 Quoted in Carroll, *American opinion*, p. 92.   59 Gwynn (ed.), *The letters and friendships of Sir Cecil Spring*, Spring Rice to Cecil, 18 May 1917, pp. 400–1.   60 Lansing, *War memoirs*, p. 277.   61 Hartley, *The Irish question*, p. 138. 62 Gwynn (ed.), *The letters and friendships of Sir Cecil Spring*, Spring Rice to Cecil, 18 May 1917, pp. 400–1.   63 YULMC, FLPP, diary, 30 April, 5 May 1917.   64 Hendrick, *Page*, ii, undated, House to Page, p. 263; ibid., Polk to House, 25 May 1917, pp. 263–4.

American opinion and arranging for letters and getting men to speak to Wilson, who spoke to Balfour.'[65]

The extent to which official US pressure contributed to Lloyd George's decisions to summon the Irish Convention, with the aim of creating a scheme for the future self-government of Ireland within the empire, and to announce the release of Irish prisoners in June 1917 remains unclear. Studies of the background to these announcements identify many factors including Lloyd George's personal support for Irish home rule, the intransigence of the Ulster Unionists, the increasing unrest in Ireland orchestrated by Sinn Féin, the bypassing of Redmond's constitutional path, the continuing diversion of British resources to Ireland and away from the war theatres and, after US entry into the war, the importance of a good relationship between Britain and the US. It was a combination of these factors that led Lloyd George to inform King George V, in early March 1917, that the cabinet had decided 'to put ourselves right with the civilized world.' By this he meant that the British government would offer immediate home rule 'to that part of Ireland that wants it', but he emphasized that no British government could 'now or at any time hand over Ulster to the rest of Ireland against its will.'[66] Two cabinet ministers, Curzon and Lansdowne, in addition to Wiseman, indicated that by May 1917 appeasing the US had become important in pursuit of the larger goal of victory in the war. The Ulster Unionists and Sinn Féin believed that the Convention was 'window dressing for the Americans' and the latter boycotted it.[67] Undoubtedly the Convention decision served a number of purposes for Lloyd George; firstly, it might find a solution to the Irish problem, secondly, Britain's image in the US might improve and thirdly, the Irish question could be set aside for a period. In the words of Liam Mellows, the Irish republican and socialist who had fled to the US after the rising, the Convention was the 'smartest piece of work the English have done for a long while.'[68]

Certainly Lloyd George's announcement immediately appealed to Wilson who 'assumed' that Plunkett would be a member of the Convention. Although he already had a channel of communication to Plunkett through House, he asked Wiseman to find some way of keeping him informed of its proceedings, in which he said he was deeply interested.[69] Not surprisingly, Wilson felt that he could not rely on Page to accurately report on Irish affairs. Page felt that the Convention represented a 'sincere effort' by Lloyd George to settle the Irish question and the settlement rested with the 'Irish themselves', specifically the Catholic Church and nationalists. In other words, he fully accepted Lloyd George's argument that

65 Londraville (eds), *Too long a sacrifice*, John Quinn to Maud Gonne, 30 May 1917, p. 197; Shane Leslie was convinced that 'we take it that we shall owe home rule to him [Wilson].' NLI, JRP, MS15236 (14), Leslie to Redmond, 18 May 1917.   66 H. Nicolson, *King George the fifth: his life and reign* (1952), p. 311.   67 Quoted in Hartley, *The Irish question*, pp. 147–8; B. Fowler, *British–American relations, 1917–1918: the role of William Wiseman* (1969), p. 159.   68 NLI, J.J. Hearn Papers, MS15986, Mellows to Mrs Hearn, 28 May 1917.   69 *PWW*, 43, Plunkett to Balfour, 3 August 1917.

if the Convention failed, the Irish would be blamed and the British government.[70] Ironically, this latter assessment was correct. The emerging Sinn Féin abstained from the Convention proceedings on the twofold grounds that it was doomed to failure and that Irishmen, not the British government, would be blamed if it failed. But in Wilson's eyes, Page's comments prejudged the Convention's proceedings, which he followed with 'interest and sympathy.'[71] Instead he must have shared Plunkett's view that the Convention 'will get the Irish question out of the way, so far as it is a disturbance to the world at large, for some years to come.'[72] At any rate, it was Plunkett who kept Wilson informed through his correspondence with House and Wiseman.

Plunkett's observations on the first meeting of the Convention, on 25 July 1917, were forwarded to Wilson for his 'confidential information.' The chairman's optimism was clear. While admitting that it was impossible to judge how far the Convention represented the Irish people 'it is generally felt to be representative of a large majority including political, agricultural, commercial and labour interests, in fact all except extremists. The Catholic Church is strongly represented. Leaders, who in the past have been bitterly opposed, are meeting for the first time.' Furthermore, the Convention was determined 'to keep on until they reach some conclusion' and Plunkett promised to forward confidential reports to Wilson and House at each stage of the proceedings.[73] Vice consul Charles Broy in Dublin also provided the State Department with reports on the context, composition and proceedings of the Convention.[74] The Convention met between 25 July 1917 and 5 April 1918. Its very existence served both British and American needs by removing the Irish problem from the US public's gaze; the timing of the Convention announcement and prisoner release coincided with the escalation of US involvement in the war and, therefore, prosecution of the war became the all-consuming issue for the US public, politicians, press and president from spring 1917 onwards. The majority of Irish-Americans turned their attention from put-

70 NARA, RG59, M580/6, 841.00/42, Page to Secretary of State, 19 May 1917.   71 *PWW*, 43, House to Wilson, 4 August 1917.   72 Ibid., 42, Plunkett to House, 1 June 1917. House passed the letter to Wilson on 19 June. Ibid., House to Wilson, 19 June 1917. Throughout the proceedings Plunkett was informed by John Buchan, director of the department of Information 'about the Irish situation in the States.' *PWW*, 43, Plunkett to Balfour, 3 August 1917.   73 Ibid., 43, Enclosure 1, Wiseman to House, 11 August 1917. The Irish Convention consisted of ninety-five representatives of nationalist and unionist viewpoints. They met at Trinity College Dublin in Ireland on 25 July 1917 and elected Horace Plunkett as chairman. In September Plunkett asked Balfour to send on a copy of his first 'secret report' prepared for King George to President Wilson but Link states that there is no evidence that it was sent to Wilson. Ibid., *PWW*, 43, Plunkett to Balfour, 17 December 1917, fn. 1. At the same time Wiseman acted as a messenger between American and British administrations and pressure groups on the Zionist question, finding a homeland for Jews. Fowler, *British–American relations*, pp. 93–4.   74 NARA, RG59, M580/6, 841.00/45/7, Broy to Secretary of State, 1, 14 August 1917. Broy attached sixteen clippings from newspapers also. On 27 August, Adams reported on the timetable adopted by the Convention and its social arrangements. Ibid., 841.00/49, Adams to Secretary of State, 27 August 1917.

ting 'Ireland first' to putting 'America first' in their everyday lives, just as Wilson had hoped would happen.

The Wilson administration and Irish-American 'loyalism'

It would be incorrect to assume from the above that the Balfour mission in spring 1917 was dominated by the Irish problem. Instead the bulk of the discussions between the two sides focused on the world situation, including the Russian revolution and other diplomatic and financial issues such as the 'blacklist and bunkering problems ... the sending of destroyers and troops' to the European war theatres.[75] Until their entry into the war, Americans had assumed that their contribution would consist of shipping, naval support, credit and materials, all of which were necessary. But Wilson and his advisers were surprised to learn from the visiting allied war missions that the Allied theatres needed food and manpower also. The US population was required to engage in the war, beginning in summer 1917. This appeal to US loyalism had direct consequences for the Irish-American community. The majority of immigrant communities, including Irish-Americans, fully participated in the war effort by joining the army, fund-raising and working in factories. Major General John F. Pershing, the veteran of America's indigenous Indian and Mexican wars, arrived in Paris in June, to establish the American Expeditionary Force (AEF). Pershing controlled his share of the western front near Verdun with only 14,500 men. Irish names appeared in the lists of the many regiments making up the AEF. One of the first units to go to the European front was the New York sixty-ninth regiment commanded by Colonel 'Wild Bill' Donovan.[76] Eighty-five per cent of the regiment was of Irish birth or parentage but its Roman Catholic chaplain, Francis Patrick Duffy, believed that the whole regiment was 'Irish by adoption, association or conviction.'[77] But many more recruits were needed; Wilson rushed the 'selective service' or conscription bill through Congress and the secretary of War, Newton D. Baker, selected 5 June as the first registration day. The administration appealed to Americans to demonstrate their patriotism and by the end of the war, 4,791,172 men had served in the armed forces.[78] Those Irish-Americans who remained at home served with the Red Cross Society, worked in local defence and fund-raising organizations and committees and on draft boards. The various Liberty Loan drives were over-subscribed. The Irish-dominated Knights of Columbus provided

75 Hendrick, *Page*, ii, Polk to House, 25 May 1917, pp. 263–4.   76 M. McLoughlin, 'Nationalism and world war one' in M. Glazier (ed.), *The encyclopedia of the Irish in America* (1999), p. 653. Donovan was awarded the Distinguished Service cross, Distinguished Service medal and the Congressional Medal of Honour. P. Foley, 'Donovan, William Joseph' in Glazier (ed.), The *encyclopedia*, p. 222.   77 J.E. Cuddy, *Irish-America and national isolationism, 1914–20* (1976), p. 144. 78 LaFeber, *The American age*, pp. 304, 305; P. Thompson, *Cassell's dictionary of modern American history* (2000), p. 456.

social facilities for US soldiers abroad through its war fund, to which former Secretary Bryan contributed, and also provided religious guidance by organizing non-commissioned priests to accompany troops into the battlefield.[79]

The reasons why the majority of Irish-Americans turned from 'Ireland first' to 'America first' were many but none were surprising. Firstly, on a personal level, the majority of moderate Irish-Americans could now demonstrate their loyalty to the United States and become more American. Secondly, political and religious leaders preached loyalism. Cardinal Gibbons who had promoted peace efforts with Wilson and Lansing in autumn 1915, reluctantly came around to the view the US would be involved and supported universal manhood training to 'safeguard the nation, build up its manhood and fuse its foreign strains.' He reacted to the declaration of war by stating that 'there must be no shirkers ... it behoves every American citizen to do his duty and to uphold the hands of the president and the legislative department in the solemn obligation that confronts us.' On 18 April 1917, the American Catholic archbishops pledged full and active support for the government so that the 'great and bold cause of liberty may triumph.' They regarded the conflict as a just war and preached patriotism throughout it.[80] Officials in the Foreign Office believed that 'as good Americans, the Catholics are as one behind their government' but they were realistic enough to accept also that,

> It can hardly be hoped that they will forget at once how they have been taught to regard England as the oppressor of Ireland; France as the country which expelled the religious orders and banished Christian teaching from the schools; Italy as the usurper of the patrimony of the Holy See; Portugal as the oppressor of the Catholic Church and Russia as the hereditary enemy of Catholicism[81]

Among the Catholic prelates who were regarded as having real sympathy for the allied cause were Cardinal Gibbons and Archbishop Ireland as was indicated in chapter one. Even Archbishop O'Connell of Boston, regarded as a 'vigorous champion of Ireland' and an arch promoter of Catholic rights, encouraged patriotism among the broad mix of old world nations in his diocese.[82] Moreover, when Pope Benedict XV appealed to the belligerents for peace in August, the US hierarchy interpreted this in ways that would allow Catholics to support the war effort and Wilson. Thus, Wilson's rejection of the papacy's call for peace negotiations did not damage him or the growing US war machine. Similarly, despite

---

79 Cuddy, *Irish-America and national isolationism, 1914–20*, p. 144.   **80** A. Sinclair Will, *Life of Cardinal Gibbons: archbishop of Baltimore*, 2 vols (1922), ii, pp. 810–15.   **81** K. Bourne & D.C. Watt (general eds), *British documents on foreign affairs* (hereafter *BDFA*), part ii, series C, North America, 25 vols. (1986–95), vii, The American press, 1920–22, Catholics papers in America, Catholics in the United States, January 1920, p. 2.   **82** Ibid., p. 4; J.M. O'Toole, *Militant and triumphant: William Henry O'Connell and the Catholic Church in Boston, 1859–1944* (1992), p. 152.

the presence of some anti-war views within its ranks, the leadership of the trade union organizations rowed in behind Wilson. In 1915, Samuel Gompers, leader of the American Federation of Labour, had urged Wilson to enter the war on the allied side.[83]

Moderate Irish-American political leadership immediately rowed in behind Wilson also. Senator Thomas J. Walsh from Montana believed that Germany had become the greatest threat to freedom of the seas, while William Bourke Cockran, who had supported US intervention in the war from its beginning, believed that Wilson's ideals had transformed the war into a 'Catholic war' which the papacy supported. Consequently, Cockran felt that Americans 'are fighting for him [the pope] and with him, behind the banner of the United States, unfurled to enforce as principles of international law the truths expressed under the leadership of Woodrow Wilson.' While Wilson might not have agreed with Cockran's interpretation of his aims, at least it allowed this life-long advocate of disarmament and constitutional Irish nationalism to fully support the war effort. Cockran and most other Irish-American politicians worked resolutely for the war campaigns, thereby providing their constituents with exemplary examples of loyalty and patriotism.[84] Similarly John Quinn admitted to being personally more interested in winning the war than in settling the Irish question.[85] These moderates, however, expected that Wilson's guiding principles would be applied to Ireland once the war was over.

For the extreme Irish-American leaders, defined by Quinn as the 'Cohalans, the Devoys, the McGuires and the Jeremiah O'Leary's who have been working with the Germans', the strategy of winning Irish freedom by working for a German victory was soon abandoned.[86] Instead, on 5 April, the day before war was declared, Clan na Gael issued a circular to its members which stated that:

> Until the US would plunge into the world war it was the duty of members to oppose the war but as soon as war is declared it is the duty of the members to stand steadfastly faithful to the USA. For over 100 years no truer sons of the US were known than the Irish and their children born here, and let no man be able to say that they did not live up to their traditions in this crisis. True it is a bitter experience that the country that we all love so well should be aligned with the arch enemy, England, the persecutor of our race, and we must consider it a bitter defeat for the cause of freedom which is sure to set the cause of Irish freedom back for many a day, but we must prove to the world and to the enemies of our

83 Gwynn (ed.), *The letters and friendships of Sir Cecil Spring*, Spring Rice to Grey, 6 September 1915, p. 280; E. McKillen, *Chicago labor and the quest for a democratic diplomacy, 1914–1924* (1996), p. 56. The opposition of the Chicago Federation of Labor is detailed in ibid. 84 J. McGurring, *Bourke Cockran: a free lance in American politics* (1948), pp. 289–300. Quoted in Cuddy, *Irish-America*, p. 141. 85 Londraville (eds), *Too long a sacrifice*, John Quinn to Maud Gonne, 17 July 1917, p. 204. 86 Ibid., John Quinn to Maud Gonne, 14 March 1917, p. 189.

race in the USA especially that the patriotism of the Irish people is not to be questioned.

It then goes on to counsel temperate language, advising members to refrain from criticizing the US government or to indulge in any word or act that could be construed as meaning that 'we are not whole heartedly with the USA from the moment war is declared.'[87] Two days after the US entered the war Clan na Gael organized a meeting in Madison Square Gardens in support of the move. John Rogers, a British intelligence agent who attended it, reported that 'little was said of Ireland, all speakers dealing with American matters in a patriotic way' while other informers recorded that Cohalan and Devoy instructed the audience to be loyal Americans working to support the war effort but not to forget that one US war aim was to preserve the interests of small nations.[88] But the radical leadership walked a tightrope; in public they had to refrain from statements or actions that might be interpreted as disloyal and unpatriotic while insisting that Wilson's aims applied to Ireland and working to achieve another rising in Ireland. For the majority of Irish-Americans, however, the choice was between being seen as a 'good' American or an enemy and few were willing to choose the latter path. Yet, many were united in their expectation that Wilson's self determination principle would be applied to Ireland in the post-war settlement. This hope was also shared and articulated in early summer 1917 by the recently released leadership of the Irish republican movement who had formed the Provisional Government of Ireland. An address to Wilson was drawn up on 18 June and forwarded to Patrick McCartan, the representative of the Irish Republic to the US. He presented it to congressional politicians on Capitol Hill, where he was received publicly by Tumulty, Marshall and Clark on behalf of Congress.[89] When confronted directly with this appeal, Wilson resumed his non-interventionist position and his inclination was not to reply to it. Polk agreed 'I think the best thing to do would be to file the papers and not reply.'[90] No reply was sent but the issue lay in wait

---

87 NLI, JMcGP, MS17502, Reports of British intelligence on Irish nationalists in United States, Memo. No. 3 Series, 13 April 1917, enclosure A from John Rogers, 5 April 1917. 'John Rogers' was one of the busiest agents. He handled a network of spies in the various Irish-American groups and forwarded reports to his superiors. S. Cronin (ed.), *The McGarrity papers: revelations of the Irish revolutionary movement in Ireland and America 1900–1940* (1972), pp. 66–7.   88 NLI, JMcGP, MS17502, Reports of British intelligence', 13 April 1917, enclosure A from John Rogers, 5 April 1917; ibid., Informer's reference 'Josephs'; ibid., Enclosure A, 12 April 1917 (39). At its meeting on 8 April, Clan na Gael pronounced that it would centre its efforts to secure an amendment to the military bill then in Congress that would prohibit US soldiers from going overseas. This failed. Ibid., Informer's reference 'Patterson'.   89 NLI, 'Ireland's appeal to America 1917'. Address presented to Congress. July 23rd'; ibid., 'America's appeal to Ireland. 1775. Two historic documents' (1917), pp. 3, 4.   90 Quoted in A.J. Ward, *Ireland and Anglo-American relations, 1899–1921* (1969), p. 151. Yet, at this time Wilson continued to show his support for Irish home rule by meeting with T.P. O'Connor and Richard Hazelton, both members of parliament on 5 July 1917, through the intervention of Senator Phelan. O'Connor expressed the thanks of the Irish Parliamentary Party,

for Wilson once the war ended. In the interim, the Wilson administration got on with winning the war not just abroad but at home also, through its repression and propaganda campaigns. Both of these had an Irish dimension; the administration had to repress Irish-American extremists who opposed US involvement in the war while the Committee on Public Information (CPI) treated events in Ireland on the one hand, as a target for suppression and, on the other, as fodder for the promotion of war.

The majority of US citizens may not have wanted a war in April 1917 but they supported Wilson's declaration of it. It had to be fought and won. However, when the war was declared Wilson admitted that he did not have a united nation behind him. Petersen and Fite suggest that a popular referendum at the time might have resulted in a 'sizeable vote' against the war in some parts of the country. Undoubtedly, the decision left many Americans 'angry and bitter', specifically these included socialists, labour agitators, pacifists, opponents of conscription and the millions of Germans, Austrians, Hungarians, Poles, Russians and other 'aliens in our midst', including Irish and Indian nationalists.[91] Even before the declaration of war, numerous government agencies, such as the Bureau of Investigation in the department of Justice, Secret Service in the Treasury Department, Military Intelligence Division, Office of Naval Intelligence and Shipping Board Intelligence, managed intelligence activities at federal, state and local levels. From 1915 onwards, as seen in chapter three, U-1 in the State Department gradually extended its authority over these agencies with the triumvirate of Polk, Auchincloss and House co-ordinating the work. Voluntary, private and semi-official organizations were also formed to suppress opposition; these included the American Defence Society, the National Security League, the American Protective League and the All-Allied Anti-German League. In addition, supporters of war, particularly Attorney General Thomas Gregory, sought legislation to combat opposition to the war throughout April and May 1917.[92]

(the home rule party), to Wilson for his sympathy for the Irish cause. Page described O'Connor as 'a professional Irishman and an MP– of somewhat the better sort.' *PWW*, 43, Page to Wilson, 3 September 1917, fn. 2; ibid., 44, fn.2, p. 134; ibid., Page to Wilson, 3 September 1917, p. 133; H. Fyfe, *T.P. O'Connor* (1934), p. 266.   **91** H.C. Peterson & G.C. Fite, *Opponents of war 1917–18* (1958), pp. 10, 12–13; J.R. Mock & C. Larson, *Words that won the war: the story of the committee on public information, 1917–19* (1939), p. 3. Indian nationalist agitation against the British empire had become a problem for the Wilson administration before April 1917. Their anti-British rhetoric, support by Irish- and German-Americans soon led to them being regarded as a threat to the US war effort. Sailendra Nath Ghose escaped to the US in 1917 and was subsequently arrested under the Espionage Act. Jeffreys-Jones, *American espionage*, pp. 108–16.   **92** G. Creel, *How we advertised America: the first telling of the amazing story of the committee on public information that carried the gospel of Americanism to every corner of the globe* (1920), p. 168; Peterson & Fite, *Opponents*, p. 15; NARA, Record Group 65 (hereafter RG65), M1085, *Investigative case files of the Bureau of Investigation, 1908–22*. Among those who opposed the espionage legislation was John D. Moore, national secretary of the Friends of Irish Freedom. He appeared also before the House Judiciary Committee on 12 April along with representatives of the Free Speech League of America, the

For example, Auchincloss warned Polk on 1 May 1917 that a bill was pending in the New York senate making it impossible for a police commissioner or a district attorney in New York to tap a telephone without first getting a court order to permit it. Auchincloss and New York Police Commissioner Woods felt that the bill had to be put aside 'for the present emergency.'[93]

Wilson eventually agreed to tighter legislation and the Espionage bill became law on 15 June 1917. Based on Mr Justice Holmes' theory of 'clear and present danger', one of its main purposes was to reduce domestic opposition to the war. But as time went on, it became clear that opponents of the war could, and indeed would, be suppressed. A further restrictive amendment to the Espionage Act was the Sedition Act signed by Wilson on 16 May 1918; it introduced fines and prison sentences for 'disloyal, profane, scurrilous or abusive language' about the US government, constitution, armed forces, uniform or flag and brought them into 'contempt, scorn, contumely or disrepute.' In addition to this federal legislation, state and municipal authorities also introduced laws to quell opposition to the war. For example, states legislated against the use of language opposed to the war effort and against union activities.[94] The final part of this jigsaw was the presence of British and French intelligence networks whose activities were tolerated by the Wilson administration.

Co-operation between the US and British authorities on intelligence matters was already well-established by February 1917 when Wiseman, now liaison officer between the British and US governments, revealed his secret service identity to Polk in the State Department. When, from December 1916 onwards, Wiseman's work began to develop along political lines, Major Norman Thwaites, who could read and speak German, took over the foreign intelligence unit of the British War Office, MI1(c) in New York city, while Colonel H.A. Packenham of the MI5 was based in the US War College Division in Washington. The scope of Thwaites' work increased over time and, following the entry of the US into the war, larger offices were taken. In March 1918, the New York office of British military intelligence was regarded by the US agencies, as well as by the British

Women's Peace Party of America. The Catholic Young Men's National Union was vigilant also and complained to Newton Baker, secretary of War, in August 1917 about the head of the British recruiting mission in Philadelphia, Colonel St John Loftus Steele whose 'slanderous comments' on events in Ireland were given 'great publicity' in the Philadelphia press. Steele stated that the 'Ulsterites desire home rule instead of Rome rule.' The Union complained that individuals who attacked the 'race or creed of the American people' and caused 'resentment' should be suppressed. The Union pointed out that Catholics supported the war with forty per cent of its members in the armed forces. The Federation of Irish County Societies complained to assistant attorney general, Charles Warner, about the same issue. He suggested that Spring Rice be asked, to ensure that recruiting officers be instructed not to use 'language which might be disagreeable to a portion of our citizens. See Mock & Larson, *Words that won the war*, pp. 23, 30; NARA, RG65, M1085, M.J. Slattery to Baker, 25 August 1917; Ibid., 841.00/48, Baker to Lansing, 4 September 1917. 93 YULMC, FLPP, box 1, file 015, Auchincloss to Polk, 1, 8 May 1917. 94 Peterson & Fite, *Opponents*, pp. 17, 18, 20; Mock & Larson, *Words that won the war*, pp. 45–6.

embassy and consulates, as the best source of information since it had been in existence longer than any of the other investigation and intelligence organizations. Packenham wrote in 1918 'our lists of suspects are more complete, and our methods of gaining information are more widespread than any department up to the present.' There was 'complete co-operation' between British intelligence and US agencies such as the respective military, police and naval intelligence divisions, the secret service, the department of Justice particularly the Bureau of Investigation, the police department and Custom House in New York city and American civil organizations fighting sedition such as the American Protective League. The heads of these organizations had access to British files and information. US intelligence organizations were equally ready to reciprocate and Packenham, who was based in Washington, felt that 'the spirit of friendly co-operation makes the work extremely pleasant and ... useful.'[95]

This co-operation took many forms. From January 1916 onwards, Indian nationalist affairs were a focus of attention for the American and British governments and eventually resulted in the Indian sedition trial held in San Francisco in March 1918. British officials in the New York office collected documents, translated them, interviewed agents and, most importantly, by arrangement with the US cable censors, scrutinized all messages sent from the US 'to persons and places in the Orient.'[96] Other examples of co-operation related to passenger control. Port control by the New York MI1c office was eventually extended to every US port. In October 1917, Wiseman was approached by officials from the US Naval Intelligence Department who suggested that British intelligence should co-operate with them in a new scheme for the detection of aliens engaged in enemy activities upon all ships leaving US ports. By March 1918, every name that came before the US authorities for permission to travel was submitted to the New York office 'to be passed upon.' Furthermore, Thwaites and Packenham had made arrangements with shipping companies operating out of US ports, both for coastal and ocean traffic, to hand over all passenger lists to the New York office before the departure of the steamers. The system was already bearing fruit and the two sides had been able to find 'enemy agents' of whom the British had lost track; in 1918, the details of approximately 1,200 passengers and crews of vessels leaving New York port were scrutinized daily. This co-operation between

95 YULMC, William Wiseman Papers (hereafter WWP), box 6, file 173, memorandum sent by General MacLachlan and Colonel Packenham to MI5, 28 March 1918; ibid., Office personnel. Also in the New York office with Thwaites were Captain Fred Lloyd, Lieutenant W.D. Boshell, Lieutenant Tom Furness, Lieutenant Lawrence Grossmith and Frederick M. Hall. Salaries were paid also to agents who were recruited directly and others employed by professional agencies. In early 1918, one of the strengths of the New York office was that Thwaites was fluent in German and it employed the services of German agents whereas none of the US offices employed Germans. Occasionally, US intelligence asked Thwaites 'to lend these men for special cases.' At this time Thwaites spent several nights in New York police headquarters examining German documents. YULMC, WWP, box 6, file 173, Expenditure, undated probably March 1918.   96 Ibid., memorandum sent by General MacLachlan and Colonel Packenham to MI5, 28 March 1918.

British and US authorities at the docks and the Custom House in New York ensured that 'undesirable' passengers could be stopped from travelling from the US to Britain. Among the crew lists in March 1918 were fourteen Hindus who were investigated by the Indian department.[97] Of course the co-operation extended to investigating the composition of cargoes to ensure that munitions were not transported to undesirable destinations. There was a constant flow of intelligence between the British and Americans agencies; by 1918 Attorney General Gregory stated 'it is safe to say that never in its history has this country been so thoroughly policed.'[98]

Irish-Americans, specifically the secret, revolutionary Clan na Gael and the more open organization, Friends of Irish Freedom, came into the radar of this surveillance structure. The former's links to German-American networks, previously detailed, combined with both organizations' anti-British focus, guaranteed attention. Such activities were now signs of disloyalty. British agents attended 'all' Irish and Indian nationalists' gatherings. By April 1917, British agents in the US operating under Wiseman's direction had infiltrated Irish-American radical organizations such as Clan na Gael itself and some of its attendants groups such as the Innisfail, Geraldine and Shamrock clubs in New York. British agents reported 'a sense of unease' among the groups as to whether the US government would take action against them due to their pro-German views and activities.[99] In Philadelphia, Joseph McGarrity's Clan na Gael work was targeted in summer and autumn 1917 by the expanding US intelligence service. Bureau Agent Todd Daniel had a contact, Wanda Fernand, a stenographer in the Austro-Hungarian consulate who told him that McGarrity was a 'bitter enemy' of Britain, 'intimate' with the former German consul in Philadelphia and that he had often given money to the consulate for relief work before the US entered the war. Daniel suggested in October that McGarrity should be 'closely watched' as he would 'sacrifice the interest of this country, in order to prejudice the English in the same way.'[1] Following this report, Daniel recruited an Irishman, Joseph P. Bryan, to gain McGarrity's confidence. Bryan was trying to avoid prison because his connections with the pro-German magazine, *Fatherland*, had been uncovered by Senator King of Utah and the Bureau of Investigation. He promised to keep trying to get an interview with McGarrity who remained under permanent surveillance by the Bureau, State Department and later Military and Naval Intelligence sections as well as by the British.[2]

97 Ibid., file 175, New York office, section v, and other activities, undated, probably 1918; ibid., file 172, Wiseman to Thwaites, 3 October 1917.   98 Ibid., file 168, Wiseman and McLachan, September 1917; Peterson and Fite, *Opponents*, p. 20.   99 YULMC, WWP, box 6, file 175, New York office, section v, and other activities, Jewish Affairs, undated, probably 1918. NLI, JMcGP, MS17502, Reports of British intelligence on Irish nationalists in United States, Memo. No. 3 Series, 22 March 1917, 12, 13, 17, 25 April 1917. Later in 1918, British surveillance covered meetings of Jews, Bolsheviks and the International Workers of the World.   1 NARA, RG65, M1085/439, 8129, Todd Daniel, 8 October 1917.   2 Ibid., 73392, Todd Daniel, 2 November 1917.

Following several Friends of Irish Freedom meetings in New York in August 1917, the city government decided to prevent the 'preaching of sedition on street corners.' The police raided a meeting on 29 August in New York and arrested several protesters for 'obstructing traffic.'[3] The FOIF had sponsored Hanna Sheehy Skeffington's speaking tour of the US which provides a further illustration of the increasing harassment of the organization. Bureau agents infiltrated her meetings and kept a dossier of reports from agents on the meetings, along with press cuttings and pamphlets, as part of their continuing investigations into the activities of pro-German sympathizers. However, the US department of Justice concluded that her lectures were 'extremely pro-Irish and anti-British but that they do not attack the United States', while Military Intelligence reports noted that 'her remarks could not be construed in any way as anti-American or anti-Ally.' Sheehy Skeffington ensured that her messages did not work against her. After April 1917, she spoke less about British brutality in Ireland and more about Irish hopes for independence from the peace settlement and she refrained from condemning America's partnership with Britain. Nonetheless, Colonel van Deman in the US War Department believed that 'utterances which would tend to foment disloyalty in this country, are made at informal gatherings. But neither agency ever had sufficient evidence to detain or arrest her, although British agents nearly managed to capture her during a journey to Buffalo, when a group of men and women posed as a welcoming committee and invited her to board a train to Canada where she could have been arrested for leaving Ireland illegally. British agents followed her from the time of arrival and, she believed, tampered with her luggage, ransacked her accommodation and interfered with lettings of hall for her meetings.[4]

By autumn 1917, 'in the name of national defence', the Wilson administration had created a system of surveillance of radicals, suspected radicals and enemy aliens including Irish-Americans.[5] It also used a discrediting tactic to highlight the anti-Americanism of these Irish-American organizations. The circumstances of the publication of the von Igel documents, seventeen months after the US Secret Service raid on the German commercial attaché's office in April 1916, had taken place, were examined in chapter three. It is sufficient to say here that the documents implicated the Clan na Gael and Friends of Irish Freedom leadership, namely McGarrity, John T. Keating (who died in June 1915), O'Leary and Cohalan in anti-American activities although these were prior to the US entry into the war. The raid was not followed up by legal proceedings against the men but the British government continued to forward to Lansing, through Page, evidence of German–Irish conspiracy in the US, even though it had taken place before April 1917. Nonetheless, the timing of the release of these documents in September 1917, on the eve of the Indian sedition trials, was calculated to con-

3 Peterson & Fite, *Opponents*, pp. 73–4.   4 Ward, *Hanna*, pp. 191, 192, 193; Sheehy Skeffington, *Impressions*, pp. 11–12.   5 Jeffreys-Jones, *American espionage*, p. 67.

vict 'by association' Irish-American nationalists.[6] US newspapers reacted immediately by branding the Clan and Friends leaders as German agents. The *New
York Times*' pillorying of Cohalan led him to fear removal from the New York
courts while the *Washington Post* article named McGarrity as 'a useful Irishman
for German purposes' which intensified surveillance of his movements.[7] In early
1918, the Naval Intelligence section picked up a rumour that McGarrity was closing up his business affairs to leave the US. The Military Intelligence division
asked the Bureau of Investigation for information because McGarrity was considered a 'most suspicious and dangerous character ... pro-German' and 'likely
to cause trouble in Ireland.'[8] He did not leave, but his founding of the *Irish Press*
newspaper in March 1918 provoked further Bureau attention.[9] McGarrity and
Cohalan escaped arrest but the von Igel incident was followed by the arrests of
O'Leary, Patrick McCartan and Liam Mellows while another Clan leader, John
T. Ryan, escaped detention by fleeing the country.[10] In 1917 and 1918 Irish-
Americans were held for trial in Seattle (Washington state), Omaha (Nebraska),
Sacramento (California), Ely (Nevada) and Spokane (Washington). Others were
detained in prisons in McNeills Island, Bellingham and Mount Vernon in
Washington state, in Iowa, Fort Leavenworth in Kansas and in Clinton prison
in Albany, New York. The seventy-seven Irish-Americans known by Frank P.
Walsh, the Kansas labour lawyer, and Cohalan to have been detained were
charged with anti-war acts and violation of the Espionage Act. Among the crimes
committed were interfering with production of copper at the White Pines company in Ely, Nevada, conspiracy to hinder the US government by inciting strikes
in the mining and lumbering regions and distribution of anti-war leaflets. Some
of them were freed but others were sentenced to deportation, imprisonment that
varied from one to twenty years, payment of fines from $500 to $30,000.[11] Mary
McWhorter, president of the Ladies' Auxiliary of the Ancient Order of
Hibernians recalled 'during the time we were in the war, under this [Espionage]
act we were deprived of every bit of our personal liberty "as a war necessity".'[12]
Packenham reported to London on the British role in these contra-espionage
events in March 1918:

> The arrests of the last weeks have been more than satisfactory, and the
> work done by the Bureau of Investigation of the US Department of Justice
> is beyond all praise. They have been amazingly well supported by the

6 Ibid., p. 116.   7 F.M. Carroll, 'Friends of Irish Freedom' in Funchion (ed.), *Irish American voluntary organizations*, pp. 120–1; NARA, RG65, M1085/439, 8129, RW Lanaleman to Bielaski, 15
October 1917.   8 Ibid., 73392, McCauley to Harrison, 28 February 1918; ibid., Harrison to Bielaski,
2 March 1918; ibid., Report, 5 March 1918, New York city.   9 Ibid., J.F. McDevitt, Philadelphia,
5 September 1918.   10 Cronin, *The McGarrity papers*, pp. 68–9; Jeffreys-Jones, *American espionage*,
p. 65.   11 American Irish Historical Society (hereafter AIHS), Daniel F. Cohalan Papers (hereafter
DFCP), box 17, folder 5, List of prisoners, undated.   12 NLI, Patrick McCartan Papers (hereafter
PMP), MS17670, McWhorter to McCartan, 15 May 1919.

Military Intelligence section of the New York and the Naval Intelligence. In most cases we have been able to supply evidence of a useful kind. Very few of the names of those apprehended are strange to us. Many of them have been on our black books for the past two years, and we were, therefore, able to supply the United States authorities with records of the activities of these undesirable aliens.[13]

But Packenham and Thwaites felt that even more successes could be had if more staff was sent from London.[14]

The US government's campaign against the 'disloyal' Irish-Americans resulted in a number of consequences. In October 1917 Wiseman believed that the von Igel incident had created an 'excellent impression' and helped to make the 'pro-Germans and their activities here very unpopular.'[15] Secondly, by the end of the year the Clan na Gael and Friends public campaigns had practically ceased.[16] Thirdly, illegal activities such as running training schools in the use of explosives and contact with Germans declined and fund-raising became more difficult. Fourthly, this decline in activity and cancellation of the 1917 Irish Race Convention by the older radicals contributed to the establishment of the Irish Progressive League (IPL) in October 1917. It brought together individuals interested in achieving the complete independence of Ireland and it aimed to ensure that Ireland was represented at the post-war peace conferences. This specific political focus differentiated the IPL from the older, apparently subversive organizations and that pressure remained on Wilson to deal with the Irish question at the end of the war.[17]

Clan na Gael and the Friends activities were also targeted by the Committee of Public Information (CPI). Wilson had established the Committee by executive order on 13 April 1917 and appointed the journalist George Creel as its civilian chairman and the secretaries of State, Navy and War as the other members. Creel wrote that it was an agency that 'would not only reach deep into every American community, clearing away confusion, but at the same time seek the friendship of neutral nations and break through the barrage of lies that kept the Germans in darkness and delusion.'[18] It became the US ministry for propaganda

13 YULMC, WWP, box 6, file 173, memorandum sent by General MacLachlan and Colonel Packenham to MI5, 28 March 1918.   14 Ibid., file 175, New York office, section v, and other activities, undated, probably 1918; ibid., Thwaites to Packenham, 9 April 1918.   15 Quoted in Ward, *Ireland and Anglo-American relations*, p. 156.   16 Peterson & Fite, *Opponents*, pp. 73–4.   17 F.M. Carroll, 'Irish Progressive League' in Funchion (ed.), *Irish American voluntary organizations*, p. 207; NLI, Papers of Peter Golden (hereafter PGP), MS17668.   18 George Creel was born in 1876 in Lafayette County, Missouri became a journalist and editor of the *Rocky Mountain News* in Denver, Colorado and was a Wilson supporter from the start of his political career. During the 1916 campaign he helped the Democratic national committee with publicity. According to Creel, he had to decline Wilson's invitation to take up a government post due to financial pressures. See G. Creel, *Rebel at large: recollections of fifty crowded years* (1947), pp. 148–56, 158; Mock & Larson, *Words that won the war*, p. 4.

with a foreign and domestic section. Wilson had only to look at the work of German and British propagandists in the US since the beginning of the war to justify his decision. By April 1917, British operations were well established in the US and Britain and were augmented in June, when press baron Northcliffe directed the second British war mission and for six months launched an extensive propaganda campaign in the US. British pamphlets, newspapers and articles were sent to American homes and newspapers. The operation peaked under the direction of Lord Beaverbrook in 1918 when the British ministry for Information was established to co-ordinate publicity activities.[19]

The CPI's tools became extensive including the use of film, radio, exhibitions, publications, public speaking, advertising and cartoons. Creel was the unofficial censor and separate divisions in the domestic section dealt with areas such as work and foreign born. From the very beginning of its existence, the 'alien in our midst' received CPI attention although the formal division was not established until May 1918 with Josephine Roche as its director. There were three units in the Foreign Section; wireless and cable service, the foreign press bureau and the foreign film division.[20] The tentacles of the Committee were to touch every group in US society, whether they were supporters of the war effort or sources of opposition.

The extent of the loyalty of 'hyphenated Americans' was a constant source of concern and holding US citizenship was no proof of that loyalty. In total the CPI attempted to reach twenty-three foreign groups. Some countries were more important than others. German-Americans were the most important with the 'subject peoples' in Austria–Hungary, particularly the Hungarians and Yugoslavs, next. At the end of the war the bureau chiefs in the Division of Work with the Foreign Born covered peoples from Scandinavia, Germany, Hungary, Italy, Lithuania, Poland, Czechoslovakia and Yugoslavia. Two methods were used by the CPI to manage these foreign born elements; suppression and persuasion. Creel used the full rigours of the Espionage Act and surveillance agencies when necessary.

In co-operation with the US Post Office, Creel monitored the loyalty content of foreign newspapers. Working with Postmaster General Burleson, Creel invoked the Trading with the Enemy Act to prohibit the use of the US mail service to offending newspapers including the *Gaelic American*, the *Irish World*, the

19 J.D. Startt, 'American propaganda in Britain during world war 1', 17–20. For further on the work of the British propaganda bureau based in London see M.L. Saunders, 'Wellington House and British propaganda during the first world war', 119–46. Arthur Willert, *The Times* correspondent in the US between 1910 and 1921, did propaganda work for the British embassy in Washington and Geoffrey Butler and John Buchan of the British ministry for Information in 1917 and 1918. He believed in January 1918 that the 'Irish situation' was a key obstacle, if not most important, in the way of full US public support for the war and 'good relations' between the US and Britain. See British Library, Manuscripts Division (hereafter BLMD), Northcliffe Papers (hereafter NP), Add. 62255, Willert to Northcliffe, 19 January 1918, 24 July 1918. 20 Mock & Larson, *Words that won the war*, pp. 8, 66–73, 74.

Freeman's Journal and the *Bull*. The *Freeman's Journal* was censored because it printed a statement by Thomas Jefferson that Ireland should be free. The *Irish World* got the same treatment due to a declaration that French people were materialistic and that Palestine would not be independent but would become a British protectorate.[21] During her speaking tours throughout the US, Hanna Sheehy Skeffington encountered the activities of the CPI. She noted that German music, prayers, books, words were all banned. 'Sauerkraut' became 'liberty cabbage', 'frankfurter' became 'liberty sausage' and German measles became American measles. She wryly concluded 'of course, one might still drink German beer under another name, and the flavour, I believe is not impaired.' She recalled her surprise at the 'childish exhibitions in the much abused name of patriotism.' Also 'Loyalty Days' were organized when immigrant communities were given the opportunity to display their love for the US.[22] Generally, Creel preferred to educate rather than coerce the foreign born and one message often used in CPI material to engender loyalty, was Wilson's doctrine of self-determination. However, it is significant firstly, that no dedicated section, division or bureau dealt with Irish-Americans and secondly, that the Wilson message was not seen by Creel and Roche to apply specifically to the Irish-American community. However, there was an Irish dimension to other themes used by the CPI to promote patriotism.

The Speaking Division was established on 25 September 1917, with Arthur E. Bestor as director. He gathered together more than 10,000 speakers who could lecture on the war in any part of the country. Among the most successful of these tours were those undertaken by men and women who had experienced the war already and those which promoted war charities or drives such as the Liberty Loans and equipment for war hospitals. Fifty men from Pershing's American Expedition Force spoke in aid of the Third Liberty Loan along with Belgian and French soldiers while British and French officials toured the larger cities. But the most 'sensational' lecture tour arranged by the Speaking Division was that of Wesley Frost who gave sixty-three addresses in twenty-nine states.[23] Frost had taken testimony in Queenstown from survivors of eighty-one vessels including the *Lusitania* and the *Arabic*, attacked by German submarines. In 1917 and 1918 he delivered a series of lectures throughout the country. His first was titled 'Devils of the deep' and another was 'The tragedy of the *Lusitania*' but he used material from the other atrocities that he ascribed to U-boat commanders or 'the jackals of the sea' as he called them, and often his talks were illustrated with slides. Apparently, the solid consul possessed a sense of drama that assured his presentations a good press. The effectiveness of his talk was helped also by the CPI bombardment of publicity in local newspapers prior to his arrival. Gradually communities came to believe that Frost had not merely observed and assisted

21 Mock & Larson, *Words that won the war*, pp. 215–16; Ward, *Ireland and Anglo-American relations*, p. 145; Peterson & Fite, *Opponents*, p. 100. 22 Sheehy Skeffington, *Impressions*, p. 18; L. Gerson, *The hyphenate in recent American politics and diplomacy* (1964), p. 15. 23 Mock & Larson, *Words that won the war*, pp. 126–9; Creel, *How we advertised America*, pp. 152–3.

the survivors but had actually participated in the military engagement. Frost's *Lusitania* speech included the following:

> It was quite black out there on the Atlantic, and in the blackness the life-boats alternately rose on the crests of the waves and sank into the black valley between. The boats carried women and children whose hair hung in icicles over their shoulders and their half-frozen bodies yielded to the rolling and pitching of the frail boats ... Meanwhile in the dark hull of the German submarine, the captain watching through the periscope finally turned his head away. Even this man, agent of Prussian cruelty, had witnessed a scene upon which he did not care to gaze.[24]

When he arrived in the Irish-American stronghold in Butte, Montana, the headline on the *Daily Post* was 'Wesley Frost, the good Samaritan of the U-Boat War, comes to Butte.' An article in Creel's former newspaper, the *Rocky Mountain News* noted 'A thousand Denverites sat in the Auditorium last night and alternately sobbed and cheered.'[25] Frost's lecture provided a dramatic account of events at the war front; other speakers talked on more mundane topics but the CPI Speaking Division lecturers, along with the Four-Minute Men who spoke on radio, spearheaded the CPI attack on popular indifference and civic apathy. Mobilizing US public opinion through this programme of censorship and counter-espionage was one part of the Committee's mission, the other centred on winning the battle abroad using propaganda.[26]

The 'fight for the mind of mankind' in enemy, allied and neutral countries was implemented through the use of the wireless-cable service, the foreign press bureau and the foreign film division which all carried information and propaganda. Other methods used were film, exhibitions, lectures, press correspondents, distinguished visitors, leaflet drops by airplanes and balloons and secret agents, among other methods. Although Creel clashed with Lansing over the CPI's foreign activities and State Department interference in its work, CPI divisions were established in England, France, Italy, Russia, Spain Switzerland, Sweden, the Netherlands, Denmark, China, Latin America, Mexico, Brazil, Argentina, Chile,

---

24 Quoted in Mock & Larson, *Words that won the war*, p. 129; YULMC, FLPP, box 34, file 740, Polk, 'Introduction'.   25 Mock & Larson, *Words that won the war*, pp. 128–9. In 1918 Frost published a book on German submarine warfare that was approved by the State Department and the British authorities. Polk wrote the introduction for it. YULMC, FLPP, box 34, file 740, Frost to Polk, 14 June 1918.   26 Mock & Larson, *Words that won the war*, p. 237. Among the other figures who took part in the loyalty drives were cardinals Gibbons, Farley and O'Connell. They appealed to Italian-American Catholics to support the allies' efforts. Also when army major Eugene F. Kinkead, head of the US Military Intelligence Labour and Sabotage unit (MI-41) encountered extreme anit-Britishness among Irish-American Catholic clergy, he reported the evidence to Cardinal Gibbons who reprimanded the priest. H.D Lasswell, *Propaganda technique in the world war* (1927), p. 122; G.J.A. O'Toole, *Honorable treachery: a history of US intelligence, espionage and covert action from the American revolution to the CIA* (1991), p. 281.

Peru and Panama. Other countries received Committee material through US embassies and legations, the Military Intelligence Division and US businesses. In January 1918, Creel was preparing to use the files of the departments of Justice and State to compile a pamphlet on 'German intrigues' and show how the German government was using 'national groups in this country such as the Irish' to stimulate anti-American activities or sentiments in other countries.[27] Creel wanted to follow the threads of these activities back to German agents located within Germany's embassies and legations.

The CPI's foreign mission aimed to persuade other nations that:

> (1) America could never be beaten; and, therefore, that it behoved them to join the winning side; (2) America was a land of freedom and democracy; and, therefore, that it could be trusted, however faithless imperialist rulers might be; (3) thanks to President's Wilson's vision for a new world and his power of achieving it, victory for the Allied arms would usher in a new era of peace and hope in which armaments could be forgotten, all mankind would gather around a council table of the nations, minorities would be released from oppression, and the sovereignty of every country would be returned to the people.[28]

The task of carrying the message to the British people, neutrals and 'weaker allies' in Europe was directed by an office based in London which was led by a succession of directors beginning with H.N. Rickey.[29] The London division had a difficult time to fulfil its British mission. Despite the common cultural bonds, British politicians, press and public were suspicious about American materialism, business and political practices and foreign policies, specifically neutrality. But along with counteracting British resentment, Wilson wanted American war aims and objectives to be better understood, particularly his post-war aims.[30]

The staff of the Committee's foreign section, in both the UK and the US, were all sensitive to these difficulties and to others relating to Ireland. The London staff employed motion pictures, photographs, pamphlets, articles and guest speakers as vehicles for US propaganda. They worked hard to send news and publicity material of appropriate length and content which would find space in British newspapers, magazines, journals or in the words of Perry Arnold 'to reach any pay dirt.'[31] By early summer 1918, ten to fifteen per cent of the news

27 YULMC, FLPP, box 2, file 128, Creel to Polk, 11 January 1918.   28 N.A. Graebner (ed.), *An uncertain tradition: American secretaries of state in the twentieth century* (1961), p. 114; Mock & Larson, *Words that won the war*, pp. 239, 247.   29 NARA, Record Group 63 (hereafter RG63), Committee on Public Information (hereafter CPI) 1-C4, folder: England, 'Report on propaganda for neutral countries', Russell, 8 August 1918.   30 J.D. Startt, 'American propaganda in Britain during world war 1' (1996), 17–20.   31 NARA, RG63, CPI 1-C4, folder: England, Arnold to Sisson, 8 August 1918; ibid., 'American propaganda in Great Britain', Balderston to Sisson, 10 August 1918; ibid., 'Report on photo situation', Russell, 8 August 1918.

articles of 100 to 1,000 words in length sent by the CPI in the US were being placed in British papers. Topics covered not just politics, but trade, technical and religious material and any human interest story involving Wilson. John L. Balderston, a journalist for the *McClure* syndicate who began to work for the CPI in London in early summer 1918 moved to expand its Scotland, northern England and Ireland services.[32] He responded to a suggestion by Horace Plunkett and Hugh Law, who was in charge of Irish-American propaganda at the British ministry of Information but was an advocate of Irish self-determination, on the advisability of 'putting out Irish-American news and articles dealing with American war aims' in Ireland.[33] The sole aim behind the Irish service was to support allied unity but the CPI had to be careful when promoting US war aims in Ireland because of the anglophobia of Irish nationalists (escalated by the threat of conscription in 1918) and on-going British government fears of German intrigue in Ireland.[34] One example of the anti-British and pro-German propaganda, 'The Sinn Féin Hymn of Hate', was widely distributed in Britain. It went as follows:

> *The Sinn Féin Hymn of Hate*
>
> God of Mercy, watching
> O'er the Irish race,
> Save our Nation's honour,
> Keep us from disgrace.
> Let thy powerful arm,
> Right o'erthrowing might,
> Lead the German Armies
> In this glorious fight ...
> Give all British soldiers
> Purest Essen steel.[35]

This evidence of Irish hatred seemed to Balderston to endanger the allied war effort, particularly during summer 1918 when Germany launched its last offensive. Balderston expanded on the bureau's aims in Ireland in letter to Paul Kennedy, who prepared the news wires in the Committee's Wireless-Cable service in New York:

> Our object in Ireland is two-fold, to exploit the traditional Irish friendship for the States and get recruits to fight for what American Irishmen are fighting for, even though they will not fight for England; and second, and more important, to persuade Irishmen that the aims for which this

32 Ibid., CPI 17-A1, folder: 'Balderston—press abroad', Anonymous, probably Perry Arnold to Creel, 7 August 1914; ibid., folder: 'Balderston-reports', Balderston to Sisson, 1 August 1918. 33 Hartley, *The Irish question*, p. 186. 34 Startt, 'American propaganda', 26. 35 NARA, RG63, CPI 1-C4, folder: 'England', enclosure in Russell to Sisson, undated, probably early August 1918.

war is fought are international and idealistic. The more war aim stuff we can get written from the American point of view the better, because the great trouble in Ireland is, that people regard this war as a British war fought to aggrandise the British empire. Of course we could not refer to England at all in our Irish propaganda, nor should we do so, but we should show them that they are taking a narrow view in concentrating on the supposed imperialist aims of England by showing them the broader world view of the situation, and thus making them a bit ashamed to stand out of the show.[36]

It was evident to Balderston from the beginning that no English channels could be used for the dissemination of 'our matter' because of the 'prejudice' in Ireland towards 'anything that savours of English government propaganda.' Accordingly, on Plunkett and Law's suggestion, he sent the first communications to W.H. Brayden, chairman of the Irish Recruiting Council believed to be a nationalist organization. But although the material secured 'considerable publicity', rumours that many Irishmen thought the articles were a front for the British ministry of Information were reported to Balderston. Consequently, John Russell was sent to Ireland during summer 1918 to investigate and report. He recommended that sending out material through the Council was a mistake and instead that a CPI agent should be sent to Ireland. Until that happened, the London bureau should distribute material directly to the Irish newspapers. Each of the editors was contacted on 14 September with a letter in which the CPI policy 'to offer to the Irish people news dispatches about the deeds of Irish-Americans at the front and sacrifices and opinions of Irish-Americans at home' was briefly explained. The letter emphasized that the Committee dealt in 'news not propaganda' and assured them that there was no 'collusion' with the British government.[37]

By late September, Balderston wanted articles from the New York office focusing on the 'heroic exploits' of Irish soldiers, with his hometown in Ireland named or the town of his people.[38] An article originating in the New York office titled 'New York pays tribute to Irish fighting men' appeared in Irish newspapers while another on 'Henry Ford' appeared in the *Cork Evening Echo* on 15 September 1918 and two days later in the *Cork Examiner*.[39] The nationalist *Freeman's Journal* printed a supplement from material about Wilson's war aims supplied by the London bureau.[40] While he was trying to influence Irish nationalist readers, Balderston quickly realized that a different approach was needed to

36 Ibid., CPI 17-A1, folder: 'Balderston—press abroad', Balderston to Kennady, 12 September 1918.
37 Ibid., folder: 'Balderston—reports', Balderston, 'Preliminary report on work of the Committee in Ireland', 20 September 1918; ibid., Brayden to Balderston undated in Balderston memo. to Perry, 22 August 1918.   38 Ibid.   39 Ibid., CPI 17-A1, folder: 'Balderston—press abroad', Report on pouches received, enclosure in Balderston to Kennady, 31 October 1918; ibid., Report from 'National War Aims Committee on stories used middle of September', enclosure on Balderston to Kennady, 7 September 1918.   40 Ibid., Balderston to Kennady, 6 December 1918.

reach unionist readers, many of whom were supporting the British war effort but were suspicious of the Americans. He asked Kennady in New York for material to placate the 'Orange element and the southern Unionists, who do not like us.'[41] By late September, the London bureau supplied material, generated in both the US and London, three times each week to thirteen newspapers (six unionist and seven nationalist) in Ireland. Balderston was encouraged that the articles were given the 'greatest prominence.'[42] Balderston was satisfied with the placement rate of its news releases and its longer articles in Irish and British press outlets. The Committee of Public Information had achieved its aims in Britain by the end of the war as its work had contributed to a more positive image of the US and greater Anglo–American harmony.[43] This success would soon decline as the realities of the post-war world materialized but in the interim Irish affairs had become part of the CPI's work both as a source of disloyalty in the US and Ireland and as material for the loyalty campaign in the US.

During the period April 1917 to September 1918, almost all radical Irish-American covert activities in the US were in abeyance at least and there was little pro-German activity to spy on in this community as substantial links between the Irish-Americans and German spies had ended by April 1917, while the remaining anti-British activity was easily monitored by the US and British authorities. It is clear that the methods used by the CPI and the other US authorities against radical Irish-Americans were no different from those used to suppress other groups, however, there may have been a difference in the intensity of application. As noted earlier, Creel did not establish a dedicated bureau to handle Irish-American disloyalty. When the Justice Department received evidence from Eugene F. Kinkead chief of the Military Intelligence Labour and Sabotage unit (MI-41) of Irish-American Catholic clergy's subversive activities, it was reluctant to prosecute because of the impact on other American Catholics. Furthermore, Jeffreys-Jones suggests that the Wilson administration did not harass radical Irish-American nationalists in the same aggressive fashion as other disloyal groups because 'from the Democratic administration's point of view, it would have been unwise' to alienate the 'politically entrenched and numerous Irish-American voters.' He offers as evidence the absence of high profile show case trials of 'Hibernian spies.'[44] Certainly, Wiseman attempted to engineer such trials in July 1918, when he requested that an official from the Irish office be sent to the US to persuade the authorities to prosecute 'one or two of the most dangerous Irish agitators' as had occurred with the Indian trials.[45] But Wilson was unwilling to interfere. At a cabinet meeting on 27 May 1918, Attorney

41 Ibid., folder: 'Balderston-press abroad', Balderston to Kennady, 3 December 1918.   42 Ibid., Balderston to Kennady, 6 December 1918.   43 Startt, 'American propaganda', 26.   44 O'Toole, *Honorable treachery*, p. 281; Jeffreys-Jones, *American* espionage, p. 116.   45 YULMC, WWP, box 1, file 74, Wiseman to Reading, 26 July 1918. According to Wiseman, it had been an official from the India Office who had collected evidence and prepared the case again the Hindu seditionists. Ibid.

General Gregory reported to the cabinet that the US Secret Service had 'caught five Irishmen busy with German spies' and suggested 'giving out facts' as requested by the British authorities, Wilson disagreed and expressed the view that Britain 'had been stupid in its dealing with Ireland and we should not be stupid likewise.' Wilson decided to 'Let the traitors be arrested and indicted and the news go from the courts and not from the Administration.'[46] If there were to be trials for the Irish, they would be genuine ones not show trials.

Other British government attempts to secure the arrests of Irish republicans in the US continued. On 19 September, Wiseman asked Arthur Murray, assistant military attaché in the British Secret Service office in New York, to investigate a notice published in the *Gaelic American* on 14 September which urged 'citizens of the Irish republic' to register with representatives of the Irish Provisional Government. Wiseman saw this as 'a flagrant and audacious breach of section 2 of the US Espionage Act.' He had been in contact with officials in the Justice Department and Military Intelligence who were prepared to take 'stringent action.'[47] Although the US authorities proceeded with the case with unofficial British help, Patrick McCartan, the representative of the Irish republic in the US, was not arrested.[48] Further evidence to support the view that there was leniency towards Irish-American activity is that out of 2,168 persons prosecuted under the espionage and sedition legislation not more than ten were Irish-Americans. Furthermore, Wilson rebuffed official British efforts to have him legitimize a smear campaign against Sinn Féin, as will be seen later, and by May 1918, the only Irish publication on a list of forty-four whose mailing privileges had been withdrawn was the *Bull*.[49] Finally, Sheehy Skeffington, a target of British and US surveillance, was surprised at American leniency. Writing after the war was over:

> We Irish exiles in the United States ... first thought that all Irish propaganda on behalf of self-determination for our small nation would have been made impossible, that our meetings would have been suppressed, and that we ourselves would be sent to prison or deported. To our great surprise nothing of the kind happened. Irish propaganda went on, if possible, more strongly than ever.[50]

Wilson even received Sheehy Skeffington in the White House on 11 January 1918 and a smuggled petition from Cumann na mBan in Ireland which claimed self-determination for Ireland.[51] The interview was held in private and, therefore, following convention she did not disclose its contents, although she stated that

46 Cronon (ed.), *Josephus Daniels*, 28 May 1918, p. 307.   47 YULMC, WWP, box 1, file 74, Wiseman to Murray, 19 September 1918.   48 Ibid., Wiseman to Murray, 21 September 1918.   49 Link et al., *American epoch*, p. 141; Mock & Larson, *Words that won the war*, pp. 215–16; Ward, *Ireland and Anglo-American relations*, p. 145.   50 Sheehy Skeffington, *Impressions*, p. 19; Gerson, *The hyphenate*, p. 15.   51 Sheehy Skeffington, *Impressions*, pp. 28–9.

Wilson had been given hope by Lloyd George that a settlement would emerge from the Irish Convention and that the president personally wanted this result. Indeed the day before the meeting, when accepting from Senator Phelan a replica of the statute of Robert Emmet recently placed in the National Museum in Washington, Wilson refused to talk about the Irish question because the Convention was still in session and Britain was an ally. Although he was 'indignant' about Phelan's 'treasonable' talk, Wilson restrained himself from reacting.[52] Despite his support for the Convention which Sinn Féin opposed, she recognized the importance of firstly, his agreeing to meet a Sinn Féiner classified as 'radical' by his own intelligence services, secondly, his willingness to discuss Ireland and thirdly, his receiving her document, which was 'unsubmitted to the British censor.' But she felt also that Wilson while he might have preferred the Irish question settled '"domestically"', he would 'see the force of having it settled internationally for the sake of the peace of the world.'[53] Sheehy Skeffington and indeed the other Irish-American organizations were not to know that Wilson had no intention of discussing the Irish question within any post-war settlement context. A few weeks later, in February, Wilson told Wiseman that 'as far as he was concerned he would not allow Ireland to be dragged into a Peace conference.'[54]

The complexity of the Wilson administration's wartime approach to Irish-Americans, made up of a mixture of restriction, toleration and mollification, was mirrored in Congress. Throughout 1918, resolutions on Irish independence were introduced in Congress while McCartan and Sheehy Skeffington were warmly welcomed by politicians and officials.[55] Nonetheless, congressional politicians kept the pressure on the State Department to investigate and weed out anti-American activity. Moreover, this radical activity must be balanced against the loyalty and patriotism of the majority of Irish-Americans. The Irish-American community did not exercise its potential to disrupt the war effort either on the factory floor or in the battlefield. Creel believed that the extent of actual disloyalty was not large enough even 'to speck the shining patriotism of the millions of Americans that we refer to as "adopted".'[56] The transition from peace to war, and neutrality to belligerence had immediate repercussions that tested Wilson's belief in democracy and opposition to imperialism. Prior to the US entry into the war, this dilemma was more clear-cut but after April 1917 the challenges were greater and forced Wilson to act on Ireland. His administration became a partner with the British empire in fighting the central powers and he needed a united nation. Consequently, he moved from showing sympathy for the Irish problem to directly

52 *PWW*, 45, A reply, Wilson, 10 January 1918, p. 560; Cronon (ed.), *Josephus Daniels*, 11 January 1918, p. 265.   53 Sheehy Skeffington, *Impressions*, pp. 28–9.   54 YULMC, WWP, box 7, file 102, Wiseman to Drummond and Balfour, 4 February 1918.   55 For example on 10 January 1918, Congressman Henry D. Flood, Chairman of the House Committee on Foreign Affairs asked Lansing for his opinion of a resolution before it, proposing the recognition by Congress of the 'right of Irish independence.' NARA, RG65, M580/6, 841.00/57, Flood to Secretary of State, 10 January 1918. 56 Creel, *How we advertised America*, p. 153.

approaching the British government, but diplomatic proprieties combined with a belief that Ireland was Britain's problem to ensure that this intervention did not go further. Instead the Wilson administration interacted with Irish-America and the Irish question in the same way as it did with other 'hyphenated' groups seeing them as a source of both loyalty and disloyalty. But there was another Irish dimension to US involvement in the war because US consuls in Ireland were charged with upholding US interests there.

The Irish theatre

Four activities occupied the greater part of Wesley Frost's and from June 1917, Charles Hathaway's time in Queenstown; trade promotion, dealing with US citizens, reporting on the Irish political situation and dealing with the consequences of the on-going submarine campaign and the presence of the US navy.

Until summer 1917, when Frost left, the Queenstown office was at the heart of the Atlantic campaigns. Upon receiving news of an individual submarine attack on US or allied shipping, the consul would send a telegram to Washington, copied to London and Dublin, and a fuller report followed later on. The telegram outlined the circumstances of the attack, whether a warning was given or not and the number of passengers and of those lost and survivors. Frost also always endeavoured to take affidavits from the American survivors to verify information and allow relatives to be contacted. The resumption of unrestricted German submarine activity on 31 January 1917 posed a most dangerous threat to US vessels on the seas. In February and March, Frost reported on the sinking of the *Eavestone, California, Turino, Mantola, Saxonian, Vedamore, Dalbeattie, Palm Leaf, Isle of Arran, Laconia, Galgorm Castle, Tritonian, Storenes, Storstad, Folia, Blenheim, City of Memphis, Lucilline, Malmanger, Neath, Crispin* and *Canadian*. His analysis of the campaign confirmed his determination to transmit the realities of the sinkings which he spoke about later on the CPI-sponsored tours in the US. He reported that 'exceedingly few lives' had been lost in proportion to the number of vessels sunk but he believed this was due more to the weather which favoured the safety of survivors and the vigilance of the British Admiralty patrols, than to any 'reasonable humanity' on the part of the German commanders, although his sense of fairness and accuracy led him to conclude:

> The conduct of different submarine commanders varies considerably. In general it would seem that no opportunities of sinking vessels are overlooked, no matter at what cost of life; but it is of course impossible to say whether submarines ever voluntarily refrain from attacking vessels, because in such instances the vessels would be unaware of the self-restraint exercised by the submarines. There is no doubt that when they can safely do so, except in the rarest cases, the submarines take pleasure in extending

every courtesy and consideration to the vessels which they destroy; but this attitude is not incompatible with a "beyond good and evil" attitude when anything is to be gained.[57]

At the end of February, Frost reported on the sinking of the *Blenheim* and confirmed the continuation of above practices. But despite the increase in the number of British naval units located in Queenstown and although there was no increase in the number of German submarines in the area, none of the latter had been destroyed.[58] The British strategy of heavily patrolling the British and Irish coastlines and dispersing traffic further into the Atlantic was unsuccessful. Frost's analysis became even more relevant after the US entered the war as the losses of life and shipping mounted up.

Although his relationship with the British authorities was tense at the time of the sinking of the *Lusitania*, he seems to have accepted that British naval officers, or at least those with whom he had contact, were 'naturally reticent' and he hesitated to pierce their 'reserve.'[59] But, not surprisingly in a small town, he had built up a network of contacts that kept him informed of activities. Thus he knew of the arrival of six US naval torpedo-boat destroyers and attendant staff two weeks before Vice Admiral Sir Lewis Bayly informed him of it on 29 April 1917. The flotilla arrived on 4 May and a further six destroyers followed two weeks later. As this was the first occasion on which British and US armed forces came into permanent co-operation, the occasion was marked by formal festivities, including a visit to the lord mayor of Cork, which Frost was particularly pleased at because 'it indicates that a great body of Irishmen have not been alienated from their esteem for the United States by the latter's alliance with the country which holds Ireland as a conquered province.'[60] More significantly, the presence of US naval forces in Queenstown gave Rear Admiral William Sims, the commander of US naval operations in European waters, further leverage to push for an increase in America's naval commitment and an alteration in Britain's naval strategy in the Atlantic waters.

Sims' headquarters were in London but he arrived in Queenstown in June 1917 to take over the command of the British and American forces temporarily from Admiral Bayly. He immediately confirmed Frost's view that British naval strategy was failing and in a letter to Page on 25 June, he wrote 'the Allies are losing the war.' Both men had already agreed that the situation facing the British off the Irish coast was a cause for alarm; in April and May they had appealed to

---

57 *FRUS*, 1917 supplement 1 the world war (1931), Frost to Sec. of State, 7 February 1917. The Cunard-owned, *Laconia*, was sunk on 25 February, six of the passengers and fourteen of the crew were Americans. Two American passengers, Mrs Mary Hoy and Elizabeth Hoy died of exposure in the boat which landed at Bantry bay, the rest of the two hundred and seventy-eight survivors landed at Queenstown.   58 *FRUS*, 1917 supplement 1 the world war, Frost to Secretary of State, 24 February 1917.   59 Ibid.   60 *FRUS*, 1917 supplement 2 the world war, 2 vols (1932), i, Frost to Secretary of State, 8 May 1917.

the US War Department and Wilson for US vessels to be diverted to the area. After Sims had experienced the situation first hand in Queenstown he appealed again to Page to telegram Lansing and Wilson for more anti-submarine craft to be sent to Queenstown: 'there are at least seventeen more destroyers employed on our Atlantic coast, *where there is no war*, not to mention numerous other very useful anti-submarine craft, including sea-going tugs etc.' Page cabled Lansing and Wilson that 'the war will be won or lost in this submarine zone within a few months.'[61] US and British accounts of the delay in increasing America's naval commitment place responsibility on the opposite side and need not concern us here.[62] Nonetheless, by July there were thirty-five American destroyers based in Queenstown and two at Berehaven, further along the Cork coastline, and the convoy system for merchant ships crossing the Atlantic began. With the U-boats gradually being controlled, allied shipping losses declined from 881,027 tons in April to half that in December 1917 and never went above 200,000 tons per month after April 1918.[63]

For the consulate staff, the arrival of the US navy destroyers in early May came at a time when they were overwhelmed by the consequences of submarine sinkings which continued into July and forced Frost to pass on the work of collecting affidavits to his vice consul, Tuck Sherman, and to the administrative assistant. Frost also asked the US consul in Liverpool to take statements from survivors who travelled from Queenstown to Liverpool. However, despite the allies gradually gaining control of the Atlantic, the consulate's workload expanded. Behind each of the welcoming ceremonies lay preparations and Frost had to liase with British authorities and local authority representatives. He and Mrs Mary Frost also entertained the recently arrived officers to tea in two instalments on 6 and 7 May.[64] In addition, there were practical arrangements to be sorted out. Frost had to arrange payment of salaries for the officers and men through local Irish banks and he revealed his astuteness when he chose the Munster and Leinster Bank instead of the Bank of Ireland. The former was the 'largest genuine Irish bank', whereas the latter was owned by 'English unionists.' He also avoided any future confusion because British naval personnel stationed in Queenstown were paid through the Bank of Ireland.[65] His sensitivity to Irish political culture, and specifically to its day-to-day manifestations, is noticeable.

---

61 Hendrick, *Page*, ii, Sims to Page, 25 June 1917, p. 282–3; ibid., Page to President, 27 April 1917, 4 May 1917, pp. 278, 280. 62 Link et al., *American epoch*, pp. 131–2; For the British view see *Lord Riddell's war diary, 1914–18* (1933), 25 October 1918, p. 375; Page's account of the delay placed himself and Sims at the heart of the matter. He felt that as both were 'so pro-British' their reports were regarded with suspicion in Washington and confirmed that Britain was attempting 'to lure American warships into European waters, to undergo the risk of protecting British commerce, while British warships were kept safely in harbour.' He believed that his decision to circumvent this problem by requesting Balfour to write directly to Wilson on 30 June was the deciding factor which intensified the American naval presence. See Hendrick, *Page*, ii, p. 283–5. 63 Link et al., *American epoch*, pp. 131–2. 64 *FRUS*, 1917 supplement 2 the world war, i, Frost to Secretary of State, 8 May 1917. 65 Ibid.

When difficulties arose in November 1917 which attracted the attention of the British ministry of Information and the US authorities, it was his successor, Charles Hathaway, who was in charge of the Queenstown office.

Hathaway was promoted from the class eight posting at Hull, England to the class seven office in Queenstown where he replaced Frost in June 1917. He remained there until December 1919. His wife, Francis Elizabeth, and son accompanied him in the Irish posting. The consul general at large, Ralph Totten, believed that both contributed 'favourably to his standing' and that his wife would be of help to him in any post to which he might be sent because of her 'adaptability and good sense.' While in Queenstown he was promoted to class six which led to his transfer to Budapest. Further promotion later led to an assignment in Bombay and a return to Ireland in 1921, this time as consul class four in Dublin, where he remained until 1927.[66]

Hathaway inherited from Frost a well-run office based in Scott's Square in the business quarter of Queenstown. Along with fulfilling the normal consular duties of promoting US trade, Hathaway identified the subjects that were 'peculiar' to his district; 'Irish politics, submarine war-fare, presence of the United States Navy, presence of many naturalized American citizens of Irish birth and in peace time constant flow of emigration to the United States.'[67] During the war years, Hathaway and his staff neglected economic work and commercial work came to a standstill.[68] When export trade between Ireland and the US resumed in 1918, it consisted of pickled mackerel, woollen cloth and books valuing $298,862.[69] In other words, trade was in exactly the same areas as it had been in the pre-1916 period. This will be examined further in chapter twelve.

The bulk of Hathaway's extra work arose from the increase in the size of the US community located in the Queenstown district. In 1914, there were twenty-eight US citizens in the district and this increased to ninety-one in 1919, most of whom were Irish born wives married to US naval personnel. It was the task of maintaining a good relationship between the US naval and local communities that became a priority for Hathaway and his staff. US naval regulations were more liberal than their British equivalents and permitted enlisted men and petty officers more shore leave. Not surprisingly, the Americans proved popular with local young women. During one of the inevitable clashes, a local man, Frederick Plummer, was killed by a US sailor, John William Parente, on 8 September 1917.[70] The consequences were manifold. On 13 November, H.E. Duke, the

---

66 His background was more that of the traditional US diplomat than of a consul as he was educated at Yale University. He entered the service in 1910 and his first appointment came in August 1911 when he was made consul at Puerto Plata, where he stayed for two years, and he then moved to Hull in England. Promotion came soon enough and, having been upgraded to a class eight consul in February 1915 and class seven in September 1916, he was assigned to Cork (Queenstown). NARA, *Register of the Department of State, 1922*, p. 127; NARA, RG59, Inspection reports on foreign service posts (hereafter IRFSP), Queenstown 1919, p. 3.   67 NARA, RG59, IRFSP, Queenstown 1919, p. 34.   68 Ibid., pp. 11, 34.   69 Ibid., p. 37.

British chief secretary for Ireland, reported to John Buchan, director of the department of Information in London, that there were 'scandalous reports' of the interaction between the sexes and an 'offended sense of propriety' among the local community, particularly among Sinn Féiners. Duke stated that feelings ran strong enough for local Sinn Féin leaders encouraged by Catholic clergy, to organize groups of vigilantes who 'marched about the streets in large numbers and interfered between sailors and women whenever they saw them together.'[71]

The British government seized on the events as proof of Sinn Féin's anti-Americanism and publicized it in the *New York Times* and *Tribune* to discredit Sinn Féin. The US department of War was alarmed to learn that Sinn Féin had 'attacked the US Navy.' Theodore Roosevelt heard about Irish-American sailors 'declining to take shore leave at Cork because of their bitter feeling as to the Sinn Féin outfit', while Sims who was already sharply critical of Irish republicanism for its allegedly pro-German activities, believed that Sinn Féin had orchestrated the attacks and subsequently denied permission for US sailors to go ashore.[72] Although Hathaway attended the inquest, his report on the event is not extant.[73] However, in late 1919, he responded to a statement from Sims that the Irish were either hostile to US forces in Ireland or assisted the enemy:

> Among a certain section of the population there was an undercurrent of resentment at the coming of the Americans – the particular friends of Ireland for many years – to the hope of "Ireland's chief enemy". It is my impression that this feeling lessened steadily as the months went on.[74]

---

70 For an account of the inquest and trial see *Cork Examiner*, 12 September 1917; ibid., 6 October 1917; *Freeman's Journal*, 12 September 1917.   71 This account is based on Hartley, *The Irish question*, p. 159. Even King George V commented to the new US ambassador, John W. Davis, on 18 December 1917, about the 'disorders in Cork caused by the American seamen getting the best of the natives with the Irish girls.' See J. Davis & D.A. Fleming (eds), *The ambassadorial diary of John W Davis: the court of St James' 1918–21* (1993), p. 11.   72 This account is based on Hartley, *The Irish question*, p. 159; Cronon (ed.), *Josephus Daniels*, 3 November 1919, p. 455. The context of Daniels' reference was an article written by Sims on Sinn Féin which provoked criticism from Daniel O'Connell, director of the Irish National Bureau. Daniels as secretary of the Navy had given Sims permission to write the article. Ibid. In contrast to Sims' reaction to the events in Queenstown, he had no difficulty in September 1918 denying that there was any basis to rumours of friction between US sailors and local populations in English ports. See BLMD, Balfour Papers (hereafter BP), Add. 49742, 'Questions asked by a party of American editors visiting the allied countries and, at their request, answered by Vice Admiral Sims, US navy, September 1918.   73 NARA, RG59 M580/1, List of documents, 841.00/5–841.2225/4455 and ibid., M580/6; *Cork Examiner*, 12 September 1917. 74 NARA, RG65, M580/6214 841.00/112, Hathaway to Secretary of State, 13 December 1919. Sims' statement provoked widespread reaction in nationalist political and press. Hathaway transmitted a resolution from Middleton Urban District Council to US Secretary Daniels emphasising that the Irish people were never 'pro-German' but were simply 'pro-Irish'. Ibid., enclosure, James J Ronayne to Hathaway, 7 November 1919. Charles McCarthy visited Ireland in summer 1918 at the invitation of Lord French, lord lieutenant of Ireland, and reported to Woodrow Wilson that 'our sailors and soldiers and the Irish population are in constant clashes.' None of the consuls

He did not refer to the September 1917 incident, which suggests that it was an isolated one. Indeed the jury foreman and coroner at the Plummer inquest agreed that 'good relations' existed ordinarily between the Queenstown people and the US sailors.[75] Nor did Hathaway identify the existence of any plan of indoctrination of US naval personnel by Sinn Féin, although there was some evidence of this. W. Le Vestal, who was from Winston-Salem, North Carolina and Pelham Naval Station, met and socialized with Esther Sheehan while his US vessel was stationed in Queenstown. Upon return to the US, he gave a speech and 'spoke for you and for Ireland, I told them how England was oppressing Ireland' and he promised to 'work to do all I can for the "Freedom of Ireland".' His letter to Sheehan was intercepted by the censor and forwarded to the US embassy in London where, in March 1919, W.L. Hurley regretted that this 'sort of propaganda' was carried to the US by a US navy employee. He also feared that it resulted from a Sinn Féin-organized anti-English campaign directed towards US sailors and soldiers in general. The British censor told him that similar 'anti-English' letters were increasing in the inward mail to Ireland.[76] Hartley recounts genuine British fears that Sinn Féin would get control of Ireland and allow a German naval base on the west coast.[77] But it is likely that the experience of Chief Petty Officer John J. O'Brien senior, who was stationed in Passage, county Cork and in Wexford between January and November 1918, was more representative. He took his shore leave in Queenstown, where he 'looked the place over' and went to the movies at the Naval Club. Following his move to Wexford, where he joined other US personnel in the intelligence section, he socialized in White's Hotel, attended local Catholic Church services, toured the locality and went dancing at Rosslare, county Wexford, ostensibly 'to investigate a German spy.'[78] He did not report any difficulties with locals either.

The Queenstown incidents, however, highlighted the increased anxiety in British government circles about Sinn Féin's growing popularity in both Ireland and the US. Eamon de Valera's electoral victory in the east Clare constituency in July 1917, was followed by other electoral successes. At Sinn Féin's first convention in October 1917, de Valera was elected president of the organization with Arthur Griffith as vice-president. Hathaway reported the growing support for Sinn Féin and described the spirit of numerous resolutions from public bodies

reported this but it would have served French's ends. Wilson ignored the report. See *PWW*, 49, McCarthy to Lansing, Memo. on Irish conditions, 12 September 1918.   75 *Cork Examiner*, 12 September 1917. The *Freeman's Journal* sensationalist account of the event suggested that there were 'occasional disturbances' between the two sides. *Freeman's Journal*, 12 September 1917.   76 HHPL, LHP, Box 103, 'Irish propaganda', Hurley to Harrison, 18 March 1919. Hurley also marked an extract in another intercepted letter from a Brother Jacobus Josephus, St Thomas Aquinas Church, Bronx, New York to Sister Dominica, Convent of Mercy, Borrisoleigh, county Tipperary dated 14 January 1919 which noted 'The American soldiers are to a man, all Sinn Féiners and openly hope that they will have a chance to go over and help the Sinn Féiners.' Ibid., 14 January 1919, 18 March 1919.   77 Hartley, *The Irish question*, p. 159.   78 NLI, MS22642, Excerpts from diary of John J. O'Brien snr., chief petty officer, US navy.

that he was asked to forward to Wilson, as one of 'bitter resentment' at British rule in Ireland, particularly following the death of Thomas Ashe on 25 September 1917 after his force feeding in Mountjoy prison in Dublin.[79] Capitalising on this support, Sinn Féin set about establishing a *de facto* government with the re-organized Irish Volunteers as the republic's army. Thus, the timing of the Queenstown incidents in November 1917 was crucial to the British authorities' campaign to undermine the burgeoning republican organization on both sides of the Atlantic.

Nonetheless, it was Hathaway and his colleagues who had the task of smoothing relations between the US naval personnel, British military authorities and the local community in Queenstown. By the end of the war, Totten was able to commend Hathaway 'for having established the most amicable relations with the local authorities' and Sims praised him for his 'excellent co-operation' with the US navy at Queenstown and his 'admirable manner.' Sims offered to do anything he could to assist Hathaway and on 26 March 1919, he cabled his views to the US department of War along with his offer of a complimentary passage on a naval vessel to the US for Hathaway and his family.[80]

The other aspect of Hathaway's performance that Totten praised was his 'excellent work in political reporting.'[81] Even though he belonged to the consular, rather than the diplomatic, part of the foreign service, Washington expected relevant information to be forwarded immediately if a consular district became politically important, as had been the case during the Easter rising in April 1916. Hathaway's political reports were repeatedly commended by the State Department and London embassy.[82] According to Totten, he was an 'unusually efficient officer' who had a large circle of friends and acquaintances in Cork city, including officials and businessmen, which would have helped him gather information. Frost had admitted to not having close relationships within the republican movement but he had been able to gather enough information to produce the informative report after the rising in 1916. Similarly Hathaway attempted to give a balanced view of developments in Irish politics. For example, on 30 March 1917, US consuls in Ireland were instructed by Skinner not to transmit to the State Department resolutions passed by public bodies, many of which supported the republican cause. Nevertheless, in October Hathaway thought it 'desirable' to transcribe three resolutions from Cork Corporation, Queenstown and Tipperary Urban District councils respectively, for the 'information' of the department 'as they seem to me very significant of the present state of feeling in this district', particularly after Thomas Ashe's death.[83] By way of comparison, in winter 1917–18 the Belfast consular staff merely forwarded a raft of newspaper clippings

---

79 NARA, RG65, M580/6, 841.00/52, Hathaway to Secretary of State, 17 October 1917. 80 NARA, RG59, IRFSP, Queenstown, 1919, pp. 11, 35, Sims to Hathaway, 26 March 1919; ibid., Cable, 26 March 1919. 81 NARA, RG59, IRFSP, Queenstown, 1919, p. 40. 82 Ibid., p. 44, 5. 83 NARA, RG65, M580/6, 841.00/52, Hathaway to Secretary of State, 17 October 1917. 84 NARA, RG65, M580/6, 841.00/53/4/5/6/7, Sharp, 7 November 1917; ibid., 841.00/58, Vice Consul Hitch, Belfast, to Secretary of State, 26 January 1918.

on the Sinn Féin convention and an eight-line telegram outlining the attitude of the local press towards the 'unwarranted and impertinent' US interference if it pressed the British government for 'Irish Home Rule.'[84] Similarly Adams' dispatches from Dublin consisted of 'newspaper clippings or copies of resolutions adopted at public meetings' and he was formally reprimanded for his 'failure to furnish reports concerning 'political disturbances and general conditions in Ireland.' The State Department wanted reports of 'actual conditions existing in your district.' It was not just the content of his reporting that was noted but the infrequency also.[85]

The need for up-to-date information was vital, particularly because the time bought by Wilson and Lloyd George through the establishment of the Irish Convention appeared to be coming to an end without a settlement package and, secondly, because Page failed to report the intricacies of the Irish situation. As noted earlier, Wilson had decided in January 1918 not to say anything about the Irish question during the Irish Convention.[86] But Page kept up the pressure on Wilson not to give in to congressional pressure, by supporting Irish independence and, therefore, bypassing the Irish Convention.[87] But Wilson's 'wait and see' Irish policy came under pressure in early April 1918 when the failure of the Irish Convention to find a solution emerged and he became embroiled in the conscription controversy.

The Herbert Asquith-led coalition cabinet first discussed the inclusion of Ireland in the Military Services Act (1918) in autumn 1915. The issue arose again after the Easter rising in 1916, when voluntary recruitment among nationalists in Ireland declined. But the respective chiefs of military and civilian affairs in Ireland, Maxwell and Duke, were worried that it would encourage support for Sinn Féin, aggravate Irish-Americans and play into the hands of German propagandists. In cabinet these worries were too strong for Tory ministers to bring in conscription.[88] In February 1917, the new prime minister, Lloyd George, supported both men's views because he feared that Irish conscription would cause 'scenes in the House of Commons, a possible rupture in American relations, which is hanging in the balance, and a serious disaffection in Canada, Australia, and South Africa.'[89] Two months later, the US entered the war and this altered

---

85 NARA, RG65, M580/6, 841.00/62, Adams [news clippings] to Secretary of State, 31 January 1918. Adams sent a resolution from Cumann Sinn Féin on 25 January 1918. Ibid., Adams to Secretary of State, 25 January 1918; ibid., Department of State to American Consul, Dublin 18 January 1918.   86 *PWW*, 44, An address and a reply, 10 January 1918.   87 NARA, RG65, M580/6, 841.00/59, Page to Lansing, 20 January 1919.   88 The above account is based on Hartley, *The Irish question*, p. 174.   89 *Lord Riddell's war diary*, 11 February 1917, p. 239. Throughout this time, the State Department received inquiries from Irish-Americans regarding their status under a proposed conscription agreement with Britain. Tom Logan of Washington worried that a recently naturalized Irish friend of his might be in danger of 'being thrown into a Ford' and sent to Ireland for military service. But Lester Wolsley, assistant solicitor, reassured Polk that the British government had released the US government from applying the treaty to Irishmen 'if we do not wish to do so thereby sparing it great embarrassment.' YULMC, FLPP, box 37, file 371, Wolsley to Polk, 2 March

the US dimension of the arguments, as Irish-Americans were signing up to fight for the allied cause. Throughout the winter of 1917, the British and French governments pleaded with Wilson for more troops. An added urgency was given to Irish conscription in March 1918 when the allies faced a severe shortage of soldiers due to the German assault along the western front and in the following month the intervention of British and French troops in the Russian civil war added to the strain.[90] Pershing recalled that at this time, it was a matter of 'common knowledge that the draft had never been enforced in Ireland' and at one meeting of the Supreme War Council, Georges Clemenceau, French prime minister, asked Lloyd George why he did not draft the Irish? The British leader replied 'Mr Prime Minister, you evidently do not know the Irish.'[91] Thus, while Wilson decided on the strength and logistics of sending more US troops to shore up the allied campaigns in Europe and in Russia, Reading, who replaced Spring Rice as British ambassador in Washington, told the Foreign Office that Irish conscription might 'disturb the unanimity of the war spirit now prevailing', a view that Lloyd George subscribed to. But the British war cabinet wanted 'an unbiased expression of the American view' and Balfour consulted House on 2 April.[92]

Balfour told House that he welcomed Wilson's recent decision to send more US troops to France and outlined the reasons why Britain could not raise more troops, namely that it would 'involve Irish problems which necessarily affect American politics.' This allocation of a role to the US government in British domestic affairs was startling and emphasized the urgency of the matter. Balfour continued that further conscription in Britain would affect the war effort by taking men from vital industries or would reduce the quality of men by making fifty years the age limit. Both measures, he believed, were severe but he felt it would be even more difficult to introduce them as 'Ireland is not even called upon to bear the burden of conscription.' But on the other hand, imposing conscription would be at 'the cost of serious disorder and possible, even, of bloodshed. This is certain.' He identified that the measure would unite the 'priests, parliament, the nationalists and Sinn Féiners' and that the only way of reducing this opposition would be to introduce home rule which 'will probably alienate Ulster and all that Ulster, Belfast and her shipyards mean where the effective conduct of the war is concerned.' The British government was in a no-win situation and Balfour was unable 'to gauge the exact part that [the] Irish question takes in American politics and now, less than ever, do I feel competent to do so. I will,

1918.   90 Ambassador Reading's views and actions on getting more US troops into Europe are examined in Reading, *Rufus Isaacs: first marquess of Reading* (1945), pp. 88–93.   91 J.J. Pershing, *My experiences in the world war* (1931), p. 122.   92 Hartley, *The Irish question*, pp. 174–5. Some Unionists opposed this consultation with the US. F.S. Oliver a critic of US politics noted 'I have just read such a document as I never thought to see an English statesman put his name to – AJB's [Balfour's inquiry] to House. He asks H[ouse]. in effect to make up the minds of the war cabinet as to whether they should or should not conscript Ireland.' Fowler, *British–American relations*, p. 159, fn. 92.

therefore, be most grateful if you will inform me of your opinion of the policy which I have outlined above and its effects on the conduct of the war viewed from America.'93 House acted swiftly, showed the letter to Wilson and replied to Balfour on 3 April, 'I am not able to advise intelligently as to the effect of conscription upon your domestic situation.' But he directly reported the contents of Wilson's handwritten reply dated 3 April, stating that enforced Irish conscription 'would accentuate the whole Irish and Catholic intrigue which has gone hand in hand in some quarters of this country with the German intrigue.'94 Wilson did not wish to stir up the becalmed Irish and German extremists.

On 5 April, Eric Drummond, Balfour's private secretary, asked Wiseman to clarify House's reply in advance of a cabinet meeting on that day. Wiseman said that House had accurately represented Wilson's view. But he disagreed with both men and believed that neither felt strongly about conscription. Instead he felt that there would be 'an outcry from Irish extremists here' but 'America's view would depend largely on how the case is presented through the press', particularly to US Catholics. Neither did he believe that 'the possibility of bad effects here should influence your decision.'95 Wiseman's views proved to be more influential with the war cabinet than those of Wilson, House and Reading. Not surprisingly, Page sided with Wiseman.96 So the British cabinet decided to introduce Irish conscription along with self-government for Ireland because the US 'would view with the greatest disfavour any attempt to apply conscription without Home Rule.'97 Three days later, Plunkett submitted the Irish Convention's majority report to Lloyd George. The Convention had failed to find a scheme for the self-government of Ireland but this was not unexpected. Skinner forwarded a copy of the report to Lansing on 17 April, and Reading presented Wilson with a copy on 8 May.98 The conscription legislation that included Ireland, was approved by the House of Commons on 16 April, without accompanying home rule legislation. On the same day, Lloyd George indicated that 'American opinion' supported the conscription bill on condition that self-government was offered to Ireland. The Long Committee was established to produce a home rule bill based on the Irish Convention's majority opinion. This dual approach was regarded as necessary by Lloyd George in order to secure US support, even though Wilson had not specified this path.99

93 YULMC, WWP, box 1, file 7, Balfour to House, 2 April 1918.   94 *PWW*, 47, Balfour to House, 2 April 1918, fn. 2.   95 YULMC, WWP, box 5, file 141, Drummond to Balfour, 5 April 1918; *PWW*, 47, Wiseman to Drummond, 5 April 1918   96 See Hartley, *The Irish question*, pp. 176–7 for Page's conversation with Balfour and support for Irish conscription.   97 Hartley, *The Irish question*, p. 177   98 The Irish Convention's proceedings and reports did not provide a blue print for a settlement although they did confront key issues – the unionist/nationalist divide, the nature of an Irish nationalist state – which would confound future generations. R.B. McDowell, *The Irish Convention*, 1917–18 (1970), pp. 179–84; NARA, RG65, M1085, 841.00/59, Skinner to Lansing, 17 April 1919.   99 J.J. Lee, *Ireland: 1912–1985* (1989), p. 39. Hartley, *The Irish question*, p. 178; See also K. Middlemas, *Thomas Jones, Whitehall diary, volume 1, 1916–25*, 3 vols (1969).

Wilson was immediately bombarded with appeals from radical and moderate Irish nationalists in the US and Ireland, to oppose conscription outright or, if it was introduced, to ensure that some form of Irish self-government accompanied it.[1] Among the appeals was one from Mary McWhorter of the Ancient Order of Hibernians who organized the 'Mothers' Mission' a group of Irish-American mothers who had sons in the US armed forces but opposed Irish conscription. Working through P.T. Moran, a past officer of the AOH and a close friend of Tumulty's, they met with the secretary and presented him with a petition of 600,000 signatures. Although Tumulty indicated that the 'stress of official business prevented' Wilson seeing them, Tumulty advised them to work through their congressional representatives.[2] The Irish Progressive League, the Irish Race Convention, the former US ambassador to Denmark, Maurice Francis Egan and US Catholic hierarchy all made representations to Wilson. On 12 April, Wilson replied to Egan, 'I realise the critical significance of the matter ... and [I] wish there were some proper way in which I could help to guide matters, but so far, unfortunately, none has opened before me.'[3]

In Ireland, Hathaway had continued to acknowledge resolutions and project the 'seriousness of the situation' to the State Department. His eight-page report, sent on 25 April, outlined the 'attitudes of the south of Ireland towards the application of conscription.' He presumed that the State Department was thoroughly informed through the newspapers of the mass meetings and general work stoppage on 23 April. He tried to explain the reasons for the outburst of popular feeling in all Ireland 'except the Protestant districts of Ulster', which involved the political, religious and labour leaders of nationalist Ireland. He concluded:

> As a demonstration of Irish nationalist unity, determination and discipline, the complete stoppage of work on Tuesday, coupled with the absolute tranquillity was very successful. It would seem to indicate that whether the Nationalists are right or wrong in the premise on which they are acting, so long as the present unity of temper persists, the enforcement of conscription would be practically impossible, and certainly not productive of any increase of force in the Allied armies ... It remains to be seen how the situation will be affected by the Home Rule proposals expected shortly to be made by the British government.[4]

Hathaway apologized for reporting on events happening outside his district but he wrote that the nationalist movement was a national one and was directed from its Dublin headquarters.[5] A week later he provided a twenty-six page letter, including typed extracts from statements made by Roman Catholic hierarchy and

---

1 Carroll, *American opinion*, pp. 108–9; Ward, *Ireland and Anglo-American relations*, pp. 161–3.   2 NLI, PMP, MS17670, McWhorter to McCartan, 3 June, 12 July 1918.   3 Carroll, *American opinion*, p. 109, p. 243, fn. 65.   4 NARA, RG65, M580/6, 841.00/72, Hathaway to Lansing, 20 April 1918; ibid., 841.00/81, Hathaway to Lansing, 25 April 1918.   5 Ibid., 841.00/81, Hathaway to Lansing, 25 April 1918.

clergy who were in the forefront of the anti-conscription movement.[6] Both reports
were regarded as important enough to be circulated beyond the Consular bureau
to the divisions of Western European affairs and Foreign Intelligence and the
office of the assistant secretary, William Phillips. Moreover, their value was
enhanced in the absence of a report from Adams in Dublin. Sharp in Belfast,
offered a view from the unionist perspectives. During April 1918, none of his
reports were longer than one page and they generally consisted of a cover note
to enclosed newspapers articles. He reported that in Belfast 'the inhabitants went
about their avocations as usual' during the anti-conscription strike. On 23 April,
he provided the first evidence of a protest against conscription in his district
when he detailed the role of the Catholic hierarchy in administering the anti-
conscription pledge signed outside Catholic churches throughout Ireland, including St Peter's Church in Belfast.[7] Both consuls provided the State Department
senior officials with an accurate and useful insight into the strength of the anti-
conscription movement in Ireland and how it augmented the Sinn Féin republicans, endangered the credibility of the home rulers unless some form of self-
governing legislation was introduced soon, and it consolidated further the
differences between nationalists and unionists.

These conclusions should also have been evident to Ambassador Page also.
But once again his interpretation of events was less than balanced as he displayed
little sympathy for those opposing conscription. However, he expected the British
government not to enforce conscription in Ireland until a home rule bill had been
passed.[8] None of this surprised official. But his information that the lord mayor
of Dublin, Laurence O'Neill, intended to visit the US to place before Wilson a
protest against the application of conscription to Ireland was shown to Wilson.[9]
O'Neill, however, needed a passport to leave Ireland and a visa to enter the US.
Once Page learned from the Foreign Office that a passport would be granted, he
requested instructions from Lansing as to whether a visa should be issued or not.
The telegram presented a problem for Lansing and he asked Wilson how he
should reply. His request to Wilson was attached to another telegram received
from a group based in Fort Morgan in Colorado who opposed O'Neill's visit or
that of 'any other anti-draft delegation' to the US.[10]

Page had not received any instructions by 1 May and he informed Lansing
that he would be issuing a visa.[11] Immediately Lansing replied that he should

6 Ibid., 841.00/82, Hathaway to Lansing, 30 April 1918.   7 Ibid., 841.00/85, Sharp to Lansing,
23 April 1918.   8 Ibid., 841.00/67, Page to Lansing, 22 April 1919; ibid., Page to Lansing, 24 April
1919. He noted that among the opponents of conscription was Bishop Cohalan of Cork and he could
not resist reminding the State Department that Cohalan was 'rumoured' to have been appointed by
the Vatican at Germany's instigation.   9 Ibid., 841.00/68, Page to Lansing, 24 April 1919; NLI,
'No Conscription. Ireland's case restated. Address to the President of the United States of America
from the Mansion House Conference.'   10 NARA, RG65, M580/6, 841.00/68, Page to Lansing,
24 April 1918; ibid., Lansing to Wilson, 25 April 1918; PWW, 46, Lansing to Wilson, 25 April
1918.   11 NARA, RG65, M580/6, 841.00/71, Page to Lansing, 1 May 1918.

'delay' this action until he received 'further instruction.'[12] Phillips asked Wilson for instructions on 3 May.[13] Since the initial request on 25 April, further appeals were made by Wiseman and Plunkett to Wilson for some statement on Ireland to support home rule and perhaps quieten the anti-conscription protests which the former believed was organized by the German-financed Sinn Féin.[14] House, however, advised Wilson not to make any statement although he wished something could be done to improve the Irish situation.[15] Wilson agreed and remained silent. However, on 4 May he replied to Phillips on the O'Neill request, 'It is plain to me that there is no way in which we can head off the lord mayor of Dublin though I think his visit is most unwise from every point of view. We can only follow the best course we can devise amongst us when he gets here. If he knew how little he was going to get out of the trip, he would stay at home!' But on the same day Wilson encountered further evidence of the excited state of Irish-America because a mass meeting of 15,000 people, representing Irish people in the eastern states, met at Madison Square Garden to resolve their opposition to conscription in Ireland and called upon Wilson, the Senate and Congress 'to use their influence to have' the conscription legislation reversed.[16] Two days later, Lansing cabled Page, 'You may visa passport for Lord Mayor of Dublin.'[17] The visit did not take place as O'Neill refused to submit the address to Viscount French, lord lieutenant of Ireland, prior to his departure from Ireland. Eventually the statement was sent to Wilson through the US embassy in London. But Page's collusion with Balfour ensured that it did not reach Wilson until 13 August, by which time the Unionists had formulated their own address for Wilson and the Irish situation was even more inflamed. The Unionist letter stated that the southern nationalists had no right to resist conscription.[18] Even though Wilson was spared having to decide whether to meet O'Neill, he was exposed to both sides of the argument on the issue of conscription for Ireland and requests for his intervention on Ireland continued to come from the two opposing sides in May 1918.

The despondent Plunkett asked Wilson to send an unofficial representative to Ireland to privately interview political leaders and inform them that if they pledged themselves to get support the war, Wilson would 'undertake, privately and unofficially, to use his good offices' with the British government in favour of the 'establishment of Irish self-government' which could subsequently discuss conscription.[19] Coincidentally, Ray Stannard Baker, the journalist turned State Department 'special agent', was in Europe to provide balanced reporting that would counteract Page's 'blatant anglophilism. He received a salary of $5,000 per annum, trav-

---

12 Ibid., Lansing to Page, 3 May 1918.   13 Ibid., Phillips to Lansing, 3 May 1918.   14 *PPW*, 46, Wiseman to House, 25 April 1918.   15 *PPW*, 46, House to Wilson, 26 April 1918.   16 NARA, RG65, M580/6, 841.00/76, Wilson to Phillips, 4 May 1918; *PPW*, 47, Peter Golden, Irish Progressive League to Wilson, 4 May 1918, p. 520.   17 NARA, RG65, M580/6, 841.00/71, Lansing to Page, 6 May 1918.   18 Ibid., M580/1, entry '9 July 1918'; Carroll, *American opinion*, p. 110, fn. 58; Ward, *Ireland and Anglo-American relations*, pp. 163–4.   19 *PWW*, 46, Plunkett to Wilson, undated probably early May.

elling expenses and a diplomatic passport. Baker was trusted by Wilson and House and sent his reports to Polk and Lansing in the State Department.[20] On 4 May, Baker sent the first of four communications from Ireland:

> I am making survey of Irish situation, seeing leaders of each important group for opinion of Nationalists, Sinn Féin, Labour and Ulsterites. Sir Horace Plunkett is assisting me. I am leaving for west of Ireland today with John Dillon. Will cable report for your information ... Situation very grave indicating possibility that American opinion may be most important factor.[21]

In each subsequent report his appeal for Wilson to openly oppose 'forcible' conscription of an 'unwilling' Irish people intensified.[22] Polk regarded Baker's letters and reports as 'invaluable' and they were passed to Lansing for Wilson's attention. Baker was never sure if Wilson actually read them although he later commented, 'Your letters at that time helped me.'[23] Baker's indirect appeal for Wilson to intervene with the British government on behalf of the anti-conscription side fell on deaf ears as did all of the others. Yet, Wilson refused to assist the British government in its attempt to discredit and suppress Sinn Féin in the US and Ireland.

The intense nature of nationalist Ireland's reaction to conscription led the British government to resort to heavy-handed tactics in order to undermine Sinn Féin's support and popularity in Ireland and the US. German–Irish collusion had been a constant concern for the relevant British and US authorities since the beginning of the war. The background to the so-called 'German plot' is well-known and originated in the British capture, on 12 April 918, of a member of Roger Casement's Irish Brigade on the west coast of Ireland after he disembarked from a German submarine with details of a German expedition to Ireland.[24] Lloyd George concluded that the 'Sinn Féinners are in league with the Germans' and he intended using the information to justify the arrests of Sinn Féin leaders and end the disturbances in Ireland. On 9 May the Long Committee supported this view.[25]

On the following day, the British government, through Page, requested the State Department to release evidence in the US proving a Sinn Féin–German

20 R.C. Bannister jr, *Ray Stannard Baker: the mind and thought of a progressive* (1966), pp. 179, 178; YULMC, FLPP, Box 1, file 030, Polk to Baker, 8 July 1918. In mid-December 1918, Wilson invited Baker to organize and head the press bureau of the American Commission to Negotiate Peace in Paris. He was appointed by Wilson to write his biography and was openly partisan towards his subject. Ibid., p. 183.   21 NARA, RG65, M580/6, 841.00/73, Baker to Polk in Page to Polk, 6 May 1918.   22 Ibid.; YULMC, FLPP, Box 1, file 026, Baker to Polk, 18 May 1918.   23 Ibid., Ray Stannard Baker; Ibid., Baker to Polk, 25 May 1918; Bannister, *Ray Stannard Baker*, pp. 179, 178. In July, Baker toured the front in France and in late August left England for Italy. At House's request, he spent September and October gathering information about the strength of the labour and socialist movements. Ibid., p. 179; ibid., 841.00/80, Baker to Polk in Page to Polk, 16 May 1918.   24 Hartley, *The Irish question*, p. 181.   25 Middlemas, *Thomas Jones*, i, 9 May 1918, p. 64. 26 *PWW*, 48, Page to Lansing, 10 May 1918.

conspiracy. Page forwarded thirty-two documents consisting of decoded telegrams, cipher letters and one wireless message that had passed between the German embassy in Washington and the German Foreign Office in Berlin between 25 September 1914 and 18 January 1917. He indicated that Lloyd George wanted the material published in the US 'in the interests of the Allied cause.'[26] Six days later, on 16 May, Page wrote again 'please let me have an answer as soon as possible as the British authorities want to publish without further delay unless our government decide to do so themselves.'[27] Yet, on the same day Baker's second report on his trip to Ireland, sent to Polk and on to Wilson, made no reference to German–Sinn Féin links and he even suggested that Wilson speak out in favour of the anti-conscription cause. On 19 May, Lansing advised Wilson:

> it would be impolitic at the present time for us to assume the responsibility for the publication of these papers. The Irish situation is very delicate and anything which we might do to aid either side in the controversy would, I fear, involve us in all sorts of difficulties with the Irish in this country.[28]

Lansing admitted to having no sympathy for Irish nationalists who co-operated with Germans and his government had previously published the von Igel documents in September, but this act would be 'construed as a direct assistance to Great Britain in the matter of conscription in Ireland' and he 'was loath to involve this country in the quarrel.' He wanted to do 'everything' to defeat a movement that weakened Britain but he was doubtful as to whether the proposed request would be 'sufficiently valuable to warrant the trouble it would probably cause over here.'[29] Wilson maintained his non-intervention policy:

> I do not think that the British government ought to use us to facilitate their fight for conscription in Ireland. I believe that the difficulties that would be created for them as well as for us by the publication in this country, by official release, would be greater than any of the alleged advantages; and I hope that you will reply to Page in that sense.[30]

On 20 May, Lansing instructed Page to inform the British government that the State Department would not help in publicising the documents.[31] US and British newspapers published details of the German plot without reference to the US government. But Admiral Reginald Hall, who co-ordinated the release of the doc-

27 NARA, RG65, M580/6, 841.00/79, Page to Lansing, 16 May 1918. 28 *PWW*, 48, Lansing to Wilson, 19 May 1918. 29 Ibid. 30 Quoted in C. Tansill, *America and the fight, 1866–1922: an old story based upon new data.* (1957), p. 267. 31 NARA, RG59 M580/1, entry 'To Great Britain, 20 May 1918'. On 19 June, the State Department inquired with the Foreign Office after de Valera's condition in prison following an intervention from Congressman Tinkham on behalf of de Valera's half-brother, Thomas Wheelwright. Carroll, *American opinion*, p. 242, n. 63.

uments in the US, noted to Reading that in the despatch he wrote for *The Times* he used the phrase 'America believes' which he hoped readers would take to mean 'Wilson believes.'[32]

In the interim, Wilson's decision seemed justified by British actions and by further information received in the State Department. On 17 May, the leaders of Sinn Féin, including Eamon de Valera, Arthur Griffith, Constance Markievicz and 150 members, were arrested and imprisoned on the charge of conspiring with the German government. Irwin Laughlin in the US embassy in London, regarded it as a 'brilliant stroke'[33] But Hathaway believed it was 'merely a piece of government chicanery.'[34] The latter's view was backed up by a memorandum denying the veracity of the German plot prepared by T.P. O'Connor and Richard Hazleton, Nationalist members of parliament, and handed by Senator Phelan to Lansing on 29 May. Lansing wrote to Wilson that day, it 'gives a new point of view to the publication of information in regard to the Sinn Féin conspiracy in this country.'[35]

Wilson made no public statement on Ireland but on 29 May told Wiseman that he 'hoped the government would not force conscription without home rule.' Wiseman tried to explain to Wilson that these were two separate problems. The president said he understood this but 'the mass of the people in America would not understand it.' He repeated his view that the US could not have publicized the German plot documents because 'it would have been regarded here [US] as too obviously helping the British government in a political situation: the people would have resented it', even though he had no sympathy for 'Irishmen either here or at home who sought German aid.'[36] Prosecuting the war was his foremost concern but he walked a tightrope balancing various interests; those of his British allies, his own administration and Irish-American Democratic voters. For moderate Irish-Americans, Wilson's assurances of sympathy for the Irish cause rang increasingly hollow and they would be put to the test again as many

---

32 *PWW*, 48, Hall to Reading, c.19 May 1918.   33 NARA, RG65, M580/7, 841.00/130, Laughlin to Secretary of State, 21 September, Report January 1–June 30 1918.   34 Ibid., 841.00/104, Hathaway to Secretary of State, 26 May 1918. The US consul in Shanghai reported on 14 May that the conscription issue in Ireland had resulted in dividing the Irish community in Shanghai. Later in December 1918, the US consul in Queensland, New South Wales reported that a large percentage of the population was more 'pro-Irish than pro-British' and he forwarded a cable from the national director representing the Hibernian Australasian Catholic Benefit Society congratulating Wilson for championing the rights of small nations and appealing to him to secure 'undivided self-government' for Ireland at Paris. Ibid., 841.00/108, Consul General, Shanghai to Secretary of State, 14 May 1918; ibid., M580/213, 841.00/108, Consul General, Queensland to Secretary of State, 14 December 1918.   35 *PWW*, 48, Memorandum on the pro-German conspiracy charge against Sinn Féin in Ireland and America, 29 May 1918 in Lansing to Wilson, 29 May 1918; It must be noted that T.P. O'Connor was hostile to Sinn Féin and the FOIF was bitterly critical of his home rule politics. Fyfe, *T.P. O'Connor*, pp. 267–8; NARA, RG59 M580/213, 841d.00/9a, Lansing to Wilson, 29 May 1918. Ray Stannard Baker informed Polk that he disbelieved the evidence which sought to discredit Irish-American support for home rule. YULMC, FLPP, box 1, 028, Baker to Polk, 28 May 1918.   36 *PWW*, 48, Wiseman to Drummond, 30 May 1918.

expected the president to champion the Irish cause during the peace settlement negotiations, as will be seen in the next chapter.

Meanwhile, in late summer 1918, Baker reported from London that the situation in Ireland had settled into an uneasy peace. But he left Polk and Wilson under no illusion about its permanence and who was responsible; 'Sinn Féin feeds upon the blunders, misunderstandings and oppressions of the British government.'[37] However, he felt that moderate Irish nationalists required US support; on 20 August he wrote; 'if any encouragement comes from America, it should support [Horace] Plunkett, [Edward] Shortt, [secretary for state for Ireland], and [James] Campbell, [lord chancellor of Ireland].'[38] Page offered a different perspective on events in Ireland. On 3 August, he facilitated the delivery of a five-page statement from James Johnson, lord mayor of Belfast, and other Unionist office holders to Lansing by having it 'embedded' into an official telegram from the embassy to Washington. The note emphasized Ulster Unionists' loyalty to the allied cause and their distance from the nationalists' German plot and opposition to compulsory recruitment. Page's anglophilism contrasted sharply with Hathaway's balanced reports. The Queenstown consul sent three reports in May, June and on 12 September; he began by apologizing for not responding 'more promptly and fully to the Department's instructions to submit a further report.' The reasons for this were first that

> the threads of the Irish political situation and action are drawn into a very tangled web and to report upon them with any degree of certainty requires not only extensive reading of current newspapers and other publications but also frequent and extended conferences with many representatives of varying shades of opinion, most of whom can not be seen in Queenstown.

Secondly, in the absence of a vice consul since 12 December 1917, he had had to attend to the daily routine of the office which made it difficult to do the necessary reading and studying and to get out of Queenstown. He recognized that such research was indispensable because 'so much of what is going on is underground and appears in the papers at most only by implication.'[39] Hathaway wrote, 'the course of events seems to have settled down to a slow contest of endurance between the will of the government and the will of the majority to defy.' He continued:

> The naked skeleton of the Irish situation … seems to be that the native Irish race, comprising three quarters of the population of the island, are

37 YULMC, FLPP, box 1, file 026, Baker to Polk, 7 June 1918.   38 Ibid., file 030, Baker to Polk, 20 August 1918.   39 NARA, RG59, M580/213, 841d.00, Hathaway to Secretary of State, 12 September 1918. Also he enclosed a booklet by Horace Plunkett titled 'Home rule and conscription' which reviewed the situation 'very sanely and comprehensively' and an anonymously penned pamphlet, 'The complete grammar of anarchy' dedicated to Sir Edward Carson.

held against their will in subjection by an alien race. While this condition continues no settlement appears to be possible ... England must either grant full Home Rule or govern by force with no pretence to other than that of the conqueror ... The situation with regard to the German plot charge by the government has not changed except that the Irish attitude of scoffing incredulity has merely strengthened with the passage of three months without the production of anything they regard as proof, and indeed even an outsider is somewhat puzzled to understand just why such definite charges of German activities should have been produced and so little heard of them afterward.[40]

His analysis was confirmed when the British authorities could not produce any evidence for the German plot at the trials of the Sinn Féin leaders in September. Nor was conscription ever implemented in Ireland and British recruitment never recovered to the pre-1916 rising levels. London's dual approach of conscription and home rule had failed. Sinn Féin organized itself to fight a general election in December 1918 on the planks of independence and full self-government, turning to the US to gather funds and political support. Opportunities for the latter appeared to be better than ever before, because allied troops had finally pushed back the German army and its civilian government had sued for peace on 3 October. Once again the nationalists in Ireland and the US targeted Wilson's proposed peace plan and the conference to be held in Paris, beginning on 12 January 1919, as one avenue through which to fulfil their aims. Even the extremist *Gaelic American* noted on 19 October, 'Irish citizens must stand by Wilson ... whose self-government and self-determination are on record.'[41]

*

From the entry of the US into the war in April 1917, Ireland intersected Woodrow Wilson's policy. Although he held a firm position of non-intervention on the Irish question, featured it in his foreign policy discussions with his advisers, officials and congressional politicians and with British diplomats and leaders in spring 1917 and spring 1918. His desire to see the Irish problem resolved arose firstly, out of a personal dislike for the heavy-handed British tactics in Ireland, secondly, from constant pressure from supporters of Ireland within Congress and thirdly, from the immediate needs of the war, namely a united nation and US–British co-operation. Wilson undoubtedly believed that he had contributed to the establishment of the Irish Convention and, despite its inherent divisions, he genuinely hoped that Plunkett would produce a settlement. The majority of Irish-Americans endorsed these views and were content, like most

---

40 Ibid., 841d.oo, Hathaway to Secretary of State, 12 September 1918.   **41** *Gaelic American*, 19 October 1918.

ethnic groups, to fall in behind his 'America first' policy. It was in that latter context that Wilson's wartime policy revealed a further Irish dimension; prosecuting the war at home meant weeding out disloyalty and consolidating loyalty. The activities of radical Irish republicans in the US and Ireland remained a target of US and British surveillance, security and propaganda agencies.

Throughout 1917 and 1918, Clan na Gael, the Friends of Irish Freedom, the Irish Progressive League and the exiled Irish republicans were under constant surveillance by US and British agencies but Wilson tolerated their activities, much to the annoyance of British officials and ministers. Neither would he assist the British government by publishing the so-called evidence of the German plot in spring 1918, when Ireland intruded into American–British affairs again. Wilson was kept well informed on the deterioration of the situation in Ireland following the failure of the Irish Convention. His many sources, both official and unofficial, provided him with nationalist, unionist and British perspectives, incorporating radical viewpoints. He had a good understanding of the complex situation and formulated his own Irish policy that wavered from the path of strict nonintervention when it suited wider objectives. By summer 1918, Wilson was firmly back on his non-interference path but by then his post-war plans had become a target for Irish republicans in Ireland and the US.

CHAPTER FIVE

Wilson, peace and Ireland, 1918–March 1920

Joseph O'Grady's useful study of immigrants' influences on Woodrow Wilson's peace policies outlines four reasons why they were able to influence the president's post-war foreign policy agenda. Firstly, Wilson welcomed pressure from the 'people', at least in public. Secondly, immigrant groups, particularly the more established immigrant communities, were organized in their lobbying. Thirdly, the war had been fought in Europe for 'freedom' and fourthly, the political balance of power between the Republican and Democratic parties meant that each side had to cater for groups whose votes might swing elections. Consequently, throughout the war, Irish lobbying competed with that of Czechs, Slovaks, Ruthenians, Poles, Jews, Italians, Germans, Magyars, south Slavs and those from the mid-European union for Wilson's attention and for US intervention in their respective territorial and sovereignty problems.[1]

Wilson's war-time Irish policy of non-intervention was formulated by himself and supported by Robert Lansing and Edward House. It was based on realistic, practical considerations tinged with varying degrees of sympathy for the Irish cause and influenced by the pressures of war. Wilson had been able to adhere to his policy as he saw fit but he had built up a store of expectations among hyphenated Americans of European origins that his peace plans, specifically his belief in the principle of self-determination, applied to their particular situations.

---

1 J.P. O'Grady, 'Introduction' in J.P. O'Grady (ed.), *The immigrants' influence on Wilson's peace policies* (1967), pp. 4–5, 18. According to O'Grady, after June 1918 when Wilson had decided to break up the Austrian empire, strong unofficial support was given by Wilson and House to the central European nationalities to resolve their problems. By late summer 1918, it seemed that the Irish and the Germans were the only groups that had failed to influence Wilson's peace plans. Ibid., p. 21. Even in October 1918, the administration supported the 'Conference of Oppressed Nationalities' meeting in Washington. Wilson and House hoped that these representatives of the central European peoples could resolve their differences and go to the Paris peace conference as a united group. Wiseman reported that they were already working with House's office. The National Archives, London (hereafter TNA), Foreign Office (hereafter FO), William Wiseman Papers (hereafter WWP), F800/225, Wiseman to Lord Reading and Eric Drummond, 3 October 1918.

Ireland and self-determination

From 1914 onwards, the immigrant groups mentioned above believed that the allies' war aims, and, more specifically, Wilson's aims, incorporated their particular demands. His elaboration of his fourteen points to Congress on 8 January 1918, included the right of 'every peace-loving nation ... to live its own life, [and] determine its own institutions' and the establishment of a league of nations 'affording mutual guarantees of political independence and territorial integrity to great and small states alike.'[2] Immigrant activists' hopes intensified during 1918 as the president continued to speak in these general, all-inclusive terms. All groups believed that the president was communicating directly with them. This was true in the case of the central Europeans and the Zionists because Wilson had decided to break-up the Austro–Hungarian and Turkish empires. Similarly, the Poles, led by Ignace Jan Paderewski, had successfully negotiated Wilson's support for Polish independence even before the US entered the war.[3] Consequently, when the war ended, the Irish-Americans had not progressed their claims despite being organized, being strident and having access to Capitol Hill and the White House. However, with congressional elections due in November and Wilson's peace-plan the sole blueprint for a post-war settlement, Irish hopes were high once again despite their failure to get Wilson's support after the Easter rising and for the anti-conscription campaign.

From January 1918 until the peace treaty was signed in June 1919, the Irish in the US and Ireland lobbied Wilson's administration directly and indirectly to have the cause of Irish independence included in the post-war settlement. Following Hanna Sheehy Skeffington's appeal to Wilson on 11 January 1918, the Friends of Irish Freedom (FOIF), the Ancient Order of Hibernians (AOH) and the Irish Progressive League (IPL) organized individual politicians, labour and religious leaders and congressional and state legislatures to petition Wilson to apply self-determination to Ireland.[4] By 19 October even his arch-enemy, John Devoy, used the columns of the *Gaelic American* to encourage all Irish-Americans to support Wilson, because he believed that 'all peoples are entitled to self-government and self-determination.'[5]

Meanwhile, Consul Edward Adams forwarded newspaper reports of a speech by Eamon de Valera 'of the Irish Sinn Féin party', delivered on 18 January 1918 at the Mansion House in Dublin, where he stated:

---

2 *The messages and papers of Woodrow Wilson*, 2 vols (1924), i, pp. 467, 471.   3 O'Grady, 'Introduction', pp. 7–13.   4 See F.M. Carroll, *American opinion and the Irish question, 1910–23* (1978), p. 114; See J.P. O'Grady, 'The Irish' in O'Grady, *The immigrants' influence*, pp. 59–63 for further details. The US Catholic hierarchy weighed in behind Wilson's plan following endorsement from Pope Benedict XV in his peace appeal in 1917. Gompers' American Federation of Labour endorsed his peace plans also and many members hoped that Irish independence would be achieved. B. McKillen, *Chicago labor and the quest for a democratic diplomacy, 1914–1924* (1996), p. 95.   5 *Gaelic American*, 19 October 1918.

We want Ireland to be set up as an independent state ... We say that if those who go about mouthing about self-determination do not take that interpretation of it, then they are hypocrites, and we tell President Wilson, in view of the statements he has made, if he does not take that view of it, he is as big a hypocrite as Lloyd George.[6]

Later in the year, Consul Charles Hathaway reported that similar sentiments had crystallized within the nationalist community. He cited in evidence the increasing press attention devoted to the Paris conference and attention paid to a speech on Ireland's right to self-determination, made on 22 October 1918 by the Roman Catholic bishop of Cork, Daniel Cohalan, to the Cork Young Men's Society. As was previously noted, the bishop was a cousin of Daniel F. Cohalan and shared the latter's anglophobia. Cohalan's address, which was titled 'The Slave – Ireland – and the objects of the war', began by focusing on the 'causes of British misgovernment in Ireland' and implied a threat of civil unrest in the absence of Irish independence.[7] This speech and Hathaway's presentation of it provoked immediate criticism from US diplomats in London. The ageing and ill Walter Page had submitted his resignation to Wilson in September 1918, but his replacement, John Davis, did not take up permanent residence in the embassy until 16 December. Instead, Page's staff, particularly Butler Wright and Irwin Laughlin, directed embassy affairs. It was the latter who complained to Lansing, on 1 November, that Hathaway's report on the Cohalan address consisted of nothing more than a reprise of 'the bishop's justification of first, his own aversion and that of many other Irish men to engaging in the war on the side of the Allies on various grounds ... his interpretation of the Dublin Rising of 1916 and his justification for it.' Laughlin also felt that Hathaway should have noted Cohalan's German connections, and specifically that he had been previously described by German Ambassador Bernstorff, as 'strongly nationalist and pro-German.' Laughlin believed that it was not necessary to seek further than this for the reasons which 'animated' Cohalan's statement.[8]

An examination of Hathaway's report suggests that Laughlin was harsh in his criticism and was probably motivated by the predominant anglophilism in the embassy. Hathaway reported the Cohalan address verbatim and stated that he felt Cohalan was 'an accurate reflector of popular opinion and reveals clearly what is passing in the minds of the people of this district.' Significantly, he confirmed that Cohalan compared the position of Ireland with that of the Czechs, Slovaks, Jugoslavs, Poles, Belgians, Serbians and others not enjoying national self-deter-

6 *Freeman's Journal*, 19 January 1918 in National Archives and Records Administrations, Maryland (hereafter NARA), Records of the Department of State relating to internal affairs of Great Britain, 1910–29, Record Group 59 (hereafter RG59), M580/6, 841.00/63, Adams to Secretary of State, 21 January 1918. 7 NARA, RG59, M580/7, 841.00/138, Hathaway to Secretary of State, 4 November 1918; ibid., M580/6, 841d.00/63, enclosure in Hathaway to Secretary of State, 28 October 1918. 8 Ibid., M580/213, 841d.00/2, Laughlin to Secretary of State, 1 November 1918.

mination and noted that Cohalan's 'manifest insistence that Ireland is exactly in the same case as they are ... [is a] line developed by Irish nationalists based on Wilson.' Moreover, Hathaway took seriously Cohalan's reference to the possibility of another insurrection in the absence of Irish self-determination. Neither had he neglected to note that the unionist press was increasingly concerned to make clear 'the error of Nationalist Irishmen' in assuming that self-determination 'will work in favour' of nationalist claims.[9] The accuracy of this commentary, made in late 1918, was soon revealed by events in 1919.

Hathaway's attempt to offer a realistic but balanced view of events in Ireland was supported also by his inclusion of a copy of the unionist *Belfast Newsletter* which he said, 'represents so clearly and succinctly the anti–nationalist view.' His synopsis of the editorial of 28 October included the point that Wilson's declarations on self-determination did not apply to Ireland because it was not a nation.[10] As indicated above, his approach was not well received in the London embassy, Laughlin believed that Hathaway was too understanding of Cohalan's arguments. This pro-nationalist jibe was often levelled at US representatives in Ireland by diplomats in London and indeed in Washington, when they felt that too much sympathy was being given to the Irish nationalist cause which in turn implied a criticism of US and British policy on Ireland. However, Hathaway was not reprimanded for the content of his report. Instead Lansing censured Wilbur Carr, director of the Consular bureau, because 'it is important for all offices to have full information about Ireland.'[11] Hathaway's reading of nationalist Ireland's expectations from the post-war peace settlement was accurate. The day after the Cohalan address, Sinn Féin sent an appeal to Wilson asserting Ireland's right to independence and representation at the peace conference, a view which was also expressed by Cohalan.[12] So, the Wilson administration was fully informed about the climate in Ireland and knew that not only did the nationalist Irish expect the peace settlement principles to be applied to their problem but that they wanted independent representation at the peace conference.

Not surprisingly, the question of US support for Irish self-determination was raised during the congressional elections in November 1918. In Pennsylvania, the Friends of Irish Freedom asked all candidates in the state 'Will you, if elected to the public office for which you are a candidate, openly and unequivocally sup-

9 Ibid., 841d.00/4, Hathaway to Secretary of State, 28 October 1918; ibid., M580/7, 841.00/138, Hathaway to Secretary of State, 4 November 1918. This point was noted also by the Irish Parliamentary Party who appealed to Wilson to apply self-determination to Ireland. Ibid., M580/7, 841.00/141, enclosure in Laughlin to Secretary of State, 17 December 1918.   10 Ibid., M580/213, 841d.00/4, Hathaway to Secretary of State, 28 October 1918; ibid., 841d.00/7, Hathaway to Secretary of State, 30 October 1918.   11 Ibid., M580/7, 841.00/146, quoted in Sharp to Secretary of State, 31 January 1919; ibid., M580/213, Lansing to Carr, 16 January 1919; ibid., Lansing to Carr, 16 January 1919; ibid., Carr minute, 17 January 1919. On 22 August 1918, Carr had reprimanded the Ireland based consuls for not reporting fully on Ireland. Ibid., Carr to Consuls, 22 August 1918.   12 Ibid., M580/213, 841d.00/24, Adams to Secretary of State, 8 February 1919.

port Ireland's claims to complete independence, the form of government to be determined by the whole male and female population of Ireland?' Eight congressional and two gubernatorial candidates, both Republican and Democrat, publicly endorsed the pledge.[13] The extent to which the Irish issue affected the election is difficult to gauge but the Democrats lost their dominance of the Congress and it was the Republicans who made gains. Certainly, the Grand Old Party benefited from Wilson's ill-judged decision to ask voters to return a Democratic Congress. Wilson had warned that the return of a Republican majority would mean a 'repudiation of my leadership' in Europe. The tactic appalled his supporters and opponents. House was 'greatly disturbed' because it was dangerous to appeal for a 'partisan congress.' Edith Wilson advised him not to 'send it out ... it is not a dignified thing to do' and Arthur Willert, *The Times* correspondent in the US, felt that it smelt of the 'president's autocracy.'[14] Republican criticism focused on Wilson's impugning of their wartime patriotism. Wilson's appeal combined with the re-uniting of the Republicans and local factors, to produce Democratic losses while his decision not to include any Republican representatives in his peace commission further alienated the opposition and also reduced their sense of responsibility for a future peace structure. The latter was intensified by the installation of the influential Republican, Henry Cabot Lodge, as chairman of the Senate Foreign Relations Committee that would accept or reject the Paris settlement.[15]

The armistice ending world war one was signed on 11 November 1918. House was already in Paris and in regular contact with Wilson, discussing the terms of the armistice and the location and conditions of the up-coming negotiations. However, after November the Republican Party was strategically placed to undo Wilson's peace-making agenda because of its congressional predominance; Lodge informed both the British and French governments that the Republicans favoured a harsher peace settlement than did Wilson. He warned against Wilson's personal ambition to be the 'THE peacemaker.'[16] On the eve of his departure for Europe, the re-emergence of the Republicans in Congress weakened Wilson's bargaining power in Paris. Both David Lloyd George and Georges Clemenceau,

---

13 Quoted in O'Grady, 'The Irish', p. 64; J.E. Cuddy, *Irish-America and national isolationism, 1914–20* (1976), p. 164.   14 C. Seymour (ed.), *The intimate papers of Colonel House, volume iv. The ending of the war, June 1918–November 1919*, 4 vols (1926–8) iv, p. 68; P. Lee Levin, *Edith and Woodrow: the Wilson White House* (2001), p. 217; British Library, Manuscripts Division (hereafter BLMD), Northcliffe Papers (hereafter NP), Add. 62255, Willert to Northclliffe, 8 November 1918. Willert had reported already that the Republicans 'do not much believe in the League of Nations.' Ibid., Memorandum on the US from 24 October to 31 October 1918.   15 W. LaFeber, *The American age: US foreign policy at home and abroad*, 2 vols (1994), ii, p 314. For the reasons why he excluded Republicans see ibid and A.S. Link et al., *American epoch: a history of the United States since 1900 volume 1, 1900–1945*, 2 vols (1987), i, p. 144.   16 Quoted in E.R. Parsons, 'Some international implications of the 1918 Roosevelt–Lodge campaign against Wilson and a Democratic congress', 154. Lodge expressed the same sentiment to Foreign Secretary Balfour. BLMD, Balfour Papers (hereafter BP), Add. 49742, Henry Cabot Lodge to Balfour, 25 November 1918.

prime ministers of Britain and France respectively, recognized this even if Wilson failed to do so.[17] Indeed both the European leaders entered the Paris negotiations in stronger positions, as they had been re-elected by their respective domestic parliaments with significant majorities. Despite the altered political landscape, Wilson was in no doubt about the immigrant groups' expectations of him in Paris.

Irish-American agitation continued right up to his departure and climaxed with the 'Self-Determination of Ireland Week' on 8–15 December. During this week, the national council of the FOIF organized meetings across the US, each publicising the same message; Ireland should have self-government. The largest was held in New York city on 10 December when over 25,000 people attended, including thousands of war veterans. Daniel Cohalan asked Cardinal William O'Connell of Boston to address the meeting at Madison Square Garden. O'Connell's lecture was titled 'Ireland: one and indivisible' and he declared, 'This war, we are told again and again by all those responsible for the war, is for justice for all ... for the inalienable right, inherent in every nation, of self-determination. The war can be justified only by the universal application of those principles. Let that application begin with Ireland.' The speech had several results; it helped confirm O'Connell as the leading Irish Catholic churchman in the US and it signalled that the Catholic hierarchy had re-entered the campaign for Irish freedom. The meeting concluded with the passage of a resolution urging Wilson to demand self-determination for Ireland at the peace conference. He received it and similar ones from fifteen other meetings while en route to Europe. Wilson took O'Connell's speech seriously and, fearing the archbishop might jeopardize Irish-American Democratic support for the settlement, he wrote a 'personal and confidential' letter to Cardinal Gibbons, the leading Catholic prelate, indicating his 'profound pleasure' to find himself 'aligned' with Gibbons on the issue. Wilson hoped this would deflect further hierarchical criticism of his 'pet project.'[18] While O'Connell was speaking in New York, Senator Edward J. Phelan, a member of the Senate Foreign Relations Committee,

---

17 G.W. Egerton, 'Britain and the "Great Betrayal": Anglo-American relations and the struggle for United States ratification of the Treaty of Versailles, 1919–20', 886–7; BLMD, D. Lloyd George, *Memoirs of the Paris conference*, 2 vols (1939), i, p. 93.   18 J.J. Splain, 'The Irish movement in the United States since 1911' in W.F. Fitzgerald (ed.), *The voice of Ireland: a survey of the race and nation from all angles by the foremost leaders at home and abroad* (1923), p. 232. O'Grady, 'The Irish', p. 65; J. McGurrin, *Bourke Cockran: a free lance in American politics* (1948), pp. 237–8; See American Irish Historical Society (hereafter AIHS), Daniel F. Cohalan Papers (hereafter DFCP), Box 13, folder 1, Cohalan to O'Connell, 17 December 1918. O'Connell also sent a cheque for $100 to Cohalan to help defray the expenses of the meeting. Ibid., Harerlin to Cohalan, 17 December 1918; J.M. O'Toole, *Militant and triumphant: William Henry O'Connell and the Catholic Church in Boston, 1859–1944* (1992), p. 233. Few among the audience would have known that one month previously O'Connell had sent a personal message to the British embassy in Washington which stated that 'as [the] principle of self-determination of peoples has been recognized by all, England could not refuse it to Ireland.' But he also indicated that he wished 'no ill to England and that he is forced to use vigorous language in order to retain control of the forces he is attempting to lead.' O'Connell had no intention of alienating the British government. O'Toole, *Militant and triumphant*, p. 234; *PPW*, 61, Wilson to Gibbons, 25 July 1919.

addressed a gathering in Philadelphia presided over by Congressman Michael Donohoe. Phelan emphasized the message that the US could not be true to its own 'ideals and traditions' if it failed to use 'its good offices on behalf of Ireland's right to self-determination.'[19]

But, what exactly was Wilson's attitude towards the Irish issue as represented by these resolutions and all the other appeals as he prepared to depart for Europe? Wilson had assured Lloyd George that he 'would not allow Ireland to be dragged into the Peace Conference.'[20] But neither could he distance himself from the Irish problem and, prior to his departure for Paris, he replied to an appeal for Irish self-determination from Senator Thomas J. Walsh on behalf of Bishop John Carroll of Montana. The president wrote on 3 December:

> I appreciate the importance of a proper solution of the Irish question and thank you for the suggestions of your letter of yesterday. Until I get on the other side and find my footing in delicate matters of this sort I cannot forecast with any degree of confidence what influence I can exercise, but you may be sure that I shall keep this important interest in mind and shall use my influence at every opportunity to bring about a just and satisfactory solution.[21]

A similar message was penned by Wilson on 3 December to Bishop Thomas J. Shahan, rector of the Catholic University of America in Washington, who had also argued in favour of Irish self-determination. In this he acknowledged that he would 'be watchful of every opportunity to insist upon the principles' but did not refer specifically to Ireland.[22] This lacuna had already been noticed by John Devoy. After Wilson's January 1918 speech, he wrote in the *Gaelic American*,'[the] one fatal defect [in Wilson's peace] terms is that they apply only to a portion of the world – that controlled by Germany and her allies – and utterly ignore all the rest.' He concluded 'Why must German imperialism be curbed and English imperialism aided and abetted?'[23]

Wilson was sympathetic to the Irish cause and hoped that an Irish settlement would be forthcoming from either the British government or the League of Nations once established but he would never allow it to damage US–British relations, which were crucial to the success of the peace conference. Tumulty believed that Wilson was convinced that to have made the issue 'a *sine qua non* would have

---

19 Splain, 'The Irish movement in the United States since 1911', p. 232.   20 A.S. Link (ed.), *The papers of Woodrow Wilson* (hereafter *PWW*), 69 vols (Princeton, 1966–94), 46, Wiseman to Drummond and Balfour, 4 February 1918. The mayoral elections were held at the same time and the Irish vote in Boston was not sufficient to prevent the defeat of Mayor James Curley, a supporter of Wilson's foreign policy, but whose administration was tainted by rumours of scandals and corruption. See T.H. O Connor, *The Boston Irish: a political history* (1995), pp. 190–1.   21 Quoted in J. Tumulty, *Woodrow Wilson as I know him* (1922), p. 401.   22 Quoted in ibid., p. 400.   23 *Gaelic American*, 12 January 1918.

been futile and foolish and might have resulted in disaster.'[24] Yet, by the time he sailed for Paris on board the SS *George Washington* on 4 December, Irish nationalists had come to believe that the Irish were included on his list of peoples who would win freedom from the settlement and that he would support the presence of an Irish delegation in the peace negotiations in Paris. The ingredients were present for a violent rupture between Wilson and Irish nationalists.

Wilson was accompanied on the voyage by the other member of the American Commission to Negotiate Peace including Lansing.[25] It was the universal nature of the tenets of Wilson's thinking that remained a concern for Lansing. Wilson accorded his secretary of State one meeting on board, on 8 December, although he often met with George Creel and John Davis who were also on board.[26] But it did little to assuage Lansing's concerns who recorded in his diary 'When the President talks of "self-determination", what areas has he in mind? Does he mean a race, a territorial area, or a community? Without a definite unit which is practical, application is dangerous to peace and stability.' Lansing believed that the principle contained 'the seeds of future trouble.'[27] This not only confirms that Lansing had been sidelined in the making of US foreign policy, but makes it clear that the secretary believed that a large gap existed between Wilson's idealistic plan and its practical application.

If Wilson expected some respite from nationalists' pressures when he arrived in Paris on 13 December, he was disappointed. Americans of Jewish, Yugoslav, Italian, central European and Irish origins sent delegations to Paris and these linked up with homeland representatives.[28] By the time Wilson and his party arrived, the parameters of the Irish problem had changed. In preparation for the upcoming general election on 14 December 1918, the Lloyd George government had restated its commitment to finding a settlement but had postponed it.[29] The consequences for the Irish Parliamentary Party (IPP) were terminal; it won just five seats in Ireland in addition to that won by T.P. O'Connor in the Scotland Division of Liverpool. Even John Dillon, who had replaced John Redmond as leader of the IPP, failed to win a seat. The Unionist Party won 26 seats while the Sinn Féin victory in 73 out of a total of 105 seats, made it the largest party in Ireland. Sharp commented from Belfast that the Sinn Féin victory represented the 'biggest and most dangerous problem the British government ever had to tackle.'[30]

---

24 Tumulty, *Wilson*, p. 404. Arthur Willert implored Northcliffe 'we must settle the Irish question before the [Paris] conference is over.' BLMD, NP, Add. 62255, Willert to Northcllffe, 15 November 1918. 25 The other members of the commission – Edward House, Wilson's adviser and chairman of the commission and General Tasker Howard Bliss – were not on board. In addition approximately 1,300 Americans represented the US at the Paris peace conference. See J. Davis & D.A. Fleming (eds), *The ambassadorial diary of John W. Davis: the court of St James', 1918–1921* (1993), pp. 5, 7, fn. 13. Joseph C. Grew was the secretary general of the commission. Tumulty did not travel and Creel was one of Wilson's private secretaries. 26 G. Creel, *Rebel at large: recollections of fifty crowded years* (1947), p. 205. 27 R. Lansing, *The peace negotiations: a personal narrative* (1921), pp. 26, 96–7. 28 O'Grady, 'Introduction', pp. 22–3. 29 Quoted in S. Hartley, *The Irish question as a problem in British foreign policy, 1914–18* (1987), p. 190. 30 NARA, RG59, M580/213,

Rather than taking up its seats in the Westminster parliament, Sinn Féin organized itself into a constituent assembly (Dáil Éireann) that met for the first time on 21 January 1919, adopted a constitution and issued a declaration of independence. Among the departments established were those dealing with foreign affairs and publicity; George Plunkett was appointed foreign minister. From this beginning, the international context to the Irish quest for independence was emphasized. Hathaway reported that Sinn Féin would make a 'dramatic appeal to the world.'[31] Indeed the republican plan was to gain recognition for the Irish republic from the Paris peace conference through publicity, fund-raising and lobbying in the US and through links with countries that had substantial Irish communities or nationalist movements. This was to be implemented immediately. Patrick McCartan, Dáil Éireann envoy to the US, informed Lansing that the 'Republic of Ireland denies the right of any foreign government henceforth to enter into negotiations or arrangements concerning the Irish people with the government of His Britannic Majesty.'[32] Prior to this, Sinn Féin had sent Seán T. O'Ceallaigh, Michael Collins and George Gavan Duffy to London to try and meet with Wilson, who was to be in the city between 26 and 31 December.[33] Wilson's own plans for going to England changed many times before he left the US but did not include a meeting with the Irish republicans.[34]

He did meet with Lloyd George and Foreign Secretary Arthur Balfour on 28 December and they discussed the peace conference, the question of freedom of the seas, the need for an international labour policy, curbing Italy's territorial ambitions and the 'grave menace of the Irish problem.'[35] The priority given to Ireland within this conversation confirms that the coincidence of the Sinn Féin victory with the peace conference posed a problem for them. However, Wilson always believed that it was not America's responsibility to find a settlement to the Irish problem within the US–British context and by the end of 1918, this belief had been extended to include the international context. Gordon Auchincloss was part of Wilson's party in London; he reported 'the trip of the President to England did a great deal of good. In the first place it has made him much more firmly disposed towards the British.'[36] Nonetheless, the new Provisional Government was idealistic and still believed that the war had been fought for the rights of small of nations, which Wilson's commitment to self-determination underlined, and that Wilson would realize this aim in the forthcoming peace settlement. Hathaway commented that the significance of the overwhelming vote

841d.oo/14, Sharp to Secretary of State, 17 January 1919.   31 Ibid., 841d.oo/12, Hathaway to Secretary of State, 5 January 1919.   32 Ibid., 841d.oo/17, McCartan to Lansing, 3 January 1919. 33 T.P. Coogan, *De Valera: long fellow, long shadow* (1993), p. 133.   34 Yale University Library, Manuscripts and Archives Collection (hereafter YULMC), Frank L. Polk Papers (hereafter FLPP), box 1, file 019, Auchincloss to Polk, 20 December 1918; ibid., 5 January 1919.   35 Lee Levin, *Edith and Woodrow*, p. 238. Lloyd George's account of the visit did not mention Ireland at all. Lloyd George, *Memoirs*, pp. 110–13.   36 YULMC, FLPP, box 1, file 019, Auchincloss to Polk, 5 January 1919.

for Sinn Féin 'should be construed as an emphatic vote for self-determination.'
He also reported that public meetings were held all over Ireland on 22 December
to pass resolutions inviting Wilson to visit Ireland.[37] Among the first acts of the
new Dáil in January 1919 was to send O'Ceallaigh to Paris to present the Irish
republic's case for recognition to Wilson and the Paris conference.

This gap between Irish republican expectations and Wilson's priorities was
not lost on John Davis. The new US ambassador had trained as a lawyer, was a
Democratic congressman and Wilson's solicitor general. He, therefore, possessed
valid political experience and a diplomatic personality, unlike his predecessor.[38]
On the one hand, Davis recognized that the reaction of the 'crowds, the speeches,
the applause and the press' to Wilson's visit to London were all that could have
been wished for.[39] But on the other hand, once installed in the embassy, Davis
set about acquainting himself with all the troubling questions in US–British diplomatic relations, specifically Ireland. And in his search for information he was
forced to complain to Lansing on 15 January that he had not received any consular reports of any value from Ireland for the previous few months. Following
this complaint, both Sharp and Adams were again reminded about previous
departmental instructions with respect to furnishing regular reports about conditions in Ireland.[40] Sharp replied defensively that he had been without a vice
consul since July 1918 and that, unlike the south and west of Ireland, his district 'had been free, singularly free' of political disturbances.[41]

Despite the patchy reporting from Ireland, Davis and his embassy staff were
kept informed on events in Ireland by other sources, including newspapers, and
he met with T.P. O'Connor on 31 December 1918. He recorded in his diary
that the former home ruler now believed that the best way to settle the question was 'to let the Sinn Féiners deliver their republic if they can.'[42] Significantly
Davis did not comment further because as a Wilson supporter, he saw no role
for Wilson in settling the Irish question, secondly, he did not share the US public's sympathy for Irish self-determination and he was highly critical of US politicians who courted the Irish vote and finally, he was bitterly opposed to the violent tactics adopted by Sinn Féin in Ireland. However, when the Anglo-Irish
war of independence broke out on 21 January 1919, he found it difficult to support Britain's Irish policy.[43] Meanwhile, his good friend Lansing, now ensconced
in Paris, still grappled with the wider application of self-determination. After

37 NARA, RG59, M580/213, 841d.00/12, Hathaway to Secretary of State, 5 January 1919.   38
Davis & Fleming, *The ambassadorial diary*, pp. xi–xiii. Davis was a close friend of Lord Reading
the British ambassador to the US. Ibid., p. 8, fn. 20.   39 Davis & Fleming, *The ambassadorial diary*,
Davis to Polk, 4 January 1918, p. 26.   40 NARA, RG59, M580/213, 841d.00/9, Davis to Lansing,
15 January 1919; ibid., 841d.00/9, Polk to Adams and Sharp, 18 January 1919; ibid., M580/7,
841.00/146, Sharp to Secretary of State, 31 January 1919.   41 Ibid., M580/7, 841.00/146, Sharp
to Secretary of State, 31 January 1919.   42 Davis & Fleming, *The ambassadorial diary*, 31 December
1918, p. 18.   43 C.J Walshe (ed.), *Notable US ambassadors since 1775: a biographical dictionary*
(1997), pp. 80–1.

the US delegation arrived in France, Lansing wrote a diary entry dated 30 December:

> The more I think about the President's declaration as to the right of self-determination, the more convinced I am of the danger of putting such ideas into the minds of certain races. It is bound to be the basis of impossible demands on the Peace Congress and create trouble in many lands.
>
> What effect will it have on the Irish, the Indians, the Egyptians, and the nationalists among the Boers? Will it not breed discontent, disorder, and rebellion ... The phrase is simply loaded with dynamite. It will raise hopes which can never be realised. It will, I fear, cost thousands of lives. In the end it is bound to be discredited, to be called the dream of an idealist who failed to realise the danger until too late to check those who attempt to put the principle in force. What a calamity that the phrase was ever uttered! What misery it will cause.[44]

His assessment that the application of self-determination would be extremely difficult was correct not only because of every politically disaffected immigrant group's belief that it had a just cause but also because of the scale of the rest of the problems facing the post-war leaders.

Delegations from twenty-seven nations met in Paris for the first time on 12 January 1919. They had to handle the consequences of the collapse of the German, Austro–Hungarian and Turkish empires, along with the consequences of the 'black cloud of the east [Bolshevism]' that threatened 'to overwhelm and swallow up the world.'[45] Disagreements soon emerged about the Rhineland, reparations, indemnities, Germany's colonies and Italy's territorial claims. Against this background, settling the Irish problem did not appear urgent to Wilson, even if he had wanted to do it. The tortuous settlement negotiations are not of direct concern to this study, except in relation to Wilson's treatment of the Irish problem and the Irish republican representatives from the US and Ireland. As soon as he arrived in Europe, Wilson started to attend pre-conference meetings, and the conference itself opened on 12 January. The gap between his principles and their application, so obvious to the US delegation and their allies, now emerged into the open. During the first period of the conference, from 12 January to 14 February, Wilson had to make concessions – particularly in relation to open diplomacy, the reparations issue and colonial mandate system – and accept that the final treaty might be flawed but he remained convinced that a soundly constructed League of Nations would resolve all issues. However, the French concept of this international organizations as being a league of victors was different from his, with the result that British support became vital to him. Auchincloss reported

---

44 Lansing, *The peace negotiations*, pp. 97–8.   45 W. LaFeber, *The American age: US foreign policy at home and abroad: volume 2 since 1896*, 2 vols (1994), ii, pp 318–9.

from Paris in early January, 'I think [Wilson] sees clearly now that it is necessary for us to play very close to the British during the coming conferences.' A
few days into the conference he wrote 'The British and ourselves are playing
very close together now and it is encouraging.'[46] Once he had secured British
support, Wilson proceeded to personally draft a covenant for the League that
would be embedded and guaranteed by the treaty.[47]

This work he undertook further alienated the already-sidelined Lansing and
the other US commissioners. In the ten-day period up to 15 February, when he
departed for the US, Wilson drafted article ten of the peace treaty, which he
called the 'heart of the covenant.'[48] It established that each League of Nations
member pledged 'to respect and preserve against external aggression the territorial integrity and existing political independence of all members of the League.'
Not only did the needs of subject peoples not receive a hearing during this first
phase, but the covenant protected the inviolability of the British empire and one
interpretation of article ten was that it prevented the US from helping Ireland
to gain independence from Britain. A further significant consequence of Wilson's
work was increased co-operation between the US and British delegations. Even
Maurice Hankey, British secretary of the peace conference and sceptic on
Anglo–American relations, recorded that Wilson and Lloyd George 'are working
most splendidly together', while the American secretaries and himself were 'as
blood brothers.'[49] This harmony did not mean that traditional concerns were sup-
planted but simply that in Paris close collaboration was required to achieve common aims.[50] Much work remained to be done before the League of Nations could
be created, but the implications of the covenant and of US–British co-operation
on the matter, soon led moderate and extremist Irish opinion into open opposition to Wilson and his plans.

46 YULMC, FLPP, box 1, file 019, Auchincloss to Polk, 5 January 1919; ibid., 16 January 1919.
47 A. Link, *Wilson: the diplomatist: a look at his major foreign policies* (1957), p. 119. Lloyd George
was petitioned also to raise Ireland's claims to self-determination before the peace conference. NARA,
RG59, M580/213, 841d.00/35, Sharp to Secretary of State, 12 March 1919, enclosure, 'Memorial
signed by 140 Irish officers of the British army sent to the prime minister for submission to the
King asking that Irish claims be brought before the conference'. The memorial drew attention to
the 200,000 of men of Irish blood and birth voluntarily enlisted in the British army in Ireland and
the large number of forces raised in the colonies and the United States of Irish birth. Not surprisingly, Sharp included also an article from the Unionist *Belfast Newsletter* describing the memorial
as 'audacious and misleading.' Hathaway believed that the memorial reflected the complexity of
Irish nationalism as these men had co-operated with England. NARA, RG59, M580/213,
841d.00/36, Sharp to Secretary of State, 12 March 1919; ibid., 841d.00/37, Hathaway to Secretary
of State, 17 March 1919.   48 LaFeber, *American age*, ii, p. 321.   49 K. Middlemas (ed.), *Thomas
Jones: Whitehall diary, volume 1, 1916–1925*, 3 vols (1969–71), i, Maurice Hankey to Thomas Jones,
18 January 1919, p. 73.   50 Egerton, 'Britain and the "Great Betrayal"', 886–7; K. Bourne & D.C.
Watt (general eds), *British documents on foreign affairs*, part II, series C, North America (hereafter
BDFA), 25 vols. (1986–95), i, The Republican ascendancy, 1919–28, Annual Report on the United
States (hereafter Annual Report) for 1919.

O'Grady, Ward and Carroll have all detailed the way in which the Irish-American campaign inside and outside Congress for US support of the Irish case at Paris, gathered pace from December 1918 onwards.[51] Frank Polk, acting secretary of State, noted that the 'anti-British campaign' was becoming 'acute' and drawing in politicians unhappy with the growing US–British closeness in Paris. He continued, 'it is extraordinary the unreasonable feeling that a number of men in Washington have on the subject of Great Britain.[52] Eight resolutions were introduced in the third session of the sixty fifth Congress which adjourned in March 1919. That introduced by Congressman Thomas Gallagher of Illinois, requesting that the American Commission present to the Paris conference 'the right of Ireland to freedom, independence and self-determination', was discussed by the House Foreign Affairs Committee in public on 12 and 13 December 1918. The hearing took testimony from sixty witnesses and received letters, telegrams, petitions, memorials and resolutions. With the exception of George L. Fox, all supported the resolution. The chairman of the committee, Congressman Henry Flood of Virginia, met Tumulty and reported that there was 'tremendous sentiment behind' the resolution and that it would pass the House by a 'big vote' if the committee reported it 'favourably.' Flood wanted Wilson's guidance as its passage 'might embarrass you' and he felt it might require diluting and redrafting to express only the view that Ireland should have the right of self-determination rather than to request official action.[53]

On 31 December, Tumulty cabled Wilson and asked 'What do you think? Is there any action with reference to Ireland you would suggest that might strengthen your hand? He [Flood] will act upon it.' Meanwhile, Phelan introduced a similar resolution in the Senate even though he was a Wilson supporter, creating an embarrassing situation for the president. Wilson's replies to Tumulty on 7 and 30 January revealed his concern. On the latter date he wrote:

> I frankly dread the effect on British public opinion with which I am daily dealing here, of a Home Rule resolution by the House of Representatives and I am afraid that it would be impossible to explain such a resolution here but I willingly trust your discretion in handling the matter at Washington. It is not a question of sympathy but of international tactics at a very crucial period.[54]

Tumulty and Polk who was familiar with Irish affairs, began to campaign to dissuade the politicians. The latter outlined his actions to Lansing in Paris on 3 February:

---

51 O'Grady, 'The Irish', pp. 82–4; Ward, *Ireland and Anglo-American relations, 1899–1921* (1969), p. 167; Carroll, *American opinion*, pp. 124–31.   52 YULMC, FLPP, box 1, file 019, Polk to Auchincloss, 20 December 1918.   53 *PWW*, 53, Tumulty to Wilson, 31 December 1918.   54 Ibid.

One proposal goes as far as requesting the President to instruct the peace
delegates to present the matter for consideration in Paris. I have been able
to delay the matter in committee for over a month, but I understand it
may be forced out this week unless I can tell the committee the President
would prefer to have it held in committee. Both sides are playing politics
with the resolution in order to get the Irish vote and I hesitate to recommend that the President interfere. I, however, feel that I should ask you
to lay the matter before him and request that you give me at earliest possible moments his views.[55]

Two days later, Tumulty cabled Wilson:

Flood says passage of some kind of Irish resolution inevitable and could
not be stopped without open and active opposition on your part and then
he believes it would pass. Found as drawn resolution was joint which
would require your approval or veto. Had him promise resolution would
be made concurrent which will require action by Senate.[56]

Wilson decided it would not be 'wise' for him to intervene but instructed
Tumulty keep up the utmost pressure to see that Congress did not act on it.[57]
Wilson's instructions were motivated by his traditional caution on the matter but,
more importantly, in January and February, the US–British relationship had
become as vital to his peace plans as having domestic support.

In Paris, Irish republicans provided Wilson with a further opportunity to
address their agenda for representation and independence. O'Ceallaigh arrived
in Paris on 8 February 1919. He set up office in the Grand Hotel and informed
all delegations of his presence. Soon afterwards he distributed a document titled
'The case for Ireland's independence' and set out to meet Wilson, 'the only one
of the American delegates who counts', to ask him to secure permission from the
British government for an Irish delegation, consisting of Eamon de Valera, Arthur
Griffith and Count Plunkett, to attend the Paris conference. Two days later he
had a meeting with a man whom he had been led to believe would be House; to
his disappointment he turned out to be only an assistant in the office of the legal
adviser to the American Commission instead. Following this failure and after
consultations with 'more highly placed friends', O'Ceallaigh decided that the only
way to approach Wilson 'with any remote hope of being received or heard, was
to tackle him boldly and publicly.'[58] O'Ceallaigh, who was working on his own

55 NARA, RG59, M580/213, 841d.00/11a, Polk to Lansing, 3 February 1919.   56 Quoted in C.
Tansill, *America and the fight, 1866–1922: an old story based upon new data* (1957), p. 307.   57
NARA, RG59, M580/213, 841d.00/16, Lansing to Polk, 15 February 1919.   58 R. Fanning et al.
(eds), *Documents on Irish foreign policy, 1, 1919–22* (hereafter *DIFP*), 3 vols (1999–), i, Seán T.
O'Ceallaigh to Cathal Brugha, 7 March 1919. O'Ceallaigh was known also as Seán T. O'Kelly. He
was a member of the First Dáil, Ceann Comhairle (Speaker) of Dáil Éireann and he assisted in

at this stage, wrote to Wilson on 11 February asking for an interview. He delivered the letter personally to the American headquarters at the Hotel Crillon. When there had been no acknowledgement or reply by 13 February, he called again but, not surprisingly, failed to see Wilson.[59] News of this failure led Hunter Sharp to remind Polk that Belfast Unionists believed that the 'internal affairs of the United Kingdom are not matters that are subject to the Peace Conference, nor are they matters on which President Wilson and Congress can urge the right of self-determination.'[60] When O'Ceallaigh called again to the US headquarters, after some trouble, he saw Herbert Hoover, US director general of relief for Europe and a member of Wilson's committee of economic advisers.[61] But Wilson would not meet with the Irish republicans and he asked Joseph C. Grew, secretary to the American Commission, to dissuade the Irish nationalists from sending any delegation to Paris.[62] Another of Wilson's private secretaries, George Creel, pointed out to republicans Wilson's belief that the conference was not a 'world court with power to hear and judge any or all complaints, but a council of victors to impose terms on the vanquished.' He stressed Wilson's interest in the Irish question but Creel felt that 'none of it softened' the Irish 'truculence.'[63]

During the following weeks, O'Ceallaigh continued to 'bombard' Wilson with Sinn Féin demands.[64] He also left his card with each member of the American delegation and called repeatedly on House. The Irish envoy was convinced that he had taken the 'right course – in fact the only course.' By early March, he had not met with Wilson, with House, with any American commissioner, with Clemenceau, president of the conference, with any other French delegate or with a representative from the smaller powers.[65] On 7 March, he recommended to Cathal Brugha, president of Dáil Éireann, 'the prospects of being heard are very slight indeed … we should … bring such pressure on the Americans owing to the difficulties that have arisen between Wilson and the Senate over the League of Nations and this opportunity must be made the most of at once.'[66] This conclusion had a basis in reality, as part of the reason why Wilson returned to the US on 15 February was to try and quell emerging opposition in the Congress and newspapers to his work in Paris and to sign legislation prior to the end of the sixty-fifth Congress on 3 March. Even though O'Ceallaigh was subsequently reprimanded by the Irish republican Executive Council for having 'bounced' Wilson into refusing to meet him, there were two consequences of his campaign. Firstly, the Irish envoy had succeeded in gathering publicity for the Irish cause.

getting George Creel to visit Ireland. See ibid.   **59** *DIFP*, i, O'Ceallaigh to Brugha, 7 March 1919. **60** NARA, RG59, M580/213, 841d.00/29, Sharp to Lansing, 27 February 1919.   **61** *DIFP*, i, O'Ceallaigh to Brugha, 7 March 1919. A report on O'Ceallaigh's attempts to meet Wilson appeared in the *Daily Mail*, 27 February 1919; J. Hoff Wilson, *Herbert Hoover: forgotten progressive* (1975), p. 170.   **62** J.B. Duff, 'The Versailles Treaty and the Irish-Americans', 586.   **63** Creel, *Rebel at large*, pp. 218–19.   **64** Ibid., pp. 218–19.   **65** *DIFP*, i, O'Ceallaigh to Brugha, 7 March 1919. O'Ceallaigh also had invited Wilson to visit Dublin on behalf of Dublin corporation but he refused. He was offered the freedom of Dublin and Cork cities but refused those also.   **66** Ibid.

Creel recalled that the 'the most clamorous of all the nationalist groups was a Sinn Féin delegation from Dublin, pressing a demand that Ireland's case be judged by the peace conference.'[67] Secondly, before he left Paris, Wilson asked Creel to go to Ireland and England 'for a look at the Irish situation.'[68] Wilson sailed for home. While he had been able to rebuff the Irish government's advances in Paris, it was quite another matter when it came to handling Irish-Americans in the US who were furious at his failure to raise Irish self-determination in Paris and, as details of the covenant leaked, their antagonism intensified and they gathered some unexpected allies.

The president had not wished to return to the US but had agreed to do so in order to fulfil his legislative duties and meet his critics. Back in Washington he met with the congressional politicians in charge of foreign relations to discuss the covenant. Many were disgruntled that the US–British delegations were 'hand in glove.' Lodge was disgruntled at not knowing what Wilson 'intends and what he means by a League of Nations.' Polk predicted that Wilson was not going to get the reaction he wanted from Congress because the Democrats were 'sore for all kinds of reasons' and the Republicans were 'just out to make it disagreeable.'[69] Indeed Lodge did not speak during Wilson's first encounter with the Republican congressmen while his colleagues indicated that the covenant a) did not recognize the Monroe Doctrine, b) excluded internal affairs from the League of Nation's authority and c) did not provide for a member nation's withdrawal. Wilson replied that these points were already covered but that 'he would be glad to make the language more explicit, and entered a promise to this effect.' It was made clear to him that these changes would be needed if the Republican-dominated Senate Foreign Affairs Committee were to approve the covenant. But of greater concern to the president was the warning from some Republicans that they would accept the peace treaty but not the covenant. Wilson 'shot back; that he would tie the peace treaty to the covenant so that both would have to be accepted or rejected together.'[70] He failed to win over the Republicans. British Ambassador Reading commented that the 'Republican element in the senate ... wishes to proclaim and emphasize to the Conference and the world that the President cannot make a valid treaty without the ratification of the senate'.[71] At his last cabinet meeting before returning to Paris, Wilson talked about the League of Nations for three hours in an 'impressive' and 'clear' manner, but Polk remained convinced that firstly, the public would only respond to Wilson himself and secondly, the Republicans' opposition was 'tremendous.' He characterized the co-operation of the establishment figure, Lodge and radical Irish-America

---

67 Creel, *Rebel at large*, p. 215.   68 Ibid., p. 214.   69 YULMC, FLPP, box 1, file 019, Auchincloss to Polk, 12 February 1918; BLMD, BP, Add. 49742, Henry Cabot Lodge to Balfour, 8 February 1919; YULMC, FLPP, box 1, file 019, Polk to Auchincloss, 18 February 1919.   70 Link et al., *American epoch*, p. 148; Quoted in Tumulty, *Wilson*, p. 346.   71 TNA, FO115.2804, Reading to Foreign Office, 4 March 1919.

on the issue in the following terms; 'It seems that cold roast Boston certainly has changed in the last few years into a first class Irish village.'[72]

On 4 March, the last day of the sixty-fifth Congress, Lodge led his Republicans in a 'bold and open attack' on the League of Nations and Wilson's war aims. He read to the Senate a declaration or round robin, signed by thirty-nine senators. It stated that the 'the constitution of the League of Nations in the form now proposed to the Peace Conference should not be accepted by the United States.' In addition, they wanted the US delegation to negotiate the peace treaty with Germany and then attention could be directed to the establishment of a League of Nations. The significance of the round robin also lay in serving notice on Wilson that more than one-third of the Senate opposed his Paris plans in their current form and that, since ratification of the treaty would require the support of two-thirds of the Senate, he should not assume approval.[73] Wilson had attended the Capitol for the closing hours of the Congress and 'found very little to do', as the Republican filibuster prevented the passage of financial legislation until the inauguration of the new Republican Congress. Following the final adjournment of Congress, Wilson circulated a statement and placed the responsibility for the 'impaired efficiency of the government' on the Republicans. He did not intend calling a special session of the Congress as it was impossible for him to be in Washington because of 'a more pressing duty elsewhere.'[74] He left behind an unstable, volatile political situation to concentrate on foreign affairs. Furthermore, he had even less political support for his peace plans, particularly the League of Nations proposal, than he had had on his original departure in December 1918, and was fully attuned to the potentially explosive nature of the Irish issue, as indicated by the path of the Gallagher motion and his last contact with Irish-America stateside.

In Wilson's absence, concern about the revival of Irish-American agitation and a mounting campaign against Wilson grew within the State Department and White House. In January 1919, the leaders of Clan na Gael and the Irish Progressive League held national meetings in support of Irish self-determination. Mary McWhorter, president of the Ladies' Auxiliary of the Ancient Order of Hibernians believed that article ten would give 'ample excuse for the re-inforcing of the Espionage Act.' She worried that 'it will become treason ... to urge the freedom of Ireland.' The leaders of the Friends of Irish Freedom were similarly disappointed about article ten and adopted a new strategy at the Third Irish Race Convention held in Philadelphia on 22 and 23 February. Among those in attendance were Republican Senator William E. Borah. The Convention decided firstly, to send messages of support to Eamon de Valera, secondly, to request Wilson to ensure that Irish self-determination was recognized and have the Irish

72 YULMC, FLPP, Box 1, folder 019, Polk to Auchincloss, 3 March 1919; ibid., 20 March 1919; ibid., 12 March 1919.   73 Link et al., *American epoch*, p. 148; Quoted in Tumulty, *Wilson*, p. 346. 74 *PWW*, 55, Diary of Dr Grayson, 4 March 1919, a statement, 4 March 1919.

case heard at the Paris conference, thirdly, to establish the Irish Victory Fund to finance political agitation in the US and Ireland and finally, to appoint a delegation to meet with Wilson prior to his departure for Paris. The seeds of future conflict within the leadership of the republican movement in the US were laid, as the Convention did not demand recognition for the Irish republic as the Provisional Government and Dáil Éireann sought and the exact uses of the victory fund were not specified. But in February 1919, the FOIF was greatly strengthened by the cross party, cross religious support it received.[75] In the State Department, Polk expected the Convention to send delegates to Paris 'to present the Irish cause' and he asked Lansing for advice on whether or not to issue them with passports, if applications were made.[76] A few weeks later, he again turned to Lansing for assistance, this time on how to reply to a resolution received from the Rhode Island legislature in favour of Wilson using his influence to obtain self-government for Ireland.[77]

Reports from Ireland suggested that the American connection remained an important dimension of the republican campaign. In a rare report on political events in Ireland, Adams detailed that during a raid by the Dublin Metropolitan Police on the Sinn Féin headquarters at 6 Harcourt Street in Dublin, on 11 January 1919, considerable literature was seized, including pamphlets designed for use among American readers, particularly military and naval men. The titles of some of the pamphlets were 'America's verdict on Easter week' and 'To the American soldiers and sailors in Ireland'. Adams noted that the latter included a piece that said 'we helped you to win your independence. Will you not help us to win ours?' Adams also reported a comment from Séan T. O'Ceallaigh 'What would the representative Irish in America say if these men left the Peace Conference having left Ireland still in bondage and slavery?'[78] In March, a minute from the division of Western European Affairs summarized the Irish situation; 'There appears to have been no radical change in the political situation in Ireland during the last two months ... so far as can be judged the people are determined to stick it out until self-determination is attained.'[79] Evidence of the depth of the concern about the Irish situation emerged from William Phillips' instruction to

75 F.M. Carroll, 'The Friends of Irish Freedom' in M.F. Funchion (ed.), *Irish American voluntary organizations* (1983), pp. 122–23; NLI, Patrick McCartan Papers, MS17670, McWhorter to McCartan, 15 May 1919; F.M. Carroll (ed.), *The American commission on Irish independence, 1919: the diary, correspondence and report* (1985), p. 4; Wilson, *Tumulty*, p. 175. Consul Sharp in Belfast reported that Belfast unionists viewed the Convention as the result of 'Irish-American Roman Catholic agitation' and not surprisingly they did not support its resolutions. NARA, RG59, M580/213, 841d.00/29, Sharp to Secretary of State, 27 February 1919.   76 Quoted in Tansill, *America and the fight*, p. 307.   77 NARA, RG59, M580/213, 841d.00/25, State of Rhode Island to Lansing, 5 March 1919; ibid., Polk, 14 March 1919. The New Hampshire and Nevada legislatures also sent similar resolutions on 25 and 26 March respectively. Ibid., 841d.00/28, New Hampshire to Lansing, 20 March 1919; ibid., 841d.00/39, Senate Joint Resolution.   78 Ibid., M580/213, 841d.00/24, Adams, 8 February 1919.   79 Ibid., Division of Western European Affairs, March 1919; ibid., 841d.00/37, Hathaway to Secretary of State, 18 March 1919.

Davis in London, to cable brief weekly summaries of events of importance in Britain arranged under general headings including 'Irish question, bolshevism and the like.' They were to incorporate reports from consuls and the military, naval and commercial attachés in London.[80]

Meanwhile, the Wilson administration had to deal with the consequences of the Irish Race Convention's agenda. The FOIF delegation had set about arranging a meeting with Wilson along with consolidating their ties to Borah and other anti-Wilson and anti-League of Nations politicians and groups.[81] From late 1918 onwards, and throughout 1919, Borah received appeals from Irish-American individuals and groups such as the Knights of Columbus, the Emmet Club and individual citizens of Butte, Montana to support the FOIF cause. As a Republican, Borah may not have seemed a natural ally but he was bitterly opposed to US involvement in the League of Nations and supported the principle of self-determination, not just for Ireland but for Egypt, India and China. His links to the hyphenate groups were balanced by his patriotism and belief in the 'preservation of American independence.' His sympathy with the Irish cause was clear; he believed 'that there will never be peace between Ireland and England until the Irish people secure their freedom.' During the following months, he corresponded with and met key Irish-Americans, including Cohalan, to discuss their strategy for the disruption of Wilson's peace plans.[82] The Wilson administration could do little about this alliance but Tumulty moved to blunt similar alliances within the Democratic Party ranks.

Not only did the National Democratic Executive Committee endorse the FOIF resolutions for Irish self-determination, but in Congress the Democratic-controlled House Foreign Affairs Committee had not abandoned the Gallagher resolution. Instead, on 14 February, the committee agreed to a watered-down version of it due to persuasion from Wilson, Tumulty and Polk and to loyalty to the Democratic Party. The committee did not ask Wilson 'to present and to urge' Ireland's case for self-determination in Paris but hoped that the conference would 'favourably consider' Ireland's claims. In other words, it did not commit Wilson in any way to any action. Chairman Flood had also managed to alter its status from that of a joint resolution to a concurrent one, which required both houses' agreement before it could be passed to the president. Congressman Mann,

---

80 Ibid., M580/7, 841.00/146a, Phillips to Davis, 10 March 1919; ibid., Polk to Davis, 7 May 1919. The embassy was to continue to send its quarterly report which provided the department with a 'wider view of international relations.' Ibid.   81 Wilson, *Tumulty*, p. 175.   82 Library of Congress (hereafter LC), Manuscripts Division (hereafter MD), William E. Borah Papers (hereafter WEBP), box 768, file League of Nations/Ireland, 1919–20, Mary Fogarty to Borah, 12 November 1918, Knights of Columbus to Borah, Petition from citizens of Butte, Montana to Borah, the Emmet Club to Borah, 29 January 1919; ibid., box 96, file General Office file, Irish question, 1920–21 (1), Borah to John E. Mullholland, 13 January 1921; ibid., Borah to G.H. Hulbert, 25 April 1921; ibid., box 768, file League of Nations/Ireland, 1919–20, ibid., Cohalan to Borah, 8 May 1919; ibid., Borah to John W. Hart, 24 March 1919.

a Republican, noted that 'it has as much chance of passing the Senate as a snowflake has in hell' and that Wilson would, therefore, never be required to act on it. The Democratic leaders of the House protected the president further by deferring the debate until 4 March, the last day of the session, which meant there would not be enough time for the Senate to debate it. However, even though the Gallagher resolution did not force Wilson to act, on 4 March the House passed it with 216 in favour and 45 against. The support of Democrats and Republicans gave a notable victory to the Irish campaigners.[83] Vice consul Karl Hitch, in Belfast, reassured Lansing that passage of the resolution had not stirred up an 'anti-American feeling' among the people of Ulster.[84]

The significance of the vote for Wilson was manifold: firstly, the Gallagher resolution had exposed within the Democratic Party a fault line between loyalty to the president and to its Irish-American constituency, which was resolved only by compromise. Secondly, it had revealed the president's lack of authority over his own party, as he had failed to prevent the resolution from leaving the House committee and being voted on. Thirdly, even though the force of resolution had been reduced and was not debated in the Senate, gaining the House's endorsement represented a significant step for the Irish campaigners and buoyed them. Fourthly, the Republicans had strengthened themselves by 'playing politics' with the Irish cause and, more importantly, Borah and Cohalan continued to work to secure rejection of the proposed settlement. Wilson's reaction to the result became evident on the evening of the vote. It also proved to be a momentous day for Wilson's peace plans in other ways.

A delegation of the Irish Race Convention led by Cohalan arrived in Washington on 25 February and requested a meeting with Wilson, Tumulty reminded the president of his promise to Bishop Shahan that he would be watchful of every opportunity to insist upon his post-war principles, which included self-determination.[85] Wilson informed Tumulty on 24 February, 'Please express my great regret that I am obliged to decline to see all delegations. Time barely suffices to transact necessary public business.' Cary Grayson, Wilson's doctor, suggests that Wilson's refusal was prompted by the insistence of the group.[86] Further appeals to Wilson to meet the delegation came from Congresswoman Jeannette Rankin and from Tumulty, who had received several requests from 'men of all races' urging Wilson to meet the delegation.[87] Tumulty persisted and

83 Wilson, *Tumulty*, p. 176; quoted in Tansill, *America and the fight*, pp. 308–9.   84 NARA, RG59, M580/213, 841d.00/45, 'American sentiment in Europe'. The Phelan resolution was buried in the Senate Foreign Relations Committee.   85 Wilson, *Tumulty*, p. 176.   86 Quoted in Tansill, *America and the fight*, p. 303, fn. 40; *PWW*, 55, Diary of Dr Grayson, 4 March 1919. During Wilson's return to the US he met with members of the Senate and House Foreign Affairs committees on 26 February 1919. They discussed the Monroe Doctrine and the meaning of article ten for Ireland in its struggle for independence. Wilson insisted that the latter was a domestic matter for Ireland and Britain. See R. Stone, *The irreconcilables: the fight against the League of Nations* (1970), pp. 60–2. 87 Carroll, *The American commission on Irish independence, 1919*, p. 5.

on 28 February he wrote to Wilson, 'regardless of what we may think of Cohalan and his crowd, there is a deep desire on the part of the American people to see the Irish question settled in the only way it can be settled – by the establishment of a Home Rule parliament in Dublin.' On 1 March, he followed this up by out-lining the danger to the Democratic Party and the president's peace programme if there was another refusal and concluded:

> You have been so busy during the past few years that you have not been able, I think, to give sufficient though to the importance of the request to receive a delegation to present a resolution with reference to Ireland's cause. Your attitude in the matter is fraught with a great deal of danger both to the Democratic Party and to the cause you represent ... Republicans are taking full advantage of this ... You know that I am not a professional Irishman but your refusal to see this delegation will simply strengthen the Sinn Féin movement in this country.[88]

These arguments finally won Wilson round and he reluctantly agreed to meet the delegation for a few minutes after his speech at the Metropolitan Opera House in New York on 4 March, before he left for France.[89]

All this Irish-American activity was closely monitored by the British embassy in Washington.[90] The consequences of the public campaigning and congressional activity were evident at both personnel and policy levels. From the time of his arrival in February 1918, Reading's role had been a limited one due to ill health, the lack of access to Wilson and the change of the centre of political activity from London and Washington to Paris from late 1918 onwards. In early 1919, Frank Polk, who regularly met Reading on both professional and personal levels, recorded that the British diplomat was not 'very busy' and that it was a 'hard position for him because the Irish are raising the devil and he hesitates to make any speeches for fear of inciting them to further outbreaks.'[91] However, Reading managed to meet Wilson on 4 March before his departure for New York and the meeting with the FOIF delegation. He confirmed to Balfour that he was satis-fied that when Wilson met the deputation he would do nothing which could com-mit him in any way to bringing the Irish question before the peace conference.[92] Reading was correct.

The meeting with the FOIF delegation started badly. The group, led by Cohalan, attended Wilson's address and afterwards waited for him backstage but Wilson insisted that he would not attend the meeting if Cohalan was present because 'he is a traitor.'[93] Tumulty told the president that Cohalan's exclusion

88 Wilson, *Tumulty*, p. 176.   89 *PWW*, 55, Diary of Dr Grayson, 4 March 1919; Wilson, *Tumulty*, p. 177; Carroll, *The American commission on Irish independence, 1919*, p. 5.   90 TNA, FO371/4245, Barclay to Balfour, 6 January 1919.   91 YULMC, FLPP, Box 1, folder 019, Polk to Auchincloss, 20 March 1919.   92 TNA, FO115/2804, Reading to Balfour, 4 March 1919.   93 *PWW*, 55, Diary

would make 'a terrible impression' and Wilson replied 'that's just what I want
to do, Tumulty, but I think it will make a decent impression on good people.'[94]
The meeting went ahead because Cohalan dramatically announced 'Ireland's cause
is of far more concern than my feelings – it is greater than any man' and withdrew.[95] The group then not only handed over their resolutions to Wilson but
asked him to take action to bring about an Irish republic at the Paris conference.
Wilson expressed his sympathy but stated that the matter was a 'domestic affair
for Great Britain and Ireland to settle themselves, and not a matter for outside
interference.' When Frank P. Walsh asked him to use his influence and secure
a hearing at the peace conference for an Irish delegation, Wilson replied, 'You
do not expect me to give an answer to this request now?' Walsh replied that he
did not and the meeting ended.[96] The Friends delegation was disappointed with
Wilson's responses and with the fruitless meeting. It confirmed their belief that
Wilson would not apply self-determination to the Irish case. Wilson's opposition, combined with the news of the outbreak of the Anglo-Irish war of independence in January 1919, pushed the FOIF, under Cohalan's direction, into a
gradual alignment with Republican opponents of the peace settlement.[97]

Wilson was so annoyed at the whole episode that he continued to discuss it
on board ship back to France. Wilson told the journalist Ray Stannard Baker
that the delegation was 'so insistent ... that I had hard work keeping my temper.'[98] In a discussion with Grayson, he told him

> that the Irish as a race are very hard to deal with owing to their incon-
> siderateness, their unreasonable demands and their jealousies. He [Wilson]
> predicted that owing to the dissatisfaction among the Irish-Americans and
> the German-Americans with the Democratic administration, unless a
> decided change was brought about, it might defeat the Democratic Party
> in 1920.[99]

During the voyage, when he read in the ship's paper, *The Hatchet*, that the leadership of Sinn Féin in Ireland threatened to use the Irish-American vote to kill
the League of Nations unless the Paris conference accorded them an Irish republic, he told Grayson that he would 'go to the mat with them – show them where
they got off in America.' Yet, at this time he was still convinced that if the British

of Dr Grayson, 4 March 1919.   **94** E. Bolling Wilson, *My memoir* (1938), pp. 242–3. The delegation consisted of former governor Edward F. Dunne, Michael J. Ryan, Bishop Shahan, Michael
Francis Doyle, Major Eugene F. Kinkead, Major John P. Grace, John J. Splain, Judge O'Neill
Ryan, Dr William Carroll, John E. Milholland, the Rev. James Grattan Mythen, Rev Norman
Thomas, Judge Goff, Bishop Muldoon, Frank P. Walsh.   **95** Quoted in Splain, 'The Irish movement in the United States since 1911', p. 234.   **96** *PWW*, 55, Diary of Dr Grayson, 4 March 1919.
97 M. Doorley, *Irish-American diaspora nationalism: the Friends of Irish Freedom 1916–35* (2005), p.
103.   **98** R. Stannard Baker, *American chronicle: the autobiography* (1945), p. 386.   **99** *PWW*, 55,
Diary of Dr Grayson, 5 March 1919.

government had hung Edward Carson for treason in 1914, the Irish problem would have been practically solved.[1] Wilson's anger about the Opera House engagement, was still manifest ten days later when he arrived in Paris; he confided to Baker that he could have told them 'to go to hell, but he realised that while that might give him some personal satisfaction it would not be the act of wisdom or the act of a statesman.'[2] Not surprisingly, once the details of the Cohalan episode reached London, Wilson's stock was raised. Lloyd George told him that the way in which he handled the FOIF delegation had given the British 'great delight.'[3] But if Wilson had hoped that his snub to Cohalan would appeal to 'decent people' and bring him support, as had happened with his rebuke to Jeremiah O'Leary in 1916, he miscalculated the depth and nature of support for the Irish cause.

Although a minority of Irish-Americans still favoured home rule or indeed direct rule, a majority supported the FOIF campaigns for self-determination and for republican representation at Paris. The protests flooded into the White House about Wilson's treatment of Cohalan, whom one writer described as 'the next President of the United States.'[4] Patrick McCartan, who already distrusted Cohalan, felt that Wilson had played into the hands of extremists by making Cohalan the 'hero martyr' of the Irish-Americans, while Peter Golden of the small but vigorous Irish Progressive League, which was dedicated to having the Irish cause presented to Paris peace conference, told McCartan on 21 March 1919:

> I never had any hope in Woodrow Wilson and it seems he has shown unmistakeably that he won't do anything. The only way he did anything for the movement was when he was forced to do so. If he and the rest are made to feel that it will be end of the [Democratic] party if they don't come across for Ireland, they may wake up. Though I fear it is late to bring pressure to bear. Indeed I was not at all disturbed at seeing the snub to our distinguished citizen nor were dozens of others. In fact between you and me the matter has caused no end of trouble here ... there is a drive on more strongly than ever against the League ... the cause is so popular now that people ... attend and advocate without any risk of being labelled this or that or the other.[5]

Similar views led to a further appeal to Wilson on republican Ireland's behalf, from within the ranks of the Democratic Party. Five Democratic senators; David Walsh (Massachusetts), Thomas J. Walsh (Montana), Peter Gerry (Rhode Island), Key Pittman (Nevada) and John Kendrick (Wyoming), wrote to Wilson on 28

---

1 Quoted in Lee Levin, *Edith and Woodrow*, p. 277; *PWW*, 55, Diary of Dr Grayson, 12 March 1919. 2 Baker, *American chronicle*, p. 385–6. 3 *PWW*, 56, Diary of Dr Grayson, 31 March 1919. 4 Quoted in Duff, 'The Versailles Treaty', 590, fn. 33. 5 P. McCartan, *With de Valera in America* (1932), p. 93; NLI, Peter Golden Papers (hereafter PGP), MS17668, Golden to McCartan, 21 March 1919.

March, calling for some progress in Paris on the 'vexing question of self-government for Ireland.' They warned him about the intensity of feeling prevailing
throughout the country and it was not only that 'the future of our party imper-
atively demands that something be done' before the conference ended 'to meet
the reasonable expectations of the Irish people' but they agreed 'that the prospect
of early ratification of the treaty by the Senate will be jeopardized otherwise.'
They recommended that, as Britain was benefiting from the peace conference
negotiations more than the US, 'she ought to be quite willing to give assurances
in some form that Ireland should at least be accorded the same measure of self-
government as is enjoyed by the favoured colonies.'[6] Their demand for Wilson
to bring about self-government for Ireland illustrated the success of the Cohalan
and Borah campaign. Wilson's dilemma emerged from his reply 'on the Irish
business' to Peter Gerry on 17 April. He said that the brevity of his note did not
indicate 'any lack of appreciation of the capital importance of the matter your
letter dwells upon. It is very much in mind and I am earnestly seeking some way
to be useful in the matter, though I must admit it is very difficult to find a way.'[7]
The reply could not have given the senators much comfort. Senator Walsh
received a telegram on 30 April from Archbishop Christie of Oregon city and
five other bishops, representing the states of Oregon, Washington, Idaho and
Montana, who appealed to him 'to urge a guarantee of self-determination for
Ireland before the ratification of the League of Nations by the US senate.'[8]
Walsh's sparse reply indicated that he had twice communicated with Wilson.[9]
But he could not offer them any hope of action. Indeed the sympathetic but non-
committal nature of Wilson's words confirmed again the latter's unwillingness to
intervene directly. But was this position in April representative of the views of
his official and unofficial advisers?

Horace Plunkett had crossed to the US in January 1919 in the hope that he
would finally win Wilson over to the settlement proposed by the Irish
Convention. He was gravely disappointed when he found that House was in Paris
with Wilson and, more significantly, that the two statesman were not as close
personally as they had been.[10] Instead he met with Polk and Phillips who told
him that 'an immediate settlement' of the Irish situation was needed to thwart
the growing opposition to the League of Nations proposal, although they did not
suggest that Wilson should intervene.[11] When Wilson returned to the US,
Plunkett tried to meet him but Tumulty replied that it would be impossible.
Instead Plunkett wrote to Wilson on 2 March:

---

6 LC, MD, Thomas J. Walsh Papers (hereafter TWP), Box 190, subject file B, c. 1913–33, Ireland
c. 1917–21, letter to Wilson, 28 March 1919.   7 Ibid., subject file Ireland, government of, resolutions on Irish freedom throughout 1919 from Irish-American organizations in Montana, Wilson to
Geary, 17 April 1919.   8 Ibid., subject file B, c. 1913–33, Ireland c. 1917–21, telegram to Walsh,
30 April 1919.   9 Ibid., Walsh to Chirstie, 20 May 1919.   10 M. Digby, *Horace Plunkett* (1949),
pp. 244–5; NLI, HPP, P6584, Plunkett to Wilson, 2 March 1919.   11 *PWW*, 55, Polk to Wilson,
6 March 1919.

Already I note the troubles of my country are being used to embarrass you. I am quite sure ... that it is extremely improbable that you would take any action in regard to Ireland which might even have the appearance of intervention in the domestic affairs of the British Isles. You may, however, see fit to make your personal wishes and that of your people privately known to the British government.[12]

Plunkett fully appreciated the sensitivities of Wilson's position and in a circuitous fashion appealed to Wilson to permit House to discuss finding an Irish settlement with himself and Lloyd George. Wilson's reply to Plunkett on 26 March maintained his position of non-interference.[13] Unfortunately for Plunkett his usefulness to both the US and British governments had passed, despite his continued aspirations to 'lead Ireland out of this morass', because he could not speak on behalf of republican nationalism. No longer were his views on Ireland representative of a majority nationalist viewpoint, nor was he acting as an intermediary between the two governments, while Lloyd George disliked his interference in the Anglo–American relationship on the Irish problem.[14] Nevertheless, Plunkett's letter confirmed the interlinking of opposition in the US to the League of Nations and the need for an Irish settlement in Paris.

The danger of the Irish issue to Wilson's position and policies in the US was also recognized by Davis in London. Unlike his predecessor, Page, he had dwelt on the matter during late 1918 and early 1919. Davis collected views from nationalist and government circles and discussed the issue at length with his staff. A further pressure on Davis and his staff to keep up to date was the State Department's insistence that it report weekly on the 'Irish question.' Following a discussion with Captain Alfred L. Dennis from the military attachè's office, and Butler Wright, he followed up by reading correspondence between House and Plunkett and Plunkett's report on the failed Convention. By early March, Davis was more critical of Ulster Unionist intransigence but felt that Lloyd George would address the Irish problem if pressurized and he was worried that if it was not settled it would be a leading issue in the next election campaign 'to the detriment of ... the president.'[15] It is doubtful if he asked Wilson to act on

12 Ibid., Plunkett to Wilson, 2 March 1919.   13 Wilson's short reply to Plunkett stated that he was 'glad to have your guidance in a most perplexing matter' and he hoped he was recovering. NLI, HPP, P6584, Wilson to Plunkett, 26 March 1919.   14 *PWW*, 55, Plunkett to Wilson, 2 March 1919; Digby, *Horace Plunkett*, p. 245.   15 Davis & Fleming, *The ambassadorial diary*, 17, 18 January 1919, 4 March 1919, pp. 34, 35, 67. Davis and Robert Skinner, US consul general in London, forwarded to Lansing requests from consuls Adams and Hathaway's for advice on how to deal with Sinn Féin messages for Wilson. Among these was one from the 'Parliament and Government of the Irish Republic' signed by de Valera, at its session on 11 April 1919. Department instructions required that no consul forwarded such correspondence to Wilson but Adams believed there were 'circumstances in the present case' which made it different and he sought advice from the London embassy. Skinner had not heard anything by 22 April and instructed Adams to abide by existing instructions. Polk later approved this course of action. NARA, RG59, M580/213, 841d.00/43, Skinner to

the matter but he was friendly with two of Wilson's inner circle, Creel and Baker, who he frequently met in London and Paris.[16]

Indeed in February 1919 Wilson had sent Creel, the former director of the Committee on Public Information, to Ireland to report on the political situation. Creel had also been encouraged to visit by Seán T. O'Ceallaigh.[17] During his visit to Ireland he met with political leaders from all sides, including Michael Collins, Harry Boland and John Dillon. It was ironic that during the war Creel had successfully vilified Irish nationalists for their German activities, but he was appalled at the political oppression, economic exploitation and religious discrimination suffered by the Irish at British hands throughout the centuries. He was surprised that, for all their 'implacability', the Sinn Féiners were 'far more reasonable' than Irish-American republicans. They listened politely to his insistence that, while Wilson could raise Ireland's case in Paris, it would be a 'meaningless gesture that could have only dangerous consequences.' Also he broadened the context of the Irish question in two ways. Firstly, he indicated that there was not a 'corner of the world' in which some group of people did not have a similar demand but the Paris conference did not have the 'power' to hear and adjudicate these appeals. Secondly, he stressed that even though the US public was sympathetic, it would not go to war with Britain on Ireland's account. He recalled that the 'disappointment in every face was plain to be seen' but he felt they accepted his argument's 'force and logic.' Nonetheless, Creel reported that Sinn Féin still wanted Wilson to bring 'personal and private pressure' on Lloyd George.[18]

After he had concluded his business in Ireland, Creel met Lloyd George again and spent three hours with him. Both men agreed on the urgency of settling the Irish problem. Creel also pointed out that 'dominion status', with an opt-out clause for the Ulster counties, rather than full independence was still acceptable to Sinn Féin' and to the lord lieutenant of Ireland, Lord French, but he was convinced that if 'nothing was done' it would harden into a demand for a republic and 'the bitterness of Irish-Americans' would find 'full expression' during the

---

Secretary of State, 17 April 1919, enclosure Adams to Skinner, 16 April 1919; ibid., 841d.00/44, Skinner to Secretary of State, 22 April 1919; ibid., 841d.00/46, Davis to Secretary of State, 25 April 1919; ibid., Polk to Davis, 7 June 1919.   **16** Davis & Fleming, *The ambassadorial diary*, 15 February 1919, 14 March 1919, pp. 57, 72.   **17** *DIFP*, i, O'Ceallaigh to Cathal Brugha, 7 March 1919, p. 9. **18** Creel, *Rebel at large*, pp. 215–22. Another Irish group who communicated with Wilson and House in Paris was the Irish League of Nations Society. Its president was National University of Ireland (NUI) Professor R. Donovan, Joseph Devlin member of parliament was vice-president, W.F. Trench and the joint honorary secretary was E.A. Ashton. Alec Wilson member of the Royal Irish Academy and justice of the peace and Trinity College Dublin professor of French literature was a committee member. Their aim was to secure a declaration of national rights for subject peoples as the basis of the League of Nations. Due to travel problems they failed to arrive in Paris before the draft covenant was signed. But they met with House and later asked him to visit Ireland which he was unable to do. See YULMC, Edward M. House Papers (hereafter EHP), box 636, file 2064, League to Wilson, 6 March 1919; ibid., Arthur Frazier, counsellor, US embassy, Paris to Ashton, 15 March 1919; ibid., Ashton to House, 18 June 1919; ibid., House to Ashton, 26 June 1919.

League of Nations fight in the US Senate. It is doubtful whether Creel's appeal to Lloyd George to settle the Irish problem carried presidential sanction, but the prime minister did grant him a lengthy meeting, and, according to George Moore, Creel made 'an impression.' On 1 March, Creel submitted his report to Wilson, who had read it by 20 March, replying that Creel's suggestions were 'very valuable and you may be sure will remain in my mind.'[19] Creel remained strongly critical of the 'professional' German- and Irish-Americans who 'incited to bellow their hatred of England' and doomed the League of Nations to failure, but after his return to the US in spring 1919, he penned a series of strongly anti-British articles that Tumulty said had a profound effect on public opinion.[20] Creel, Davis and Plunkett did not ask Wilson to act on behalf of Ireland at the Paris conference but each emphasized to him in one way or another the importance of resolving the Irish problem for him, for his party and for the success of his peace plan.

American Commission on Irish Independence

When Wilson returned to Paris on 14 March, Ireland was still on his mind but, despite all the warnings about its potential to sink the settlement and the League of Nations, settling it was not an immediate concern. Instead the president was gravely disappointed with House's leadership in his absence. Wilson felt that his chief adviser had undermined his liberal principles by compromising on reparations and territorial adjustments.[21] Although House had kept Wilson informed by telegram throughout the month of his absence, Wilson felt that he had to retrieve lost ground and to revisit the covenant and treaties in order to protect US domestic and foreign interests, specifically immigration and tariff policies and the Monroe Doctrine. In the following weeks, Wilson excluded House and the other American commissioners and worked himself into exhaustion, making concessions to cover Republican demands and to protect his cherished covenant. He capitulated and permitted French occupation of the Rhineland for fifteen years, a US guarantee of France's borders with Germany, German demilitarization, the insertion of the war guilt clause (although the total amount of reparations was settled by a commission), that Italian territorial claims to Adriatic lands would be settled after the conference and that security concerns would predominate over self-determination for eastern Europe in the face of the Bolshevik threat.[22] In the midst of this tense and delicate situation the American

19 Report of Lloyd George meeting in Davis & Fleming, *The ambassadorial diary*, 4 March 1919, p. 67; Creel, *Rebel at large*, p. 221. O'Ceallaigh complained to Cathal Brugha, President of Dáil Éireann, that he never heard anything about Creel's visit and did not see his report. See *DIFP*, i, O'Ceallaigh to Cathal Brugha, 7 March 1919.   20 Creel, *Rebel at large*, p. 226; Duff, 'The Versailles Treaty', 594.   21 E. Plischke, *Diplomat in chief: the president at the summit* (1986), p. 99.   22 Link

Commission on Irish Independence (ACII) arrived in Paris on 11 April firstly, to secure safe conduct for the Sinn Féin leaders, Eamon de Valera, Count Plunkett and Arthur Griffith, to Paris and, if this failed, to present the Irish case for self-determination themselves before the conference and secondly, to promote the idea of an Irish republic.[23] The timing could not have been worse.

Smarting from the disappointment of the New York meeting with Wilson the officers of the Irish Race Convention decided to send three Irish-Americans to Paris.[24] They were a distinguished group. The chairman was Frank P. Walsh, the labour lawyer and joint chairman with former President Taft of the War-Labour Board. Michael J. Ryan was also a lawyer, a former solicitor for Philadelphia city, a Public Service commissioner and the unsuccessful Democratic candidate for the governorship of Pennsylvania. He was the only one of the three to have been formally involved in Irish-American nationalist activities as president of the United Irish League of America. But the most prominent member was Edward F. Dunne, educated in Trinity College Dublin, a solid Democrat who had been a lawyer, judge, mayor of Chicago and governor of Illinois.[25] A characteristic of the ACII was that none of them had been involved in opposing Wilson's re-election in 1916 as Cohalan had been. Consequently, the group had a national prominence in orthodox politics and were of good character. But it was less these characteristics that led Wilson to authorize the granting of passports to the group and more the involvement of the British ambassador. Reading discussed the issuing of passports and visas to the group with Wilson on 4 March. He indicated that the British authorities would 'not refuse' to grant visas if applications were made. Wilson agreed that it would be 'unwise to adopt any such policy or for the US government to refuse passports.'[26]

et al., *American epoch*, p. 148; LaFeber, *American age*, ii, pp. 321–4. Ireland provided evidence of the growing Bolshevik threat also. Reports from the US consular agent in Limerick and Hathaway in Queenstown led Davis to conclude that the Limerick 'political' strike 'was essentially Bolshevik and, therefore, not primarily Sinn Féin or trade unionist in character.' However, Hathaway saw it as a political strike against the British government. Hathaway reported on the declaration of policy by the National Executive of the Irish Labour Party and Trade Union Congress in late May and confirmed that both were 'definitely anti-capitalist but not incendiary.' In late June, Sharp in Belfast reported that four men had been arrested and convicted of unlawful assembly specifically preaching 'extreme Russian revolutionary doctrine.' NARA, RG59, M580/213, 841d.00/00/48, Davis to Secretary of State, 6 May 1919; ibid., 841d.00/54, Hathaway to Secretary of State, 19 May 1919; ibid., 841d.00/55, Hathaway to Secretary of State, 20 May 1919; ibid., 841d.00/00/68, Sharp to Secretary of State, 30 June 1919.   **23** Carroll, 'American commission on Irish independence', p. 18.   **24** For a full account of the composition and activities of the American Commission on Irish Independence in Paris and Ireland see Carroll, *The American commission on Irish independence*; F.M. Carroll, 'The American commission on Irish independence and the Paris peace conference of 1919' (1985), 103–19.   **25** NARA, RG59, M580/213, 841d.00/00/51, Adams to Secretary of State, 16 May 1919. The group was accompanied by Patrick Lee who was connected to Clan na Gael in New York. Ibid.   **26** TNA, FO115/2804, Reading to Foreign Office, 4 March 1919; Duff, 'The Versailles Treaty', 592, fn 41; Funchion, 'American commission on Irish independence', p. 18; Davis & Fleming, *The ambassadorial diary*, 19 May 1919, p. 99.

The ACII arrived in Paris on 11 April and was met by O'Ceallaigh, who had been joined by George Gavan Duffy, Dáil Éireann envoy to France.[27] Once the Irish-Americans had settled in at the Grand Hotel, they set about putting pressure on Wilson to get safe passage from the British government for the Sinn Féin delegation to travel from Ireland to Paris in order to present their case. In the first few days, they received a call from Lincoln Steffens, an American magazine writer who offered to show Walsh through the official channels in Paris. Both men called on Ray Stannard Baker who, Walsh felt, was 'very friendly.' He assured Walsh that he would convey any message to Wilson at any time and he offered to help in arranging an interview with the president for the Commission if they wished. Walsh met William C. Bullitt, the State Department official who was a member of the Current Intelligence Department of the American Commission, and the latter contacted Lloyd George's secretary, Philip Kerr, on behalf of the Irish-Americans. On 15 April, Bullitt reported to Walsh that Lloyd George would probably give passports to the Sinn Féin leaders but would not permit them to appear before the conference. Later that day, Walsh had a cordial meeting with House who agreed to meet them again. The ACII followed up on these actions with a letter to Wilson on 16 April setting out their demands. They reminded him that if he did intervene he would earn the 'grateful appreciation of millions of our fellow-citizens' and they asked for a meeting with him.[28]

Baker, who sympathized with the Sinn Féin cause, was true to his promise and Wilson read the letter and agreed to meet Walsh on 17 April. The reasons behind Wilson's decision are difficult to identify: perhaps they related to the reports on the deteriorating conditions in Ireland and reasonableness of the Sinn Féin leadership that he received from Baker and Creel or to the pressures emanating from US domestic politics or Walsh's personal standing in the Democratic Party. Nonetheless, the circumstances of Walsh's meeting with the president placed the Irish issue in a wider context. Walsh's appointment was the fourteenth of eighteen engagements which Wilson fulfilled that day. These included meetings with representatives of other minor nations and principalities who all presented their 'just claims.' Yet, the fact that he was prepared to meet Walsh represented progress for the Irish-Americans.[29] Walsh presented the Commission's requests for safe conduct for the republican leaders, a hearing before the conference and an Irish republic. Wilson indicated that he had twice talked with Lloyd George about the Irish situation and that he had urged upon him the

27 The Irish group were accompanied by Victor Collins and Joseph Walsh who comprised the staff of the Irish missions. AIHS, DCP, Box 1, folder 9, Diary of the American commission on Irish independence, p. 3. George Gavan Duffy was a member of the First Dáil, an Irish Republican envoy to France in 1919–20 and roving envoy in Europe in 1920–1. 28 AIHS, DCP, Box 1, folder 9, Diary of the American commission on Irish independence, pp. 6–10; Steffens and Baker had worked together on *The American magazine*; *PWW*, 57, Walsh, Dunne, Ryan to Wilson, 16 April 1919. 29 Carroll, *The American commission on Irish independence*, p. 11; *PWW*, 57, Diary of Dr Grayson, 17 April 1919.

importance of an early settlement, with which Lloyd George had agreed. Regarding the request that the Sinn Féin delegation appear before the conference, Wilson indicated that the problem was that no group had appeared before the larger assembly or smaller committee and that he did not know if it was feasible. But he agreed that Walsh could go to House 'at once and say to him that we think it wise and proper that these three gentlemen should be permitted to come to Paris and for him to take the matter up with Lloyd George, or with whomever he thought best and see if he could not bring it about.' Wilson also indicated that once agreement had been reached on the peace settlement, he would say to Lloyd George that Irish-Americans were 'intense' about the Irish problem and that a settlement was vital to US–British relations.[30] Wilson's promise to act on the Irish question, albeit in the future, combined with his offer of House's help on the passage issue, represented substantial progress for the Irish-American delegation, particularly after the low point of the New York meeting and the failure of the Dáil Éireann mission to contact Wilson. The Irish-Americans' mission seemed close to success.

House met with Walsh, Ryan and Dunne on 18 April, expressed his 'warmest sympathy', indicated he had repeatedly urged Lloyd George to find a settlement and promised to ask the British leader for 'safe conduct' for the Irish representatives. Later in the day Bullitt invited Walsh to meet with himself and Philip Kerr.[31] On the same day, the ACII wrote to Cohalan 'things proceeding in quite satisfactory manner. We have had interview with the President and Colonel House and hope to have something to report very shortly.'[32] Expectations were high within the Irish-American delegation and among journalists that House would issue a statement on the passports during his usual press briefing on Sunday 20 April. However, he cancelled the briefing. When Walsh met House the following day, the latter intimated that he expected to hear from Lloyd George and it 'looked mighty feasible.' Walsh also learned from Bullitt that 'something favourable is going to happen for Ireland.'[33] House had several meetings with Lloyd George at this time concerning the Irish question, not least because, as he told Plunkett, 'it has now become almost as much of a political issue in America as in England.'[34] During a meeting on 21 April, Lloyd George agreed with House that he should see the Irish-American delegates to discuss with them 'the question of bringing to Paris the delegates from the so-called "Irish Republic".'[35] House also contacted Wiseman to investigate getting passports for the Sinn Féin group. The Foreign Office officials told Wiseman that they would be willing to

30 AIHS, DCP, Box 1, folder 9, Diary of the American commission on Irish independence', 17 April 1919, pp. 39–45.   31 Ibid., 18 April 1919, p. 46.   32 Ibid., Box 17, folder 5, Walsh, Dunne, Ryan to Cohalan 18 April 1919.   33 AIHS, DCP, Box 1, folder 9, Diary of the American commission on Irish independence, 19, 20, 21 April 1919, pp. 47, 48, 49. The ACII also met with representatives of other delegations seeking independence from the British empire including the Egyptian delegation and the Lithuanian delegates. Ibid., 21 April 1919, p. 51.   34 NLI, HPP, P6584, reel 2 of 2, House to Plunkett, 25 April 1919.   35 PWW, 57, Diary of Colonel House, 21 April 1919.

give them passports but they preferred getting Lloyd George's consent.[36] The prime minister's meeting with the Irish-Americans was delayed due to the pressure of conference work, which irritated the group. In the interim de Valera sent a message to the Irish-American delegation suggesting that they visit Ireland. [37] Lloyd George gave permission and, with House's support, their US passports were provided with visas by the British authorities to permit them travel to Ireland, even though there was some disquiet in the State Department about the possible repercussions of their visit in the US.[38] When Wilson had agreed to issue passports to the Irish-Americans in March, he had instructed Polk to issue them for France only, and to emphasize that they 'would not be permitted to go to England or Ireland.'[39] But once Lloyd George had agreed to allow the delegation to visit Ireland, House instructed the US embassy in Paris to amend the passports.[40] The delegation arrived in Dublin on 3 May 1919 to begin a ten-day tour of Ireland.

They met with political and religious representatives of nationalist Ireland, spoke publicly about the purposes of their visit to France, supported Irish independence, criticized British rule in Ireland and implied that their presence had official British and US government sanction.[41] The resultant newspaper publicity and furore caused by their visit was such that on 6 May, when the delegation was still in Ireland, Davis cabled US headquarters in Paris to inquire about the status of the visit which he would have opposed as 'their presence must do far more harm than good. Ireland at this time is no place for irresponsible oratory.'[42] Sharp confirmed that there was 'bitter resentment' among unionists that Lloyd George had permitted the visit and had promised to meet the Irish-Americans.[43] Three days later, on 9 May, when the delegation was still in Ireland, Lloyd George wrote to House complaining that he had allowed the group to go to Ireland at House's request and on his guarantee that they were 'responsible

36 *PWW*, 58, House to Wilson, 9 April 1919.   **37** AIHS, DCP, Box 1, folder 9, Diary of the American commission on Irish independence, 29 April 1919, p. 55. Cohalan had suggested a visit to Ireland also. See New York Public Library (hereafter NYPL), Frank P. Walsh Papers (hereafter FPWP), box 124, Cohalan to Walsh, 28 March 1919.   **38** AIHS, DCP, Box 1, folder 9, Diary of the American commission on Irish independence, 1 May 1919, p. 58; Carroll, *The American commission on Irish independence*, p. 12; YULMC, FLPP, Box 26, file 328, Polk to Davis, 16 May 1919.   **39** *PWW*, 58, A memorandum by Gordon Auchincloss, 15 May 1919; NARA, RG59, M580.00/149a, Polk to Davis, 16 May 1919.   **40** YULMC, EHP, box 203, file 2/674, Arthur Frazier, US Counsellor to Peace Commission, to US passport bureau, 1 May 1919.   **41** Carroll, *The American commission on Irish independence*, pp. 12–13. Walsh believed that the 'fires on the hillside' that welcomed them confirmed that the 'sacred fire was still burning in the hearts of the people after all these thousand years of darkness.' See LC, MD, Thomas J. Walsh Papers (hereafter TJWP), Box 32, Frank P. Walsh, 'Windows alight in Connaught', *America*, 7 June 1919, pp. 225–6; B. Nelson, 'Irish Americans, Irish nationalism and the "social" question, 1916–1923', 167.   **42** Davis & Fleming, *The ambassadorial diary*, 6 May 1919, p. 95.   **43** NARA, RG59, M580/7, 841.00/149, Davis to Secretary of State, 19 May 1919. Sharp's comments were of 'considerable interest' to the division of Western European Affairs and were passed on to Assistant Secretary William Phillips. Ibid., M580/213, A. Bliss Lane, Division of Western European Affairs to Phillips, 17 June 1919.

men' who had given 'excellent service to the Allied cause' during the war. He then detailed his version of the visit and concluded that it was impossible for his government to permit 'inflammatory speeches ... to be delivered' and indicated that he intended publishing the letter.[44] On the same day, House presented 'the facts' to Wilson, blamed Lloyd George, firstly for not meeting or writing to the Irish-Americans in Paris to indicate whether he would permit the Sinn Féin group come to Paris and, secondly, for giving them visas to travel to Ireland. House wanted to know if he should reply to the prime minister and what he should say.[45] In his short reply to Lloyd George, also on 9 May, House restated his refusal to take any responsibility for the episode.[46] Gordon Auchincloss, a staff member in Wilson's immediate circle, agreed: 'Walsh, Dunne and Ryan ... are acting like the devil, but it is George's own fault.'[47] Wilson was also in contact with Lloyd George on 12 May to discuss the matter and the prime minister promised to send him copies of the *Freeman's Journal* that carried Walsh and Dunne's speeches.[48] The contemporary accounts of the events, recriminations and misunderstandings before and after the visit are contradictory. Essentially it seems that the visit was stage-managed by the Sinn Féin leadership with the Irish-Americans expressing the expected sentiments of support for the republic and independence from Britain. Unbelievably, Lloyd George, Wilson, House and their respective officials in Paris had not expected the Irish-American delegation to behave in a partisan way and each side disavowed any responsibility for it.[49]

Lloyd George immediately curtailed the Irish-Americans' itinerary in Ireland.[50] The American Commission completed its visit on 12 May by issuing an inflammatory statement to the newspapers, which Adams immediately forwarded to Washington.[51] On receipt of it, Polk recommended to Auchincloss in Paris that the situation should be outlined to the press so that all would know that 'the British have brought this trouble on themselves by visaing their passports for England and Ireland.' The following day he reiterated the same position to Davis in London. Clearly, Polk did not know that Wilson, with Lloyd George's approval, had authorized House to facilitate the delegation's visit to Ireland and that it was House who arranged the extension of the US passports to include Britain and France. Not surprisingly House opposed Polk's suggestion that a public statement should be issued.[52] But when the Irish-Americans published an open letter to

---

44 *PWW*, 58, Lloyd George to House, 9 May 1919. The visit was raised also in both the House of Commons and House of Lords on 14 and 22 May respectively.   **45** *PWW*, 58, House to Wilson, 9 May 1919.   **46** Ibid., House to Lloyd George, 9 May 1919.   **47** YULMC, FLPP, box 1, file 022, Auchincloss to Polk, 12 May 1919.   **48** *PWW*, 59, House to Lloyd George, Kerr (Lloyd George's secretary) to Wilson, 12 May 1919.   **49** Carroll, *The American commission on Irish independence*, pp. 12–16. Also see *PWW*, 59, Correspondence throughout and 'Report on conditions in Ireland with demand for investigation by the peace conference'. 3 June 1919.   **50** *PWW*, 59, Lloyd George to House, 10 May 1919.   **51** NARA, RG59, M581/213, 841d.00/51, Adams to Lansing, 16 May 1919.   **52** *PWW*, 59, Polk to Auchincloss, 13 May 1919; NARA, RG59, M580/7, 841.00/149a, Polk to Davis, 16 May 1919; *PWW*, 59, House memorandum, 15 May 1919; YULMC,

Wilson on 20 May, in which House featured as having told them Lloyd George would grant safe conduct to the Sinn Féin group, an annoyed House issued a denial to the press associations and also notified Lloyd George.[53] When the Irish-Americans returned to Paris on 16 May they faced a changed atmosphere and the earlier good will built up with Wilson, House and Bullitt on the US side and Lloyd George, Wiseman and Kerr on the British side, had been dissipated.

Nonetheless, on 17 May the ACII launched a further round of appeals for the safe conduct of the Sinn Féin delegation to the peace conference. They met with House and wrote to Lansing and Wilson.[54] Wilson personally drafted a reply on 22 May:

> ... although it had not been possible to extend official assistance to these gentlemen, every effort had been made to bring them into friendly communication with the British representatives here and through these friendly offices Mr Lloyd George had consented to see them. But that the utterances which they had made while in Ireland had been of such a character as to give the deepest offence to those with whom they were seeking to deal and had rendered it impossible for us to serve them any further. In brief the statement (which you can easily elaborate, with House's assistance) ought to show that the whole failure of their errand lies at their door and not ours ... I think on the whole it would be better to send the answer which is here suggested than the rather formal one which you sent me.[55]

It is significant that his note was written on the day when former Ambassador Reading visited him. Reading updated Wilson on the Republicans' campaign to use the issue of the recognition of the Irish republic as a weapon to defeat the League of Nations in Congress. Wilson 'listened carefully' and immediately took steps to get all the facts dealing with the situation. At the same time, the president received similar information on the situation in the US from Polk.[56] Thus, even though he was aware of the increasingly explosive nature of the Irish situation at home, he still penned the toughly worded reply to the Irish-Americans.

House, however, toned down Wilson's reply which stated that in view of the 'situation', the American commissioners had decided that 'any further efforts' on behalf of the Irish-Americans would be 'futile and, therefore, unwise.'[57] The letter should have indicated the end of the ACII's mission and Ryan did return to America on 24 May. However, Walsh and Dunne continued to lobby for passports for the Sinn Féin leaders. They wrote again to Lansing on 26 and 27 May, to Wilson on 28 May, and to each of the five members of the American

EHP, box 203, file 2/674, Frazier to US passport bureau, 1 May 1919.   53 *PWW*, 59, Diary of House, 21 May 1919.   54 Carroll, *The American commission on Irish independence*, Walsh et al. to Lansing, 17 May 1919, p. 92; ibid., Walsh et al. to Wilson, 20 May, 1919, p. 93.   55 *PWW*, 59, Wilson to Lansing, 22 May 1919.   56 Ibid., Diary of Grayson, 22 May 1919; ibid., fn 2.   57 Ibid., Lansing to Walsh, 24 May 1919.

Commission to Negotiate Peace to remind them of their duty as public representatives to present full information on Ireland to the peace conference prior to the conclusion of a treaty with Germany.[58] Wilson also received more than thirty cables from Irish-American organizations, each complaining about article ten of the covenant.

By the end of May 1919, as the terms of the peace treaty were finalized and circulated to the smaller nations, the issue of gaining US Senate approval for the treaty became more urgent for Wilson. News from home confirmed that the Republicans continued to lead the opposition to it. Polk wrote to Auchincloss 'I wish the President was coming home a little sooner, confidentially as people are getting restless.' A few weeks later he warned that, as well as opposing the treaty, the 'Republicans are very resentful of the fact that Lloyd George has been getting on pleasantly with the President.' He felt that the bonds between the Republicans, 'the extreme Irish and even ... the Germans' were tightening every day Wilson was absent.[59] The news provoked discussions within Wilson's circle in Paris as to whether submission of the treaty to the Senate could be avoided.[60] By the end of May, supporters of the treaty were openly fearful about its approval by the Senate. Tumulty cabled Wilson on 26 May to emphasize that every Republican member of the new Senate Foreign Relations Committee was 'openly opposed to Treaty ... There is a decided reaction against the League, caused, in my opinion, by dissatisfaction of Irish, Jews, Mediterranean, Poles, Italians and Germans.' He identified other reasons for the opposition as being Wilson's absence from the US, a lack of publicity for US gains in Paris and information on 'so-called compromises.' Although Tumulty was not disturbed by the reaction against the League of Nations, considering it inevitable, he advised that only a dedicated campaign spearheaded by Wilson could defeat the 'vicious drive' against it.[61] Despite all the difficulties, Tumulty had faith in Wilson's power of persuasion, as did the president himself and, therefore, as the proceedings moved towards a close in Paris, his attitude towards the Irish-Americans both in Paris and the US remained uncompromising and even hardened, if that was possible.

On 29 May, Baker recorded a conversation with Wilson about Ireland. Baker told him of a phone call that he had received from Louis Marshall, the Jewish-American leader, and of his assertion that 'all oppressed minorities in the world, religious or political' would be for the League to which Wilson replied:

"All the minorities except the Irish."
"Yes", I [Baker] said, 'the Irish seem unhappy. Walsh and Dunne are in my office every day with a new letter or manifesto."

58 Carroll, *The American commission on Irish independence*, Walsh to Lansing, 26, 27 May; ibid., Walsh to Wilson, 28 May 1919; ibid., Walsh to Henry White, 27 May 1919. 59 YULMC, FLPP, box 1, file 022, Polk to Auchincloss, 21 April 1919; ibid., 5 May 1919. 60 Tumulty, *Wilson*, p. 401; Davis & Fleming, *The ambassadorial diary*, 20 March 1919, p. 74. 61 *PWW*, 59, Tumulty to Wilson, 26 May 1919.

"I don't know how long I shall be able to resist telling them what I think of their miserable mischief-making," said the President, almost savagely. "They can see nothing except their own small interest. They were at first against the League because it contained a reference to the interference of outsiders with the 'domestic affairs' of other nations, thinking that it prevented Irish-Americans from taking part in Irish affairs. Now they are attacking Article X because they assert that it limits the right of revolution. As a matter of fact Article X safeguards the right of revolution by providing that the members of the League shall respect and preserve the integrity of nations only against 'external aggression'."[62]

Wilson, who was already disgruntled with the ACII in Paris, now began to identify his Irish-American opponents as a source of serious opposition in the US to the treaty. Moreover, the intertwining of the Republicans and the Irish-Americans at home intensified the pressure for him to do something for the Irish. On 29 May, Senator Borah introduced a resolution to the Senate which urged the American Commission to secure a hearing for the Sinn Féin delegates before the peace conference.[63] When Baker met Wilson two days later, the latter spoke of '"these mischief makers" Walsh and Dunne and the trouble they are endeavouring to stir up in America.' Indeed, Walsh had kept in constant contact with Cohalan.[64] The president's negative view of the ACII was shared by Lansing, House and American Commissioner Henry White who described them as 'meddlers.'[65]

By 24 May, Walsh had accepted that there was no chance of the Sinn Féin delegates being allowed to appear before the peace conference, decided to adopt another approach and penned a letter to Wilson which requested the opportunity for the two Irish-Americans to present the case themselves.[66] The request was ignored. It was a strategy which was not only unacceptable to the American negotiators but was unrealistic, mainly because the 'Big Four' were engaged in negotiations on the four final but vital points of reparations, the League of Nations, Upper Silesia and the military occupation of the Rhine. Walsh's request had also been superseded by the passage of the Borah resolution in the Senate on 6 June by a vote of 61 votes in favour with only 1 opposing. Now Wilson was officially obliged to act on the Irish case, but he knew that any delay in signing the treaty might prove fatal to it and endanger Anglo–American relations.[67] It

62 Baker, *American chronicle*, pp. 434–5.   63 M. Hopkinson, 'President Woodrow Wilson and the Irish question', 101.   64 *PWW*, 59, Diary of Ray Stannard Baker, 31 May 1919; *DIFP*, i, O'Ceallaigh to Dublin, 24 May 1919, pp. 15–16. Walsh told O'Ceallaigh, on 24 May, 'the fight must be transferred to the United States.' Every detail of their trip was reported in the *Gaelic American*.   65 A. Nevins, *Henry White: thirty years of American diplomacy* (1930), p. 454; *PWW*, 59, Walsh and Dunne to Wilson, 28 May 1919; ibid., diary of House, 31 May 1919; ibid., 60, Walsh to Wilson 2 June 1919. 66 *DIFP*, i, O'Ceallaigh to Dublin, 24 May 1919, pp. 15–16; *PWW*, 59, Walsh and Dunne to Wilson, 31 May 1919.   67 *PWW*, 60, Polk to Lansing, 6 June 1919. One senator voted against, John Sharp Williams from Mississippi, the champion of Anglo-Saxon America, who declared, 'I consider it

was against this background of intense pressure that Wilson used his final meeting with the ACII to publicly vent his true feelings on the Irish situation.

Before that meeting took place, an anxious Tumulty urged Grayson on 7 June
to emphasize to Wilson 'the real intensity of feeling' about the Irish question.
He felt it was 'growing every day and is not at all confined to Irishmen.' He
wished Wilson 'could do just a little for I fear reaction here upon League of
Nations.' Wilson replied the following day:

> The American Committee of Irishmen have made it exceedingly difficult,
> if not impossible, to render the assistance we were diligently trying to ren-
> der in the matter of bringing the Irish aspirations to the attention of the
> Peace Congress. By our unofficial activity in the matter we had practically
> cleared the way for the coming of the Irish representatives to Paris when
> the American committee went to Ireland and behaved in a way which so
> inflamed English opinion that the situation has got out of hand, and we
> are utterly at a loss how to act in the matter without involving the gov-
> ernment of the United States with the Government of Great Britain in a
> way which might create an actual breach between the two. I made an effort
> yesterday in this matter which shows, I am afraid, the utter futility of
> future efforts. I am distressed that the American committee should have
> acted with such extreme indiscretion and lack of sense, and can at the
> moment see nothing further to do.[68]

It is evident that Wilson believed that he and the other commissioners had been
active on the passport matter on behalf of the US citizens, and were close to success. But Wilson, like Lloyd George, blamed the Irish-Americans for ruining
these efforts and preventing any future actions on it. It was also clear that he
would only act unofficially on behalf of the Irish and that that such action would
always be in the context of the wider US–British relationship, which was so central to his Paris strategy. In the short term, at least, he valued British support in
Paris more highly than Tumulty's warnings about alienating the Irish-American
voter. Tumulty restated his arguments on 9 June when he wrote 'I hope you will
not allow indiscretions of Walsh and others to influence your judgement against
Ireland. Lloyd George's mistakes in handling this will be his undoing; for it has
in it the elements of a revolution. It is our own political situation here and the
facts of the treaty itself that concern me.'[69] It was Tumulty, with his finger on
the pulse of public opinion and his contacts in the Irish community in the US
and Ireland, rather than Wilson, who had isolated himself in Paris, whose judgement was to be proved correct.[70]

ill-advised and none of our business.' See E. Cuddy, '"Are the Bolsheviks any worse than the Irish?":
ethno-religious conflict in America during the 1920s', 15; G.H. Haynes, *The senate of the United
States: its history and practice*, 2 vols (1960), i, p. 983.   68 *PWW*, 60, Tumulty to Grayson, 7 June
1919.   69 Ibid., Tumulty to Wilson, 9 June 1919.   70 Arthur Willert told Lord Northcliffe, 'it is

There had been numerous opportunities for Wilson to discuss a hearing on Ireland with Lloyd George, Clemenceau or Orlando during the conference which could have gone a long way towards appeasing Irish-Americans and serving Tumulty's needs.[71] Indeed Wilson's unwillingness to embarrass the British government was recognized by Lloyd George who felt that Wilson has been 'eminently fair' every time any Irish question was mentioned to him' and this did not change when it came to handling the Borah resolution.[72]

House described the resolution supporters as 'irresponsible politicians', while Wilson regarded it as an infringement on British sovereignty and 'an unfriendly act' and was annoyed that the Irish representatives in Paris and the US were trying to place his administration 'in a false light' before the US public. He had no intention of permitting the Borah resolution to annoy the British government or the delicate balance of US–British relations at the conference. Nevertheless, the president approached Lloyd George on 9 June, during a meeting of the Council of Four and asked him 'whether it would embarrass him if the matter were to be brought up before the Big Four.' Lloyd George told Wilson that he 'could not consent to hear the Irish in any way' because a parliamentary crisis would be precipitated in London and 'it would be very likely that the government would be overthrown.' Wilson told him that he 'appreciated his approach in the matter very much, and that in any action he would take, he would be careful not to embarrass the Premier.'[73] The following day Wilson discussed the matter with Lansing and the other American commissioners who recommended that they would write to Clemenceau asking him 'to lay' the resolution 'before the peace conference.'[74] Wilson agreed with this minimum strategy, and on 16 June he forwarded the resolution to Clemenceau, who did not act on the matter.

Wilson's final meeting with the Irish-American delegation took place on 11 June. It was a 'very frank and open' meeting that deeply affected Walsh and left Dunne in tears by the end of it. When Walsh pressed him about applying self-determination to Ireland he replied that it was the 'great metaphysical tragedy of today' and came close to admitting that he had not fully thought through the implications of self-determination, something which Lansing had identified in December 1918.[75] The meeting ended as badly as that of 4 March and afterwards

no exaggeration to say that the Irish are now more active against us than they have ever been and those whose business it is to know say that all over the place the old German activities are starting again ... you can realise the effect of this with senators ... the Peace conference has, on the one hand, tried to let virtually every oppressed nationalist in Europe have "self-determination" and, on the other hand, has not hesitated to interfere with nationalist independence ... the demand will grow that the convenience of the [British] empire be allowed to go hang ... I find sane and friendly people ... taking this line.' See BLMD, NP, Add. 62255, Willert to Northcliffe, 13 June 1919. 71 See for example *PWW*, 60, Hankey's notes of a meeting of the council of four, 11 June 1919, 11.00 am, 5.45 pm. 72 Ibid., Diary of Grayson, 9 June 1919. 73 YULMC, EHP, box 91, file 3141, House to Plunkett, 13 June 1919; *PWW*, 60, Diary of Grayson, 12 June 1919; ibid., Diary of Grayson, 9 June 1919. 74 *PWW*, 60, Wilson to Lansing, 10 June 1919; ibid., American commissioners to Wilson, 10 June 1919. 75 At the Irish-Americans' meeting with Lansing on 6 June they gave him

Wilson spoke of the continued 'trouble' the Irish-Americans were making for him.[76] Despite his sympathy for the Irish cause, the Irish-Americans' behaviour had greatly irritated him. In early summer 1919, Wilson's policy of non-intervention in the domestic affairs of Britain and Ireland, prompted by diplomatic concerns, personal annoyance and a continued opposition to hyphenism, remained intact. This final meeting with Wilson ended the ACII's mission, although the members continued writing letters to the American commissioners, presenting petitions and resolutions passed by the American Federation of Labour and the US Senate. They also threatened to work towards the failure of the treaty in the US unless they were heard at the conference. Walsh and Dunne departed for the US on 20 June, thereby ending the Paris phase of the Friends of Irish Freedom campaign for recognition of self-determination for Ireland.[77]

The Irish-American delegation had failed in its mission to get passports for the Sinn Féin leadership or to get a hearing of Ireland's case at the peace conference for either the Irish leadership or themselves. Dunne concluded that it 'was in part a failure, and partly a big success'.[78] O'Ceallaigh wrote to Cohalan and Devoy that the mission was successful with many achievements.[79] By this time the Anglo-Irish war of independence was gathering pace and O'Ceallaigh measured the mission's success in terms of its publicity and propaganda value, believing that since the ACII's arrival in Paris 'there is not a part of the world, no matter how distant, in which the cause of Ireland has not been advertised.'[80] In Ireland, Hathaway recorded that the ACII visit provided an immense fillip to the Sinn Féin movement as a whole while on an individual level, Patricia Lavelle, a Sinn Féin member, recalled 'I remember less of what they said than what they meant to us, something outside of Ireland herself and working for her freedom.'[81]

Carroll queries whether the Irish-American group was really interested in getting a hearing at the peace conference at all or whether they were just gaining publicity.[82] Undoubtedly the publicity value for the fledgling Sinn Féin government of the Irish-Americans' activities in Paris and Ireland was immense. Sharp was convinced that the visit combined with the Senate resolution endorsed the Sinn Féin movement and strengthened its cause to the extent of carrying the

a copy of their report on Ireland which detailed in highly charged language the atrocious conditions prevailing there, particularly in Mountjoy prison in Dublin. It was published in Ireland and the US. The attendant publicity led the British government to issue a ten-page rebuttal. *PWW*, 60, Diary of Grayson, 11 June 1919, see also Hearings before the Committee on Foreign Relations, pp. 835–8; LC, RLP, vol. 43, report of an interview Lansing with Walsh, 6 June 1919.   76 *PWW*, 60, Diary of Edith Benham 11 June 1919.   77 Walsh and Dunne wrote to Clemenceau again on 27 June but did not receive a reply. The Irish Race Convention sent John A. Murphy and L.S. Trigg to Paris on 28 June and they took over from Walsh and Dunne lobbying and writing letters until the end of August. Carroll, *The American commission on Irish independence*, pp. 19–20.   78 Dunne, 'Ireland at the Paris Peace Sessions' in Fitzgerald, *The voice of Ireland*, p. 224.   79 AIHS, DFCP, Box 13, folder 4, Ó'Ceallaigh to Cohalan, 27 June 1919.   80 Ibid.   81 NARA, RG59, M580/214, 841d.00/71, Hathaway to Lansing, 11 July 1919; P. Lavelle, *James O'Mara: a staunch Sinn Féiner* (1961), p. 136.   82 Carroll, *American opinion*, pp. 136, 257, fn 41.

'reign of crime' in the south of Ireland into his Ulster district.[83] However, Carroll's judgement may be somewhat harsh. Firstly, it minimizes the appeal which Wilson's war aims, particularly self-determination, held for many ethnic minorities. Secondly, representatives of many groups had flocked to Paris in the hope of getting a hearing from the conference as a whole, or from delegates of the 'Big Four', for their claim to self-determination. But, in addition, each of the nationalist groups that claimed independence recognized the importance of publicising its respective cause and gathering allies. The republican Irish in America and Ireland were no different and were the best at self-publicity anyway. Nonetheless, if the success of the Irish-American and Sinn Féin representatives' mission in Paris is measured in terms of publicity then it was successful, but in terms of fulfilling their specific aims it failed. Davis commented in June that the ACII's visit to Ireland had raised 'the hopes' of Irish republicans about winning self-determination and caused 'considerable apprehension' within the London administration, but he thought it too early to say what the 'real results' would be.[84]

Some consequences were immediate. When details of Wilson's final interview with the Irish-Americans were published in the US, Wilson's stock with Irish-America fell to its lowest point. The signing of the treaty of Versailles on 29 June did not improve the situation. It was, and could only be, a compromise between Wilson's fourteen idealistic and often impracticable points and the demands of the allied governments. It represented less than he sought and more than his opponents wished. Furthermore, the treaty seemed to be a victory for Britain and confirmed Wilson's anglophilism, particularly when it emerged that the British empire would have six votes in the proposed League of Nations assembly and the US one. Tumulty and Baker suggested that taking into account all the other claims for self-determination that were being put to Wilson at the time, he had paid a substantial amount of attention to the Irish case.[85] But this did not translate into action as it did for other previously subject peoples. Baker recalled that on 27 June, the day before the treaty was signed, Wilson told the press correspondents that 'all things considered, the Treaty adheres more ... to the Fourteen points than I had a right to expect ... Think of the positive achievements of the peace – the newly liberated peoples, who had never before dared dream of freedom, the Poles, the Czechoslovaks, the Slavs, the peoples of Turkey.'[86] The Irish-Americans felt betrayed, while the German-Americans believed the treaty's terms to be too harsh, the reparations payments too large

---

83 NARA, RG59, M580/213, 841d.00/59, Sharp to Secretary of State, 10 June 1919. Walsh notes that numerous attempts were made to discredit the Irish-American group both at the time and later. One of the most influential was the published diary of Lieutenant Colonel Stephen Bonsal, a military adviser to the American Commission, who implied that the Irish-Americans were drunk and violent in Ireland. For further see J.P. Walsh, 'Woodrow Wilson historians vs. the Irish', 55–65. 84 Ibid., M580/7, 841.00/159, Davis to Secretary of State, 26 May 1919.   85 Duff, 'The Versailles Treaty', 598.   86 Baker, *American chronicle*, p. 453.

and the war guilt clause unjust and the Italian-Americans were furious at the loss of Fiume to Yugoslavia. To other Americans, the Shantung settlement, which gave German territory in China to Japan, appeared to favour the latter as did article ten, the most contentious part of the covenant.[87] But the Paris episode undoubtedly confirmed that the most effective instrument by which the Irish sympathizers had achieved results remained the US Congress and not the presidency or indeed the State Department.

Irish-America and the fate of the peace settlement

Wilson arrived back in the US on 8 July. He believed that he could persuade the US public and politicians to support the treaty by appealing to their patriotism and loyalty. Lansing put it in harsher terms, saying '[Wilson] is going back with blood in his eye and his loins girded for battle.'[88] The president expected that his personality and powers of persuasion would win public opinion to his side and overcome his treasonous Irish-American opponents. But he told Baker on 31 May and Edith Benham, Mrs Wilson's secretary, on 11 June, that if Irish-America continued to make 'trouble', he had 'one terrible weapon' to use against them. He would publicize documents to show that opposition to the League of Nations was inspired by the Roman Catholic hierarchy and Vatican authorities.[89] This threat to introduce the religious card and, by extension, the patriotic card into the debate about the peace settlement to frighten off non-Catholics from opposing it, revealed his determination to face down his opponents by using all manner of tactics necessary.

Wilson's return was greeted by the cheers of the crowd along Fifth Avenue in New York city, but Congress was not so easily mesmerized by his presence. The German-, Italian- and Irish-Americans had cemented their ties with the Republicans and disaffected Democrats, in order to defeat the treaty and particularly the League. There was no organized front, but as the Senate, and specifically the Foreign Relations Committee, was the key forum, Borah and Lodge, the committee chairman, led the anti-treaty opposition there. Twelve Republican irreconcilables resolutely opposed the new international organizations, primarily because it undermined the Senate's constitutional authority over foreign policy and represented the abandonment of US non-involvement in European affairs. Wiseman, who had returned to the US in July 1919, described their position as 'violently anti-British and anti-European generally.'[90] It was fortuitous for the two senators that the fight coincided with Wilson's difficulties with the Irish-American delega-

87 J.M. Blum, *Joe Tumulty and the Wilson era* (1951), p. 181.   88 YULMC, FLPP, box 3, file 304, Lansing to Polk, 4 June 1919.   89 *PWW*, 59, Diary of Baker, 31 May 1919; ibid., 60, Diary of Edith Benham, 11 June 1919.   90 L.E Ambrosius, *Woodrow Wilson and the American diplomatic tradition* (1987), p. 174.

tion in Paris. Borah became a link between the Irish-Americans and the irreconcilables in Congress. Significantly, he never promised Cohalan that the Republicans
would adopt the Irish cause in return for his support. But, in the interim, Borah
went on speaking tours throughout the US during spring 1919 to counteract support for the treaty and League of Nations. Wherever possible he spoke to Irish-
Americans and was in daily contact with Cohalan throughout the campaign.[91]

A further reason for Irish-American mobilization against the Paris proposals
centred on Eamon de Valera, who had arrived undetected in the US on 11 June,
much to Ambassador Davis' surprise.[92] But Polk and Roland Lindsay in the
British embassy, who discussed de Valera's presence many times during June,
agreed on the importance of not making a 'martyr of him.' Both believed that
the Irish leader had entered the country illegally and Polk set about investigating the circumstances of that event.[93] Nonetheless, de Valera's unveiling was
orchestrated by the FOIF on 23 June, at a press conference at the Waldorf
Astoria Hotel in New York. His first public statement in the US began

> I am in America as the official head of the Republic established by the
> will of the Irish people in accordance with the principle of self-determi-
> nation ... We shall fight for a real democratic League of Nations, not the
> present unholy alliance which does not fulfil the purposes for which the
> democracies of the world went to war. I am going to ask the American
> people to give us a real League of Nations, one that will include Ireland.
>   I well recognise President Wilson's difficulties in Paris. I am sure that
> if he is sincere, nothing will please him more than being pushed from
> behind by the people for this will show him that the people of America
> want the United States government to recognise the Republic of Ireland.[94]

In addition to gaining recognition for the republic from the US government,
the Sinn Féin leader wanted to float a Dáil Éireann loan on the New York stock
exchange and win Irish-American support for the economic development of
Ireland.[95] His first statement seemed to align him with Wilson. Lindsay believed

91 Ward, *Ireland and Anglo-American relations*, p. 194.   92 NARA, RG59, M580/213, 841d.oo/58,
Davis to Secretary of State, 23 June 1919. A hint of the 'German plot' was revived when US Minister
Stovall reported from Berne that the German press reported de Valera's movements before his arrival
in the US. Ibid., 841d.oo/60, Stovall to Secretary of State, 1 July 1919.   93 NARA, RG59,
M580/213, 841d.oo/58, Polk to Davis, 25 June 1919; *BDFA*, i, Lindsay to Curzon, 28 June 1919.
Ray Stannard Baker told Frank Polk on May 1918 that de Valera's 'history makes him a hero.'
YULMC, FLPP, box 37, file 371, Baker to Polk, 18 May 1918.   94 Quoted in McCartan, *With de
Valera*, p. 145; *Gaelic American*, 29 June 1919.   95 Doorley, *Irish-American diaspora nationalism*, pp.
105–12. There was even a song published in his honour, 'There'll never be a League of Nations
without Ireland'. J. Bowman, 'De Valera on Ulster, 1919–20: what he told America', 4. Even in 1962
de Valera felt that Cohalan had prevented him from addressing the US Congress. University College
Dublin Archives (hereafter UCDA), Éamon de Valera Papers (hereafter ÉVP), P150/1100, 19
November 1962, Recollections by de Valera of his American mission, June 1919 to December 1920.

that de Valera's presence would not strengthen the 'temporary alliance' that had arisen between the Republicans and the Irish-Americans over the League of Nations.[96] But in mid-July, Wiseman believed that de Valera's arrival would adversely affect Wilson's fight for the settlement.[97] Tumulty also warned Wilson, on 25 June, that de Valera's arrival 'is going to intensify feeling and Republicans will take full advantage.'[98] Tumulty's analysis was right. One week after his press conference, de Valera embarked on a nation wide speaking tour organized by the Friends. He met representatives from politics, religion and educational interests and made seventeen public speeches, delivered numerous addresses and received extensive coverage in Boston, Chicago, New York and San Francisco newspapers. On 30 June in Manchester, New Hampshire, the Irish president described the treaty as a 'mockery.' But he did not object to the principle underpinning article ten, so long as it was 'based on just conditions from the start.' This reasoning confused many Irish-Americans who saw the settlement as pro-British.[99] By 11 July, Lindsay regarded de Valera's presence as a 'menace' and worried that Congress could force Wilson to intervene on Ireland.[1] De Valera did attempt to get his views 'conveyed' to Wilson but suspected that he would not 'change.' He was correct but the Irish president continued to hope and, therefore, refrained from attacks on Wilson and his administration, unlike his hosts.[2] But it was difficult to remain aloof. When Cohalan brought de Valera to the Congress, Democratic Senator Thomas Walsh took umbrage that 'they came so see none of us [Democrats], but confided their purpose and aspirations to Borah.'[3] Although de Valera favoured a non-partisan approach to achieve his aims he permitted Cohalan to act as a conduit between himself and Congress until March 1920, thereby approving the Republican alliance with nationalist Irish-America.[4]

Tumulty was hopeful that the US public was largely supportive of Wilson and his proposals. He had reported to Wilson the defeat of the Knox resolution and the adoption by the American Federation of Labour of a resolution favouring the League of Nations. But, ominously, he also noted that the resolution contained a reservation in favour of independence for Ireland, included at Frank P. Walsh's insistence.[5] In addition, 32 state legislatures and 33 state governors supported it as did a majority of the nation's newspapers. But it was the alignment in the Senate which was crucial to Wilson. Not only had he not included senators as part of the American Commission in Paris but he had permitted the inter-

96 BDFA, i, Lindsay to Curzon, 28 June 1919.   97 Ambrosius, Woodrow Wilson, p. 234.   98 PWW, 61, Tumulty to Wilson, 25 June 1919.   99 K. O'Doherty, Assignment America: Éamon de Valera's mission to the United States (1957), pp. 49–50; Coogan, De Valera, pp. 145–9.   1 BDFA, i, Lindsay to Curzon, 11 July 1919.   2 DIFP, i, Dáil Éireann report on foreign affairs, 19 August 1919; ibid., de Valera to Griffith, 21 August 1919.   3 MD, LC, TJWP, Box 190, Walsh to Scanlon, 14 October 1919.   4 DIFP, i, Eamon de Valera to all members of the cabinet (Dublin), 10 March 1920.   5 The Knox resolution sought to limit the peace conference to deciding on the treaty with Germany only and not the League of Nations. PWW, 61, Tumulty to Wilson, 21 June 1919. The issue of Irish independence was a source of disagreement between Irish nationalists such as Walsh and Gompers at four AFL annual conventions between 1918 and 1921. See McKillen, Chicago labor, p. 117.

linking of the Treaty of Versailles with the covenant of the League of Nations, even though he knew it would be unacceptable to a majority of the Senate Foreign Relations Committee.[6] Firstly, it entailed the abandonment of the Monroe Doctrine, specifically it failed to ensure that US interests were adequately protected. Secondly, article ten, relating to territorial integrity, threatened to minimize the Senate's authority to declare war and potentially could commit the US to involvement in quarrels that did not concern them. The third factor was the vagueness of article eleven, which, in Wilson's words, stated that 'every matter which is likely to affect the peace of the world is everybody's business.' Consequently, in July 1919, 43 of 47 Democrats supported the treaty and only 16 Republicans opposed it, while the majority of the Republicans supported ratification if the treaty was amended to protect US interests. In other words, more than two-thirds of the Senate favoured ratification and US membership of the League of Nations. However, it was the 16 irreconcilables who dominated the Senate Foreign Relations Committee and were succeeding in stalling ratification during July and August, while at the same time campaigning against it.[7]

Wiseman visited Washington at this stage where he met with members of the Wilson administration and leading Republicans. He identified three lines of attack on the treaty within the Republican Party. There were the extremists, led by Borah and Hiram Johnson, who were 'violently anti-British', entirely opposed to the League of Nations and against any US participation in foreign affairs, thus constituting the 'most troublesome body' in 'American politics at the moment.' The second group was the reservationists, led by Lodge and Philander C. Knox, who were primarily inspired by 'personal hatred of Wilson' but were only 'reluctantly anti-British.'[8] The third group comprised of the majority of the Republican Party who had not yet committed for or against the settlement. Lodge's role was significant to events. He had believed Wilson to be an appeaser during the Mexican revolution and the German submarine attacks in the early days of the war.[9] But he was also an American nationalist who represented Boston with its strong Irish-American vote and his dilemma was apparent in a note he sent to Henry White in July 1919:

> Wilson's attitude has forced the Irish question to the front. The resolution of sympathy for Ireland, demanding a hearing – which I think their representatives were entitled to – was brought about by Wilson's attitude and it may assume a very much more serious aspect. You know what the Irish vote is in this country. As far as I can make out, they are bitterly opposed to the League, and the fate of the Democratic party in the northern states is in their hands. They are having great meetings and all pronouncing against the League.[10]

6 Haynes, *The senate*, pp. 598, 696.   7 Link, *American epoch*, p. 150.   8 YULMC, WWP, box 9, file 213, Wiseman to Malcolm, 1–2 July 1919.   9 Ward, *Ireland and Anglo-American relations*, p. 195; LaFeber, *American age*, pp. 326–7.   10 Nevins, *Henry White*, p. 445.

Wiseman believed that Wilson could force the Senate to ratify the treaty without amendment or reservation. But he recognized that 'all' Irish-Americans complained that Wilson had lost a 'unique' opportunity by not pressing their case at the peace conference. Wiseman felt that this permitted the 'extremists' to steer Irish-America against the treaty.[11]

When Wilson formally presented the treaty to the Senate chamber on 10 July, it was not as a project upon which he wanted advice but as a 'completed instrument.' He was in a triumphant mood. He urged and expected prompt and unqualified approval of the 'hope of mankind.'[12] Wilson also offered his 'services' and 'information' to the Foreign Relations Committee but many weeks passed before the committee showed any interest in meeting with him.[13] After Wilson left the chamber, the first action of the Senate was to order the removal of secrecy from the treaty and refer it to its Foreign Relations Committee, which now consisted of ten Republicans and seven Democrats, with the result that the committee was packed with men opposed to the League of Nations. The removal of secrecy resulted in the printing of the treaty, in arrangements being made by the committee for public hearings and in the decision that the vote on the treaty would be held in open session.[14] Daniel T. O'Connell, director of the Friends of Irish Freedom national bureau in Washington, had also been lobbying Republican senators on the committee to grant a public hearing on the treaty question. No Democrat was advised of the plan.[15] By now Wilson believed that 'Irish extremists' were deliberately trying to wreck the treaty.[16]

Edward Grey, former British foreign secretary, who was in Washington as temporary ambassador of the British government during the hearings, attended some of the sessions. He commented on the high quality of the debate, but senators also took the opportunity of open sessions, the presence of the press and recording into the *Congressional Record* to talk to the galleries and to address their own and constituents' issues.[17] A complex array of forces was lined up against Wilson during the summer hearings: a Republican-dominated Senate, the hyphenates and the Hearst newspapers. Testimony was presented on behalf of Albania, Estonia, Fiume, Greece, Hungary, India, Ireland, Yugoslavia, Latvia, Lithuania and the Ukraine.

The Irish hearing took place on 30 August and, of the committee members, all the Republican senators except McCumber attended, but only two of the Democrats, Swanson and Pittman, were present. One hundred and fifteen Irish-Americans presented themselves before the committee. Also present was a group of British-Americans, who presented a written document which did not oppose

11 YULMC, WWP, box 9, file 213, Wiseman to Malcolm, 1–2 July 1919; Lee Levin, *Edith and Woodrow*, p. 321. 12 Link, *Wilson: the diplomatist*, p. 131; Haynes, *The senate*, p. 584. 13 Haynes, *The senate*, pp. 602, 700. Later on in August, when he met the fifteen Republican senators, each told him the treaty could not pass without some reservations. Ibid. fn 1. 14 Ibid., pp. 669, fn. 3, 700. 15 D.T. O'Connell, 'Irish influence on America's foreign policy' in Fitzgerald, *The voice of Ireland*, p. 237. 16 YULMC, WWP, box 1, file 11, Wiseman to Balfour, 18 July 1919. 17 Haynes, *The senate*, pp. 669, fn. 3, p. 700.

or support the treaty but protested at Sinn Féin and Irish-American organiza-
tions 'thrusting' the Irish question into the Senate hearings. De Valera did not
attend. The influential Republican career diplomat who had been in Paris, Henry
White, objected to Cohalan's demand that de Valera be granted a hearing because
Irish aspirations had 'nothing to do with the making of peace.' But Lodge replied
that 'neither did the Monroe Doctrine come within the jurisdiction of the Peace
Conference.'[18] Eight Irish-Americans spoke at the hearing, including Frank P.
Walsh, Michael J. Ryan and Edward F. Dunne. Each gave an account of their
problems when trying to get a hearing for the Irish cause in Paris and of the
dreadful conditions in Ireland. They also presented their correspondence with
the American commissioners and the British delegation in Paris but said nothing of the efforts made by Wilson, House and Lansing on their behalf.[19]

At the end of a long day, the hearing concluded with a statement from William
Bourke Cockran, the New York politician: 'If, after having entered this war for
the cause which Mr Wilson defined when he appeared before both houses of
Congress, there should be a betrayal of the blood which was shed to make that
cause triumphant, the loss not to Ireland alone, but to the whole world, would be
a calamity immeasurable, irreparable.' Lodge described the speech as 'one of the
greatest speeches ever delivered inside the walls of the Congress.'[20] The Irish testimony was impressive and Walsh later recalled that the senators expressed their
sympathy for the Irish cause and praised them for opposing the League.
Interestingly Irish men were also involved in some of the other cases. Dudley F.
Malone presented the Indian case to the committee, while Frank P. Walsh coached
Joseph W. Folk, a former governor of Missouri, who presented Egypt's case. A
statement supporting the treaty was submitted on behalf of Irish unionists.[21]

Most of the witnesses who were called condemned or criticized the treaty,
but no testimony was sought to help explain the purpose of international co-
operation to prevent war. Nor did Wilson elucidate his position to the committee members. It was not until after 19 August that he began to meet the senators.[22] However, even when he talked with supporters, he did not offer much
practical help on how best to proceed.[23] Senator Thomas J. Walsh met Wilson
on 16 July and they discussed Ireland and the treaty fight. Walsh, like Tumulty
and House, was concerned about the 'formidable opposition' that had built up

18 D.J. McCarthy, 'The British' in O'Grady, *The immigrants*, p. 105; L. Gerson, *The hyphenate in
recent American politics and diplomacy* (1964), p. 103.   19 Carroll, *The American commission on Irish
independence*, pp. 23–5. Frank P. Walsh requested Lansing to have the Irish Commission's report
transmitted by the State Department to the Senate but Lansing refused to do so. Instead it was read
into the *Congressional Record* by senators. NARA, RG59, M580/214, 841d.00/99, Walsh to Lansing,
26 August 1919; ibid., 841d.00/100, Walsh to Lansing, 19 September 1919; ibid., 841d.00/101,
Lansing to Walsh, 20 October 1919.   20 'The cause of Ireland and its relations to the League of
Nations. Statement by Hon W. Bourke Cockran Before the Committee on Foreign Relations of the
United States Senate. 30 August 1919' (reprint, 1919).   21 Ward, *Ireland and Anglo-American relations*, p. 198.   22 Haynes, *The senate*, p. 716.   23 Duff, 'The Versailles Treaty', 598.

against the League and he wanted Wilson to make a public gesture towards the Irish-Americans. Wilson replied, 'I am not sure that it would be wise at the present time to act.'[24] He did not tell Walsh that at this time House was meeting with Edward Grey in Washington and both men agreed that Ireland must get home rule.[25] Even though House and Wilson were not as close as they had been in March 1919 and Grey received little support from the British government for his views on Ireland, the House–Grey meetings could have been presented to Wilson's struggling political allies as another attempt by the Wilson administration to help find a settlement for Ireland.[26] Instead, in mid-summer 1919, Wilson still believed that the peace proposals would be approved and he doggedly stuck to non-intervention on Ireland. Neither was he affected by reports of the escalating war of independence in Ireland sent by Hathaway and Sharp.[27]

The FOIF leadership, however, was buoyed by news of the intensification of the war of independence in Ireland. The Irish Victory Fund totalled $1,005,080.83 by 31 August and not only financed de Valera's speaking tour in the US but also paid for the printing and distribution of anti-League pamphlets, posters, advertizements, cables and letters to newspapers, politicians and the State Department.[28] This lobbying led Lansing to ask Wilson for a reply to the volumes of letters on the Irish question being received in the department and to clarify the exact nature of US policy on Ireland. No direction was received. Nor did Wilson give any hope to his loyal supporter Senator James D. Phelan, in California, who complained to him, on 31 August, that 'the Irish are in a fair way to leave the Democratic Party.' Unsurprisingly, this view heartened Lodge.[29]

---

24 *PWW*, 61, Walsh to Wilson, 17 July 1919; Carroll, *American opinion*, pp. 145–6. Walsh introduced his resolution to the Senate on 17 October at the urging of Michael Francis Doyle, the Democratic Party activist, in order to try and forge an alliance of moderate Democrats and Republicans. But it was too late by then and it was opposed even by the FOIF and did not come up for a vote.   25 NARA, RG59, M580/214, 841d.00/78/12, Note, 8 August 1919.   26 Egerton, 'Britain and the "Great Betrayal"', 892–3.   27 NARA, RG59, M580/214, 841d.00/71, Hathaway to Lansing, 11 July 1919; ibid., 841d.00/75, Sharp to Lansing, 17 July 1919; ibid., 841d.00/82, McAndrews to Secretary of State, 9 August 1919; ibid., 841d.00/90, McAndrews to Secretary of State, 17 September 1919. Hathaway highlighted the prohibition by the military authorities of a celebration of American Independence Day organized by the Cork Sinn Féin Executive for 4 July. Also he reported that the SS *Ashburn* ship owned by the US Shipping Board flew the Sinn Féin flag entering and departing the harbour of Queenstown. The incident attracted considerable attention with crowds of people turning up to cheer and wave flags. In view of the seriousness of the matter, the captain, William F. O'Brien, was deprived of his command and placed on the 'desirable list' of captains. Ibid., 841d.00/83, J.R. Ditmars to Lansing, 6 September 1919.   28 See AIHS, Friends of Irish Freedom Papers (FOIFP), Box 2, folder 2, Office of the National Secretary-statement regarding problems over use of funds. Also resolutions in favour of Irish independence were presented in the Congress. NARA, RG59, M580/214, 841d.00/89, House Joint Resolution No. 11, 12 August 1919.   29 LC, RLP, vol. 45, Lansing to Wilson 22 August 1919; Phelan quoted in Hopkinson, 'President Woodrow Wilson and the Irish question', 106. Wilson did not respond to a letter from Frank P. Walsh either. Writing on behalf of the American Commission on Irish Independence, on 16 August, Walsh suggested that a changed League of Nations with a joint secretariat which precluded the possibility of British dominance would be acceptable and secondly, he complained that the

By the end of August, it was clear that Wilson's strategy was faltering; firstly, he had failed to turn his opponents.[30] Secondly, the Senate hearings had generated great publicity, mostly unfavourable, about Wilson's behaviour in Paris and had fed doubts inside his own party about US obligations under the treaty which the Democratic State Committee of Massachusetts interpreted as supporting British policy in Ireland.[31] On 4 September, Lodge's Senate Foreign Relations Committee had passed forty-five amendments and four reservations to the peace treaty with the aid of the vote of Democratic Senator John K. Shields of Tennessee.[32] A final concern for Wilson was that the campaign against the League was gathering momentum outside Congress, largely as a result of Irish-American efforts. Wilson was forced to change his approach. He abandoned the carrot approach and took up the stick.[33] He had originally mooted a speaking tour in late July but Lansing and Democratic senators advised against it 'believing he could win more support' by staying in Washington.[34] On the night before the trip, Lansing still opposed it 'He [Wilson] starts off tomorrow night "to carry the war into Africa" ... I think that the President ought to be in the closest touch with Congress at this critical time and this means to be here in Washington. However, he has made up his mind and will leave as planned.' Not only did Lansing believe that Wilson was needed in Washington to defend the settlement against the 'fanatical' Republicans but he felt that the public was more interested in domestic issues such as the 'high cost of necessaries, strikes, industrial unrest, profiteering and similar subjects', than in the covenant and the treaty.[35] Even though the signs did not bode well for Wilson's mission, on 3 September he launched a nation-wide tour that lasted three weeks and covered 8,000 miles. He delivered more speeches than he had ever done before, even during election campaigns. His message was simple; he explained the provisions of the treaty and its purposes, answered criticisms about its harshness to Germany, the Shantung settlement and the damage to US interests and admitted that the treaty was not perfect but said that the weaknesses were balanced by its achievements such as the collective security system implemented through article ten. Finally, he reminded the public about US responsibility to provide world leadership.

When the tour began, Wilson was advised to make some special advances towards Irish-Americans, not only because of their opposition but also because stories of British oppression in Ireland were being widely publicized at the time.

State Department with British government support, had prevented John A. Murphy one of the Irish-American delegation who remained in Paris from going to London. Wilson, on Tumulty's advice, did thank Cardinal Gibbons for his support on the League. *PWW*, 62, Walsh to Wilson 16 August 1919; *PWW*, 61, Tumulty to Wilson, 25 July 1919; ibid., Wilson to Gibbons, 25 July 1919. **30** *PWW*, 61, Wiseman to Balfour, 18 July 1919. **31** Ibid., 62, O'Leary to Wilson, 26 July 1919. **32** Ambrosius, *Woodrow Wilson*, p. 174. **33** Link, *Diplomatist*, p. 140; Rear Admiral C.T. Grayson, *Woodrow Wilson, an intimate memoir*, second edition (1977), p. 95. **34** *Papers relating to the foreign relations of the United States* (hereafter *FRUS*), The Paris Peace Conference, 1919, 13 vols (1942–7), xi, Lansing to Polk, 31 July 1919. **35** YULMC, FLPP, box 9, file 314, Lansing to Polk, 2 September 1919.

However, he could not do so. Along with defending article ten, Wilson, when asked during his stop over in San Francisco on 17 September, about not hearing the Irish case in Paris, replied that the peace conference 'had no jurisdiction over any question of that sort which did not affect territories which belonged to the defeated empires.' His reply to a question about self-determination for Ireland was:

> My position on the subject of self-determination for Ireland is expressed in Article XI of the Covenant, in which I may say I was particularly interested because it seemed to me necessary for the peace and freedom of the world that a forum be created to which all peoples could bring any matter which was likely to affect the peace and freedom of the world.[36]

His speeches also attacked 'the hyphen' groups who had opposed the US government during the war and now wanted to destroy the League. In Denver he stated that 'the hyphen is the knife that is being stuck into this document.'[37] His feelings towards the Irish issue had not changed, even though he could have referred to House's presence in London where he discussed Ireland with Lloyd George, Grey and Balfour. But he had resisted all pressure to date to interfere in the domestic British problem and, even in his hour of need, he adhered to that approach.

It is difficult to know what effect Wilson had on the public. Every stage of his trip was counteracted by a publicity campaign organized by the Friends. Cohalan and the FOIF leadership had already placed full-page advertizements in newspapers of each city where he spoke. De Valera's speaking tour of the US had also resumed and senators Borah and Johnson respectively embarked on their speaking tours while the Hearst-owned newspapers maintained their opposition to the League and highlighted the Irish case. But the feeling grew within the Wilson camp that if the public reception could be translated into pressure on senators, their opponents might be defeated.[38]

Wilson had delivered thirty-six formal speeches in just twenty-three days and the effort took its toll. On 25 September, at Pueblo, Colorado, Wilson collapsed and returned to Washington immediately. On 2 October, he suffered a stroke

36 *PWW*, 63, 16 September 1919, p. 304.   37 Quoted in Ward, *Ireland and Anglo-American relations*, p. 206.   38 J.J. Splain, '"Under which King?" The tragic-comedy of President de Valera's errors in the United States' in Fitzgerald, *The voice of Ireland*, p. 243. De Valera received expenses totalling $26,748.26 from the Irish Victory Fund on 5 July, 26 September 1919 and 9 January 1920 towards his speaking tour. AIIHS, FOIFP, Box 2, file 2, Office of the National Secretary-Statement regarding problems over use of funds. See Blum, *Tumulty*, p. 211. The US State Department almost inadvertently accorded the Sinn Féin government formal recognition at this time. The Irish leadership requested Vice-President Marshall to send its thanks to the Senate for passage of the resolution of sympathy with Ireland for a government of their own choice in June. Marshall asked Wilson for advice and Wilson's instructions were interpreted to imply recognition for the Sinn Féin government. The letter was altered before it was returned to Marshall with Wilson's instruction that it would not be transmitted to the Senate. See NARA, RG59, M580/214, 841d.00/91, Marshall to Wilson, 29 August 1919; ibid., Lansing to Marshall, 1 October 1919.

which paralysed his left side. He could no longer arouse public support for the settlement, nor counteract the highly organized opposition either outside or inside Congress. He was removed from politics at the time when the Senate was moving towards the ratification vote. During September and October, the FOIF maintained pressure on the administration with letters and petitions demanding that the US government fulfil its wartime aims of making the world safe for democracy and that it recognize the Irish republic.[39] Senators were specifically targeted. Each senator was sent a list of twelve questions including 'Are you in favour of the League as submitted by President Wilson?' When Senator Joseph Frelinghuysen of New Jersey showed signs of supporting the League, Cohalan organized the posting of over seventy thousand cards, each demanding the defeat of the treaty and each signed by a New Jersey voter.[40] A second source of pressure came from the 'red scare', which gained momentum between June 1919 and January 1920. Ironically, the public's fear of bolshevism was exacerbated by Wilson himself. During his speaking tour he argued that only the League of Nations could defeat Lenin's apostles. Unfortunately for him Americans interpreted this as meaning that US membership of the League would increase contacts with bolshevism.[41] *The Times* journalist Arthur Willert who worked closely with British diplomats in the Washington embassy, concluded 'the President's tour was not a success. He was unable to counteract the effect of the chief lines of Republican ammunition ... then there is Ireland and other irritants.'[42]

On 19 November 1919, after many hours of negotiation, the US Senate moved to vote on the treaty. The vote on the treaty with Lodge's fourteen reservations was 41 voted in favour and 51 against, including the Democrats, on Wilson's instructions. The Senate voted down the treaty without reservations, by 38 to 53 votes. In neither vote did the treaty command the two-thirds majority required for ratification and the Senate adjourned until the new session in early December. Wilson's strategy had failed.[43] In the immediate aftermath of the vote, Cohalan wrote to Borah 'Heartiest congratulations. Greatest victory for country and liberty since Revolution largely due to you.' Borah replied on 22 November,

> You have rendered in this fight a service which no other man has rendered or could have rendered. Your country will always be under a debt of gratitude to you. In addition to that too much cannot be said in honour of the Irish people who have helped to make this great fight. Of course some people will say that they did it because of their dislike for England but I know

39 NARA, RG59, M580/214, 841d.oo/95, Ladies Auxiliary, Ancient Order of Hibernians to Lansing, 16 October 1919.   40 See AIHS, DCP, Box 1, folder 9, Questionnaire.   41 LaFeber, *The American age*, p. 329. A further dimension to the role of labour was that organized labour in Massachusetts changed its official policy to one of opposition on 8 September 1919 which strengthened senators Lodge and Walsh's opposition. R. Jeffreys-Jones, 'Massachusetts labour and the League of Nations controversy in 1919', 397.   42 BLMD, NP, Add. 62255, Willert to Northcliffe, 1 October 1919.   43 LaFeber, *The American age*, p. 329; Link et al., *American epoch*, p. 151.

from my experience during the last six months that they did it because of their love of America. Second, because of their profound sympathy for the country of their birth or their ancestors, and third because of their belief that this whole scheme was a scheme of oppression.[44]

From some viewpoints Borah's analysis was accurate. The Irish-American propaganda campaign had been highly organized, was nation-wide and had incorporated both congressional and public dimensions. Almost $750,000 of the Irish Victory Fund financed the campaign and the messages consistently related to American patriotism, self-determination for the Irish, recognition of the Irish republic, criticism of British policy in Ireland and outright opposition to the settlement. The Irish-American campaign had helped in the fight. But there were other factors also; the German and Italian agitation, the decision by Borah and Lodge to use the Irish issue in their campaign and the prevalence of an anti-British sentiment which Grey commented on in his dispatches to Curzon after his arrival in Washington.[45] In other words, the combination of hyphenism, Americanism, isolationism and anglophobia created a front which Wilson could not break down and his unwillingness to compromise made defeat on the treaty inevitable.

Nonetheless the Senate defeat on 19 November was not the end of the matter. After all, five-sixths of the Senate favoured a settlement of some sort, while public pressure, mainly by peace groups and international organizations, forced the Senate to reconsider the treaty again in March 1920, much to Cohalan's annoyance. In the interim the Irish issue intruded on congressional business in the form of the Mason legislation which attempted to get a congressional appropriation for a US diplomatic presence in Ireland. Following public hearings on 12 and 13 December 1919, the legislation was eventually buried in the House Foreign Affairs Committee, a move that was supported by the new secretary of State, Bainbridge Colby, on Wilson's instructions.[46]

De Valera wrote to Arthur Griffith on 26 March 1920 that 'the Mason bill has no chance of passing.' But the Irish leader tried to salvage something from it and he worked with Mason to reword a resolution which merely sympathized with the 'aspirations of the Irish people for a government of their own choice.' De Valera felt that the new resolution 'is not of course quite as good as the Bill would be, but as there was no hope whatever that the Bill would pass, and as time was pressing all our friends here, even the Judge [Cohalan] consider this move wise.'[47] Mason and de Valera worked to gather the votes to support this

44 LC, MD, WBP, Box 550, Cohalan to Borah, 19 November 1919; ibid., Borah to Cohalan, 22 November 1919.   45 Ambrosius, *Woodrow Wilson*, p. 235.   46 De Valera did not attend the hearings because he believed it was a matter to be determined by Americans but his presence added force to the republican arguments presented at the hearings. US Congress, House of Representatives, Committee on Foreign Affairs, Hearings on H.Res. 3404, T*o provide for the salaries of a minister and consuls to the Republic of Ireland*, Friday, 12 December 1919, 66th Congress, 2nd Session, 1920, pp. 72–3; *BDFA*, i, Annual Report for 1920, p. 54.   47 O'Doherty, *Assignment*, p. 88; *DIFP*, i, de Valera

watered-down resolution and, according to British Ambassador Geddes, for a time there was a danger of a debate in the House. Polk wrote to his friend, Davis in London; 'every one is playing politics with it, and I see every prospect of my chief [Colby] and the House Committee getting into a fine old jam.' But the House Speaker Gillett, a Democrat, intervened and opposed all efforts to force a debate. The subject was dropped by the end of the year.[48]

The Mason bill failed but the seeds were laid for future attempts to win diplomatic recognition and representation for Ireland. On this occasion, Colby and Geddes were relieved at the result, and both were critical of congressmen who placated their Irish constituents by supporting any pro-Irish resolutions without wishing them to go further.[49] For de Valera and Cohalan political, public and press attention compensated somewhat for the failure of the Mason legislation and other Senate resolutions.[50] The forces of Irish-America during the final days of the sixty-sixth Congress, however, did achieve one significant victory, the passage of the Gerry resolution in the Senate. Again it occurred with Republican support and in the context of the final battle on the League of Nations.

After the defeat of the peace settlement in Congress in November 1919, international organizations, peace groups, religious groups and labour organizations, who claimed to represent twenty million Americans, and individuals such as the moderate Republican Taft and Democrat Bryan, demanded that Wilson and Lodge resolve their differences. British and French representatives indicated that they wanted US acceptance of the treaty, albeit with reservations, rather than a total rejection and US exclusion from the League of Nations. The extent to which Wilson was involved remains unclear as consensus appears to exist that his wife, his physician, and his personal secretary protected him from visitors and correspondence and, according to Lansing, even made policy. Indeed Lazo's work on the Jenkins incident appears to confirm that this group wielded authority if not power. Polk described Wilson as 'distinctly better but apparently he only takes up a few things that are pending.'[51]

The president now experienced the full weight of the desire for compromise. Tumulty warned him, on 2 January 1920, 'that we can no longer adhere to the

to Griffith, 26 March 1919, pp. 56–7. De Valera's role in drafting the watered down version became a matter of dispute as de Valera denied his role. McCartan and McGarrity were furious at the passage of another meaningless measure. Coogan, De Valera, p. 177.   48 BDFA, i, Annual Report for 1920, p. 54; YULMC, FLPP, Box 2, file 129, Polk to Davis, 26 May 1920.   49 BDFA, i, Annual Report for 1920, p. 54.   50 The Cohalan–de Valera dispute escalated over the Mason legislation also. Doorley, Irish–American diaspora nationalism, pp. 116–17; BDFA, i, Annual Report for 1920, p. 54. On 4 May, a telegram addressed to Lloyd George by eighty-eight representatives protesting against the imprisonment of Irish men without trial and urging that they be tried without unreasonable delay. Ibid.   51 Link, Diplomatist, p. 152; D. Lazo, 'Lansing, Wilson and the Jenkins incident', 177–98; Blum, Tumulty, pp. 214–6; YULMC, FLPP, box 2, file 128, Polk to Davis, 17 January 1920. King George V even commented to Davis in London later on in March that he felt Wilson's dismissal of Lansing was severe and resulted from Wilson's 'long seclusion' during which 'the world has moved ahead and he [Wilson] did not realise all that had taken place.' See Davis & Fleming, The ambassadorial diary, 11 March 1920.

position that we have taken in the matter of the Treaty. The people of the country have the impression that you will not consent to the dotting of an "i" or crossing of a "t".' He urged Wilson to come to some agreement with the 'mild reservationists' or to produce a line of defence that would blame Lodge for the defeat. House, who was convinced that the treaty would be ratified, pursued a similar line, although his influence with the president had waned considerably. Moderates within both sides attempted to negotiate a compromise during December 1919 and January 1920 and Lodge's opposition, particularly to article ten, weakened. The final decision on the next move rested with Wilson.[52]

But Wilson refused to compromise. As Link notes, since November 1919 'his intransigence had been compounded by personal bitterness and by the growing conviction that rejection of the treaty was preferable to a dishonourable ratification.' During the final months from January to March 1920 Wilson refused to yield on article ten. Instead he hatched a plan that astounded his advisers and political allies. He intended to make the presidential election a single issue one. Not only was this unheard of but Wilson's belief that he could recover from his paralysis and win an unprecedented third term in 1920 was unacceptable to Democratic Party bosses.[53] Even his supporters, realizing the strength of opposition and the political realities of the upcoming presidential elections, wavered in their loyalty. Senator Thomas J. Walsh described their dilemma. 'We must either allow Lodge to triumph and see Article X emasculated, or we must join with the irreconcilables and kill the treaty.'[54]

The treaty came before the Senate again on 9 February and, by the beginning of March it appeared that defeat was inevitable. Even the French ambassador, Jules Jusserand, had produced a draft that had reservations protecting US interests and congressional control of foreign policy, specifically in the event of war. He hoped these would be favourably received by key Republican senators, his own superiors and the British government.[55] Although Lloyd George believed that Wilson had walked himself into the trouble with the Senate because he insisted upon the covenant and the creation of a 'fixed and formal organization', he told Davis on 6 February, at a meeting in 10 Downing Street, that he did not want Wilson to think that he had deserted him during his treaty fight. He stated that if the Senate added reservations to the treaty 'that would be the business of the United States alone so long as we are not asked to expressly agree to them – the latter it would be difficult to do.' He denied Borah's alleged remark that he had wired Grey approving the Lodge reservations.[56] Davis felt that the British

52 Cuddy, *Irish-Americans*, p. 216; Davis & Fleming, *The ambassadorial diary*, 2 January 1920; Link, *Diplomatist*, p. 152. For Grey's contact with Lodge at this time see Egerton, 'Britain and the "Great Betrayal"', 904–6.   53 Link, *Diplomatist*, pp. 152, 153; LaFeber, *American age*, p. 350. House's sidelining was particularly evident in June 1920 when the State Department cabled Davis in London to say that a forthcoming visit by House was without government sanction. Davis & Fleming, *The ambassadorial diary*, 17 June 1920.   54 Quoted in Cuddy, *Irish-Americans*, p. 220.   55 Link, *Diplomatist*, p. 131.   56 Davis & Fleming, *The ambassadorial diary*, Memo. of conversation with the

public favoured US ratification.[57] But despite overtures from the British, the French and appeasing Republicans, Wilson would not budge and the addition of a fifteenth reservation merely increased his intransigence.

Introduced by Rhode Island Democrat Senator Peter G. Gerry on 18 March, the reservation stated:

> In consenting to ratification of the treaty with Germany the United States adheres to the resolution of sympathy with the aspirations of the Irish people for a government of their own choice, adopted by the Senate, June 6, 1919, and declares that when self-government is attained by Ireland, a consummation, it is hoped, is at hand, it should be admitted as a member of the League of Nations.[58]

It supported the principle of self-determination and Irish independence and urged the prompt admission of a self-governing Ireland into the League of Nations. Lodge fought hard to oppose the sweeping support for self-determination or at the least to limit it to Ireland, but in this election year he could not get support. Senators Sterling and Frank B. Kellogg, a future secretary of State, opposed it and the latter believed it would alienate the British government by interfering with its domestic affairs. But Hitchcock, minority leader of the Democrats and a loyal Wilsonian, endorsed the reservation as did five Democratic Irish-American senators – Gerry (Rhode Island), Phelan (California), John K. Shields (Tennessee), David I. Walsh (Massachusetts), Thomas J. Walsh (Montana) and the irreconcilable Republicans. Opposition came from reservationist Republicans, including Lodge and future president Warren Harding, and southern Democrats, but it was not strong enough to defeat the reservation. Lodge's position revealed his dilemma; on the one hand, he had gloated over the Irish support garnered by the Republicans on the settlement, but on the other, he was genuinely concerned about the effect of the prominence of the Irish question on Anglo–American relations. Reservation fifteen was adopted by a vote of 38 votes to 36 with 13 not voting.[59]

Haynes wrote of the Gerry reservation: 'more incongruous or meddlesome it would be hard to find in the entire record of the Senate's amendments and reservations upon treaties.'[60] The addition of the fifteenth reservation may be seen as evidence of the Republicans unwillingness to accept ratification on any basis because if Wilson had indicated any willingness to accept the treaty another reservation would have been added. However, it was inspired by a Democrat and supported by the irreconcilables and by over half the Democrats present, including

Prime Minister, 6 February 1920.   57 Ibid., 30 November 1919, 5 December 1919; ibid., p. 141 notes.   58 Quoted in Haynes, *The senate*, p. 669, fn. 2.   59 Ambrosius, *Woodrow Wilson*, p. 249; Carroll, *American opinion*, p. 147; Haynes, *The senate*, p. 669, fn. 2; W.C. Widenor, *Henry Cabot Lodge and the search for an American foreign policy* (1980), p. 327, fn. 120.   60 Haynes, *The senate*, p. 669, fn. 2; Bailey described it as the 'acme of legislative absurdity'. T. Bailey, *Woodrow Wilson and the great betrayal* (1945), pp. 263–4.

Hitchcock.[61] A further interpretation of the Gerry reservation was that it was administration inspired, being a way of exposing the fallacious nature of Republican support for the Irish cause in the Senate. Tansill suggested that Gerry hoped that this last minute move would appease Irish-Americans.[62] He may have been correct and perhaps it can best be regarded as a response to Irish-American pressure in an election year. During early 1920, the same FOIF forces that supported the Mason legislation bombarded congressional politicians and the administration with letters and petitions urging Irish self-determination (by then outdated as a majority of Irish people had already selected Sinn Féin as their government) and rejection of the treaty. Nonetheless, Democrats were most susceptible to such influence. Some establishment Americans supported this view, albeit for an opposite reason. William Edward Dodd, the historian, recalled with disgust that Lodge 'was more than once on the point of adopting the treaty, when the Irish, Italian and German influences, speaking always through the Irish of Massachusetts took him in hand.'[63] The FOIF targeted senators with Irish-American backgrounds and constituents.[64] Over half the Democrats present for the vote on the Gerry reservation took the opportunity to restate their credentials on Ireland.

Not surprisingly, the voting alignments changed again on the following day. The Democratic senators were instructed by Hitchcock to oppose ratification of the treaty with the fifteen reservations. Twenty-one defied him and, therefore, Wilson, and voted in favour. Twenty-three Democrats abided by instructions and voted with Borah's irreconcilables by voting 'no'. In the final Senate vote on the treaty with fifteen reservations, 49 voted in favour and 35 against. As the vote in favour was less than the two-thirds required for ratification of a treaty, it fell.

Not surprisingly, the Irish-Americans and Irish republicans again claimed a victory. Cohalan congratulated Senator Johnson on his 'splendid work' and backed him for the Republican presidential nomination.[65] The Sinn Féin government naturally welcomed the Gerry reservation and the defeat of the treaty, Arthur Griffith told the Dáil that both resulted from 'de Valera's work.' He continued 'the reservation written into the peace treaty made it quite clear that the League of Nations could only be adopted with Ireland as a consenting party.' De Valera, in the US, regarded the Gerry reservation as another step 'in keeping the Irish claim [to independence] before the Congress.' Like his government colleagues, he viewed both developments as evidence of the strength of Irish-American influence on both Democratic and Republican politics.[66]

*

61 Widenor, *Henry Cabot Lodge*, p. 335.   62 Hopkinson, 'President Woodrow Wilson', 108; Tansill, *America and the fight*, p. 372.   63 *PWW*, 67, Dodd to Alexander Frederick Whyte, 9 January 1921. 64 AIHS, FOIFP, Box 2, file 2, Office of the National Secretary – Statement regarding problems over use of funds; Cuddy, *Irish-Americans*, p. 219; O'Connell, 'Irish influence on America's foreign policy', p. 236.   65 Coogan, *De Valera*, p. 179.   66 Carroll, *American opinion*, p. 148; *DIFP*, i, Dáil Éireann report on foreign affairs, Dublin, June 1920, pp. 72–3.

A combination of unique regulations, that afford the US Senate constitutional powers in foreign treaty-making, and unique circumstances outside Congress brought the Senate and executive into inevitable opposition with each attempting to assert its authority on the treaty of Versailles and the League of Nations. It has been noted previously that Irish activism was the best organized and most effective of the ethnic agitation in the US at the time, but this alone could not account for the defeat, despite the belief of Friends of Irish Freedom, Sinn Féin and historians such as Link, Adler and Stone that this was the case.[67] Indeed, even in Massachusetts it has been suggested that the Irish factor was not the 'root cause' of opposition to the League, which also lay in non-Irish factors such as the desire for peace and prosperity. McKillen suggests that local labour groups often strongly immigrant in composition, saw the League as a tool of oppression for workers and nationalities.[68] The interests of Lodge and his reservationists and of Borah and his irreconcilables coincided with those of the hyphenates, specifically the Irish, Germans and Italians. Both sides' needs were served by the alliance. But Wilson also shared responsibility for the failure of his peace plans. His intransigence, obstinacy, under-estimation of the opposition forces and personal hatred of Lodge resulted in his inability to listen to his advisers and allies.[69]

The question as to whether Lloyd George would have accepted the fifteen reservations remains unanswered, as he was never faced with the decision. Although his conversation with Davis took place prior to the passage of the Gerry reservation, it is probable that Lloyd George would have accepted all fifteen reservations as the price for US ratification of the treaty and involvement in the League of Nations. It is equally difficult to decide whether Wilson could have stomached raising the fifteenth reservation with Lloyd George. The issue of Irish nationalism had long been an irritant in Anglo–American relations and an embarrassment at times, but in 1919 and early 1920 it forced itself into the centre of US foreign and domestic politics. At the very least it contributed to the destruction of Wilson's peace plans for the settlement of a critical international issue and resulted in Wilson believing the Irish-American leaders to be among 'these evil men' who destroyed his peace plans.[70] It remained to be seen whether the strange alliance between Irish-Americans and the Republicans would hold, influence the outcome of the 1920 presidential election and bring some rewards for the increasingly disunited republicans in the US and Ireland.

---

67 Link, *Wilson, the diplomatist*, p. 133; S. Adler, *The isolationist impulse: its twentieth-century reaction* (1957), p. 85; Stone, *The irreconcilables*, p. 102.   68 Jeffreys-Jones, 'Massachusetts labour', 398–9; Widenor, *Henry Cabot Lodge*, p. 342, fn. 190; McKillen's work on the short-lived Cook County Labor Party indicates that its opposition to the League of Nations was motivated by the belief that it would perpetuate the oppression of workers and national ties and would not end British imperialism. McKillen, *Chicago labor*, pp. 133, 151.   69 Ward, *Ireland and Anglo-American relations*, p. 213; see Link, *Diplomatist*, pp. 153–4 on Wilson's intransigence; Link, *American epoch*, p. 152.   70 Stannard Baker, *American chronicle*, p. 474.

CHAPTER SIX

The final challenges to Wilson's Irish policy, March 1920–January 1921

Woodrow Wilson's response to the failure of his peace plans was to set about making the presidential election 'a solemn referendum' on the treaty and, despite his health problems, he wanted to be the Democratic Party's standard bearer in the election for an unprecedented third time. Instead the first post-war election became a referendum on which party should 'preside over the design of the new political fabric, and in what pattern in would be stitched together.'[1] US domestic policy is not a central concern of this work but US foreign policy does not exist in isolation. Both are intertwined. Consequently, Wilson's hope for a single-issue election ignored the economic and social problems that most US citizens faced daily.

During 1919 and 1920, inflation and unemployment rose because of the ending of wartime controls, the shortages of consumer goods and the return of millions of troops from the European war theatre. More than four million workers went on strike in 1919, primarily to either maintain or increase wartime wage gains. There were strikes in major industries such as textiles, railroads, steel, mining and the police and these fed the public mood of 'anti-radical hysteria' and exploded into the 'red scare.' Race riots also occurred, resulting from the migration of African-Americans from southern to northern states to work in the factories during the war years. Although Wilson's progressive agenda still emerged in legislative terms, with the General Leasing and Powers Acts of 1920, the female suffrage and prohibition amendments, these were not sufficient to combat the stresses of the period. It was in this situation that Wilson attempted to lead his party into the election and to fight it on a single foreign policy issue.[2]

Party conventions and presidential election

On 5 March 1920, Roland Lindsay, counsellor and chargé d'affaires in the British embassy in Washington, informed Foreign Secretary Curzon that 'as the elec-

---

1 D.R. McCoy, 'Election of 1920' in A.M. Schlesinger et al., *History of American presidential elections 1789–1968*, 4 vols (1971), iii, 1900–36, p. 2349.   2 A.S. Link et al., *American epoch: a history of the United States since 1900 volume 1, 1900–1945*, 2 vols (1987), i, pp. 152–62; McCoy, 'Election of 1920', p. 2350; J.M. Cooper, jr., 'Thomas Woodrow Wilson' in M.L. Urofsky (ed.), *The American presidents* (2000), p. 301.

tion campaign draws near there are increasing signs of an approaching anti-British campaign ... it is impossible to exaggerate the extent to which the Irish question and the Irish vote dominates this situation.' He was in no doubt '[that] the Irish vote in America is enormous, well disciplined and easily swayed by anti-British sentiment, and that at moments of crisis American politicians even against their convictions will bid for it.'[3] Election time was one of those moments and given the prominence of the Irish question inside and outside Congress in spring 1920, combined with the escalating Anglo-Irish war of independence, it was not surprising that Lindsay expected the Irish question to figure prominently at the respective party conventions, in the platforms and during the campaign.

The Republican convention was held in Chicago on 8–13 June. In the struggle for the presidential nomination, the main contenders were General Leonard Wood, Frank O. Lowden, governor of Illinois, Calvin Coolidge, governor of Massachusetts, Senator Warren G. Harding of Ohio and Senator Hiram Johnson of California. The race was tight and it was no easier to agree on a platform. The resolutions committee produced one that condemned the Wilson administration, promised much and praised the achievements of the Republican-dominated Congress. On the League of Nations, Elihu Root's compromise supported an 'international organisation ... based upon international justice.' It was ambiguous, but this was necessary if it was to satisfy the irreconcilables and reservationists within the party.[4] It had to leave the door open to either US isolation or involvement in future collective security arrangements. Promises were made to curb inflation and the cost of living, control profiteering, reduce the number of strikes and lock-outs, encourage private ownership of railroads, impose laws to limit immigration to those 'whose standards are similar to ours' and exclude Asians, recognize African-American voters and protect women and children in industrial work. McCoy describes the 1920 platform as 'the most conservative document' written by a convention in twenty years. The liberal and reforming impulses of Progressive Republicans were written out of it and when they spoke during debates they were heckled and defeated.[5]

The resolutions committee had also considered proposals from the supporters of Daniel Cohalan and Eamon de Valera, whose relationship had finally disintegrated on 19 March over money, authority and strategy.[6] De Valera was advised by Frank P. Walsh, William Bourke Cockran, Bishop Michael Gallagher of Detroit and others not to attend Chicago, but he insisted on going as his aim was to gain recognition for the elected government of the Irish republic. However, although he had not attended the Senate hearings on either the League of Nations

3 K. Bourne & D.C. Watt (general eds), *British documents on foreign affairs* (hereafter *BDFA*), part 11, series C, North America, 25 vols. (1986–95), i, The Republican ascendancy, 1919–28, Lindsay to Curzon, 5 March 1920.   4 McCoy, 'Election of 1920', p. 2356.   5 Ibid.   6 See M. Doorley, *Irish-American diaspora nationalism: the Friends of Irish Freedom, 1916–35* (2005), pp. 116–21; for the Cohalan version see C. Tansill, *America and the fight for Irish freedom, 1866–1922* (1957) pp. 369–96; and the de Valera version see T.P. Coogan, *De Valera: long fellow, long shadow* (1993), pp. 173–5.

or Mason legislation because he did not want to intrude into US domestic affairs, at Chicago there was no chance of 'offending America' that he 'did not take.' De Valera believed that it was his duty as president of Ireland, and now as leader of the anti-Cohalan faction, to use every opportunity to work for his aims, but Cohalan, who had close ties to Borah, Lodge and Johnson, believed that the convention would not endorse an Irish resolution because of the recent defeat of the Mason bill in Congress. He felt that endorsement would leave the party open to press charges of anti-Britishness, and it would be contrary to the party's opposition on foreign entanglements. Instead Cohalan called for a statement in favour of self-determination for Ireland. The Republicans had previously adopted an Irish plank in 1892 but this had not committed it to action. On 9 June, the resolutions committee defeated de Valera's resolution and approved Cohalan's. Nevertheless de Valera publicly opposed Cohalan's plank because it failed to demand diplomatic recognition of the Irish republic and eventually it was dropped from the final platform.[7] Consequently, the Cohalan–de Valera divide spared the future Republican administration any commitment to act on Ireland's behalf. As Auckland Geddes, the recently-appointed British ambassador in Washington, noted, 'the incident illustrates in an interesting manner the immense influence Irishmen can have on American politicians if they proceed wisely; and how ready American politicians are to withdraw themselves from that influence if they can find some colourable pretext for doing so.'[8] The Irish tactics had backfired and left both factions with nothing from the convention. Consul Frederick Dumont, Adams' replacement in Dublin, confirmed to the State Department on 16 June that Sinn Féin 'found it difficult to believe that the ... Convention ... had refused the plank prepared by her leader, and was disgusted with the plank incorporated in the platform as to Ireland.'[9] Indeed, the Dáil Éireann report on foreign affairs noted 'it is clear ... that the party are not prepared to declare themselves definitely for recognition.'[10] The optimistic tone in the latter comment revealed the gap between the perception and reality of the strength of ties between Irish-America and the Republican Party and shows how far the alliance during the League of Nations fight was one of expediency.

After the platform was approved, the Republican delegates moved on 11 June to choosing their presidential nominee. The candidates ranged from progressive

7 Doorley, *Irish-American diaspora nationalism*, p. 128; R. Fanning et al. (eds), *Documents of Irish foreign policy, volume 1, 1919–22*, 3 vols (hereafter *DIFP*) (1998–), i, Dáil Éireann Report on Foreign Affairs, Dublin, June 1920; A.J. Ward, *Ireland and Anglo-American relations* (1969), pp. 220–1; Coogan, *De Valera*, p. 179; J.J. Splain, '"Under which King?" The tragic-comedy of President de Valera's errors in the United States' in W.F. Fitzgerald (ed.), *The voice of Ireland: a survey of the race and nation from all angles by the foremost leaders at home and abroad* (1923), p. 248.   8 The National Archives, London (hereafter TNA), Foreign Office (hereafter FO), 371/4550, Geddes to Curzon., 16 June 1920.   9 National Archives and Records Administration, Maryland (hereafter NARA), Records of the Department of State relating to internal affairs of Great Britain, 1910–29, Record Group 59 (hereafter RG59), M580/216, 841.00/214, Dumont to Secretary of State, 16 June 1920; McCoy, 'Election of 1920', pp. 2363–66.   10 *DIFP*, i, Dáil Éireann report on foreign affairs, Dublin, June 1920.

to conservative on the issues of law and order, national defence, the League of Nations and prohibition. On economic issues, there were few differences between the candidates, who all supported private enterprise, lower taxes and minimal regulation of business. On the tenth ballot the only potential candidate who had not been eliminated was Harding. His nomination was, therefore, declared unanimous on 13 June and his vice-president was to be Calvin Coolidge, 'the law and order man.' Harding had emerged because each of the other candidates had as much opposition as support and because his supporters waged a clever campaign, soliciting second and third choice promises of votes which were eventually cast in favour of their candidate after first choices had been eliminated. Finally, Harding was considered weak and could be managed. As one senator put it 'We have a lot of second raters. This man Harding, is not a world beater, but we think he is the best of the bunch".' Coolidge was selected because he was the best known and most respected of the vice-presidential nominees. The Republicans had selected two 'safe and sane' men to fight the election and it was now the Democrats' turn.[11]

Three factions fought for control of the Democratic platform and presidential candidacy in the convention which began in San Francisco on 28 June; 'the Wilsonites representing the administration; the Bryanites representing the "Drys", the isolationists and the remnants of the agrarians; and the bosses of the big cities – Charles Murphy of Tammany Hall, Thomas Taggart of Indiana and George Brennan of Illinois – representing themselves.' The contenders were William McAdoo (former secretary of the Treasury and Wilson's son-in-law), A. Mitchell Palmer (attorney general), James Cox (governor of Ohio), William Jennings Bryan (former Democratic Party leader and secretary of State) and Woodrow Wilson, the incumbent in the White House. From the beginning of the convention, it was clear that the race was even tighter than that of the Republicans, not least because most of the delegates were not tied to any one candidate. But before the decision-making started, the process of writing the platform took place and it was as important as the nomination.[12]

Disagreement revolved around four issues; the League of Nations, prohibition, Irish independence and a bonus for war veterans. Wilson's views were already known as he had forwarded to the resolutions committee planks that concentrated on the League of Nations but did not have any other proposals. Between 28 June and 2 July, the committee worked to frame a document that was finally presented to the delegates on 2 July. Not surprisingly, it condemned the Republicans and praised Wilson's administration. The League of Nations was endorsed and the document advocated the immediate ratification of the treaty without reservations which would dilute its integrity. Thus, Wilson's wishes were accorded with on the League, but the platform left the way open for acceptance

11 McCoy, 'Election of 1920', pp. 2357–61; H. Eaton, *Presidential timber: a history of nominating conventions, 1868–1960* (1964), p. 273.   12 McCoy, 'Election of 1920', pp. 2361–63.

with reservations. On the other issues, it promised a revision of the tax system to introduce greater equity and justice, government savings and an end to profiteering and it upheld farmers' and workers' right to organization and collective bargaining while decreeing that no damaging labour strikes would be permitted. Assistance to soldiers, the return of railroads to private ownership and the principles of free speech and a free press were upheld but there would be no toleration of propaganda threatening to national security and Asian immigration would be restricted. The platform said nothing on prohibition, an indication of the stalemate between the 'drys' and the 'wets' on the issue.[13]

The Cohalan faction decided not to attend San Francisco, believing there was no hope of getting a plank recognizing the Irish republic. A Republican victory was seen as being inevitable and would soon bring recognition if Johnson became president and Borah secretary of State in the new Republican administration.[14] Their first instinct proved to be correct. De Valera met with the Democratic Party resolutions committee on 29 June but his plank, which would commit the US to recognition of Irish independence, was defeated by 31 votes to 17. [15] However, there was some support for an Irish plank from a variety of corners. Before the convention Wilson had ignored the issue in his platform but Tumulty, along with Mitchell Palmer and senators Gerry, Glass and Thomas J. Walsh, appealed to him for assistance in framing a plank endorsing Irish aspirations for national self-determination. The group felt that it would make the League of Nations and the Democratic Party more attractive to the Irish voter in November. Wilson ignored the request.[16] House also expressed his worries about the need to secure the Irish vote for the party to the British diplomat Gloster Armstrong.[17] Pressure for an Irish plank of some sort also came from other sections of the party, including the powerful bosses, Murphy, Taggart and Brennan, who were 'perfectly frank' in their demand that 'as the icing on the shamrock, they wanted a platform plank declaring in favour of Irish independence.'[18] An unnamed senator on the resolutions committee, perhaps Senator Edward Phelan, a firm Wilson supporter, produced a weak, lacklustre plank which expressed sympathy for the aspirations of Ireland for self-government and was endorsed by the committee.[19] De Valera and his advisers prepared another proposal which did not demand formal recognition of the republic but simply asked for the continuation of the US policy of recognizing any nation that established a government by the free vote of the people. The resolutions committee agreed to present this milder plank to the convention as a minority report where it was defeated by a vote of 665? to 402?. The delegates finished the session by merely expressing sympathy with Irish aspirations.[20]

13 A.S. Link (ed.), *The papers of Woodrow Wilson* (hereafter *PWW*), 69 vols (1966–94), 65, A news report, 6 June 1920; McCoy, 'Election of 1920', pp. 2362–63.   14 Splain, '"Under which King?"', p. 249.   15 T.E. Hachey, 'The Irish question: the British foreign office and the American political conventions of 1920', 105.   16 J.M. Blum, *Joe Tumulty and the Wilson era* (1951), p. 242.   17 TNA, FO371/4550, Armstrong to Foreign Office, 21 June 1920.   18 Eaton, *A history of nominating conventions*, p. 283.   19 *PWW*, 65, A news report, 6 June 1920.   20 Hachey, 'The Irish ques-

For traditional and practical reasons, sympathy for the Irish problem remained strong within the Democratic Party, but not so strong as to tie the party or presidential candidate to any action on the matter. Cohalan was highly critical of de Valera's actions at both conventions and regarded the failure to secure an Irish plank as a defeat. His only hope now lay in a Republican victory in the presidential elections, albeit one without an Irish dimension to the platform.[21] De Valera believed that the Democratic Party had underestimated 'the great volume of public sentiment in this country behind the demand for justice in Ireland.'[22] It remained to be seen whether that sentiment would materialize on voting day. In the meantime, the split between the Cohalan and de Valera factions was absolute and de Valera set about getting control of the Friends of Irish Freedom and eventually establishing a rival organization.

Agreeing the final Democratic platform was as laborious as the nomination process that began on 30 June. William McAdoo was the favourite candidate, but he had complicated matters by refusing to have his name presented to the convention on 18 June out of 'filial respect.' Wilson still harboured plans to be renominated if there was a deadlock, even though Tumulty and other advisers counselled against this. By 2 July, the door was finally closed on a third term for Wilson. The bosses who controlled the key states opposed Wilson's candidature from the beginning because they had had enough of 'Wilson and idealism … they wanted a man in the Harding image who would "go along".' Wilson was informed that there was no deadlock and that either McAdoo or James Cox would succeed. On 5 July, Cox was victorious at the forty-fourth ballot. He chose Franklin Delano Roosevelt (under secretary of the Navy) as vice-presidential candidate. The Democrats' presidential ticket was 'balanced between the mid-western, boss-backed, non-Administration man Cox and … Roosevelt, the anti-Tammany, Administration man from the populous east.'[23]

After the completion of the two conventions, Geddes felt that Cox was an unknown figure who relied on Ohio Democratic Party backroom boys for support and that Harding was representative of a similar coterie. He was not impressed by either candidate, did not see much difference between the parties except on the League of Nations, and did not believe that polling day would stymie the prevalent 'state of moral collapse.' However, he felt that from the British point of view something had been gained from the conventions; 'it has been possible to avoid an Irish plank that matters in either platform.'[24] Geddes was relieved at this because of the increasing levels of anti-British activity. Against

tion', 104–5.   21 *Gaelic American*, 3 July 1920.   22 Quoted in Coogan, *De Valera*, p. 183.   23 McCoy, 'Election of 1920', pp. 2363–66; Eaton, *A history of nominating conventions*, p. 283; Link et al., *American epoch*, pp. 160, 162. Despite the disappointments of the conventions, de Valera recalled in 1962 that he had managed to get a proposal for recognition adopted by the Progressive Party. University College Dublin Archives (hereafter UCDA), Eamon de Valera Papers (hereafter EVP), P150/1100, 'Recollections by de Valera of his American mission, June 1919 to December 1920', 19 November 1962.   24 *BDFA*, i, Geddes to Curzon, 13 July 1920.

a background of war in Ireland and the prominence of Sinn Féin personalities in the US, embassy officials reported continuous Irish lobbying and agitation. Following the congressional activity on the League of Nations, Mason, Gerry and other resolutions, news of conditions in Ireland, specifically in the prisons, had begun to spread and this resulted in congressional interest and in Colby's involvement. In April, the embassy in Washington was subjected to 'Sinn Féin' picketing while June and September saw the burning of the Union Jack flag in many parts of the US, including both Washington and New York. Geddes was 'very surprised' by the amount of concern manifested in 'official circles' over the flag burning incident on 2 June. Indeed Colby felt strongly enough about it to apologize to Geddes 'for this act of a small and unrepresentative group of persons.' Geddes believed that many of these 'ill-considered actions' of the Irish in the US 'did more harm than good to the cause which they were endeavouring to promote.'[25] Nonetheless, this underlying view that Irish agitation could never be effective enough with the US public and politicians to force Britain's hand in Ireland, was balanced by an acceptance that it presented ammunition to extreme elements in the US who could use it to serve their own ends. At the very least it augmented the persistent anti-British sentiment in the US and destabilized Anglo–American relations. By July, Roland Lindsay was convinced that an Irish settlement would remove the sole continuous source of disorder in Anglo–American relations.[26] But in mid-summer, at a time when British actions in Ireland were producing powerful material for Irish republican propaganda and lobbying campaigns in the US, the political clout of the Irish movement had been weakened. The Cohalan/de Valera divide had given both the Democrats and the Republicans an escape route on the issue of recognizing the Irish republic and committing the next president to action on Ireland's behalf. Harding and Cox prepared to enter the presidential campaign but they remained cautious of the potential power of the Irish-American voters just as Lindsay had predicted. The Irish question was not an official part of the presidential campaign but both candidates were drawn into comment on it.

Harding, as an experienced politician and newspaperman, launched his campaign on 22 July in Marion, Ohio and ran an effective campaign, even though he was not as widely known or thought to be as intelligent as his opponent. His speeches lacked intellectual consistency but they appealed to voters. He knew

---

25 Ibid., Annual Report for the United States (hereafter Annual Report) for 1920, pp. 54–8. Gertrude Corless, an editorial writer wrote 'We picketed the embassy on Good Friday to remind Great Britain and the State Department of the crucifixion of Christ and to call attention that Ireland was being crucified.' J. Doyle, 'Striking for Ireland on the New York docks' in R.H. Bayor & T.J. Meagher (eds), The New York Irish (1996), p. 361. From 1914 to 1921, State Department officials regarded the burning of the British flag as a serious activity but the Solicitor's Office could not find any law under which to prosecute the mainly republican Irish and Irish-American culprits. NARA, RG59, M580/1, entry 'indignities and insults to British flag in US', see entry for 9 June 1920.   26 BDFA, i, Lindsay to Curzon, 11 July 1919.

that many Americans were tired of Wilson and war and wanted assurances that the Republicans would return the country to stability, to 'normalcy.' His rhetoric appealed to big business and to those living in urban and rural areas who believed in traditional values. Coolidge adopted a low-key approach to the campaign not straying too far from New England. Unlike Harding and Coolidge, Cox and Roosevelt co-ordinated their campaign from the beginning, taking the field on 7 and 9 August respectively and embarking on an extensive nation-wide speaking tour. But the Democrats faced a number of difficulties; firstly, they did not begin to organize a campaign machine until after the convention, secondly, they had less money than the Republicans with $2.3 million as against $8 million and thirdly, party headquarters were less well organized than those of their opponents. They were also hampered by the recent congressional losses, by public tiredness of or down right opposition to Wilson and, finally, by Wilson's own physical inability to participate in the campaign. Consequently, from the beginning the Democratic campaign was weakened and Cox had to adopt an aggressive approach that Coolidge said, on 18 September, was characterized by 'coarser and coarser methods, wilder and wilder charges.' On 23 September, Ambassador John Davis, who had returned from London to the US to give his resignation to Colby, noted in his diary, 're. campaign, situation desperate.'[27] House commented to Horace Plunkett in late September, 'there is little or no chance for the Democrats to win the coming election.'[28]

Except for Harding's commitment to farmers and big business, neither presidential candidate offered concrete proposals on economic and social issues. The Republican also emphasized the return to representative government from Wilson's 'one-man government.' Both handled cautiously the prohibition issue and the Volstead Act because of their varying records on it and the 'wet/dry' division in their respective parties. Both supported ratification of the nineteenth amendment to permit all women to vote in the upcoming election. Cox dodged the issue of Asian immigration by saying that the Californian authorities should take a leading role in any decision.[29] Harding again rode the wave of opposition to aliens and Catholics by declaring himself, in September 1920, in favour of stronger controls on immigration. He favoured an 'America First' policy that would admit only immigrants who could be easily assimilated into US society.[30] Journalist H.L. Mencken wrote, on 26 July 1920, 'It seems to be quite impossible for any wholly literate man to pump up any genuine enthusiasm for either of them.'[31]

27 McCoy, 'Election of 1920', pp. 2370–72; R.H. Ferrell, *The presidency of Calvin Coolidge* (1998), pp. 16–7; J. Davis & D.A. Fleming (eds), *The ambassadorial diary of John W. Davis: the Court of St James' 1918–1921* (1993), 23 September 1920.   28 National Library of Ireland (hereafter NLI), Horace Plunkett Papers (hereafter HPP), P6584, House to Plunkett, 25 September 1920.   29 McCoy, 'Election of 1920', pp. 2370–72; F.M. Carroll, *American opinion and the Irish question, 1910–23: a study in opinion and policy* (1978), p. 162.   30 R.K. Murray, *The Harding era: Warren G. Harding and his administration* (1969), p. 267.   31 M. Moos (ed.), *H.L. Mencken: a carnival of Buncombe*

When the question of independence for Ireland arose, as it did on 23 September, Harding showed himself to be representative of the traditional Republican view that the Irish problem was a domestic British one in which the US had no role, even though he expressed sympathy for the cause of Irish freedom.[32] But the hollowness of the latter bland statement was revealed by his Senate voting record on Ireland, which the Democratic national committee immediately published. One pamphlet noted that 'on every roll call Senator Harding, Republican candidate, has voted against the principle of self-determination for Ireland.'[33] Despite this, the *Gaelic American* advised readers to vote for Harding 'as the surest method of defeating Woodrow Wilson and all he stands for.'[34] Meanwhile, Cox pronounced himself in favour of the Wilsonian principle of national self-determination and declared that the Irish people deserved to be independent, if they so wished.[35]

However, Ireland arose again within the context of the contentious issue – the League of Nations. Both men struggled to find a position acceptable to the irreconcilables, reservationsists and League supporters on both sides. In early October, Harding announced himself in favour of an association of nations which might perhaps be the League of Nations and which would not damage Americans' constitutional rights, but he constantly referred to the 'sinister possibilities' of article ten. Harding's position was strengthened when important pro-League Republicans supported him, resulting in endorsement by both wings of the party. By way of contrast, Cox's position appeared inconsistent. In the initial stages he favoured the election as a referendum on the League. He emphasized to Tumulty that 'there is no question but that the real issue is the League of Nations. Domestic problems should be presented by other speakers than the candidate.'[36] Throughout the summer months, John Devoy in the *Gaelic American,* warned his readers that Cox 'was a mere puppet of Woodrow Wilson' and, if elected, would draw the US into the League of Nations. Moreover, in early September he charged that Cox did not understand that the covenant would mean the continued 'subjection [of] the peoples of Ireland, of Egypt, of India, of Shantung and Korea.'[37] By October, Cox was trying to woo back the disillusioned Irish-American voters by emphasizing that the League covenant could not force the US to assist British policy in Ireland. On 2 October, he promised an audience in Kansas city that he would appeal to article eleven of the treaty if the Irish problem was not solved by the time of his inauguration in March 1921. Cox hoped that this low-key promise would retrieve the Irish vote. Tumulty asked to him to go further and indicate how the League could help Ireland's case, but the promise raised alarm bells in London, where Lloyd George spoke 'rather bit-

(1956), p. 15.   **32** *The Times,* 24 September 1920.   **33** TNA, FO371/4554, Enclosure in Armstrong to British embassy, Washington, 5 November 1920.   **34** *Gaelic American,* 18 September, 16 October 1920.   **35** McCoy, 'Election of 1920', pp. 2370–72; Hachey, 'The Irish question', 106.   **36** Quoted in M. Hopkinson, 'President Wilson and the Irish question', 108.   **37** *Gaelic American,* 17 July, 11, 18 September 1920.

terly of the speeches which Cox had made ... on the subject of an independent Ireland and the League of Nations.' The prime minister warned Davis that if Cox was elected and 'attempted anything of the sort Great Britain would have been compelled to reply "that after all Ireland was our business"', a view which Davis agreed with.[38]

Wilson intervened once in the election campaign, on 3 October, when he declared that US entry into the League was vital to save the nation's honour and denied that there was anything in the covenant which 'interfered with or impaired the constitutional arrangements of the great nations.'[39] Devoy described this as an 'absurd statement', published to gain Irish support for Cox, who was pledged to bring the US into the 'English-controlled League of Nations.'[40] Instead it was Bainbridge Colby who defended the League of Nations in addresses throughout the country. Another national figure who intervened in October was Cardinal Gibbons who declared his support for the League to 'safeguard the order of human society.'[41] Meanwhile, Cox changed his position again on 20 and 22 October, denying that he fully supported Wilson's League plan. Democratic voters were even further confused when Cox announced, on 25 October, that he would work with the Senate to ratify the treaty.[42]

Cox's inconsistency on the League did little to enhance his candidacy and neither did the wild statements that he resorted to towards election day on 2 November. Both candidates became the subject of personal slurs. Davis, who was still in the US in late October, wrote 'How attractive to run for office in the USA; Harding assailed as a man of mixed blood, Cox charged with illegitimacy and his relations with his first wife made the subject of slander.' Neither man impressed. Both were compromise candidates and neither was exceptional, but Harding and Coolidge won a great popular victory with 16 million votes as against 9 million for Cox and Roosevelt, while the electoral college vote was 404 to 127 respectively. Thirty-seven states voted Republican this time, including Boston, Baltimore and New York where voters abandoned the Democrats, many of whom were not surprised.[43]

Both before and after the election, there was a widespread belief in republican and British circles that a disproportionately large number of Irish and German voters had deserted the Democratic Party and produced the Republican victory. Devoy wrote that men who had never voted a Republican ticket in their lives discarded their party ties to vote for Harding, the anti-League candidate.[44]

---

38 McCoy, 'Election of 1920', pp. 2380–2; Ward, *Ireland and Anglo-American relations*, pp. 222–3; E. Cuddy, '"Are the Bolsheviks any worse than the Irish?": ethno-religious conflict in America during the 1920s', 18; Carroll, *American opinion*, p. 162–3; Davis & Fleming, *The ambassadorial diary*, memo. of conversations with the Prime Minister, 13, 14, 15 November 1920.   39 McCoy, 'Election of 1920', p. 2382.   40 *Gaelic American*, 9 October 1920.   41 A. Sinclair Will, *Life of Cardinal Gibbons: Archbishop of Baltimore*, 2 vols (1922), ii, pp. 838–9.   42 McCoy, 'Election of 1920', pp. 2380–2; Ward, *Ireland and Anglo-American relations*, pp. 222–3; Carroll, *American opinion*, pp. 162–3; Davis & Fleming, *The ambassadorial diary*, 3 November 1920.   43 Davis & Fleming, *The ambassadorial diary*, 30 October 1920; McCoy, 'Election of 1920', pp. 2380–4.   44 *Gaelic American*, 13

Unsurprisingly Dumont reported from Dublin that the Sinn Féin press asserted that Harding's victory resulted only from Irish-American voters and that Irish-American organizations 'will bring this to his attention once he assumes office.'[45]

In this context, Burchell's study of electoral data for seven states, Massachusetts, New York, Pennsylvania, Ohio, Illinois, Missouri and California, chosen for the size of the electoral vote, the size of the Irish and German communities and their geographical location, is revealing. He concluded that firstly, the Irish were not 'directly and disproportionately responsible' for the swing from the Democrats in these states. Secondly, he found that a combination of economic and social issues caused by eight years of Democratic leadership and policies influenced Democratic voters and that voter apathy led to greater abstentions among Democratic voters in these states. The press was not slow to make connections either; the *New York Times* pronounced against 'the taxes, the unrest, multitudinous harassments that were the progeny of war.' The *New York Tribune* complained about 'extravagance, incompetence, and narrowness' in the Wilson administration while the *New York World* attacked the 'Wilson autocracy, impudent, intolerant, dictatorial … czarism.' In other words, hostility against the wartime control of government was linked to rising prices, high unemployment and labour unrest. Consequently, it would have required a very strong Democratic candidate to defend the party and defeat these forces, which Cox was not.[46]

Burner's work on districts with the highest immigrant populations in New York, Chicago and Boston supports the view that voters of 'foreign stock' fell away from the Democratic Party. Although the defection was temporary, it is clear that domestic and not foreign issues affected voter turnout and choice.[47] Cox's failure to persuade the public that their lot would improve if they voted Democrat and Harding's success in talking up the Republicans' ability to return to 'normalcy', prosperity and progress persuaded many to vote Republican. Such rhetoric was as effective with the Irish-American voter as it was with any other type of voter and the swing to Harding was so large that many other Democratic voters obviously felt the same.

British diplomats were keenly interested in the election results. Geddes commented that 'for the first time on record, an electoral campaign has been conducted in the United States without the political "crimes" of England being

November 1920.   45 NARA, RG59, M580/218, 841d.00/314, Dumont to Secretary of State, 28 January 1921. It is difficult to assess the effect of the news of the death of Terence MacSwiney, the Sinn Féin lord mayor of Cork city, who died on hunger strike on 25 October, on the Irish-American voter. The case attracted huge publicity in September and October as will be seen later. 46 R.A. Burchell, 'Did the Irish and German voters desert the Democrats in 1920? A tentative statistical answer', 153–65. In St Louis despite the decision by St Louis Friends of Irish Freedom to abandon the Democratic party on 13 October 1920, the city's only 'Irish ward' voted with Governor Cox. M. Sullivan, 'Fighting for Irish Freedom. St Louis Irish-Americans, 1918–22' in J.B. Walsh (ed.), *The Irish: America's political class* (1976), pp. 203, 205.   47 D. Burner, *The politics of provincialism: the Democratic party in transition, 1918–1932* (1970), pp. 18, 70, 71. The efficiency of the Republican Party's election machine contributed to Harding's victory also.

dragged into the fray.'[48] His first secretary, R.L. Craigie, discounted a *New York Times* editorial view that the Irish and German vote had swung to the Republicans because of their ethnic interests.[49] But it was the impact of Harding's victory on the wider Anglo–American relationship that was of most concern. Both diplomats expected Harding to keep the US aloof from world affairs, particularly the League of Nations, and to avoid 'entanglements.'[50]

After receiving these worrying reports from the embassy in Washington, Lloyd George asked Davis to interpret the results in terms of America's relations to international affairs. Davis had agreed, at Colby's request, to stay on in London as US ambassador until January 1921. He was well placed to offer some analysis as he was a Democratic insider, had been a presidential candidate for a short time in June and had been in the US during the final stages of the campaign. However, he was unable to answer Lloyd George's questions but suggested that he not pay too much attention to Harding's campaign speeches 'since he occupied a difficult position in his effort to please all wings of his party.' But both men agreed that the dominant motive in the campaign was 'the popular desire for change.'[51]

Meanwhile, Wilson remained at the helm of government and served out his term until March 1921 or, as Davis put it, the outgoing administration 'could only patch the holes in the roof.'[52] Undoubtedly the fulfilment of his domestic policy was already hampered by the Republicans' control of Congress, but he reminded Colby 'it is clearly not the Constitutional right of Congress to direct the President to do anything whatever, particularly in regard to foreign affairs.'[53] Colby, acting on Wilson's directions, not only defended the League of Nations but maintained the policy of thwarting Japanese expansion in Manchuria, which led to the Washington conference in 1921. He began the policy of non-recognition of the Soviet Union, made a good will tour of Latin America and initiated troop withdrawal from Mexico, which paved the way for the Bucareli agreement in 1923.[54] As a result of the Anglo-Irish war of independence, Colby and Wilson also faced challenges to the administration's Irish policy. US consuls in Ireland were reporting an expanding US dimension and there were issues arising from private American relief operations in Ireland and around the release of US prisoners from British jails. There was also the problem of the US administration's response to the cases of Terence MacSwiney and Donal O'Callaghan. All of these arose out of the British government's handling of the Irish problem between 1919 and 1921.

48 *BDFA*, i, Geddes to Curzon, 15 November 1922.   49 Ibid., Craigie to Curzon, 5 November 1920.   50 Ibid., Annual Report for 1921, p. 137.   51 Davis & Fleming, *The ambassadorial diary*, memo. of conversation with the Prime Minister, 13, 14, 15 November 1920.   52 Ibid.   53 *PWW*, 66, Wilson to Colby, 2 September 1920.   54 J. Findling, *Dictionary of American diplomatic history* (1980), p. 113.

US representatives report on the Anglo-Irish war of independence

At the beginning of 1919 there were still three consuls in Ireland. These were in Belfast (Hunter Sharp), Dublin (Edward Adams) and Queenstown (Charles Hathaway). In addition there was one vice consul (George Hitch) in Belfast, one (John McAndrews) in Queenstown and a deputy consul (George B. Dawson) and two vice consuls (John F. Claffey, George van Dyne) in Dublin. John Dinan was still US consular agent in Limerick and, indeed, provided an important report on 'bolshevik' activities in the area while Philip O'Hagan was agent in Londonderry. 1919 saw changes in the personnel with Adams being replaced by Frederick Dumont and Hathaway eventually replaced by Mason Mitchell. The war years had expanded consular roles and brought new challenges for these men. Some had responded and some had not. Adams was in the latter category while Hathaway was in the former. The Queenstown consul devoted his time to the presence of the US navy in the port, the Irish political situation and the results of the torpedo-doing of merchant vessels. In June 1919, he was described by Consul General at Large Ralph Totten of the consular inspection unit, as a 'more than usually efficient officer' and rated 94 out of 100 marks. Totten concluded 'this officer has handled a rather difficult situation in a tactful and efficient manner. He has made many friends and has written a number of excellent and most useful political reports which have been several times commended by the embassy at London. He has co-operated cordially with the American naval authorities and has been universally well spoken of.'[55] Hathaway had greatly enhanced his professional reputation in the service. But just as the consular service in Ireland was re-adjusting to peace-time conditions and returning to trade extension and promotion work, along with the regular bureaucratic duties (especially those associated with emigration to the US), they found themselves involved in a clash between the forces of republicanism, unionism and imperialism and then later in the midst of an actual civil war. Both had complicated repercussions for the US that required the greatest of vigilance on the parts of these consular officers and Davis in London.

Although the Anglo-Irish war of independence had not featured in the US presidential election, events in Ireland intruded upon Wilson's agenda during his last months in office. In August 1919, McAndrews had noted in his second report on Irish conditions that the previously bitterly 'anti-Irish' *Times* newspaper had, on 24 July, offered a scheme for an Irish settlement based on the establishment of two state legislatures, one for Ulster and the other for the rest of Ireland. McAndrews felt that this indicated conclusively the desire of English 'men of repute' for an Irish settlement because of its bearing on the 'larger question of an Anglo–American alliance.'[56] Elements of *The Times* plan emerged in Lloyd

55 NARA, RG59, Inspection reports on foreign service posts (hereafter IRFSP), Queenstown, June 1919, pp. 39, 1,2, 5.   56 NARA, RG59, M580/214, 841d.00/82, McAndrews to Secretary of State, 9 August 1919.

George's legislative response to the Irish crisis, which was influenced also by the conclusions of the Irish Committee. Lloyd George told Davis and C.P. Scott, editor of the *Manchester Guardian*, on 30 November that he planned for two separate parliaments and a federal council, although control over customs would remain in London. Scott immediately noted that, since Sinn Féin would refuse to take the oath of allegiance, the plan would fail, a point that had escaped Davis, who focused on Sinn Féin's approval of the general principle. Nonetheless, Lloyd George felt sure of his position because of the continued existence of the coalition government which included Conservatives. So, on 22 December, he introduced 'The Better government of Ireland Bill' to the British House of Commons.[57]

On the following day, Davis cabled the State Department to report that the proposal had been favourably received in the British press, because there was general agreement that some effort had to be made to 'solve definitely' the Irish question. But he felt that the financial clauses would be the sticking point.[58] Meanwhile, in Dublin, Dumont who had only been in Dublin a few weeks agreed to meet with Arthur Griffith, president of the Irish republic, if there was no publicity. He found the Irish president to be 'a man of Irish lower middle class' who had a 'good deal of the Irish air of mysticism ... ungroomed, dour, sullen, unenthusiastic ... difficult to talk to. Griffith's opinion was that there 'is nothing for Irishmen in the English Premier's proposals ... they are made to affect and mislead opinion in America.'[59] But it was Griffith's views on the role of the US that Dumont highlighted to his masters. Griffith believed that an Irish settlement was

> a vital factor in the American political situation; that the Irish-American vote is the backbone of the Democratic party; and that the Catholic Church in America, dominated as it is by Irish, can force America through politics into a position where she would be willing, even if she is not at present, to help Ireland obtain her freedom if that is to be the only solution ... [H]e appears to be rather certain that the sympathy of America would be with Ireland even if she resorted to open rebellion to obtain her freedom.[60]

It is clear that Dumont did not have much personal regard for Griffith, viewing him as an obsessive politician who lacked an international perspective and that he disagreed with his analysis of the strength of Irish-America. However, the US consul did go to some lengths to ensure that Griffith's response to the Lloyd George plan was transmitted to Washington uncensored and he recognized him as being president of a Sinn Féin republic that had majority support in Ireland.

57 Davis & Fleming, *The ambassadorial diary*, 30 November 1919.   58 NARA, RG59, M580/214, 841d.00/107, Davis to Secretary of State, 23 December 1919.   59 Ibid., 841d.00/115, Dumont to Secretary of State, 23 December 1919.   60 Ibid., 841d.00/119, Dumont to Secretary of State, 2 January 1920.

Dumont's dispatch elaborated on his own opinion on the US dimension of the Irish conflict also and, unlike his predecessor, he proffered advice to the State Department that were it possible to stop all communications with the US, Sinn Féin would 'slowly die out.'[61] This report drew the attention of officials in the division of Western European Affairs, who heavily marked this latter comment. Carr was asked to commend Dumont 'highly for this excellent and comprehensive report.'[62] Dumont's beliefs, in January 1920, can be summarized as follows: firstly, the nationalists' rejection of the dual parliament settlement was significant, particularly as the Irish situation was at a 'dangerous' point, secondly, de Valera's approval of a settlement was vital, as it would bring along majority approval, and thirdly, the US administration could once again be dragged in to finding a settlement to the Irish question.[63]

The fourth home rule bill passed its second reading on 29 March 1920. Ulster Unionists voted with the government and there was no parliamentary opposition to it from Sinn Féin, the Nationalist Party or the Labour Party. While the British government debated and discussed the legislation, a war continued in Ireland. Between January 1919 and July 1921, the British government flooded the country with 40,000 soldiers, 7,000 Black and Tans and 6,000 Auxiliaries.[64] Plunkett provided House with a personal viewpoint on 1 December 1919,

> The state of Ireland is becoming desperate. We have the largest civil police per head of population in the world, with full military equipment. A huge army of occupation is engaged in the futile attempt to protect the civil population from the civil police ... never in my memory ... have life and property in Ireland been so insecure[65]

The State Department and the White House received regular reports of the escalating war from Davis, Dumont, Sharp, Mitchell and McAndrews. These reports provided up-to-date information and analysis of events, particularly of the US dimension, details of the number of raids by the Irish Republican Army (IRA), the police and the army, the numbers killed, injured, arrested and imprisoned, in addition to conducting their normal business.[66]

Hathaway in particular became a 'valuable outpost' but he departed for Budapest in January 1920. His experience would have been invaluable to the

61 Ibid. Dumont indicated to the department that he would not be sending newspaper editorials because they were 'uninteresting reading', were public property anyway and provided only a 'feeling of the moment.' Also he worried that the newspapers did not provide sufficient information on police raids. Ibid.   62 NARA, RG59, M580/214, 841d.00/119, Carr to Dumont, 14 February 1920. 63 Ibid., Dumont to Secretary of State, 2 January 1920.   64 J.J. Lee, *Ireland: 1912–85, politics and society* (1989), p. 43.   65 Yale University Library, Manuscripts and Archives Collection (hereafter YULMC), The papers of Colonel E.M. House (hereafter EHP), box 91, file 3141, Plunkett to House, 1 December 1919. Plunkett invited House to act as a mediator, an offer he repeated again during the Anglo-Irish war of independence. Ibid.   66 See NARA, RG59, M580/215.

State Department in interpreting the next phase of the Anglo-Irish war of independence which began in January 1920. Although McAndrews soon showed some sympathy for the 'long neglected and mistreated people' and Dumont maintained his contacts with Griffith, the latter leaned increasingly towards the British view of events as articulated by the British military and civil authorities in Dublin, although his work was commended by the State Department.[67] In the northern counties, Sharp provided a unionist perspective. In early 1920 the war escalated, with IRA raids and ambushes. The British government responded by recruiting former British soldiers and sailors and unleashing the Black and Tans and the Auxiliaries on the republicans and their supporters. Within six months, the IRA had killed fifty-five policemen and destroyed hundreds of police barracks.[68]

The escalation of the violence created a number of problems for the US. First there was the issue of arms. On 27 January 1920, Davis sent an urgent telegram to Colby to report that 3,000 rifles of US manufacture had been landed on the county Clare coast in the previous two weeks. The information was passed from the office of the under secretary to that of the attorney general and the divisions of Foreign Intelligence and Foreign Commerce.[69] But when Dumont investigated he was informed by the authorities in Dublin that they looked upon the story was 'as a canard.'[70] In April 1920, Davis passed on a report of an attempt to bring arms to Ireland from Germany from the US military attaché in Berne, Switzerland, to 'our friends' in the Foreign Office.[71] Soon enough in 1921, other reports of arms being shipped from the US for the IRA would prove to be true and troublesome for the US–British relationship (see chapter eight). A second aspect to the US entanglement in the Irish war related to the provision of protection for any US citizens caught up in the war or their property. From January 1919 onwards, the police and military authorities raided private homes to get hold of men suspected of sedition and of being leaders in proscribed activities and societies. In early 1919, Hathaway had raised the question of possible protection for US residents threatened with damage from seizure of their property by the authorities with Davis. But the expected injury did not materialize and the Queenstown consul was not required to take any action.[72]

Dumont believed that there were approximately 1,500 naturalized Americans in Ireland in February 1920, and that there were a further 1,500 in Ireland who

67 Ibid., 841d.00/142, Mitchell to Secretary of State, 10 February 1920; ibid., 841d.00/180, Carr to Dumont, 1 May 1920.   68 'Anglo-Irish War' in S.J. Connolly (ed.), *The Oxford companion to Irish history* (1998), p. 15.   69 NARA, RG59, M580/214, 841d.00/123, Davis to Secretary of State, 27 January 1920.   70 Ibid., 841d.00/125, Davis to Secretary of State, 30 January 1920.   71 Ibid., 841d.00/178a, Colby to Davis, 17 April; ibid., 841d.00/179, Davis to Colby, 21 April 1920. In July, Ambassador Davis cabled Secretary Colby to inform him that the British authorities had arrested James Barry, a seaman on board the SS *New York* recently arrived in Southampton from the US on a charge of bringing firearms into Britain. Also he had documents on him indicating that he was a courier between Irish-American groups in the US and Sinn Féin in Ireland. NARA, RG59, M580/216, 841d.00/212, Davis to Secretary of State, 9 July 1920.   72 Ibid., IRFSP, Queenstown, June 1919, p. 35.

had no passports but claimed US citizenship either by birth or naturalization.[73] However in February 1920, he reported that in Dublin eleven people had been arrested by the military authorities during the previous ten days, and that one of these was John Patrick Atkins, born in New York city, who had registered with the consulate as a US citizen. Consequently, he claimed the protection of the consulate. Although Dumont doubted Atkins' right to protection, he rang the police and military authorities and asked to be furnished with the charges and that Atkins be given a speedy trial. On the following day, Atkins was released, being told that it was a case of mistaken identity and that no charges would be filed against him. Atkins' brother, a British subject who Dumont maintained was prominent in Sinn Féin, was not released.[74] It is clear that Dumont was not particularly anxious to get involved; indeed he came to believe that the Irish were naturally 'restive' and that even after freedom was secured, there would be 'lawlessness.' He was also highly critical of the Roman Catholic hierarchy's tolerance of the IRA's outrages.[75] Not surprisingly, in early 1920 he was more than willing to support a suggestion from the British under secretary for Ireland, John Anderson, and the general officer commanding-in-chief, Nevil Macready, that they would welcome it if an effort were made by the State Department to limit the issuance of passports for naturalized citizens of the US who had been born in the provinces of Munster and Connacht to as small a number as possible during the 'present disturbed conditions in Ireland.' Dumont supported the request because those provinces were 'overwhelmingly Sinn Féin in sympathy and it behoves naturalized Americans visiting them to be most circumspect in their conduct.'[76] He readily reported the rumour that members of a secret Irish-American order had murdered the lord mayor of Cork, Tomás MacCurtain, on 20 March because of his opposition to IRA attacks on barracks and murders. But he felt that most Irish-Americans in Ireland were opposed to the murders that were being carried out by the IRA.[77] This deprecation intensified as Dumont built up his network of contacts in British circles. He received most of his intelligence

---

73 Ibid., RG59, M580/215, 841d.00/147, Dumont to Secretary of State, 20 February 1920.   74 Ibid., M580/215, 841d.00/147, Dumont to Secretary of State, 20 February 1920.   75 Ibid., M580/214, 841d.00/135, Dumont to Secretary of State, 27 January 1920. By way of contrast in February 1920, Vice Consul McAndrews reported on the economic shape of a new Irish republic and the opportunities for US commerce. Wilbur Carr asked him to elaborate on the trading relations between Ireland and the US and British policy. NARA, RG59, M580/215, 841d.00/142, McAndrews to Secretary of State, 10 February 1920; ibid., Carr to McAndrews, 10 April 1920; ibid., Supplementary Sheets; ibid., 841d.00/180, Dumont to Secretary of State, 5 April 1920.   76 Ibid., M580/215, 841d.00/147, Dumont to Secretary of State, 20 February 1920.   77 Ibid., 841d.00/180, Dumont to Secretary of State, 5 April 1920. The Coroner's jury indicted the RIC for causing MacCurtain's death but Dumont refused to accept the evidence which he put down to pressure from the Cork nationalist community. After MacCurtain's death, Vice Consul McAndrews received resolutions of sympathy from Waterford Corporation, Kerry County Council and Bandon Town commissioners. Ibid., M580/215, 841d.00/191, Dumont to Secretary of State, 21 April 1920; ibid., M580/216, 841d.00/201, McAndrews to Secretary of State, 11 May 1920.

from within Dublin Castle, specifically from the army staff in the commander-in-chief's office and the intelligence section, where staff also checked out the accuracy of newspaper reports for him.[78] Increasingly he displayed more sympathy for the plight of the British administrators and military and police chiefs in Dublin Castle than for the Sinn Féin leadership. In October, he was described by Mark Sturgis, a British civil servant in the under secretary for Ireland's office, as 'a very pleasant, interesting' man.[79] At the same time, Dumont indicated to the State Department that he had direct contact with the leaders of Sinn Féin. His supposed neutrality would be tested when he attempted to intervene personally in the war, as will seen later.[80]

But in spring 1920, the violence continued. Despite Dumont's personal views, his reporting could be incisive. For example, in April he reported changes in the British administration in Dublin Castle; namely a) that Macready replaced Frederick Shaw as commander-in-chief of the British army in Ireland with authority over the Royal Irish Constabulary (RIC) and the Dublin Metropolitan Police, b) that Hamar Greenwood replaced Ian MacPherson as chief secretary for Ireland and c) that the intelligence sections of the army, RIC and police were to be combined into one unit and he concluded:

> But the policy of the government is unlikely to change with the superseding of heads, at least while Lord French [lord lieutenant of Ireland] remains. These had to go to make the failure of the British government's plans seem to be their fault rather than the effect of a policy from London that constrained them, that was short of vision, and lacked intuition and the power to synthesise, and to reason from cause to effect.

The changes did not effect an improvement in the situation. Dumont shared the Castle view that political interference from London was preventing military success, but as the vicious circle of repression and outrage continued, he came to believe that the only solution left was dominion home rule.[81] This was not what was being debated in the House of Commons, where a limited form of home rule legislation provided two parliaments but did not give Ireland control of its own financial, foreign and defence affairs. In Belfast, Consul George H. Barringer continued Sharp's pro-unionist viewpoint and represented it as a reasonable one. He described Edward Carson's speech on the home rule legislation in the House of Commons debate 'as noteworthy for its sincerity as well as its effectiveness.' Barringer felt that if the bill was passed 'Ulster would make the best of it' and still be 'loyal' to the empire.[82] Ambassador Davis recognized the legislation for

78 Ibid., M580/215, 841d.00/180, Dumont to Secretary of State, 5 April 1920. 79 M. Hopkinson (ed.), *The last days of Dublin Castle: the diaries of Mark Sturgis* (1999), p. 62. 80 NARA, RG59, M580/215, 841d.00/180, Dumont to Secretary of State, 5 April 1920. 81 Ibid. 82 Ibid., 841d.00/196, Barringer to Secretary of State, 30 April 1920.

what it was; 'a compromise between the Dominion home rule proposals and the modified post-war attitudes of the Ulster Unionist Council.' He was particularly interested in the support the bill was receiving from *The Times* and the *Daily Mail* which had both implacably opposed any measure of self-government for Ireland ten years earlier.[83] Consequently, Davis was surprised to receive Dumont's view that 'full dominion home rule' might work. He felt that a political solution was not possible but he was not the man on the ground, where the situation gradually deteriorated as the spring wore on.[84]

On 21 April, Dumont reported the military authorities' measures to prevent another Sinn Féin rising, which was rumoured to be planned for Easter Monday. It did not happen and instead the Sinn Féin leadership launched a series of attacks on state offices and police barracks on 3–4 April.[85] Meanwhile Barringer contentedly reported from Belfast that the Sinn Féin outrages were carried out on a minor scale in the northern counties, due to the presence of the military and police in Belfast and its vicinity and their 'vigilance' in the predominantly Roman Catholic, Londonderry. He also reported the arrests of Sinn Féin men and their removal, on 10 April, from Belfast and Londonderry prisons to English jails.[86] This latter action came after approximately 100 political prisoners in Mountjoy prison in Dublin began a hunger strike on 4 April to demand political status. News of the strike soon spread. Barringer reported 'very little sympathy' for them in Belfast, except among the minority nationalist community. Neither was there a general work stoppage in support of the hunger-strikers in Belfast or Londonderry, as happened in the rest of Ireland, although he reported considerable fighting between the police, military and civilians in Londonderry and rioting at night.[87] Despite the patchy support in the northern counties, appeals for the men's release gathered pace.

On 12 April, Dublin City Council agreed to send a memorial outlining the circumstances of the hunger strike to the consuls of the US, France and Italy. It was delivered to Dumont on 13 April by the lord mayor, the high sheriff and relatives of the hunger strikers. Dumont proffered the official line, namely that he could not accept the memorial. If they wanted it to reach the US government it should be presented through the British ambassador at Washington because he, as consul, did not have a diplomatic function.[88] Although he was technically correct, other consuls found ways to accede to similar requests. Dumont was also asked to use his personal influence with the Dublin Castle authorities to secure the release of the hunger strikers. But he explained that he had 'no influence' as an individual and that any requests made by him would be considered only because he was US consul, explaining that this would lead to 'trouble' for the

83 Ibid., 841d.00/184, Davis to Secretary of State, 13 April 1920.   84 Davis & Fleming, *The ambassadorial diary*, 19 May 1920.   85 NARA, RG59, M580/215, 841d.00/191, Dumont to Secretary of State, 21 April 1920.   86 Ibid., 841d.00/196, Barringer to Secretary of State, 30 April 1920.   87 Ibid.   88 Ibid., 841d.00/191, Dumont to Secretary of State, 21 April 1920.

consul not only with the British government but with his own government as well. The delegation were dissatisfied with Dumont's replies and indicated that, since he refused to pursue a course dictated by the 'ordinary instincts of humanity', they would appeal 'over his head to the American ambassador' in London. Dumont punctured this hope by indicating that, in 'all probability', the ambassador would give the same reply as he had. Dumont described the interview as 'courteous', but said that in view of the situation in Dublin the pressure brought to bear on him was 'heavy.' Later in the day, he received a delegation from the Wicklow Urban District Council who sought to present a memorial and request his intervention. He gave the same reply, but some members of the committee 'were rather ugly.' It was not clear if these were the men who claimed to be US citizens but, whether they were or not, Dumont was taken aback by the strength of feeling. Neither the Italian nor the French consul was visited in person by the respective delegations.[89] Dumont had resisted republican pressure but clearly his position still accorded him a certain standing in republican circles. He kept a close watch throughout the events and met Griffith again on 14 April. Griffith told him that a settlement was imminent and by that evening eighty five men, including forty political prisoners, were released unconditionally.[90]

Dumont's sympathies were clearly with the British side. Having discussed the release of the hunger-strikers on 14 April, and the arrests of more republicans later on in the same day, he informed Colby that the British military authorities in Ireland had 'no intention' of coming 'into conflict with the Irish people.' But he pronounced that it was acceptable for the British leaders to contemplate the use of airplanes armed with machine guns 'to terrify the people making the trouble.' At this difficult time, evidence of Dumont's standing with the British administration emerged. On 16 April, he and his wife were invited to dinner by French. Such an invitation was not unusual, as foreign consuls were a part of the official social circle in Dublin, but on this occasion the Dumonts were the only guests present along with French, Macready and their respective aides-de-camps and wives.[91] Significantly, after the dinner Dumont reported to Washington the great concern in Britain at the 'freedom with which the propaganda for an Irish republic is allowed to be carried on in the United States' even while recognizing that it was an election year.[92]

Public opinion in the US and liberal opinion in Britain was less accepting of the situation in Ireland. The State Department and administration began to feel the strength of Irish-American pressure to intervene. Newspapers reported details of the general conditions, specifically those pertaining in Mountjoy jail in Dublin.[93] Agnes Newman, Roger Casement's sister, cabled Wilson and Tumulty on 12 April, to appeal for US intervention on behalf of Irishmen 'dying of star-

89 Ibid.   90 Ibid.   91 Ibid., M580/215, 841d.oo/191, Dumont to Secretary of State, 21 April 1920.   92 Ibid.   93 NARA, RG59, M580/215, 841d.oo/193, Phelan to Secretary of State, 24 April 1920.

vation' in Mountjoy.[94] A few days later, Lloyd DeMarst, president of the Loyal Coalition, cabled Colby to counteract the republican pressure and urge the State Department not to intervene in British domestic policy but it was the Sinn Féin viewpoint that was influential in Congress in this election year.[95] On 15 April, a select committee, representing one hundred members of the House of Representatives, met with Colby to appeal for immediate action by the US government 'for the amelioration of the condition of Irish political prisoners now lying in English jails.' The conference was followed by the submission of a signed five-page letter expanding on and justifying their request.[96]

Senator Phelan, on behalf of John D. Cantwell, bishop of Monterey, brought an individual case to Colby's attention. On 24 April, Phelan asked Colby to get details of the whereabouts of the 'unaccused and untried man', Walter Cantwell, the bishop's elder brother, who had been arrested in an RIC raid on suspected Sinn Féin families. Colby told Phelan that many other cases had been received by the State Department and that where such persons were British subjects, the department was not in a position to make representations to the British government protesting against the 'alleged arrest and ill-treatment' of individuals who were not US citizens.[97] Colby was adhering to the usual legal and diplomatic procedures but the negative publicity appeared to pay off. Dumont reported that French and Macready were ordered by the London government to do everything possible 'to conciliate Americans and American opinion.'[98]

94 Ibid., 841d.00/175, Agnes Newman to Wilson, 12 April 1920; ibid., Agnes Newman to Tumulty, 12 April 1920.   **95** Ibid., 841d.00/177, DeMarst to Colby, 16 April 1920.   **96** Ibid., 841d.00/192, Select Committee to Colby, 15 April 1920.   **97** Ibid., 841d.00/193, Cantwell to Phelan, 22 April 1920; ibid., Phelan to Colby, 24 April 1920; ibid., Division of Western European Affairs, no date. Neither did the State Department intervene when the master of the SS *Panhandle State* decided not to call at Queenstown because the British Admiralty had closed the port to passenger vessels. The ship was in mid-journey and six passengers complained through the lawyer, Rossa F. Downing, a member of FOIF. In a letter to Colby on 24 September 1920, Downing reminded him that 'England is not at war with the United States, therefore, British ports are open to American shipping ... there is no plague in the vicinity of Cork Harbour, or any other Irish port ... Britain will not admit that Ireland is at war with her; nor is Ireland at war with the United States. Ireland welcomes American tonnage, both passenger and cargo.' Colby received advice from Fred K. Nielsen, the State Department solicitor indicating that the opening or closing of a port was a matter of domestic policy but more significantly Nielsen reminded Colby that 'we have not recognised the belligerency of Ireland and, therefore, cannot dispute the British government's right to close a British port.' He recognized that the question of whether a representation should be made to the British government was one of 'policy' but he understood that US commercial interests were 'hampered very little' by the closure. No further action was taken and a 'careful' reply to Downing was drafted. Colby instructed Admiral S.S. Benson, chairman of the US Shipping Board to direct the master of the SS *Panhandle* not to call at Queenstown on the east-bound voyage but to do so on the west-bound provided there were no restrictions. Downing complained again on 10 October with but policy remained unchanged. NARA, RG59, M580/218, 841d.00/307, Downing to Secretary of State, 24 September 1920; ibid., Nielsen to Colby, 28 September 1920; ibid., 841d.00/328, Benson to Colby, 22 September 1920; ibid., 841d.00/309, Downing to Colby, 11 October 1920.   **98** Ibid., M580/215, 841d.00/191, Dumont to Secretary of State, 21 April 1920; ibid., 841d.00/197, Dumont

But in late May, Dumont was under no illusion but that Ireland was moving towards a 'collision.'[99] He accepted that the British policy in Ireland, particularly the use of the Defence of the Realm Act and imprisonment without trial, was responsible for much of the unrest and he accepted that the use of the hunger strike was inevitable; 'the truth is that they were deprived of liberty without being brought to trial for any offence against the law and that imprisonment under such conditions is repugnant to the sense of justice of unprejudiced persons.' Yet, he stated that Sinn Féin statements in Ireland and the US about prison conditions were 'equivocal' because, according to his sources, the prisoners had destroyed the furniture and windows in the cells.[1] In the US, criticism of British actions in Ireland continued. Dumont did his best to thwart reports originating in Ireland. In mid-May, he reported that William MacDonald, a former professor at Brown University and contributor to the liberal journal, the *Nation*, was travelling throughout Ireland and interviewing various persons in order to get a correct understanding of the Irish situation. Dumont pointed out to the State Department that he had only met Sinn Féin leaders and no Unionists. MacDonald had justified this on the grounds that Sinn Féin represented the 'proletariat' but Dumont concluded that, as a consul, he had met many like MacDonald, who 'love the proletariat only in print' and stay at the 'best hotels and travel first class.'[2] The *Nation* maintained its support for the Irish cause and in September 1920 was instrumental in establishing the American Commission on Conditions in Ireland which will be examined later in this chapter.

An increase in Sinn Féin attacks on police barracks, tax offices and court houses convinced Dumont that the British government either had to give Ireland full dominion home rule, with absolute control of its own revenues, or apply rigid military rule, with an army of not less than 300,000 men to ensure peace but not future prosperity in Ireland.[3] Dumont's views mirrored those of Davis in London, and foreshadowed the contradictory approach adopted by the British government in Ireland for the following fourteen months. On the one hand, the coercion policy was intensified, while on the other, peace initiatives started in summer 1920.[4]

One attempt at conciliation involved Edward House. It was not just Sinn Féin nationalists who looked to the US for official assistance. So also did moderate nationalists. In early summer 1920, Horace Plunkett requested his friend, House

to Secretary of State, 14 May 1920. After Hamar Greenwood, the new chief secretary for Ireland, arrived the Dumonts were again invited to dinner to meet him on 7 May.   99 Davis & Fleming, *The ambassadorial diary*, 31 May 1920.   1 NARA, RG59, M580/215, 841d.oo/197, Dumont to Secretary of State, 14 May 1920. After other meetings with Griffith, he forwarded to the State Department and discussed with Ambassador Davis, Griffith's warnings that Sinn Féin 'intend that America shall come into this thing ... It makes no difference to us how much trouble we may create in America' to illustrate Sinn Féin's naïve hope in US intervention. Davis & Fleming, *The ambassadorial diary*, 31 May 1920; NARA, RG59, M580/216, 841d.oo/209, Dumont to Secretary of State, 15 June 1920.   2 NARA, RG59, M580/215, 841d.oo/197, Dumont to Secretary of State, 14 May 1920.   3 Ibid.   4 Ibid., M580/216, 841d.oo/198, Davis to Secretary of State, 17 May 1920; M. Hopkinson (ed.), 'Introduction' in Hopkinson (ed.), *The last days of Dublin Castle*, p. 7.

who was then in London, to consider acting as a mediator between the sides in the Anglo-Irish war. He wanted him to visit Ireland on an excuse, meet Sinn Féin people and subsequently report to Lloyd George, who would ask him to negotiate. House did not baulk at the idea and replied that 'I see great possibilities in the suggestion of a mediator and for the reasons you give'. Plunkett promised to 'work quietly to bring this about.'[5] But the idea went no further for a number of reasons. Firstly, Plunkett had little actual influence with Sinn Féin, secondly, he was an ill man, thirdly, House was no longer influential with Wilson, whom he had not seen since June 1919, or with Lloyd George and finally, there was more fighting to be done in Ireland before the two sides moved towards negotiation.[6]

In May and June 1920, Dumont reported a reduction in the numbers of deaths, which he believed arose from a decision by Sinn Féin to appease US opinion but which Macready believed resulted from the extra British soldiers in Ireland. But the riots, attacks and raids on public buildings persisted. Sinn Féin continued to mete out justice through its own court system and by mid-July the consul stated that the situation 'gets worse day by day' throughout the country. Describing himself as an 'impartial observer', his reference point was always the Sinn Féin-orchestrated violence, while he believed that the British forces 'held themselves in check under the most irritating conditions.' For example, he devoted one page of a report to undermining an account which originally appeared in the Sinn Féin organ, *Irish Bulletin*, and was reprinted in other Irish and English newspapers, which claimed that a divisional commander of the British army in Munster had announced a 'shoot to kill' policy in Listowel, county Kerry, if the public did not co-operate with the army. However, Dumont accepted that the Black and Tans did not have the same disciplinary standards as the army.[7]

5 NLI, HPP, P6584, Plunkett to House, 25 June 1920; ibid., House to Plunkett, 27 June 1920; ibid., Plunkett to House, 1 July 1920; YULMC, EHP, box 91, file 3141, Plunkett to House, 10 July 1920; NARA, RG59, M580/215, 841d.00/197, Dumont to Secretary of State, 14 May 1920.   6 NLI, HPP, P6584, Plunkett to House, 10 September 1920. In 1920, Plunkett also appealed to his friend, the moderate Irish-American John Quinn to get involved in Ireland again. He asked him to fund a 'first class weekly journal and the conduct of a national propaganda' campaign dedicated to shaping public opinion in Ireland, Britain and the US in favour of an Irish constitution along dominion lines. Both men believed that Sinn Féin's demands for a republic were unwise. The journal was the resurrected *Irish Statesman*. B.L. Reid, *The man from New York: John Quinn and his friends* (1968), pp. 512–13.   7 NARA, RG59, M580/216, 841d.00/209, Dumont to Secretary of State, 15 June 1920; F. Costello, *The Irish revolution and its aftermath, 1916–1923: years of revolt* (2003), p. 78; NARA, RG59, M580/216, 841d.00/214, Dumont to Secretary of State, 14 July 1920. Dumont continued to report on the state of the labour movement in Ireland particularly signs of 'bolshevism'. But he did not support a State Department proposal that consuls reject applications from known bolsheviks for US visas because in the context of Ireland, it would target Sinn Féin members and lead to protests from Irish-Americans. However, in October he wondered whether members of the Irish Transport and General Workers' Union 'brought up on teachings' of James Connolly were 'fit subjects for admission as immigrants' into the US. Ibid., M580/216, 841d.00/209, Dumont to Secretary of State, 15 June 1920; ibid., M580/217, 841d.00/237, Dumont to Secretary of State, 15 September 1920; ibid., 841d.00/248, Dumont to Secretary of State, 15 October 1920.

Even Macready admitted to Henry Wilson, chief of the imperial general staff, that the '"Black and Tans" officers are a most cut throat lot of men and that they terrorise a town or a countryside just as much as the S[inn].F[éin]s.'[8] It was the composition of these new recruits that soon worried State Department officials. In August, Colby cabled Davis to investigate Hearst press reports from Dublin that a new 'secret service army' had been enlisted for duty in Ireland, with orders to 'take terrorist chiefs dead or alive.' Colby had heard that it consisted of 'many Americans who had served in British or Canadian forces and who are being instructed by Scotland Yard and Army Intelligence officers.'[9] Davis did not confirm or deny this rumour but he was able to deny that 'expert gunmen shipped from the United States with bogus passports' had killed an RIC inspector in Belfast at the end of August 1920.[10] In Dublin, Dumont made no reference to US citizens composing part of the new recruits to the British military. Recent research indicates that just ten of the 13,732 of the Black and Tans and Auxiliaries gave their birthplace as the United States.[11]

Dumont's fears of a worsening military situation were soon realized.[12] Davis attended the House of Commons on 5 August for the final reading of the Restoration of Order in Ireland bill and he described the debate as a 'sham battle', as all present knew the government had enough votes to pass it.[13] He opposed the imposition of 'martial law' in Ireland but remained bitterly anti-Sinn Féin. In these last few months of his tenure, he was disappointed that he could not do anything about the deteriorating situation and felt his mission was impotent after the November election results.[14] On 9 August, the act became law and extended the war-time emergency powers and empowered courts martial to try a wide

8 Imperial War Museum, London (hereafter IWM), The diaries of Field Marshall Sir Henry Wilson (hereafter HWD), DS/Misc/80, reel 9, 1–1–1920 to 22–12–1921, 6 September 1920. 9 NARA, RG59, M580/216, 841d.00/210a, Colby to Davis, 18 August 1920. Prior to this on 21 June, Norman Davis, acting secretary of State, instructed Ambassador Davis in London to check out reports received by the US Military Intelligence Division that murders in Ireland were being committed by 'imported American gunmen' of Irish extraction. On the following day, Davis reported the British authorities' categorical denial. Ibid., 841d.00/205a, Davis to Davis, 21 June 1920; ibid., 841d.00/206, Davis to Davis, 22 June 1920. 10 Ibid., M580/216, 841d.00/221, Davis to Secretary of State, 24 August 1920. Davis also forwarded, at Shane Leslie's request, copies of twenty statements made by owners of private houses in Ireland that had been raided by the British army in summer 1920. Ibid., M580/218, 841d.00/321, Davis to Secretary of State, 24 June 1920; ibid., 841d.00/322, Davis to Secretary of State, 16 July 1920. 11 Ibid., M580/216, 841d.00/209, Dumont to Secretary of State, 15 June 1920; W.J. Lowe, 'Who were the Black-and-Tans?', 49. 12 Ibid., M580/217, 841d.00/232, Dumont to Secretary of State, 28 September 1920. He reported on Plunkett's ill-fated peace conference, held in the Dublin on 24 August, but boycotted by representatives of republicanism, labour and unionism. Dumont described Plunkett as 'politically bankrupt' and his political opinions were valued only in the US. Ibid. 13 Davis & Fleming, The ambassadorial diary, 5 August 1920; ibid., June–August 1920. Davis was impressed by reports from the departments of Local Government, Foreign Affairs, Home Affairs, Trade and Commerce, Agriculture, Forestry and Fisheries and Irish that were submitted to the Sinn Féin parliament, for their 'ability and effort to conduce a government with all customary forms.' Ibid., 10 August 1920. 14 Ibid., 11 December 1920.

range of offences, increased the powers of the military authorities and suspended *habeas corpus*.[15] Griffith appealed to Wilson to intervene and likened the Irish situation to Belgium's in 1914.[16] However, one arrest in late summer 1920 swung the focus of the US representatives' attention from Ireland back to Washington and tested Wilson's policy of non-interference on Ireland.

The MacSwiney case

Dumont believed that the Restoration of Order in Ireland Act was a 'confession of the complete failure of British civil authority in almost all of Ireland' and noted a 'considerable increase' in the activities of the government troops and police on one side, and Sinn Féin sympathizers on the other, in the 'guerrilla warfare' in Ireland. Among the 'special outrages and acts of aggression', that he noted, were the murder of Mr Craig, the county inspector for Cork East Riding and the arrest on 12 August of the lord mayor of Cork, Terence MacSwiney. Dumont continued that MacSwiney was known to the military authorities, the police and the press as the Sinn Féin commandant in Munster and at the time of his arrest he had an RIC secret code message book in his possession along with secret messages. Dumont understood from his contacts within the military that there was more evidence against MacSwiney, but that it was held back and would be used to arrest other Sinn Féin activists.[17] MacSwiney was found guilty of sedition on 16 August and imprisoned in Brixton prison in London on 18 August. Dumont was in no doubt about MacSwiney's guilt and finished his note by stating that MacSwiney was on hunger strike that would not end until his release. By 31 August, he was in a critical condition and members of his family and the Roman Catholic chaplain were continually present in the prison, fearing his death.[18] MacSwiney's case became an international *cause célèbre* and, against the background of the presidential election, Irish and Irish-American republicans looked to the Wilson administration for help. His brother, Peter J. MacSwiney, who was a US citizen resident in New York city, requested Colby on 18 and 21 August to make 'such diplomatic representations as will prevent the murder of my brother by the English government.'[19] Colby replied, on 24 August, that from precedents established it was not possible to protest to the British government against the arrest and imprisonment of a non-US citizen. The same reply was sent to MacSwiney's sister, who was resident in St Genevieve's College in North Carolina and had asked for intervention if 'America was sincere in her war aims.'[20] Colby's

15 S. Connolly, 'Restoration of Order in Ireland Act' in Connolly, *The Oxford companion*, p. 483; S. Connolly, 'Anglo-Irish War' in ibid., p. 15.   16 Davis & Fleming, *The ambassadorial diary*, 31 May 1920.   17 NARA, RG59, M580/217, 841d.oo/232, Dumont to Secretary of State, 20 August 1920.   18 Connolly, 'Terence MacSwiney' in Connolly, *The Oxford companion*, p. 339.   19 NARA, RG59, M580/216, 841d.oo/217, MacSwiney to Secretary of State, 18 August 1920.   20 Ibid., Colby to MacSwiney, 24 August 1920; ibid., 841d.oo/219, MacSwiney to Colby, 22 August 1920; ibid.,

rebuff did not see the end of the campaign to secure US government intervention on behalf of MacSwiney and on 6 September Peter MacSwiney appealed to
Wilson as the campaign gathered momentum.[21]

The conservative *New York Times* provided bulletins on MacSwiney's condition on 13, 16, 19 and 31 August.[22] On 21 August, Dumont took the unusual
step of sending a cable directly to Colby; 'Mr Griffith informs me that if Lord
Mayor of Cork dies in prison it will be impossible to avoid gravest consequences
in spite of leaders disapproval.'[23] Cardinal O'Connell in Boston also implored
Colby 'in the name of humanity' to do everything to prevent MacSwiney's death.
Norman Davis, under secretary of State, replied that the government could not
protest to the British government because the lord mayor of Cork was not a US
citizen.[24] Among the other letters sent to Colby and Wilson were those from
Bishop Turner of Buffalo, on behalf of 250,000 Catholics who appealed to Colby
to intervene, Patrick McCartan, envoy of the Irish Republic to the US and Frank
P. Walsh.[25] The latter pleaded with Wilson, 'if you could see your way clear to
make direct official or personal appeal to Mr Lloyd George, we feel sure that
this tragedy would be averted.' Having read it, Wilson simply initialled it and
instructed it be acknowledged and filed. Most of the correspondence was acknowledged, but Colby specifically directed Robert Woods Bliss not to acknowledge
the petition from McCartan because it would have meant recognizing the Sinn
Féin government in Ireland.[26] Nonetheless, the campaign continued.
Congressional politicians such as Congressman John Q. Tilson from Connecticut,
on behalf of the John Dillon Literary Club, forwarded letters from constituents
requesting intervention.[27] In New York, Archbishop Patrick J. Hayes presided
over a memorial mass.[28] On 2 September, Tumulty passed a telegram to Wilson
from 'a very good Irish friend of ours', George Brennan. Brennan had emerged
as leader of the Democratic Party in Chicago and he grandly predicted that 'the
League of Nations will be ratified in November if the President will make friendly

---

Alvey A. Adee to MacSwiney, 24 August 1920.   **21** Ibid., M580/217, 841d.00/223, MacSwiney to
Wilson, 6 September 1920.   **22** *PWW*, 66, p. 89, fn 1.   **23** NARA, RG59, M580/216, 841d.00/218,
Dumont to Colby, 21 August 1920. Griffith cabled Wilson directly also on 24 August. Ibid.,
M580/217, 841d.00/227, Griffith to Wilson, 24 August 1920; ibid., 841d.00/231, Dumont to Colby,
26 August 1920.   **24** Ibid., 841d.00/223, O'Connell to Colby, 26 August 1920; ibid., Colby to
O'Connell, 26 August 1920.   **25** Ibid., 841d.00/225, Turner to Colby, 1 September 1920; ibid.,
841d.00/228, McCartan to Colby, 1 September 1920; ibid., Adee to Bliss, 10 September 1920. Initially
at least, not all Irish-Americans were swayed by the MacSwiney case. John Quinn, was suspicious
of Sinn Féin, refused to believe that he was not being fed in secret and believed the situation to be
a piece of 'Chinn–Feign' performance. He had not forgiven Irish-American extremists for 'going to
bed with the Germans' during the war. Reid, *The man from New York*, p. 512.   **26** *PWW*, 66, Walsh
to Wilson, 1 September 1920.   **27** NARA, RG59, M580/217, 841d.00/229, Tilson to Colby, 3
September 1920. In New York, a strike on the West Side docks prevented the loading of cargo on
British ships but failed to prevent passenger liners from sailing. Doyle, 'Striking for Ireland on the
New York docks' in Bayor & Meagher, *The New York Irish*, p. 371.   **28** M.E. Brown, 'Hayes, Patrick
Joseph Cardinal' in M. Glazier (ed.), *The encyclopedia of the Irish in America* (1999), p. 380.

representations to the Premier or King for Terence MacSwiney. He will also rehabilitate himself with the Irish people by this act.' Wilson replied to Tumulty on the same day, 'This is more than futile; it is grossly impertinent. I wish I knew some way to rebuke it. It is a piece of confounded impudence.' On the same day, Colby reported to Wilson a 'crescendo [of] pressure' on the State Department in the form of letters, telegrams personal calls and picketing on behalf of MacSwiney.[29] Colby set out the choices for Wilson:

> It is needless for me to even mention the entire absence of legal justifica-
> tion for any representation or action on our part. MacSwiney is a British
> subject, in jail as the result of the infraction of a British law, and the judge-
> ment of a presumably competent tribunal. Even on "humanitarian
> grounds" – the basis of most of the appeals to which I have referred –
> there seems to be a lack of support for any intervention, as the man is the
> victim of himself and no one else.
>   And yet – his death would be deplorable, and its effect not easy to esti-
> mate in advance.[30]

Colby's reaction reflected a mixture of influences: traditional State Department thinking on Ireland and the use of legalistic argument to justify official non-inter-vention. But, significantly, Colby was also well acquainted with the Irish cause due to his contacts with Irish-America and Hanna Sheehy Skeffington, among others, and finally, he was from the progressive wing of the Democrats. Perhaps it was the latter two motivations that led him on 2 September to offer Wilson a possible solution:

> The thought occurred to me that I might take advantage of my acquain-
> tance with the officials of the British embassy to express, in the most infor-
> mal and friendly way, our concern for the effect on public opinion of a
> successful martyrdom, and the hope that the British government might
> find a way to avert the man's death, without too great a sacrifice of con-
> sistency.
>   Or – is the subject one which I had best let alone?[31]

There is no evidence to suggest that Wilson instructed Colby, or indeed Davis in London, to intervene in the case even though it occurred in the middle of the

29 *PWW*, 66, Walsh to Wilson, 1 September 1920; ibid., Tumulty to Wilson, 2 September 1920; Brennan telegram, 2 September; ibid., Colby to Wilson, 2 September 1920. In St Louis, All Soul's Day on 31 September 1920 was renamed MacSwiney Day. Sullivan, 'Fighting for Irish freedom', p. 194.   30 *PWW*, 66, Colby to Wilson, 2 September 1920. In October, Patrick McCartan detailed for Secretary Colby the 'murder of unarmed civilians, the sacking of towns and the destruction of creameries' that occurred in Ireland between 1 January 1919 and 12 October 1920, the secretary directed that no reply was to be made. NARA, RG59, M580/218, 841d.00/304, McCartan to Secretary of State, 14 October 1920.   31 *PWW*, 66, Colby to Wilson, 2 September 1920.

election campaign.[32] Instead he held firm on his Irish policy. The anguish continued for Peter MacSwiney. The republican Liam Mellows commented 'it is painful to watch poor Peter [MacSwiney] feverishly watching the papers for a gleam of hope.'[33]

With no sign of assistance from Wilson and his administration and with MacSwiney's condition worsening, Davis worried about Dumont's safety in Dublin. Griffith had visited the consul on 24 September and had indicated that in two weeks time events would occur that would force the US government 'to show definitely what side it was on ... that Sinn Féin was determined to win if she forced the whole world into another great war.' Dumont sent a copy of the conversation to Davis in London who, reading between the lines, immediately cabled Colby that it was 'not impossible that something might happen to him [Dumont] as Sinn Féin is desperate,' although he felt that the consul had 'kept on consistently good terms with both British and Sinn Féin.'[34] Nothing happened to Dumont but Terence MacSwiney died on 25 October 1920. Britain's draconian security policy continued and Dumont reported a 'ring of steel' around Dublin city. Rather than forcing conformity such measures aroused ever more intense civilian opposition in Ireland, while in the US, the persistent newspaper publicity and criticism of British policy increased the pressure on the administration to act. Following a demonstration and speech by Katherine Hughes, in American League Park in Washington one week after MacSwiney's death, the crowd marched in silence to the White House. Bureau of Investigation agents reported that 'there were no disorders of any sort' and the police did not intervene. For seventy-four nights the protest was repeated and on the last night a US soldier, Captain Purcell, presented a memorial to Wilson from one thousand war veterans asking him to recognize the Irish republic.[35] In San Francisco, a memorial service was held on 31 October. Bureau agents reported that before the meeting a procession of about 5,000 people and approximately 500 cars had gone through the city.[36]

---

32 Ward, *Ireland and Anglo-American relations*, p. 231; Davis & Fleming, *The ambassadorial diary*, August to October 1920.   33 NLI, J.J. Hearn Papers, MS15986, Mellows to Hearn, 1 September 1920.   34 NARA, RG59, M580/217, 841d.oo/238, Davis to Colby, 29 September 1920; ibid., 841d.oo/oo/243, Dumont to Secretary of State, 28 October 1920.   35 Ibid., 841d.oo/259, Dumont to Secretary of State, 12 November 1920; For a discussion of the agitation in Washington DC see R.F. Downing, 'Men, women and memories' in W.G. FitzGerald, *The voice of Ireland*, p. 219. Dumont reported that one of the eleven prisoners on hunger strike in Cork prison who died on 25 October 1920 was Joseph Murphy who claimed US citizenship by reason of his American birth. Also he reported the hanging of Kevin Barry on 1 November 1920 in Mountjoy jail in Dublin which provoked 'intense feeling' among republicans but Dumont accepted that he was guilty. Ibid., NARA, Investigative Case Files of the Bureau of Investigation, 1908–1922, Record Group 65 (hereafter RG65), M1085/ reel 921, General Intelligence Report, no. 7, 5 December 1920; ibid., 13 December 1920.   36 NARA, RG65, M1085/ R920, Weekly Intelligence Report-San Francisco District to Hoover, 1 November 1920.

At the heart of this republican agitation was Eamon de Valera, who was still in the US making speeches and raising funds that were monitored by Bureau agents and British diplomats. Indeed de Valera had solidified his hold on the majority of Irish-American opinion and had attempted to sideline Daniel Cohalan and the Friends of Irish Freedom, by establishing the American Association for the Recognition of the Irish Republic (AARIR). Along with Harry Boland, Dáil Éireann representative to the US, he designed the AARIR with its headquarters in Washington, to undertake political and propaganda work.[37] Boland saw the AARIR as central to the future republican strategy in the US. Prior to the presidential election on 2 November, he told de Valera

> America must make peace, and my opinion is that no matter which Party wins on Tuesday next there will be either a League of Nations or an International Court of Justice. Therefore, the force of Irish-American opinion should be organised and definite plans laid immediately for the conducting of the campaign to secure that in any international agreement to which America may commit herself Ireland must be recognised in that agreement.[38]

The US and British governments, along with their agents on the ground in the US, watched these activities closely. US Bureau agents reported a 'split' in the Pádraig H. Pearse, Washington branch of the Friends of Irish Freedom and on 28 November it went over to the AARIR. But, as was indicated previously, neither of the governments interfered with de Valera because his martyrdom would not help either side.[39] However, the recently appointed Geddes was more sensitive to the heightened anti-British criticism by the US press and public.

Geddes arrived in Washington in March 1920 to face a difficult situation: Wilson had already established a pattern of aloofness from the diplomatic corps and this gulf was now increased due to the president's poor health. Most of Geddes' contact with the administration was with Polk and Colby, both of whom from November 1920 onwards were in caretaker mode only.[40] But of greater significance for the effectiveness of Geddes' work was the bitterness and hostility that he encountered in the press and Congress on the issues of British policy in Ireland and the repayment of war debts.[41] The latter will be examined in chapter nine but it was Ireland that mainly concerned him in late 1920.

37 National Archives of Ireland (hereafter NAI), Early Series (hereafter ES), Box 27, file 158, de Valera to Harry Boland, 30 May 1921.   38 Quoted in David Fitzpatrick, *Harry Boland's Irish revolution* (2003), p. 191.   39 Ward, *Ireland and Anglo-American relations,* p. 235; See NARA, RG65, M1085/R921, General Intelligence Report, no. 7, 5 December 1920.   40 *BDFA,* i, Lindsay to Curzon, 19 February 1920; J.C. McKercher, *Esme Howard: a diplomatic biography* (1989), p. 272.   41 G.H. Stuart, *The Department of State: a history of its organisation, procedure and personnel* (1949), p. p. 251; S. Bemis (ed.), *The American secretaries of state and their diplomacy* (1929), p. 218; B. Willson, *Friendly relations: a narrative of Britain's ministers and ambassadors to America (1790–1930)* (1934), pp. 329–30.

Geddes delivered many speeches during 1920. Some of them attracted the attention of Irish-American protestors and made Geddes nervous for his personal security. Polk did not think anything would happen to him but he gave instructions for a secret service agent to accompany him everywhere. Polk wanted to be on the 'safe side' and he admired Geddes because he showed a 'good deal of discretion' when Irish-American agitation was high.[42] Geddes continued to speak in public and in November 1920 against the backdrop of the MacSwiney protests, at an American Chamber of Commerce dinner in New York, he pleaded for Anglo–American friendship and co-operation.[43] But, later in the month, reports of the events of 'Bloody Sunday' in Dublin on 21 November, when thirteen mostly British intelligence officials, three republican prisoners and twelve people attending a football match in Croke Park were killed, combined with escalating anti-British sentiment provoking Geddes to seek a change in the British and US governments' hands-off position on de Valera. On 28 November, Geddes wanted to take a 'strong line' with the US government and seek de Valera's expulsion.[44] William Tyrell, now working in the Foreign Office, advised caution and instructed Geddes to collect evidence for the request but he felt 'we have to deal, not only with a government that exercises but a feeble control over the local bodies, but also with an administration which is discredited.'[45] Geddes could not resist responding to a statement by de Valera published in the *New York Times* on 23 November. He told Under Secretary of State Norman Davis

that while the British government understands that the Federal government has no control over the municipalities in the United States, and hence their official receptions to de Valera, it was impossible to get the British public to understand this ... they had, however, been considerably concerned about de Valera's recent statement ... he desired to know if this government had taken notice ... if they were contemplating doing something about it, or felt that it could, or that it would be expedient to do something. That it had occurred to him that the raising of funds in the United States and permitting them to Ireland in furtherance of a revolution, and statements inciting assassination, would at least justify, if not make it incumbent on this government, to deport at least any alien connected with such activities.

But Davis's reply revealed the continuing dilemma facing the Wilson administration, he

jokingly told the Ambassador that the Irish question was almost as great a source of embarrassment to this government as to his own government,

---

42 YULMC, Frank L. Polk Papers (hereafter FLPP), box 2, file 129, Polk to Davis, 26 May 1920. 43 Willson, *Friendly relation*, pp. 329–30. 44 TNA, FO371/4554, Geddes to Foreign Office, 24 November 1920. 45 Ibid., Tyrell, 30 November 1920.

and that as we have many more Irish than they have we might be justified in looking at it from one standpoint, to complain to the British government for the reflex action in the United States caused by the trouble in Ireland.[46]

When Davis said he would think it over, Geddes replied that his government might decide to file a complaint which would force a formal response from the administration. However, it is clear that while Davis was equally irritated by Irish republican agitation in the US he came close, on this occasion, to criticising British policy in Ireland, treating it as a source of the US administration's ongoing difficulties on the issue. Nevertheless, deporting de Valera was never an option for the US authorities. Indeed Special Agent Caskey confirmed to J. Edgar Hoover, head of the General Intelligence Division (formerly the radical division) in the Bureau of Investigation, on 12 December that State Department 'officials generally admit that the situation has assumed very delicate angles.'[47] By late December, it was too late to deport the Irish leader. De Valera had secretly left for Ireland, but this did not signal a reduction in the pressure on the administration because the public hearings of the American Commission on Conditions in Ireland were underway.

American Commission on conditions in Ireland

On 29 September 1920, Davis warned Colby that Sinn Féin intended sending a representative to testify before a US-based commission of inquiry into the situation in Ireland. This Commission was organized by Oswald Garrison Villard, editor of the *Nation* magazine and relative by marriage to W.J. Moloney, a New York doctor and Irish nationalist propagandist. Villard invited every US senator, governor, mayor of a large city, college presidents, prominent university professor, religious representatives, metropolitan newspaper editor and prominent citizens to establish a 'Committee of One Hundred' and form a commission comprising eight members to inquire into conditions in Ireland.[48] William MacDonald, former Brown University professor and journalist, who had visited Ireland earlier in 1920, was secretary of the Commission and he informed Colby on 30 October that the Commission of US citizens had been established and that it would not interfere in any part of the British jurisdiction.[49] Closely watched

---

46 Quoted in Ward, *Ireland and Anglo-American relations*, p. 235.   47 NARA, RG65, M1085/R921, General Intelligence Report, no. 8, for the week ending 12 December 1920.   48 *The American commission on conditions in Ireland: interim report* (1921), p. 1. The Commission comprised L. Hollingworth Wood (chairman), Frederick C. Howe (vice-chairman), Jane Addams, James H. Maurer, Major Oliver P. Newman, Senator George W. Norris, Rev. Norman Thomas, Senator David I. Walsh.   49 NARA, RG59, M580/217, 841d.00/247, MacDonald to Colby, 30 October 1920; *BDFA*, i, Annual Report for 1921, p. 55.

by Bureau of Investigation agents, the Commission decided to hold a series of public hearings at which witness statements from both sides would be heard, while a sub-committee was delegated to visit Ireland.[50] It was to be impartial in its proceedings and the British government, Unionists and, to use Dumont's words, 'convinced Sinn Féiners' were all invited to provide witnesses. British diplomats were convinced that the main idea inspiring Villard's plan was enmity to Britain, combined with advertising his newspaper.[51] Dumont, was in no doubt either about its partiality, specifically in that the story of British reprisals would be told but not the 'murders by Sinn Féin.'[52] Carroll has examined the establishment and work of the Commission in general but it is the interaction of the US administration with it that is of concern here.[53]

The first set of public hearings was to take place on 19 and 20 November with subsequent ones on 9, 10, 11, 15, 18, 21, 22 and 23 December and 13, 14, 19, 21 January 1921. Before they could begin three issues regarding the methodology to be used by the Commission had to be resolved; firstly, would the Irish-based witnesses be permitted by the British authorities to leave Ireland, secondly, would the US authorities permit them entry and thirdly, would the British authorities permit the Commission to visit Ireland to gather evidence. All three questions drew in the Wilson administration in its final days. On 27 September, MacDonald asked Geddes for an assurance that no impediments would be placed in the way of persons from Ireland travelling to the US to give evidence and that there would be no reprisals. Geddes, having consulted with the Foreign Office, believed there was no point in preventing any witnesses from leaving Ireland to appear at the hearings. Geddes replied to MacDonald on 23 October, 'the British government will refuse no one a passport to the United States on the ground that he or she desires to give evidence on either side before your committee … I may add that nothing will be done by the British government to encourage the holding of this enquiry or to assist witnesses to appear before the committee.'[54] Once it was clear that the British authorities would issue passports, Colby instructed Dumont and Davis to cable the State Department with the names of the Sinn Féin representatives who would be attending, the name of the steamship and the date of sailing. This they did.[55] The information was passed from the State Department to the US department of Labour and onwards to its immigration officers at the various ports of entry on the Atlantic and Gulf coasts in the event that 'aliens', as Louis Post, assistant secretary called them, would

50 *The American commission on conditions in Ireland: interim report*, p. 2.   51 *BDFA*, i, Annual Report for 1920, p. 55; NARA, RG65, M1085/R921, General Intelligence Report, no. 4, 14 November 1920.   52 NARA, RG59, M580/217, 841d.00/259, Dumont to Secretary of State, 12 November 1920.   53 F.M. Carroll, '"All standards of human conduct": The American commission on conditions in Ireland, 1920–21', 59–74.   54 TNA, FO371/4552, Geddes to Foreign Office, 7 October 1920; *The American commission*, appendix a, Geddes to MacDonald, 23 October 1920.   55 NARA, RG59, M580/217, 841d.00/238, Colby to Davis, 1 October 1920; ibid., 841d.00/249, Davis to Colby, 3 November 1920.

attempt to gain entry to the US.[56] Davis followed this up with a cable to Colby outlining the specific sailing arrangements of John Derham, Denis Morgan, Muriel MacSwiney and Mary MacSwiney, but he did not know about the departure of Donal O'Callaghan for the US.[57]

O'Callaghan was lord mayor of Cork and he arrived in Newport News, Virginia on 4 January 1921 as a stowaway on a US ship, SS *West Canon*. He did not have a passport and was denied entry by the US immigration officials with the result that the case aroused 'much public comment', to the dismay of the British embassy in Washington.[58] He was accompanied by Peter MacSwiney who was in possession of a visaed passport. O'Callaghan told the immigration inspector that he was a 'seaman'. Under a 1918 act and the president's proclamation on 8 August 1918, seamen were not required to have passports and, therefore, he came under the jurisdiction of the department of Labour and once his identity and nationality was checked to the satisfaction of the immigration officials, he was allowed to land in the US on parole. He was closely watched by Bureau of Investigation agents as he proceeded first to New York and afterwards to Washington, where he gave evidence before the American Commission.[59]

Meanwhile the immigration inspector's report and a request for a decision as to whether or not the passport regulations would be waived arrived on Norman Davis's desk in the State Department on 7 January 1921. It was immediately clear to him that the State Department's jurisdiction had been usurped. O'Callaghan had no passport, was not a 'seaman' and, therefore, under the 1918 legislation, the secretary of State had the sole power to grant or refuse permission to enter or depart the US. Davis immediately rang secretary of Labour, William B. Wilson, to ascertain 'his reasons for taking such action.' Wilson explained that 'on account of the political and other embarrassing aspects of the question he thought the best way to dispose of it was to grant a parole' pending the decision on a passport. When asked if he would deport O'Callaghan, who had entered the US illegally without a passport. Wilson would not answer.[60] Davis recommended the following course to President Wilson on 7 January 1921,

> It would seem, therefore, that unless the policy of the Department is reversed and an exception made of this case, it is my duty to refuse entry to O'Callaghan and to order his deportation. This case has already received considerable publicity, and any action is going to cause more publicity.[61]

56 Ibid., 841d.00/246, Post to Colby, 29 October 1920.   57 Ibid., 841d.00/249, Colby to Davis, 3 November 1920; ibid., 841d.00/252, Colby to Davis, 17 November 1920.   58 *BDFA*, i, Annual Report for 1921, p. 140.   59 NARA, RG65, M1085/R921, General Intelligence Report, no. 11, for week ending 17 January 1921; ibid., no. 12 for week ending 24 January 1921.   60 *PWW*, 66, Davis to Wilson, 7 January 1921; Findling, 'Norman Hezekiah Davis' in *Dictionary*, p. 134.   61 *PWW*, 67, Davis to Wilson, 7 January 1921.

W.B. Wilson had also outlined his views to the president and argued for greater discretion to make exceptions to the rules in the awarding of passports.

This was not the US administration's first contact with O'Callaghan. Prior to his departure for the US, the Cork lord mayor had, on 12 December 1920, cabled Livingston Farrand, director of the American Red Cross, requesting aid to help with the distress and destitution in Cork caused by the burning of the city by British forces. Farrand consulted with the State Department, the British embassy, the Foreign Office and the British Red Cross. The American Red Cross did not normally consult with the State Department or the governments involved when deciding whether or not to dispatch aid but, according to Norman Davis, the society felt that the Irish case 'presents conditions of such a peculiar nature that there is a grave risk of the Red Cross involving America in a national controversy foreign to our interests.' Geddes regarded this and other appeals as being motivated by propaganda and he persuaded Ferrand to refuse direct aid and to inform O'Callaghan that he had contacted the British Red Cross who would give financial assistance, if needed. Farrand also informed Mary MacSwiney that the American Red Cross would only act in the case of a widespread disaster. Mrs Peter Golden of the Irish Progressive League equated the Irish situation with that of Cuba, Belgium and Siberia, where the American Red Cross had acted. On 30 December, the British Red Cross reported that it had made all necessary arrangements for relief work in Ireland and there was no need for the American Red Cross to get involved, while President Wilson replied to Davis, 'I think it would be extremely unwise for the Red Cross to respond to the appeal ... It would be an international act of the most questionable sort, and I hope that you will express in my name if you choose, our sense of its unwisdom at this time.' In late December, Farrand decided not to act but pressure from Irish-America forced a re-consideration in 1921 which will be discussed in chapter eight.[62]

So the US administration had a substantial amount of information about the circumstances of O'Callaghan's case. President Wilson intervened and, in these post-election days, opposed Secretary Wilson's request to exercise discretion in O'Callaghan's favour. President Wilson regretted that a difference of opinion had arisen between the two departments with regard to the 'stowaway, O'Callaghan.' But he

> did not concur in the conclusions of your argument about making more liberal exceptions to the rules regarding passports ... Exceptions inevitably lead to vagueness in administration and to complaints of favouritism.

62 Ibid., 66, Davis to Wilson, 15 December 1920; ibid., Wilson to Davis, 16 December 1920; *BDFA*, i, Annual Report for 1921, p. 56. O'Callaghan had also cabled Ambassador Davis in London on 14 December 1920 for help to end the British tyranny in Ireland. NARA, RG59, M580/217, 841d.00/274, O'Callaghan to Davis, 14 December 1920; F.M. Carroll, 'The American committee for relief in Ireland, 1920–22', 31.

I, of course, do not wish to interfere with the legal jurisdiction of the Department of Labour, and I think it would be very unwise to make an exception in the case of O'Callaghan. In the present state of Ireland, we should have a whooping lot of stowaways descending upon us if we admit them without passports. I think passports are particularly necessary in the present disturbed state of the world.

In other words, if future aliens without properly visaed passports sought admission to the US, they should be denied admission unless the secretary of State specifically waived the passport requirements. Moreover, he had no intention of facilitating the arrival of republicans from Ireland. However, in order to save the face of his secretary of Labour, it was decided that this ruling should not apply to the O'Callaghan case and that he should continue to be regarded as a 'seaman' and be permitted to remain in the US until 11 February 1921. W.B. Wilson yielded to his president but he wrote again to Norman Davis, reasserting his right to admit O'Callaghan permanently. But he stated that he had decided against such a course 'in the present circumstances.' The matter did not end there and, following a cabinet meeting on 18 January, W.B. Wilson, Davis and the president met at the White House to discuss the case. Not surprisingly the president supported Davis in his decision that O'Callaghan had to leave the US by 11 February. W.B. Wilson ordered O'Callaghan to report to Norfolk and ship out from there.[63] Predictably, the *Sinn Féiner* reported 'The Irish people are not surprised at the determination of the State Department to deport Lord Mayor O'Callaghan. They look upon it as a dying kick of the Wilson administration from which they have long since learned to expect very little consideration.'[64]

O'Callaghan testified before the Commission on 13 and 14 January and his presence was widely publicized, although not all comment was supportive. The *New York Times* attacked W.B. Wilson and his 'law breaking Department' for allowing O'Callaghan to enter the US illegally. O'Callaghan's republican supporters suggested that the State Department's deportation decision confirmed its anti-Irish bias. But a different argument was presented by the AARIR delegation in its appeal to Norman Davis during their meeting in late January. They represented the lord mayor as a political refugee whose life would be in danger if he returned to Ireland. Davis did not agree. Nonetheless, the State Department was in a quandary; O'Callaghan's presence had generated a lot of publicity and if he was deported to Ireland and was then arrested there, it could be embarrassing for the US government. A headline in the *Gaelic American* on 29 January screamed 'Wilson's last kick at Ireland' and outlined how the decision to deport would deliver to the British government 'an Irish enemy whom it wants to lay its hands on, so that it can wreak vengeance upon him.' Davis was concerned

---

63 *PWW*, 67, Davis to President, 7 January 1921; ibid., Wilson to Wilson, 12 January; ibid., W.B. Wilson to Davis, 17 January, in fn. 1, p. 53; ibid., fn. 1, p. 53. 64 *Sinn Féiner*, 22 January 1921.

enough by the new argument and perhaps by Dumont's detailed reports of the British view that 'the "murder gang" of Sinn Féin must be hunted down and destroyed' to contact the British embassy about O'Callaghan's fate should he return to Ireland. On 31 January, he met with Craigie to ascertain unofficially whether there was any likelihood of O'Callaghan being arrested on his return and whether O'Callaghan had applied for a passport to go to the US but had been turned down.[65]

Shortly after that meeting, on 1 February 1921, the Democratic Senator Thomas J. Walsh from Wisconsin wrote to Colby about the case. On behalf of his constituents he inquired 'as to how the action which has been taken in the case of Lord Mayor O'Callaghan, denying him the right to remain in this country at will, can be harmonised with the theory that political refugees may freely seek this country as an asylum.' Colby replied on 8 February, insisting that the deportation decision was determined by law and was not 'dictated' by any views on the Irish question. Two days later Walsh appealed the deportation decision again, on the grounds that it must have been written by a clerk in the State Department because it was 'entirely uncandid if not misleading'.[66] But W.B. Wilson's reply to Walsh on 5 February, made it clear that he had exercised discretion towards O'Callaghan by permitting him to land and allowing him time to find a vessel for reshipment and that it was Colby who declined to waive the passport requirements.[67] However, as indicated above, it was Davis, now acting secretary of State, and President Wilson who had decided to exclude O'Callaghan.

In the meanwhile, Curzon authorized Craigie to repeat the British government's undertaking that no proceedings would be instituted against any person who had appeared before the American Commission in the US. He further denied that O'Callaghan had been refused a passport by his government, saying it had not received an application for one. On 4 April, O'Callaghan's appeal to the State Department, asking to remain as a political refugee, was rejected. However, he was not forced to leave the country in accordance with the original decision. Geddes interpreted this to mean that the British government's assurance on his security was 'insufficient' for Wilson and Davis. By this time O'Callaghan was less in the public view and he returned to Ireland in April by signing on as a seaman, ironically on board one of the US Shipping Board vessels.[68] Wilson had

65 *The American commission on conditions in Ireland: interim report*, pp. 39–41; Findling, 'Davis, Norman Hezekiah', p. 134; *BDFA*, i, Annual Report for 1921, pp. 140–1; NARA, RG59, M580/217, 841d.00/239, Dumont to Secretary of State, 12 November 1920; *Gaelic American*, 29 January 1921.
66 Library of Congress (hereafter LC), Manuscripts Division (hereafter MD), Thomas J. Walsh Papers (hereafter TJWP), Box 190, subject file c1913–33, file Justice Dept., misc., Walsh to Colby, 1 February 1921; ibid., Colby to Walsh, 8 February 1921; ibid., Walsh to Colby, 10 February 1921
67 LC, TJWP, Box 190, subject file 1913–33, file Justice Dept., misc., Wilson to Walsh, 5 February 1921   68 *BDFA*, i, Annual Report for 1921, p. 141. The State Department decided that a political refugee was defined as one who is being sought by a foreign government for a political offence. Inasmuch as the British government had made no request for the surrender of O'Callaghan, the

gone as far as he could to deport O'Callaghan. Against the background of the Anglo-Irish war, he did not want to make O'Callaghan more of a hero than he already was for republican Irish-Americans, but neither would he fuel anti-British campaigns in the US. This reasoning also informed the administration's position on another aspect of the American Commission's work.

In mid-November, MacDonald, secretary to the American Commission, applied to the British embassy in Washington for visas for a sub-committee to go and investigate conditions in Ireland. Also at this time, Colby began to receive letters of support for, and criticism of, the work of the Commission. Reverend L.M. Powers, an American 'with no interest in Ireland', wrote on 26 November that he 'trusted' Colby 'would make it possible for responsible men to visit Ireland and to report to us on their findings.' While Mary E. Nicol, writing on 28 November, told Colby that Irish republicans should not be allowed 'to stir up trouble' in this country.[69] On the British side, Geddes recommended to the Foreign Office that permission be given, while Hamar Greenwood, the chief secretary for Ireland, wrote in late November, 'I certainly object to any foreigner or foreign committee meddling in Irish affairs in Ireland.' MacDonald was informed of the decision on 8 December.[70] The Commission did not give up on the matter. Within a week of receiving the refusal, Colby received a letter from ten senators who asked that he protest to the British government on the grounds that it was a 'violation of the right of free communication between the liberty-loving people of two democracies'. They also drew parallels between the work of the American Commission and that of the 'Bryce Commission on atrocities in Belgium.'[71] Congressman Mason went so far as to cable a protest to the president of the League of Nations.[72]

State Department ruled that he was not a political refugee. On 10 April, Warren Harding's new secretary of Labour, James J. Davis, upheld his predecessor's, Secretary Wilson's ruling which declared O'Callaghan to be an alien seaman. Under that order O'Callaghan had to leave the US within a reasonable time defined as sixty days, the time allowed a seaman to find a vessel. NARA, RG65, M1085/R921, General Intelligence Report, no. 22 for week ending 15 April 1921.   69 Ibid., RG59, M580/217, 841d.00/256, Powers to Colby, 26 November 1920; ibid., 841d.00/257, Nicol to Colby, 28 November 1920. The sub-committee consisted of Arthur Gleason, journalist and writer, James A. Maura, president of the Pennsylvania State Federation of Labour, Oliver Newman, journalist and former commissioner in the District of Columbia and the Rev Norman Thomas, editor of the World Tomorrow. Ibid., RG59, M580/218, 841d.00/301, Hitchcock to Secretary of State, 18 December 1920.   70 The American commission, pp. ii–vi, 1–4, appendix a; Carroll, '"All standards of human conduct"', 62.   71 NARA, RG59, M580/217, 841d.00/260, Senators G.W. Norris, T.J. Walsh, J. Irwin, R. La Follette, J.E. Ransdell, D.I. Walsh, A.J. Gronna, G.E. Chamberlain, D.N. Fletcher, J.N. Shields to Colby, 15 December 1920. Dumont was able to provide the State Department with further information in January 1921 confirming the prejudiced nature of the Commission, not only would it just examine Irish reaction to British policy but Senator Fletcher's daughter was married to Lionel Smith-Gordon, a 'leading' Sinn Féiner. Ibid., M580/218, 841d.00/314, Dumont to Secretary of State, 28 January 1921.   72 Ibid., RG65, M1085/R921, General Intelligence Report, no. 8, 12 December 1920.

On 11 January 1921, four days after recommending to President Wilson that O'Callaghan be deported, Norman Davis replied to the senators. He stated that the other commissions were 'evidently very different from that of the persons who desire to investigate conditions in Ireland.' Neither did he 'feel certain' that the refusal of the visas involved 'an unfriendly or discriminatory attitude against the government of the United States.' The State Department could not question the British government's judgement to refuse admission because the US government would not do so in a reversal of the situation. Senator Thomas J. Walsh appealed the decision but Davis refused to intercede.[73] The American Commission got on with the work of collecting evidence without visiting Ireland, while Wilson and the State Department's reputations as anti-Irish and pro-British were further confirmed, at least in the eyes of republican Irish-Americans. It was ironic, therefore, that the last months of the Wilson administration saw a direct intervention by a representative of his administration, albeit without authority, in the Anglo-Irish war of independence.

A US consul mediates in Ireland

The incoherence of the British military, political, propaganda and legislative strategy in Ireland was apparent throughout the period 1918 to 1921. Mutual reprisals had continued. In 1920–1, there were 525 deaths in the British forces and approximately 1,000 were injured and between January and July 1921, at least 750 IRA fighters and civilians died.[74] In late September 1920, Henry Wilson commented, 'The Black and Tans, RIC are painting Ireland red.'[75] Towards the end of the year, Lloyd George and Hamar Greenwood, believed that Sinn Féin and the IRA were weakening and would soon be beaten. Both men discussed the issue with Davis and 'thought the "murder gang" [IRA] [was] slowly but surely being rounded up'. Indeed, Dumont was now using similar language and referred also to the 'murder gang ... being hunted down man by man.' But in November he felt that both the extremists and moderates in Sinn Féin would not accept a settlement that did not give them self-determination for all Ireland whereas Davis, Lloyd George and Greenwood believed that the sentiment 'in favour of some settlement was getting a chance to show itself.' This shared view that republican Ireland would accept the Better Government of Ireland bill, thereby partitioning Ireland and establishing separate parliaments in Dublin and Belfast with self-government powers, was erroneous.[76] The British misunderstanding of repub-

73 Ibid., RG59, M580/217, 841d.00/266, Davis to Norris, 11 January 1921; LC, TJWP, Box 190, subject file c1913–33, file Justice Dept., misc., Walsh to Davis, 14 January 1921. The State Department had previously refused a passport to one member of the Commission, James H. Maurer, president of the State Federation of Labour because of his anti-government speeches. Ibid., RG65, M1085/R921, General Intelligence Report, no. 8, 12 December 1920.   74 'Anglo-Irish War', p. 15.   75 IWM, HWD, DS/Misc/80, reel 9, 1-1-1920 to 22-12-1921, 28 September 1920.   76

lican Ireland's view of the British legislation combined with its military strength led the government to intensify the military campaign and incorporate a policy of reprisals.[77]

On 21 November, the IRA launched a campaign to destroy the British military intelligence network in Dublin, partly in response to the hanging of Kevin Barry and Terence MacSwiney' death. The events of 'Bloody Sunday' resulted in deaths on both sides and continued retaliations.[78] Davis wrote to his friend Polk, 'at this instant, Ireland holds the centre of the stage and I go to the House of Lords this afternoon to hear the opening of the debate on the pending home rule bill. The hideous murders of Sunday in Dublin are in everyone's mind and the British temper is hardening rapidly.'[79] Davis had no solution to offer that would ameliorate these difficulties, but his subordinates in Ireland reacted differently to the situation. William Kent in Belfast welcomed the co-operation between the auxiliaries, the military and the police to ensure an 'effective armed force' which was suppressing 'all serious disorders throughout the region.'[80] Dumont in Dublin became embroiled in a mediation effort.

Hopkinson has detailed the intensifying of efforts to secure a truce and a peaceful settlement in autumn 1920. The calls for peace came from liberal and conservative quarters both inside and outside the British cabinet, from the dominions, from Irish-American ecclesiastics and from the leadership of the IRA and Sinn Féin amongst others. In October, influential newspapers such as Northcliffe's conservative *Times* and *Daily Mail* and C.P. Scott's liberal *Manchester Guardian* carried articles supporting a peace settlement. October also saw the Cockerill and Moylette initiatives. In late November and throughout December, the Australian archbishop of Perth, Joseph Clune, conducted shuttle diplomacy between representatives of the republican movement and the British government in Dublin and London.[81] The Clune mission was noted with interest by US intelligence agents but another of these peace-making efforts involved the US government through Dumont's efforts.[82] Although this interjection took place during what was technically the Wilson presidency, in practice it was in an interregnum period. More importantly, it emphasized the permanent belief held by the leadership of republican Ireland that the US government could have a meaningful role in solving the on-going conflict with the British government.

Davis & Fleming, *The ambassadorial diary*, memoranda of conversation with the Prime Minister at Trent Park on 13, 14, 15 November 1920; NARA, RG59, M580/217, 841d.00/239, Dumont to Secretary of State, 12 November 1920.   77 Lee, *Ireland, 1912–85*, pp. 47, 42–3. See also Hopkinson, *The last days of Dublin Castle* for another British view that Sinn Féin was weakening.   78 F. Costello, *The Irish revolution and its aftermath, 1916–1923: years of revolt* (2003), pp. 92–6.   79 YULMC, FLPP, box 2, file129, Davis to Polk, 23 November 1920.   80 NARA, RG59, M580/217, 841d.00/270, Kent to American Embassy London, 7 December 1920.   81 M. Hopkinson, *The Irish war of independence* (2002), pp. 180–1; Coogan, *De Valera*, pp. 191, 197, 218. For further on the peace moves see Hopkinson, *The Irish war of independence*, pp. 180–6.   82 NARA, RG65, M1085/ R920, Weekly Intelligence Report-San Francisco District to Hoover, 20 December 1920.

Dumont had struggled to provide impartial accounts of events in Ireland. His own experience on the ground combined with his reliance on the intelligence he gained from the military and police authorities in Dublin Castle were sufficient for him to justify the excesses of the RIC, the Black and Tans, the Auxiliaries and the British army. Instead he reserved criticism of the British side for the government in London with its 'wait and see' approach.[83] His familiarity with the British authorities in Dublin Castle had continued into late 1920. Mark Sturgis recounted two examples of Dumont's partiality to British officials. Firstly, Davis had made a complaint to the Foreign Office in London about British interference with US consular business. Sturgis recorded '[Wednesday 13 October] hell of a wire from FO [Foreign Office], the American Ambassador objecting to 'Dublin District' having 'raided' a letter from US Consul London to US Consul Dublin – the latter had tea with [Major General Gerald] Boyd yesterday and thought it a very good joke but I suppose we must apologize.' A few weeks later Sturgis wrote 'one of the dead Shinns is said to be an American citizen and Dumont has formally protested.'[84] Dumont's complaints were pro forma and lacked intent. But Ambassador Davis had 'no doubt that if the Castle were consulted he [Dumont] would be charged with having fallen under the influence of Sinn Fein – the usual fate of officers in such a position.'[85] Despite his personal and professional sympathy for the British side, which became a problem later on for the Sinn Féin leadership, as US consul in Dublin Dumont had an important status which accorded him an intermediary role in December 1920.

On 6 December, Dumont cabled Davis in London to say that when he arrived into his office earlier that morning he found 'one of the leaders of the Irish Republican Army' waiting for him 'to ask my unofficial good offices.' He told Dumont that the IRA was 'willing to meet representatives of the British army in Ireland in order to confer regarding an armistice and the political and military terms on which the Irish question should be settled satisfactorily to both parties.' This 'well-known' individual was subsequently named by both Henry Wilson and Mark Sturgis as Keating, a Dublin shop keeper. When Dumont had assured himself that Keating was in a 'position to speak for his party and of his good faith', he called at Dublin Castle to see Nevil Macready. The latter was absent in London and instead he met Major General Boyd who was in charge of the Dublin military district. Boyd agreed to meet the 'Irish leader' to discuss the 'Irish situation.' Guarantees of personal safety were given by both sides and it was agreed that the meeting would take place on neutral ground. On the same day, Dumont brought the two men to the Shelbourne Hotel for lunch, having

83 Ibid., RG59, M580/217, 841d.00/239, Dumont to Secretary of State, 12 November 1920. His reports in 1920 included copies of Irish republican papers, *Irish Bulletin* and *An Tóglách* but he believed that republican details of British actions were generally exaggerated whereas he never advised caution about the accuracy of British reports on republican acts. 84 Hopkinson, *The last days of Dublin Castle*, pp. 56, 67. 85 Davis & Fleming, *The ambassadorial diary*, 19 November 1920.

put in place the necessary precautions to prevent newspaper attention. After lunch, they went to Dumont's private apartment in the hotel where they talked for two hours in his presence. Both men agreed that Macready would be asked to meet an IRA delegation and that if he agreed to do so, a list of these leaders with their addresses would be given by the IRA to Dumont for transmission to Macready. Boyd insisted that no man would be included who was guilty of the assassination or murder of individuals in the British forces in Ireland, but it was agreed that, as ambushing was a part of warfare, involvement therein would not exclude participation in the conference. The IRA delegation would not be arrested pending the conference and if the conference failed, the IRA men would not be liable to arrest for the following two weeks.[86]

Costello and Hopkinson have detailed the varying levels of commitment both within and between the British and republican Irish sides to achieving a truce and settlement. It is, therefore, in the context of the Clune mission that the Dumont intervention must be treated. On 1 December 1920, Clune had held discussions with Lloyd George, who had asked him to meet the Sinn Féin leaders in Mountjoy prison. In the following days he discussed the possibility of a truce with Arthur Griffith and Eoin MacNeill, who were both in jail, Michael Collins, who was on the run and John Anderson, Andrew Cope and Mark Sturgis of the Dublin Castle administration. But the peace-making was complicated. On 3,4, and 5 December resolutions by Galway County and Urban District councils called on Dáil Éireann to seek a truce while Fr Michael O'Flanagan, acting secretary of Sinn Féin, sent a cable to Lloyd George indicating that Sinn Féin wanted to make peace.[87] Dumont, however, was told by Keating that 'any settlement made by O'Flanagan will be repudiated by them because 'no faction of Sinn Féin' except the IRA leadership, 'can, as Mr Lloyd George expresses it, deliver the goods … the IRA alone … makes and has made opposition to the British rule in Ireland practical.' He felt that the IRA leaders were afraid of 'betrayal' by the Sinn Féin politicians and the Catholic Church hierarchy. However, Keating was convinced that if the IRA leadership and the British military could 'agree on terms', political and military, all opposition to British rule would disappear.[88] Boyd made it clear that he could not come to any arrangement, except that he promised to report to Macready and that Keating would not be arrested. In Macready's absence from Dublin, Boyd brought the agreed terms to Henry Wilson in London where he also met Macready. Wilson was an Irish Unionist who disapproved of the Black and Tans' excesses but, as noted above, favoured the repressions policy. Following the meeting Wilson recorded in his diary, on 8 December 1920,'the rebel army was distrustful of L[loyd]G[eorge] … and, therefore, wanted to come to an arrangement with our soldiers.' The three sol-

86 NARA, RG59, M580/217, 841d.00/268, Davis to Secretary of State, 8 December 1920; ibid., 841d.00/279, Dumont to Davis, 6 December 1920 in Dumont to Secretary of State, 17 December 1920.   87 Hopkinson, *The Irish war of independence*, p. 183; Costello, *The Irish revolution*, pp. 112–13. 88 NARA, RG59, M580/217, 841d.00/268, Davis to Secretary of State, 8 December 1920.

diers had a 'long discussion' and agreed that it was 'not out of the question to hold "parley" with rebel commanders', particularly as Lloyd George was already 'in touch' with Michael Collins.[89]

Meanwhile, Davis reacted to Dumont's actions. He was not disposed to censure Dumont on the matter; 'I approve your action in the matter.'[90] But he warned him that now that the parties had been brought in contact, Dumont should not permit himself to be involved in 'any further course of negotiations.' The ambassador also telegraphed Colby with Dumont's account of the contact, while a copy of the message was sent to President Wilson.[91] Davis also felt obliged to inform Curzon and his permanent under secretary, Eyre Crowe. Davis did not expect any 'tangible result' to flow from Dumont's action but he felt that 'it seems to indicate a rift in the ranks of Sinn Féin itself.'[92] Davis' conclusion was accurate as nothing came of the Dumont measure or any of the other peace measures at this time.

Events had already bypassed Dumont's efforts. Greenwood had left Dublin on the evening of 6 December. On the following day, he announced in the House of Commons that no amnesty would be granted to the 'murder gang.' Later that evening he told Henry Wilson that he would be telling Lloyd George 'on no account to dream of talking of an armistice or peace with the rebels.' Thus, Wilson knew of Greenwood's position before he met Macready and Boyd on 8 December and also knew that it was Lloyd George who was directing Britain's policy on Ireland.[93] Lloyd George hardened his position and insisted that IRA arms be given up prior to any truce. Griffith and Collins rejected this demand, with the former questioning whether Lloyd George truly wanted peace at this time. Instead, on 9 December, Lloyd George announced a new approach to Ireland, 'the double policy': to encourage efforts towards peace but at the same time intensify the war. The results were immediate, with the burning of large parts of Cork city, shootings and, on 27 December, the imposition of martial law in counties Cork, Tipperary, Limerick and Kerry. Lloyd George's policy was based also on the view of British military commanders in Ireland that the peace efforts signalled a weakening within republican ranks. Davis' endorsement of the hardening of British policy was evident from the instruction he sent to Dumont on 10 December 'to pipe down on his Sinn Féin negotiations'.[94] In the cauldron of London politics the pro-British Davis continued the ambassadorial tradition of not wittingly embarrassing his hosts but, on the other hand, he was sensitive to the implications of continuing repression in Ireland for his own country.[95]

89 IWM, HWD, DS/Misc/80, reel 9, 1–1–1920 to 22–12–1921, 8 December 1920; K. Jeffrey, 'Wilson, Sir Henry' in Connolly, The Oxford companion, p. 593.   90 NARA, RG59, M580/217, 841d.00/279, Davis to Dumont, 9 December 1920 in Dumont to Secretary of State, 17 December 1920.   91 NARA, RG59, M580/217, 841d.00/268, Davis to Secretary of State, 8 December 1920.   92 Davis & Fleming, The ambassadorial diary, 8 December 1920.   93 IWM, HWD, DS/Misc/80, reel 9, 1–1–1920 to 22–12–1921, 7 December 1920.   94 Hopkinson, The Irish war of independence, p. 183; Davis & Fleming, The ambassadorial diary, 10 December 1920.   95 Davis & Fleming, The

Davis' instructions to Dumont were not questioned by Wilson or Colby. The failure of the peace efforts and further extension of martial law ensured that no talks would be successful until July 1921. Henry Wilson commented, 'we are all agreed that martial law is the thing and that any question of a truce ... would be fatal.'[96]

It is difficult to gauge the extent of Dumont's standing with the leadership of republican Ireland at this stage. Dumont reported later that Greenwood's sudden departure from Dublin combined to the intensification of British policy, led Keating to conclude, 'not unreasonably – that again faith had been broken'. But contact with Keating did not break down and Dumont wrote that it took him a full week 'to show' Keating that Greenwood 'knew nothing about the terms.'[97] In April, Dumont was still in contact with Keating who asked him to mediate with Eoin MacNeill in prison. Mark Sturgis in Dublin Castle regarded Keating as a 'peaceful Shinner' and facilitated the request because he felt 'must keep this [contact] dangling.'[98]

However, outside these mediation efforts Dumont devoted his time to reporting on the escalating events and identifying the consequences for the new Harding administration in Washington. Along with the other US consuls in Ireland, he had to deal with the consequences of the conflict. In Belfast, Kent shared with other 'law-abiding citizens' his support for the British policy, including the reprisals measures and extension of martial law. Similarly he found himself providing assistance for three US citizens arrested by the authorities. One was charged with being an 'American gunman' of Irish extraction who was found guilty of committing an 'atrocious murder', the other arrived into Belfast on a US vessel and carried 'seditious correspondence.' A third US citizen of Catholic persuasion asked for Kent's 'official intervention' to get compensation for the burning of his summer house which he had mistakenly bought in a Protestant neighbourhood. Kent knew better than to get involved and the complainant was advised that he must rely on the orderly processes of the law. The third issue that concerned Kent was the revival of the traditional consular business, particularly US trade with the region so that he was pleased to report in December 1920 the presence of US vessels in Belfast docks while people were again emi-

ambassadorial diary, 11, 15 December 1920.   96 IWM, HWD, DS/Misc/80, reel 9, 1–1–1920 to 22–12–1921, 29 December 1920.   97 Ibid., M580/218, 841d.00/314, Dumont to Secretary of State, 28 January 1921. In mid-March 1921, Dumont was approached by a Mr Ford to help secure the release of his sister Mrs J.W. Lindsay of Leemount House, Peake, county Cork, who had been kidnapped by Sinn Féin on 12 March. The area was a hot bed of military and insurgent activity and she was suspected of giving information to the local British authorities on the IRA men who had engaged in an ambush at Peake and had been subsequently shot and executed. Dumont does not detail his involvement but stated 'it has been found impossible to get any trace of her hiding place.' He does not appear to have engaged in negotiations with the IRA leadership as Michael Collins, whose men controlled the district, admitted later that the case was not referred to him and that he regretted Mrs Lindsay's execution due to her advanced years. NARA, RG59, M580/218, 841d.00/339, Dumont to Secretary of State, 22 March 1921; Costello, *The Irish revolution*, p. 47. 98 Hopkinson, *The last days of Dublin Castle*, pp. 161, 165.

grating to the United States. Many were going to relatives but he felt, most were 'fleeing from the disorders of Ireland, the dangers, the depressed conditions resulting in the difficulties in securing employment.' He was exercising great vigilance to exclude the 'undesirable classes.'[99]

Mitchell, like Dumont, had developed close relations with the British military authorities in Cork through meetings and correspondence with General E.P. Strickland, divisional commander and his staff. But unlike Dumont, he openly acknowledged that it 'was a pleasure to report of the continued courtesies both official and personal that have been accorded by his administration to the writer.' Similarly he was sufficiently acquainted with Admiral Reginald Tupper, commandant of the Queenstown base, to arrange a courtesy visit with visiting Americans later in March 1921 as will be seen in chapter eight. But Mitchell did not allow these relationships to influence his judgement.[1] On 19 December 1920, he reported that, 'the condition of things in this consular district of Munster, both from the political and economic standpoint, could scarcely be worse, and there seems unfortunately no immediate prospects of an improvement so far as can be judged.' He lodged also two complaints with Strickland on behalf of US citizens who had been 'maltreated and robbed' by the 'Black and Tans.' Of greater significance for the State Department was his belief that 'strong appeals for relief will be made to the United States for people made destitute by the [Cork] fire.'[2] Clearly, he was unaware that Lord Mayor of Cork Donal O'Callaghan, had already contacted the American Red Cross and indeed left for the United States to appear before the American Commission on Conditions in Ireland. The provision of relief for Ireland had become a political issue in the US. Soon enough it would intrude into the Harding administration's relationship with the British government (see chapter eight).

Meanwhile on 23 December 1920, the House of Lords approved the Better Government of Ireland Act which partitioned Ireland and allowed the London government control over defence, foreign policy and, vitally, finance, served to strengthen republican resolve to continue the war and indeed provided Sinn Féin with a humanitarian dimension to their US campaign.

Wilson and Ireland: an overview

On voting day in November 1920, Ray Stannard Baker had lunch with Wilson and noted that

99 NARA, RG59, M580/217, 841d.00/278, Kent to Secretary of State, 14 December 1920; ibid., M580/218, 841d.00/281, Kent to Secretary of State, 21 December 1920. 1 Ibid., M580/218, 841d.00/323, Mitchell to Secretary of State, 3 March 1921; ibid., 841d.00/330, Mitchell to Secretary of State, 9 March 1921. 2 Ibid., M580/217, 841d.00/272, Mitchell to Secretary of State, 19 December 1920.

There began outside of the White House, the slow, single-file parade of a group of sympathisers with Irish freedom. They were demanding of the broken old man that he straightway free Ireland. The patriotic faith of men in heroes and supermen. The idea that someone who has spoken true words can magically do for them what they can only do for themselves. This also was the very core of the tragic events at Paris; of the persistent idea that the world can be made over by the word of one man of whom they would make a god, or perchance a president. And when their prayer is not answered, they turn upon him and rend him.[3]

The daily marches continued into January 1921 and although they were observed by Bureau agents, the police did not intervene.[4] Wilson's tenure as the twenty-eight president of the United States ended on 4 March 1921 and the Wilsons retired to 2340 S Street, North West, Washington. Irish nationalists in the US and Ireland had hoped the Democratic president would, firstly, support the fight for Irish freedom, secondly, after 1916 recognize the new republic and its government, thirdly, after 1918 gain a hearing for it at the Paris peace conference, fourthly, temper British policy in Ireland during the Anglo-Irish war of independence and finally, assist in specific circumstances. But he had failed them on all counts by allying with Britain in world war one, by not officially criticising the British government for permitting the executions of the leaders of the 1916 rising, by not recognizing the republic, by not supporting self-determination for Ireland, particularly in Paris and by remaining aloof during the war of independence. Despite his understanding of the Irish cause he was influenced always by the larger picture, namely the re-ordering of the world system and, therefore, his priority was US relations with Britain. Even when he permitted officials such as House, Lansing and Tumulty to intervene he would not embarrass the British government. Thus, since Wilson formulated his own foreign policy, his position on Ireland was mainly one of non-interference, except when US interests were at stake, for example upon entry into world war one and when US legislation demanded it, particularly in order to protect US citizens' interests abroad. But his personal lack of sympathy for the Irish nationalists hardened, particularly when Irish-America forged links with Germany between 1914 and 1917 and the League of Nations failed. In addition, he personally disliked Cohalan and Devoy and when this was combined with the hyphenism and anti-Americanism which they seemed to represent, there was little chance of Wilson acting on Ireland's behalf.

The advice the president was given on Ireland by his advisers and secretaries of state rarely ran contrary to his own views. He emasculated the role of the secretary of State. Tumulty walked a tightrope between keeping an eye to the needs of the Irish-American voter and avoiding being labelled a 'professional Irishman.'

3 R. Stannard Baker, *American chronicle: the autobiography of Ray Stannard Baker* (1945), p. 484.
4 NARA, RG65, M1085/ R92, General Intelligence Report, no. 11 for week ending 17 January 1921.

House, who kept in contact with Plunkett and Leslie and occasionally tried to work on Ireland's behalf, did so within the wider context of international relations. Both Baker and Creel were asked by Wilson to report on Ireland but little direct action followed. At any rate, Tumulty's relationship with Wilson deteriorated from 1916 onwards and House's from March 1919. Among the president's diplomatic and consular representatives, Page was so anglophile that his usefulness to the State Department and Wilson was recognized as being limited by 1914, while Davis described himself as a liberal who opposed martial law in Ireland but was hostile to republicans in Ireland and the US. As a consummate diplomat, US interests predominated with him. As late as 8 February 1921, and against the background of the war of independence, Davis was appalled at Senator David I. Walsh's statement that he would introduce a resolution into the Senate for the recognition of Irish independence. Davis wrote 'What madness! It might easily lead to a rupture of diplomatic relations at the least.'[5] Yet, he was in no doubt that British mishandling of the Irish question was linked to the level of Irish-American agitation in US domestic politics; he encouraged the visit to the US by Grey and the prince of Wales in late 1920 in order to educate the US public. On the eve of Davis' departure as ambassador in early 1921, he commented to King George V about the trouble caused by the Irish 'you send over to us.'[6] Davis also oversaw a closer relationship between officials in the US embassy and the Foreign Office which, according to William Tyrell, brought nothing but 'golden opinions' of him.[7] This tie would work against him in the eyes of some Irish-American voters when he was nominated as the Democratic presidential candidate in 1924.[8]

The quality of US consular officials in Ireland between 1913 and 1921 varied enormously and largely reflected the state of flux that the State Department was undergoing before and after the war. The State Department was fortunate to have as consuls in Queenstown first Wesley Frost and then Charles Hathaway, who was a capable, professional officer able to deal with the consequences of US neutrality and subsequent involvement in the war. The well intentioned but amateurish Charles Adams, in Dublin, was unable and unwilling to fully dispense his duties, particularly during and immediately after the 1916 rising. His replacement, Frederick Dumont, however, adopted a professional approach to the posting, although his neutral status became compromised. Yet, during the Anglo-

5 Davis & Fleming, *The ambassadorial diary*, 8 February 1921. 6 Ibid., 5 March 1921. According to William Phillips, assistant secretary of State, the success of the royal visit was evident from positive press coverage, enthusiastic crowds and in New York, 'the Irish gave the Prince a hearty cheer whenever he passed.' W. Phillips, *Ventures in diplomacy* (1952), pp. 46–7. 7 YULMC, EHP, box 111a, file 3869, Tyrell to House, 29 April 1920. 8 Beckles, *American ambassadors*, p. 466; Findling, 'Davis, John William' in *Dictionary*, p. 133. Within the embassy, he re-organized the size and structure of the staff. Also he replaced the circumlocutory method of letter writing with a telephone call in the interests of greater co-ordination and efficiency in routine affairs. He also maintained personal and professional contact with the consular officials in Ireland unlike his predecessor.

Irish war of independence he showed signs of initiative that ran contrary to the Wilsonian policy of non-interference on Ireland.

In an era when the president accorded all decision-making power to himself in foreign policy terms and could operate independently of the State Department, the Wilson presidency was a lost opportunity for the Irish-Americans in many ways. As O'Grady notes, the Polish-Americans, operating through House, were successful in getting Wilson to agree to fight for Polish freedom as early as November 1915. The Jewish-Americans, working through Louis Brandeis, were able to write Wilson's policy on Palestine. The Central Europeans and the Mid-European Union ethnic groups did not influence Wilson until after the settlement, by which time Wilson had agreed to recognize these new states anyway. The Hungarian-Americans were also able to reach him to persuade him of their national differences. Wilson's decisions on these cases were strongly influenced also by the outcome of the war, defeat of the central powers and balance of power issues. Nevertheless, there was the third division, the Italian-American and the Irish-Americans. Neither of these groups could persuade Wilson to assist with their problems even though it might be said that the Irish had the most effective of all the machines for influencing public and political opinion[9] Effectively, it appears that Wilson's personal grasp on foreign affairs on so many levels worked against the Irish cause. Even at the end of his tenure Wilson had definite views on Ireland. Less than two months before he retired from office in March 1921, he gave an interview to the historian, William Edward Dodd, for his book, *Wilson and his work*. Dodd subsequently quoted the president: "'Oh, the foolish Irish. ... Would to God they might have all have gone back home.'"[10] If this is true, and there is no reason to disbelieve it, Woodrow Wilson believed that Irish nationalists' quest for self-determination defeated his cherished project and ideals both abroad and at home.

9 J.P. O'Grady, Introduction' in J.P. O'Grady (ed.), *The immigrants' influence on Wilson's peace policies* (1967), pp. 28–9.   10 *PWW*, 67, Dodds to Le Whyte, 9 January 1921.

CHAPTER SEVEN

The Harding presidency, foreign policy and Ireland, March 1921

On 9 January 1921, William Edward Dodd wrote 'And now Harding, who won by appealing to these [Irish and German] elements, in much the same way Wilson did, must defeat the purposes of the better element of his party by pleasing them or defeat himself, and make his administration one continued row, by displeasing them.'[1] Dodd, like the Sinn Féin leadership, believed that Irish-America had voted for Harding but Irish-America was not a homogenous voting bloc and even if many did vote for the Republican candidate, they were influenced more by domestic factors, the force of Harding's personality and the desire for change than by Irish issues. Despite the widespread sympathy among the United States public, politicians and press for the Irish republicans fighting for self-determination in the on-going Anglo-Irish war of independence, and although Roland Lindsay, chargé d'affaires in the British embassy in Washington, could say that 'most Americans are now anxious to be fair' to the Irish, President Harding had not committed himself to intervention upon taking up office.[2] However, from an Irish republican perspective, Harding, as a new president with a Republican Congress, had the opportunity to embark on a new direction in his Irish policy and to have his new secretary of State and diplomatic and consular representatives implement it. Any change in policy would depend on the president's own views on foreign policy, and specifically on policy for Ireland, along with his interaction with the forces that had brought him to office.

Path to the presidency

Harding's victory marked the end of eight years of Democratic rule. He became the twenty-ninth president with one of the greatest popular vote majorities, winning 60.4 per cent of the total, while his Democrat opponent, James M. Cox, polled 35 per cent. Despite a level of popular support that was greater than either

1 A.S. Link (ed.), *The papers of Woodrow Wilson* (hereafter *PWW*), 69 vols (1966–94), 67, William Edward Dodd to Alexander Frederick Whyte, 9 January 1921.   2 K. Bourne & D.C. Watt (general eds), *British documents on foreign affairs* (hereafter *BDFA*), part 11, series C, North America, 25 vols. (1986–95), i, The Republican ascendancy, 1919–28, Lindsay to Curzon, 11 July 1919.

of Wilson's victories, Harding lamented 'My God, this is a hell of a place for a man like me to be.' For if Wilson'.a background, beliefs and personality prepared him to assume the highest office in the land, Harding's did not. H.L. Mencken, the caustic journalist, characterized him in July 1920 as 'simply a third-rate political wheel-horse, with the face of a moving-picture actor, the intelligence of a respectable agricultural implement dealer, and the imagination of a lodge joiner.'[3]

Harding was born on 2 November 1865 in Blooming Grove in eastern Ohio, to Phoebe Elizabeth Dickerson and George Tyron Harding. His family's origins specifically African-American antecedents, dogged him throughout his political career and formed the basis of a whispering campaign during the presidential campaign. Will Hays, Harding's campaign manager in 1920, emphasized his candidate's lineage as being 'the finest pioneer blood, Anglo-Saxon, German, Scotch-Irish and Dutch.' However, this description of Harding's place in the racial pecking order was controversial.[4] By the time Harding was born in 1865, his parents were established within the middle-classes in Ohio which became the Republican centre of gravity, producing six out of ten presidents from 1865 to 1920 and voting solidly Republican from 1868 to 1908.[5]

The Harding household was a Republican, and also a strait-laced Christian, one. After graduating as a schoolteacher in 1882, Warren worked for one term which he described as the hardest job he had ever done. Two years later, he and two friends bought the *Star* newspaper in Marion, Ohio. Soon he became editor and sole owner of the paper from which he would embark on a political career.[6]

These early years revealed a young man with a gregarious, out-going personality who was little interested in intellectual matters. He suffered from chronic insecurity which has been attributed to his genealogy, his family's financial worries, his personality and constant psychological and physiological ill health. His marriage in 1891 to Florence Mabel Kling DeWolfe, a divorced mother of one child, lasted both their life times despite his extramarital affairs. He entered politics in 1892 and although he was beaten as the Republican candidate for county auditor, politics continued to interest him, but this was less from an ideological motivation and more because he was bored with running a newspaper, albeit a successful one.[7]

The combination of his family background and his own mainstream views led him into Republican Party politics. The Democrats held no attractions for him

---

3 R.F. Martin, 'Warren Gamaliel Harding' in M.I. Urofsky (ed.), *The American presidents* (2000), pp. 304–5; M. Moss (ed.), *H.L. Mencken:.a carnival of Buncombe* (1956), p. 15.   4 Quoted in P. Johnson, *A history of the American people* (1997), p. 557. There were allegations that Harding's grandmother, Elizabeth Madison, had been an African-American as was his paternal grandfather.   5 P. Thompson, *Cassell's dictionary of modern American history* (2000), pp. 154–5, 352; Johnson, *A history of the American people*, p. 546; A. Sinclair, *The available man: the life behind the masks of Warren Gamaliel Harding* (1965), p. 27. Harding also became director of a bank, a lumber company, a phone company, a building society and an insurance agent.   6 R.K. Murray, *The Harding era: Warren G. Harding and his administration* (1969), pp. 6–7.   7 Ibid., p. 8.

and throughout his life he regarded them as 'bunglers, depression creators, dem-
agogues, place-hunters and generally incapable of living up to the responsibilities of power.'[8] Politics interested him for another reason; the simple need for
convivial, varied and interesting company and pursuits. During the 1890s, he
spoke at party meetings throughout the state and developed a reputation as a fine
orator. He was elected in 1899 to the first of two terms to the Ohio senate and
became a firm friend and political associate of Harry Daugherty, who would
become attorney general in his cabinet but would eventually discredit his administration. In 1903 Harding became lieutenant governor of Ohio and in 1914 was
swept into the US Senate on a Republican wave. During the campaign, Harding
defeated the Progressive candidate, Arthur L. Garford, and the Democrat candidate, Ohio Attorney General Timothy S. Hogan. As will be seen later, the campaign was dirty, centring on Hogan's Roman Catholicism and his Irish background. Although Harding did not personally indulge in these attacks, he
benefited from them and enjoyed a 100,000 vote majority in the election.[9]

The characteristics of his approach to politics were formed in these early years.
As a state legislator, he defended protectionism, was concerned about the 'new
immigration', distrusted organized labour, a position which had become a hall-
mark of the GOP, and became uncertain about prohibition. He revealed a conservative moderate streak but more significantly, he had become a politician of
compromise and conciliation. He did not take dogmatic positions and instead
adopted the role of mediator which would characterize his political life. When
he reached the US Senate in 1914, he spent sixty per cent of his time in the
Senate and did not vote on any issue which was damaging to his Ohio constituents.[10] His response to the outbreak of world war one in August 1914 was
to go on a two months' hunting trip to Texas.[11] Throughout the following five
years, he introduced 134 bills, most of which dealt with Ohion issues and none
with national matters. He voted along GOP lines – favourable to business and
hostile to labour. He supported woman's suffrage after it became popular and
favoured individual states voting on the prohibition amendment, thus avoiding
having to take a stance on it in the Senate.[12]

His position on foreign policy was similar; he supported US entry into the
war and made many patriotic speeches during the period. He was unenthusiastic about the Versailles settlement because it had little to offer the US. As was
indicated in chapter five, during the League of Nations fight he was among
Lodge's reservationists rather than Borah's irreconcilables. So, in both foreign
and domestic policy matters, Harding avoided controversy, playing the role of
mediator and it was his 'charm and congeniality', rather than his oratory, intelligence or hard work, which impressed his colleagues and won him the Republican

8 R.C. Downes, *The rise of Warren Gamaliel Harding, 1865–1920* (1970), p. 265.   9 Murray, *The Harding era*, p. 8.   10 Ibid., pp. 10–11.   11 S.A. Cuneo, *From printer to president: the story of Warren G. Harding* (1922), p. 87.   12 E.P. Trani & D.L. Wilson, *The presidency of Warren G. Harding* (1977), p. 35.

presidential nomination in July 1920.[13] Nonetheless, he won the election and became president.

From the beginning of his tenure, Harding's interpretation of the presidency was closer to that of William McKinley than of Wilson. He did not intend to be the sole formulator and implementer of policy and instead left that to his cabinet, advisers, party leaders and Congress. He would adopt the role of co-ordinator and facilitator. He appreciated the importance of having clever men in his cabinet, the civil service and the judiciary. When he was choosing his cabinet, during December 1920 and January 1921, he consulted the 'best minds', but there was little agreement on the right candidates. On 12 January 1921, the *New Republic* asked, 'Will Harding surround himself by a group of men of large calibre, like Hughes and Hoover, or will he sink to the depths with Senator Fall and Daugherty?'[14] He chose both types. Andrew Mellon became secretary of the Treasury, Herbert Hoover secretary of Commerce, Henry C. Wallace secretary of Agriculture, Edwin Denby secretary of the Navy and Charles Evans Hughes secretary of State. However, political necessity insisted on the reservation of cabinet seats for the friends who had helped him to gain the presidency and who he felt he could trust. He chose drinking and poker-playing cronies such as Harry M. Daugherty (attorney general), John W. Weeks (secretary of War) and Albert B. Fall (secretary of the Interior). Daugherty was his Ohio campaign-manager and had promised Harding that he would protect him from the 'influence-peddlars' who would crowd into Washington from Ohio. He boasted to the journalist Mark Sullivan, 'I know who the crooks are, and I want to stand between Harding and them.' Daugherty was no Edward House but Harding trusted him, a choice that was to prove fatal. His choice of Fall was popular in Congress but proved to be another mistake. Yet, Harding also resisted strong pressure from the Ohio Republican Party and from advisers, ironically including Daugherty, to appoint more Ohion men, not just to the cabinet but to federal committees and judgeships.[15]

British Ambassador Geddes delayed reporting to Foreign Secretary Curzon about the various phases of cabinet-formation until 25 February 1921, when he reported that Harding had 'met with more than usual difficulty in constituting a cabinet agreeable at once to Congress and to the Republican Party organization.'[16] Geddes had misgivings about the suitability of some members of the Harding cabinet, but they were balanced by respect for others, particularly Hughes, and by a feeling of hope after the period of political deadlock that marked the closing months of Wilson's administration.[17] Overall Harding displayed both good and bad judgement in his cabinet appointments and was influ-

13 Martin, 'Warren Gamaliel Harding', p. 306. 14 *The New Republic*, 12 January 1921. 15 Martin, 'Warren Gamaliel Harding', p. 308; Murray, *The Harding era*, pp. 303, 112, 118. William Phillips, under secretary of State, recalled that most of Harding's evenings were spent 'playing poker with his cronies ... and imbibing more than was good for him.' W. Phillips, *Ventures in diplomacy* (1942), p. 55. 16 *BDFA*, i, Geddes to Curzon, 25 February 1921. 17 Martin, 'Warren Gamaliel Harding', p. 308; Murray, *The Harding era*, pp. 303, 112, 118.

enced by both personal and political factors. His style of governing also differed
from Wilson's. Harding accorded each cabinet member considerable independence in formulating policy and running their own affairs. Decisions were rarely
taken at the cabinet table and instead resulted from individual meetings. Thus,
government was less by collective decision-making and more by 'presidential syn-
thesis of the ideas of his cabinet secretaries.'[18] He also hoped to co-operate with
the Republican-dominated Congress. In effect government would be through co-
operation and facilitation rather than personal domination.

Harding and foreign policy

While Harding may have been a man of mediocre intelligence who was bereft of
original thinking and who swayed with the majority popular positions, his guiding principles were a belief in American nationalism and patriotism. He set out
his agenda in his inaugural address on 4 March 1921. Just like Wilson, he
expected to concentrate on domestic and not foreign affairs. Among other proposals, he suggested legislation that would increase tariffs, reduce taxes and cut
government spending. All measures were influenced by the various factions within
his party and designed to appease them.

The weakest part of Harding's speech dealt with foreign policy, Harding
stated:

> The recorded progress of our republic, materially and spiritually, in itself
> proves the wisdom of the inherited policy of non-involvement in old world
> affairs. Confident of our ability to work out our own destiny, and jealously
> guarding our right to do so, we seek no part in directing the destinies of
> the old world. We do not mean to be entangled. We will accept no respon-
> sibility except as our own conscience and judgement, in each instance, may
> determine.[19]

The isolationist streak was obvious. Despite this statement and his hometown
image he had informed himself about foreign affairs and assumed a policy stance
prior to becoming president. Firstly, he had travelled more than Wilson. He had
been to Egypt, the Mediterranean, Italy, Germany, Switzerland and the Caribbean
before becoming a US senator in 1914. In 1915, he travelled to Hawaii and in
May 1919, joined the Senate Foreign Relations Committee. Prior to his inauguration in March 1921, he visited Panama and Jamaica. The visits, whether for
private or Senate business, at least made him more than aware of the extent and
nature of US foreign relations and responsibilities and limited his parochialism.

---

18 Martin, 'Warren Gamaliel Harding', p. 308.   19 Quoted in P.R. Moran, *Warren G. Harding
1865–1923: chronology-documents-bibliographical aids* (1970), p. 27.

By the day of his inauguration, it was evident that his views on foreign affairs were informed by his belief in nationalism and in protecting US rights and security abroad. Although he opposed Wilson he spoke in favour of war with Germany in 1917 and in the sixty-fifth Congress he voted for war and for espionage legislation. His anti-Germanism had to be tempered by the predominance of German-American votes in his constituency. His isolationism was balanced by his version of internationalism. It was this ambivalence which weakened the speech. He continued,

> Our eyes never will be blind to a developing menace, our ears never deaf to the call of civilisation. We recognise the new order in the world, with the closer contacts which progress has wrought ... We crave friendship and harbour no hate. But America, our America, the America built on the foundation laid by the inspired fathers, can be a party to no permanent military alliance. It can enter into no political commitments, nor assume any economic obligations which will subject our decisions to any other than our own authority.[20]

He would direct the US into conference with other nations to achieve disarmament, establish a world court, aid in the economic recovery of Europe and prevent another war. US involvement in the post-war international system would be on US terms and it would not be through the League of Nations. Harding's belief in American greatness and pre-eminence underpinned his views throughout his life and, while he saw a coherence to these views, not all agreed.[21] One British commentator described it as 'the most illiterate statement ever made by the head of a civilised government', while Davis described it as 'a fearful and wonderful piece of English.'[22] Harding expanded on the themes in this address when he met Congress on 12 April. He urged Congress to declare peace with former enemies and declared that there had to be an 'orderly funding and gradual liquidation' of war debts and the US would 'have no part' in the League of Nations. Instead he aimed 'to associate nations to prevent war, preserve peace and promote civilization.' America's aspiration, indeed, the world aspiration, was an association of nations.[23]

Certainly, Congress was surprised by the speech, not just because it covered virtually every domestic and foreign difficulty facing the nation but because there was something in it for all shades of political opinion. It appealed to and offended liberals, progressives and conservatives, opponents and proponents of the League of Nations and bureaucrats. For others, even within the Republican Party, there was relief that at least there were policies on some issues and that even if there were not solutions there was an appreciation of difficulties. Others such as former secretary of State Elihu Root did not have the 'slightest idea of what

20 Ibid., pp. 27–8.   21 Downes, *The rise*, p. 339.   22 Quoted in Moran, *Warren G. Harding*, p. 27; J. Davis & D.A. Fleming (eds), *The ambassadorial diary of John W. Davis: the Court of St James, 1918–21* (1993), p. 410.   23 Quoted in Moran, *Warren G. Harding*, p. 35.

Harding's foreign policy is to be.' The *New York World* reported, in January 1921, that Geddes was returning to London to outline Harding's plans, but suggested that he should inform Harding of them first.[24]

It fell to Charles Evans Hughes to make sense of Harding's foreign policy and to cope with the resulting challenges. Hughes' cabinet appointment was one of the earliest that Harding made.[25] When he introduced Hughes to the press on 19 February 1921 he declared: 'from this time on, gentlemen, you will get our news as to the foreign relations of the United States from the State Department.'[26] It was clear that, unlike his predecessor, Harding did not intend to provide the initiative in foreign affairs and it was Hughes who took over that mantle. Oswald Garrrison Villard, owner and editor of the liberal organ, the *Nation*, writing on 9 March criticized Harding's appointments as lacking international knowledge and favoured Knox instead of Hughes as secretary of State.[27] Yet, the Democratic *New York World* endorsed Hughes, although, as Michael A. Kelly, a retired Irish-American soldier, explained this had less to do with his 'personal worth, but rather ... it sees in him a man to perpetuate the principles of Wilsonism in our foreign policy.'[28]

Hughes had practiced and taught law until 1907, when he was elected Republican governor of New York. Between 1910 and 1921, he was an associate justice of the Supreme Court and was a failed presidential challenger to Wilson in 1916. His background, therefore, revealed little experience of diplomacy and foreign relations. But what he lacked in practical experience he made up for with a 'ruthless intelligence' and he believed firmly in international co-operation. William Phillips, who became his under secretary and whose office adjoined Hughes', recalled that Hughes 'took a lawyer's delight in plumbing the depths of any problem.' He described his boss as a 'towering "Washington monument".' Hughes certainly shared Henry Cabot Lodge's reservations about the League of Nations but he believed that the US had 'to establish a *Pax Americana* maintained not by arms but by mutual respect and good will and the tranquilizing processes of reason.'[29] Nonetheless, if Hughes' interpretation of international relations was to be legalistic, his presence in cabinet was balanced by the presence of Hoover who might also have been considered for the State Department post. Hoover had international experience and offered a more nuanced ideological approach to foreign policy that linked it with domestic policy.[30] Prior to accepting Harding's offer of secretary of Commerce, however, Hoover had insisted that he be involved in foreign policy decisions.

24 Davis & Fleming, *The ambassadorial diary*, 29 November 1920, 22 January 1921.   25 M.J. Pusey, 'Charles Evans Hughes', book review, 417; Murray, *The Harding era*, pp. 96–7.   26 G.H. Stuart, *The Department of State: a history of its organisation, procedure and personnel* (1949), p. 259.   27 *Nation*, 9 March 1921.   28 *Sinn Féiner*, 5 February 1921.   29 J. Findling, *Dictionary of American diplomatic history* (1980), p. 230; Phillips, *Ventures in diplomacy*, p. 55; C. Evans Hughes, *The pathway to peace* (1925), p. 159.   30 Hoover had risen from poverty to economic and political power as an engineer and millionaire and this had taken him to Australia, China, Latin America and Russia.

This placed the new secretary of Commerce at the centre of the foreign policy-making process. But Harding also permitted secretaries Henry Wallace, in
Agriculture, and Albert Fall, in Interior, to contribute and allowed each to establish a separate, albeit short-lived, foreign service in their respective departments.
Disagreements over territory between these departments and the State
Department would soon emerge.[31] Ireland offers one case study of these conflicts
as indicated in chapter twelve. The difference between the Harding and Wilson
administrations in terms of sources of foreign policy is pronounced. Not only did
Harding adopt a more low-key approach to the formulation of foreign policy but
he did not have any single special adviser, such as House, and while he became
involved in certain issues, as will be seen, he permitted other cabinet members
and their departments to have a strong voice in the process as well. However,
when it came to the implementation of policy, Harding's ambassadorial appointments were influenced by the same factors as Wilson's.

After eight years out of office, the Republican faithful deluged Harding with
requests for posts, while the president also had certain political debts to repay.
First choice for the office seekers was a cabinet post that was followed in prestige by an ambassadorial one, particularly that to the Court of St James in
London. Davis tendered his resignation again on 13 January 1921 and Harding
accepted it on 6 March 1921. His successor was to be Colonel George B. Harvey,
former editor of the *New York World* and owner and editor of *Harvey's Weekly*.
Indeed the *Louisville Courier Journal* described him as a 'journalistic rough neck
… bumptious, unstable, sensational and loose of tongue.' Throughout the war,
he used his magazines, *Harper's Weekly* and *Harvey's Weekly*, to attack first,
Wilson's war and post-war policies. He was an adviser to Borah's irreconcilables
and influential in the Republicans' choice of Harding to oppose Wilson for the
presidency.[32] Prior to Harding's inauguration, Harvey resided in the Harding
household.[33] The reward for his service was immediate.[34]

He had also been Director General of Relief for Europe and a member of Wilson's committee of
economic advisers. He split from Wilson due to article ten of the League of Nations charter, which
he believed prevented the US leadership from using its economic, military and political power as
it thought fit. In other words, he was not an isolationist but a 'diplomatist', who favoured a policy
of 'independent internationalism', whereby America could construct a new world order where its
interests could thrive Prior to the party convention meetings in summer 1920, Robert Lindsay in
the British embassy backed Hoover to be a contender for the presidential nomination for either the
Republican or Democratic parties. *BDFA*, i, Lindsay to Curzon, 19 February 1920.   31 H. De
Santis & W. Heinrichs, 'United States of America: the Department of State and American foreign
policy' in Z. Steiner (ed.), *Foreign ministries of the world* (1982), p. 582.   32 Findling, *Dictionary*,
p. 211; Stuart, *The Department of State*, p. 262; W. Fletcher Johnson, *George Harvey: 'a passionate
patriot'* (1929), pp. 174–80, 217. Harvey had not always been a Republican and had supported
Democrat presidential candidate Grover Cleveland in 1892 and Woodrow Wilson between 1906 and
1913. He was friendly with Joseph Tumulty but broke with Wilson because the latter disliked his
journalistic methods.   33 Yale University Library, Manuscripts and Archives Collection (hereafter
YULMC), Frank L. Polk Papers (hereafter FLPP), box 2, file129, Polk to Davis, 16 December
1920.   34 Findling, *Dictionary*, p. 211; Stuart, *The Department of State*, p. 262. Nor did Harvey's

It was Harvey's lack of polish and unpredictability that appealed to some Irish-Americans. An editorial in *The Monitor* on 16 April noted

> Our ambassadors to England have in many times past furnished, as a rule, many striking examples to which the disease of anglomania can carry one. Chosen for the most part from the wealthy snoocracy of this country, they have thought it necessary to cultivate "good will" by exhibiting sycophancy as disgusting as it was futile.
>
> From Rufus King in the early days of the Republic who acted as a British Secret Service agent, to Walter Page, who declared that "America was English-led and English-ruled." The long roll of ambassadors has been far from edifying.
>
> One wonders, therefore, whether we are going back to the days of real Americanism in the choice of Colonel Harvey as our representative in the Court of St James. If one may judge by the following article and the accompanying cartoon taken from his [*Harvey's*] *Weekly* in 1919 it would look as if the position will be held by one worthy of treading in the footsteps of the men of the past who would not let the English "pull the wool over their eyes."[35]

The article included a piece which had supported calls for an inquiry into conditions in Ireland published in the new ambassador's newspaper, *Harvey's Weekly*, in early 1919.[36] The piece had not gone unnoticed by British diplomats either in 1921. It was included in the weekly review of Irish activities sent by Harry Gloster Armstrong, the British consul general in New York, to the Foreign Office where R.H. Hadow in the American department commented; 'The *Monitor* brings up past utterances of Colonel Harvey and ... [one] wonders what he will say as ambassador.'[37] Hadow's comment was prophetic and echoed others within the US diplomatic service. Harvey's appointment was not unreservedly welcomed in the London embassy for both personal and professional reasons. Undoubtedly, with Davis' imminent departure and the flaring up of his asthma, the pace of work had declined: the arrival of the new ambassador was eagerly awaited to revive it. Boylston A. Beal, a senior official in the US embassy in London bemoaned Davis' departure; 'we shall all be heart-broken ... the time seems very short now.' Nor did he like changes, 'which are always horrid and such a complete overturn leaves

---

addiction to alcohol endear him to many, least of all Hughes. M.E. Pusey, *Charles Evans Hughes*, 2 vols (1963), i, p. 418. Senator George Norris was the only Republican to oppose Harvey in the senate confirmation vote. Norris claimed that Harvey had used 'disreputable and dishonourable' methods to drive his enemies from public life and that he could not function as an effective diplomat. R. Lowitt, *George W. Norris: the persistence of a progressive, 1913–33* (1971), p. 140.   **35** The National Archives, London (hereafter TNA) Foreign Office (hereafter FO), 371/5645, Gloster Armstrong to Foreign Office, 19 April 1921.   **36** Ibid., *The Monitor*, 16 April 1921.   **37** Ibid., FO371/5645, R.H. Hadow, 3 May 1921.

one in rather a gasp.' He hoped that Harvey would leave the 'social side of the embassy work' to the diplomats, as he 'did not feel that he [Harvey] has quite the social flair to understand many of the finer points.' Harvey's political instability aroused Beal's concern who admitted to being 'pro-British in my sympathies.' Beal concluded, on 7 March 1921, 'the future will decide.'[38] Harvey was left in place during Harding's term of office despite many gaffes.[39]

During his tenure, Hughes avoided making or suggesting political appointments. At the same time, he had to deal with the consequences arising from the right of the president to use the upper echelon of foreign service positions for political and personal purposes and the reassertion, particularly by Republican business interests inside and outside Congress, that the foreign service should be shaped to serve US needs, which they perceived as being their own. It will be seen in later chapters that the 'diplomacy as a business' debate raged on between 1921 and 1923, leading to a compromise whereby the Rogers act amalgamated the diplomatic and consular services into the Foreign Service with a common entrance examination, rank, pay and retirement system. However, both services remained 'functionally separate' and from that time on fought over control of the reformed department. Hughes led the reorganization process, which was not finalized until 1924.[40] At the same time, after the stasis of the last months of the Wilson era, under Hughes' direction the State Department began to reassert itself within the decision-making process on foreign policy.[41]

It was, therefore, within the context firstly, of this developing departmental machinery, secondly, of independent internationalism and thirdly, of the open-door policy whereby the new government would not brook any discrimination against US business interests abroad, that Harding, Hughes and Hoover acted to deal with the main challenges to the US reordering of the world economic, political and military order. These included war debts, reparations, disarmament, the Japanese threat in the east and fear of an expanding bolshevik revolution. William Wiseman, the former British intelligence chief who visited Washington in spring 1921, provided the Foreign Office with the insight that US foreign policy was in an 'uncomfortable, but not necessarily unsatisfactory chrysalis stage. [Harding's] desire to do the right thing is counteracted by the play of prejudices.'[42]

---

38 Herbert Hoover Presidential Library (hereafter HHPL), William R. Castle Papers (hereafter WRCP), Box 3, file: England 1920–5, Beal to Castle, 4 February 1921, 25 October 1921, 7 March 1921.　39 In two cases his actions caused difficulty for the administration first when he questioned the veracity of Lord Curzon and on a second occasion when he attempted to progress negotiations with Britain over the funding of war debts which nearly broke up the discussions. B. Glad, *Charles Evans Hughes and the illusions of innocence: a study in American diplomacy* (1966), p. 136.　40 Heinrichs, Jr, *Joseph Grew*, pp. 99, 103–4.　41 Pusey, *Charles Evans Hughes*, i, pp. 412–13.　42 YULMC, The papers of William Wiseman (hereafter WWP), box 4, file 110, Wiseman to Tyrell, 21 May 1921. Wiseman returned to banking in 1921 when he joined a Wall Street firm.　43 Trani & Wilson, *The presidency of Warren G. Harding*, p. 110; Murray, *The Harding era*, pp. 132–3.

While Harding admitted that foreign policy was not a priority for him and although Hughes set the pace on foreign policy, the two talked almost every day and returning ambassadors reported to both of them. Furthermore, Harding's notes and comments on Hughes' reports suggested a careful reading at the very least and, depending on the region involved, the president also took an active part in setting policy.[43] He was determined to improve relations with the central and southern American countries in order to protect US interests and also to distance himself from Wilson's interventionist approach. According to Murray, Harding involved himself in this normalization process both through personal direction to Hughes and through the appointment of personal emissaries.[44] Meanwhile, Hughes and Hoover moved to limit Japanese horizons further by entangling it in disarmament treaties, breaking its 1902 treaty with Britain and making it reliant on Wall Street financiers.[45]

When it came to the Union of Soviet Socialist Republics (USSR), Harding, prior to his inauguration, had expressed a willingness to reverse Wilson's policy of non-recognition and resume diplomatic and trade relations. Two weeks after the inauguration the Soviet president, Mikhail Kalinin, requested a normalizing of the relationship. There were strong forces within US society in support of both positions. The American Legion, the Roman Catholic Church and the American Federation of Labour (AFL) opposed bolshevism, while US business interests such as General Electric, General Motors and the Ford Motor company viewed the Soviet Union as a fertile market for their goods. Nonetheless, when the Soviet request was discussed at the cabinet on 25 March 1921, Hughes and Hoover opposed it and Harding acquiesced, although in July the cabinet agreed to distribute relief aid to deal with the famine conditions in the USSR. Hughes' non-recognition position held albeit side by side with the expansion of US business and banking in the USSR.[46]

Harding also involved himself in the Middle East, although the official policy was one of 'non-involvement.' He sanctioned Hughes and Hoover's imple-

---

44 The following is based on Murray, *The Harding era*, pp. 327–60. Regarding southern America, Harding promoted US friendship with Peru, Argentina, Chile, Brazil, Venezuela and the Caribbean and negotiated the Colombian treaty (April 1921), which strengthened the US position in Colombia's oil fields. Harding and Hughes also acted as peace brokers in disputes between Costa Rica and Panama and Chile and Peru respectively, while the Central American conference hosted by Harding in Washington in late 1922 aimed to bring political stability to the region. Through their actions Harding and Hughes reinterpreted the Monroe Doctrine and expressed it as a defensive, rather than an offensive policy. He sent General James A. Ryan and Emer Dover to Mexico, much to Hughes' annoyance. In Cuba he used General Enoch H. Crowder as his personal representative, while in Haiti he requested Hughes to send Sumner Welles, chief of the Latin American division in the State Department, to carry out a survey of its status. In July 1921, he made the disastrous appointment of General John H. Russell as special commissioner and ambassador extraordinary to Haiti to carry out Welles' recommendations. In July 1922, the President sent a special bipartisan Senate committee, headed by one of his oldest senate friends, Senator Joseph Medill McCormick (Illinois), to Haiti.   45 Findling, *Dictionary*, pp. 515–16; LaFeber, *American age*, pp. 337–8.   46 Murray, *The Harding era*, pp. 349–51; LaFeber, *American age*, pp. 347–8.

mentation of the 'open door' policy which permitted US oil interests to expand their activities and reduce the allies' influence in the region. Protecting and progressing US economic considerations, rather than US humanitarian interests, predominated in Harding's agenda for the region. Even when Christians were attacked by Turks in Anatolia in mid-1922 and the White House and State Department were inundated with requests for US intervention to protect the Christians, Harding insisted that the US would not intervene militarily. Significantly for Ireland's case he cautioned the public against being overcome by the 'emotionalism' of the case and warned the State Department about raising false hopes.[47]

It is Harding's view and position on US–European relations, particularly those with Britain, which are of central concern to this study. Despite Harding's contact with Europe, he was never as interested in Europe as he was in central and southern America or the Middle East. Murray suggests Harding was confused by the complicated diplomatic and economic issues involved in the European situation.[48] Consequently, he left the formulation of European policy in the hands of Hughes and of US ambassadors in key capital cities who moved immediately on war debts, reparations, and disarmament matters, but delayed in handling US relationships with the League of Nations and international institutions more generally. The latter trend, particularly US withdrawal from the Reparations Commission in February 1921, led Davis to note that 'the links with Europe are getting few.'[49] All of these issues formed part of the US relationship with specific European countries in one degree or another during the Harding era.

Auckland Geddes had a long talk with John Davis on 8 February 1921 about the state of relations between their respective countries. Geddes believed that there was a visible hardening of British sentiment against the US and he felt that George Harvey would have a difficult time in London. On the other side, he believed there was growing opposition to Britain in the US and he felt that he would not be around to see 'Anglo-American affairs ... serene again.'[50] Wiseman supported Geddes' view. He met with Hoover, Lodge and other senators and public figures in May 1921 and felt that, although the US 'now sits impotent among her money bags', a majority of the US public, merchants and financiers believed that they were 'done in the eye by their British rivals' over the League of Nations and in financial and commercial terms. Wiseman gave Tyrell other reasons why the Foreign Office should not expect too much from Harding on Anglo-American co-operation; firstly, he said that the 'hyphenates are as active as they were before the war. The Irish tilt at Anglo-American relations with increased venom', secondly, there were divisions within the Republican Party between protectionists and free traders, isolationists and supporters of US mem-

47 Murray, *The Harding era*, pp. 355–60; LaFeber, *American age*, p. 346.   48 Murray, *The Harding era*, p. 360.   49 Davis & Fleming, *The ambassadorial diary*, 18 February 1921.   50 Ibid., 8 February 1921.

bership of an altered League of Nations and thirdly, there was nervousness about an impending 'financial panic.' He concluded that the British government needed to settle, or at least explain, the various questions that were worrying Americans and stirring up US opinion such as the Anglo-Irish war of independence, the Anglo-Japanese alliance, oil, equal access for the US and European victors in the mandated territories, war debts and the Panama Canal tolls issue.[51] As usual the Foreign Office played down the Irish factor because 'we must always reckon with Irish hostility in the US', but, until November 1921 at least, these issues dominated the correspondence of the British embassy in Washington with the Foreign Office in London and that of US embassy in London with the State Department.[52]

Early exchanges between the two administrations on the Anglo-Japanese alliance and secondly, on the tariff question suggested fewer points of agreement. Since 1918, the US government had regarded Japan as being its only naval rival in Asia and the 1902 Anglo-Japanese alliance was regarded as a threat to US security and additionally if the US and Japan ever came to fight each other, the alliance might mean that the US also had to face Britain. These fears contributed to the resumption of US naval shipbuilding as soon as Harding assumed office but also to forces favouring the reduction of the US naval budget. Hughes made the termination of the alliance one of his objectives.[53] This was supported by a campaign which used the newspapers and congressional debates to pressure the British government to end the alliance when it came up for renewal later in 1921. Geddes reported to Curzon that the Harding administration viewed the alliance as an 'unfriendly act' and that renewal of it would be 'disastrous.'[54] But the alliance was a cornerstone of British policy in the Pacific region.

In 1921, Wiseman and Geddes described for the Foreign Office the growth of US interest in the tariff question. Both showed that the post-war trading boom and spending had given way to industrial depression, a slump in trade, rising prices and unemployment thereby strengthening the protectionist movement. Republican politicians, producers and manufacturers feared foreign competition and demanded drastic tariff revisions, particularly for cereals, peanuts, potatoes, rice, wool, sugar, meat and tobacco. Opponents of protectionism, including bankers with international interests, exporters and owners of shipping companies, found some respite in one of Wilson's last acts as president. On 3 March, he had tried to stem the flow of protectionism by vetoing the Emergency Tariff

51 YULMC, WWP, box 4, file 110, Wiseman to Tyrell, 21 May 1921.   52 TNA, FO371/4550, Sperling, 15 April 1920.   53 Pusey, *Charles Evans Hughes*, ii, pp. 491–2. On 22 March 1921, Frank P. Walsh, legal counsel to the AARIR had linked Ireland to the debt issue. He submitted to the Senate Judiciary Committee which was then investigating foreign loans, a memorandum purporting to show that the net cost of maintaining the British military in Ireland was sufficient to pay one-half of the annual interest on Britain's debt to the United States. *New York Times*, 23 March 1921, *Washington Post*, 23 March 1921.   54 *BDFA*, i, Annual Report for 1921, p. 137.

bill. Nonetheless Geddes was convinced that the bill would 'almost certainly' be re-introduced after the next Congress met. Moreover, Dr Page, Chairman of United States Tariff Commission, told him that he favoured a 'bargaining tariff' that authorized his commission to impose certain duties without special legislation.[55] The consequences for British and imperial trade of the US administration building tariff walls were significant. According to the US department of Commerce, the US imported approximately $35.2 million direct from Ireland in 1919 and exported approximately $15.7 million.[56] Consequently, as early as 19 January 1921, Diarmaid Fawsitt, Dáil Éireann consul in New York, wrote to owners of businesses in Belfast who traded with the US to request their views on the effects of increased US tariffs on their business. Replies were to be sent to Fawsitt in New York. Consul Kent advised the businessmen in his Belfast district to ignore the letter but the issue would not go away so easily.[57] By mid March 1921, the South African government complained to the Colonial Secretary, Winston Churchill, about the effects on the South African wool trade of the proposed re-imposition by the US government of the 1909 customs tariff. Churchill supported the complaint and requested that 'His Majesty's Ambassador at Washington may be asked to take action.' Hadow, in the Foreign Office, minuted 'this will not influence the US much.' Curzon agreed.[58] It was clear from Geddes' despatches that diplomacy would have little or no part to play in what was regarded by the Harding administration as a domestic economic problem.[59] Harding's indecision combined to the political imperative of 'preserving a conciliatory attitude towards both parties' and attending to the needs of US business, set the boundaries on the tariff agenda for US–British relations throughout Harding's tenure. Protectionism was interlinked with the other issue that dominated the relationship; the repayment of Britain's war debts to the US. Hadow put it succinctly on 21 April, 'it is hard to see ... how Europe is to pay interest on her loans while every effort is made to kill her trade with the USA.'[60]

During world war one, Wilson had permitted US bankers to loan between four and five billion dollars to Britain in financial support, but even before Harding assumed office he had indicated that he would adhere to Wilson's position, namely that the US would not consider any debt-funding scheme.[61] The allies' hope of reducing their US debts or linking them with inter-allied debts and reparations was not possible. US public and political opinion endorsed Wilson

---

55 TNA, FO371/5670, Geddes to FO, 7 January, 6 April 1921; YULMC, WWP, box 4, file 110, Wiseman to Tyrell, 21 May 1921.   56 Quoted in 'Note on American trade with Ireland, restrictions on American travel', National Archives and Records Administration, Maryland (hereafter NARA), Records of the Department of State relating to internal affairs of Great Britain, 1910–29, Record Group 59 (hereafter RG59), M580/218, 841d.00/309, Rossa Downing to Secretary of State, 11 October 1921.   57 Ibid., 841d.00/316, Kent to Secretary of State, 9 February 1921.   58 TNA, FO371/5670, Colonial Office (hereafter CO) to FO, 17 March 1921, Hadow 22 March 1921.   59 Ibid., Geddes to Curzon, 6 April 1921.   60 Ibid., Haddow, 21 April 1921.   61 P.A. Grant, 'President Warren G. Harding and the British war debt question, 1921–3', 479.

and Harding's position on the issue and wanted America's debtors to make direct repayment. In April 1921, one of Harding's first cabinet meetings unanimously favoured full repayment of all war debts. Hughes regarded the debts issue as a political problem, Hoover as a trade one and Mellon as a fiscal matter, but each agreed the debts had to be repaid.[62] Thus, in March 1921 there was a standoff between the US and Britain, with the former refusing to consider cancellation, reduction or substitution of the debts and Britain reluctant to acknowledge its validity. When Geddes discussed the matter with Harding in early 1921, the latter said that of course the debt could not be paid in goods 'which would lower the standard of American living, nor in services such as shipping.' But when Geddes asked 'How then?' the president replied 'We must find a way'.[63] Finding a way became a serious irritant in the US–British relationship. The resolution of the debt question began in December 1921, when Harding delivered his first state of the union address and urged Congress to settle the on-going problem.[64] Much negotiation and compromise occurred stretching the relationship to its limits (see chapter eight).

The final feature of the US–British diplomatic requiring attention in March 1921 was Ireland. In December 1920, Boylston Beal in the US embassy in London wrote to Castle; 'Ireland and unemployment are so much nearer and blacker than anything else that not much time or thought is left for other worries.' Beal did not personally support the British government's policy of reprisals in Ireland but could justify it to himself on the grounds that 'if such retaliation were too much repressed it might be that the loyal troops might be difficult to keep in hand.'[65] Beal's superior, the departing Davis, agreed. When Davis met King George on 5 March 1921, at Buckingham palace, for a farewell lunch, the latter proceeded to talk 'in a very serious fashion' about Anglo–American relations and focused on navy expansion and the 'Irish situation.' As was indicated previously, Davis also took the matter seriously and at one stage in his tenure, had regarded finding a solution to the on-going Anglo-Irish war of independence as being one of his responsibilities. However, by early 1921 he had come to accept the inevitability of continued warfare in Ireland and his lack of influence. One of his last attempts to thwart the Sinn Féin efforts occurred prior to his departure. In February, he facilitated the transmission of information from British intelligence to the Bureau of Investigation.[66] British–American co-operation on halting arms shipments to the republicans in Ireland did not bear fruit until later in 1921 and even then it was more through luck than design, as will be seen in chapter eight. In the interim, Davis prepared to leave London and, on the topic of Ireland at least, he

62 Murray, *Harding era*, pp. 361–2.   63 Davis & Fleming, *The ambassadorial diary of John W. Davis*, 8 February 1921.   64 Grant, 'President Warren G. Harding', 485–7.   65 HHPL, WRCP, box 3, Beal to Castle, 28 December 1920.   66 NARA, RG59, M580/218, 841d.00/299, Davis to Secretary of State, 4 February 1921; ibid., 841d.00/314, Davis to Secretary of State, 24 February 1921; ibid., 841d.00/315, Colby to Davis, 25 February 1921.

fully agreed with King George's view; 'how can we raise the white flag, when the country is in the grip of a gang of outlaws and murders?'[67] During his time in office, Davis discussed the Irish question widely and kept up to date on developments there through the US consular network and contacts in London. This was more than some of his predecessors did. Yet, he followed the other ambassadorial tradition of coming to sympathize with the British position and adhering to a non-intervention policy while wishing fervently that a settlement would be reached. In March 1921, it remained to be seen whether Harding and Hughes regarded Ireland as a live issue in the US foreign policy agenda. Moreover, the poor state of American–British relations provided republicans in the US and Ireland with much ammunition to help promote their interests.

Harding, Ireland and foreign policy

Prior to becoming president, Harding's contact and exposure to Irish-related matters were influenced by his political and personal allegiance and practices. Ohio remained his base throughout most of his life and it was a state not readily identifiable with the Irish community, unlike other north eastern states or California. However, from the time when Ohio was declared a state in 1803, the Presbyterian Irish or Scotch Irish, as Harding's grandparents' generation were, had arrived to farm the land and build their churches, schools and colleges. They valued hard work, religion and education. Many of the clergy and citizens, including Harding's parents, were active in the anti-slavery movement that culminated in the formation of the Republican Party in Ohio in 1854 by which time most of the Scotch Irish had been integrated into the mainstream of US life. But the state was representative of the diversity of its immigrant population and, by the time of Harding's birth in 1865, had a significant Catholic Irish presence.[68]

The building of canals and railroads throughout the state brought in the Catholic Irish who swelled the populations of Cincinnati, Cleveland, Dayton and other growing Ohio cities. Unlike their Presbyterian counterparts, most of the Catholics were manual labourers who lived in shantytowns and earned reputations for drunkenness and disorderly behaviour. They encountered discrimination on economic, racist and religious grounds, but, as was the case elsewhere, they gradually emerged from poverty and established organizations to assist new arrivals, protect themselves and support campaigns back in Ireland.[69]

---

67 Davis & Fleming, *The ambassadorial diary*, 5 March 1921.   68 T.F. Campbell, 'Ohio' in M. Glazier (ed.), *The encyclopedia of the Irish in America* (1999), pp. 730–1.   69 Campbell, 'Ohio', pp. 730–1. By the 1860s Judge Dennis Dwyer of Dayton assisted in the establishment of the Irish Catholic Benevolent Union to help needy immigrants. More importantly was the identification of the Catholic Irish with all shades of political activity in Ireland. Delegates from Cincinnati representing Ohio attended a national convention of repeal organizations held in Philadelphia in February 1842, while the Fenian Brotherhood at its Chicago meeting in November 1863 established a centre

The Catholic Irish-American allegiance in Ohio was to the Democratic Party which, by mid-century, opposed the anti-Catholicism and anti-immigration policies of the Know-Nothing Party and subsequently, of the Republican Party. These policies, combined to the anti-Catholic and anti-Irish attitudes of Republican newspapers throughout Ohio, repulsed the Catholic Irish voter.[70] By 1900, in Marion, Ohio, the *Marion Star* and its editor, Harding, represented the Republican Party in the county. At this time several of his political beliefs were being formed, such as suspicion of foreign immigration, support for American nationalism and distrust of unions, which pitched him directly against many Catholic Irish-Americans. Nor was he averse to riding the wave of anti-Catholicism which characterized Ohio's politics and society in the last decades of the nineteenth and beginning of the twentieth centuries.

Religious prejudice was deeply embedded in the state.[71] By the turn of the century there were five Catholic newspapers in the state of Ohio, all of which were regarded by British officials as 'pro-Irish' and 'anti-British', but it was not until 1910 that the first Catholic Irish-American won state office.[72] Timothy S. Hogan, a lawyer, who worked on behalf of dissenters and women, was elected to the post of attorney general. Four years later, he lost the race for the US Senate to Harding, whose campaign included a strong anti-Irish and anti-Catholic tinge. One poster plastered throughout the state stated 'Read the *Menace* and get the dope, go to the polls and beat the Pope.'[73] The *Menace* was a notorious organ of Catholic baiters. It claimed a circulation of over a million in 1912 and every issue was sensational in its anti-Catholic attacks.[74] Harding was not associated with these tactics but undoubtedly he benefited greatly, winning the seat with a large majority.[75]

Even though Harding had emerged from this establishment background and had little in common with Catholic Irish-America he possessed other political beliefs and personal characteristics that reduced this gulf. From 1920 onwards, his belief in appeasement and mediation as political methods, combined with his personal ability to effect compromise, made him an appealing candidate not only for Republicans voters but also for Democratic ones, including Catholic Irish-

---

in Ohio to create a state organization which was sufficiently strong to host a national congress in January 1865. In 1882, the Cleveland branch of the Ladies' Land League was severely criticized by Bishop Richard J. Gilmour who threatened excommunication to any women participating in the league. But moderate, non-violent Irish-American nationalists who welcomed Charles Stewart Parnell's constitutional approach joined the Irish National League of America and the Irish Parliamentary Fund Association which was organized in Cincinnati by Mayor John Byrne on 24 January 1885. Its sole aim was to finance Parnellite candidates' electoral path to the British House of Commons. Just over twenty years later, the Ancient Order of Hibernians held a convention in Cleveland in 1884. An anti-Parnellite Irish National Federation of America emerged in Cleveland in February 1892. See M. Funchion, *Irish American voluntary organizations* (1983), pp. 28, 46, 61, 108, 109, 117, 185, 204–5, 220, 222, 237, 238, 239.   70 Campbell, 'Ohio', p. 733.   71 Sinclair, *The available man*, p. 54.   72 *BDFA*, vii, The American press, 1920–22, Catholic papers in America, February 1920, pp. 10–11.   73 Campbell, 'Ohio', p. 733.   74 E.A. Moore, *A Catholic runs for president: the campaign of 1928* (1956), p. 15.   75 Murray, *Harding era*, pp. 13–14.

Americans. So, while Harding had few, if any, positive contacts with Catholic Irish-America prior to 1914, at the same time he was a realist who could jettison personal convictions if they stood in the way of political survival.[76]

Chapter six revealed that his congressional voting record between 1915 and 1919 reflected the needs of his Republican voters and party machine back in Ohio and that he toed the party line on Ireland. During the 1920 presidential campaign, his voting record on Irish matters was published by his Democratic opponents in order to discredit his expression of sympathy for the cause of Irish freedom. Like most of his party colleagues, he regarded the Irish question as a domestic matter for the British government to solve. The League of Nations controversy saw Harding's first significant contact with the Irish question. As a member of Borah's irreconcilables, he was part of a faction that included Daniel Cohalan and the Friends of Irish Freedom (FOIF) and helped defeat the League of Nations. Later in the year, despite the failure to have a plank on Irish freedom inserted into the Republican convention, Dumont reported from Dublin that the Sinn Féin leadership there believed that Harding was 'really in favour of Irish freedom' and had voted for it in Congress.[77] In fact, Harding had been inconsistent. In March 1920, he had opposed the Gerry reservation but supported the amended treaty while on 6 June 1920 he had abstained in the vote on David Walsh's Senate resolution that expressed sympathy with the aspiration of the Irish people for self-government.[78]

During the 1920 presidential campaign he had little to say about Ireland beyond bland statements of support for Irish freedom, and analysis of the results concluded that some Irish-Americans voted as Americans first and that this led them to side with Harding. Nevertheless, Irish-American republican activists were optimistic. Immediately after the November result, John Devoy in the *Gaelic American*, believed that the 'six million majority of the American people' mandated him to 'take steps leading up to the formal recognition of the Republic of Ireland.'[79] Frank P. Walsh, now legal counsel for Eamon de Valera's American Association for the Recognition of the Irish Republic (AARIR), shared these hopes:

> The Irish effort is going better in America than at any time in its history
> ... The new administration takes office on 4th of next month ... While
> we cannot hope for anything immediate and definite from them, never-
> theless they cannot be as wrong headed as the present administration and
> at least we will have a new and fresh ground for our activities. I am
> extremely hopeful of the future.[80]

76 R.A. Burchell, 'Did the Irish and German voters desert the Democrats in 1920? A tentative statistical answer', 156; Murray, *Harding era*, pp. 10–11.   77 NARA, RG59, M580/216, 841d.00/209, Dumont to Secretary of State, 15 June 1920. Andrew Mellon along with Henry Clay Frick helped fund Borah's 'irreconcilables' campaign against the League of Nations. H. O'Connor, *Mellon's millions: the biography of a fortune: the life and times of Andrew W. Mellon* (1933), p. 116.   78 *Washington Post*, 24 September 1920.   79 *Gaelic American*, 20 November 1920.   80 Quoted in M. Hopkinson,

Unsurprisingly, Cohalan believed that 'Mr Harding has far more commonsense and far less credulous vanity than Mr Wilson had, and Senator Hughes towers head and shoulders over Mr Wilson's ludicrous State Department.'[81] Within Irish republican circles, two days after Harding's election Harry Boland, Dáil Èireann representative to the US, was 'convinced that we can bring sufficient pressure to bear in Washington so as to secure a square deal for Ireland.'[82] His colleague, Mary MacSwiney, another Sinn Féin representative in the US, believed she had obtained evidence of Harding's commitment to Irish recognition. During Harding's consultations on cabinet-formation, he called in a friend, Colonel Mather, who proceeded to question the president-elect about his attitude on US official recognition of the Irish republic. According to MacSwiney, Harding said he had 'no fixed ideas on the subject' and that if Congress voted for it, he would 'put no obstacle in the way.' She was convinced of the efficacy of the lobbying path because of Mather's information. On 15 February 1921, she advised James O'Mara, trustee for the Dáil Èireann loan in the US, to 'concentrate on lobbying at congress as much as possible ... [you] should not leave a day without getting after the people who have a vote.' [83] These Irish-American and Irish republicans hoped that Harding would recognize the Irish republic and perhaps intervene in the Anglo-Irish war of independence and they watched closely the composition of Congress and the new cabinet for any opportunities to garner support.

Immediately, the Dáil Èireann mission in Washington began to focus on a strategy to win recognition from the new Congress and administration. Joseph Begley noted Harding's 'repeated' statement that there would be much closer co-operation between the legislative and executive branches of government than during Wilson's tenure. Consequently, Begley was hopeful that this might offer a 'favourable prospect for Irish interests' because 'the incoming executive may be more amenable to congressional influence than was Mr Wilson.' For Begley, the point to be determined was whether Irish interests would be better served by solely demanding direct action by Congress on the Irish question or by linking the Irish question with issues which were important to the American public and politicians. He felt that 'England will be more embarrassed by the latter policy than by the former.' Frank P. Walsh agreed with him and together they drew up a list of US foreign policy issues: 'Panama Canal tolls, cable censorship, shipping, English debt and oil.' They also wanted to draw up a handbook to explain

'President Wilson and the Irish question', 108, 110.   81 American Irish Historical Society (hereafter AIHS), Daniel F. Cohalan Papers (hereafter DFCP), Box 1, folder 5, Cohalan to Hoving, 1 March 1921. As governor of New York between 1907 and 1910, Hughes had encountered the full force of Tammanay Hall, particularly Boss Charles Murphy who defeated much of his reformist programme. Pusey, *Charles Evans Hughes*, i, p. 173; D. Burner, *The politics of provincialism: the Democratic party in transition, 1918–1932* (1970), pp. 24–5.   82 Quoted in David Fitzpatrick, *Harry Boland's Irish revolution* (2003), p. 191.   83 University College Dublin Archives (hereafter UCDA), Mary MacSwiney Papers (hereafter MMP), P48A/115, MacSwiney to James O'Mara, 15 February 1921. The Sinn Féin loan issue will be examined later in this chapter and in chapter thirteen.

the Irish context of these issues for distribution to all members of the new Congress, while individual branches of the AARIR would be requested to adopt resolutions in favour of a 'great navy programme' not reduction and to galvanize public opinion within states, particularly the newly enfranchized woman voters. Senator Thomas Walsh suggested working at local level and was 'particularly insistent' that senators only paid attention to resolutions and petitions from within their own states.[84]

The approach of exploiting an Irish dimension in US foreign policy and using local support to pressurize congressional representatives was not new. After all, the relationship between US isolationism and anti-British hostility had brought Cohalan, John Devoy, the Friends of Irish Freedom and the Republican Party into a coalition that helped defeat Wilson's Paris settlement. Despite the subsequent split in Irish-America between Cohalan's FOIF and de Valera's AARIR, 'Americanism' continued to prevail with Cohalan, through his support for the anti-British campaigns of other organizations such as the non-partisan All American National Council (AANC).[85] But despite Cohalan's impressive network of contacts with US politicians, particularly Borah, his effectiveness as leader of Irish-American had been eroded because of the split with de Valera and his power base, the Friends, faced competition for financial and congressional support with the establishment of the Dáil Éireann mission and the AARIR in late autumn 1920. The AARIR, under the direction of Dáil Éireann representatives, put Irish and not Irish-American needs firmly to the fore as will be seen.

Prior to Harding's installation as president, Harry Boland, Joseph Begley, O'Mara, Miss Rosser and other workers in the Dáil Éireann missions in Washington and Chicago, along with the AARIR, particularly Frank P. Walsh and Peter Golden, worked hard to gather information about the composition of the new Congress, specifically looking for those on the congressional foreign relations committees and other politicians who might be sympathetic to the Irish cause and willing to link with the republicans on common issues. Miss Rosser, in the Washington Office, reported to O'Mara that Congressman Mason 'has high hopes of the appointment of several real Americans' to the foreign relations committees. She concluded 'if that means anything, we can all hope.'[86] Among the congressional figures that MacSwiney deemed 'alright' on the Irish issue were Republican senators George W. Norris and Asle J. Gronna and Democrats George E. Chamberlain, Joseph Irwin, Joseph E. Ransdell, Duncan U. Fletcher, John K. Shields and Gilbert M. Hitchcock. All had signed the appeal sent to

84 UCDA, Eamon de Valera Papers (hereafter EVP), P150/1124, Report. Activities of Washington Office, week ending 29 January 1921. Begley also asked for Erskine Childers to be sent to the US as a representative with plenipotentiary powers. Ibid.   85 AIHS, DFCP, Box 1, folder 6, AANC, *Bulletin*, 16 November 1922; ibid., folder 5, Johannes Hoving, President AANC to Cohalan, 30 September 1921; see also folder 7.   86 UCDA, EVP, P150/1175, O'Mara to Rosser, 3 March 1921; ibid., Rosser to O'Mara, 12, 25 March 1921. See also Fitzpatrick, *Harry Boland*, pp. 136–7. Another 'Washington veteran' who advised Boland was Republican journalist John E. Millholland. Ibid.

Acting Secretary of State Davis for visas to be given to the American Commission. Other senators to whom republican representatives could look to for support were Democrats David I. Walsh and Thomas J. Walsh and Republicans William E. Borah, Robert La Follette, Joseph I. France and Medill McCormick along with Republican congressmen William E. Mason and Stephen G. Porter.[87] Thus, irrespective of the resurgence of the State Department within the decision-making process on foreign policy and the wish of State Department officials to restrict access to the president, politicians still had to be responsive to their constituents' demands and were important conduits for activists. As early as February 1921 Senator David I. Walsh of Massachusetts was prepared to introduce a resolution for the recognition of Irish independence into the new Senate, as was Senator La Follette.[88]

But the question for Boland, O'Mara, MacSwiney, Begley and the AARIR leaders was whether public opinion could be galvanized to put pressure on the new Republican-dominated but factionalized Congress, not just to propose, debate, and refer the question of Irish recognition to Senator Lodge's Senate Relations Committee but to force it through to resolution stage and produce a response from Harding.

It was the possibilities offered by Harding's cabinet that the *Sinn Feiner* newspaper highlighted:

> All sorts of rumours are afloat as to the probable personnel of Mr Harding's cabinet. The strings are being pulled behind the scenes. "Deserving" Republicans want everything their own way. They desire a cabinet of amenable politicians, men who will be at the beck and call of the corporations and other big interests ... The people who elected him should have first consideration. No element contributed so much to the Republican victory in the Presidential election as the Irish.
>
> Will the new Chief Executive take cognisance of these facts in picking candidates for his cabinet? Will he see that the Irish element is represented therein? Perhaps Mr Harding has not given these aspects of the situation proper consideration. The Irish element throughout the country should insist on proper representation in the new cabinet. Hitherto they have been content to go the polls, cast their votes, and then allow themselves to be forgotten or ignored in the selection of candidates for important offices at Washington.[89]

---

87 Library of Congress (hereafter LC), Manuscripts Division (hereafter MD), William E. Borah Papers (hereafter WEBP), box 96, 137; LC, MD, The La Follette Family Collection, Robert La Follette (hereafter RLF), series B, box 94, box 184. Borah was corresponding with Cohalan and the AARIR about Ireland while La Follette was in contact with Frank P. Walshe of the AARIR.   88 UCDA, MMP, P48A/115, MacSwiney to James O'Mara, 15–20 March 1921.   89 *Sinn Féiner*, 22 January 1921.

It transpired that none of his cabinet appointments had Irish antecedents except for Andrew Mellon and Harry Daugherty.[90] More significant was the spread of religious affiliation within his cabinet: Mellon and Hays were Presbyterians; Evans Hughes and Davis were Baptist; Weeks was Unitarian; Daugherty was Methodist; Hoover was Quaker; Wallace was United Presbyterian; Denby was Episcopalian and Albert Fall was unaffiliated.[91] Harding's private secretary was his childhood friend George B. Christian junior, who had lived next door to him in Marion, Ohio and was also Methodist. No Catholic was appointed, which seems to give weight to the view that a silent anti-Catholicism continued to pervade US society and reinforce the boasts of the Ku Klux Klan that it would control both the Democratic and Republican conventions in 1924.[92] Yet, it is difficult to assert that Harding was anti-Catholic, for Catholics were often found in the Democratic Party rather than in the Republican Party and, later on, he supported Daugherty's choice of the Roman Catholic William J. Burns as chief of the Bureau of Investigation despite much criticism, including that of religion.[93] Harding's appointments were dictated by pragmatism and political patronage.

Irish-American republicans reacted predictably to the cabinet composition. The FOIF organ, the *Irish World* asked, on 30 April 1921,

> What have we gained by the change? President Harding is a simple minded man, ignorant of world affairs and easily misled by those in whom he trusts. In Secretary Hughes we have another of the sanctimonious breed. The whole cabinet is English and imperialistic.[94]

Even though John Devoy in the *Gaelic American* also found these appointments unpalatable for the same reasons, his criticism was deflected by a surprise move on Ireland on Harding's part which will be examined later. However, by December 1921 Devoy was more forthcoming, charging the cabinet with being under the influence of pro-British interests in the Republican Party.[95] Despite the absence of any obvious supporter at the Harding cabinet table, activist republicans did have some indirect contact with his administration.

Harry Daugherty, the Ohioan lawyer who orchestrated Harding's presidential campaign and regarded himself as Harding's chief adviser, became attorney general. Daugherty had Irish antecedents but regarded them as more of a liability than a help to him.[96] While there is no evidence that Daugherty had direct

90 W.D. Griffin, *The book of Irish-Americans* (New York), p. 274.   91 Murray, *Harding era*, p. 108.
92 Moore, *A Catholic runs for president*, p. 27.   93 M. Small, *Democracy and diplomacy: the impact of domestic politics on US foreign policy, 1789–1994* (1996), p. 68. Neither Harding's executive or private papers include significant correspondence with the US Catholic hierarchy particularly Cardinal O'Connell who was the most powerful US prelate due to Cardinal Gibbons' death on 24 March 1921. H.M. Daugherty, *The inside story of the Harding tragedy in collaboration with Thomas Dixon* (1932), pp. 105–6.   94 *Irish World*, 30 April 1921.   95 *Gaelic American*, 3, 17 December 1921.   96 Quoted in Murray, *Harding era*, p. 26.

contact with Irish-American organizations or issues. Begley wrote to James O'Mara, 'the man in the cabinet for us to reach is Attorney General Daugherty ... Our friends in Ohio should be urged to keep in political communication with Daugherty.' Also Daugherty was friendly with Joseph Scott and Edward L. Doheny, two wealthy, influential republican sympathizers. By 30 March 1921, Miss Rosser had made contact with his staff to set up a meeting with him.[97]

Officials in the evolving Irish departments of Foreign Affairs and Publicity in Dublin also welcomed the use of the good offices of Scott and Doheny. An anonymous note titled 'Foreign propaganda' said that while Dáil Éireann had a diplomatic presence in every continent, '5 per cent of the ruling classes govern most countries.' Consequently, the assistance of wealthy Irish in the US was needed in order to get at the 'individual official.'[98] Scott from Los Angeles was a member of the AARIR, but more significantly he was a Republican who had canvassed the western states for his friends Harding and Daugherty. When Harry Boland discovered this, he immediately wanted Scott to present Ireland's case for independence to Harding. Writing to O'Mara, on 4 April 1921, he said, 'if Scott were here he could go up to the White House and see the president without appointment and could also be received at any time by the members of the cabinet.'[99] It was not until July 1921, after the truce in the Anglo-Irish war of independence was announced, that Scott's important contacts provided access to the White House, as will be seen in chapter eight.

Another important connection between republicans and Harding's circle arose from Doheny's links with Albert Fall, secretary of the Interior. Doheny's parents were Irish born and he was a nephew of the Young Irelander Michael Doheny. Fall and Doheny met as young prospectors and became fast friends. Both struck rich and, while Doheny became an oil millionaire, Fall went on to become a politician and senator. By 1920, Doheny had already come to the attention of the British. On 17 March, Mortimer, the British consul in Los Angeles, warned his superior that Doheny was 'probably the richest man in California ... and is dealing a good deal with the British government, so I think you should know that he is and always has been in sympathy with the Fenians ... I am quite sure that he wants watching.'[1] In fact, Doheny had not been active in Irish-American affairs until he donated $10,000 to Irish republican bond-certificates. When the Foreign Office learnt of this on 13 April, the British Admiralty was informed immediately that Doheny, who would be dealing with them on oil contracts, was an Irish republican sympathizer. Rowland Sperling in the American department hoped that 'an association with a grasping monopoly ... will not benefit in the long run the Irish in America.'[2] In November, Doheny's connection with Ireland was consolidated when he was

97 UCDA, ÉVP, P150/1175, Begley to O'Mara, 30 March 1921; Daugherty, *The inside story*, p. 198.   98 National Archives of Ireland (hereafter NAI), Department of Foreign Affairs (hereafter D/FA), Early Series (hereafter ES), Box 27, file 158, anonymous, undated.   99 J. Maher, *Harry Boland a biography* (1998), p. 144.   1 TNA, FO371/4550, Mortimer to Ross, 17 March 1920.   2 Ibid., Sperling, 15 April 1920. Doheny was president of the Pan-American Oil company. The

elected president of de Valera's AARIR.[3] Doheny's influence with Daugherty and Fall would prove to be useful to the AARIR and the Dáil Éireann representatives. As the AARIR and Dáil Éireann envoys prepared themselves to infiltrate the new administration and Congress, during the period January to March 1921 there was an escalation in publicity in the US for the Irish cause.

During the first two months of 1921, the US dimensions to the Anglo-Irish war of independence were brought home to the in-coming administration and Congress by a number of sources. In January and February, the American Commission on Conditions in Ireland continued to hold sittings and to examine witnesses who, according to the British embassy, 'indulged in violent orgies of anti-British denunciation.'[4] A more nuanced view of the testimony came from one of the Bureau of Investigation special agents. F.G. Caskey who attended the hearings in December 1920. Following Mary MacSwiney's testimony, he believed that 'neither she nor anyone else in Ireland expected the United States to go to war with England over Ireland, but that it is expected that Americans will help Ireland with moral and financial aid.' Caskey was more affected by other witnesses. He described Muriel MacSwiney as having a 'pleasing personality' and said that her testimony 'about English reprisals and the violence of the Black and Tans was far more impressive than that of her sister-in-law,' while he thought that four former members of the Royal Irish Constabulary gave 'very unbiased testimony, which showed how England used methods beyond the pale of civilized nations.' Testimony from P.J. Guilfoil of Pittsburgh, whose point of view seemed to be 'entirely American', told of absolutely unjustified attacks against an innocent Catholic priest which he had witnessed.' Caskey's balanced reports were forwarded to J. Edgar Hoover who was in charge of subversive activities in the Bureau of Investigation, and they formed part of a growing dossier on Sinn Féin activism which will be examined in chapter eight.[5]

The American Commission intended to publish its report in March 1921, but in the interim a further report outlining the excesses of British military policy in Ireland was published by the British Labour Party in late January and this brought more criticism of British actions in US newspapers and journals. Oswald Garrison Villard's the *Nation* published the report on 26 January and endorsed its findings that the Cork city fires in December 1920 were started by British

relationship between Fall and Doheny remained close but by the end of 1921, the Teapot dome scandal which implicated Fall in the sale of state-owned oil-rich land to Doheny had serious legal, economic and political implications for both men, as well as for Harding.　3 Trani & Wilson, *The presidency of Warren G. Harding*, p. 183; TNA, FO371/4550, Embassy to Foreign Office, 27 March 1920; ibid., Ross to Embassy, 17 March 1920; J. Harrell, 'Doheny, Edward Laurence' in Glazier (ed.), *The encyclopedia*, p. 216; F.M. Carroll, 'American Association for the Recognition of the Irish Republic' in Funchion, *Irish American*, pp. 9–11.　4 *BDFA*, i, Annual Report for 1921, pp. 139–41. 5 NARA, Investigative Case Files of the Bureau of Investigation, 1908–1922, Record Group 65 (hereafter RG65), M1085/ reel 919 (hereafter R), General Intelligence Report, no. 8 for week ending 12 December 1920.

forces.[6] Another liberal periodical, the weekly *New Republic*, described the report on 23 January 1921 as a 'convincing indictment of the brutal and stupid military policy in Ireland.'[7] Although these periodicals did not have circulations equivalent to the daily newspapers, they were read mainly by the educated classes and, therefore, had some currency.[8] However, a more publicized protest against British rule in Ireland was the escalating economic boycott directed by the labour bureau of the American Commission against British-made goods. The *Sinn Féiner* covered every action of the boycott because its general manager, Patrick J. Meehan, had initiated the campaign. The newspaper published lists of English firms selling English manufactured goods and insurance and lists of US firms selling equivalent US-made goods and services. Individual Irish-Americans were asked to boycott English goods sold in the large department stores and salesmen and saleswomen, especially those of Irish origin, recommended US goods in preference to English ones when buyers asked for the latter. Although opposed by the American Federation of Labour and initially derided as ineffective by British diplomats in the US, the topic increasingly dominated despatches from the New York consulate and Washington embassy to the Foreign Office. The boycott also attracted the attention of the Loyal Coalition, founded in 1920 by Lloyd Demarest and others who wanted to combat the influence of Irish nationalists in US and to revive the wartime Anglo-American alliance.[9]

On 24 January, the Loyal Coalition held a mass meeting in Boston to protest, among other things, about the boycott of British goods. The principal speaker was Rear Admiral William Sowdon Sims, who still disliked Sinn Féiners. He denounced the boycott as un-American.[10] This opposition only served to galvanize republican Irish-America and its sympathizers even more and, on 17 February, Armstrong drew the attention of Foreign Office officials to the continuance of the boycott of British goods. In mid-March, the consul general reported that the boycott dominated the Irish-American press and Hadow in the Foreign Office described it as a 'vigorous' drive against British trade. It was not until late April that Armstrong reported a decline in the boycotting of British

---

6 *Nation*, 26 January 1921.　7 *The New Republic*, 23 January 1921.　8 Patrick McCartan, Dáil Éireann envoy forwarded a copy of the British report to out-going Secretary Colby on 17 January 1921. He likened British military actions in Cork city to their burning of Washington DC and the presidential residence in 1814. Once again the letter was not acknowledged and the direction from Colby's office was 'file.' NARA, RG59, M580/218, 841d.00/302, McCartan to Secretary of State, 17 January 1921.　9 E. McKillen, *Chicago labor and the quest for a democratic diplomacy, 1914–24* (1996), p. 179; F.M. Carroll, *American opinion and the Irish question 1910–23: a study in opinion and policy* (1978), pp. 200–1. The Loyal Coalition launched a series of public lectures and newspaper articles promoting Anglo–American friendship, warning the government against the dangers of Irish-American influence to that diplomatic relationship, denounced the American Commission on Conditions in Ireland and protested against Irish resolutions in Congress. Ibid., pp. 170–1.　10 *Sinn Féiner*, 5 February 1921. Mitchell reported from Queenstown that the speech was 'favourably' received by British military and naval officers and caused 'bitterness' among the Irish people. NARA, RG59, M580/218, 841d.00/311, Mitchell to Secretary of State, 3 February 1921.

goods.[11] Neither an official, nor even an unofficial complaint against the boycott was lodged with the State Department by the British government. Armstrong explained the dilemma to the Foreign Office on 10 February; 'this situation is a difficult one, and it would be hard to prove discrimination as the salesman would justify himself by stating that as an American, being employed in an American house, he was justified in pursuing native goods against imported ones, more especially in view of American labour being employed on native goods.'[12] Undoubtedly the effectiveness of the boycott lay less in the actual decline in sales of British goods in the US market and more in its publicity value. US secret service agents reported to the department of Justice on the course of the boycott and those involved, but the US government did not intervene.[13] From March 1921 onwards, its value to republican Irish-American as a publicity tool was surpassed by the attention given to the relief of distress in Ireland campaign.

With de Valera's return to Ireland in late December 1920, the 'star turn' of the AARIR recognition and fund-raising campaigns had left the US, but Mary MacSwiney, the second 'greatest propagandist', Patrick McCartan, envoy of the Republic of Ireland, and Harry Boland spearheaded the AARIR drive. The focus of their work and that of their supporters would be on relief for Ireland and the recognition of the republic issue was given a back seat. Mason Mitchell's reports confirmed the loss of houses, commercial property and jobs for the State Department.[14] The main US news agencies and newspapers ensured that the details of the arrests, burnings and destruction in Ireland were widely disseminated to the US public. Consequently, when Mary and Muriel MacSwiney arrived in Washington on 7 December 1920 to testify to the American Commission, they were greeted at the train station by fifteen thousand men and women who escorted them in 'silent march' to their accommodation. A few days later, after news of the burning of Cork city by the Black and Tans came through to the US, Mary MacSwiney had made her first public address at the Central High School, where thousands of dollars were subscribed to the 'Relief of Mallow Fund'.[15] This was among the first events in a nation-wide campaign for relief

---

11 TNA, FO371/5643, Armstrong to Curzon, 17 February 1921; ibid., FO371/5644, R.H. Hadow minute on Armstrong, 20 April 1921.   12 Ibid., FO371/6542, Armstrong to Curzon, 23 January 1921; ibid., 10 February 1921; *Sinn Féiner*, 22 January 1921, 5 February 1921.   13 NARA, RG65, M1085/R920, Weekly Intelligence Bulletin-San Francisco District for week ending 27 November 1920; ibid., 9 January 1921.   14 Donal O'Callaghan's testimony to the American Commission reported that the loss of property in Cork city totalled twenty million dollars. *The American commission on conditions in Ireland: interim report* (1921), pp. 40–1; NARA, RG59, M580/217, 841d.00/272, Mitchell to Secretary of State, 19 December 1920.   15 Frank P. Walsh quoted in Fitzpatrick, *Harry Boland*, p. 198; R.F. Downing, 'Men, women and memories' in W.F. Fitzgerald (ed.), *The voice of Ireland: a survey of the race and nation from all angles by the foremost leaders at home and abroad* (1923), p. 219; NARA, RG65, M1085/R 921, General Intelligence Report, no. 8, 12 December 1920; ibid., RG59, M580/218, 841d.00/300, McCartan to Secretary of State, 14 January 1921; ibid., 841d.00/302, Kent to Secretary of State, 17 January 1921; Fitzpatrick, *Harry Boland*, p. 194.

funds for Ireland. The organizers soon found that these appeals were more potent with more Americans than had been previous campaigns for support for armed resistance to the British authorities in Ireland and for recognition of the republic. Even British diplomats, who constantly underplayed the popular appeal of Irish campaigns, wrote that in the early months of 1921 there was a 'marked increase' in the humanitarian appeals for support for the women and children who were said to be starving and homeless as a result of political struggle in Ireland. They saw this 'subtle' form of propaganda calculated to appeal to a much larger field of sentiment than the earlier appeals on behalf of 'armed resistance to the British crown.'[16] By March 1921, three principal relief organizations had emerged: the Irish White Cross Society, the American Committee for Relief in Ireland (ACRI) and the Quaker Committee of Friends. The interaction of the Harding administration with this relief effort will be examined in chapter eight.

As Harding prepared for his inauguration, which was to be on 4 March 1921, the State Department continued to receive reports about the situation in Ireland from the US consuls with one in particular, that detailed the US dimensions to the problem, reaching Hughes' desk within a few weeks of his installation as secretary of State. In mid-January, as the details for implementing the Government of Ireland bill were worked out by the Lloyd George government, the 'troubles' continued in Ireland, with martial law imposed in eight southern counties. Kent was satisfied with the 'peace and good order' in Ulster which distinguished the province from upheaval in the rest of the country. Like the unionist community, he was not concerned that it was maintained with British troops and auxiliaries supporting the local police, that roads were closed and that a curfew was in place. When he did report serious disturbances, on 2 March, he emphasized that they had occurred in the 'remote county of Donegal. Here the Sinn Féin and Roman Catholic population is in the majority.'[17] His counterpart in Queenstown, Mason Mitchell, revealed a more balanced and less benign view of events; while accepting that martial law brought protection, he felt that in spite of these measures 'shocking conditions in southern Ireland are still in force.' He also said that on 5 January he had been forced to complain again to Major General Strickland, divisional commander of southern Ireland, about the bad behaviour, including disrespect for the US flag, of British troops towards the US crew on the *Lake Fontana* during a search for guns.[18] A few weeks later Mitchell almost became a victim of the on-going war. On 28 February, he left Queenstown with Mr

16 *BDFA*, i, Annual Report for 1921, pp. 141–2.   17 NARA, RG59, M580/218, 841d.00/292, Kent to Secretary of State, 12 January 1921; ibid., 841d.00/325, Kent to Secretary of State, 2 March 1921.   18 Ibid., 841d.00/293, Mitchell to Secretary of State, 19 January 1921; ibid., 841d.00/308, Mitchell to Colby, 7 February 1921. However, Strickland did provide Mitchell with a copy of his instructions to his officers on how to operate martial law in the southern counties of Ireland. Not surprisingly Strickland wanted the US government to be advised of his policy in dealing with the difficult Irish situation. Mitchell added no further comment. Ibid., M580/218, 841d.00/323, Mitchell to Secretary of State, 3 March 1921.

Mulligan, head of the Ford factory in Cork city, and Mr Hertz, the US agent of the Moore and McCormack Shipping line, to go to Cork by car. They encountered three British army lorries with troops but did not hear any command to stop and so kept driving. However, the officer in command then ordered the soldiers to 'make ready' to fire and only reversed it after Mr Pelly, manager of the Hibernian Bank in Cork city, who happened to be passing recognized Mitchell and shouted 'for god's sake, don't shoot, that is the American consul in that car.' Mitchell was in no doubt that his life had been endangered.[19]

In Dublin, Dumont offered his usual analysis of the situation. At the end of January 1921 he confirmed that the 'present situation had been brought on by Sinn Féin sympathizers themselves' who were located in Ireland, Britain, India, Africa and the US. He illustrated his point with the example of the British Labour Party Commission which, he pointed out, had met only representatives of Sinn Féin, some of whom were supporters also of the 'Russian Soviet type of government' and that the Commission members spent only one hour with the British authorities. But of greater concern to him was the support received by Sinn Féin in the US. He believed that Griffith wanted to unite Irish-American republican supporters with anti-British feeling on the 'oil question' in US foreign policy. His oblique mention that Arthur Griffith felt that 'it could be handled from California to advantage' suggests that Dumont may not yet have known about Doheny's connection with de Valera's AARIR. Dumont's information was considered noteworthy in the office of the third assistant secretary in the State Department. Of even greater import was his warning that Irish-American voters expected Harding to act on Ireland once he assumed office[20]

Dumont also identified a second US dimension to the situation. Between October and August 1920, Sinn Féin had received $1,700,000 in subscriptions to its American Loan Certificate drive and had raised approximately £200,000 in Ireland. Dumont believed that by March 1922 the Irish funds totalled £110,000 and the American funds $1,272,000. He thought the monies were being used firstly, 'entirely for propaganda' in the US, secondly, to pay the 'flying columns' in Ireland and finally, to support the dependent families of dead or imprisoned republicans in Ireland. But he thought it impossible to see how money could be raised to carry on for another twelve months. Dumont was offering not only his own views on the subject but also those of Nevil Macready, the military commander in Ireland. Dumont had met Macready a few days previously and the latter had told him that he needed 100,000 men to 'restore Ireland to its pre-war condition', which Dumont interpreted as meaning 'to repress the Sinn Féin movement.' These resources were unavailable and instead Macready pinned his hopes

19 Ibid., 841d.00/327, Mitchell to Secretary of State, 1 March 1921. 20 Ibid., 841d.00/314, Dumont to Secretary of State, 28 January 1921. In March Dumont elaborated on the revival of emigration from Ireland. His report and those of other consuls elsewhere, were later used to support anti-immigration forces dominating Congress which will be discussed in chapter twelve.

on Sinn Féin funds growing 'low.' It was in this context that Dumont's sup-
posedly unbiased view slipped. He continued:

> this is one of the reasons that they are so suspicious of American relief in
> the shape of money gifts to Irish societies and individuals, and particu-
> larly to the disposition of the funds raised by the American Committee
> for the Relief of Distress in Ireland ... The situation is one of danger to
> the peace and well-being of the United States. The activities of Irish-
> Americans are well worth investigating, particularly the activities of those
> who are more loyal to Ireland than to America.[21]

The implications in Dumont's report that republican-organized fund-raising for
Irish relief in the US and Ireland was anti-British and that US funds collected
for relief purposes might be used to shore up Sinn Féin's military campaign
against the British government ensured that Dumont's report was passed from
the consular section to William Castle's division of Western European Affairs,
who sent it on to Hughes' office. On 15 April, G. Howland Shaw directed
Hughes' attention to this 'particularly interesting report on conditions in Ireland',
including his account of 'the activities of ... American relief workers already in
Ireland.' Immediately, Hughes wrote to Harding, suggesting that he would 'be
interested in reading' the enclosed sections dealing with relief in Ireland: a copy
was also sent to Hoover.[22] Dumont's document came to Hughes' attention at a
key time when he was dealing with the consequences of a decision by Harding
and Hoover to support the Irish relief campaign.

*

At first glance, the Harding administration contained few supporters of the Irish
cause. Despite the widespread view among Irish republicans in the US and
Ireland, neither Harding, his cabinet or party had any obvious loyalty to them.
Yet, no administration operates in isolation and, just as Democratic politicians

---

21 Costello regards Dumont's report as 'impartial' and astute. F. Costello, *The Irish revolution and
its aftermath, 1916–1923: years of revolt* (2003), p. 123–4.   22 The Warren G Harding Papers (hereafter WGP), series 4, 1921–3, misc. files, roll 180, Hughes to Harding, 16 April 1921. Dumont at
this time also received a complaint from a US citizen Mary Farrell who was visiting a house in
November 1920 when the British army allegedly raided it. She complained to Dumont and sought
compensation from the British authorities. The consul had to pursue the matter with the chief secretary's office in Dublin Castle which investigated the matter. Andrew Cope's reply to Dumont on
6 December 1920 appeared to admit liability and the matter was passed to Ambassador Harvey in
London who brought it to the attention of the Foreign Office. It transpired that the British army
had not been involved and that she was owed nothing but the matter was not resolved until
December 1921 by which time Dumont had been replaced. TNA, FO371/5715, Cope to Dumont,
6 December 1920; Anderson to Under Sec of State, 20 December 1921, Harvey to Curzon, 9
December 1921; Tyrell to US Chargé d'Affaires, 4 January 1922.

needed Irish-American votes, so too did Republicans. Late 1920 and early 1921 saw the face of the Irish cause alter from an appeal to the US public for recognition of the Irish republic to an appeal for humanitarian aid. Consequently, the attraction of images and news of distress among women and children in Ireland combined with continuing suspicion of British foreign policy motives provided Irish and Irish-American republican activists in the US with a new opportunity to approach the Harding administration in its earliest days.

Although the new administration, and specifically Secretary Hughes, was not interested in Ireland and expected to maintain the Wilsonian policy of non-interference, he was faced with a number of pressing Irish matters. Specifically, he had to decide how to respond firstly, to a new fund-raising campaign in the US for the relief of Irish distress and to Dumont and Harvey's information, which threw doubts on the use of those funds in Ireland, secondly, to the publication of the *American commission on conditions in Ireland interim report* and thirdly, to British government concerns about the continuing anti-British agitation on issues such as the economic boycott of British trade, republican fund-raising, war debts and disarmament. Just as the Irish republicans in 1919 and 1920 had gathered unexpected allies by linking the US role in the post-war settlement to the Irish problem, so they intended at this time to tie Ireland to the wider concerns of US foreign policy and carve out similar links. The new administration had little time to settle in before it had to respond in a variety of ways to these Irish and British problems. Moreover, Harding surprised observers by engaging with the Irish problem almost immediately.

CHAPTER EIGHT

Harding, Irish relief aid and recognition, spring 1921

The American Red Cross Society which had taken advice from President Wilson, the British embassy, the Foreign Office and the British Red Cross Society, refused to act on appeals from Donal O'Callaghan, the lord mayor of Cork city, and James G. Douglas of the Dublin Society of Friends for aid for the citizens of Cork, after parts of the city were burnt on 6 December 1920. Rowland Sperling in the Foreign Office commented; 'I don't know why any relief should be given to those "on the run" when it is our policy to burn the houses and contents of persons withholding information about attacks on the military and police.'[1] His colleague, Horace J. Seymour agreed and hoped that 'this will close the matter.'[2] However, it did not and British Ambassador Geddes in Washington telegraphed an anxious message to the Foreign Office; 'the situation as regards Irish affairs is now most menacing. There is a lull in the cruder forms of Sinn Féin propaganda and an increase in humanitarian appeals for women and children who are said to be starving and homeless as a result of the political struggle in Ireland.'[3]

During the early months of 1921, in the interregnum before Harding and the new Congress took office, a wider section of the US public began to appeal for the provision of relief for Ireland and this soon became a matter of contention between the US and British administrations.

American Committee for Relief in Ireland

By the end of December 1920, it had become evident to Irish-Americans that the American Red Cross and the State Department would not respond to appeals for assistance for Ireland and this led to their taking matters into their own hands. Special Agent F.G. Caskey reported that Irish societies in Washington were urged

---

1 The National Archives, London (hereafter TNA), Foreign Office (hereafter FO), 371/5663, Stanley to Seymour, 10 January 1921, Sperling 13 January 1921, Ferrand to Stanley 7 January 1921, Seymour to Stanley 14 January 1921. 2 TNA, FO371/5663, Stanley to Seymour, 10 January 1921, Sperling 13 January 1921, Ferrand to Stanley 7 January 1921, Seymour to Stanley 14 January 1921. 3 Ibid., Geddes to Curzon, 5 May 1921.

not to contribute to the American Red Cross because it was not sending aid to Ireland, while W.M.J.A. Maloney, the former British army surgeon who had a medical practice in New York city, was unsuccessful in his attempt to send a ship with relief supplies to Ireland.[4] Consequently, the Irish Relief Board initiated a campaign throughout the US for the relief of starving women, children and old people in Ireland. The campaign was supported by posters showing distressed conditions said to be caused by British policy in Ireland. Clergy of all denominations were invited to get involved.[5] Simultaneously, the Irish Relief Committee of Philadelphia, the Red Cross Unit of the Ladies' Auxiliary of the Ancient Order of Hibernians, the Irish Progressive League and the New York council of the American Association for the Recognition of the Irish Republic (AARIR) organized a cargo of supplies of foodstuffs and clothing to be carried on the SS *Honolulu*. It also took flour purchased by the Dáil Éireann consul in New York, Diarmuid Fawsitt, on Eamon de Valera's directions.[6] Then at the end of January 1921, as a protest against the refusal of the American Red Cross to help the Irish cause, three hundred nurses and members of the American Red Cross resigned and formed the first American union of the Irish White Cross Society. It organized a ball to raise funds which were passed to the organization in Ireland.[7] Maloney changed this piecemeal approach.

On 11 December 1920, five days after the burning of Cork city and amid widespread publicity, Maloney organized a luncheon party in the Bankers' Club in New York city for potential supporters of the Irish cause.[8] Plans were made to establish a national organization, the American Committee for Relief in Ireland (ACRI), to raise $10 million countrywide and to administer the distribution of supplies in Ireland. Geddes was alarmed at the proposed campaign because he felt that this 'particular form of propaganda' had proved more effective than any other attempted by the Irish-American campaigners. He suggested to the Foreign Office that steps be taken immediately to counteract its effects, and specifically

4 National Archives and Records Administration, Maryland (hereafter NARA), Investigative Case Files of the Bureau of Investigation, 1908–1922, Record Group 65 (hereafter RG65), Microfilm (hereafter M) 1085/Reel 921 (hereafter R), General Intelligence Report, no. 8 for week ending 12 December 1920; F.M. Carroll, 'American committee for relief in Ireland' in M. Funchion (ed.), *Irish American voluntary organizations* (1983), pp. 26–7.   5 K. Bourne & D.C. Watt (general eds), *British documents on foreign affairs* (hereafter *BDFA*), part 11, series C, North America, 25 vols. (1986–95), i, The Republican ascendancy, 1919–28, Annual Report for the United States (hereafter Annual Report) for 1920, p. 56.   6 *Sinn Feiner*, 8 January 1921.   7 *BDFA*, i, Annual Report for 1921, p. 142. Dr Gertrude Kelly became the first president of the New York branch and Miss Katherine O'Brennan was appointed secretary. Among the patronesses of the ball were Mrs John Hylan, Mrs Harriet Stanton Blatch, Miss Katherine Leckie, Mrs Frederick C. Howe, Mrs Frank P. Walsh. The Irish White Cross Society was organized to cope with the distress and destitution resulting in Ireland from the war. Its membership included representatives of all religions and political parties except unionism, Geddes described the Irish White Cross Society as 'purely Sinn Féin in character'. Ibid., *Report of the Irish White Cross to 31 August 1922* (1922), p. 34.   8 Carroll, 'American committee', pp. 26–7.

that they should publicize how the British authorities were relieving any cases of genuine distress that might exist. This did not occur and instead, with the worsening situation in Ireland, the ACRI campaign expanded and its effectiveness was intensified.[9]

The American Committee was to be non-political and non-sectarian in character and its work was to be organized along the lines of Herbert Hoover's relief work in Belgium during the war.[10] Among the founders were Maloney, Judge Morgan J. O'Brien, Cardinal Gibbons, Edward L. Doheny, Senator Thomas J. Walsh and Bishop Gallagher of Detroit. They appointed an executive committee comprising O'Brien as chairman, Judge Richard Campbell as secretary, and John J. Pulleyn, president of the Emigrants' Industrial Savings Bank, as treasurer. Doheny donated $10,000 and promised to underwrite the project up to $247,000. Even before the organization was fully established, Maloney cabled $25,000 to Douglas, who had become a trustee and treasurer of the recently established Irish White Cross Society in Dublin.[11] The executive committee of the ACRI eventually consisted of twenty-three Irish-Americans.[12] Between January and March 1921, the committee established a national council consisting of prominent Irish-Americans and Americans, thereby emphasizing the organization's non-partisan and non-denominational profile. The 250 strong membership included twenty-three state governors, three former cabinet members and prominent members of the judiciary, legislature, trade union movement, churches, business, professions, the press and education. The organization spread into each state, where prominent locals headed fund-raising efforts. By mid-March, local and national structures were put in place. Bureau of Investigations agents who monitored the ACRI's work believed on 19 February, that the Washington relief committee was 'making a serious attempt ... to keep itself free from all political influence' and was 'not conducting any propaganda so far as can be learned and is entirely what it purports to be, a relief committee.' One measure of the organization's success at this stage was that Geddes raised the issue again with the Foreign Office and the State Department.[13]

Geddes first informed Foreign Secretary Curzon about the establishment of the ACRI on 27 December 1920 and reported again on 5 March 1921, when he noted that Cardinal Gibbons and senators Walsh and Phelan were involved. He

9 BDFA, i, Annual Report for 1920, p. 56.   10 Carroll points out that the provision of relief for Ireland was different to the Belgium operation because it started in Europe, involved US diplomats and much of the relief was government-supplied. F.M. Carroll, 'The American committee for relief in Ireland, 1920–22', 30–1.   11 Carroll, 'American committee', pp. 26–7.   12 Report of the Irish White Cross, p. 17.   13 Ibid., pp. 17–21, 37–42; Carroll, 'American committee', pp. 27–8; F.M. Carroll, American opinion and the Irish question 1910–23: a study in opinion and policy (1978), pp. 167–8; A.J. Ward, Ireland and Anglo-American relations, 1899–1921 (1969), p. 241; NARA, RG65, M1085/R921, General Intelligence Report, no. 16 for week ending 19 February 1921; ibid. no. 17 for week ending 26 February 1921. Borah also supported the campaign. LC, MD, WEBP, box 96, general office file Irish question 1920–21 (January to May) (1), Borah to GH Hulbert, Idaho, 25 April 1921.

wrote that it was appealing for funds 'on an ostensibly non-political and purely humanitarian basis' and, indeed, the British consul general in Chicago had been invited to attend a dinner under the committee's auspices. Geddes advised him to decline the invitation but he warned Curzon, 'in view of the committee's activities, it seems necessary to issue circular instructions to His Majesty's Consular Officers.'[14] But in early March, it was not just the American Committee's success in appealing to the US public and raising money for Irish relief which disturbed Geddes and his colleagues in London but also that it had secured endorsements from within the Harding administration. Prior to becoming US secretary of Commerce on 3 March 1921, Herbert Hoover, who had organized America's wartime relief operations in Europe, particularly in Belgium, had been approached by the ACRI executive with a request to associate his European relief organization with work to be done in Ireland. Hoover endeavoured 'to guide the people interested in it in such manner as would not cause international feeling.' He suggested to the relief committee that it should secure the services of Captain John F. Lucey, formerly associated with the commission for relief in Belgium, to manage the fund-raising in the US. Lucey was in place by 11 March 1921 and Hoover offered him strategic advice. He suggested that it would be 'a good thing' if he could secure the agreement of the American Friends Service Committee (AFSC), a Quaker organization, to help distribute the aid in Ireland on the grounds that 'such an arrangement would be very much in the cause of world peace for obvious reasons' and that the Society of Friends was well-known to the British government 'for their pure objectivity.'[15]

As Lucey got on with the work, Hoover assisted the Irish cause by contacting Secretary Hughes on 11 March, reiteratimg that the ACRI fund-raising sought to alleviate 'human misery' and that it was unrelated to 'politics or propaganda.' He tentatively suggested to Hughes that he make some informal inquiry of the British authorities to facilitate the relief work in Ireland.[16] Hoover's arguments were persuasive and he raised the matter with the British ambassador on the morning of 17 March, the day when the American Committee formally launched its fund-raising drive with a promotional brochure titled *A summons to service from the women and children of Ireland*. It compared Irish difficulties with those of Belgium and appealed to 'all Americans' for assistance in giving relief that would be 'solely humanitarian, absolutely non-sectarian and strictly non-political.'[17] Prior to the meeting, G. Howland Shaw, Hughes' executive secre-

14 TNA, FO371/5663, Geddes to Curzon, 5 March 1921. 15 Herbert Hoover Presidential Library, West Branch (hereafter HHPL), Commerce Papers (hereafter CP), Box 345, Ireland 1922–26, Hoover to Hughes, 11 March 1921. James A. Healy, assistant secretary of ACRI and a member of the New York Stock Exchange, wrote about ACRI also to Lewis Straus who had worked with Hoover in Belgium. HHPL, Lewis L. Strauss Papers (hereafter LLSP), file 'Healy', Healy to Strauss, 4 August 1921. 16 Ibid. 17 M.J. Pusey, *Charles Evans Hughes*, 2 vols (1963), i, p. 412; HHPL, CP, Box 345, Ireland 1922–6, Fletcher on Hoover to Hughes, 11 March 1921; TNA, FO371/5663, Geddes to Curzon, 7 March 1921.

tary, penned a note to Hughes signalling a potential source of embarrassment for the department on the matter. Shaw reminded Hughes that at the end of January the ACRI had requested passports for a delegation to go to Ireland. The department had been informed that the men had been selected at the request of representatives of the Irish Society of Friends and that their relief work in Ireland would be in co-operation with the Irish Society. Shortly after the passports were issued, the American Friends Service Committee wrote to the State Department stating that they had no connection whatever with the ACRI workers who were about to leave for Ireland. Shaw also reminded Hughes that Hoover was 'anxious' to ensure that the Irish relief work be 'placed exclusively in the hands of the American Friends Service Committee ... the authentic Quaker relief organization which has done so much and such excellent work in Europe.'[18] Hoover, Shaw and Harry Fletcher, Hughes' under secretary, supported the campaign but wanted its organization controlled by the non-aligned Friends' groups and not ACRI.

Two interpretations of the Geddes–Hughes meeting on 17 March emerged. Firstly, Hughes wrote to Hoover later in the day indicating he was 'glad' to say Geddes saw no reason to doubt that his government would accept the American Friends Service Committee distributing relief in Ireland. Geddes had suggested that the American committee should work with their British counterparts although he did tell Hughes that Ireland 'had never been more prosperous than it is today' and that where relief was needed – 'in the slums of the cities, and patches here and there' – it was being provided.[19] Geddes' version of the meeting, also telegraphed to Curzon on 17 March, reported Hoover's proposal but omitted the statement of his support for it. Instead he said that he believed it 'essential that some official statement should be made on the subject' as he was convinced that the 'movement to raise funds for Irish relief is assuming considerable proportions and is by far the most dangerous form of anti-British propaganda.' His plan was to undermine the ACRI campaign and, consequently, the need for any relief in Ireland. While the Foreign Office consulted with the Irish Office about Geddes' request for a statement about conditions in Ireland, the contributions began to reach the ACRI, as did the most important endorsement of all.[20]

Once in office, Harding was swamped by the demands of the presidency: at its first meetings his new cabinet was unable to agree on the administration's priorities. Between 3 March and the special session of the sixty-seventh Congress on 11 April he also worked to appease the farmers and business blocs who demanded tariff revision and tax reform and on his message for Congress, in addition to dealing with numerous requests from office-seekers.[21] Coinciding with this was an increase in correspondence requesting his help with the Irish relief campaign. He received letters and telegrams from supporters and representatives

18 HHPL, CP, Box 345, Ireland 1922–6, Shaw to Hughes, 17 March 1921.   19 Ibid., Hughes to Hoover, 17 March 1921.   20 TNA, FO371/5663, Geddes to Curzon, 17 March 1921.   21 R.K. Murray, *The Harding era: Warren G. Harding and his administration* (1969), pp. 124–5.

of the ACRI and from congressmen. Among them were four significant communications: on 17 March, Senator Borah forwarded a telegram from 'a very able young man in our state' and member of the Idaho state legislature, Donald A. Callahan, requesting Harding's endorsement of fund-raising 'to relieve starving women and children of Ireland.' Harding's private secretary, George Christian, said that he would bring it to Harding's attention. Two days later Senator Lodge, chairman of Senate Foreign Relations Committee, also passed on a letter from the Massachusetts committee for Irish relief, with a covering letter which stated 'you understand, of course, that it is sometimes very difficult to refuse to transmit such communications, although we shall not trouble you unless we find it necessary.' Clearly, this was one of those occasions. On 21 March, Harding received an appeal from within his own state. William F. Hoehn, the director of Ohio committee for Irish relief, wrote to him because 'you are one of us' and he believed Harding was 'in sympathy with all humanitarian effort.' Hoehn wanted both an 'expression of approval' for their fundraising campaign and a contribution to the cause. Two days later Judge Morgan J. O'Brien, cabled Harding for an endorsement of a performance at the New York Metropolitan Opera House on 3 April to help 'the pathetic conditions of women and children in Ireland.'[22]

The arguments that influenced Harding's response to the ACRI's appeal were domestic ones. Firstly, he regarded the Irish problem as being a domestic British matter. Secondly, although he had only been in office a few weeks, he had already born some criticism from Irish-America by endorsing General Ackman and Admiral Dunn's refusal to allow US military personnel to march in uniform during the anniversary of the British evacuation of Boston parade in Boston, which coincided with St Patrick's Day and involved the AARIR. This decision provoked the headline 'Harding adheres to Wilson Irish policy' in the *Michigan Citizen* on 26 March. Thirdly, the appeals made to him were from prominent, loyal, American citizens, including his secretary of Commerce, who were themselves supporting the non-political humanitarian effort. Harding did not seem to know that the American Friends Service Committee wanted nothing to do with the ACRI.[23] Additional factors related to his endorsement of the China famine

---

22 Library of Congress (hereafter LC), Manuscripts Division (hereafter MD) William E. Borah Papers (hereafter WEBP), box 96, file General office file, Irish question 1920–21 (Jan. to May), (1), Borah to Harding, 17 March 1921; ibid., Christian to Borah, 17 March 1921; *Irish World*, 2 April 1921; Warren G. Harding Papers (hereafter WGHP), series 4, 1921–3, misc. files, roll 180, Presidential executive file 135, folder 2, Lodge to George B. Christian, secretary to the president, 19 March 1921. The ACRI asked Colonel Edward House to serve as honorary vice chairman of the national organization which he declined. See Yale University Library, Manuscript and Archives Collection (hereafter YULMC), The Papers of Colonel E.M. House (hereafter EHP), box 127, file 4529, Lucey to House, 16 March 1921.   23 TNA, FO371/5663, Geddes to Curzon, 31 March 1921; WGHP, series 4, 1921–3, misc. files, roll 180, Presidential executive file 135, folder 2, Harding to Harrigan, 17 March 1921; *BDFA*, i, Annual Report for 1921, p. 141. General Pershing, Harding's army chief of staff had also antagonized Irish-Americans by comments made at an All-American meeting in New York in mid-March that were widely publicized as anti-Irish in the *Irish World*

relief work and Harding felt that he 'could not refuse to extend his patronage to their undertaking.'[24]

Harding's genuine humanitarianism and his dislike of disharmony appear to have predominated over a wish to stamp out hyphenism or any diplomatic concerns. On 26 March, he wrote to O'Brien and wished the committee

> the fullest measure of success ... The people of America never will be deaf to the call for relief on behalf of suffering humanity, and the knowledge of distress in Ireland make quick and deep appeal to the more fortunate of our own land, where so many of our citizens trace kinship to the Emerald Isle.[25]

Not surprisingly, O'Brien immediately acknowledged Harding's 'great kindness ... effective and splendid support.'[26] The contrast between this action and Wilson's non-interference Irish policy was obvious to all Irish-Americans of whatever political hue. Martin Campbell wrote to Harding 'as a Democrat who voted for the Republican ticket for the first time' in 1920, thanking him 'for the stand you have taken.'[27] Harry Boland, the Dàil Éireann envoy, welcomed the 'moral

---

and other Irish-American newspapers. One correspondent to Harding described the chief of staff as 'this English Sir Pershing'. *Irish World*, 2 April 1921; WGHP, series 4, 1921–3, misc. files, roll 180, Presidential executive file 135, folder 1, Canning to Harding, 22 March 1921. On 16 March 1921, Alice Stopford Green, Violet Russell, Ellen Smith-Gordon, Susan L. Mitchell and Augusta Gregory cabled Mrs Florence Harding and appealed 'through you to the thirty million women of America for sympathy with the women of Ireland ... the women of Ireland plead, in this message to their sisters in America that they lend emergency relief to enable the women and children of Ireland to survive the present ordeal.' See TNA, 371, 6542, letter to Mrs Harding, 16 March 1921; LC, MD, Thomas J. Walsh Papers (hereafter TWP), box 190, subject files c. 1913–33, McCoy to ACRI, New York, 16 March 1921.   24 TNA, FO371/5663, Geddes to Curzon, 31 March 1921; WGHP, series 4, 1921–3, misc. files, roll 180, Presidential executive file 135, folder 2, Hughes to Christian, 29 March 1921. A devastating drought hit north China in 1920. President Wilson issued a declaration in support of the America China Famine Fund and Harding urged popular support of it on 21 March 1921. It raised $7,750,420 in funds along with investigating and reporting on the extent of the famine. Hoover, *An American epic*, iii, p. 411; WGHP, series 4, 1921–3, misc. files, roll 180, Presidential executive file 135, folder 1, Senator Morris Sheppard to Harding, 24 March 1921; ibid., John F. Harrigan, AARIR, to Harding, 16 March; HHPL, CP, Box 345, Ireland 1912–26, Shaw to Hughes, 17 March 1921. Harding may not have been aware of an anonymous communication that was sent to the British embassy threatening the lives of several people including General George Squiers and G. Howland Shaw, Secretary Hughes' executive secretary. This was passed to the Bureau of Investigation and in February and March 1921, agents tried to trace the writer of the letter. See NARA, RG65, M1085/R921, General Intelligence Report, no. 20 for week ending 26 March 1921.   25 Quoted in *Report of the Irish White Cross*, p. 38.   26 WGHP, series 4, 1921–3, misc. files, roll 180, Presidential executive file 135, folder 1, O'Brien to Harding, 29 March 1921. Many celebrities such as John McCormack gave benefit concerts for the cause. Donations came from the US Catholic Church and Pope Benedict XV contributed 20,000 lire. See *Report of the Irish White Cross*, pp. 37–42.   27 WGHP, series 4, 1921–3, misc. files, roll 180, Presidential executive file 135, folder 1, Campbell to Harding, 29 March 1921.

support' of the president, while Mary MacSwiney saw it as a stepping-stone towards official recognition of the Irish republic.[28] The *New York Times* editorial on 2 April found parallels with Cuba:

> It is interesting to recall that President McKinley, who strongly opposed to the very last intervention by the United States in Cuba, warmly welcomed an effort to raise a million dollars for the relief of the *reconcentrados*.
>
> As it turned out, this fund did in the end help to expose the age-long misgovernment in Cuba. But President McKinley called it benevolent intervention.[29]

Others, however, were not as pleased by the decision and it was not long before Geddes officially raised the matter with Hughes, thereby giving the Irish situation a similar status to that of the repayment of war debts and tariff issues in its impact on Anglo–American relations.

Harding and Hoover's endorsements were widely publicized in the US, Ireland and Britain, with the Irish-American newspapers making considerable political capital out of it. The consequences were immediate and soon afterwards similar approvals came from Vice-President Coolidge, secretary of War J. Wingate Weeks, General Leonard Wood, William J. McAdoo, former secretary of the Treasury, Bernard Baruch, former director of the War Industries Board, James W. Gerard, former ambassador to Germany, Josephus Daniels, former secretary of the Navy, Franklin K. Lane, former secretary of the Interior, Samuel Gompers, president of the American Federation of Labour, and the anti-British newspaper magnate, William Randolph Hearst, who was also a close friend of Doheny.[30] Some just gave moral support but others made financial contributions or took active part in the fund-raising. McAdoo delivered a speech at an ACRI dinner in New York on 26 May, where he congratulated O'Brien and the committee 'on what they have done, and on what the American people have done, for suffering women, children, babies and infirm people in this hour of Ireland's distress.' Although McAdoo emphasized the non-political aspect of the work, he hoped that 'a way would be found … for the realisation of Ireland's just aspirations' after 'seven centuries of heroic struggle for Ireland.'[31] The British view was offered by Hadow; 'what was obviously a one-sided committee is now being exploited as a "non-partisan American" one.'[32] The scenario which Geddes had warned Curzon about on 17 March began to emerge: the ACRI had successfully

28 National Archives of Ireland (hereafter NAI), Department of Foreign Affairs (hereafter D/FA), Early Series (hereafter ES), Box 27, file 158, Boland, 15 April 1921; J. Mooney Eichacker, *Irish republican women in America: lecture tours, 1916–25* (2003), p. 133.   29 *New York Times*, 2 April 1921.   30 TNA, FO371/5646, Armstrong to Foreign Office, 13 May 1921; *BDFA*, i, Annual Report for 1921, p. 143.   31 National Library of Ireland (hereafter NLI), Joseph McGarrity Manuscript, MS 17524(3), Speech, 26 May 1921.   32 TNA, FO371/5663, Hadow 29 March 1921.

gained official approval for its work highlighted the destitution in Ireland caused by British policy and had increased anti-British hostility in the US.

The British counter-offensive began on 30 March. Geddes met Hughes on 30 March for an hour-long meeting on Ireland. He pointed out that Hoover's 'equivocal' attitude and Harding's endorsement of the ACRI relief scheme was causing a misunderstanding on the British side. Hughes clarified that the president's attitude with regard to Ireland was 'that there must be no interference by the United States in a purely British internal affair.' He said that Harding had clearly demonstrated his position in his refusal to allow US military personnel participate in the evacuation day parade at Boston but Hughes added that the president felt he could not 'refuse to extend his patronage to a strictly non-political work such as charity and humanitarian effort.'[33]

In reply, Geddes pointed out

> that whatever the President's motives were, the result of his action was to convince well-meaning but ill-informed Americans that there was such widespread distress in Ireland that it was necessary for them to send relief, also to convince the Irish that they need not despair of securing help from America and, therefore, to stiffen their attitude, and finally, to convince the British public that the sympathies of the United States government were with Sinn Féiners, especially when in addition to the President, Mr Hoover and Mr Weeks, both members of the cabinet allowed their names to be used in connection with the movement.[34]

Geddes concluded by deploring the administration's 'apparent lack of caution.' According to the ambassador, Hughes was 'considerably perturbed by the President's action and undertook to speak to him about it.'[35] Hoover, when questioned by a British diplomat, admitted that he had in the first instance encouraged the ACRI. But his sole purpose had been to keep the movement in the hands and under the control of 'really reputable people' so as to ensure that the money was spent on genuine relief work.[36]

A few days later, Geddes had the chance to directly raise the issue with Harding who said that he was 'sorry' that his endorsement had been understood as 'supporting the Sinn Feiners' and he offered to help the situation. Geddes suggested that Harding might state publicly that the US had 'no political interest in Ireland' and did not support extremist elements. The president responded 'I could not say that politically, it would be impossible, but it is true.'[37] Harding was not in a position to retract his endorsement, even though he had virtually acknowledged to Geddes that he had made a mistake. Given that Hughes had

33 Ibid., Geddes to Curzon, 31 March 1921; *BDFA*, i, Annual Report for 1921, pp. 142–3.   34 TNA, FO371/2673, Geddes to Curzon, 31 March 1921   35 Ibid.   36 *BDFA*, i, Annual Report for 1921, p. 143.   37 TNA, FO371/5663, Geddes to Curzon, 5 April 1921

known of Harding's decision beforehand and believed the latter's reasons to be quite acceptable, it seems that he had not anticipated the British reaction to the Harding endorsement or seen it as being anti-British until Geddes pointed the difficulties out. The British ambassador certainly blamed the 'new and quite inexperienced administration' for the 'President's indiscretion.' He suggested to Curzon that they had a choice of either making a formal protest, in which case there 'was a risk of a man of the President's temperament taking umbrage at what he would regard as a foreign crisis and doing something more indiscreet to show his independence' or they could accept that the 'action taken today will prove sufficient.' He himself favoured the later option. Curzon endorsed his official's advice that the only 'effective line for us to take is to leave it to the American administration to deal with it, unless or until their action in the matter become provocative to us.'[38] In order to counteract the effectiveness of the ACRI campaign, the Foreign Office reversed an earlier decision not to comment and instead instructed the embassy to issue two statements which had been agreed by Curzon and Hamar Greenwood, chief secretary for Ireland.[39]

On 31 March the *Washington Post* and on 1 April the *New York Times* carried the embassy statement which dealt with the 'widespread misapprehension' that existed in regard to the ACRI fund raising and pointed out that banking and trade statistics and tax returns showed that Ireland as a whole had never been more prosperous. Apart from 'cases of genuine unemployment common to all countries at the present moment, and apart from the unhappy but normal poverty of the slums of towns, every case of distress and destitution is due to the effects of the Sinn Féin rebellion.' The British administration in Ireland said that it did not believe that there was any need for American charity in Ireland but it would place 'no unnecessary difficulties in the way of any charitable organization which is constituted on a strictly non-political basis and deals in an impartial spirit with any case of Irish distress brought before it.'[40] On the following day, a second statement was issued in reply to the publication on that day of the interim report of the American Commission on Conditions in Ireland, which indicted British rule in Ireland. Hadow in the Foreign Office, described the report as 'good propaganda and well thought out' but said that its 'anti-British' personnel and methodology inevitably meant that its 'conclusions must ... be biased.'[41] Similarly, Kent reported Ulster unionists' indignation about its contents which bore the 'earmarks of Sinn Féin inspiration.'[42] The embassy statement followed these lines. It rebutted the Commission's findings by stating that Ireland was not devastated but prosperous, that Britain's policy of reprisals in

---

38 Ibid., 31 March 1921. Although William Tyrell hoped that Geddes would remember that he now had a lever over Harding if he ever complained about 'foreign interference with his own actions.' Ibid. 39 TNA, FO371/5663, Seymour 23 March 1921. 40 *Washington Post*, 31 March 1921; *New York Times*, 1 April 1921. 41 TNA, FO371/5663, Hadow, 15 April 1921. 42 NARA, RG59, M580/218, 841d.oo/348, Events of importance period 13 April to 20 April 1920, American consulate, Belfast to Secretary of State, 20 April 1921.

Ireland resulted from Sinn Féin murders, that the Irish Republican Army (IRA) was illegal and that Sinn Féin did not command total nationalist support. Finally, the report was described as being 'biased and wholly misleading' both in detail and conclusion.[43] Both statements were widely publicized but Geddes was disappointed that they had not aroused the degree of interest expected because of the coverage of Cardinal Gibbons' funeral on the previous day, 30 March, in Baltimore. The ACRI responded to the embassy offensive through Andrew L. Hickey, its executive secretary and Frank P. Walsh. Hickey assailed the statements as being an attempt to interfere with the raising of funds for Irish relief while Walsh challenged Geddes to appear before the Commission and prove his statements. Nevertheless, the relative prominence afforded the embassy statements by the important east coast newspapers, combined with the 'intemperate retort' from the ACRI, led Geddes to suggest to the Foreign Office that his future requests for information on Ireland should be met more promptly.[44]

British hopes that the actions of 30 and 31 March would undermine the ACRI fund-raising campaign were not realized. Now that it had been endorsed by Harding and other distinguished people money flowed into the ACRI. On 5 May, Geddes reported that $2 million had been paid and $3–4 million pledged to the cause.[45] Even the American Red Cross, after consultation with the State Department on 28 March, overcame its earlier opposition and donated $100,000 to the ACRI.[46] By mid-April, Geddes was describing ACRI activities as a 'formidable movement' and was worried that the boycott of British goods would spread from New York to Philadelphia and the southern states.[47] The Conservative member of parliament Sir Frederick Hall asked in a parliamentary question, whether any protest had been addressed to the US government over the activities of the ACRI and other anti-British organizations. The reply was that a protest had not been made but that another press statement 'with true facts' had been issued to all US newspaper correspondents in London and sent to Geddes on 14 April for distribution.[48] Moderate Irish-American nationalists involved with ACRI such as John Quinn, reacted to these 'lying statements' from the embassy by circulating 'among friends whose opinions were likely to matter' George Russell's essay 'The inner and outer Ireland', which he called 'one of the wisest and sanest things on the Irish question.'[49] The Irish republican perspective was offered by Joseph Begley on 1 April 1921, 'All in great form here – good

43 TNA, FO371/5663, Geddes to Curzon, 1 April 1921; *BDFA*, i, Annual Report for 1921, p. 140. 44 TNA, FO371/5663, Geddes to Curzon, 1 April 1921; NARA, RG65, M1085/R921, General Intelligence Report, no. 24, for week ending 7 April 1921; *New York Herald*, 31 March 1921.   45 TNA, FO371/5663, Geddes to Curzon, 5 May 1921.   46 NARA, RG59, M580/241, 841d.48/19, Memo. 28 March 1921.   47 TNA, FO371/5644, Hadow, 11 April 1921.   48 Ibid., FO371/5663, Parliamentary Question, 21 April 1921; ibid., A.W.G. Randall, News Department, 26 April 1921. Hall became honorary treasurer of the Metropolitan Division of the National Unionist Association in 1923. See *The Times*, 5 February 1923.   49 B.L. Reid, *The man from New York: John Quinn and his friends* (1968), p. 513.

news all the time.'[50] Neither Geddes' informal protest to Hughes nor the British counter propaganda campaign proved effective and the dollars continued to flow to the ACRI, while the question of how the money was to be distributed in Ireland posed difficulties for both governments.[51] Throughout spring 1921, Ireland remained a principal cause of tension in US–British relations.

The American Committee for Relief in Ireland proposal to the State Department

While the fund-raising continued in the US, ACRI had sent a delegation to Ireland in January 1921 to examine conditions in Ireland and to make arrangements for the effective disbursal of US aid. Clemens J. France acted as chairman and Samuel Duff McCoy as secretary of the delegation, which was also known as the Quaker Committee of Friends. The inclusion of six Society of Friends members helped confirm the ACRI's non-political intentions but, as was noted previously, this did not give it the approval of the American Friends Service Committee.[52] They stopped in London on their way to Ireland and called on Hamar Greenwood, chief secretary for Ireland, who gave them a letter for John Anderson, joint under secretary for Ireland, which they would present after they had completed their investigations. US embassy staff suggested that they meet Dumont immediately upon their arrival in Dublin.

The group arrived in Ireland on Saturday, 12 February, and the meeting with Dumont took place the same day. The latter had followed the relief campaign in the US. He expressed surprise at Harding's endorsement of the ACRI because he felt that Sinn Féin was determined to make 'the question of relief a political and not an economic one' and because the Irish White Cross Society was a 'Sinn Féin movement.' Dumont was partly correct in that the Society's executive committee and standing council consisted of republicans in addition to nationalists and its main figure, James G. Douglas was a leading member of the Dublin Society of Friends. Nonetheless, he impressed upon the delegation that they were on a 'delicate mission which might not be altogether pleasing to the British

50 University College Dublin Archives (hereafter UCDA), Eamon de Valera Papers (hereafter EVP), P150/1175, Begley to O'Mara, 1 April 1921. 51 TNA, FO371/5663, Geddes to Curzon, 5 May 1921; ibid., Foreign Office, 21 April 1921, Wallis to Broderick, 9 March. 1921. 52 Its members were Samuel Duff McCoy, a journalist who had worked with the *Philadelphia Ledger* and the American Red Cross, Clemens J. France, brother of Senator Joseph I. France of Maryland and six members of the Society of Friends; Walter C. Longstreth, a lawyer, R. Barclay Spicer, former head of the Friends Service Committee to the Baltic states, William Price, an architect from Philadelphia, Philip W. Furnas, a housing expert and former member of the Friends Relief Unit in France, John C. Baker, an agricultural expert and former member of the Friends Relief Unit in France and Oren Wilbur, a farmer. See *Report of the Irish White Cross*, p. 39; Carroll, 'The American Committee for Relief in Ireland', 32.

authorities in Ireland' and 'insisted' that they immediately call on Anderson and Macready, rather than wait until the end of their visit. On Monday, 14 February, Dumont discussed the matter with Andrew Cope and Mark Sturgis in Dublin Castle. Sturgis privately recorded that if the ACRI delegation was 'properly handled' they could do 'much good.' He felt that their funds could help in rebuilding, providing food and was a 'good safety valve for American-Irish money.' But they could '*not give money*' and Sturgis wanted to prevent S[inn] F[éin] from capturing them.'53 A short time later, Dumont arranged a meeting between the delegation and Anderson, emphasising that it was done 'informally and unofficially'; thereby distancing himself and the US government from the delegation. Anderson told the delegation that any relief work to be done must have his permission and that of the military authorities. This was confirmed by Macready, who instructed the delegation not to distribute financial assistance in certain districts in case it helped Sinn Féin. He did not object to relief in kind or to the rebuilding of houses and factories, unless they had been destroyed by military orders. He advised the delegation to travel to Belfast and the west of Ireland, saying he would decide whether relief could be given to the martial law areas in the interim.54 Dumont agreed with Anderson and Macready that the delegation and their funds should not fall under Sinn Féin control and that it was vital to prevent them from strengthening Sinn Féin's anti-British propaganda campaign in the US regarding conditions in Ireland.55

Much to Dumont's annoyance, the delegation did not take Macready's advice and instead stayed in Dublin, with the result that by the end of the week he believed they were 'thoroughly in the hands of the Irish White Cross.' The delegation then departed for Belfast, where Consul William Kent was coincidentally 'out for the moment' when they called on him.56 Dumont was particularly alarmed when they travelled to the martial law counties in the south, a journey which Macready had not sanctioned, although some went to the west of Ireland as he had suggested. When the news of the delegation's arrival in Cork reached Macready's office in Dublin Castle, he dispatched Brigadier-General J. Brind, his chief of staff, to call on Dumont and ask why they had gone there 'in violation of their understanding' with the Castle authorities. Dumont wired Mason Mitchell in Queenstown, 'that it was advisable to keep in touch' with the delegation.57

When they arrived in Cork, Mitchell ensured that they met Major General Edward Strickland, commanding officer of southern Ireland, in Victoria Barracks, who had been informed about the delegation by Macready's office. Again the delegation explained the purposes of their visit, specifically as it pertained to

53 NARA, RG59, M580/218, 841d.oo/351, Dumont to Secretary of State, 23 April 1921; M. Hopkinson (ed.), *The last days of Dublin Castle: the diaries of Mark Sturgis* (1999), 14 February 1921. 54 NARA, RG59, M580/218, 841d.oo/339, Dumont to Secretary of State, 22 March 1921. 55 Ibid., 841d.oo/331, Skinner to Secretary of State, 15 March 1921. 56 Ibid., 841d.oo/348, Events of importance period 13 April to 20 April 1920, American consulate, Belfast to Secretary of State, 20 April 1921. 57 Ibid., 841d.oo/339, Dumont to Secretary of State, 22 March 1921.

Cork, where they wanted to loan sums of money at a low rate of interest to those who had sustained losses due to the burning of creameries in rural districts and businesses and homes in the city. They emphasized that the purpose of their visit was by no means political, being purely philanthropic on behalf of Irish-Americans. Mitchell reported to the State Department that Strickland was 'favourably impressed' with the object of their mission but that he had asked what arrangements were to be made to ensure that the monies went towards 'peaceful purposes' and not to the 'enemies of the crown.' France replied that they had carefully chosen 'responsible and reputable business men in Cork' to work with. Strickland again indicated his support for their relief aims and, on Macready's instructions, gave orders that permits and passes be issued to the two men in order to facilitate their work in the martial law area. The delegation also met Admiral Sir Reginald Tupper, commander of the Queenstown naval base, who offered to give them a tour of the naval yard at Haulbowline island which they declined. Mitchell recorded that the delegation acknowledged the courteous treatment accorded them by the representatives of the British military and naval authorities in the Cork region. Among their other formal meetings was one with the Cork Harbour Board and a tour of Cork harbour.[58] In his report to the State Department, Mitchell did not query the delegation's motivation and accepted the assurances they had given Strickland about the distribution of money. Unlike Dumont, Mitchell did not infer that refusing the boat trip provided evidence of their anti-Britishness.[59] Indeed, on 1 March he facilitated the transmission of a telegram by the delegation to incoming President Harding and the US Senate, requesting support for the ACRI's fund-raising appeal to rehabilitate Irish industry.[60] Harding refused the request. Instead Mitchell was instructed to tell McCoy and France that 'while the President was always sympathetic in cases of distress he did not consider it opportune to issue the appeal requested at the present time.' Mitchell complied with the instruction.[61]

The delegation went back to Dublin, coming back into Dumont's jurisdiction. He was delighted to report to Hughes that, at a meeting attended by the delegation, Macready, Anderson, their staff officers and Dumont, all 'understood' firstly, that the distribution of relief such as rebuilding creameries would be permitted, but not 'money relief', secondly, that the rebuilding would be supervised by a 'mixed committee composed of genuine American business men and Irish business men' and thirdly, that the Irish White Cross Society could not control the expenditure of ACRI funds although certain ACRI members 'as individuals might be put on the mixed committee.' Dumont believed the delegation to be well intentioned but 'in ignorance of the depth of feeling between the political

58 Ibid., 841d.00/330, Mitchell to Secretary of State, 9 March 1921. 59 Ibid., 841d.00/339, Dumont to Secretary of State, 22 March 1921. 60 Ibid., 841d.00/330, Mitchell to Secretary of State, 9 March 1921. 61 WGHP, series 4, 1921–3, misc. files, roll 180, Presidential executive file 135, folder 2, Mitchell to Hughes, 13 April 1921; ibid., Hughes to Christian, 6 May 1921.

factions in Ireland' and he seemed pleased about their 'embarrassing position' at the above meeting. However, he was sufficiently astute to realize that the delegation's return to the US would not signal the end of the ACRI's relief work in Ireland. In a long letter to Butler Wright in the US embassy in London, he warned him about the true intentions of the ACRI, saying, '[its] whole object is to use Protestant Americans to get Irish-American aid to Sinn Féin sympathizers, if not to Sinn Féin itself.'[62] The theme predominated in his dispatch to the department on 22 March and he went to warn Hughes that the delegation would look for State Department backing to overcome the deal agreed with Macready.[63]

Before examining the consequences of Dumont's warning to the State Department, it is appropriate to examine his role during the ACRI delegation's visit to Ireland. Macready believed Dumont to be 'well posted in all that was going on' and thought that he maintained 'an admirably correct attitude, [Dumont] had no use for his countrymen's charitable filibustering expedition.' Indeed Macready's view on the state of Ireland heavily influenced Dumont's report to Washington on events in Ireland from 22 March to 23 April, that again confirmed the Irish were 'not in the last stages of starvation' and that 'relief was not required from non-British sources.'[64] From the Sinn Féin side, three aspects of the delegation's visit merited Eamon de Valera's attention. Firstly, he opposed the understanding reached at the last meeting between the delegation, Macready and Anderson, on the grounds that this would restore property to 'capitalists.' Instead he wanted to establish 'co-operative industries.'[65] Secondly, he believed that Macready's refusal to have the Irish White Cross Society distribute funds was evidence of latter's intention 'to starve the people into submission.' Furthermore, if the Irish White Cross did not distribute the funds he wanted 'men with backbone' on the American committee, who would stand up to the British authorities.[66] Thirdly, as he wrote to Harry Boland in the US on 7 March:

---

62 NARA, RG59, M580/218, 841d.00/339, Dumont to Secretary of State, 22 March 1921; ibid., 841d.00/351, Dumont to Wright, 29 March 1921 in Dumont to Secretary of State, 23 April 1921. Dumont was horrified to read in republican newspapers on 30 March that Senator William S. Kenyon of Iowa 'the close personal friend of President Harding' was coming to Ireland unofficially at Harding's request to investigate the situation in Ireland and would return to Washington in time for the opening of the next Congress, at which it was to be presented to Congress. The consul was relieved when Kenyon did not turn up. Ibid., 841d.00/351, Dumont to Secretary of State, 23 April 1921.   63 Ibid., 841d.00/339, Dumont to Secretary of State, 22 March 1921.   64 General The Rt. Hon. Sir Nevil Macready, *Annals of an active life*, 2 vols (1924), ii, pp. 540–1. Often Dumont incorporated the weekly review of the Irish situation issued from Dublin Castle without reference to the source while Kent in Belfast always credited the source. Dumont legitimated Dublin Castle's accounts of military raids on IRA gatherings. One example was a raid on a dance in Bruff, county Limerick that Dumont described as an 'IRA Company dance.' See NARA, M580/218; ibid., 841d.00/351, Dumont to Secretary of State, 23 April 1921.   65 NAI, D/FA, ES, Box 27, file 158, de Valera to Boland, 7 March 1921, no. 4.   66 Ibid., de Valera to Boland, 28 February 1921, no. 3; ibid., file 160, de Valera to Boland, 17 March 1921, no. 1.

Dumont, the American consul here, who is not regarded as very favourable to us, has been their [the ACRI delegation] guide naturally, and not a little I fear their tutor. Their task is exceptionally difficult, for, of course, they have no idea of the real attitude of the British government here.[67]

De Valera regarded Dumont's partiality towards the British as a threat to Sinn Féin and a few weeks later he warned Boland again that Dumont 'is regarded as being a great danger here. I wish we had a sympathetic man.' He went further this time 'Do you think it could be managed?'[68] Following further evidence of his pro-British stance, both Boland and O'Mara worked in the US to have him removed from the Dublin post.[69] In September, Stephen O'Mara, who had replaced his brother James as trustee for the Dáil Éireann loan in the US, also predicted a change of consul in Dublin and on 27 December 1921, Charles Hathaway who was now a class four consul, was commissioned to the US consulship in Dublin.[70]

Despite Dumont's contact with Sinn Féin in late 1920 and early 1921 and his intermediary role at that time, the Dáil Éireann leadership saw his attempts to interfere with the American Committee's relief work and his pro-British views as being sufficient reason to have him removed. They believed that it was their representations to Harding that had accomplished this. However, in the absence of a record explaining the change and given Hughes' commendation of his work in July 1921, it is more likely that Dumont was in line for promotion to consul

---

67 Ibid., de Valera to Boland, 7 March 1921, no. 4.   68 Ibid., de Valera to Boland, 30 April 1921, no. 6.   69 Ibid., Box 16, file 105(14), Ernest Blythe to D O hEigeartaigh, 24 May 1921, Box 9, file 62 (2), Childers to Foreign Affairs, 30 June 1921. By August 1921, Dumont believed that his consulate office and private apartment in the Shelbourne Hotel had been searched by 'unknown persons' at various times and that he was being watched. He implied that this was the work of republicans. NARA, M580/218; ibid., 841d.00/441, Dumont to Secretary of State, 9 August 1921. The Dáil government learnt from a US visitor, John F. Moore, that Dumont described Sinn Féin as a 'gang of gunman' and was urged to seek his removal because he was 'doing England's work.' See NAI, D/FA, ES, Box 27, file 158, Boland to de Valera, 20 July 1921; D. Fitzpatrick, *Harry Boland's Irish revolution* (2003), p. 199; NAI, D/FA, ES, Box 27, file 158, Stephen O'Mara to Robert O'Brennan, 30 September 1921.   70 NAI, D/FA, ES, Box 27, file 158, O'Mara to Robert O'Brennan, 30 September 1921. De Valera did not request the replacement of US consul William Kent in Belfast despite his obvious partiality with the British side and closeness to the Unionist community in his jurisdiction. Kent gushed about the 'right royal day' when King George V opened the Northern Ireland parliament. But despite the closeness that both Kent and Dumont displayed towards the British side in Ireland, appearing to be close to Sinn Féin led Mason Mitchell, US consul in Cobh, into trouble with his superiors in Washington. The *Irish Independent* reported on 3 October 1921 that Mitchell and Vice Consul Flood were seen chatting to Harry Boland, the Irish 'ambassador' to the US, prior to his departure for the US. Carr cautioned Mitchell on 8 November to use the 'utmost care to avoid any action which may result in such comments … which might possibly be construed by the public as indicating a partisan attitude on the part of your office.' NARA, RG59, M580/218, 841d.00/388, Kent to Secretary of State, 22 June 1921; ibid., M580/225, *Irish Independent*, 3 October 1921; ibid., 841d.01B11/8, Carr to Mitchell, 8 December 1921; *Register of the Department of State, 1922* (1922), p. 125.

general, a position which was not available in any of the Irish postings. After he left Dublin, he became consul general in Frankfurt. However a further interpretation is that following the announcement of the truce in July 1921 and the signing of the Anglo-Irish treaty on 6 December 1921, signalling the withdrawal of British personnel from the civil and military administration, Ireland entered into a new phase of its political life which posed different challenges for the US consul in Dublin. Hathaway was highly regarded by State Department officials also and, having had previous experience of Ireland during the difficult war years, was more suited to the new situation ahead.

Until Dumont's departure, the Dáil Éireann leadership remained suspicious of his links to the Dublin Castle authorities and of his efforts to divert ACRI funds from their control. Meanwhile, McCoy and the ACRI leadership in the US decided to make a direct approach the State Department to progress their plans. Upon his return to the US in April 1921, where the ACRI had collected almost four million dollars for Irish relief, McCoy had met Howland Shaw in the State Department, to explain that the British authorities had reneged on a promise to allow non-partisan relief to be distributed in Ireland because the ACRI had decided to work with the Irish White Cross Society. McCoy proposed an elaborate plan for the creation of a relief organization to operate in Ireland and requested that the State Department firstly, request the British government to permit the new organization to be established in Ireland and secondly, supervize the distribution of the funds in Ireland as it had done in Belgium during the war. Shaw was sufficiently convinced by McCoy to draw up a plan for Irish relief that gave the State Department a central role, but William Castle doubted whether it would be wise for the Department to approve any particular plan of relief work. Both men agreed that Hughes should discuss the whole question with Geddes, which he did on 4 and 5 May.[71]

Prior to this meeting, Hughes had received information that questioned the non-political nature of McCoy's visit and of the whole ACRI relief operation in Ireland. Firstly, by 17 March 1921 Hoover and Hughes both knew that the American Friends had distanced itself from the ACRI project. Secondly, in mid-April Christian Herter, Hoover's secretary, informed Howland Shaw that Lucey had resigned from the ACRI on account of the 'anti-British tone which is rapidly becoming associated with that organization and with its activities.' Hoover also withdrew his support.[72] Thirdly, Dumont's report, penned on 22 March reached Hughes' desk on 15 April. In a covering note to Hughes, Howland Shaw

71 *Report of the Irish White Cross*, pp. 15–17; Carroll, *American opinion*, p. 197; NARA, RG59, M580/241, 841d.48/35, -/38, Memo. of McCoy and Shaw conversation 21 April 1921; HHPL, Commerce Papers, Box 345, Ireland 1922–6, Shaw to Hughes, 29 April 1921; *BDFA*, i, Annual Report for 1921, p. 144.   72 HHPL, Commerce Papers, Box 345, Ireland 1922–6, Shaw to Hughes, 15 April 1921. Although de Valera believed that American consular cables from Dublin to Washington were tampered with by the British authorities. NAI, D/FA, ES, Box 27, file 158, de Valera to Boland, 28 February 1921, no. 3.

wrote 'you will be interested by the account given by Mr Dumont concerning the activities of Senator France's brother and other American relief workers already in Ireland.'[73] Along with warning the State Department about the consequences of the delegation's visit to Ireland, Dumont's comments that Ireland was 'prosperous', that US aid lay unused in a Cork warehouse and that 'money gifts' might be used by Sinn Féin to prolong the war by continuing to pay the 'monthly wage' of the 'Flying Columns' and the 'gunmen', were marked by Shaw for Hughes and Harding's attention. Dumont's report undermined the ACRI delegation's work.[74] On the following day, Hughes forwarded extracts of Dumont's report to Harding, noting 'I think that you will be interested in reading the enclosed extracts from the report of Mr Dumont ... with respect to relief in Ireland.' On 20 April, Harding penned a non-committal reply: 'I need not say ... that I hold it to be a highly interesting document.'[75] Immediately, Hughes asked the US consuls in Dublin, Cork and Belfast to provide more information on conditions in Ireland and on the need for relief. Mitchell's next reports on 5 and 17 May did not refer to the general situation but focused on land tenure and fatalities on both sides in the war. Further reports from Dumont, dated 23 April, 29 April and 17 May, and from Kent in Belfast, dated 20 and 30 April, unsurprisingly confirmed the view that famine was not impending, that US relief aid for Ireland was unnecessary and that US money would only fall into Sinn Féin hands, thereby prolonging the war with Britain.[76]

Another source came Hughes' way questioning ACRI's use of the US donations. On 20 April, in a personal note, Herter passed on to Howland Shaw the concerns of the American Red Cross about the uses of the ACRI's relief funds, including the Red Cross donation of $100,000, in Ireland. Herter had already suggested to the US relief organization that they should ask ACRI about its plans for distribution of the monies.[77] The possession of Dumont's information, Herter's queries and Hoover's withdrawal confirmed to Hughes that the official endorsement of the ACRI campaign was misplaced.

Harding had already begun to distance himself from ACRI activities. On 21 April and 6 May, the New York ACRI branch invited him to attend a play, titled *Ireland arisen*, by the Irish Amateur Players in New Jersey and to provide a signature on a baseball for a raffle. At the same time the ACRI branch in New

73 HHPL, Commerce Papers, Box 345, Ireland 1922–6, Shaw to Hughes, 15 April 1921; Consul Kent's 20 April report from Belfast confirmed Dumont's view about the 'prosperous' state of Ireland and that the ACRI report was 'deliberately invented'. His report did not go beyond the Western European division. NARA, RG59, M580/218, 841d.00/348, Events of importance period 13 April to 20 April 1920, American consulate, Belfast to Secretary of State, 20 April 1921.   74 HHPL, Commerce Papers, Box 345, Ireland 1922–6, Shaw to Hughes, 15 April 1921.   75 Ibid., Hughes to Harding, 16 April 1921; NARA, RG59, M580/218, 841d.00/392, Harding to Hughes, 20 April 1921. Dumont received a commendation from Wilbur Carr. NARA, RG59, M580/218, 841d 00/392, Hughes to Dumont, 2 August June 1921   76 NARA, RG59, M580/241, 841d.48/22a, 22b, 22c, Carr to Dumont, Mitchell and Kent, 11 April 1921; for reports see NARA, RG59, M580/218.   77 HHPL, Commerce Papers, Box 345, Ireland 1922–6, Herter to Shaw, 20 April 1921.

Jersey asked for a 'line of encouragement' and a flower from the White House to raffle. All such requests were refused and attention was drawn to his earlier endorsement.[78] Of greater significance was a request, on 28 April, from L. Hollingsworth Wood, a liberal New York lawyer and chairman of the American Commission on Conditions in Ireland, for a five-minute interview with Harding to allow him present its interim report which supported the ACRI campaign.[79] On this occasion Harding referred the request to the State Department for information and advice.[80] In a hand-written note Harry Fletcher replied 'I would not advise receiving this man personally. It will be played up as anti-British and certainly cannot help the USA in any way.' But ever conscious that criticism might be levelled at the administration, Fletcher's formal reply to Harding suggested that Harding could invite Wood to send him a copy of the report.' The suggestion was adopted and Christian sent it to Wood on 6 May.[81]

Hughes, however, had little choice but to raise the ACRI proposal with Harding.[82] Undoubtedly, the ACRI action had placed the State Department, in Geddes' words, 'on the horns of a dilemma' because

> The Department has always been very unwilling to depart from the position that Ireland and the Irish question must be regarded as an integral part and an internal question of the United Kingdom. On the other hand, to refuse to move would bring on the heads of the government not only the wrath of the Irish, but of all those many influential persons who had subscribed to the fund under the belief that the President and the Vice-President when they endorsed the appeal, knew what they were talking about.[83]

Hughes and Geddes discussed the matter unofficially on 4 and 5 May. Hughes did not record the meeting but Geddes' cables kept the Foreign Office fully informed. Hughes informed Geddes that he did not wish to communicate the ACRI's scheme to him officially and instead he outlined its general aims and handed him a copy of the document. On the one hand, Hughes made it clear to Geddes that the administration considered Ireland and its affairs to be British internal matters. The latter accepted that the State Department was 'very unwilling to depart from this position.' On the other hand, both men agreed that if the State Department refused the ACRI's proposal it would bring criticism on the administration not just from Irish-Americans but from those Americans who had subscribed millions of dollars to the ACRI fund because its non-partisan stance

78 WGHP, series 4, 1921–3, misc. files, roll 180, Presidential executive file 135, folder 2, Smith to Harding, 21 April 1921; ibid., Brady to Harding, 6 May 1921, 26 April 1921; ibid., Harding to Smith, 28 April 1921; ibid., Christian to Brady, 7 May 1921.   79 Ibid., Wood to Christian, 30 April 1921.   80 Ibid., Christian to Fletcher, 30 April 1921, Fletcher, 2 May 1921, Christian to Wood, 6 May 1921.   81 Ibid., Christian to Fletcher, 30 April 1921, Fletcher, 2 May 1921, Christian to Wood, 6 May 1921.   82 Carroll, 'The American Committee for Relief', 45.   83 TNA, FO371/5663, Geddes to Curzon, 5 May 1921.

had been endorsed by Harding, Coolidge, Hoover and Weeks and might desta-
bilize the government leading to Hughes' resignation and replacement by the
anti-British Albert B. Fall, secretary of the Interior. Geddes further reported
Hughes' belief that if there were was a formal British refusal to accept the relief
proposal, a majority would be found in Congress to support a resolution for
recognition of the Irish republic.[84] After the meeting, Geddes was convinced that
the Harding administration's inexperience had led it into the difficult position.
In the third of three communications sent to the Foreign Office on 5 May
(including a copy of Dumont's report of 22 March), he wrote that the

> Secretary of State is consistently excited by [the] position in which he
> finds himself and today put into my hands original documents forwarded
> to him by American Committee for Relief in Ireland and told me of his
> dilemma and difficulties and also that he did not know what was the best
> thing to do.[85]

While it is doubtful if the dignified and statesmanlike Hughes was 'excited', it
is true that the State Department was thrown into a quandary, but Geddes and
Foreign Office officials in London were also alarmed. He wanted instructions on
whether to inform Hughes that the Irish question was 'purely internal', whether
he should tell him that the British government would only accept the proposal
direct from the ACRI, or whether he should accept the proposal from Hughes.
He advised the Foreign Office to refuse to receive the proposals from the State
Department or to discuss the relief of Ireland with the State Department. Instead
the British side should deal directly with the ACRI representatives in London,
thereby removing the problem from the level of Anglo–American diplomatic relations. This course, he said, would 'annoy [the] State Department but will ...
relieve the rest of the American cabinet.'[86]

It is clear from the above exchanges that both men viewed the matter of relief
for Ireland as having the potential to damage US–British relations. While the
British deliberated over their reply, the wider context of US–British relations
between March and June 1921, influenced their discussions on and decision about
the ACRI proposal.

The wider context to the ACRI proposal

Hughes' reference to recognition was significant because while ACRI was directing the fund-raising campaign, the Dáil Éireann mission and the AARIR were
supervising the recognition campaign. The Irish republicans' demand for US

---

84 Ibid. For another view see Carroll, 'The American committee for relief', 30–49.   85 TNA,
FO371/5663, Geddes to Curzon, 5 May 1921.   86 Ibid., Haddow, 5 May 1921.

recognition of the republic was not the only case of its type facing the Harding administration. On the issue of the Philippines, the Harding administration reversed Wilson's stand and refused to recognize Philippine nationalists' independence claims, imposing Leonard Wood as governor general. The same geopolitical and business interests dictated recognition of Cuba, with the creation of an ambassadorial post at Havana in late 1922.[87] The Hungarian-Americans were disorganized and disunited during the war and failed to produce a leader either in the US or Europe. As early as June 1919, Wilson had recognized their claim to be a separate nation and the Harding administration's need to end the state of war between the United States and the central powers resulted in recognition of Hungarian independence through the treaty signed at Budapest on 29 August 1921.[88] The American-Hungarian Federation wrote to Harding on 6 September 1921, expressing 'appreciation' of the re-establishment of peace between the two countries and 'gratitude' for aid sent to Hungarian 'sufferers.'[89] Polish sovereignty, based on the consent of the people, had been recognized by Wilson as early as December 1916 and was subsequently enshrined in the post-war treaties agreed by the Harding administration in summer 1921.[90]

The Wilson administration had been meticulous in its refusal to accord official recognition to the Irish republic, but, as was seen in chapter seven, the new administration and Congress offered renewed hope to activists and supporters of the Irish cause. The official propaganda campaign for recognition was organized by the Benjamin Franklin Bureau in Chicago led by James O'Mara, it would soon be subsumed into the Irish National Bureau in Washington. The latter was managed by Judge John Goff and its literary activities were directed by Katherine Hughes, a Canadian. It supplied political and literary articles to Catholic papers and sympathetic politicians free of charge. The Foreign Office believed that this material found 'ready acceptance.'[91] Meanwhile, individual AARIR groups, such

---

87 R.K. Murray, *The Harding era: Warren G. Harding and his administration* (2000), pp. 344–7, 331–2.   88 J.P. O'Grady, 'Introduction' in J.P. O'Grady (ed.), *The immigrants' influence on Wilson's peace policies* (1967), pp. 17, 28; Murray, *The Harding era*, p. 139.   89 Warren G. Harding Papers (hereafter WGHP), Series 4, 1921–3, Secretary of State, roll 144, Presidential executive file 20, Enery Pal to Harding, 6 September 1921.   90 O'Grady, 'Introduction', p. 17.   91 Ibid., Geddes to Curzon, 5 May 1921; F.M. Carroll, 'American Association for the Recognition of the Irish Republic' in Funchion, *Irish American*, p. 10; NAI, D/FA, ES, Box 2, file 158, de Valera to Boland, 30 May 1921. Indeed de Valera faced criticism in the Dail in March 1921 about the high expenditure of the US mission and he advised O'Mara and Boland to slim down the US organization, concentrate its efforts in Washington, not to spend more than $100,000 in the next year and instead hand over political and propaganda functions to the AARIR. Boland and James O'Mara were to concentrate on raising first $1 million and later $20 million through a loan drive. The Benjamin Franklin Bureau in Chicago went out of existence in early summer 1921 and its work taken over by the AARIR and the Dáil Éireann mission in Washington. Although Boland does not fully set aside the lobbying role as will be seen. NAI, D/FA, ES, Box 27, file 158, de Valera to O'Mara, 24 March 1921, de Valera to Boland, 30 May 1921; *BDFA*, vii, The American press, 1920–22, Catholic papers in America, February 1920, pp. 10–11; NAI, D/FA, ES, Box 27, file 170, Boland to de Valera, 20 July 1921.

as the Patrick Henry Council in New York state, organized appeals to the federal and state congresses and mailed pamphlets to every newspaper in England demanding recognition of the Irish republic.[92] The Bureau of Investigation maintained a watchful eye on AARIR meetings throughout the country.[93] Another source of pressure was Joseph McGarrity. Despite the division in Clan na Gael between himself and John Devoy, he reorganized Clan na Gael to support the IRA in Ireland and the work of the Dáil Éireann mission in the US. In March 1921, he still maintained the support of sympathetic Republican and Democratic politicians such as Borah, Shields, Reed and Norris for his meetings and publicity activities.[94]

Once Congress convened, the lobbying operated at local level and in Washington DC. Senator Thomas Walsh and Frank P. Walsh of the AARIR, had decided upon a strategy to promote the recognition issue in Congress. Senator Walsh believed that he should keep 'still' and the 'speech-making [should] be done by senators who could not be accused of being moved by racial sympathies or prejudices.' Consequently, he preferred that Norris, Borah and La Follette, who were on the progressive wing of the Republican Party, assume this role in spring 1921. Meanwhile, he worked to get the support of other senators and provided MacSwiney and the other republicans with the names of other 'Washington men' to approach.[95] She expected US recognition to be achieved by 24 March and that recognition by other countries would follow by '24 April', Easter Monday.[96] The timing was unrealistic but on 15 April Harry Boland was able to report to de Valera that they had secured 'first place' in the Senate and House of Representatives calendars for Irish resolutions and they had about twenty more resolutions which would be introduced by various members.[97] A total of eight resolutions on Ireland was introduced into Congress between March and November 1921. By mid-April, resolutions had been adopted by the Illinois and Minnesota state legislatures and Boland hoped that more would follow and that there would be a revival of the Mason bill. He noted that 'the atmosphere round

92 NLI, JMcGP, MS 17524(1), Josephine Crick to Joseph McGarrity, 25 May 1921.   93 For surveillance of Mary MacSwiney and AARIR see NARA, RG65, M1085/R921–4, Weekly Intelligence Reports and General Intelligence Reports.   94 NLI, JMcGP, MS 17524(1), J.E. Mullholland to McGarrity, 9 March 1921, McGarrity memorandum, 20 March 1921. By late 1921, the AARIR claimed a membership of 700,000 and to be the main representative body of Irish-America at the expense of the FOIF.   95 LC, MD, TWP, box 190, file: Ireland, government of, Walsh to William Johnson, 27 April 1921; ibid., Walsh to Patrick Meany, 25 April 1921. Walsh described Norris' speech as 'very eloquent and exhaustive.' Ibid., Walsh to A Leighton, 22 June 1921. UCDA, Mary MacSwiney Papers (hereafter MMP), P48A/115, MacSwiney to James O'Mara, 15–20 March 1921. Walsh wielded significant influence in the Democratic Party, becoming permanent chairman of the Democratic national convention from 1924 until 1933, and was approached to become the party's presidential candidate in 1924. Sobel, *Coolidge*, p. 258; also see Library of Congress (hereafter LC), Manuscripts Division (hereafter MD), Thomas J. Walsh Papers (hereafter TWP) for evidence of his interest in Irish affairs.   96 UCDA, MMP, P48A/115, MacSwiney to O'Mara, 11 February, MacSwiney to Boland, 12 February 1921.   97 NAI, D/FA, ES, Box 27, file 158, Boland to de

Washington is fairly friendly.'[98] Included among the resolutions were those sponsored by J.J. Kindred in the House to establish a US diplomatic service in Ireland and by Senator Norris protesting against 'violations and indignities committed by British forces against the Irish people in their struggle for independence', along with one introduced by La Follette.[99] It was the latter's efforts that Geddes highlighted in his annual report for 1921.[1]

La Follette had opposed both US entry into world war one and the League of Nations. In 1921, he was in contact with the AARIR and it was Frank P. Walsh who suggested that he introduce a recognition resolution. On 25 April 1921, La Follette told the Senate 'that the independence of the Republic of Ireland ought to be recognized by the Government of the United States of America.'[2] Frank P. Walsh described the speech as a 'very able and helpful ... a splendid presentation of the controversy.'[3] On the other hand, Geddes thought it long but noted to the Foreign Office that although the Senate was not well attended, the public galleries and the corridors were crowded. At the end of the speech, the resolution was referred to the Senate Foreign Relations Committee chaired by Senator Lodge.[4] Neither the La Follette resolution nor the other resolutions were given hearings or reported from the respective foreign relations committees, and MacSwiney's deadline for securing recognition passed. There are two main reasons why the congressional and state legislature activity on the recognition issue did not and would not achieve anything concrete. In the first place most, if not all, of Congress believed that, in Borah's words, 'the Irish question should not be permitted to stir up strife in this country and lead us into war.' Secondly, Irish-American politicians such as Thomas J. Walsh had to tread carefully when promoting the issue. He acknowledged that his 'kind and admiring friends in Montana have been a little impatient' because he had not made a speech in the Senate on recognition for Ireland. Yet, following the La Follette resolution, he had been criticized by a constituent, F.B. Gillette from Hinsdale, Montana, for his 'continued advocacy of the intervention of the United States into the domestic affairs of Great Britain in the matter of the Irish question.' Replying to Gillette on 17 May, Walsh defended his support on humanitarian grounds but acknowledged that the 'Sinn Féin Dáil' had not secured such 'exclusive control' of Ireland as to justify 'our government in recognising it.'[5]

Valera, 15 April 1921.   98 *Congressional Record*, 67th Congress; 1st session, vol. 61, Index; ibid., pp. 639–51. NAI, D/FA, ES, Box 27, file 158, Boland, 15, 27 April 1921.   99 R. Lowitt, *George W. Norris: the persistence of a progressive, 1913–33* (1971), p. 142. Norris' interest in Ireland arose from his hostility towards imperialism. Ibid.   1 *BDFA*, i, Annual Report for 1921, p. 141.   2 LC, MD, TWP, box 190, file: Ireland, government of, Walsh to M.T. O'Brien, 4 May 1921; LC, MD, The La Follette Family Collection, Robert La Follette (hereafter RF), series B, box 94, subject file Ireland, part iii, Senate Resolution, 67th Congress, 1st session, p. 178.   3 LC, MD, TWP, box 190, file: Ireland, government of, Walsh to William Johnson, 27 April 1921; Walsh to M.T. O'Brien, 4 May 1921.   4 *BDFA*, i, Annual Report for 1921, p. 141.   5 LC, MD, WEBP, box 96, general office file Irish question 1920–21 (January to May) (1), Borah to GH Hulbert, Idaho, 25 April 1921; ibid., Walsh to M.T. O'Brien, 4 May 1921. Some senators appeared to have

It was not surprising, therefore, that by late May, MacSwiney was experiencing difficulty in arranging meetings even with sympathetic congressmen, who thereby revealed their priorities. Vivian Pierce, an AARIR organizer, wrote to her on 18 May describing the efforts she had gone to in order to arrange a series of meetings with key senators for the Irishwoman. Senators David Walsh, J.K. Shields and Johnston were already amenable to her approaches but Borah had told Pierce that he had to deal with the Naval bill before he could meet MacSwiney and even then Pierce suggested that MacSwiney 'jog him along' on the appointment. Senator Frank B. Brandegee was 'too busy', leading Pierce to suggest that MacSwiney and her secretary, Catherine Flanagan, go to Capitol Hill without making any appointments and 'call out the senators', which meant asking for 'a friendly Senator, such as Senator Walsh' first and then asking him 'to help get out all the others.'[6]

A second part of the Pierce strategy and that of the Dáil Éireann mission involved winning over the members of the Senate Foreign Relations Committee to the Irish side. Lodge had been re-nominated as chairman of the committee on 18 April 1921 and remained in that position until his death on 9 November 1924, when Borah took over. During Lodge's tenure irreconcilables on the committee included Lodge, Brandegee, Johnson, McCormick, Moses, Borah and two new senators Shields and New, while the internationalist members were McCumber, Kellogg, Wadsworth, Hitchcock, Swanson, Pomerene, Pittman and McCumber.[7] On 18 May, Pierce suggested to MacSwiney that Congressman Kindred and Senator Shields might help to get Senator Key Pittman of Nevada 'on our side.' She offered no hope of getting Lodge's support; 'I think no Senator save perhaps Senator Lodge would refuse' to meet MacSwiney.[8] Not only would Lodge not meet MacSwiney but, despite his previous alliance with Cohalan and the FOIF on the League of Nations issue, he had no intention of promoting the Irish nationalist issues with either his committee, the State Department or the executive. Certainly he felt obliged to pass on protests and petitions from his Irish-American constituents in Massachusetts to the State Department, but he made it clear that he did not expect any action to ensue and his committee would

been influenced by information received by Senator Fletcher of Florida from his daughter, Ellen, and son-in-law, Lionel Smith-Gordon who supervised the Sinn Féin land bank and lived in Dublin. The couple were critical of British rule in Ireland. Consul Dumont in Dublin had identified the connection to the State Department. LC, MD, TWP, box 190, file: Ireland, government of, Walsh to FB Gillette, 17 May 1921; Carroll, *American opinion*, p. 273n. Harding received recognition resolutions from the Wisconsin legislature in early June. NARA, M580/219, 841d.01/26, Assistant Secretary of State, Wisconsin to Harding, 3 June 1921.   6 UCDA, MMP, P48A/156, Pierce to MacSwiney, 18 May 1921. But accessing friendly politicians did not mean automatic support. Pierce told MacSwiney that Senator Johnson was 'strong on the republic' but felt that that he could not argue for recognition 'when it is still so weak.' Ibid.   7 B. Glad, *Charles Evans Hughes and the illusions of innocence: a study in American diplomacy* (1966), pp. 140-1.   8 UCDA, MMP, P48A/156, Pierce to MacSwiney, 18 May 1921.

not assist either. He reacted to La Follette's innocuous resolution for a peaceful end to the London negotiations, introduced to the Senate on 22 November 1921, in the following words; 'it is being referred to the Foreign Relations Committee and it will stay in the Committee a damn long time.'[9]

When the republicans tried to bring the recognition campaign directly to Hughes and Harding in May they also found their doors closed. MacSwiney tried to get an interview with Hughes but failed because he had 'made it a rule not to see non-Americans on political matters.'[10] Instead, he permitted her to meet his third assistant secretary, Robert Bliss, and his secretary, Howland Shaw, on 14 May, because, as MacSwiney explained to de Valera a few days later, Hughes 'evidently wanted to hear if I had anything new to say without committing himself to giving an interview.' In the course of the interview with Bliss it emerged that what Hughes really wanted to find out was whether there was any hope that the Irish republicans 'would compromise' with the British in the war in Ireland. Not knowing that movements in that direction were imminent in order to reach a truce, she indicated that there was no chance and also told Bliss 'that we could hold out indefinitely, certainly for four years on a conservative estimate.' The significance of the 'four years' timeframe did not pass unnoticed by Bliss for a number of reasons. It meant that the Irish question would remain an issue in US politics while contradicting the impression circulated by Cohalan, that Sinn Féin was 'only a faction' and Dumont's belief that the IRA was in dire need of money. In late May, she correctly analysed the State Department's policy on Ireland, namely that it should avoid direct contact and 'fight shy of interviews' with Irish republicans in order to avoid any further British criticism. Shaw's report of the meeting confirms that the State Department 'was by no means unfamiliar' with the request for Irish recognition but it would require 'careful and deliberate study.'[11] Following this low-level contact between MacSwiney and the administration, Hughes was even more determined to ensure that the recognition campaign was not brought directly to the president. However, this was not straightforward because once again Harding had acted independently of his secretary.

On the eve of the opening of the sixty-seventh Congress on 9 April, the Washington Bureau of Investigation reported that Harding had received MacSwiney and Catherine Flanagan.[12] During this meeting, Harding had suggested that she call on him at another time. Not surprisingly, MacSwiney followed this up with a formal request, on 25 May, for an unofficial and private meeting with the president to discuss the 'situation in Ireland' with him. Her letter to Harding spelt out her position; 'in seeing me you are not seeing a diplomat, an accredited envoy or any one seeking publicity.' This statement was disin-

9 New York Public Library (NYPL), Frank Patrick Walsh Papers (FPWP), Box 28, Walsh to James O'Mara, 30 April 1921.   10 UCDA, MMP, P48A/115, MacSwiney to de Valera, 20 May 1921. 11 Ibid., NARA, RG59, M590/219, 841d.01/27, Office of the Secretary, E.H. Shaw, Memorandum of conversation with Miss Mary MacSwiney, 14 May 1921.   12 NARA, RG65, M1085/R921, General Intelligence Report, no.2 4, for the week ending 7 May 1921.

genuous, as the *raison d'être* for her visit to the US was to assist in the public campaign to gain recognition of the Irish republic. The following day Harding solicited Hughes' advice. The latter penned a two-page reply. He was surprised to hear that the president had met MacSwiney previously and had issued a personal invitation to her and he advised Harding not to meet her again, invoking procedural and diplomatic arguments. Hughes said that the State Department was trying to make it an 'invariable rule' that foreign prominent persons either in or out of office should be presented only by the diplomatic representative of the countries from which they came. He felt sure Harding would see the logic of this 'for otherwise political agitators, opponents of administrations abroad, those who wish to make political capital out of their visits to the president' would be seen and result in seriously impairing 'relations which we much seek to maintain with foreign governments.'[13] Mary MacSwiney's case fitted into all these categories. Hughes was undoubtedly irritated at his ignorance of Harding's invitation to MacSwiney and at the bypassing of the State Department on foreign affairs matters. Throughout his tenure, Hughes closely watched Harding's remarks on foreign policy, even assigning a State Department official to monitor the president's press conferences. Murray suggests that these unplanned interviews and remarks on foreign affairs presented difficulties for Hughes which occasionally produced rumours of his resignation.[14]

On this occasion, Hughes spelt out the implications for US–British relations of a meeting with MacSwiney:

> Of course the president will understand the difficulty of the situation. In all that pertains to Ireland there is nothing with respect to which British opinion is more sensitive and nothing that we can do which would be more significant in Great Britain than to have any dealings with those who, from the British point of view, are citizens of Great Britain and cause their government a great deal of difficulty. Of course, the question of governmental relations is quite distinct from a question of personal interest or sympathy.[15]

While not overstepping the boundaries of his position, Hughes was criticising the president's impromptu style. The point was taken in the White House and on 31 May MacSwiney was informed that she could not be granted an official meeting with Harding 'unless the request was made by the British ambassador.' She replied that she could not apply to the 'representative of my brother's murderers and my country's enemy' in order to meet Harding, which seemed to justify Hughes' arguments.[16] The Hughes line was also used in the following days

13 WGHP, series 4, 1921–3, misc. files, roll 180, Presidential executive file 135, folder 2, MacSwiney to Harding, 25 May 1921; Hughes to Christian, 28 May 1921; Christian to MacSwiney, 31 May 1921.   14 Murray, *The Harding era*, p. 132.   15 WGHP, series 4, 1921–3, misc. files, roll 180, Presidential executive file 135, folder 2, Hughes to Harding, 28 May 1921.   16 Ibid., Christian to MacSwiney, 31 May 1921.

to reply to requests for meetings from Donal O'Callaghan, lord mayor of Cork and Lawrence O'Neill, lord mayor of Dublin.[17]

Less than a week later, Harding sent out another negative message to Irish republicans in the US and Ireland. On 7 June 1921, the anglophile Rear Admiral William Sims delivered a speech to the English-Speaking Union in London. Sims was already a target of Irish-American newspapers for the allegations, made in his memoirs, *The victory at sea*, that during the war Irish nationalists collaborated with Germans, US sailors dating Irish girls had been attacked on the streets of Cork city and Irish nationalists were still attempting to break the Anglo–American alliance. The offending speech included the following piece:

> There are many in our country who technically are Americans naturalised and born there, but none of them American at all. They are American when they want money but Sinn Féiners on the platform. They are making war on America today. The simple truth of it is that they have the blood of English and American boys on their hands. They are like zebras, either black horses with white stripes, or white horses with black stripes. But we know they are not horses, they are asses. But each of these asses has a vote, and there are lots of them.

Protests from Irish-America flowed into the Congress, the Navy department and the White House including from Harding's close friend, Senator Medill McCormick who was 'bristling with indignation' at the 'jackass' speech.[18] Not all opposed Sims. He received support from the *New York Times*, the *New York Herald*, the *Christian Science Monitor* and from many critics of the Irish republican cause. W.H. Haskins, from Canton, Ohio, telegraphed the president on 14 June, 'speaking on behalf of millions of Americans, Admiral Sims expresses our opinion on the Irish question.'[19] Sims cut short his trip, returned to the US and, according to Senator Walsh, received a metaphoric 'slap on the wrist' from Denby and had an 'altogether pleasant visit' with Harding. He returned to the Naval College, where he served out his term of office until his retirement in 1922, although he was never promoted to full admiral.[20]

The furore over the Sims 'jackass' speech had highlighted the hostility present in parts of US society towards hyphenated-Americans and Catholics.[21] Thus,

17 Ibid., O'Callaghan to Harding, 24 May 1921; ibid., Hughes to Christian, 27 May 1921; ibid., Christian to O'Callaghan, 31 May 1921; ibid., Hughes to Christian, 28 May 1921.   18 F.M. Carroll, 'The Admiral Sims Incident. Irish-Americans and social tensions in the 1920s', 338; WGHP, series 4, 1921–3, misc. files, roll 180, Presidential executive file 135, folder 3, McCormick to Christian, 16 June 1921, Foley to Harding, 11 June 1921.   19 Ward, *Ireland and Anglo-American relations*, p. 247; WGHP, series 4, 1921–3, misc. files, roll 180, Presidential executive file 135, folder 3, W.H. Haskins to Harding, 14 June 1921.   20 Carroll, 'The Admiral Sims Incident', 342; *Congressional Record*, vol 61, part 4, 67th Congress, 1st session, 20 July 1921, p. 4017.   21 Carroll, 'The Admiral Sims Incident', 344; E. Cuddy, '"Are the Bolsheviks any worse than the Irish?": ethno-religious

less than three months after the Harding administration had been installed, it was understood by the US-based representatives of Dáil Éireann, by the AARIR leadership and also by de Valera, that it was unlikely that the Harding administration would again respond favourably on the issues of Irish relief and recognition. MacSwiney believed that de Valera was pessimistic about winning recognition when he returned to Ireland in December 1920.[22] By May 1921, he confirmed to Boland that he did not believe that US recognition would be won, except in a crisis in which America's own interests were involved. Instead he directed Boland to focus activities on fund raising for Ireland, to educate the US people about Sinn Féin policy and to maintain the link between the Irish republicans in Ireland and in the US. He also set out a retrenchment plan for the offices in Chicago and New York and the staff in order to cut down expenditure. Boland was to be replaced by James O'Mara as Dáil envoy in Washington. Before returning to Ireland in August 1921, Boland reported dejectedly to de Valera 'the first bloom of enthusiasm' has faded from the recognition campaign.[23] The two men accepted that it was unlikely that a recognition resolution would be passed by Congress or win Harding's support. They were unaware that the Irish relief and recognition campaigns were the subject of US–British relations at the highest level and that there would be a surprise turn to events.

In London, the British government was formulating its response to the ACRI proposal which had been presented by Hughes to Geddes. Sperling in the Foreign Office, took comfort from his belief that whatever majority there may be in Congress for Irish recognition, it 'can only be given by the President.' But he believed that Hughes wanted the British to accept the ACRI proposal 'to help him out' of his dilemma.[24] His colleague Haddow felt that opposition to the ACRI proposal would create a congressional majority in favour of recognition of the Irish republic which Harding would not oppose.[25] It was the views of William Tyrell, assistant under secretary of state to Curzon, which held greatest weight among Foreign Office officials and with Curzon. For him the question was one of principle:

> [A]re we going to allow American relief to be applied to Ireland? Our position, hitherto, has been that there is no distress in Ireland calling for such an exceptional measure of relief. If we adopt ... Geddes' suggestion to receive the proposals ... (whether it be done through the State Department or not, is really a matter of minor importance which would hardly justify us in antagonising the State Department), we run the risk of giving away a key position besides landing ourselves in endless trouble with the American relief committee. It seems to me our best chance is to stick to our key position and make it quite clear that the situation in Ireland does not justify

conflict in America during the 1920s', 22–5.   22 UCDA, MMP, P48A/115, MacSwiney to de Valera, 20 July 1921.   23 NAI, D/FA, ES, Box 27, file 158, de Valera to Boland, 30 May 1921; Fitzpatrick, *Harry Boland*, pp. 204, 203.   24 TNA, FO371/5663, Sperling, 6 May 1921.   25 Ibid., Haddow, 5 May 1921.

His Majesty's government in accepting the American offer. This agitation has been cleverly contrived by the Irish, as it appeals to the emotional side of the American, and creates a political issue disguised as a philanthropic one. I would, therefore, submit that we should advise ... Geddes for his guidance, that we cannot countenance any such proposal, and that if is communicated to him through the State Department he should reply that ... the situation in Ireland would not warrant the application of such relief.[26]

Unlike Geddes and Hughes, Tyrell did not link the relief and recognition issues, sharing a long-held view in the Foreign Office that British diplomats in Washington tended to exaggerate the extent of congressional support for Irish political causes and presidential willingness to interfere on Ireland. Nor was he concerned that the relief campaign had attracted the support of distinguished people in the US, including the president and some of his cabinet. Tyrell suggested that the approval of the Irish office was needed for his suggestion and further evidence should be provided to substantiate the statement that there was no such distress in Ireland. At the end of Tyrell's memorandum Curzon noted, 'I agree with the course recommended above.'[27] Hamar Greenwood and Edmund Talbot, the new lord lieutenant, in the Irish Office approved Tyrell's proposal. From Dublin Macready denied that the Irish 'were in the last stages of starvation' and stated that 'relief was not required from non-British sources.'[28]

The Geddes cables were circulated to the British cabinet and on 9 May Curzon drafted a memorandum in response. In it he noted that the 'American proposal is in the main political in character, constitutes an unwarrantable interference with the government of a foreign state' and would be 'indignantly rejected had it been made in analogous circumstances to the American government, and ought to be firmly though politely refused.'[29] On the following day, the cabinet set aside Geddes' warnings about the consequences for Anglo–American relations if Fall replaced Hughes and agreed with the Foreign and Irish offices' view that there was no need for relief in Ireland. Curzon was authorized to communicate these views to Geddes.[30] This decision reflects the hard-line approach on Irish matters prevalent in the cabinet at the time. On 12 May, two days after the decision on the ACRI proposal, the cabinet voted against offering a truce to Sinn Féin, although Winston Churchill worried that 'we are getting an odious reputation' and 'poisoning our relations' with the US.[31] For the following six weeks, until King George V delivered his speech at the opening of the Northern Ireland parliament on 22 June, signalling the cabinet's decision to seek a negotiated settlement, the war in Ireland continued unabated.

26 Ibid., Tyrell, 6 May 1921.   27 Ibid., Curzon, 7 May 1921.   28 Ibid., Curzon to the Cabinet, 9 May 1921; Macready, *Annals of an active life*, ii, pp. 540–1. Talbot was identified to be Unionist in his sympathies. NARA, RG65, M1085/R921, General Intelligence Report, no. 24, for week ending 7 April 1921.   29 TNA, FO371/5663, Curzon to the Cabinet, 9 May 1921.   30 TNA, Cabinet Records (hereafter Cab.), 23/25, C. 36/1/4, Cabinet minutes, 10 May 1921.   31 Quoted in F. Costello, *The Irish revolution and its aftermath 1916–23: years of revolt* (2000), p. 212.

Nonetheless, Curzon replied to Geddes on 11 May, expressing 'considerable surprise' at receiving the proposal because there was no need for 'foreign' relief in Ireland. Alluding to the ACRI proposal, he continued that such 'a proposition was not one which any British government would consider compatible with its dignity to sanction.'[32] Geddes met Hughes on 23 May, when the latter acknowledged that the ACRI proposal was 'entirely unacceptable' to the British government who had the right to reject it. Yet, he wanted Geddes to explain to London that the complete rejection of the proposals would provoke anti-British feeling among existing contributors to the ACRI, who might appeal to Harding again and create a difficult situation.[33] Hughes observed that he and Harding 'were only too anxious to prevent any further bitterness between the two countries arising out of the Irish question' but that it was a matter over which neither the president nor himself had any control. According to Geddes, Hughes went on to suggest that the British government might recommend to ACRI to approach some well-known British relief agency, presumably the British Red Cross, with the idea that it should administer the ACRI funds in Ireland. After the meeting Geddes warned Curzon that 'formidable agitation' would result once the British refusal became known, including the possibility of congressional recognition of the Irish republic. He reminded Curzon of the British government's earlier 'undertaking', issued through the Washington embassy on 30 March, that it would place 'no unnecessary difficulties' in the way of relief work in Ireland. Geddes believed that there was some merit in the idea that the British government might meet with representatives of the ACRI in London to discuss 'some method of administering the fund' in order to soften the shock of refusal.[34]

In the Foreign Office, Sperling opposed any 'further concession', but his superior Tyrell agreed with Geddes that, not because of a threat of a recognition resolution but because Harding and Hoover were involved, 'we shall have to make some concession.' Tyrell requested an opinion from the Irish Office. Like Sperling this opposed any concessions because of ACRI links to the Irish White Cross Society, a 'purely rebel organization.' Ironically, part of its evidence for this assertion was Dumont's report dated 22 March, a copy of which Geddes had obtained from the State Department and sent back to the Foreign Office. In other words, the Irish Office tried to use information gathered by one part of the State Department to undermine and embarrass another part of it. The Irish Office had decided that the earlier guarantee of non-interference in ACRI work 'no longer holds' and that James Craig of the Ulster Unionists would not sanction any foreign relief for Northern Ireland. Greenwood only felt himself able to sanction Geddes' compromise that the British Red Cross could become involved.[35]

32 TNA, FO371/5663, Curzon to Geddes, draft telegram, May 1921.   33 LD, Charles Evans Hughes Papers (hereafter CEHP), box 157–8, Memorandum of interview with the British ambassador, 23 May 1921.   34 BDFA, i, Annual Report for 1921, p. 145; TNA, FO371/5663, Geddes to Curzon, 25 May 1921.   35 TNA, FO371/5663, Irish Office, 3 June 1921.

The Irish Office's hard line response divided the Foreign Office and forced Curzon to intervene and, in his own words, he 'infused a certain amount of water into the strong water of the Irish office and [made] it less heady'.[36] On 6 June, Curzon instructed Geddes to restate to Hughes that the British government would not 'place any unnecessary obstacles' in the way of 'genuine' relief efforts, that relief was not needed, that the ACRI was linked to the Irish White Cross Society and that the ACRI proposal could not be entertained. Hughes and Geddes' suggestion that ACRI funds might be entrusted to the British Red Cross and to representatives of Irish interests but not to Roman Catholic clergy or to unionists, could be offered to the Americans if Geddes thought it 'would ease the situation.' The instructions were for Geddes' guidance in his 'unofficial and confidential conversations' with Hughes, but they could form the basis of a public statement if needed.[37] Before Geddes could act on Curzon's instructions three developments in June altered the context of the relief issue linking it to the recognition issue and more generally affected the political relationship between the US and Britain. These related to the renewal of the Anglo–Japanese alliance, the discovery in Hoboken, New Jersey, of arms and ammunition destined for the IRA in Ireland and the Anglo-Irish war of independence.

Chapter seven noted US opposition to the Anglo–Japanese alliance due to its threat to US security in the Pacific region. In mid-June, political interest in the issue intensified because of US newspaper coverage of the imperial conference's discussions about renewal. On 23 June, the State Department issued a somewhat indignant communiqué denying a rumour that it was being kept informed by the British government of its plans for renewal of the alliance and that the US government had received assurances in the matter. On the same day, Geddes called on Hughes, who stated that he viewed the renewal of the alliance in any form with 'disquietude' and that it would provoke public criticism of the British.[38] He added that one consequence of this anti-British feeling would be a congressional debate on a resolution calling for the recognition of the Irish republic. Geddes did not feel that this reference merited inclusion in his annual report for 1921 but the State Department *aide-mémoire* mentioned that the

> Secretary also told the Ambassador that he had been advised that a resolution for the recognition of the Irish Republic would be introduced in Congress; that the resolution in the Secretary's opinion would not pass but that it would be debated; that undoubtedly in the debate any relation between Great Britain and Japan could be seized upon by the enemies of Great Britain as indicating a desire to support the policy in the Far East to which this government was committed, would give great aid and comfort to those who were opposing such a resolution.[39]

36 Ibid., Sperling, 3 June 1921; ibid., Tyrell, 4 June 1921; ibid., Curzon, 5 June 1921.   37 Ibid., Sperling, 26 May 1921; ibid., Tyrell, 26 May 1921; ibid., Curzon 5 June 1921; ibid., Curzon to Geddes, 6 June 1921.   38 *BDFA*, i, Annual Report for 1921, p. 138.   39 *Papers relating to the*

Pusey, Ellis, Duroselle, Roskill and Carroll all interpreted Hughes' remarks about the Irish resolution as a serious threat of US intervention in Ireland unless the British ended the Anglo–Japanese treaty.[40] However, another reading of it might be that Hughes, who was furious about a possible renewal, simply used the strongest cards in hand – the threat of Irish-America – to exert pressure on the British. It is highly unlikely that he was serious because by 23 June his Irish 'card' had been undermined both by the discovery of arms and ammunitions in the US destined for the IRA and by movements toward a truce in Ireland.

Special Agent J.T. Fleurney's report for the week ending 18 June noted:

> British agents at Hoboken, New Jersey, have seized a shipment of machine guns at the port alleged to be consigned to the Sinn Féin organization in Ireland by Irish sympathisers in this country and claim that this substantiates the charge often made that there is "constant gun-running" from this country to Ireland.[41]

The Bureau of Investigation's Washington office subsequently investigated George G. Rorke and Frank Menkling, who were 'alleged accomplices' in the arms shipping.[42] Rorke was a known arms-dealer, a member of the Protestant Friends of Ireland and an acquaintance of Harry Boland while Menkling was an official of the Auto-Ordnance Corporation, which made the guns, and was Thomas Fortune Ryan's secretary. Ryan, a millionaire, had contributed to Irish causes, including the ACRI, and was the financial-backer of the Auto-Ordnance corporation.[43] It is probable that Boland began to order sub-machine-guns for the IRA campaign in Ireland from this company in late December 1920, using Rorke as his intermediary. Small numbers of US weapons had been imported into Ireland for some time but more powerful weapons were needed by the end of 1920. The Thompson sub-machine gun filled the requirement because it was easily available under US gun laws and it was powerful.[44] Shipments were successfully delivered to Michael Collins in Ireland in early May and on 11 July shortly before the truce.

Boland and his co-conspirators, Liam Pedlar, Laurence de Lacy and Joseph McGarrity, decided in late May or early June, to send another instalment of arms to Ireland in one shipment. According to Hart, this decision was facilitated by the chartering of the SS *East Side* by the Irish White Cross Society to buy coal with

foreign relations of the United States (hereafter *FRUS*), 1921, 2 vols (1936), ii, memo. of conversation between the Secretary of State and the British Ambassador (Geddes), 23 June 1921, pp. 314–16; NARA, RG59, M580/225, 841d.01/28/12, Note, 23 June 1921.   40 Pusey, *Hughes*, ii, p. 492; L. Ethan Ellis, *Republican foreign policy, 1921–1933* (1968), p. 94; J. Duroselle, *From Wilson to Roosevelt: foreign policy of the United States, 1913–1945* (1968), p. 158; S. Roskill, *Naval policy between the wards, 1919–29*, 2 vols (1968), i, p. 293; Carroll, 'The American committee for relief', 47.   41 Ibid., General Intelligence Report, no. 29, for week ending 18 June 1921.   42 Ibid.   43 Fitzpatrick, *Harry Boland*, p. 212; Peter Hart, 'The Thompson submachine gun in Ireland revisited', 161; J. Bowyer Bell, 'The Thompson submachine gun in Ireland, 1921', 99–100.   44 Hart, 'The Thompson submachine', 162. Hart suggests the gun was unsuitable to the type of warfare being conducted in Ireland.

ACRI funds and ship it to Dublin. The vessel, owned by the US Shipping Board and operated by the Cosmopolitan Shipping company, left New York for Hoboken, New Jersey (a known arms smuggling centre) on 8 June. Its departure was delayed due to an engineers' strike. Four days later the guns, parts and ammunition, sewn into sacks and labelled as legs of lamb, were delivered to the *East Side*. There is some dispute about how the guns were discovered. According to the US customs office report of 18 June, Marine Superintendent Brodie of the Cosmopolitan Line received information that packages had been loaded on board the vessel and, on Sunday, 12 June, searched the vessel but found nothing that was not on the manifest. Brodie alerted US customs officers and a second search took place on 13 June that turned up the guns. The customs officers searched the ship and discovered the guns, which had been moved to the engine room.[45] The newspapers quickly picked up the story and on 17 June, the *New York Times* reported:

> Customs officials, department of Justice agents, Hoboken detectives, US district authorities, representatives of Williams [Laurence de Lacy], Williams himself, and reporters thronged the corridors of the Hoboken police station all day ... Government agents stared with suspicion at representatives from other federal departments and refused to give their names to reporters or discuss their interest in the case.[46]

Hart insists that, contrary to Agent Fleurney's report British agents were not involved in detecting the seizure. If so, neither were US agents involved, although both sides had received information about the Auto-Ordnance order and other gun-running activities. In February and March, Ambassador Davis transmitted information received from British intelligence to the State Department about gun-running organized from Roxbury, Massachusetts and Pawtucket, Rhode Island.[47] But on 3 June, George Harvey was reliably informed that Sinn Féin was trying to import the Thompson sub-machine gun sold by Auto-Ordnance Corporation. He asked to be informed if any had been shipped to Ireland or England and if anything was being done to stop the shipments.[48] The telegram was read by Henry Fletcher on the same day and he immediately minuted it 'for action' and requested that an acknowledgement be sent to Harvey, a course approved by Hughes.[49] Thus,

---

45 NARA, RG59, M580/R218, 841d.00/374, H.C. Stuart Special Deputy Collector to Secretary of the Treasury, 18 June 1921. Hart maintains that the sacks were left lying on the dockside and on 13 June were opened by a cook who reported his news to the ships' stewards and on to the port superintendent. Hart, 'The Thompson submachine', 162. The role of union workers, particularly dockers and seamen, in the US and Britain in facilitating the delivery of people, arms, equipment and other packages to Ireland in this period is worthy of further study.   46 *New York Times*, 17 June 1921 quoted in Hart, 'The Thompson submachine', 163.   47 NARA, RG59, M580/218, 841d.00/299, Davis to Secretary of State, 4 February 1921; ibid., 841d.00/231, Wright to Secretary of State, 31 March 1921; ibid., 841d 00/366, American Consul in Charge, London to Secretary of State, 28 May 1921; ibid., 841d 00/358, Wright to Secretary of State, 4 May 1921.   48 Ibid., M580/218, 841d 00/360, Harvey to Secretary of State, 3 June 1921.   49 Ibid., M580/218, 841d

it would appear that both governments had prior warning about the Hoboken shipment. Bureau surveillance commenced on Rorke and Menkling but neither government had exact information about either the transportation of weapons from New York to Hoboken or the movements of the SS *East Side*.

As the various interested agencies and parties descended on Hoboken to claim ownership of the cargo there were repercussions in Washington. Agent Fleurney had not identified the important link between the arms and the ACRI but the Hoboken discovery appeared to confirm ACRI's connections to Sinn Féin as predicted by Dumont and Greenwood in Dublin.[50] Consequently, the endorsement given by Harding and Hoover to the relief campaign which they had thought non-political and humanitarian, now seemed thoroughly misguided.

A further consequence of the discovery was that it confirmed, much to Hughes' embarrassment, the existence of an arms trade between a private company in the US and the IRA in Ireland. He immediately launched an inquiry into the matter. Dumont was ordered to 'send all specific information which you may be able to obtain as to the introduction of American funds into Ireland, particularly when, in your opinion, these funds are to be used for the purposes of the Republican Army.'[51] On 20 June, he received a report from the special deputy collector in New York on the Hoboken events of 12 and 13 June and offering the co-operation of his department.[52] On the same day, Harvey informed Hughes that British intelligence indicated that recent raids in Ireland had turned up instructions on how to use the Thompson machine-gun and 'they, accordingly, assumed that shipments of this gun would soon be on the way' to Ireland. This was flimsy evidence and Harvey was

00/360, Fletcher, 3 June 1921.   **50** Ibid., M580/241, 841d 48/27, Dumont to Hughes, 17 May; ibid., M580/218, 841d.oo/381, Dumont to Hughes, 9 June 1921. On 9 June, he reported 'only one logical conclusion can be reached, and that is that it is not the intention of these [relief] organizations to do other with their funds than to put them at the disposition of the opponents of the British government in Ireland.' Ibid. Carroll notes that Dumont's allegations are difficult to believe without full financial information on the operation of the Dáil government. Also Dumont admitted in August 1921 while there were twelve republican fund-raising projects, that he had found 'little information' to prove that ACRI funds were used by the IRA. The *Report of the Irish White Cross Society* details the expenditure but not the names of the recipients but this does not mean that Douglas channelled money into the hands of revolutionaries. Furthermore, as de Valera launched the bond drive in America, almost $2 million lay unused in the bond-certificate account. Ultimately, the flow of ACRI funds was interrupted between July and August 1921. In total $4,907,102.70 was sent to the Irish White Cross Society between 7 January 1921 and 28 June 1922 comprising fifty-four instalments of $00,000 approximately. In summer 1921, Dumont continued his campaign to discredit ACRI by informing the State Department that if the Anglo-Irish peace efforts failed, it was 'not at all unlikely' that the US representatives of ACRI would be 'ordered out of the country or be deported.' He was referring particularly to Clemens J. France, brother of Senator Joseph France. Carroll, *American opinion*, p. 277, n. 47; NARA, RG59, M580/218, 841d.oo/411, Dumont to Secretary of State, 9 August 1921; *Report of the Irish White Cross*, pp. 28–31. Ibid., NARA, RG59, M580/218, 841d oo/402, Dumont to Secretary of State, 22 July 1921.   **51** NARA, RG59, M580/218, 841d oo/381, Hughes to Dumont, 11 July 1921; ibid., 841d.oo/372, Fletcher to Secretary of the Treasury, 1 July 1921. Ibid., 841d.oo/370, Hughes to Harvey, 21 June 1921.   **52** Ibid., 841d oo/371, Moyle to Hughes, 20 June 1921.

asked to secure 'certified or photostat copies of papers referred to.'[53] In the interim, Hughes received a 'semi-official' letter from Geddes, which noted the press reports of the Hoboken seizure and asked 'for any information with which you may be able to furnish me on the subject ... I should also be glad to learn how it is proposed to dispose of the guns etc.'[54] There was some debate within the State Department about what reply should be sent. Castle advised Hughes as follows:

> This case of the seizure of certain machine guns destined for Ireland bids fair to last for some time and it seems to me only appropriate that the letter of the British Ambassador should be acknowledged. The Department of Justice has sent one more batch of evidence which adds little or nothing to the report I made a few days ago. It merely increases the belief that Mr Rorke who bought the guns knew where they were going and for what purpose they would be used and that he probably paid for them with money collected from Sinn Féin sympathisers in this country.[55]

Significantly, Castle did not identify the ACRI as the actual source of the funds and neither did other US and British officials. Hughes replied to Geddes that a 'very careful investigation of this matter is now being conducted' and that as soon as 'definite conclusions' had been reached, he would be 'glad to let him know the result.'[56] Hughes had an awkward interview with Geddes on 29 June.[57]

Hoboken caused many problems for Hughes, not least of which was a semi-official complaint from the British. There were unsaid accusations of US collusion with the IRA which made US intervention in Ireland even more unlikely than it already was. Fortunately for Hughes, two announcements on 11 July calmed a difficult situation for the State Department and for the US administration generally. The Hughes/Geddes meeting on 23 June had concluded with both men agreeing to examine the possibility of a declaration of policy on the Pacific region by the US, British and Japanese governments. On the following day, Hughes told Geddes that he had discussed the matter with Harding and that they were hopeful that, through this tripartite approach, the 'difficulties in America' which he regarded as 'certain to attend a renewal of the Anglo–Japanese treaty, might be avoided.'[58] Soon the idea of an international conference to consider Asian security and the limitation of armaments emerged from the imperial conference in London and took hold with British and US leaders.[59] This led, on

---

53 Ibid., 841d.00/370, Harvey to Hughes, 20 June 1921.   54 Ibid., M580/218, 841d 00/379, Chilton to Hughes, 17 June 1921.   55 Ibid., 841d 00/380, Castle to Hughes, 27 June 1921.   56 Ibid., 841d 00/379, Hughes to Geddes, 28 June 1921.   57 The guns remained in a Brooklyn army base until November 1925 when they were handed over to the 'owner's agent', Joseph McGarrity. Despite Hughes and Geddes' efforts and a long legal case, the Thompsons began to arrive in Ireland, but not until 1931. Hart, 'The Thompson submachine', 164, 168.   58 *BDFA*, i, Annual Report for 1921, p. 138; Pusey, *Charles Evans Hughes*, ii, p. 492.   59 The origins of the idea to hold a conference remain a matter of dispute as both governments claimed ownership of it. However, Hoag admits that it was as much a

11 July, to Harding's inviting the interested powers to attend what became known as the Washington Conference, which will be examined in chapter nine.[60]

Simultaneously events were moving swiftly on Ireland and further supported the interpretation that even as Hughes seemed to threaten intervention on Ireland, it held little real potency. Elections in mid-May in Ireland gave Sinn Féin 72 per cent of votes cast and mediation efforts to end the war of independence were intensified in London and Dublin. Field Marshall Sir Henry Wilson had come to the 'very clear opinion' on 7 June that 'England was going to lose Ireland' and in the following weeks King George V's speech at the opening of the Northern Ireland parliament on 22 June signalled the breakthrough.[61] Influenced by the South African prime minister, General Jan Smuts, who acted as intermediary between de Valera and Lloyd George, the king spoke about the need for peace and reconciliation. Following further negotiations, a truce was signed on 9 July between the British military authorities in Ireland and the Sinn Féin leaders and this came into effect on 11 July. De Valera and Lloyd George agreed to meet in London on 14 July.[62] The impact in the US was immediate. Geddes recorded that from the end of June onwards the 'anti-British agitation' became less noticeable with a 'distinct falling off … in the interest taken by the American public in Irish affairs.'[63] Similarly, the Washington Bureau of Investigation report for the week ending 9 July concluded that 'Sinn Féin activities are seemingly dormant here at the present time.'[64] This weakening of public support for Irish relief and recognition reduced the pressure on Congress to act on Ireland and made it less likely that a resolution on Ireland would be passed. Yet, Hughes had progressed two of his foreign policy objectives, those on disarmament and the Anglo–Japanese treaty, and had received the added bonus of the Irish question being removed from US–British relations.

The penultimate question to be treated here is whether there was a US dimension to the British cabinet's decision to seek a solution to the Anglo-Irish war of independence? In December 1920, during British cabinet discussions on a truce, it was recognized that an escalating situation in Ireland might 'even attain such gravity as to bring on us the intervention of the United States of America.'[65] This possibility did not result in any tempering of British military actions in Ireland. One month later, in January 1921, as public condemnation of British policy in Ireland increased Lloyd George discussed the *détente* question with Andrew Bonar Law, leader of the British Conservative Party, specifically referring to Geddes'

British idea as it was American. But the Harding administration was influenced into calling a conference by popular pressure for disarmament. See C. Leonard Hoag, *Preface to preparedness: the Washington Disarmament Conference and public opinion* (1941), p. 79n. 60 Pusey, *Charles Evans Hughes*, ii, pp. 491–2. 61 Imperial War Museum, London (hereafter IWM), The diaries of Field Marshall Sir Henry Wilson (hereafter HWD), DS/Misc/80. reel 9, 1–1–1920 to 22–12–1921, 7 June 1921. 62 M. Hopkinson, *The Irish war of independence* (2002), pp. 195–6. 63 BDFA, i, Annual Report for 1921, p. 139. 64 NARA, RG65, M1085/R921, General Intelligence Report, no. 32, for week ending 9 July 1921. 65 K. Middlemass (ed.), *Thomas Jones, Whitehall diary: Ireland 1918–25*, 3 vols (London, 1921) iii, p. 48.

'most gloomy account of the situation in America' and continuing, 'in the interests of peace with America I think we ought to see de Valera and try and get a settlement.' Not surprisingly, Bonar Law immediately tried to undermine Geddes' view saying that Eric Geddes', the ambassador's brother, believed that 'Auckland is apt to be panicky and ... what he says ought to be taken with a grain of salt.' Lloyd George retorted 'if we take it with a salt cellar full, it is still seriously serious.'[66] The latter did not actively pursue a truce until the end of May 1921, by which time others in the cabinet shared his fears about the US administration. At a cabinet meeting on 12 May, Laming Worthington-Evans, minister for the War Office, worried about postponing the Irish elections because of the 'effect' in the US. Churchill was always sensitive to the possibility of official US intervention. Even in the opposition ranks, Bonar Law believed by this stage that there should be consistency between Britain's European policy of self-determination and its Irish policy so that 'no American can say [it] is unfair.'[67] US opinion mattered to these politicians and also to Foreign Office officials, who constantly reassured themselves that the US government would not intervene in Ireland, although Harding's endorsement of the ACRI and Hughes' threat of intervention on Ireland, demonstrated they could never be fully confident of this.

However, one should not exaggerate the influence of US public and official opprobrium on the British government's decision to move towards the truce in June and July 1921. A representative of the Dáil Éireann mission and AARIR, Joseph Scott, eventually managed to meet Harding on 14 July, the meeting coming about through the intervention of Harry Daugherty and bypassing all diplomatic protocol.[68] There is no record of this meeting but, according to Boland, 'Harding [said] that he had already had three interviews with [Ambassador] Geddes and that he urged the Ambassador to impress on the British government the importance of settling the question.'[69] The ever-conciliatory Harding did not tell Scott that he and Hughes had expressed to Geddes their regret over the 'bitterness' caused by the Irish question in Anglo–American relations.[70] Instead, the president told Scott that he wanted a 'just settlement' to emerge from the truce negotiations and that he had asked Harvey to notify the British government informally that he was anxious to see a settlement.[71] Harding's messages to Geddes and Harvey do not equate with official intervention. Moreover, the voluminous literature on the war of independence indicates that the US dimension was just one factor among others in both sides' move towards a truce. Other influential reasons related to both sides' genuine desire for peace, their respective military strength and the inevitability of negotiations.[72]

66 Ibid., p. 49. Eric Geddes was minister for Transport from 1919 to 1921.   67 Ibid., pp. 63–7.   68 Murray, The Harding era, p. 421; WGHP, series 4, 1921–3, misc. files, roll 180, file 135, folder 3, Daugherty to Christian, 14 July 1921.   69 NAI, D/FA, ES, Box 27, file 158, Boland to de Valera, 20 July 1921.   70 BDFA, i, Annual Report for 1921, p. 145.   71 Hopkinson, The Irish war of independence, pp. 195–6; J. Maher, Harry Boland a biography (1998), pp. 144–5; NAI, D/FA, ES, Box 27, file 158, Boland to de Valera, 20 July 1921, Boland to Robert Brennan, 20 July 1921.   72 J.J. Lee, Ireland. 1912–85, politics and society (1989), p. 47. The matter still remains one for discussion among histo-

What was the fate of the ACRI proposal? On 6 June, Geddes received Curzon's reply, which confirmed the British government's refusal to accept the ACRI proposal but permitted him to suggest to Hughes that the funds could be entrusted to the British Red Cross, with co-opted members representing Irish interests. The ambassador was relieved that by the end of June US public interest in Irish grievances had considerably weakened because of the beginning of the truce negotiations. Consequently, he reported that the 'pressure' on the State Department to insist on the institution of the ACRI proposal had 'apparently slackened.' He heard nothing further from Hughes about the relief proposal and it was never officially communicated to him.[73] The British permitted the distribution of ACRI relief funds in Ireland through the Irish White Cross Society into 1922, despite their many misgivings.[74] The ACRI proposal and recrudescent recognition agitation in Congress had served Hughes' needs well. Despite his own misgivings, he had raised the relief issue with Geddes and voluntarily raised the recognition issue thus according both an importance in the US–British diplomatic relationship. The two announcements on 11 July were a coincidence but as a result the Irish question, in all its guises, regained its lowly status in the Harding administration's foreign policy agenda.

*

During the first four months of the Harding administration, the Irish lobby had achieved more success than it had for a long while, much to the concern of British officials. The latter explained it in terms of an inexperienced administration, unstable Congress and the unpredictability of Harding's personality. Nonetheless, the Irish gains were substantial. Not only had they managed to win Harding's endorsement and that of members of his cabinet for the ACRI campaign but Hughes had

rians. The anglophobe historian, Charles Tansill suggested that the British government agreed to negotiate the truce with Sinn Féin in order to a) appease US official and public opinion and b) prepare the way for an Anglo–American agreement on ship construction in order to keep parity of size between the respective navies. On the other hand, MacDonagh believed that Irish-American influence on British policy in Ireland in mid-1921 was exaggerated. More moderate interpretations came from Mansergh, Hachey, Ward and Hopkinson who regarded the persistent Irish-American military and financial support for the Irish cause as influential with Lloyd George's decision to seek peace. Costello accords with Churchill's emphasis on assuaging public opinion as a significant factor in the negotiation decision on the British side. Carroll also sees links between the two momentous announcements on both sides of the Atlantic on 11 July 1921 of the Washington Conference on limitation of armaments in November 1921 and the truce in the Anglo-Irish war of independence. See C. Tansill, *America and the fight for Irish freedom, 1866–1922: an old story based upon new data* (1957), pp. 423–6; Ward, *Ireland and Anglo-American relations*, pp. 252–3; TNA, FO 371/5621, Disarmament conference; O. MacDonagh, *Ireland* (1968), pp. 128–9; N. Mansergh, *The Irish question, 1840–1921: a commentary on Anglo-Irish relations and on social and political forces in Ireland in the age of reform and revolution* (1975), p. 304; T. Hachey, 'The British Foreign Office and new perspectives on the Irish issue in Anglo-American relations, 1919–21', 12–13; Carroll, 'The American committee for relief', 49; A.J. Ward, 'America and the Irish problem, 1899–1921', 89–90; Costello, *The Irish revolution and its aftermath*, p. 221.   **73** *BDFA*, i, Annual Report for 1921, pp. 145.   **74** *Report of the Irish White Cross*; Carroll, 'The American committee for relief ', 49.

formally raised the recognition and relief issues with the British ambassador and the propaganda, fund-raising and arms-dealing were officially tolerated.

However, there is a wider context to be considered. Firstly, Harding's endorsement of the ACRI campaign in spring 1921 represented the height of his interest in Irish affairs. He never recognized the new republic but, motivated largely by personal and humanitarian factors, he assisted the Irish relief campaign. However, even this grand gesture on Ireland was not special if it is compared to his actions to ameliorate famine conditions in the USSR, which involved the introduction of legislation and the establishment of the American Relief Administration in December 1921. The Harding administration also helped to evacuate women and children from Constantinople in September 1922, following the Turkish onslaught in Anatolia.[75] In all three cases, Ireland, USSR and Anatolia, public emotions ran high and there was pressure on Harding to act, but the degree of intervention was tempered by US foreign policy interests.

The last time a US secretary of State had officially raised Ireland with a British counterpart was in May 1917, when Robert Lansing had discussed it with Arthur Balfour. On both occasions the reasons for doing so were comparable, namely that wider US interests were at stake. In 1917, it was done to unite the US public behind US entry into the war and in 1921 to promote US foreign and security policy in the Pacific, not because of a belief in the importance of the Irish issues.

For Hughes, handling the Irish-Americans in spring 1921 must have confirmed some of his views on the formulation of US foreign policy. Two of his core beliefs were that public opinion was the ultimate source of US foreign policy and that public consensus could overcome the divisive effect of the separation of executive powers. However, in later speeches he indicated that public opinion should be informed and moderate and that it should not prevent a secretary of State from solving problems. He further accepted that there were special difficulties in reaching public consensus. One of these was that Americans were drawn from 'many races and countries' and were 'still bound by ties of sentiment and interest to many lands.'[76] His experience of Irish-Americans during spring and early summer 1921 may have contributed to the evolution of his views on foreign policy-making. At any rate, the announcements on 11 July 1921 of the truce and of the beginning of negotiations were warmly welcomed by Harding and Hughes in the hope that it would remove America's Irish difficulty and smooth the course of US–British relations. A report from the pro-unionist Kent in Belfast to the State Department on 6 July stressed the dangers of complacency in believing that the Irish question was fully removed from US–British affairs. Although they were becalmed in summer 1921, republicans in the US and Ireland still had an active agenda, which would involve the Harding administration.

75 Harding, *The Harding era*, pp. 348–50, 357; WGHP, series 4, 1921–3, roll 144, file 20, folder 8, State Department to Harding, 23 January 1921; ibid., Hughes to Harding, 30 January 1922.   76 Glad, *Charles Evans Hughes*, pp. 144–5; C. Evans Hughes, 'Some observations on the conduct of our foreign relations', 369; quoted in Glad, *Charles Evans Hughes*, p. 144.

CHAPTER NINE

Official US interest in Ireland: recognition and treaty making, July 1921–August 1923

By summer 1921, there was relief within the Harding administration that the Irish republicans and the British government had agreed to a truce and negotiations. The majority of the US press, public, politicians and Catholic Church welcomed the truce.[1] The general remission in agitation on Irish affairs reduced both the pressure on the State Department to act on Irish matters and the temperature of the US–British relationship. In the State Department, Secretary Hughes and his officials resumed the traditional cautious indifference on Irish issues. Nevertheless, republican activists in the US did not cease their work. Consequently, Hughes and his staff still had to handle Irish matters, some were of a minor nature but others were not.

---

1 Cardinal William Henry O'Connell on behalf of the US Catholic hierarchy sent a message of support to Cardinal Michael Logue, archbishop of Armagh and primate of Ireland. Samuel Gompers, leader of the American Federation of Labor with its sizeable Irish-American base, did not comment but he refused in mid-June and October 1921 to support either side in the Anglo-Irish conflict. National Archives and Records Administration, Maryland (hereafter NARA), Records of the Department of State relating to internal affairs of Great Britain, 1910–29, Record Group 59 (hereafter RG59), Microfilm (hereafter M) 580/225, 841d 01/37, Mitchell to Secretary of State, 24 September 1921; National Archives of Ireland (hereafter NAI), Department of Foreign Affairs (hereafter D/FA), Early Series (hereafter ES), 27/158, Boland to Brennan, 20 July 1921; D. Doyle, 'The Irish and American labour, 1880–1920', 42–53; NAI, D/FA, ES, 27/168, Boland to Gompers, 27 October 1921.   2 Hughes did help Frank P. Walsh to travel to Ireland. Walsh applied to the British embassy in Washington for a visa but was refused. Immediately, he appealed to Hughes. Geddes informed Curzon that the State Department was 'anxious' to avoid a 'disagreeable incident.' Geddes felt that Walsh was 'unlikely to do much harm in England' but he would 'undoubtedly cause trouble in the United States' if the application was refused. Walsh was awarded a visa and left for Ireland on 23 July. Fears that he would upset the peace talks proved unfounded. Subsequently in an article in the *Nation*, he acknowledged that there were 'decent Englishmen in Ireland' such as Andrew Cope. The National Archives, London (hereafter TNA), Foreign Office (hereafter FO) 371/5633, Geddes to Curzon, 20 July 1921; *Nation*, 12 October 1921.

The impact of the truce on the republicans' agenda

If the US government was unwilling to recognize the republic and its representatives prior to the truce, it had even less reason to do so afterwards.[2] Even so Mary MacSwiney remained hopeful of recognition but felt that it would not come before the Washington conference in November 1921.[3] This view was shared by Boland who had decided that, as a result of the 'peace parley we deemed it expedient' to postpone the hearing on the Norris resolution before Lodge's Senate Foreign Relations Committee and also 'gave notice of delay' on the La Follette resolution. In common with Peter Golden, and presumably also with Norris and La Follette, Boland considered it more important to permit the London conference to develop 'without embarrassment from here.' He assured Robert Brennan in Dublin that the American Association for the Recognition of the Irish Republic (AARIR) personnel were watching 'keenly the trend of events' and that no opportunity 'will be missed by them in furthering Ireland's cause or in strengthening the hands of Ireland's representatives at the peace parley.'[4] For Vivien Pierce, in the AARIR, the truce undermined the congressional campaign for recognition and she felt that the future of a resolutions would depend on the results of the negotiations.[5] She was correct because Eamon de Valera changed his position on the direction the recognition campaign should take in the US while he was at the London talks.

On 28 July, he instructed Robert Brennan to 'be ready to make a vigorous effort' towards seeking simultaneous recognition from a number of countries, including France, Germany, Italy and the US. Ireland's foreign representatives were to be instructed to go about achieving it immediately, while public appeals would follow 'if the negotiations break down.' A further set of instructions was sent to the respective missions abroad; it contained the most controversial of the recent British proposals relating to status and control of territory and an Irish critique of them, so that envoys could 'properly inspire' the press in respective countries and defeat in advance the 'misrepresentations' which would be attempted by the British government.[6] De Valera was preparing for a breakdown in negotiations. The timing of de Valera's decision was unfortunate in the context of the US at least.

On 4 August, prior to Boland's departure from the US for the opening of the second Dáil in Dublin, he outlined to de Valera the effect of the truce on political lobbying:

> Our (very) best friends in the senate have a perfect alibi and find it very difficult to secure action on Ireland's behalf just now. I am practically in the same position myself, as I have been very careful not to make any statements that might in any way embarrass the present negotiations.[7]

3 University College Dublin Archives (hereafter UCDA), Mary MacSwiney Papers (hereafter MMP), P48A/115, MacSwiney to de Valera, 20 July 1921.   4 NAI, D/FA, ES, 27/158, Boland to Brennan, 20 July 1921.   5 UCDA, MMP, P48A/115, Pierce to MacSwiney, 11 July 1921.   6 NAI, D/FA, ES, 14/96, de Valera to Brennan, 28 July 1921, Brennan to Boland, 5 August 1921.   7 Ibid., 27/159,

Not only was there a drop in congressional support for the recognition issue in July, but once it had broken up for the summer recess in August the task had become impossible. Outside Congress most Americans interested in Ireland regarded the truce as the beginning of the end of Ireland's problems.[8] Boland wrote that without exception, the American press had hailed the negotiations with 'great relief' and would support a 'compromise.' Nonetheless, Boland endeavoured to fulfil de Valera's new instructions by contacting McFarland of the Hearst newspaper organization and Moore of the *Pittsburgh Leader,* to ask them to wage a press campaign in favour of US recognition.[9]

The decline in support for Irish-American republican activities was most obvious in the fate of the largest organization, the AARIR. In mid-September, O'Mara described the AARIR in Washington to be 'at sixes and sevens.' The local membership had declined from ten thousand to three and he was very worried about the success of the recognition campaign and the bond drive. On the latter topic, he had previously warned Robert Brennan, on 19 August, 'it is becoming more difficult every day to count on a bond drive this Fall' and, again, on 14 September, 'it is going to be difficult to carry it through successfully under present conditions.' He felt that recognition would only come if there was a 'whole time man on the job here – either myself or somebody else from home.' He believed that without that kind of direction 'things are inclined to fall to pieces', as none of the local committee of the AARIR could afford to give the 'time and attention' which was required for the work.[10] During summer 1921, against a background in which there was decreasing public and political interest in Ireland, a weakening of the AARIR in terms of membership, structure and effectiveness, uncertain negotiations in London and infrequent updates on the state of those talks, O'Mara struggled to fulfil de Valera's orders to win recognition and as importantly, to prepare for the second bond drive. Such difficulties were not identified, however, in Robert Brennan's report on foreign affairs, dated 10 August 1921. Instead he concluded that reports from the US continued to be 'encouraging, the Irish cause is gaining in sympathy and support there each day.'[11] The gap between republicans in Ireland and those in the US was more than just a matter of geographical distance; it reflected, as usual, a misreading of the situation by some of the Dublin-based leadership. Events in September further illustrate this.

Both de Valera and Lloyd George had set out their proposals in July and August and serious differences existed over the continuation of partition, the compatibility of an independent republic and dominion status, including continued British military and naval presence in the twenty-six counties, free trade and Ireland carrying its share of the British war debt. A return to conflict appeared

Boland to de Valera, 4 August 1921.   8 See UCDA, George Gavan Duffy Papers (hereafter GGDP), P152/265, James E. Murray, Director for Montana, AARIR to Frances J. Horgan, 10 July 1922. 9 NAI, D/FA, ES, 27/158, Boland to de Valera, 4 August 1921.   10 Ibid., Stephen O'Mara to Brennan, 14 September 1921.   11 Ibid., 4/4/2, Foreign Affairs Report, 10 August 1921.

a possibility in early September and de Valera turned to the US for political and financial assistance.[12]

The Sinn Féin leader feared that a resumption of war in Ireland would prevent the remainder of the American Committee for Relief in Ireland funds from being sent there. The transmission of remittances had ceased on 8 July because of the truce. But in early September, Clemens J. France requested the executive committee to resume the transmission of ACRI relief funds and supplies to Ireland. This started on 8 September when instalments were sent on a weekly basis until the ACRI was wound up on 31 August 1922. Gloster Armstrong kept a close eye on the activities and on 23 September notified the Foreign Office that £250,000 was being forwarded to France. But he believed that de Valera had given assurances that it would be used for relief purposes only, although he reminded the Foreign Office about possible links between the ACRI funds and the arming of the IRA[13] Curzon, however, did not ask the US government to act.

It was not so easy for Stephen O'Mara to fulfil the political dimension to de Valera's request. On 9 September, he wrote to Hughes asking him to intervene with the British government on the contentious issues. He stated that one of the main obstacles to agreement was the demand by the British government 'for naval control of the ports of Ireland ... and the land of Ireland for military air service' and he attempted to make it relevant to US security interests. He pointed out that the Irish side objected to these demands on 'her own account ... [and] because such measures are interpreted in Ireland as being in fact directed against the United States.'[14] William Castle brought the letter to Hughes' attention on 12 September, 'as it possibly is the first in a long series we shall have from the so-called "Diplomatic Representative of the Republic of Ireland".' He advised Hughes that 'under no circumstances' should it be acknowledged. As an aside, he thought Hughes might be interested in the

> rather amusing statement of the writer that Ireland is opposed to naval control in the ports of Ireland by Britain, and to the use of land in Ireland for the Military Air Service – not because the Irish themselves object, but because they consider this as directed against the United States. This is, on the whole, the most far-fetched propaganda that I have seen.[15]

12 F. Costello, *The Irish revolution and its aftermath 1916–23: years of revolt* (2000), pp. 236–8. 13 Ibid., FO371/5651, Armstrong to Foreign Office, 23 September 1921; F.M. Carroll, *American opinion and the Irish question 1910–23: a study in opinion and policy* (1978), pp. 282 fn.5, 277 fn. 45; *Report of the Irish White Cross to 31 August 1922* (1922), pp. 28–9; TNA, FO371/5652, Armstrong to Foreign Office, 7 October 1921. Armstrong noted that the arms were heading for India also. Ibid. 14 NARA, RG59, M580/225, 841d.01/32, O'Mara to Hughes, 9 September 1921. 15 Ibid., Castle to Hibbs, 12 September 1921. The use of the term 'so-called' was significant as the prefix was applied by officials in the State Department and the Foreign Office throughout 1921 when they were faced with requests for clarification about the status of the Dáil Éireann diplomatic and consular representatives. British Consul General Armstrong in New York wanted the Foreign Office to complain to the US

Hughes read the minute, noted it and did not recommend any action other than that suggested by Castle.[16] Hughes would not be drawn into the Irish negotiations and neither would he recognize the republic even by replying.

O'Mara followed up his letter to Hughes with one to Harding on 21 September. This stated that a 'crisis' in the negotiations between Britain and Ireland had been reached where 'action upon your part would be decisive.'[17] A cable from the national headquarters of AARIR also requested 'a simple word or action' from Harding to prevent a 'renewal of war.'[18] Although O'Mara did not expect to meet Harding, he met a friend of Harding's in Pittsburgh, who agreed to pass on his request to Harding and to alert the president to the overarching influence of 'die-hards' in Lloyd George's cabinet who would obstruct a settlement for Ireland. O'Mara then wrote directly to Harding's secretary, George Christian, informing him that there was someone meeting Harding on 22 September who would raise the matter with him. O'Mara told Christian that 'the President will in consequence desire' to read his letter. O'Mara suggested, therefore, that 'you ... have it on hand.' The strategy failed; George Christian passed the letter to Castle and no further action ensued.[19] Yet, O'Mara believed that Harding had 'made representations' on Ireland's behalf to Lloyd George who had modified his position in consequence.[20] Between 7 and 12 September 1921, the Irish and British leaders continued to disagree about de Valera's insistence that the British government recognize the existence of an Irish republic before a conference could be convened. This insistence became a major obstacle to further progress and was only resolved when de Valera dropped the precondition and not because of any action on the part of Lloyd George.[21] Even though O'Mara believed otherwise, Harding did not intervene on this issue or on any other aspect of the Anglo-Irish deliberations in the lead up to the talks on 11 October.[22]

But the momentum went out of the Irish republican campaign for recognition in mid-summer 1921 and other strategies were revived which were specifically designed to influence US foreign policy to Ireland's benefit. Prior to his departure for Ireland, Boland identified the three questions of concern to US politicians and officials: '1. The proposed funding of the war loan. 2. Disarmament. 3. The Anglo-Japanese alliance.' Boland believed that each had the potential to re-ignite anti-British feeling within Irish-America, to embarrass the British government and to pressure the US government into recognition.[23]

government about the republicans using the formal titles 'envoy', 'consular service', but he failed. Tyrell decided that the best course was 'to let sleeping dogs lie.' NARA, M580/218, 841d.00/385, Castle to Dearing, 15 July 1921; TNA, FO371/5651, Armstrong to Foreign Office, 2 September 1921; ibid., H. Seymour, 20 September 1921.   16 NARA, RG59, M580/225, 841d.01/32, annotated note, 12 September on O'Mara to Hughes, 9 September 1921.   17 Ibid., M580/225, 841d.01/35, O'Mara to Harding, 21 September 1921.   18 Ibid., 841d.01/34, AARIR to Harding, 22 September 1921.   19 Ibid., M580/225, 841d.01/35, O'Mara to Christian, 22 September 1921; NAI, D/FA, ES, 27/158, O'Mara to Brennan, 30 September 1921.   20 NAI, D/FA, ES, 27/158, O'Mara to Brennan, 30 September 1921.   21 Costello, *The Irish revolution*, p. 238.   22 NAI, D/FA, ES, 27/158, O'Mara to Brennan, 30 September 1921.   23 Ibid., 27/159, Boland to Brennan, 20 July 1921.

War debts and Ireland

The Harding administration had adopted the Wilson line on war debts, which was that full repayment was required from debtor countries. The difficulty lay in finding a procedure for repayment. By mid-July 1921 congressional discussion of Treasury Secretary Mellon's first recommendation was in full swing. Mellon had recommended to Harding that Congress grant 'full plenary powers' to his department in order to deal with the problem on a case-by-case basis.[24] Boland and Geddes each reported home that the proposal met with strong opposition in the Senate for a variety of reasons.[25] Congress was dominated by the Republicans but it was divided by different factions along partisan, ideological and regional lines. However, its members were united against any attempts to reduce Congress' role in policy formulation and decision-making. Secondly, both the House Ways and Means Committee and the Senate Finance Committee agreed that Mellon would be 'too lenient' when finalizing the repayment agreements.[26] From Boland's perspective, Mellon's arrangement would not be to Ireland's advantage either because 'all the negotiations will be held in secret.' This meant that public criticism could not be offered and Ireland's 'friends' in the Senate could not make 'pertinent remarks on the proposed funding of England's debt to Britain's embarrassment.'[27]

Boland believed that Harding and Mellon would defeat Congress, so in late July the ailing AARIR began campaigning against Mellon's recommendation. State conventions passed resolutions against it and forwarded their protests to congressional politicians.[28] Boland felt that this was the only way in which 'our American sympathisers can effectively strengthen the hands of Ireland's representatives at the peace parley.'[29] The Irish envoy reported to de Valera on 4 August that only the anti-British Hearst press and a few progressive senators supported by the Irish-American organizations were 'fighting vigorously against the proposed bill.' He did not hold out much hope as the bill met only 'slight opposition' in the Senate Finance Committee.[30] This committee produced majority and minority reports and the latter, signed by Robert La Follette, Andrieus A. Jones, James A. Reed, Furnifold M. Simmons, Peter C. Gerry and David I. Walsh, insisted that all war debts be repaid on harsh terms and that the sums be decided by Congress. Geddes detected an 'Irish influence' at work but reassured Curzon on 9 September that 'no real importance is attached to it.' He met with Mellon to discuss the matter and although the secretary felt that 'Irish machinations' might have been influential with the senators, Mellon attached no significance to the minority report either.[31]

24 Murray, *The Harding era*, p. 362.   25 NAI, D/FA, ES, 27/159, Boland to Brennan, 20 July 1921; TNA, FO371/5662, Geddes to Curzon, 30 June 1921.   26 Murray, *The Harding era*, p. 362. 27 NAI, D/FA, ES, 27/159, Boland to Brennan, 20 July 1921.   28 Library of Congress (hereafter LC), Manuscripts Division (hereafter MD), William E. Borah Papers (hereafter WEBP), box 96, file General office file, Irish question 1920–21 (May to October), (1), Idaho State AARIR Convention, 11 October 1921.   29 NAI, D/FA, ES, 27/159, Boland to Brennan, 28 July 1921.   30 Ibid., Boland to Brennan, 4 August 1921.   31 TNA, FO371/5662, Geddes to Curzon, 24 August, 9 September,

Eventually Harding and Mellon accepted that Congress would not agree to their proposal. They agreed to an amendment that placed authority in the hands of a commission of five members, including two approved by the Senate.[32] Congress passed the World War Foreign Debt Commission Act in February 1922. The Commission was empowered to make settlements not Congress, but only insofar as these were in accordance with certain agreed restrictions; the period of repayment to end no later than 15 June 1947, the interest rate could not be less than 4.25 per cent per annum, each debtor state had to repay its own debts and an agreed repayment schedule could not be revised or changed at a later date.[33] The decision had mixed results for the Irish republicans' agenda.

On the one hand, the Commission that met for the first time on 18 April 1922, was a select group, initially consisting of Mellon, as chairman, secretaries Hughes and Hoover, Senator Reed Smoot and Congressman Theodore Burton. Consequently the predominance of cabinet representation ensured that there were no opportunities for sympathetic politicians to link Britain's Irish policy with repayment arrangements. On the other hand, the 'big three' of the cabinet all agreed that US debtors would have to repay their war debts and that the payments schedule would not be lenient, even though this did not turn out to be the case in practice as each of the debtors ended up negotiating a separate agreement none of which conformed with the 1922 statute.[34] However, the Commission adhered to the specific principle that Britain would have to pay which was a key aim for the Dáil Éireann mission, AARIR and Irish-American newspapers and a vigilant Congress watched from the sidelines.[35]

The anti-British Hearst press kept up the pressure on the Commission to exact full repayment from the British government. But once the issue had been removed from the public domain in early October, the AARIR's plan to 'storm congress' and demand that 'America insist upon the payment of the foreign debt' failed to materialize.[36] Irish-American newspapers and the *Nation* reminded readers of the links between the repayment conditions and the progress of the continuing Anglo-Irish peace moves. In the pages of the *Nation*, Lincoln Colcord and Frank P. Walsh outlined a widely held view that one of the economic reasons behind Lloyd George's decision to propose a truce in Ireland was the hope that the Harding administration would treat its debt case with benevolence.[37] Not surprisingly, this view was also held in some circles in Ireland. The taxpayers who read the *Irish Times* were informed that any additional pressure on the British economy would

13 September 1921.   32 NAI, D/FA, ES, 27/159, Boland to Brennan, 20 July 1921; TNA, FO371/5662, Geddes to Curzon, 17 October 1921. According to Boland, the 'full pressure' of the AARIR was brought to bear against the Mellon proposal and was influential in the revision of the proposal. NAI, D/FA, ES, 27/158, Boland to de Valera, 30 November 1921.   33 Murray, *The Harding era*, p. 362.   34 P.A. Grant, 'President Warren G. Harding and the British war debt question, 1921–3', 479–80.   35 *Nation*, 5 October 1921.   36 NARA, Investigative Case Files of the Bureau of Investigation, 1908–1922, RG65, Microfilm (hereafter M) 1085/Reel921 (hereafter R), General Intelligence Report, no. 40 for week ending 3 September 1921.   37 *Nation*, 5, 12 October 1921.

have repercussions for Ireland and that, after all, Britain and Ireland had lost about a million men in defeating Germany; the writer asked, 'Will she [the US] now insist upon her pound of flesh?'[38] Few seemed to focus on the possibility that Irish taxpayers might have to shoulder a portion of the British war debt in any future settlement with Britain. This latter idea had become a sticking point during the Anglo-Irish treaty negotiations in October and article five of the result-ant treaty stated that the Irish Free State assumed 'liability for the service of the Public Debt of the United Kingdom.'[39] Even after the treaty provisions includ-ing article five, were known, republicans in Ireland and the US focused on the political implications of the British debt question and how benevolent terms revealed the Harding's administration 'pro-British' instincts.[40]

When the British debt agreement was eventually agreed by Congress in February 1923, John Devoy, in the *Gaelic American*, commented that Harding had 'won an easy victory … on England's own terms.'[41] Stanley Baldwin recognized that there was no more to be gained and recommended to the British cabinet the acceptance of the final proposals.[42] In the British debt agreement the amount to be repaid was $4,604,128,085.74 over a period of sixty-two years. For the first ten years, the annual rate of interest was established at three per cent and for the remaining fifty-two years, the figure was three and one-half per cent. Herbert Hoover later calculated that the concessions made to the British resulted in a reduc-tion of about thirty per cent of the sum owed.[43] The level of British satisfaction was evident in the new British ambassador to the US, Esmé Howard's description of the settlement as the 'outstanding event of the year' which had 'greatly added to British prestige in the US.[44] From the British perspective, therefore, this was just one issue that contributed to an improvement in its relations with Washington by 1923. In the eyes of radical republicans in the US and Ireland, the Harding government's handling of the debt issue confirmed its 'slavish pro-British policy.'[45]

The Washington disarmament conference and recognition of the Irish republic

In September and early October 1921, the influence of the Dáil Éireann mission on the war debts issue was minimal and had been fortunate in coinciding with

38 *Irish Times*, 19 January 1922.   39 K. Middlemass (ed.), *Thomas Jones, Whitehall diary: Ireland 1918–25* (1971) iii, 24 June 1921, p. 80; *Nation*, 5, 12 October 1921; R. Fanning et al. (eds), *Documents on Irish foreign policy*, 3 vols (1998–) (hereafter *DIFP*), i, Final text of the articles of agreement for a treaty signed between Great Britain and Ireland, p. 357.   40 Ibid., Smiddy to Duffy, 4 May 1922. 41 *Gaelic American*, 10 March 1923.   42 J. Barnes, *Baldwin: a biography* (1969), p. 147.   43 Grant, 'President Warren G. Harding and the British war debt', 485.   44 Murray, *The politics of normalcy*, p. 60; TNA, FO371/9635, Annual Report for the United States for 1923, pp. 3, 4–5.   45 *Gaelic American*, 31 March 1923; E. McKillen, *Chicago labor and the quest for a democratic diplomacy, 1914–24* (1996), p. 184. For further on the debt issue see chapter thirteen.

congressional interests, but a more orchestrated campaign targeted the second 'American question' – the naval disarmament conference – in late October and November. Mary MacSwiney had believed in July that as long as the work of the Harding administration was dominated by preparations for the disarmament conference in November, recognition of Irish independence would not be achieved. But she felt that the conference could offer further opportunities to promote the recognition campaign and again disturb US–British diplomatic relations by embarrassing Britain on the Irish question. She favoured pickets by Sinn Féin representatives from Ireland, 'men of Irish birth and descent, especially those who were wounded if possible, and the mothers and sisters of men who lost their lives in the war of small nations … on the style of suffrage pickets.'[46] By early August, after a visit to Washington where Harry Boland met with 'men who are pretty close to official America', he had been led to believe that the disarmament conference was 'fraught with great possibilities.' Not only might the conference deal with the question of Harding's campaign idea of an 'association of nations', thereby re-igniting the League of Nations issue but, more importantly, if the London negotiations were still pending 'the English will find it very easy to sit in at Washington undisturbed by Irish-American agitation.' He argued that if the Anglo-Irish talks were to break down it should come within a reasonable time before the November conference in order to prevent the British from misrepresenting the situation there and undermining the Irish-American protests. Boland feared that in the 'anxieties of the moment' de Valera might have 'lost sight of the importance' of the forthcoming conference.[47]

The potential of the conference for this purpose became even clearer to the Dáil Éireann mission when they received de Valera's warnings about the deadlock in the London talks, the possibility of a return to war and the importance of accurately representing the Irish viewpoint. Joseph Begley immediately linked the Anglo-Irish and disarmament issues. He felt that Lloyd George would want to keep the talks going until after the Washington conference, because if

> British terrorism was in full swing in Ireland at the time of the conference even the most unthinking American would see England's hypocrisy in talking of "Blessed Peace and Disarmament". But with the peace negotiations actually going on in Ireland [Lloyd] George will be in a position to say in effect "Well we are doing our best and we are now assured of peace in Ireland".

46 UCDA, MMP, P48A/115, MacSwiney to de Valera, 20 July 1921; NAI, D/FA, ES, 27/158, Memorandum of Katherine Hughes included in O'Mara to de Valera, 19 August 1921.   47 NAI, D/FA, ES, 27/159, Boland to de Valera, 4 August 1921. He informed de Valera the following day that Jane Addams who was also a member of the American commission investigating conditions in Ireland, was likely to be a member of the US delegation to discuss disarmament. Ibid., 5 August 1921.

Begley reported that 'many Americans here' shared his view and recalled Lloyd George pulling 'the same trick' at the time of the Irish Convention in 1917–18.[48]

De Valera was slow to respond to the suggestion of targeting the disarmament conference which led O'Mara to complain to him that they needed more specific directions.[49] Boland sailed for Ireland on 13 August to attend the opening of the Second Dáil, leaving Stephen O'Mara in charge of diplomatic and financial affairs in the US. O'Mara wanted de Valera to send out immediately an envoy to co-ordinate liaison with senators, the press, the AARIR and the activities surrounding the Washington conference. On 31 August, he reminded de Valera that 'all our friends in this country believe that a big effort should be made during the ... conference.'[50] Bureau of Investigation agent J.T. Flourney, working out of the Washington office, reported for the week ending 3 September:

> Preparations for the descent upon Washington by the Irish of America during the conference on limitations of armaments, in case the present peace negotiations with the British government fail, were divulged at a meeting of the Padraig H. Pearce [branch] of the American Association for the Recognition of the Irish Republic held at Gonzaga Hall.[51]

The AARIR began its propaganda campaign by printing feature-length articles, circulating petitions and leaflets calling for the biggest US fleet possible to be built and denouncing British imperialism. Before the conference began Begley took heart from a request received from the Japanese embassy in Washington for a copy of de Valera's pamphlet, 'Request for recognition', and for other literature on Ireland. He sent them a packet of material and was pleased that they wished to be 'well-posted for the coming disarmament conference.' O'Mara also received instructions from Robert Brennan in Dublin, to have a resolution put through Congress by senators Johnson, La Follette and Borah 'providing that the conference shall be limited to disarmament but embrace grave questions at present affecting the peace of the world.'[52]

O'Mara was rejoined by Harry Boland in early October. The latter's return journey was observed from when he left Queenstown to his arrival in New York by US consular, intelligence and immigration officials in addition to the British consul general in New York.[53] The Dáil mission proceeded to work on three

48 Ibid., 27/158, Begley to Brennan, August 1921.   49 Ibid., 27/170, O'Mara to de Valera, 19 August 1921.   50 Ibid., 27/158, O'Mara to de Valera, 31 August 1921; ibid., O'Mara to Brennan, 2 September 1921.   51 NARA, RG65, M1085/R 921, General Intelligence Report, no. 40 for week ending 3 September 1921.   52 UCDA, ÉVP, P150/1174, Report of activities, Washington Office, July 1921; ibid., P150/1213, Brennan to O'Mara, 28 September 1921.   53 NARA, RG59, M580/225, 841d 01B11/8, Mitchell to Secretary of State, 3 October 1921. Boland informed Hughes that he had arrived in Washington as representative of the Republic of Ireland and 'should it please' Hughes to give him 'an audience', he would be 'happy to present his credentials.' Fletcher read it and asked for it to be filed. Castle counselled Fletcher that a reply not be sent because it would be

fronts: firstly, it wanted to secure a resolution in the next Senate session centring on the question of the importance of a 'free Ireland' to the world and urging Harding not to discuss all questions relating to the future peace of the world
at the Washington conference until the Irish question was settled. Secondly, representatives of the mission and of the AARIR worked together to draw up a
memorandum on naval disarmament in the hope of submitting it to Harding.[54]
Thirdly, O'Mara and Boland drafted a letter dated 19 October to Harding indicating that the British delegation did not represent the Irish republic and that
the latter would not be 'bound by any understandings, covenants or contracts
which may be entered into by the British delegates.'[55] The letter did not demand
representation at or admission to the conference, in accordance with Dáil instructions on 30 September. O'Mara, however, had drawn up plans to be implemented
in the unlikely event of the Irish republic being accorded a seat. It would be filled
by an AARIR delegation from a different US state each day and each of these
representatives would ask new questions about Ireland, while outside the formal
meetings a mission official would lobby US politicians.[56]

The letter was not sent to Harding because de Valera did not sanction it.[57]
It is unlikely that Harding would have replied, both because the Dáil Éireann
mission did not have formal diplomatic status and because recognition had become
an issue for the British and US governments in the context of the conference.
During the summer, the US government had deliberated about the invitation list
and the agenda for the conference. By early August, Britain, Italy, France and
Japan had agreed to attend and Harding had also invited China, Belgium, the
Netherlands and Portugal. The presence of the latter group was necessary because
of their interest in Far East matters. The two governments had also agreed that
the British delegation would represent the dominions instead of separate invitations being issued. This produced objections from Jan Smuts, prime minister of
South Africa, because it was unfair to the dominions and unhelpful to the Irish
negotiations.[58] Eventually he agreed with Lloyd George that it was too late to
approach the US and gave full powers to a representative in the British delegation to sign the disarmament agreement on behalf of South Africa.[59] The case
served to highlight to the US government the dangers of prematurely recognizing the Irish republic while its status inside or outside the empire remained unde-

'published.' Connolly's presence as consul in New York was formally communicated to Hughes by
Frank P. Walsh. NARA, RG59, M580/225, 841d 01B11/7, Boland to Secretary of State, 17 October
1921; ibid., Castle to Fletcher, 28 October 1921; ibid., Walsh to Secretary of State, 29 October 1921;
ibid., M580/225, 841d 01B11/10, Assistant Commissioner General to J.P. Doughton, 31 October
1921; ibid., Acting Commissioner of Immigration to Commissioner General of Immigration, undated;
ibid., 841d 01B11/8a, Dearing to Attorney General, 20 October 1921.   **54** NAI, D/FA, ES, 27/170,
Boland to Brennan, 21 October 1921.   **55** Ibid., 27/158, Boland to Harding, 19 October 1921.   **56**
Ibid., O'Mara to Brennan, 14 September 1921.   **57** See *DIFP*, i, p. 201, n. 1.   **58** TNA,
FO371/5623, Colonial Office, 24 November 1921.   **59** Ibid., FO371/5622, Note, 28 October 1921;
ibid., FO371/5624, Foreign Office to Balfour, 10 December 1921.

cided. But the US administration had ensured that the representation issue in general and other criticisms attracted minimal public support.

Hughes and Harding recognized the extensive public and political interest in naval reduction by allocating representation to both at the conference.[60] The president appointed a four-man team consisting of Hughes, former secretary of State Elihu Root, Senator Henry Lodge, chairman of the Senate Foreign Relations Committee and Senator Oscar Underwood, the Democratic minority leader and also a member of Lodge's committee, to form the US delegation. At the same time he also appointed an American Advisory Committee (AAC), comprising twenty-one members, to assist the team and represent the interests of the public under the categories of finance, labour, commerce, agriculture, church and geography. Thus, he tied vested-interest groups, pressure groups and powerful individuals into the conference from its beginning.[61] By the time it opened on 12 November, public support was firmly behind the conference, particularly after Hughes' opening speech offered to scrap 846,000 tons of US ships and recommended that the British do away with 583,000 tons and the Japanese, 450,000.[62] Boland felt that Hughes' proposal secured the 'overwhelming support of the American press and the spirit favouring disarmament is widespread in this country.'[63] Throughout the following twelve weeks, the vast majority of people in the US, public, press and politicians alike, awaited the treaties, hoping that they would guarantee a reign of peace.

This almost nation-wide support for disarmament and an agreement led Boland and the AARIR to alter their strategy on the conference. Boland had gauged the atmosphere in Washington and believed that Lloyd George would receive a 'tremendous reception here.' Consequently, he had decided that 'any counter-demonstration on our part would not serve our cause', unless, of course, the London talks, which had begun on 11 October, collapsed.[64] Instead of organizing demonstrations Boland drafted another letter to Harding on 25 October, asking for representation at the conference, pointing out that Ireland was the 'key to the Atlantic' and had a 'peculiar' interest in naval policy, restating that Ireland could not be bound to the results of the conference if it did not participate and stressing the importance of the presence of smaller nations.[65] This letter was not sent either, because de Valera did not approve it.[66] Boland admitted to Robert Brennan that it was 'very difficult' to decide on the best approach because with

60 K. Bourne & D.C. Watt (general eds), *British documents on foreign affairs* (hereafter *BDFA*), part 11, series C, North America, 25 vols. (1986–95), i, The Republican ascendancy, 1919–28, Geddes to Curzon, 21 September 1921.   61 C. Leonard Hoag, *Preface to preparedness: the Washington disarmament conference and public opinion* (1941), p. 126.   62 Murray, *The Harding era*, p. 151.   63 NAI, D/FA, ES, 27/170, Boland to Brennan, 30 November 1921.   64 Ibid., Boland to Brennan, 21 October 1921. In the end, Lloyd George did not turn up because of the on-going Irish discussion which he felt could cause the fall of the government at any minute. T.H. Buckley, *The United States and the Washington conference. 1921–1922* (1970), p. 65.   65 NAI, D/FA, ES, 27/158, Boland to Harding, 25 October 1921.   66 See *DIFP*, i, p. 202, n. 1.

the negotiations going on in London, 'all public men here are very chary of taking action.'[67]

During the course of the disarmament conference what little opposition there was centred around firstly, the Hearst press, which Boland praised for standing alone in waging a 'very vigorous campaign against the limitation of armament and favouring a "big navy" for America', secondly, the Daniel Cohalan-led Friends of Irish Freedom, who maintained a 'vigorous campaign' against Hughes' proposal and the possibility of an Anglo–American alliance, and thirdly, the AARIR campaign, which focused on the 'freedom of Ireland' as a prerequisite to any agreement on arms limitation.[68] The final part of the opposition was the Dáil Éireann mission. The latter's strategy was confined to supplying the conference delegates with propaganda literature about Ireland, including the *Irish Bulletin*, which reported on the London conference, meeting unnamed 'officials' and researching for an article for the *Washington Post*.[69] The discussions with the Japanese delegation did not result in any further action but the French envoys were 'distinctly favourable' towards Ireland. One unofficial representative of the French government approached Boland about the possibility of securing the good will of Irish-American opinion on behalf of France. He asked Boland to draw up a memorandum on the power and influence of the Irish-American lobby in US foreign policy, specifically mentioning the peace and debt settlement issues, which would be submitted to the French delegation. Before Boland could complete it this unnamed man was recalled to France.[70]

Another obstacle that the Dáil, AARIR and Friends activists encountered was that British prestige in Washington was growing by the day and the US–British relationship deepening. In Washington, Arthur Balfour headed the British delegation which included his publicity officer, *The Times* correspondent, Arthur Willert, and Lord Riddell, who represented the British press; both of these met the US press every day.[71] It helped also that Balfour was clear in his own aims and those of the conference, which he reiterated to Curzon on 24 November; 'Let me emphasise the fact that it was never possible for this conference to do

67 NAI, D/FA, ES, 27/158, Boland to Brennan, 27 October 1921. 68 Ibid., 27/170, Boland to Brennan, 30 November 1921. The *Sinn Feiner* newspaper was in no doubt that the real aim of the conference was an 'Anglo-American alliance' and also that the London negotiations on Ireland would exercise a 'strong influence' on the Washington conference. In a later edition, the publication offered more than rumour as evidence of an alliance, namely that Geddes was receiving daily reports on the London negotiations and the reference by US Ambassador Harvey in a speech on 3 November to the Liverpool Chamber of Commerce where he contemplated 'a closer political relationship of Great Britain and America.' *Sinn Féiner*, 29 October, 12 November 1921. 69 NAI, D/FA, ES, 27/158, Boland to Brennan, 27 October 1921; ibid., Boland to de Valera, 30 November 1921. The second bond drive was launched on 15 November 1921 in Washington DC and Illinois. 70 Ibid., 27/156, Boland to Brennan, 30 November 1921. Consul Joseph Connolly in New York, was struck also by the 'definite ... well organised ... astute' British propaganda campaign throughout the US at this time. See J.A. Gaughan, *Memoirs of Senator Joseph Connolly (1885–1961): a founder of modern Ireland* (1996), pp. 212–13. 71 TNA, FO371/5625, Balfour to Prime Minister, 17 November 1921.

more than promote two objects: settlement of the Far East and diminution of naval armaments.'[72] These matters dominated their work. Despite opposition from the British Admiralty, Balfour quickly came to accept Hughes' ten-year moratorium on shipbuilding and his ratio of capital ships. The realities of Britain's weakened economy, its inability to compete in an arms race and the beneficial impact of the Hughes formula on the British navy, led his government to accept the idea of naval parity and a realignment of relations in the Far East.[73]

Balfour's reports to the Foreign Office at the end of November are noteworthy in two respects; firstly, he worried that the 'French can wreck' the naval plan and secondly, he noted the remarkable improvement in the Anglo–American relationship due to America's 'generous statesmanship.'[74] Harding shared his views on the latter. Writing to US Ambassador Harvey in mid-December he felt 'things have been going along finely' and he was 'everlastingly grateful for the cordial assistance' which both the British and the Japanese had given to the conference work. He stated that they had been 'more than helpful and always very considerate.'[75] The most embarrassing moments of the conference came from Harding's unpremeditated remarks, on 26 November, about creating an 'association of nations' and later, on 20 December, when he denied that the four-power pact included the main islands of Japan. The president's view was widely broadcast around the world, the conference was thrown into confusion and the White House issued a complete retraction.[76]

Outside these incidents, the conference proceedings went smoothly with a mixture of private and public sessions. Neither Hughes nor Harding's correspondence suggests any Irish dimension to the political discussions. Equally, the work of the representative AAC did not produce any protest on behalf of republican Irish-America.[77] Individual republican Irish-Americans may have remained hostile and suspicious of British motives in the London negotiations but many were impressed by British participation in the Washington conference. Most believed that the consequences of the disarmament deliberations would have a more immediate impact on their lives, in terms of taxation and security, than the London negotiations. During the conference the Committee on General Information (CIG), on behalf of the advisory committee, conducted regular polls of 185 newspapers. The sole delegation about which great disappointment was expressed in news and editorial articles was that representing France, due to its opposition to the application of the Hughes formula to all categories of ships. More than thirteen million appeals and resolutions were also received by the CIG. Strongest public criticism was reserved for the US, Japanese, French and

72 Ibid., Balfour to Foreign Office, 24 November 1921.   73 H. Temperley, *Britain and America since independence* (2002), pp. 116–17.   74 TNA, FO371/5624, Balfour to Foreign Office, 24 November 1921.   75 Warren G. Harding Papers (hereafter WGHP), Series 4, 1920–3, Presidential Personal Files, roll 228, file 60, Harding to Harvey, 15 December 1921.   76 M.J. Pusey, *Charles Evans Hughes*, 2 vols. (1963), i, pp. 498–9; TNA, FO371/5624, Reuters telegram, 26 November 1921; Tyrell, 26 November.   77 Hoag, *Preface to preparedness*, pp. 126–7.

Italian delegations, because of their preference for retaining the submarine as a defensive weapon essential for national security, whereas the British delegation favoured 'total and final abolition', as did the majority of the public and press.[78]

By the end of November, Boland seems to have abandoned all hope that Ireland's case for recognition would be progressed at the conference.[79] The only significant Irish dimensions to the Washington conference were that firstly, Lloyd George was absent due to the London negotiations', secondly, de Valera was worried that if the British got 'what they want' in Washington, it meant 'war to the knife against us' and thirdly, Harding's careless remark about the 'association of nations' revived the League of Nations idea.[80]

De Valera's comment came at a time when Ulster Unionist intransigence about all-Ireland parliamentary arrangements was becoming firmly set and the possibility of resuming war in Ireland was in the air. Consequently, his fears about the consequences for Ireland of British success in Washington were heightened. It is doubtful if he was aware of Lloyd George's view on the Washington dimension to the London talks, which was opposite to his own. Among the many strategies which the British government suggested in order to circumvent the Ulster Unionist Party resistance to involvement in an all-Ireland parliament was that even though the unionists could not be forced into accepting an all-Ireland parliament, his government might advise King George that neither could the republic be because of opposition from the dominions, the Labour Party and the 'US would break up [the] Washington Conference [and] go on building ships.'[81] He feared that failure in London would lead to problems in Washington. But this was only one of several suggestions made during a critical stage in complex negotiations. Three days earlier he had even considered resignation, and in the following days threats and persuasion were employed to move the Irish republicans and Ulster unionists towards agreement.[82]

So it is against this background, that the seriousness of de Valera's and Lloyd George's comments about the Washington conference factor in the London negotiations must be read. Meanwhile in Washington, there was no Irish dimension to the US or British negotiating positions at the conference. The British delegation was pleased with the direction of the Washington conference. The *Gaelic American* commented that Hughes and Balfour had guaranteed 'the territorial integrity of the British empire and its mastery of the seas.'[83] By the beginning of December, when the Washington conference still had two more months to run, Balfour was so hopeful that British interests had been served that he seriously considered returning to London, as did Riddell.[84] Moreover, Balfour's sole

78 Ibid., pp. 129, 132, 133, 134.   79 NAI, D/FA, ES, 27/170, Boland to Brennan, 30 November 1921.   80 TNA, FO371/5622, Sylvester to Geddes, 4 November 1921; NAI, D/FA, ES, 27/159, de Valera to Boland, 29 November 1921.   81 Quoted in Costello, *The Irish revolution*, p. 263.   82 K. Middlemass (ed.), *Thomas Jones: Whitehall diary, volume 1, 1916–25*, 3 vols (1969), i, pp. 176–7.   83 *Gaelic American*, 26 November 1921.   84 TNA, FO371/5624, Hankey to Grigg, 3 December 1921; ibid., 371/5625, Lloyd George to Riddell, 13 December 1921.

query on 6 December, following the receipt of a telegram from Lloyd George with a synopsis of the Anglo-Irish treaty, was whether it would 'necessitate any change in [the] formula of quadruple treaty.' He congratulated Lloyd George on his achievement even though he was personally opposed to the treaty until the very end.[85] Another member of the British delegation in Washington was Maurice Hankey. Throughout November and December he corresponded with Thomas Jones, Lloyd George's private secretary, who sometimes acted as an intermediary between the two sides in the London negotiations. There is no evidence from that correspondence of any Irish dimension to the Washington discussions and, indeed, when Maurice Hankey, Cabinet secretaty, heard news of the signing of the Anglo-Irish treaty, he seemed genuinely surprised and cabled Jones 'the Irish news seems too good to be true ... it really is a marvellous achievement.'[86]

It is highly unlikely that Harding and Hughes would have disrupted the Washington proceedings over Irish issues. Instead both de Valera's and Lloyd George's remarks reflected their long-distance view of events in Washington and a certain paranoia arising out of the tense Anglo-Irish negotiations.[87] There is no evidence of a direct link between the Washington conference and proceedings in London.[88] For the Irish representatives on the ground in Washington, the conference in was a disappointment as they failed to achieve any of their aims. Indeed, US and British representatives developed a cordial relationship during the conference and even Harding's controversial reference to an 'association of nations' received a mixed reaction from the Dáil Éireann mission. Boland hoped

---

85 Ibid., FO371/5625, Lloyd George to Balfour, 6 December 1921; Balfour to Foreign Office, 9 December 1921; S.H. Zebel, *Balfour: a political biography* (1973), p. 274.   86 Middlemass, *Thomas Jones*, i, 7 December 1921, p. 184.   87 Throughout the period of the London negotiation, Geddes warned that along with the launch of the second bond drive, Irish extremists in America might be preparing for 'trouble-making' in Ireland. Similarly Armstrong in New York reported on 21 October, 4, 18 and 25 November on Sinn Féin preparations for gun-running to Ireland on the SS *JL Luckenbach*. TNA, FO371/5633, Geddes to Foreign Office, 29 November 1921; ibid., FO371/5653, Armstrong to Foreign Office, 21 October 1921, 4 November, 18 November 1921.   88 Ward, *Ireland and Anglo-American relations*, p. 252. Balfour's biographers make no link between the two sets of negotiations except to record his agreement with the settlement and his congratulations to Lloyd George. See B.E.C. Dugdale, *Arthur James Balfour: first earl of Balfour*, two vols (1939), ii, p. 149; S.H. Zebel, *Balfour: a political biography* (1973), p. 274; K. Young, *Arthur James Balfour: the happy life of the politician, prime minister, statesman and philosopher, 1848–1930* (1963). Neither is there any reference in the relevant Foreign Office files on the United States. Yet, many Irish-Americans believed that Harding played a part in producing the London settlement. A telegram from Redmond Kiernan on 7 December, said that the 'treaty must have had your approval' and that Harding must claim credit. Christian thanked him for his 'cordial expressions.' Undoubtedly US opinion was one of many factors influencing Lloyd George's decision to negotiate, others were the financial cost, the chaotic state of the military authorities, the lack of co-ordination between police and army, the underestimation of the IRA's military capacity, the futility of the counter-violence strategy and its impact on the British public. WGHP, Series 4, 1921–3, misc. files, roll 180, Presidential executive file 135, folder 3, Kiernan to Harding, 7 December 1921, Christian to Kiernan, 13 December 1921: K.O. Moran, *Consensus and disunity: The Lloyd George coalition government 1918–22* (1979), p. 131.

that the establishment of an 'association of nations' would provide the Irish republic with an opportunity to be independently represented but acknowledged that
a friendly US–British relationship at the heart of a new multilateral organization
was unwelcome.[89]

In mid to late November, Boland's strategy shifted firmly back to the Senate
and the fight for recognition of the republic; he hoped that Ireland's 'friends' in
the Senate might be of assistance again.[90] Geddes noticed that 'knowledge of the
cordial relations ... between the British and American delegations is beginning
to percolate through to the public and is causing utmost irritation in the German
and Irish camps.' He reported a renewal of 'virulent attacks' by the Friends and
AARIR on the Harding administration 'to bring [it] back to the more beaten
paths through pressure on the Senate and the House.' Democrat Senator William
King of Utah, warned a member of the British embassy staff that, when Congress
reassembled, they could expect several resolutions in favour of US recognition
of the republic of Ireland. Geddes warned that 'matters will require most delicate and careful handling if a closer relationship ... is to be evolved out of the
present favourable tendencies of the Administration.'[91] Once Congress reconvened the republican lobbying resumed, but there was a change in its force. On
22 November, the La Follette-sponsored a resolution simply expressed the hope
that the London negotiations would result in peace for Ireland and Britain and
begged the question if the British government 'recognised fully' the 'de facto'
status of the Dáil Éireann government then why could the US government not
do the same.[92] The wording was agreed beforehand between La Follette and
Frank P. Walsh. The resolution did not require any presidential action.[93] Geddes
cabled London on 29 November:

> During the last two days there have been distinct indications that the Irish
> extremists who have been on the whole quiescent during the Irish nego-

---

89 NAI, D/FA, ES, 27/170, Boland to Brennan, 30 November 1921. Geddes feared that Harding's
remark would be taken up by former opponents of the League of Nations in order to embarrass the
president and undermine the conference's work. He told the Foreign Office that the 'Irish and other
propagandists are already taking this line.' The FOIF had begun a campaign of 'virulent attacks'
on the Harding administration. TNA, FO371/5624, Geddes to Foreign Office, 30 November 1921;
ibid., 371/5625, Geddes to Curzon, 30 November 1921. Geddes kept the pressure on the State
Department also in relation to the Hoboken seizure. In November he sent three notes to Secretary
Hughes offering to provide witnesses and documentation in connection with indictments for the
Hoboken seizure case. NARA, RG59, M580/219, 841d.00/454, Hughes to Attorney General, 30
November 1921.   90 NAI, D/FA, ES, 27/170, Boland to Brennan, 30 November 1921.   91 TNA,
FO371/5625, Geddes to Curzon, 30 November 1921; BDFA, ix, The Washington conference and
its aftermath, 1921–25, Geddes to Curzon, 30 November 1921.   92 Congressional Record, 61, 9, 67th
congress, 1st session, 22 November 1921, p. 8117.   93 LC, MD, The La Follette Family Collection,
Robert La Follette (hereafter RF), series B, box 184, subject file Ireland 1921, part iii, Memorandum
for Senator La Follette. Senate Resolution on Peace Negotiations between Great Britain and Ireland;
ibid., box 94, Special correspondence, 1922, Frank P. Walsh, Walsh to La Follette, 8 January 1922.

tiations in London are again becoming active. Meetings are being held to raise funds for the republican movement. Energetic attempts are being made to embarrass [the US] administration regarding [the] conference. Statements are being circulated through the mail and published in the press that having captured the State Department, Great Britain is manipulating the conference ... in the past activity on their part has more than once preceded attempts at trouble-making in Ireland.[94]

Two days later, Armstrong reported from New York that the AARIR leaders were using all their influence with senators to gather support for the La Follette resolution.[95] The Foreign Office advised caution. William Tyrell described the situation as 'delicate' but believed that it was for the Americans 'to move in this matter, we should sit tight.'[96] He was proved correct.

At the same time, Harding began to receive AARIR-inspired letters and petitions requesting him to recognize the Irish republic, forwarded by politicians such as senators Lodge and Pomerene and Congressman Brennan. George Christian received the following advice from the State Department: 'write the usual letter.'[97] The standard reply stated that the 'present circumstances' were not opportune for Harding to receive a petition.[98] Even when the president came under pressure to meet fifty AARIR delegates, representing different parts of Ohio, his home state, he refused to do so.[99] And if he required evidence of support from Ohio for non-intervention on Ireland, he also received it. Patrick J. Shouvlin advised Harding against interfering in Ireland and James Witherow warned him that the 'Catholic Irish' were preparing to rush the La Follette resolution through Congress.[1] Despite the best efforts of Dáil and AARIR activists

---

94 TNA, FO371/5633, Geddes to Foreign Office, 29 November 1921. Ironically, between 28 November and 3 December, it was not the Irish republicans but the British government that threatened the Irish delegation with a return to war in Ireland, if it did not accept its final terms. See T. Wilson (ed.), *The political diaries of C.P. Scott, 1911–28* (1970), pp. 403, 407. 95 TNA, FO371/5654, Armstrong to Foreign Office, 2 December 1921. 96 Ibid., 371/5624, Geddes to Foreign Office, 30 November 1921, Seymour, 1 December 1921, Tyrell, 1 December 1921. 97 WGHP, Series 4, 1921–3, misc. files, roll 180, Presidential executive file 135, folder 3, Christian, 7 December 1921. 98 Ibid., Christian to Brennan, 6 December 1921, to Lodge, 6 December, to Pomerene, 3 December 1921. It is unlikely that La Follette forwarded to Harding the fifteen-page document present in his papers that constructed a scenario if the State Department was to become involved in Anglo-Irish negotiations. The anonymous document probably from the AARIR, suggested that the negotiations should take place in The Hague in the Netherlands and it concluded with the fictional scenario; 'A few minutes later the American minister was cabling Washington: First session Anglo-Irish peace conference just closed. Agreement along lines suggested by Department seems certain. Work begun on formulation treaty'. LC, MD, RF, series B, box 184, subject file Ireland, 1921, part 111, Ireland 1921, anonymous document. 99 WGHP, Series 4, 1921–3, misc. files, roll 180, Presidential executive file 135, folder 3, Congressman William Morgan to Harding, 5 December 1921, Christian to Morgan 6 December 1921. Other requests for meetings to present petitions came from Congressman A. Stephens, a member of the Committee on Naval Affairs, dated 6 December 1921. The standard reply was sent by Christian on 6 December. 1 Ibid., Newton Fairbanks to Harding, 5 December

in November and early December 1921, the existence of US–British amity at both a political and popular level ensured that they had little real chance to progress their political agenda in Congress or the White House.[2] Ironically events in London at the beginning of December 1921 completely altered the parameters of the recognition campaign.

Throughout late summer and autumn 1921, US consuls in Ireland had reported regularly to the State Department on the course of Anglo-Irish negotiations. In August, William Kent had not been fully supportive of the truce because it 'mocked and betrayed' the 'devoted forces of the crown.' He was also worried that, if the truce broke down, the 'men who were at the back of the murder conspiracy' would have to be rounded up again. At this time, Mason Mitchell in Queenstown was reporting that most southern Irish were 'favourable towards acceptance' of a settlement and had an 'aversion ... to again resort to force of arms' in the event that 'no settlement' was reached.[3] Dumont agreed, but added his usual caustic remark that 'de Valera is playing politics.' He maintained this pessimistic theme in subsequent reports and provided the insightful comment that 'no Irishman of good class, except a few intellectuals, is a member of the Dáil.'[4] By mid-October, fears of a breakdown in the negotiations were widespread throughout the country and reflected in the reporting. Kent exonerated the Ulster Unionists from any responsibility and held out little hope of a settlement.[5] Ambassador Harvey fanned the flames of fear of a resurgence in republican violence when he reported, at the end of November, that he had 'learnt confidentially' of a theft of arms from Windsor Barracks by 'Sinn Féiners.'[6]

As Ulster Unionist opposition, particularly on the issue of an all-Ireland parliament, intensified, Kent suggested that the Northern Ireland government was showing a responsible attitude when its ministry for Home Affairs took over the maintenance of law and order for the Ulster counties while Belfast city local authority 'took practical steps' to provide housing. This approval contrasted with his references to Sinn Féin, whose members were, he believed, associated with

---

1921; ibid., Nelson to Harding, 9 December 1921, Witherow to Nelson, 6 December 1921, Christian to Nelson, 10 December 1921.   2 It was on the grounds of US friendship with Britain that Senator Watson of Georgia objected to Senator Thomas J. Walsh's request to have inserted into the *Congressional Record* a resolution passed by Dáil Éireann on 17 August 1921, which expressed Irish gratitude to the US people for their 'warm support' in purchasing the bonds during the first Dáil loan drive. *Congressional Record*, 62, 1, 67th congress, 2nd session, 6 December 1921, p. 34.   3 NARA, RG59, M580/218, 841d 00/410, Kent to Secretary of State, 10 August 1921; ibid., M580/225, 841d.01/31, Mitchell to Secretary of State, 29 August 1921.   4 Ibid., M580/219, 841d 00/420, Dumont to Secretary of State, 18 August 1921; ibid., 841d.00/428, Dumont to Secretary of State, 24 August 1921. Dumont also provided a photograph of the first public session of Dáil Éireann on 16 August 1921 which he noted was reported on by journalists from several US newspapers. He left the consulate in autumn 1921 and no report was sent to the State Department between the end of August 1921 and early 1922. Ibid., M580/219.   5 Ibid., 841d.00/442, Kent to Secretary of State, 19 October 1921; ibid., 841d.00/452, Kent to Secretary of State, 16 November 1921.   6 Ibid., 841d.00/449, Harvey to Secretary of State, 23 November 1921.

'gunmen and bombers.'[7] The consul was attempting not only to confirm the ability and legitimacy of the northern government as a functioning unit but also to ensure that if the talks broke down blame would be laid at Sinn Féin's door. Kent's report on 7 December 1921, the day following the signing of the treaty, was cautious in tone because, he admitted, it was too early to 'estimate the effect of this agreement upon the public mind of Ulster or to forecast its action.' However, he noted as 'significant' Lord Birkenhead's remark that the choice offered Ulster was between 'idealism and material interests.' At this stage Kent thought that the proposed settlement appeared to the 'best solution possible.'[8] Mitchell was the first US consul to attempt to provide a synopsis of the salient points of the treaty for his administration, particularly in regard to the status of the proposed political unit, which he described as 'the Irish Free State ... similar to the Dominion of Canada ... it will include "Ulster" and will have full fiscal autonomy. Ulster will have the right to leave the state within one month.'[9] Harvey wrote to Harding, describing the settlement as a victory for Lloyd George and also for Birkenhead, the lord chancellor, who had broken with his Conservative Party colleagues when he signed the treaty.[10] Not everyone in the US, or indeed Ireland, saw it in such clear-cut, simplistic terms.

When the news of the treaty broke in the US, the Irish representatives in Washington and New York were inundated with inquiries by telephone and in person from ordinary people and journalists seeking information and views. Joseph Connolly, who had replaced Fawsitt as consul in New York, released a steadying message that outlined the facts but did not offer comment and urged a 'quiet waiting until all the issues were clear.' In Washington, Boland issued a statement welcoming the agreement that 'restores Ireland to the comity of nations.' Both men paid tribute to the Irish-American support.[11] Fitzpatrick and Carroll have detailed the American and Irish-American reaction to the news of the treaty. US newspapers' welcome of the settlement was noted by Geddes and Boland.[12] At first Cohalan denounced it and Devoy's *Gaelic American* called it a 'surrender.' Three days after the treaty was signed, the FOIF held a convention in the Hotel Astor in New York. It had been organized for weeks in advance and both men used it to back away from their opposition to the treaty, realizing by now that de Valera was against it.[13] In January 1922, after the Dáil approved the treaty and

7 Ibid., 841d.00/456, Kent to Secretary of State, 23 November 1921.   8 Ibid., 841d.00/461, Kent to Secretary of State, 7 December 1921.   9 Ibid., M580/245, 841d.01/47, Mitchell to Secretary of State, 7 December 1921.   10 WGHP, Series 4, 1920–3, Presidential Personal Files, roll 228, file 60, Harvey to Harding, 19 December 1921.   11 Gaughan, *Connolly*, pp. 222–3; Maher, *Boland*, pp. 167.   12 *BDFA*, i, Geddes to Curzon, 8 December 1921; D. Fitzpatrick, *Harry Boland's Irish revolution* (2003), p. 256; Carroll, *American opinion*, pp. 177–83; *Irish Independent*, 6, 9, 11 January 1922. 13 American Irish Historical Society (hereafter AIHS), New York, US, Daniel F. Cohalan Papers (hereafter DFCP), 'Biographical note'; M. Doorley, *Irish-American diaspora nationalism, 1916–35* (2005), pp. 141–17; T. Golway, *Irish rebel: John Devoy and America's fight for Ireland's freedom* (1998), pp. 298–9.

positions were clearer, the Friends and the Devoy wing of Clan na Gael accepted that the Irish Free State was a 'stepping stone to the great dream of a republic.'[14]

Boland's position was similarly clarified in the days after the treaty announcement. By Thursday, 8 December, his response had become more cautious. In the evening, along with O'Mara, he met with wealthy Irish-Americans, AARIR leaders and sympathetic politicians. The Irish republicans' speeches betrayed their disappointment and reservations about the settlement but neither rejected it outright.[15] At the dinner there was great rejoicing and the senators 'sang hallelujahs.' Senator Thomas J. Walsh noted that 'it was the unanimous opinion that the agreement brought substantial freedom to Ireland and ought to be accepted.' Furthermore, he felt that Irish-Americans should not encourage opposition to it while they were safe in the US. On 17 December, the AARIR National Executive met with more than a hundred delegates, representing almost every state, and endorsed the treaty. Doheny said he 'was delighted with the result of the Irish peace negotiations' and Frank P. Walsh thought 'it was a big step forward.'[16] Doheny now believed the AARIR's task to have been completed but others did not.

As more details of the treaty emerged, the republican movement divided. Some accepted membership of the commonwealth, the oath of allegiance to the British crown, British military and naval presence in Irish ports, a twenty-six county state and the promise of a boundary commission to examine the border while others would accept nothing less than a thirty-two county independent republic. Supporters and opponents of the treaty emerged during the parliamentary debates in late December and early January until the Dáil voted on 7 January 1922 to ratify the treaty by sixty-four votes in favour and fifty-seven against (including those of the recently-returned Harry Boland, Stephen O'Mara and Mary MacSwiney). De Valera resigned as president and removed his supporters from the Dáil. The refusal of a large section of Sinn Féin and the IRA to accept the settlement laid the foundations of the civil war that was to follow six months later. In Britain, despite Conservative opposition, the treaty was ratified by an act of parliament on 31 March 1922.

The Harding administration did not issue a public statement in response to the announcement of the Anglo-Irish treaty, although an article in the pro-treaty *Irish Independent* implied that the president favoured its ratification. In Dublin, acting US Consul Charles A. Bay met with Michael Collins in City Hall and

14 Golway, *Irish rebel*, p. 301; J.J. Splain, '"Under which King?" The tragic-comedy of President de Valera's errors in the United States' in W.G. Fitzgerald (ed.), *The voice of Ireland: a survey of the race and nation from all angles, by the foremost leaders at home and abroad* (1923), pp. 253–4. 15 Fitzpatrick, *Harry Boland*, pp. 257–8; R.F. Downing, 'Men, women and memories. A review of thirty years' sympathy and labour for the Irish cause' in Fitzgerald (ed.), *The voice of Ireland*, p. 221. 16 Quoted in Carroll, *American opinion*, p. 180; Maher, *Boland*, pp. 165–7. The American Committee for Relief in Ireland was not wedded to the republican side, ACRI quickly defended the treaty as the best hope for social stability in Ireland. Carroll, *American opinion*, p. 182.

congratulated the provisional government.[17] Nonetheless, it was not until October 1922 that Secretary Hughes asked his officials to clarify the position of the new Irish entity, which will be examined later in this chapter. This is not to say that the developments in Ireland were ignored. The central concerns for State Department officials related to firstly, the effect of the treaty on its diplomatic relationship with the British government, secondly, the impact it would have on the Irish-American public and, finally, whether it would lead to protests and agitation. From 6 December onwards State Department officials in Washington noted the ratification process of the treaty, beginning with the approval of the British parliament on 16 December 1921 and that of Dáil Éireann on 7 January 1922. Both the treaty and the new Irish Free State constitution were validated and approved by the 'Provisional Government' in Dublin on 21 September 1922. William Castle accepted that the Irish Free State had the same 'constitutional status with the community of nations known as the British empire' as the dominions of Canada or Australia.[18] In other words, on Irish matters the US government would continue to deal with the British ambassador in Washington, at least until otherwise requested by the British government and monarch. At an informal level, as will be seen, representatives of the new Irish Free State were received by State Department officials though they may not always have been welcome visitors.

If the State Department and the British embassy had hoped the treaty would signal the disappearance of Irish agitation in the US they were to be disappointed. On 8 December, two days after the announcement of the treaty, Geddes wrote,

> There are already signs that there may possibly be a half-hearted demand amongst extremists for the establishment of an Irish diplomatic representative in Washington accompanied perhaps by a continued, if attenuated, demand for complete independence of Ireland. Such echoes will arouse no echoes amongst representative American opinion, which since negotiations started has been deeply impressed by the attitude of His Majesty's Government, and regards settlement as a signal triumph for statesmanlike compromise.[19]

Geddes was warning the Foreign Office against complacency. Horace Seymour and William Tyrell in the Foreign Office agreed with him, but the latter hoped that Irish extremists would have 'less sympathy … on the part of the general public.'[20] This was true but the experienced Geddes later identified two reasons why Irish agitation would never disappear fully. Firstly, he believed there was

---

17 *Irish Independent*, 11 January 1922; *Irish Times, Irish Independent*, 14 February 1922.   18 NARA, RG59, M580/219, 841d.01/54, Castle, October 1922.   19 *BDFA*, i, Geddes to Curzon, 8 December 1921.   20 TNA, FO371/5715, Geddes to Foreign Office, 8 December 1921; ibid., Seymour, 9 December, Tyrell, 9 December 1921.

such a thing as the '"habit"' of opposition and he felt that it was 'so highly developed' amongst the Irish-Americans, especially in so far as anything British was concerned, that it would probably persist. A second reason was that US politicians wishing to secure or retain 'Irish votes' always exercised the 'utmost caution' to avoid earning a reputation of being in the 'slightest degree "pro-British" in sentiment.'[21] As Geddes had predicted, the congressional debates on the Washington treaties provided the next opportunity to test these reasons.

The Harding administration had successfully resisted AARIR, Friends and Dáil mission pressure to recognize the First Dáil and to interfere in Anglo-Irish negotiations throughout the period July to December 1921. Its own policy of non-interference in Ireland and that inherited from Wilson remained intact. Nor was there any real pressure to act on Ireland from within Congress. Yet, many Irish-Americans believed that Harding had intervened. In fact Harding's respect for the British government had increased over the course of the Washington conference. To the Harding administration, the Anglo-Irish treaty meant little in reality, except that it intensified the hope that republican agitation on recognition and fund-raising might cease. In early 1922, having signed the bill establishing the World War Foreign Debt Commission, Harding's main foreign policy concern was to secure congressional approval for the Washington treaties.[22] It remained to be seen whether the previous alliance that defeated Wilson's peace settlement would emerge again.

The treaties and making of peace in the US and Ireland

On 6 February 1922, Harding addressed the closing session of the Washington conference. The resulting five-power treaty limited the sea power of the US, Britain and Japan according to an agreed formula, the four-power treaty replaced the Anglo–Japanese alliance and the nine-power treaty, which enshrined the open door principle into international law and guaranteed the territorial integrity of China, went to the Senate.[23] The main sources of opposition to the disarmament conference, namely the Hearst press, the Friends and the AARIR/Dáil mission, again attempted to block the passage of the treaties.

In early 1922, a poll of newspapers by the *Literary Digest* indicated that the majority of newspapers favoured ratification. It was concluded that the 'people are more significantly united on the proposals of the conference than they have been on any similar issue.' The Hearst press were the sole organs of opposition.

21 *BDFA*, xiv, Annual Report for the United States (hereafter Annual Report) for 1922, p. 7.   22 P.R. Moran (ed.), *Warren G. Harding, 1865–1923: chronology – documents – bibliographical aids* (1970), pp. 10–11.   23 W. LaFeber, *The American age: United States foreign policy at home and abroad since 1896*, 2 vols (1989), ii, pp. 340–1.

Buckely's analysis of the coverage by the *San Francisco Examiner*, Hearst's favourite newspaper, reveals a persistent theme; the four-power treaty would weaken the US navy and strengthen the British and Japanese navies.[24] This message was much less effective in late 1921 and early 1922 than it had been in 1919, because there was a pro-British climate due to the Anglo-Irish treaty and, more significantly, because of British support for disarmament. The Irish-inspired opposition faced the same hurdle and a further one; the divisive impact of the London treaty.

One immediate result was that the direction and leadership provided by the Dáil mission was weakened. Harry Boland and Seán Nunan returned to Ireland at the end of 1921, leaving Connolly in New York, and Begley and Pedlar in Washington, as the sole agents of the republic in the US. Connolly and Begley dedicated themselves firstly, to keeping the Irish-Americans united behind the pro-treaty forces, particularly the AARIR, in order to maintain an unbroken line of unity in the US ranks of the republican movement, secondly, to dissuading the AARIR leadership from interfering in the on-going Dáil debates on the Anglo-Irish treaty and thirdly, to fending off inquiries from Wall Street investors, who were 'very much alive and very keen on placing money in Ireland.' Connolly warned Michael Collins on 12 December 1921 that 'they are ... so insistent and occasionally so insidious that I feel every precaution should be taken to prevent exploitation.'[25] Connolly received no direction from the dividing department of Foreign Affairs until 13 February 1922, when he was told by an unnamed official, perhaps Acting Secretary Joseph Walshe, 'If you see work to be done which nobody else is doing, fire away and do it.'[26] For these reasons Connolly had little time to organize opposition to the Washington treaties and neither had Begley in Washington.

Begley's survey of the political situation in Washington in early March devoted most attention to American and Irish-American attitudes to the London treaty. On the subject of the four-power treaty he noted in passing that 'the fight ... is now under way in the senate and strong opposition has developed' but that 'it is the general opinion here that the measure will go through early in May if not before.'[27] Securing support for the London treaty consumed most of Begley's time and he had resigned himself to the passage of the Washington treaty. There was no reference to Irish-American agitation or to his activity on the matter. Nor would it be a priority for the in-coming Timothy Smiddy, who replaced Boland as official representative of Dáil Éireann in March 1922. Smiddy's instructions

---

24 Buckley, *The United States and the Washington conference*, pp. 172–3.   25 Gaughan, *Connolly*, pp. 224–5; NAI, D/FA, ES, 27/158, Connolly to Collins, 12 December 1921.   26 NAI, D/FA, ES, 30/195, Unnamed official in Foreign Affairs to Connolly, 13 February 1922. By this stage, the department was in a state of confusion as the government split was mirrored in the division in the nascent diplomatic service. Charles Gavan Duffy replaced George Plunkett as minister for Foreign Affairs, Robert Brennan, the under secretary, sided with de Valera and resigned to be replaced by Joseph Walshe. *DIFP*, i, pp. xii–xiii.   27 NAI, D/FA, ES, 28/176, Begley, 6 March 1922.

from the pro-treaty minister for foreign affairs, Charles Gavan Duffy, contained no mention of the Washington treaties but emphasized the importance of uniting Irish-Americans and getting them solidly behind the pro-treaty Irish government and its policies.[28] There were sound financial and political reasons why Irish representatives on both sides should focus on uniting Irish-America. At a meeting on 4 February 1922, the AARIR National Executive met in New York and overruled the resolution of 17 December 1921 and AARIR members were given the choice of contributing to the Irish Republican Defence Fund or being expelled from the organization. The AARIR had split and its membership declined from its high point of 750,000 to 75,000 in 1922, with the majority supporting the Irish Free State.[29] While the AARIR underwent this internal process of re-alignment, it was left to the quiescent pro-treaty FOIF to oppose the Washington treaties.

Before its Washington convention in February 1922, Cohalan informed Lindsay Crawford, the Sinn Féin representative in Canada,

> We will continue to be uncompromising in favour of absolute independence … we are having a very important conference in Washington … to see if the people cannot be aroused against these proposed treaties in the same way in which they were awakened against the League of Nations. It will be difficult to do it with the same measure of success, but I think it can be done.[30]

At its convention the FOIF reaffirmed its 'America first and then Ireland' priorities. It was committed to pre-empting British interference in US concerns and protecting US sovereignty which resulted in its close co-operation with, and links to, the All American National Council.[31] Cohalan penned a pamphlet titled *Senator Lodge: past and present* for the council, in which he insisted that the Washington treaties 'embroiled the United States in Europe, in the balance of power and the fate of dynasties' and turned it into a 'a colony once again.'[32] Cohalan's expectations of the Republican administration in regard to progressing the Irish cause were well and truly dissipated by now, as were Devoy's. The latter commented that Harding's foreign policy 'is infinitely worse and more dan-

---

28 Ibid., 30/199, Gavan Duffy to Smiddy, 10 March 1922. Smiddy was asked to broach the issue of Irish membership of the League of Nations which was so forcefully opposed by Irish-America during the Wilson years and to make contact with representatives of other British dominions. He was not asked to pursue the repayment of debt issue even though under article five of the 1921 treaty the Irish Free State assumed 'liability for the service of the Public Debt of the United Kingdom.' Ibid.; *DIFP*, i, Final text of the articles of agreement for a treaty signed between Great Britain and Ireland, p. 357. 29 Downing, 'Men, women and memories', pp. 221–2. The 'American Friends of the Irish Republic' was established. 30 AIHS, DFCP, box 3, folder 16, Correspondence, Lindsay Crawford, Cohalan to Crawford, 23 February 1922. 31 Splain, '"Under which King?"', p. 254. 32 AIHS, DFCP, box 8, folder 11, Correspondence, H.C. Lodge, April 1922, D.F. Cohalan, *Senator Lodge: past and present* (1922).

gerous to American interests than Wilson's invective was.'[33] In early 1922, the Friends lobbied senators to reject the four-power and later the five-power treaties on the grounds that they would emasculate the US battleship force and make the US a 'mere vassal of England.'[34] Once the Washington treaties arrived in the Senate, the Friends hoped to find common ground with enough senators to defeat them, as it had done on the League of Nations issue.

Hughes left the country for a holiday in Bermuda and on 10 February, Harding appeared before the Senate asking for ratification of the conference treaties. Soon after he left the chamber, two of the 'outstanding figures' on the US delegation took up the task of ensuring their safe passage.[35] Lodge denied that the treaties involved any surrender of sovereignty, national interest or Senate prerogatives. He had a majority in Congress but required two-thirds of the vote for the treaties to be approved.[36] His co-delegate, the Democrat Senator Underwood, emphasized the strong public support for Senate approval. Harding wrote to Harvey in London, 'I am hoping, very much, that we shall have the sanction of the Senate, to our conference agreements before the 10th March.'[37] It was soon clear that the main target of opposition would be the four-power treaty. Following the approval of the Yap treaty, which gave title over the Pacific mandates to the Japanese government, on 1 March, it emerged that a shift of four or five votes might result in the defeat of the four-power treaty.[38]

Harding's optimism about a quick passage of the treaty soon dissipated. The Senate Foreign Relations Committee and the Senate floor became the centres for most of the key debates. Among its main detractors were senators Borah, Johnson and Reed who had criticized the treaty prior to its submission to Congress and had revived anti-League of Nations arguments. Reed jibed at Lodge, 'I remember that another President had a plan and insisted that it was America's plan and he, too, I suppose, thought it ought not to fail. Yet, with all the sagacity he possessed, the Senator from Massachusetts sought to bring that to failure because it was wrong.'[39] Nor could Johnson and Borah accept that the Japanese and British governments would give up the advantages of the Anglo–Japanese alliance for the agreement. They believed that there must have been another secret deal between the US and Britain. They also suggested that the treaty undermined the US government's freedom to go to war because it would have to confer with the other signatories.[40] The figure of Ambassador Harvey also became a target for

33 *Gaelic American*, 15 April 1922.   34 Carroll, 'Friends of Irish Freedom' in M. Funchion (ed.), *Irish American voluntary organizations* (1983), p. 125; *Gaelic American*, 3 December 1921.   35 WGHP, Series 4, 1920–3, Presidential Personal Files, roll 228, file 60, Harding to Harvey, 15 December 1921.   36 Murray, *The Harding era*, p. 158; A.J. Ward, *Ireland and Anglo-American relations, 1899–1921* (1969), p. 253.   37 WGHP, Series 4, 1920–3, Presidential Personal Files, roll 228, file 60, Harding to Harvey, 18 February 1922.   38 Buckley, *The United States and the Washington conference*, p. 178. The three Republican senators who voted against the Yap treaty were Borah, Joseph Irwin and Hiram Johnson. Robert La Follette was one of four absent. Ibid., p. 178, n. 29.   39 Quoted in Murray, *The Harding era*, p. 160.   40 Buckley, *The United States and the Washington*

the opponents of the treaties, who argued that the British or Japanese had drafted the treaty rather than the US delegation. Consequently, the London-based Harvey was attacked by senators Reed and Harrison and in Hearst's newspapers as the culprit in this scenario on the grounds that he was 'pro-British.' There were calls for his resignation, which he felt served only to strengthen his position and influence with Curzon. The president reassured Harvey that the importance of his critics had 'been discounted long ago' and he once again praised 'our British friends.'[41] Harding's private sentiments would not have endeared him or the treaty to his opponents, including the Friends.

The FOIF was small in numbers and within Congress operated through Cohalan's Senate contacts but its message was simple. By mid-March, its argument that the treaties were pro-British was 'so vocal' that Democrat Senator John Williams of Mississippi, who supported Wilsonianism, attacked the organization from the Senate floor. During the debates on 14 and 15 March, he fumed that these 'newborn hyphenated Americans come up and tell me what is "American" and "un-American" … what they mean was something "un-Irish" and we might just as well be plain about it.' This suggestion that the FOIF was more Irish than American revived the wartime disloyalty charges made against Cohalan.[42] Harding became worried about the possible fate of the Washington treaties. He complained to Harvey on 22 March 1922,

> You understand, of course, what impels the disagreeable oratory. It is wholly the feeling that the friendly relations of this country to Great Britain are inimical to Irish interests and, therefore, unlikely to be helpful in appealing to the Irish vote in this country. The situation is made apparent from many angles. It has even led some of our good friends to wobble a bit in the senate in dealing with the four-power treaty which is to come to a vote on Friday of this week.[43]

He need not have worried. The supporters of the treaties were well organized and their arguments outweighed those of their opponents. Firstly, all members of Harding's administration supported the treaties and availed of every opportunity to praise them. Secondly, a committee for treaty ratification canvassed

conference, p. 179.   41 WGHP, Series 4, 1920–3, Presidential Personal Files, roll 228, file 60, Harvey to Harding, 10 March 1922, Harding to Harvey, 22 March 1922, 14 June 1922; ibid., Harvey, 18 February 1922. The controversial Harvey had adapted well to ambassadorial life, even writing a gushing letter to Harding describing the opening of parliament in early February 1922 and detailing King George V's role as 'done handsomely, even splendidly, as well befitted the head of this great empire.' Also he came to admire Arthur Balfour, who returned to London to effectively take over running the Foreign Office from the ill Curzon. WGHP, Series 4, 1920–3, Presidential Personal Files, roll 228, file 60, Harvey to Harding, 7 February 1922.   42 Buckley, *The United States and the Washington conference*, p. 173; E. Cuddy, '"Are the Bolsheviks any worse than the Irish?": ethno-religious conflict in America during the 1920s', 20–1.   43 WGHP, Series 4, 1920–3, Presidential Personal Files, roll 228, file 60, Harding to Harvey, 22 March 1922.

public opinion on the treaties and reported to Congress that they had the support of the churches, civic organizations, educational institutions, pacifist groups, women's groups and the labour movement.[44] Thirdly, the president had overestimated the extent to which Irish and Irish-American republicans were in a position to exploit the Irish factor with congressional politicians, even though congressional elections were due in November 1922. Cohalan and the Friends' anti-British rhetoric did not evoke sufficient support from the wider Irish-American public, or from Ireland's 'friends' in the Senate, to re-create the front that had defeated the League of Nations. Both Lodge and Underwood maintained control over their troops.

In the final Senate vote on 24 March on the four-power treaty, 67 senators (35 Republican and 12 Democrats) voted for ratification and 27 voted against (23 Democrats and 4 Republicans). The 4 dissenting Republicans were senators Borah, Johnson, La Follette and Joseph I. France of Maryland, all sympathetic to the Irish cause. Johnson believed noted that if Wilson had sent the treaty to the Senate, there would have been 40 Republican votes against it instead of 4.[45] But it was not. It had been sent by a president whose bipartisan congressional policy combined with public support to outweigh the disparate opposition. From the beginning of the Senate discussions, Lodge and Underwood had co-operated to secure its passage. Secondly, Harding, unlike Wilson, was willing to compromise and accept the Brandegee reservation which calmed concerns about collective action. Thirdly, in Begley's words, the senators' action reflected 'the general attitude of the American people [which] seems to be entirely in favour of the disarmament treaties. They have had enough of war.'[46]

Despite the victory, Hughes and Harding had learnt a lesson. In a letter to a friend, Judge Hiscock, Hughes wrote on 24 March,

> I am at a loss to understand how those who have attained the high position of Senator can permit themselves to indulge in reckless characterization of other peoples and to manifest in a manner so injurious to the conduct of our foreign relations their opposition to the work of the conference. There is certainly cause for anxiety when the results of the most earnest endeavour under American auspices came so near to defeat at the hands of the senate.[47]

By 1 April, the five-power treaty, including the armaments limitations, had been endorsed by the Senate. All resistance had collapsed. Harding acknowledged that there had been a fight and that 'Irish interests' and the 'Irish vote' existed but

---

44 Buckley, *The United States and the Washington conference*, pp. 174–5. Some naval experts opposed it but did not do so in public, while Samuel Gompers, the AFL leader was later shocked to discover the level of unemployment that resulted from a reduction in naval construction. Ibid.   45 Quoted in Murray, *The Harding era*, pp. 160–1.   46 NAI, D/FA, ES, 28/176, Begley, 6 March 1922.   47 Quoted in Pusey, *Charles Evans Hughes*, i, p. 500.

he had won. Certainly, the links survived from the Wilson days between the Irish, Irish-Americans, irreconcilables and other Democrats. But in 1922 Irish-American voters were just as swayed by disarmament arguments as any other ethnic group and, at the same time, they were divided on the Anglo-Irish treaty. Harding had little or nothing to fear from their political influence.

The Washington conference and the passage of the treaties was regarded by Harding as the zenith of his administration's efforts in foreign policy, even though an enforcement procedure had not been built into the treaties and the US remained psychologically and politically aloof from international entanglements such as the League of Nations or Genoa conference.[48] At the end of April 1922, with all the Washington treaties successfully through Congress, Harding was satisfied with 'our position at the moment in relation to the remainder of the world.'[49] The arms race was apparently under control, the state of hostility between the US and its world war one adversaries had been ended, the Anglo–Japan alliance had been untangled and Harding's lenient approach to the question of war debts was accepted by the Senate. None of it was palatable for Cohalan who wrote, in May 1922, that Harding 'found us first among equals and he has made us almost as dependent on England's will as any of her colonies.'[50]

In his domestic policy, Harding could point to reduced taxes, increased tariffs, more assistance and protection for farmers and restricted immigration. But voters were unhappy about Harding's handling of the coal and railroad strikes and his vetoing, on 19 September 1922, with Senate backing, of a bill that would have given war veterans a bonus. The Republican Party's links to big business sat uneasily with some who had voted for him in 1920, including disaffected Democrats. The *Gaelic American* commented 'the financial interests secured immediate control of Harding,'[51] while Dáil Éireann envoys were concerned about US big business from another perspective.

---

48 In his opening speech to the Washington conference, Harding had referred to the meeting as a prelude to an 'association of nations' and later in November he referred to 'annual meetings' of such an organization. But in the face of revived anti-League of Nations opposition particularly from Borah and Johnson along with no encouragement from Hughes, he soon left the matter die. Harry Boland's hope that Ireland would gain recognition of its republican status at such an organization, therefore, was dashed also. Neither did Harding attend the Genoa conference on the economic reconstruction of central and eastern Europe held on 10 April 1922, instead Ambassador Child attended as an 'unofficial observer.' This international forum merited little or no attention from the FOIF or the Irish mission representatives as another forum to get recognition for the republic. However, the Friends of the Irish Free State in New York city sent a round-robin letter on 10 February 1922 to Harding and others, seeking assistance to help the Irish Free State 'to take her place among the nations of the earth at Genoa.' The letter was filed in Harding's office. Murray, *The Harding era*, p. 351; WGHP, Series 4, 1921–3, misc. files, roll 180, Presidential executive file 135, folder 3, FOIFS to Harding, 10 February 1922.   49 WGHP, Series 4, 1920–3, Presidential Personal Files, roll 228, file 60, Harding to Harvey, 24 April 1922.   50 *Gaelic American*, 20 May 1922.   51 *Gaelic American*, 13 May 1922.

Economic opportunities in the emerging new state

After the signing of the Anglo-Irish treaty, it was the Harding administration's relationship to economic and financial interests, namely Wall Street bankers and producers that provided one context for Washington's ties to Ireland. The link between the Republican Party and business groups has been documented elsewhere. Suffice it to say that secretaries Hughes and Hoover co-operated with private individuals who provided loans to foreign governments and protected US manufacturers' dominant position within certain markets such as rubber, coffee and potash. So long as US dollars were not given to America's enemies or spent on war industries, but were instead granted to allies and friends, private enterprise had official endorsement. The cry that 'Wall Street ran the government' and, specifically the State Department, led Francis Huntington Wilson, the former under secretary of State, to note that 'any student of modern diplomacy knows that in these days of competition, capital, trade, agriculture, labour and state craft all go hand in hand if a country is to profit.'[52] There was great scope for the expansion of trade between the United States and Ireland in both directions. In 1919, Ireland's total exports had been £176 million of which £174 million went direct to Britain and the rest to other countries, particularly the United States. More than half of the total exports were agricultural products, particularly animals, food, drink and tobacco. Of the manufactured goods, more than half were linens, most of which went to Britain for the home market or re-export and to the United States. In terms of imports, £132 million came from Britain and £26 million from other countries, mainly the United States and Canada.[53] In 1921 and 1922, against a background of difficult conditions, US and Irish representatives on both sides of the Atlantic attempted to increase these economic ties.

US consular reports from Ireland regularly noted openings for US investment for example, the burning of Cork city and the development of hydro-electricity.[54] However, during the Anglo-Irish war there were concerns within the State Department about co-operating in business which might 'conceivably cause trouble' with Britain. But it was not considered to be a 'sufficient reason to hold back' from supporting the judgement of the consular officers in such matters.[55] The signing of the treaty did not make it any easier for the consuls to expand US trade with Ireland and neither were they too interested in doing so once the

52 LaFeber, *The American age*, ii, pp. 341–2.   53 NARA, RG59, M580/219, 841d.00/462, Kent to Secretary of State, 14 December 1921.   54 Ibid., M580/248, 841d.6463/1, Kettle to Dumont, 30 July 1921. The expanding US communications industry had included Ireland in its network also by late 1921. On 28 November 1921, the State Department presented a licence for Harding's signature for the International Telephone company to operate a cable between San Juan, Ireland, Washington, Vancouver and British Columbia and others from the Bell Telephone company and New York Telephone company. WGHP, Series 4, 1921–3, Secretary of State, roll 144 file 20 folder 7, 28 November 1921.   55 NARA, RG59, M580/248, 841d.6463/1, Castle, 3 September 1921; ibid., Carr to Dumont, 5 October 1921. Hoover recommended A.J.J. Fifer of London for the work.

civil war started on 28 June 1922. Kent's economic reports focused less on openings for US trade and investment in Ireland and more on presenting the Ulster unionist argument supporting the 'economic inter-dependence' of the British and Irish economies and suggesting the dangers of breaking that link.[56] John Gamon arrived in Cobh (formerly Queenstown) in early 1922 and devoted the following year to collecting commercial and trading information, rather than actually promoting trade.[57] It was only after March 1923 that US consuls in the new Irish Free State became active on the commercial front. This is explored in chapter twelve along with the impact of the US tariff wall.

Unsurprisingly, the signing of the treaty produced a different situation for the Dáil Éireann representatives. Connolly had been surprised to find in October 1921 a network of shipping companies, importers, exporters and agents in place, all linking the US and Ireland. He quickly settled into developing these trading links, pursuing business contracts and negotiating deals. He and his staff of seven secured valuable contracts for Irish exporters, although they also experienced many problems on the Irish side. Irish suppliers were often slow in handling correspondence or in giving detailed answers to queries. Another difficulty was that shipping agents in Ireland failed to properly pack and despatch their goods as well as to include all the documents necessary to ensure quick and orderly delivery of the goods to the US. Problems with the varying quality and delivery of butter exports to the US and the discovery that 150 barrels of herrings contained whiskey led to Connolly publicly warning Irish authorities that they might lose US markets and lead to longer customs delays. Connolly recalled that it was almost impossible to get Irish shippers to realize that the US importers were 'exacting', that they were used to getting their goods in 'proper' condition and that the US port authorities did not release the goods unless the necessary documents were available. He felt that despite these irritations and although the Irish mission was not officially recognized by the US administration, his office was steadily gaining ground and influence, whether or not it was increasing trade.[58] The signing of the treaty, however, increased the number of queries from US investors, although in the short term it diverted Connolly and Begley's attention from economic to political matters.

As early as 12 December Connolly cabled Michael Collins, minister for Finance, in Dublin: 'Finance offers. Advise no action being taken pending inquiries and advice from here.' That same day he had received numerous inquires regarding investments in Ireland. One was from Farson sons and company, offering to underwrite a loan of $20 million to the new state, which led him to telegraph Collins directly. Connolly felt that 'Wall Street is very much alive and very keen on placing money in Ireland' but he warned against US

---

56 Ibid., M580/219, 841d.00/462, Kent to Secretary of State, 14 December 1921.   57 NARA, RG59, Inspection reports on foreign service posts (hereafter IRFSP), Cobh, Ireland, May 1924, p. 30.   58 Gaughan, *Connolly*, pp. 212–13; *Irish Independent*, 6 February, 24 May 1922.

exploitation of the unstable situation. Until early December 1921, his policy had been to tell US inquirers that he had no official direction, that peace was not an 'established fact' and that they ought to go 'very slow.' Other reasons influenced his cautious approach, specifically the view that 'quite a number of these people imagine that the whole Irish race is pauperized and that we can do nothing for ourselves without Wall Street money.'⁵⁹ Previously, the astute consul had pointed out to Ernest Blythe, minister for Trade and Commerce, that 'Wall Street's activities in Cuba and Poland are likely to result in much evil for those countries.'⁶⁰ He worried about the power of the 'almighty' dollar in Ireland, fearing that US financial investment might open the door to US control of the new Irish state. But it was not surprising that US business people should view Ireland as an opportunity for investment, given the constant fund-raising and bond drives which the republican movement had engaged in since 1918 and the attendant publicizing of British destruction of Irish resources.⁶¹ One of the reasons why the newly-established Friends of the Irish Free State (FOIFS) had appealed to Harding, in February 1922, for recognition of the Irish Free State was that as well as bringing about 'peace and harmony', the US would be able to help develop the resources of the Irish Free State.⁶² The chairman of the FOIFS at this time was Senator Royal S. Copeland and the secretary was Francis J. Lowe and among its board of governors were Daniel B. O'Neill of the Cunard Line company, Alexander Steele of the American Oil corporation, and John S. Lewis, a publisher.⁶³

Lewis had met Harding in Ohio some years previously. By April 1922 he had considerable work on hand 'in connection with the development of ... commerce' with the new Free State and, in a letter to Harding on 10 April, he stated 'it appears that the United States obtains less than 1 per cent of this trade which

---

59 NAI, D/FA, ES, 27/158, Connolly to Collins, 12 December 1921.   60 Ibid. Also at this time Connolly cautioned intending Irish emigrants against travelling to the US because of unemployment. *Cork Examiner*, 17 January 1922.   61 Gaughan, *Connolly*, pp. 225–6; *Irish Independent*, 25 February 1922. The American belief in the 'power of the dollar' caused Connolly further annoyance. Some time after the treaty was signed, McGarrity suggested to Doheny that half a million dollars should be raised, 'send each of the parties an equal half of the fund to run the election and then let the Dáil get together and decide their future.' Connolly thought the suggestion not just 'fantastic but quite ridiculous.' He argued that money had 'no bearing whatever on the issue and could have no effect on the minds and outlook of the members of the Dáil.' He refused to be involved in McGarrity's approach to Doheny and the scheme was eventually dropped but he was left bewildered 'to try and think how they could imagine that dollars had or could have the slightest influence on the position at home.' Ibid.   62 WGHP, Series 4, 1921–3, misc. files, roll 180, Presidential executive file 135, folder 3, FIFS to Harding, 10 February 1922.   63 NAI, Department of the Taoiseach (hereafter D/T), S series files (hereafter S), 2246, Armstrong to Secretary of State, 8 February 1923 forwarded to Healy by Devonshire, 5 March 1923. Armstrong reported Lowe's involvement to the Foreign Office. Suspicion of such plans led Robert Monteith, an 'Easter week exile', to believe that American 'moneyed and capitalist interests' supported the Anglo-Irish treaty in order to 'permit American investment in and exploitation of the new Irish state.' Carroll, *American opinion*, p. 183.

runs over a billion and a half dollars a year.' He was 'reliably informed' that Harding was about to appoint a 'Trade Commissioner of the Irish Free State' and he stated his support for his friend and FOIFS colleague, Lowe, who had been endorsed by some of the largest manufacturing concerns in the United States. The president's office immediately sought direction from Hoover's office.[64]

In the interim, Lowe had written to Harding on 17 March 1922 to request the appointment as trade commissioner because he wanted to undertake a study of the Irish trade situation. He included his passport to have it stamped with his commission. C.H. Huston, the acting secretary of Commerce, replied on 28 March, that his department was not planning to take on an additional man for trade promotion work in Ireland. Huston explained that the staff in the London embassy were equipped to do the work and that there was a shortage in funds to employ additional trade representatives.[65] However, Lowe did not give up and indicated to Huston that not only did he have influential commercial connections but he would be able to get sufficient congressional support for a special bill to establish the position.[66] The latter was news to Huston, who replied on 12 April that the Commerce appropriations bill had already been passed by Congress and a special bill would encounter difficulties in view of the enormous legislative programme confronting Congress. He would contact him again if such a bill were passed.[67] Hoover endorsed this response in a letter to Harding's secretary, George Christian, on 22 April. Ever mindful of securing new trade openings and despite criticism over his endorsement of the relief project, Hoover added that, if Congress voted funds, his department would be 'only too glad to send a man to Ireland as soon as conditions seem to warrant the expenditure.'[68]

Although it seemed that Lowe was interested in expanding trading links between the US and Ireland, he was also motivated by having previously been refused entry to the consular service.[69] Nevertheless, his request demonstrates that there was a certain level of interest within commercial circles in expanding American–Irish trading links and it was mirrored by a similar request from Clemens J. France of the American Committee for Relief in Ireland. Within two weeks of the signing of the Anglo-Irish treaty in December 1921, France wanted the US government to help stabilize the Irish situation by upgrading the US consular representative in Dublin to a consul general 'with broad powers' to strengthen the commercial ties between Ireland and the US.[70] Needless to say, such an appointment would have given official recognition to the Free State, and the time was not yet right for this or for a growth of economic and financial ties between the two countries.[71]

64 WGHP, Series 4, 1921–3, misc. files, roll 180, Presidential executive file 135, folder 3, Lewis to Harding, 10 April 1922, Christian to Hoover, 11 April 1922. 65 Ibid., Huston to Lowe, 28 March 1922. Lowe also wrote to Michael Collins offering to renew trade relations between the US and Ireland. *Irish Times*, 17 February 1922. 66 WGHP, Series 4, 1921–3, misc. files, roll 180, Presidential executive file 135, folder 3, Lowe to Huston, 3 April 1922. 67 Ibid., Huston to Lowe, 12 April 1922. 68 Ibid., Hoover to Christian, 22 April 1922. 69 Ibid., Lowe to Huston, 13 April 1922. 70 Carroll, *American opinion*, p. 182. 71 The *Irish Independent* reported that US daily news

'Poacher turned game-keeper': defeating the irregulars in the US

In early 1922, the US administration, people, press and politicians were more interested in events at home than in those in Ireland. Begley sent back to Dublin an overview of US attitudes to the treaty. He indicated that the ordinary American press and people were generally

> overwhelmingly in favour of the proposed Free State. Those who were always more or less friendly, favour it on the old principle of half a loaf being better than no bread. The hostile pro-British press is heartily in favour of it regarding it chiefly as a triumph of British statesmanship and hoping that now at last they are rid of the eternal tiresome Irish question.[72]

Newspapers such as the *New York Times*, *New York World* and *New York Tribune* fell into the later category because their editors now felt their pro-British stance was justified. Begley reported division among the Irish-American people and press 'on the same ratio as the people at home; a preponderance in favour of the treaty.' In New York, Joseph McGarrity's *Irish Press* and the *Sinn Féiner* remained staunchly republican and anti-treaty. John Devoy's *Gaelic American* now attacked de Valera even more viciously than before while Robert E. Ford's *Irish World* denounced the pro-treatyites. Begley concluded that on the whole the Irish-American attitudes was 'wait and see.'[73] However, beginning in March 1922, Irish-America, interested Americans and US agencies came into closer contact with the opposing sides in the Irish situation, due to the arrival of different sets of individuals representing the pro-treaty Provisional Government and the anti-treaty Sinn Féin party.

The British embassy's 1922 annual report noted the arrival in mid-March of two 'Republican "delegates"', Austin Stack and J.J. O'Kelly 'whose mission was to work against the Free State' and who wanted also to enlist the support of Daniel Cohalan and John Devoy.[74] This Cumann na Poblacht delegation, as it was known, was expanded with the arrival in May of two more anti-treatyites, Constance Markievicz and Kathleen Barry, who similarly wanted to gather support and money for the anti-treaty republican cause.[75] On the same ship as Stack and O'Kelly were representatives of the pro-treaty Provisional Government, James O'Mara, Piaras Béaslaí and Seán MacCaoilte. The British embassy recorded the purpose of their visit as being to 'explain the constitution and aims of the Free State.' They had a wider remit; to win support for the 1921 treaty and the Free State and to raise money to fight the June general election. Both groups embarked

papers carried regular articles on the industrial resources of Ireland. *Irish Independent*, 25 March 1922.　72 NAI, D/FA, ES, 28/176, Begley report, 6 March 1922.　73 Ibid.　74 *BDFA*, xiv, Annual Report for 1922, p. 7.　75 UCDA, EVP, P150/1272.

on nation-wide tours that served to highlight the divisions within the republican movement, confuse Irish-Americans and weaken the Irish-American movement.[76]

Although Gavan Duffy, minister for Foreign Affairs, hoped that the signing of the treaty would have the effect of opening up 'everywhere many portals formerly closed to us through fear of England' and in early February 1922, he instructed the pro-treaty representatives in the US, Timothy Smiddy and Denis McCullough, to work 'to widen the circles of Irish influence', Collins gave more specific instructions to Smiddy. He directed him to prepare the way for Ireland's entry into the League of Nations, achieve official US recognition of the Free State, unite Irish-Americans and respond to requests from the Dublin government for information on the amendments to immigration legislation. According to Connolly, it was 'the national political situation' which was 'by far the outstanding objective of our work.'[77] Consequently, during the rest of 1922, Smiddy dedicated himself to gaining complete authority over the Irish-American organizations and the Dáil funds, thereby excluding the anti-treatyites from both and to countering anti-treatyite activism in the US. First he had to establish control over the personnel, Irish representation and space recently occupied by Harry Boland as the Dáil Éireann envoy to the US.

Smiddy found a largely anti-treaty staff in place in the Washington and New York offices and indeed, during the first two weeks after his arrival in late March, he was unable to start work or meet his staff.[78] This situation, he felt, necessitated personnel changes so that 'old traditions may be broken and the work set up on new conditions.'[79] There was the stenographer at Washington who was a 'gossiper', in the 'service of the Dáil' and 'almost useless' to Smiddy. She was replaced.[80] Also in the Washington office was Begley, who Smiddy described as a 'left Republican' but who was also 'impartial in the opinion of those for and against the treaty.' Denis McCullough also found Begley 'very helpful', but Begley opposed the treaty and he left the service in late April.[81] Possibly a greater threat to Smiddy was James O'Mara, who was based in the New York office and who Smiddy disliked. He described his behaviour at one meeting in New York, as 'ungentlemanly … discourteous and un-Irish.' Fortunately for the envoy O'Mara fell out with de Valera and returned to Ireland, where he resigned his trusteeship of the Dáil Éireann funds along with his Dáil seat. He was replaced as trustee by his brother, Stephen.[82] The other significant person in the New York office was Connolly.

76 NAI, D/FA, ES, 48a/116, Scott to MacSwiney, 10 May 1922.   77 NLI, Art Ó Briain Papers, MS8421(10), Foreign Affairs memorandum, no. 1, 1922; Gaughan, *Connolly*, p. 239; NAI, DFA, ES, 30/199, Smiddy to Gavan Duffy, 30 May 1922. Smiddy had been a professor of economics in University College, Cork. He promised to send on a bill introduced by Senator Shortridge to control immigration into the US which will be examined in chapter eleven.   78 NAI, D/FA, ES, 30/199, McCullough to Gavan Duffy, 14 April 1922.   79 Ibid., 8 May 1922.   80 Ibid., Smiddy to Gavan Duffy, 20 May 1922.   81 Ibid., 5 April 1922; ibid., McCullough to Gavan Duffy, 14 April 1922.   82 Ibid., Smiddy to Gavan Duffy, 5 April 1922; ibid., McCullough to Gavan Duffy, 14 April 1922.

His dedication to his job was soon clear to Smiddy who regarded Connolly as a 'very shrewd observer and of very good judgement.' He had been helpful to the envoy and was so 'impartial' in his political views that Smiddy was not quite sure 'whether or not he is pro-treaty.'[83] By the end of the summer, Connolly was no longer content with the political aspects of his work and Smiddy's alliances.[84]

Smiddy's problems with O'Mara and, to a lesser extent, with Connolly highlighted a further part of his authority problem; this time arising from the separation of the trade and diplomatic services. Smiddy was answerable for his actions to his minister, Gavan Duffy, and ultimately to the Provisional Government of the Irish Free State. James O'Mara had claimed that he was not answerable to Smiddy but to his brother Stephen, while Connolly reported mainly to Ernest Blythe, minister for Trade and Commerce.[85] Connolly believed that 'an imaginary protocol which drew an equally imaginary line between the *Corps Diplomatique* and the consular service' existed and would be respected by Smiddy.[86] This was not the case. Smiddy sought advice on this situation from M.M. Mahoney of the Canadian department of External Affairs and he read the Rogers bill. The bill provided for the amalgamation of the US diplomatic and consular service, a structure which Smiddy favoured for Ireland. He believed that, for reasons of 'practical expediency', the consular service should come under the authority of the diplomatic representative. By early 1923, he was overseeing the work of Connolly's successor as trade representative in New York, Lindsay Crawford.[87]

Another obstacle that Smiddy encountered was that of physically gaining control of the New York office space. O'Mara would not allow Smiddy to occupy the New York office and insisted that his office was in Washington. Consequently, Smiddy had to get Collins to send him a wire establishing his authority over both offices.[88] McCullough described Smiddy as being left 'high and dry' in the Waldorf Hotel in New York, being unable to get into the offices in New York or Washington.[89] It was not until O'Mara left for Ireland, in early April 1922, that Smiddy could really begin operations. The accommodation problems did not disappear completely. On 1 December 1922, Smiddy was informed by de Valera, in his role as president and minister for Foreign Affairs of the anti-treaty government (the second Dáil) formed on 25 October 1922, that he was to be replaced by Laurence Ginnell as official representative of the Irish republic in the US. He was to hand over control of the offices, funds, staff, documents,

---

83 Ibid., Smiddy to Gavan Duffy, 5 April 1922.   84 Gaughan, *Connolly*, p. 240. NAI, D/FA, ES, 30/199, Smiddy to Gavan Duffy, 15 May 1922. Smiddy reported on anti-treatyite gun running activities on the east coast of the US on 3 December 1922. UCDA, Desmond FitzGerald Papers (hereafter DFP), P80/385, Smiddy to FitzGerald, 3 December 1922. The representatives in the New York office in January 1922 were Lindsay Crawford, acting consul and L.P. Byrne a trade agent in New York and Smiddy was in the Washington office.   85 NAI, D/FA, ES, 30/197, Connolly to Cosgrave, 7 December 1922.   86 Gaughan, *Connolly*, pp. 229, 230, 233.   87 NAI, D/FA, ES, 32/211, Smiddy to FitzGerald, 6 February 1923.   88 Ibid., 30/199, Smiddy to Gavan Duffy, 5 April 1922.   89 Ibid., 30/199, McCullough to Gavan Duffy, 14 April 1922.

equipment and other property of the republic in Washington and New York.[90] Obviously Smiddy did not comply. Real and potential threats to his person and professional status emerged immediately. On 29 December, the rumour of a supposed threat by Ginnell that he would go the US 'to look after Professor Smiddy, reached the office of Free State President William T. Cosgrave.' It was suggested to Cosgrave that if Smiddy wished 'some protection' it should be obtained for him, as Ginnell could always rely upon a 'violent crowd of communists.'[91] The threat did not materialize even though Ginnell arrived at New York on 28 December 1922. The British embassy 1922 report recounted with some delight that as

> envoy of the Irish Republic to the United States …[Ginnell] … proceeded to take possession of the "consulate" premises, and informed Mr Daniel J. McGrath, who styles himself Irish vice-consul, that he was authorised to effect the seizure of the "consulate" on behalf of the Irish Republic. McGrath refused to vacate the premises, which were "besieged" by Ginnell and his associates for some twenty-four hours, to the enormous satisfaction of the American press.[92]

Daniel J. McGrath called the New York police and had the largely female group of fifty 'Irregular invaders' evicted. These anti-treatyite AARIR women promptly appealed for help to Mayor John Hylan, who replied that the 'Free State was the legal occupant of the premises … the law must be observed in this country and we must stop being ridiculous.'[93]

Other anti-treaty representatives and missions also complicated life for Smiddy and McCullough who cabled home, 'chaos in America and complete discrediting of whole position.'[94] He was right. Following the visit of the anti-treaty Stack, Barry and Markievicz in April–May, the second half of 1922 saw Muriel MacSwiney and Linda Kearns touring the US to raise funds for the Irish Republican Soldiers' and Prisoners' Dependants' Fund.[95] The Markievicz tour did not receive an enthusiastic reception from Irish-America or the wider American public, in marked contrast to that which had greeted previous visits before the truce was negotiated in summer 1921.[96] One of the main reasons was the deteriorating situation in Ireland.

The pro-treaty side won a majority in the Irish general election on 28 June and remained as the Provisional Government until 5 December, when the first

90 Ibid., 28/178, de Valera to Smiddy, 1 December 1922.   91 Ibid., 30/200, McGrath to Cosgrave, 29 December 1922.   92 *BDFA*, xiv, Annual Report for 1922, p. 8.   93 NAI, D/FA, ES, 30/200, Smiddy to External Affairs, 1 January 1923, 3 January 1923.   94 *DIFP*, i, 'Cavehill' [McCullough] to Dublin, c. 31 March 1922.   95 Smiddy reported on Muriel MacSwiney's US activities in September and December 1922. NAI, D/FA, ES, 26/175, Smiddy to FitzGerald, 18 September 1922, 3 December 1922.   96 J. Mooney Eichacker, *Irish republican women in America: lecture tours, 1916–25* (2003), p. 154; *BDFA*, xiv, Annual Report for 1922, p. 7.

Irish Free State government officially came into being. Soon after the elections the civil war started between the Irish Republican Army (IRA), also known as the irregulars, and the forces of the Provisional Government. It continued until 30 April 1923 and after Britain, the US became the 'next most important' centre of irregular activities abroad.[97] Immediately, US consuls provided the State Department with important insights.

Kent emphasized the 'state of anarchy prevailing in southern Ireland.' He detailed the political, economic and social upheavals and even concluded that 'there is a psychological side to the attitude of the southern Irish, who from long habit are still inclined to sympathise with anyone who can be called a rebel' and had an innate love of fighting. He reported on the 'unfit' state of the Irish Free State army who would soon be defeated in the civil war by the irregulars who were supplied with 'money and materials' not from an 'American origin' but from a 'Bolshevik origin.' They would, therefore, overthrow the Free State government and supplant it 'with some form of Soviet government, modelled upon that existing in Russia, and controlled and directed by working men.'[98] Such views played on widespread public concern in the US about the spread of communism, while also stressing the contrast between the two parts of Ireland.

By way of contrast, Kent reported 'a condition of absolute political quietude prevails' in northern Ireland and there was widespread evidence of economic recovery. The 'one shadow' which marred the solitude arose from the possibility of a boundary settlement that would deprive the northern government of a portion of 'its territory because a part of the people living there worship God after different religious forms from those practiced by another portion.' He insisted that the 'Ulster people' were law-abiding and the absence of social crimes reflected the 'promotion of sobriety and decency' that clearly contrasted with the southern Irish temperament but compared well with the prohibitionist sentiment that predominated in US society at the time. Kent also appealed to the business ethic prevailing in the Harding administration when he noted, on 7 February 1923, 'the government of Northern Ireland is a business government, composed of business men.'[99] He presented a picture of a Northern Ireland entity characterized by stable government and economic prosperity while the reverse pertained in the Irish Free State.

Hathaway's reports from Dublin, although less opinionated, drew an equally gloomy picture of the abilities of the Irish Free State government to establish its

97 E. O'Halpin, *Defending Ireland: the Irish State and its enemies since 1922* (1999), p. 22.   98 NARA, RG59, M580/220, 841d.00/580, Kent to Secretary of State, 17 January 1923; ibid., 841d.00/582, Kent to Secretary of State, 24 January 1923; ibid., 841d.00/583, Kent to Secretary of State, 31 January 1923.   99 Ibid., 841d.00/582, Kent to Secretary of State, 24 January; ibid., 841d.00/583, Kent to Secretary of State, 31 January 1923; ibid., 841d.00/577, 3 January 1923; ibid., 841d.00/574, Kent to Secretary of State, 13 December, 1922; ibid., 841d.00/584, Kent to Secretary of State, 7 February 1923. Kent identified county Donegal to be the location where illegal alcohol was mainly produced. It was part of Ulster but not of the northern state. In other words, it offered further proof of the reprobate character of the southern population.

authority and create the conditions for economic and social progress. Throughout late 1922 and early 1923, he described a picture of government impotence, frequent irregular outrage and criminal anarchy and held out little hope of an end to the conflict. Even the work of the consulate was disrupted by the fighting in central Dublin in early July and Hathaway relocated the office to the Shelbourne Hotel, in the south of the city, for eight days, as the public could not access it and the security of employees was at risk.[1] He supported the government's hard line policy towards the irregulars but shared with Kent the belief that the Irish psyche preferred conflict. He explained to the State Department that the Free State government's unpopularity was due firstly, to its use of executions and reprisals in the civil war and secondly, to the 'centuries old sympathy of the average southern Irishman for anybody who is against the government.' He predicted on 3 February 1923 that 'chaos [was] in sight.'[2] He was unaware that the irregulars could not sustain the guerrilla warfare.

Did these reports go beyond the consular bureau? Both Hathaway's and Kent's political reports were passed to the divisions of Western European Affairs and Political and Economic Information. Castle recommended that an 'instruction of commendation' be sent to Hathaway for his 3 February report.[3] While the report was well thought out and not sensational, it is clear that Hathaway shared with Kent stereotypical notions about the southern Irish predilection for violence. The information provided by these men, and by John A. Gamon in Cobh, confirmed to the State Department that the Free State government, rather than the irregulars, offered the greatest opportunity to secure peace and prosperity for the new state and informed its response to efforts to entangle it in the on-going civil war.

The presence of Muriel MacSwiney in the US proved to be a useful propaganda tool for the anti-treatyite Sinn Féin side who tried to revive the AARIR organization and increase its finances. They received a fillip for their campaign when details about her sister-in-law Mary MacSwiney's imprisonment in Ireland were publicized. The latter had opposed the London treaty and was inflexible in her opposition to it. During the civil war she toured Ireland, speaking on behalf of the republic and criticising the treaty and the leaders of the Free State and British governments. Eventually, in November 1922, she was arrested and imprisoned without charge in Mountjoy jail. She went on hunger strike and Cumann na mBan launched a publicity campaign to gain her release.

On 14 November 1922, along with eight AARIR women, Muriel MacSwiney picketed the British embassy in Washington. They denied the legitimacy of the

1 Ibid., M580/219, 841d.00/531, Hathaway to Secretary of State, 10 July 1922; ibid., M580/220, 841d.00/585, Hathaway to Secretary of State, 3 February 1923. Another officer was sent to the US consul general in London to get money because of the bank closure. Gamon in Queenstown extended 'some measure of protection' to US citizens during the recent 'civil disorders.' Ibid., IRFSP, Cobh, 1924, p. 15.   2 Ibid., M580/220, 841d.00/585, Hathaway to Secretary of State, 3 February 1923. 3 Ibid., note on Hathaway to Secretary of State, 3 February 1923.

Provisional Government and demanded Mary's release. On 25 November, the *Irish World* carried a photograph of Muriel carrying a placard which read 'England murdered my husband, Terence MacSwiney. Will America permit the English Free State to murder his sister, Mary MacSwiney?'[4] The women were arrested by the police even though the ambassador was absent from the embassy at the time. The police action contrasted with its inaction during a similar demonstration in April 1920.[5] When the case came to court, on 15 November, the defendants were represented by John F. Finnerty, president of the AARIR.[6] It was dismissed because the evidence 'did not measure up to the intent of the law.' The British diplomats were pleased at the arrests and disappointed about the dismissal which had occurred because, it seemed to Henry Chilton, 'demonstrations of this character, if unattended by any riotous or disorderly behaviour are not considered to infringe the Federal statute in question.'[7] Next the irregulars turned directly to the Harding administration for help.

In the following two weeks, Peter MacSwiney, a brother of Mary, wrote to Harding requesting a meeting. He wanted the president to make 'friendly representations' to effect her release from confinement by the 'English government through the so-called Irish Free State.' The matter was immediately referred to Hughes who advised Harding against meeting him. He also suggested that MacSwiney be advised that the president 'feels that he is unable to take a step which might be regarded by the British government as an interference by the American executive in purely British affairs.'[8] After twenty-four days on hunger strike and persistent publicity in Ireland and to a lesser degree in the US, Hathaway reported from Dublin that Mary MacSwiney had been removed to a nursing home from which she was eventually was released.[9] Muriel returned to fund-raising for the irregulars in the US, until de Valera recalled her to Ireland and asked Hanna Sheehy Skeffington and Kathleen Boland to complete her work.[10] Sheehy Skeffington arrived in the US in October 1922 and stayed until

---

4 *Irish World*, 25 November 1922; TNA, FO371/7266, Chilton for Geddes to Foreign Office, 17 November 1922.   5 Ibid. The Reuters journalist in the *Irish Times* report emphasized that they would not be going on hunger strike. *Irish Times*, 16 November 1922.   6 James E. 'Red' Murray replaced Edward Doheny as president of the AARIR in May 1922 because Doheny supported the treaty. Murray's efforts to bring both sides together led to his replacement by Finnerty who with Peter Golden kept the AARIR behind de Valera throughout the civil war. But with waning membership and public support they were unable to enliven the organization. Carroll, 'The American Association for the Recognition of the Irish Republic' in Funchion, *Irish American*, p. 11.   7 TNA, FO371/5622, Chilton to Foreign Office, 17 November 1922.   8 WGHP, Series 4, 1921–3, misc. files, roll 180, Presidential executive file 135, folder 3, Note of correspondence, undated. Muriel had cabled Harding also 'to save the life' of Mary. It was not acknowledged. NARA, RG59, M580/219, 841d.00/556, MacSwiney to Harding, 8 November 1922.   9 NARA, RG59, M580/220, Weekly report from American Consul to Secretary of State, 13 December 1922.   10 Eichacker, *Irish republican women*, p. 166; Muriel's departure from New York for France on 7 July 1923 was recorded by the vigilant British consul general in New York. NAI, D/T, S3346, Armstrong to Foreign Office, 13 July 1923 forwarded by Devonshire to Healy, 23 July 1923.

May 1923. The effect of her visit on the work of the Free State representatives is shown by a report sent by Smiddy in the Washington office to Dublin on 20 April 1923

> It is announced here that Mrs Sheehy Skeffington is about to return to Ireland soon. She has been the most active of publicists in the USA for the Irregulars and has circulated everywhere the most atrocious lies about the Free State.
>
> She says when she returns to Ireland she will probably be put in Mountjoy where she will hunger strike and as she will not be allowed to die she will be released.
>
> Is it possible or feasible to prevent her entering the Free State?[11]

She was not excluded from re-entry to Ireland. Her work and that of the other anti-treaty missions had inconvenienced the Irish Free State mission but had highlighted Sinn Féin's weakened support base. In late 1922, Congressman Basil M. Manley advised Frank P. Walsh against lobbying Congress on behalf of the Irish republican movement, because it had no chance of success and would reveal the weakness of their cause in the US.[12] In early January 1923, the AARIR executive, which remained behind de Valera, decided not to launch a fund-raising campaign or a new bond-certificate drive.[13] By mid-April the irregular threat to Smiddy and his mission had been much reduced, as de Valera cancelled the existing credentials of all anti-treaty organizers, collectors, representatives and propagandists in the US and issued new ones and as he decided that irregular headquarters were to be located at 8, Forty First Street, New York and all other places declared non-official.[14] De Valera hoped that both measures would weed out individuals who undermined the anti-treaty cause and also those who had become too closely associated with communism, particularly the supporters of the labour leader, James Larkin. For Smiddy, de Valera's decision to establish a separate representation in the US gave his mission greater legitimacy as the true representatives of the Irish Free State and distanced it even more from the irregulars.[15]

11 NAI, D/T, S2236, 'Sinbad' [Smiddy] to FitzGerald, 20 April 1923.   12 Carroll, *American opinion*, p. 186.   13 Carroll, 'The American Association', p. 11. The republicans faced more difficulties when the Free State government initiated legal proceedings to recover $2,500,000 worth of Irish bond-certificates lying in New York banks. An injunction was awarded to the government which froze all access to the fund and the matter was not fully resolved until 1931. See chapter thirteen for further.   14 NAI, D/FA, ES, 28/181, Smiddy to FitzGerald, 11 April 1923. 15 James Larkin, the labour leader who founded the Irish Transport and General Workers' Union in 1909, was in the US since 1914 after the failure of the Dublin lockout by owners. While in the US he spoke at anti-British meetings, and was a delegate to the founding meeting of the American Communist Party. In 1920 he was arrested for 'criminal anarchy' and imprisoned in Sing Sing prison. P. Collins, 'Larkin, James' in S.J. Connolly (ed.), *The Oxford companion to Irish history* (1998), p. 302.

Smiddy used other weapons to defeat the irregular threat in the US. The creation of the Irish Free State had led to substantial co-operation and consultation between the British, Irish and US authorities in the US on administrative, constitutional and security issues among other matters. By November 1922, Colonial Secretary Victor Cavendish, duke of Devonshire, was regularly forwarding Foreign Office reports from British officials in Washington, Boston, Portland and New York to Timothy Healy, the governor general of the Irish Free State, for distribution to President Cosgrave and his administration, particularly the ministers for External Affairs, Justice and Defence. This information covered reports of arms shipments to Ireland, the details of 'the interminable procession of Irish republican enthusiasts', copies of Irish-American newspapers, and details of propaganda and fund-raising meetings throughout the US attended by Irish and Irish-American irregulars.[16] Even after the Free State government was established on 6 December 1922, it remained 'very much obliged' to the Colonial Office for supplying it with any information about irregular activities in the US, particularly in connection with the shipment of arms and movement of persons between Ireland and the US.[17]

It was this kind of 'unnatural alliance with the friends of imperialist Britain' and Smiddy's 'ruthless ... campaign' against the irregulars combined with the 'shadow of uncertainty at home' that led to Connolly's resignation as consul general in New York. He was disappointed by Smiddy's surveillance of the anti-treatyites, particularly their publicity and propaganda tours, the gun-running activities and the co-operation that had developed between Smiddy, the British embassy and US intelligence, immigration and police officers.[18] The end of the war had not seen an end to US surveillance of 'foreign agents, Japanese affairs, Mexican affairs, Negro activities, radical matters, Sinn Féin affairs, strikes' by agents of the Bureau of Investigation and War Department Military Intelligence Division. J. Edgar Hoover head of the Radical Division in the Bureau, worked on the assumption that 'radicalism was alien and that aliens were behind radicalism.'[19] His boss, William J. Burns, wished to 'drive every radical out of the country and bring the parlour Bolsheviks to their senses.'[20] Sinn Féin, the FOIF,

16 NAI, D/T, S3346, Devonshire to Healy, 13 December 1922, 30 January 1923, 7 February 1923, 27 February 1923, 3 April 1923, 9 April 1923. The reporting continued into 1924. The quotation is from Armstrong's report of 26 February 1923.   17 Ibid., Secretary, Defence to Secretary, External Affairs, 5 January 1923; *DIFP*, ii, Healy to Devonshire, 12 January 1923; ibid., Healy to Devonshire, 21 April 1923.   18 Gaughan, *Connolly*, pp. 230–9; *Irish Times*, 25 November 1922.   19 R. Jeffreys-Jones, *Cloak and dollar: a history of American secret intelligence* (2002), p. 92; NARA, RG65, M1085/R919, General Intelligence Report, no. 4, for the week ending 14 November 1920, [table of contents]. During the 1920s the State Department's intelligence co-ordination activities declined and in 1927 Secretary of State Frank B. Kellogg abolished U-1. G.J.A. O'Toole, *Honorable treachery: a history of US intelligence, espionage and covert action from the American revolution to the CIA* (1991), p. 336.   20 K. O'Reilly, *Hoover and the UnAmericans: the FBI, HUAC and the red menace* (1983), p. 17.

the AARIR and the Larkin Defence League all came under this 'radical' category. Agents reported on meetings of Irish-related organizations, clubs, societies and individuals and also on newspaper coverage of their activities. Among the prominent individuals on whom dossiers were collected and maintained were Frank P. Walsh, Daniel Cohalan, Eamon de Valera, Harry Boland, Donal O'Callaghan, Mary and Muriel MacSwiney, Hanna Sheehy Skeffington and Anna Walsh, sister-in-law of the late Tomás MacCurtain, lord mayor of Cork. These reports were communicated by Bureau and Military intelligence agents throughout the US to the departments of Justice and War and on to the State Department's intelligence co-ordination unit known as 'U-1'.[21]

In early December 1922, Smiddy met with Sherman Burns, head of the 'most efficient' International Detective Agency in the US and son of the Bureau chief. Smiddy wanted an investigation of the movements of Robert Briscoe, 'a Dublin Jew' and anti-treatyite, whom he suspected of having bought guns in the US on behalf of the irregulars. He also asked Burns to find out 'if there are any guns going to Ireland from the principal ports on the east coast.' Burns replied that guns could be 'easily procured', not least because New York dockers would oblige the imprisoned trade union leader, James Larkin, who Smiddy believed was 'in league with the Irregulars.'[22] Burns was well acquainted with the mechanics of gun-running to Ireland because the Bureau utilized the services of private detective agencies and because the US department of Justice and attorney general's office had devoted much time in 1921 and 1922, to gathering evidence in connection with the Hoboken arms and ammunition case to be presented to the grand jury in Trenton, New Jersey.[23]

21 NARA, RG65, M1085/R83, 919, 920, 924 Weekly Intelligence Reports and General Intelligence Reports. The Bureau acted also on a complaint from Representative G.H. Tinkham of Massachusetts protesting against a sign on a window near the British embassy reading 'America. Why continue relations with England a country of assassins?' The Washington Bureau was able to report that the sign was there for six months but 'an effort would be made' to have it removed. One week later, it was reported that the house was occupied by Margaret V. Geagan, Martha E. Geagan and Mary A. Geagan and that an attempt was made 'to find some law or police regulation' which would prohibit the sign but no such law was found. Consequently, the Washington office 'was at a loss to know what action it can take on the matter.' Ibid., M1085/R921, General Intelligence Report, no. 21, for week ending 17 April 1921; ibid., no. 23, for week ending, 24 April 1921. Among Harding's more controversial appointments was that of William J. Burns as chief of the US Bureau of Investigation in Attorney General Daugherty's department of Justice. Jeffreys-Jones, *Cloak and dollar*, p. 79. K. O'Reilly, *Hoover and the UnAmerians: the FBI, HUAC and the red menace* (1983), p. 17. Smiddy discussed James Larkin with Castle also. Both men agreed that Larkin, the preacher of 'bolshevism', would not have 'any great effect in Ireland.' NARA, RG59, M580/220, part. 111, 841d.00/615, Castle to Hughes, 15 August 1923.   22 UCDA, DFP, P80/385, Smiddy to FitzGerald, 3 December 1922.   23 See NARA, RG59, M580/219, 841d.00/470. The British navy seized a shipment of guns on the SS *Seattle Spirit* in Tralee bay, county Kerry. The US consul at Cobh informed the State Department that the ship had been cleared at New York port and the arms were for the IRA. Ibid., 841d.00/514, Skinner to Hughes, 8 June 1922. In March 1920, it became necessary for the State Department to warn the British that the US government could not tolerate the sabotage

Burns' agents secured the services of an 'informant' to use against Larkin and his 'Irish agitators' and they watched Briscoe for the next few weeks. The information passed to Smiddy prepared him for the AARIR invasion of the consulate on 1 January 1923 and he sent information to the ministry for External Affairs in Dublin about the possible shipment of guns from the US to Ireland and the names of those involved.[24] At this stage he asked his minister, Desmond FitzGerald, if he might appoint an organizer of intelligence who would direct and report on the activities of the secret service agents he had employed. While he awaited a reply, the Irish envoy did not just collect information about possible arms and armaments shipments for transmission home but decided to see what could be done to stop a) the arrival of irregulars, b) their efforts to recruit Irish-Americans for fighting in the Irish civil war and c) fund-raising in the US, by working with the Bureau of Immigration, the departments of Labour and Justice and the New York police.[25] Subsequently, Smiddy's work received government approval and he was placed in charge of the operation.[26]

By January 1923, Smiddy was employing Burns' agents, who were working simultaneously for the Bureau of Investigation, to link the 'Reds with the Irregulars.' Bureau agents reported on the connections in the US with 'communists and Irregulars' of James Larkin, Peter Larkin, Patrick McClellain, Muriel MacSwiney and Hanna Sheehy Skeffington.[27] The communist links of employees in the New York consulate were monitored by the Bureau also following a request from Smiddy.[28] The visit of Horace Plunkett to the US and his address at a meeting in New York on 8 February provided Smiddy with another opportunity to inform US authorities about irregular agitation and to note its links to radicalism. Smiddy was warned by his agents about a disruption by Irish 'radicals and ... communists' who, along with 'a waterfront "tough element"', were intending to break up the meeting. He duly informed the New York police, who turned up in force to prevent disruption inside the hall.[29] Smiddy hoped that

activities of *agents provocateur*. Consequently, the British spy office in New York would have to go underground because its activities had been, in the words of Frank Polk, the under secretary of state and head of U1, 'too well advertised and the Irish and others were sure to make trouble'. But he was not so unpragmatic as to insist on a complete closure and it was re-established under cover of the British passport control office. Major Norman Thwaites who ran the New York office of British intelligence during the war was replaced by Maurice Jeffes and others continued into the inter-war period. NARA, RG59, M580/1, entry 20 September 1920'.   24 NAI, D/FA, ES, 28/185, Smiddy to FitzGerald, 6 January 1923; 15 January 1923; UCDA, DFP, P80/385, Smiddy to FitzGerald, 26 January 1923.   25 NAI, D/FA, ES, 28/185, Smiddy to FitzGerald, 6 January 1923. 26 Ibid., Letter Books, Washington 1923–4, Walshe to Smiddy, 12 March 1924; ibid., 10 February 1923.   27 Ibid., 15 January 1923.   28 Ibid., ES, 28/109, Smiddy report, undated but between early December and 15 January 1923. Indeed Larkin's brand of communism was too radical for some republicans. One of Smiddy's agents reported that Hanna Sheehy Skeffington said at a private meeting that a 'middle ground' would have to be found between de Valera and Larkin. She favoured the establishment of a 'co-operative commonwealth.' UCDA, DFP, P80/385, Smiddy to FitzGerald, 11 May 1923.   29 NAI, D/FA, ES, 29/190, Smiddy to FitzGerald, 19 February 1923, informants' report undated. The extremist nature of the irregular agitation was further supported by a refer-

any links uncovered between irregulars and communists could be 'raised' in the upcoming general election in Ireland and used to benefit the Free State side.[30] The Cosgrave government agreed with him and sanctioned $6,000 to fund his 'secret service' requirements, including recruiting a reliable seaman working the Atlantic routes to act as an informant.[31]

During 1923, the main focus of Irish, US and British co-operation was on the prevention of guns and ammunition being shipped to the irregulars in Ireland and the case of James Larkin. Armstrong reported to the Foreign Office, on 18 January, and to the Free State government, that the recently-arrived irregulars, Seán Moylan and Michael Leahy, had claimed, at a meeting in New York, that the 'IRA had sufficient arms and ammunitions at least until May.'[32] Consequently, in the early months of 1923 it was clear that if the supply from the US could be curtailed, an end to the upheaval in Ireland might be in sight. The informants and agents employed by Smiddy and Armstrong provided them with a flow of information about possible shipments to Ireland. In February, Armstrong's report that a 'new bomb-throwing device', manufactured in the US, was being acquired in New York for the irregulars was circulated to the Free State police, while Smiddy was asked by his minister, Desmond FitzGerald, to investigate rumours of a 'submarine' being sent to the irregulars.[33] In addition to cutting-off supplies of weapons, the co-operation centred on a close surveillance by Bureau agents of Joseph McGarrity's movements and the capturing of two 'known gun-runners', Laurence Hoover and H.H. Pickford. In March 1923, the US department of Justice asked Smiddy to obtain details on Hoover, who had 'made contracts' in Washington to have guns delivered to irregulars.[34]

In the early months of 1923, joint activity also centred on James Larkin who opposed the Anglo-Irish treaty and who Smiddy feared would become 'the rallying ground for a fresh assault' on Ireland, although he also saw him as useful propaganda tool illustrating the link between de Valera's irregulars and communism.[35] Larkin had been found guilty of the charge of 'criminal anarchy' on 3 May 1920 and had been sentenced to imprisonment for five to ten years. By 1922 he was due for release pending the hearing of an appeal against his sentence.[36] Before Smiddy's

ence in his informant's report that outside the hall the screaming of one hundred 'maddened' women 'armed with eggs' was 'demoniacal.' Ibid.   30 Ibid., 28/185, Smiddy to FitzGerald, 15 January 1923. Smiddy also reported that following the execution of Liam Mellows, the irregulars contemplated a murder attempt on Auckland Geddes, Smiddy and Cohalan. Ibid., 6 January 1923.   31 DIFP, ii, Brennan to Smiddy, 1 February 1923; NAI, D/T, S3346, Smiddy to FitzGerald, 20 April 1923.   32 UCDA, DFP, P80/385, Armstrong to Foreign Office, 18 January 1923.   33 NAI, D/FA, ES, 28/185, Smiddy to FitzGerald, 13 December 1922; ibid., Armstrong to Foreign Office, 8 February 1923, 7 March 1923; ibid., Director of Intelligence to Lt J.F. Feeney, assistant commander, Claremorris Command, 6 April 1923; ibid., Diarmaid OhEigeartaigh to FitzGerald, 16 March 1923.   34 UCDA, DFP, P80/385, Smiddy to FitzGerald, 26 March 1923.   35 NAI, D/FA, ES, 28/185, Smiddy to FitzGerald, 15 January 1923; J. Deasy, Fiery cross: the story of Jim Larkin, Irish labour history society, studies in Irish labour history, 9 (2004), p. 10.   36 E. O'Connor, James Larkin (2002), pp. 64–5; M. O'Riordan, 'Larkin in America', 52–3.

arrival in the US, Armstrong in New York and Geddes in Washington had kept an eye on the Larkin case with the co-operation of the State Department. After his arrival in 1922, Smiddy co-operated to ensure that every possible step was taken to prevent the 'dangerous agitator' as Castle described him, leaving the US and returning to Ireland where he might influence the outcome of the election against the government. Hughes even dispatched Castle to meet with Governor Miller to prevent Larkin getting a pardon. After Larkin's first release on 6 May 1922, the secretary telephoned J. Edgar Hoover in the department of Justice to keep Larkin under surveillance in New York pending a Supreme Court decision which eventually returned him to prison again on 10 July.[37]

The labour man was eventually released on 17 January 1923 with a free pardon from the newly elected Democrat governor of New York, Al Smith.[38] A few weeks later Smiddy cabled the department of External Affairs 'Keeping intimate contact Larkin movement. He expressed himself … as bitterly hostile to President and members of Free State government. That he was going home soon.' Smiddy offered his minister the choice of Larkin being allowed by the US immigration authorities to leave voluntarily, which would mean he could return to the US or Smiddy could have him deported at once.[39] Smiddy and Armstrong's agents lost contact with Larkin in February. Both thought that he had returned home and were surprised when Larkin arrived in Washington in late March with $15,000 from his supporters in Chicago to buy a vessel to transport food and clothing to the 'distressed people' in Ireland.[40]

By early April, Smiddy's surveillance operation on Larkin appeared to be working again. His secret service agents had, on 24 February, helped Justice officials to intercept ammunition intended by Larkin and his group for the irregulars in Ireland that was being moved from New Jersey to New York. The federal authorities indicted the individuals who were arrested because it was illegal to move ammunition or guns from one state to another without a licence.[41] His second objective was achieved also when he was informed by a Justice official that they had succeeded in getting the department of Labour to deport Larkin because of his 'inflammatory' speeches in favour of the 'Reds.'[42] The head of the detective division of the New York police department, with whom Smiddy had

37 TNA, FO371/7266, Geddes to Foreign Office, 5 May 1922; Tyrell, 5 May 1922; Geddes, 8 May 1922; Home Office, 9 May 1922; ibid., Geddes to Foreign Office, 5 May 1922; NARA, RG59, M580/218, Hughes note; ibid., Castle to Hughes, 9 May 1922; LC, MD, Leland Harrison Papers, Box 12, Castle to Harrison, 6, 9 May 1922; TNA, FO371/7266, Armstrong to Geddes, 10 May 1922; Geddes, 9 June 1922; Armstrong, 13 October 1922.   38 O'Connor, *James Larkin*, pp. 65–7.
39 NAI, D/FA, ES, 28/181, Smiddy to External Affairs, 2 February 1923.   40 Ibid., 28/181, Smiddy to FitzGerald, 30 March 1923l; ibid., 29/190, Smiddy to FitzGerald, 12 May 1923; ibid., D/T, S3346, Armstrong to Foreign Office, 19 March 1923. Smiddy also received information on Larkin from Constantine E. Maguire who was a US government official and supporter of the Free State.   41 Ibid., D/FA, ES, 28/181, Smiddy to FitzGerald, 11 April 1923, 28/184, Smiddy to FitzGerald, 20 April 1923.   42 Ibid., D/T, S3346, 'Sinbad' to FitzGerald, 20 April 1923, attachment, undated 'Intelligence'.

established a working relationship, described to him Larkin's arrest and transfer to the US immigration authorities for deportation from Ellis Island but said that the prisoner was entitled to be bailed and to have a hearing before the board of immigration inspectors 'to show cause why he should not be deported.'[43] Larkin was eventually deported on 21 April because of his communist speeches and links and due to 'his Irish activities.'[44] Nevertheless the attention paid by various US agencies and British diplomats and then Smiddy to the case, particularly to its communist connections, had kept it before Justice officials.

In early April 1923, the irregulars were in difficulties in Ireland due to large-scale internment and arrests and Smiddy reported from Washington that irregulars in New York and Philadelphia had ceased trying to send large quantities of arms and ammunitions.[45] He spent $4,016 on 'special intelligence' in February and March 1923, but Joseph Walshe in External Affairs felt it was worth it and sent his 'congratulations' on the 'results' of his intelligence work.[46] Smiddy continued his work, meeting with Hoover to discuss prosecuting irregular gunrunners. Unfortunately for Smiddy, there was no US law against the export of arms to a 'friendly' country even if they were known to be used against that country's government. Hoover told him that if the arms were accompanied by men organized to use them for an indictable offence, the activity would come under the heading of an 'expeditionary force.' The absence of a law against the export of arms rendered Smiddy's work 'difficult.'[47] But this did not prevent him or the British from continuing to push for US government action. Even though the irregular chief of staff, Frank Aiken, had declared a ceasefire in the civil war on 30 April, British intelligence indicated that the irregulars in the US were planning to import guns and ammunition into Ireland. Sperling in the Foreign Office believed that this afforded grounds for prosecution by the US authorities and he ordered Geddes to give Smiddy every assistance in pressing the US government to institute proceedings against the US-based irregulars for gun-running.[48]

Seán Moylan, a former director of operations and minister on the irregular side, was acting as a liaison officer with Joseph McGarrity's Clan na Gael to arrange for

43 Ibid., attachment, undated Police Department of New York City. Larkin told the head detective that he did not wish to return to Ireland but, in case he did, his address would be Liberty Hall, [Dublin]. He preferred to go to Palestine and settle there. Ibid. The case of Michael Laffan, an influential irregular, brought Smiddy into contact with the department of Justice. The envoy asked FitzGerald on 20 April, if he wanted Laffan deported from the US. Also he indicated that John F. Finnerty appealed to Justice not to deport Laffan as he would probably be executed if he returned to Ireland. Ibid., D/T, S3346, 'Sinbad' to FitzGerald, 20 April 1923; Armstrong to Foreign Office, 27 April 1923.   44 UCDA, DFP, P80/385, Smiddy to FitzGerald, undated.   45 NAI, D/FA, ES, 28/181, Smiddy to FitzGerald, 11 April 1923.   46 Ibid., Letter Books, Washington 1923–4, Accountant's Office, 31 October 1923; ibid., Walshe to Smiddy, 3 March 1923.   47 Ibid., ES, 28/184, Smiddy to FitzGerald, 20 April 1923. Smiddy indicated he met with the assistant director of the Bureau of Investigation who was Hoover. Coolidge promoted Hoover to director in April 1924.   48 NAI, D/T, S3346, Sperling to Geddes, 7 May 1923.

the purchase of weapons in Germany and recruit experienced men to fight in Ireland.[49] From the time he arrived Armstrong's and Smiddy's agents monitored his presence and gathered evidence for a possible prosecution including photographs of documents captured by British intelligence in England.[50] On 11 May, Geddes went further and wrote to Hughes to inform him that Moylan was purchasing arms and munitions and asking 'that he be deported ... if it is found he entered US unlawfully.' The letter was passed to Attorney General Harry Daugherty who instructed the agents already watching Moylan, to get evidence for a deportation. William Phillips, under secretary of State, was able to tell Geddes on 15 June that Daugherty had agreed to strengthen his orders and to have Moylan apprehended and handed over to the department of Labour for deportation.[51] Efforts to find Moylan failed and he eventually returned to de Valera's side in Ireland.[52]

Irregular supporters in the US were in no doubt about the depth of co-operation between British and Irish authorities at this time. In late March 1923, McGarrity reported to de Valera, 'the detective agencies are doing a big business ... the British or British colonials from Ireland [Smiddy's agents], the paid detective agencies here and Uncle Sam's men.'[53] Martin Howard, secretary of the New York city branch of the AARIR, published his views in the *Irish World*, on 9 May:

> We are aware that the British embassy here after consultation with the Free State authorities in Ireland instructed their Secret Service Department to keep a close watch on the activities of ... all ... leading Irish Republicans in this country and to send regular reports of her meetings and lectures to the British ambassador ... we are also aware that the reports requested by the Free State from the British Secret Service in this country have been furnished to the Free State government from their agent here, and have been received at their Dublin headquarters.[54]

This description of the interaction between the British and Irish Free State authorities was mostly accurate. But it failed to make it clear that it was part of on-going British and US surveillance of Irish 'radicals' in the US or that Smiddy was operating a secret service network of his own. The effectiveness of the British–Irish co-operation is difficult to gauge. Clearly, irregular organizers in the US were aware of the respective secret service operations but this was just one factor in the

---

49 S. Cronin (ed.), *The McGarrity papers: revelations of the Irish revolutionary movement in Ireland and America 1900–1940* (1972), p. 135.   **50** NAI, D/T, S3346, Armstrong to London, 27 April 1923, 18 January 1923; ibid., 'Sinbad' to FitzGerald, 20 April 1923, attachment, undated, 'list of names of Irregulars active here'; ibid., 27 April 1923, Healy to Devonshire, 21 April 1922; UCDA, DFP, P80/385, Director of Intelligence to FitzGerald, 11 April 1923; NAI, D/FA, Letter Books, Washington 1923–4, Walshe to Smiddy, 17 April 1923; NAI, D/T, S3346, Sperling to Geddes, 7 May 1923.   **51** NARA, RG59, roll 580.220, part ii, note from British embassy, 11 May 1923; NAI, D/T, S3346, Philips to Geddes, 15 June 1923.   **52** NAI, D/T, 3346, Alvey A. Adee, State Department to Henry Getty Chilton, British Embassy, 3 July 1923, sent to Healy on 23 July 1923.   **53** UCDA, EVP, P150/1191, McGarrity to de Valera, 25 March 1923.   **54** *Irish World*, 9 May 1923.

reduction of irregular fund-raising and gun-running activities in the US in 1923. Others related to decreasing financial and political support from Irish-American organizations, the further splintering of nationalist organizations, specifically the AARIR, and the increasing legitimacy and standing that Smiddy garnered for the Free State government, particularly on the recognition issue.

The fight for recognition of the Irish Free State

In addition to dealing with the practical difficulties of establishing his mission in the US and thwarting irregular activities, Smiddy tried to progress the recognition issue. When he first arrived in the US, he notified Hughes in accordance with the procedure regulating the arrival of foreign representatives. Although Hughes did not formally reply to Smiddy, the envoy met with William Castle through the intervention of Frank P. Walsh and Michael F. Doyle, the Philadelphia lawyer who defended Roger Casement and occasionally worked for the State Department.[55] Smiddy found that Castle was 'very sympathetic' and wished 'every success' to the establishment of the Irish Free State. Castle offered to help the Irish envoy 'at any time' and Smiddy reported to his minister in Dublin in late April 1922, that the avenue was opened for the establishment of 'orthodox' diplomatic relations as soon as the Free State was established.[56] Consequently, he did not progress the recognition issue with the US administration because he believed it would come automatically after December 1922. A clearer view of the US administration's position on the matter soon emerged. From a political perspective, Hughes considered himself to be one of the 'friends of Ireland.' He believed that with two governments in place in Ireland, 'it was unfortunate that neither … are … able as yet to assure safety to the people.'[57] The view was in line with his consuls' reports from Ireland. Greater clarity of Hughes' and Harding's position came in autumn 1922. Following a request by William A. Fitzgerald, general editor of the 'Ireland a nation' publication based in Dublin, to Harding and Hughes on 20 September 1922, the legal position was

55 NARA, RG59, M580/225, 841d.01B11/11, Castle to Hughes, 21 March 1922; ibid., 841d.01B11/12, Castle to Hughes, 22 March 1922. The creation of the Free State also provided the opportunity for other individuals to try and gain advantage. In January 1923, Claude Dawson, a US consul general in Tampico, Mexico requested the State Department to check out the identity and status of M.J. Keaf, who purported to be a Free State representative. A special agent of the State Department based in New York discovered that he was unknown in Irish or British circles and R.S. Sharp concluded that he was more of a 'confidence man than a bona fide representative'. Ibid., M580/225, 841d.01B12/-, Dawson to Hengstler, 19 January 1922; ibid., Sharp to Hengstler, 25 January 1922; ibid., Hughes to Dawson, 25 January 1922.   56 NAI, D/FA, ES, 30/199, Smiddy to Gavan Duffy, 28 April 1922. Smiddy's relationship with the US official was not so close as to enable him to spell the American's name correctly. In his dispatch home he referred throughout to 'Cassels' instead of Castle. Ibid.   57 NARA, RG59, M580/219, 841d.00/519, Hughes to Thomas E. Newberry, 10 July 1922.

defined. Fitzgerald wanted a message of greeting from the president and a welcome 'to the new Irish Free State on her formal entry into the comity of nations.'[58] Before it reached Harding's desk, George Christian turned to Hughes for advice.[59] Frederick Sterling, a State Department official, advised Hughes that the Free State *de facto* status was that of a dominion, just like Canada and that the Irish Free State had 'no more of a national status' than did Canada or Australia.' He suggested asking US Ambassador Harvey to ask the British government whether Ireland was to have a status 'for purposes of international intercourse different from the Dominions' and if Harding should comply with Fitzgerald's request.[60]

In London, the ambassador informally approached the Foreign Office and on 17 October replied to Hughes: 'status of Ireland indeterminate … in my opinion it is inadvisable to comply with request.' Hughes agreed and advised Christian on the following day, 'I think it perhaps it would be better to ignore the request altogether and not answer the communication.'[61] The president agreed.[62] However, following the establishment of the Irish Free State in December 1922, Cosgrave formally notified Hughes of the 'full legal establishment' of the new state.[63] Harding returned a message of good will through Geddes thereby providing a *de facto* recognition at least.[64] The administration was more forthcoming when asked to supply a New Year's message for publication in the nationalist *Freeman's Journal*. Hughes replied that Harding 'expressed his sincere hope of this government that the people of the Irish Free State, to whom so many Americans are bound by ties of kinship and affection may enjoy the blessings of peace, prosperity and happiness.'[65] Harvey in London endorsed these views.[66] Within three weeks of the establishment of the Free State, Hathaway provided Washington with an overview and biographical sketches of the new government. He pointed out that

> all these men took part in the armed resistance to England, that all have been in prison, that only one is past fifty and only two others have reached forty years, that they have all risen from the ranks of the common people of Ireland and that they are all of the Roman Catholic religion, like the great majority of their countrymen. They were all Sinn Féiners, and it is believed, nearly all members of the Irish Republican Brotherhood, the secret fighting organization.[67]

58 WGHP, Series 4, 1921–3, misc. files, roll 180, Presidential executive file 135, folder 3, FitzGerald to Harding, 20 September 1922.   59 Ibid., Christian to Hughes, 2 October 1922.   60 NARA, RG59, M580/225, 841d.01/54, Sterling to Hughes, 6 October 1922; WGHP, Series 4, 1921–3, misc. files, roll 180, Presidential executive file 135, folder 3, Hughes to Christian, 7 October 1922. NARA, RG59, M580/225, 841d.01/54, Sterling to Hughes, 6 October 1922.   61 WGHP, Series 4, 1921–3, misc. files, roll 180, Presidential executive file 135, folder 3, Hughes to Christian, 18 October 1922; NARA, RG59, M580/225, 841d.01/55, Harvey to Hughes, 17 October 1922.   62 On 21 September 1922, Harding signed the joint congressional resolution favouring the establishment in Palestine of a national home for the Jewish people.   63 NARA, RG59, M580/225, 841d.01/56, Hathaway to Hughes, 8 December 1922.   64 Ibid., Hughes to Gedddes, 28 December 1922.   65 Ibid., 841d.01/58, Hughes to American Consul, Dublin, 12 January 1923.   66 Referred to in NAI, D/FA, ES, 28/175, Smiddy to FitzGerald, 8 December 1922.   67 NARA, RG59,

His sketch of the individuals' capabilities and his reminder of their shared revolutionary background, did not offer much confidence to his political masters in the State Department about the capacity of the new government to handle the challenges ahead. He emphasized that the Irish government wanted 'separate control of its foreign affairs' and had a 'keen' interest in separate diplomatic representation. He noted also that the Free State government would be pressured towards these positions by 'their Republican opponents.' Hathaway expected the case for recognition of the new Free State to be promoted at the imperial conference in October 1923 and by an application to the League of Nations.[68]

Smiddy did not wait that long to regularize his position.[69] He sent two documents to External Affairs which showed that during the previous four or five months many events had made him realize the 'imperative necessity' of obtaining recognition. He detailed three in particular:

(1) to render ineffective the activities of the Irregulars and their supporters in this country.

(2) It will have a very satisfactory effect on the settlement of the suit that is pending the court.

(3) It will aid us considerably in coping with the activities of the Irregulars by giving us direct access to the State Department and helping us to obtain an embargo on the exportation of arms to the Irish Free State.[70]

All were related to the national question and a few weeks later, Smiddy received further evidence of the urgency of the matter. His agents had ascertained from their 'most reliable informants, public officials, congressmen and senators as well as foreign diplomats', that there was a 'well-organised plan afoot' led by irregular Joseph McGarrity, to prevent US official recognition of the Free State. Significantly other opponents of recognition identified by Smiddy were 'certain representatives of another foreign nation', presumably Geddes.[71] For these reasons Smiddy had prepared, during April and May 1923, the ground for an application to the US government. Early in the month he reported that the bulk of

M580/224, 841d.002, Hathaway to Secretary of State, 27 December 1922.   68 Ibid., M580/225, 841d.01/63, Hathaway to Secretary of State, 24 April 1923. The US government was not alone in seeking clarification from the British government about the status of the Free State. Patrick McGilligan, secretary to James MacNeill, Free State high commissioner in London, was told by Lionel Curtis of the Colonial Office that his government had received queries from governments where Free State representatives were maintained about the status of such agents particularly in connection with the issuing of passports and the appointment of consuls. *DIFP*, ii, UCDA, P4/503, McGilligan, 4 March 1923.   69 NAI, D/T, S3346, Armstrong to Foreign Office, 27 April 1923; ibid., S1983A, Walshe to Granard, 3 February 1923.   70 Ibid., D/FA, ES, 29/192, Smiddy to FitzGerald, 12 May 1923.   71 Ibid., 28/185, unnamed memorandum, 'Recognition of Irish Free State', 26 June 1923, unsigned report, 28 June 1923. Senator Medill McCormick passed on a copy of a letter from a constituent to Hughes on 30 May 1921, pleading for the US administration to hold elections in Ireland to allow people chose between the 'so-called Free State and the existing Republic.' NARA, RG59, M580/225, 841d.01/60, enclosure in McCormick to Hughes, 30 May 1923.

the US newspapers were on the whole 'favourable' to the Free State.[72] Secondly, he raised the matter with M.M. Mahoney, Canadian representative in the US, because that dominion had managed in 1920 to get British agreement for the appointment of a minister plenipotentiary in Washington and was considering further action in 1923.[73]

The new Irish government responded to pressure from Smiddy by initiating the formal process of applying for official US recognition and appointing a minister plenipotentiary by approaching the British government. In the interim, Smiddy was to be appointed 'agent of this ministry for the purpose of studying the methods of public administration in the United States and looking after financial interests of the Irish Free State.' The British government was further asked to make Smiddy's position known to the State Department and the British ambassador in Washington.[74]

Smiddy continued his campaign to regularize his position. In December 1922 and January 1923, he had pushed FitzGerald to secure an end to the Free State policy of executing irregular prisoners because he felt that such actions undermined the Free State's credibility in the US.[75] During April and May 1923, he promoted the recognition issue with his political contacts and learnt that Senator Lodge believed that if an application was made with the sanction of the British government, it would be very favourably received. Smiddy had also employed the retired ambassador to London, John Davis, as a legal adviser on the bond litigation and he asked him to find out Hughes' view on the matter, arming him with a six-page memorandum on the subject. As Hughes was away from Washington, Davis met with William Phillips, who unofficially told him that the US government would place 'no obstacle in the way of the recognition' of the Free State. The latter also indicated that the Canadian and Australian governments were also expected to apply for recognition, which suggests that Hughes did not wish the Irish government and its supporters to interpret the assent as preferential treatment for Ireland.[76]

Smiddy's 'confidential and trusted informants' were also working on the recognition matter by infiltrating irregular networks and counteracting their propaganda against the appointment.[77] In July, the recognition campaign picked up the support of Patrick Joseph Hayes, archbishop of New York, who generally avoided

72 NAI, D/FA, ES, 29/189(4), Smiddy to FitzGerald, 5 April 1923.   73 Ibid., ES, 32/211, Smiddy to FitzGerald, 6 February 1923; ibid., D/T, S1983, Diarmaid O'Hegarty to MacNeill, 19 October 1923. Crawford had also discussed the matter with unnamed Canadian officials.   74 Ibid., D/FA, ES, 31/200, Walshe to Smiddy, 1 February 1923; DIFP, ii, NAI, D/FA, D1976, FitzGerald to Healy, 1 February 1923.   75 NAI, D/FA, ES, 28/175, Smiddy to FitzGerald, 8 December 1922; ibid., 29/189 (4), Smiddy to FitzGerald, 23 January 1923; ibid., 28/185, Smiddy to FitzGerald, 20 April 1923; ibid., 29/178, Smiddy to FitzGerald, 10 May 1923.   76 NAI, D/FA, ES, 29/192, Smiddy to FitzGerald, 12 May 1923. Smiddy met with W.L. MacKenzie King, the Canadian prime minister, in early May 1923 to discuss the matter of separate representation in Washington for the respective dominions. At this stage King was 'quite satisfied with the existing relationship.' NAI, D/FA, ES, 29/190, Smiddy to FitzGerald, 12 May 1923. For further on the Canadian role see chapter eleven.   77 Ibid., ES, 28/185, Unnamed memorandum, 26 June 1923.

shows of political leadership.[78] The onset of the summer recess in Congress undoubtedly stalled the recognition campaign as did a coincidence of other events. Firstly, the British government led by Bonar Law collapsed in May which necessitated a general election at the end of the year, secondly, Cosgrave decided to hold a snap election on 27 August, thirdly, the Irish Free State's department of External Affairs concentrated its resources on preparations for admission to the League of Nations which was secured in September and on attendance at the imperial conference in London in October and finally, Harding died unexpectedly on 2 August. Consequently, by the time the Irish Free State government revived the recognition matter in October, when Cosgrave requested Eoin MacNeill, in London, to sound out the British government on the 'possibility of our having an Ambassador at Washington', the political landscape had changed in the US and Britain.[79]

Harding and Ireland: an overview

Harding had entered office intending to concentrate on domestic policy following the League of Nations and Treaty of Versailles debacle and was not elected to be active in foreign affairs. Ironically, he had greater experience than Wilson of the world outside the US, having travelled widely and having been a member of the Senate Foreign Relations Committee but he certainly did not have an ideologically inspired world-view of foreign affairs as Wilson had. He promoted American nationalism and protecting US rights abroad, mixing isolationism with internationalism. This ambivalence characterized his approach both to the presidency, where he wanted to be a conciliator and a facilitator and to his cabinet nominees. He worked through taking advice from men whom he considered to be the experts in specific areas while also allowing them autonomy. In the case of foreign policy, Harding fully supported Hughes and his team of diplomats, who immediately moved to settle the peace treaties with former enemies, the war debts, reparations and arms limitation matters. As part of this programme US–British relations improved dramatically between March 1921 and August 1923. This development was assisted by a weakening in Irish activities both inside and inside the White House.

During this period, Harding, who had no connections with nationalist Irish-America except through the League of Nations campaigns, provided support to the Irish relief campaign on humanitarian grounds. His action was followed by endorsements from other cabinet members. Once this extraordinary action had been interpreted by the Irish and British sides as political support for the republican cause and when anti-British agitation escalated, both Harding and Hughes reverted to a cautious policy on non-involvement, but not before Hughes had officially raised the Irish question with Geddes, albeit to achieve other policy

78 M.E. Brown, 'Hayes, Patrick Joseph' in M. Glazier (ed.), *The encyclopedia of the Irish in America* (1999), p. 380; NAI, D/FA, ES, 28/185, Unknown to Smiddy, 10 July 1923.   79 NAI, D/T, S1983, O'Hegarty to MacNeill, 17 October 1923.

aims. Nonetheless, it was the first time since 1917 that it had been discussed at this level. Throughout the rest of 1921, Harding played both anglophobe and anglophile cards but once the Anglo-Irish treaty came on the horizon, he weighed in fully behind it. When issues relating to recognition arose Hughes looked for guidance from the Foreign Office and he also controlled the already limited access of Irish-America to the president. This reduction of Irish-America power in the White House mirrored the situation outside. The ending of the war of independence, the split over the Anglo-Irish treaty and the subsequent civil war, divided republicans in the US as well as in Ireland. Consequently, in a situation where the majority of Irish-American politicians, public and press supported the treaty, believing Michael Collins' view that it represented a step along the path to full independence, and where most abhorred the civil war, it was only a minority who continued to agitate and contribute to irregular fund-raising, gun-running and propagandizing. For the majority of Irish-Americans and interested Americans, the Irish question was resolved and they, therefore, devoted themselves mainly to domestic affairs from 1923 onwards.

US representatives in Ireland faced many challenges in the period 1921 to 1923. Dumont had intervened as a mediator, though without official sanction, Kent totally supported the Ulster unionist position, while Mitchell and Hathaway attempted to provide balanced views on events in Ireland. They co-operated with and were respected by the British authorities, particularly Dumont who acted as a mouthpiece for the British administration in Dublin Castle. Soon Dumont came to be regarded by Irish republicans as 'pro-British', but this did not apply to the other US consuls. Instead they were regarded as important figures whose views were respected. The contrast between Dumont and his successor was soon evident. Hathaway struck up a working relationship with FitzGerald, Free State minister for External Affairs which was noted by Castle and Hughes.[80]

The consequences of the Anglo-Irish treaty for the Washington, London, Dublin diplomatic relationship were immediately evident in terms of co-operation on the ground in the US. Although US recognition of the Irish Free State had still not materialized, it existed in a *de facto* way illustrated by Harding's note and British diplomats working relationship with Smiddy in the US. Increasingly the every-day work of improving economic, commercial and trading links would dominate their attention, as would the on-going affairs of immigrants and emigrants, which will be examined in the following chapters. Despite a positive early engagement, Republican Warren Harding's Irish policy was little changed from that of Democratic Woodrow Wilson. Ultimately it was one of minimal or non-existent interference, despite the best efforts of Irish-American nationalist supporters. Nonetheless, it is worth recalling from chapter seven that in 1932 de Valera still viewed Harding in positive terms. The myth that Harding, on behalf of republican Ireland, had intervened with the British government still persisted.

80 NARA, RG59, 580.220, part. 111, 841d.00/615, Castle to Hughes, 15 August 1923.

CHAPTER TEN

The Coolidge presidency, foreign policy and Ireland, August 1923

Five days after Calvin Coolidge's election as mayor of Northampton city [in 1910] by a margin of only 187 votes, he wrote to his father that the results showed that Calvin Coolidge received 400 Democratic votes, and added: 'bless their honest Irish hearts'.[1]

When the news of Calvin Coolidge's appointment as thirtieth president of the US became known, few people knew anything about him. Reporters scrambled to get information about the new president.[2] He had not gone beyond the limited boundaries of the office of vice-president. At social and speaking engagements he had served as an able stand-in for Harding, presided over the Senate without major controversy and attended cabinet meetings. Although Harding broke with precedent to establish this last practice his vice-president brought little to the meetings. His tenure had been largely uneventful and unremarkable as befitted the office.[3] Coolidge stated 'While I little realised it at the time, it was for me a period of most important preparation. It enabled me to be ready in August 1923.'[4]

In his first article on 'Calvinism', H.L. Mencken wrote that Calvin Coolidge was above all a 'far more cunning and realistic politician' than Harding had been. Mencken expected government to function in a 'silent and inoffensive manner' and said that Congress 'will not be belaboured with denunciations and beseechings.' He acknowledged Coolidge's strength of character but wondered whether

---

1 R.C. Garvey, 'Coolidge and the Northampton Irish: a strange alliance', 71. 2 On the night of 2 August 1923, Calvin Coolidge, the United States vice-president, was holidaying at his family home in Plymouth Notch, Vermont, along with his wife, Grace Anna, and two children, John and Calvin. He was awakened by his father who told him that President Harding had died. A little while later his father, who was a notary public, administered the oath of office to his son. C. Coolidge, *The autobiography of Calvin Coolidge* (1929), pp. 173–5. Coolidge's autobiography is the first starting point for a study of the president. A comprehensive essay on the historiography of the Coolidge presidency may be found in R.H. Ferrell, *The presidency of Calvin Coolidge* (1998), pp. 223–33 and in the end notes in R. Sobel, *Coolidge: an American enigma* (1998), pp. 421–33. There is a useful discussion on conflicting views of Coolidge in S.M. Stern, 'William Allen White and the origins of the Coolidge stereotype', 57–68; R.H. Ferrell, 'Calvin Coolidge: the man and the myth', 11. 3 J.R. Greene, 'Calvin Coolidge and the vice-presidency: his introduction to Washington politics', 73–6. 4 Coolidge, *The autobiography*, p. 164.

he would survive the scandals of the Harding administration and whether he could secure his own position sufficiently within his own party to be assured of nomination in 1924.[5] If Mencken, a seasoned political observer, was doubtful whether Coolidge could survive beyond 1924, most other observers among the press, politicians and the public knew much less about the former vice-president and awaited his actions. Nonetheless, Coolidge was not without a great deal of practical experience of a solid Republican sort that he had built up prior to 1921.

Path to the presidency

Calvin Coolidge was born on 4 July 1872 and wrote that his family were of 'English Puritan stock ... a hardy self-contained people.' The Coolidges had prospered and by 1872, his father owned a post office, a store and land. His mother's family came from Scotch, Welsh and English stock and her mother's were mainly of the 'old New England stock.'[6] His early life was shaped by the values of a small-town, bible-reading, Yankee and Republican family and community.

According to Coolidge, there were approximately two hundred and fifty qualified voters in Plymouth Notch, of whom not more than twenty-five were Democrats with the rest Republican. However, the leaders of this small community were united in ensuring good and fair government and were less riven along party lines. In his autobiography, he noted occasions where common sense, fairness and equality prevailed rather than political partisanship.[7] Throughout his childhood he received a practical education in the importance of public duty, democracy and good governance:

> By reason of what I saw and heard in my early life, I came to have a good working knowledge of the practical side of government. I understood that it consisted of restraints which the people had imposed upon themselves in order to promote the common welfare.[8]

Like Woodrow Wilson, Coolidge grew up in an environment where reading was ingrained and he similarly developed an interest in history and law. He was admitted to the bar in 1897 and set up a practice in the same year. Coolidge's family background and his belief that entering public life would make him a better lawyer led him to become a member of the Republican City Committee. In December 1898 he was elected as one of the three Republican members of the Northampton Common Council.[9]

5 H.L. Mencken, 'Calvinism. 3 September 1923' in M. Moos (ed.), *H.L. Mencken: a carnival of Buncombe* (1956), p. 68.   6 Coolidge, *The autobiography*, pp. 5, 7, 12, 13. His parents were John Calvin Coolidge and Victoria Josephine Moor. His father's family had come from Massachusetts to Plymouth Notch, Vermont, around 1780.   7 Ibid., pp. 21, 22, 23, 25. He notes that women were given a vote on school questions in both the district and town meetings.   8 Ibid., p. 25.   9 His

Given his upbringing, his choice of political party was not surprising and soon enough his reputation for working hard on behalf of the party and for possessing sound judgement resulted in promotion. In turn he became Northampton city solicitor (1899–1902), Massachusetts state legislator (1906–08), mayor of Northampton (1910–11), Massachusetts state senator (1912–15), lieutenant governor (1916–18) and governor of Massachusetts (1919–21). His political philosophy was also honed and his circle of supporters established throughout this period.

Sobel characterized the period 1899 to 1906 as a time when Coolidge represented conventional Republicanism but held no firm position on any issue and revealed little enthusiasm for the political issues of the day.[10] This was also the period when the future president was diligently working for the party on the ground, building a legal career and establishing a home with Grace Goodhue, whom he married in 1905. Furthermore, the posts he held at that time were largely administrative and, therefore, offered few opportunities to display political views. Nonetheless, they added to his reputation as a solid, diligent, clever individual.

However, his term in the state legislature revealed sympathy for 'progressivism', although he hated labels and refused to be categorized.[11] His voting record on national issues included support for women's suffrage and for direct election of senators to the US Senate to remove them from the influence of states' interest groups. At state level, he supported legislation introducing a six-day working week for labourers, a limit on hours of work for women and children, and pensions for families of firemen and schoolteachers. Coolidge instinctively voted for measures that would protect workers.[12] He also supported Governor Curtis Guild's measures to reform the civil service, reduce the state's debt and economize in government spending.[13]

This mix of belief in fair and good government with conservative financial thinking was also reflected during his time as mayor. Between 1910 and 1911 he reduced the city debt by $90,000, increased the salaries of teachers and launched a programme of public works. He also held firm to the belief that it was more important to implement existing laws fairly than to introduce rafts of new legislation.[14] As he moved into the state senate in 1912, he was firmly in line with progressive Republicanism and when the Republican Party shifted ground towards conservatism in the following years, he moved with it, albeit cautiously.[15]

Foreign policy featured little in Coolidge's world of Massachusetts state politics but this changed somewhat with the outbreak of world war one and, later, with US entry into the war. Coolidge recalled, 'the whole nation seemed to be endowed with a new spirit, unified and solidified, and willing to make any sacrifice for the cause of liberty.' His speeches exuded patriotism and he constantly

father and grandfather served as peace officers in Plymouth Notch, Vermont, for almost seventy-five years. His father was also a public notary, justice of the peace and served in the state legislature. Coolidge, *The autobiography*, pp. 86, 87.   10 Sobel, *Coolidge*, p. 60.   11 Quoted in Sobel, *Coolidge*, p. 62.   12 Ferrell, *The presidency*, pp. 10–11.   13 Sobel, *Coolidge*, p. 63.   14 Quoted in Sobel, *Coolidge*, p. 65.   15 Coolidge, *The autobiography*, p. 112; Quoted in Sobel, *Coolidge*, p. 97.

urged the public to contribute 'men, money and supplies' for the war fronts.[16] In the last year of the war he was elected as governor of Massachusetts. It was his handling of a strike by policemen in Boston later in 1919 that established his 'law and order credentials and helped pave his path towards the vice presidency.[17]

Against a background of increasing radicalism and fear of bolshevism, such actions brought much support to his side, although Coolidge carefully avoided 'red-baiting' and insisted that state intervention was needed only at times of emergencies and that he favoured minimal government. As governor, he prided himself on having reduced the number of state departments from 118 to 18.[18] Thus, it was not surprising that, in the maelstrom of the 1920 Republican national convention in Chicago, Coolidge was nominated as Warren Harding's running mate in the presidential election although he did not deliver a speech, did not outline an agenda and did not even attend. Harding was nominated by the party's political bosses but the party selected Coolidge as its vice-presidential candidate.[19]

After twenty-three years in public office, the following two years were the least eventful of his career. This changed on 2 August 1923. But Coolidge was prepared for the highest office in the land. He had run for office nineteen times and won seventeen of these contests and had served at state and national level since 1898. He had extensive political experience. Thus, the reporters who scrambled to get information about the new president in early August 1923 found out about a man who was a professional politician and an experienced administrator, was widely-respected among the public and politicians, had a cohesive political philosophy and held definite views about the role of the president.

As a lawyer, meticulous administrator, politician and vice-president, Coolidge had formulated ideas about the duties and responsibilities of the presidency. He had also watched Wilson's attempts to unite the separate executive and legislative branches of government and Harding's opposition to such moves. Coolidge's approach in 1923 can be characterized as minimalist.[20] He believed firstly, that the primary function of government was to enforce the rule of existing law and then to legislate but only insofar as this served to enable local communities. Secondly, he never felt it was his duty to attempt 'to coerce senators or representatives, or to take reprisals. The people sent them to Washington.'[21] Coolidge

16 Coolidge, *The autobiography*, p. 121.   17 His electoral success was due to his record on state issues, his conventional rhetoric on the war, strong Republican Party backing, a weak Democratic candidate in Richard Long and the public perception of him as a solid, honest and able man. The details of the strike are not central to this study but in Coolidge's words, 'the trouble arose over the proposal of the policemen ... to form a union and affiliate to the American Federation of Labor.' He regarded this action as illegal. Subsequent events between January and September 1919 provided Coolidge with the opportunity to demonstrate his 'law and order' credentials by calling in additional state troops to deal with the strikers on 9 September 1919 and by informing Samuel Gompers, head of the union, that the workers could not be reinstated because 'There is no right to strike against the public safety by any body, any time, any where.' Ibid., pp. 127, 133.   18 Ibid., p. 135.   19 Sobel, *Coolidge*, p. 158.   20 P. Johnson, 'Calvin Coolidge and the last Arcadia' in J. Earl Haynes (ed.), *Calvin Coolidge and the Coolidge era: essays on the history of the 1920s* (1998), p. 6.   21 Coolidge,

intended to let the sixty-eighth Congress, dominated by Republican Party leaders, enact its legislative programme without direction from him. However, the success of this approach depended on agreement between president and Congress on legislation and this was not guaranteed even when the president's party dominated Congress. Nevertheless, the people had also sent him to Washington, although not as president, and in the discharge of his duties he believed there was 'one rule of action more important than all others. It consists in never doing anything that some one else can do for you.' However, in order to secure success this rule had an important corollary; 'It is not sufficient to entrust details to some one else.'[22]

Like Harding, Coolidge intended to gather around him such men of sufficient ability who could solve problems that arose in their respective jurisdictions. Unlike Harding, who delegated because he believed that others were more intelligent and better informed than he, Coolidge believed in the concept as a way of better governance. For him the president was at 'the centre of things, where no one else can stand' and Coolidge would not shirk making 'final judgements', if needed. He had a crystal clear view of the extent of the president's authority and responsibilities. Following his minimalist system of government, he would act with restraint and 'wait to decide each question on its merits as it arises.' This approach also suited his reserved, quiet personality. Yet, as revisionist historians have noted, this limited view of the presidency did not equate with laziness or stupidity. Coolidge worked longer hours than others of his time, he was the last president to compose his own speeches, he held 520 press conferences, an average of almost eight per month, and delivered more speeches than any of his predecessors.[23]

Just as the president's relationship with Congress was crucial so the key to the success of his delegation would lie in the composition of his cabinet. As Coolidge had sat in on cabinet meetings for two years he knew the abilities of the Harding appointees and decided to retain all cabinet members.[24] However, by the end of the Coolidge tenure on 3 March 1929, only four of the original cabinet remained.[25]

The autobiography, p. 232.   **22** Ibid., p. 196.   **23** Ibid., pp. 196, 198–9. For further on the details of his day see ibid., pp. 200–4; Sobel, *Coolidge*, pp. 239, 242, 243; Stern, 'William Allen White', pp. 57–68.   **24** All, except secretary of the Treasury Andrew Mellon, agreed to stay on in office. After their first meeting on 3 August, Mellon told Coolidge, 'Mr President, I neglected to tell you that I had come to resign'. Coolidge replied 'Forget it.' Mellon was central to Coolidge's plans. Both shared firstly, a philosophy of reducing taxes and debts and secondly, the belief that 'the chief business of the American people is business.' Following secretary of State Hughes' resignation in 1925, to return to a lucrative private legal practice, Coolidge regarded Mellon as his 'prime minister.' Quoted in Sobel, *Coolidge*, p. 242. H. O'Connor, *Mellon's millions: the biography of a fortune: the life and times of Andrew W. Mellon* (1933), p. 123; R.K. Murray, *The Harding era: Warren G. Harding and his administration* (1969), p. 500. J.W. Johnson, 'John Calvin Coolidge, 1923–1929' in M.I. Urofsky (ed.), *The American presidents* (2000), p. 315. Harding described Mellon as 'the ubiquitous financier of the universe.' Coolidge retained all Harding's appointees to commissions and boards at least until 1925. R.K. Murray, *The Harding era: Warren G. Harding and his administration* (1969), p. 500.

Coolidge's style of governing demonstrated his concept of the presidency. Not only did he delegate as much as possible to department heads but there were less cabinet meetings than during the Harding regime. Each cabinet member was asked if he had any problem he wished to lay before Coolidge, 'after entire freedom of discussion, but always without a vote of any kind, I accustomed to announce what the decision would be.' Coolidge recalled 'there never ought to be and never were marked differences of opinion in my cabinet. As their duties were not to advise the president, they could not disagree among themselves.' But he 'rarely failed to accept their recommendations.'[26] Naturally there were occasions when members intervened in other departments' affairs. Perhaps the best example was Hoover who had wide interests, including restructuring the executive branch of government, foreign affairs, agriculture after Henry Wallace's departure and the treasury.[27] Ultimately all the cabinet had supported the Harding agenda that Coolidge now adopted and each recognized Coolidge's excellent administrative skills and attention to detail. Nonetheless, Coolidge's reticence, brevity or silences and shyness kept his cabinet colleagues and political associates guessing about his true intentions.

Coolidge, however, reversed the Harding style of open-access to himself and the White House.[28] Yet, he entertained more than Harding and inaugurated the White House breakfasts which were attended by congressional members. He admitted, 'we did not undertake to discuss matters of public business at these breakfasts, they were productive of a spirit of good fellowship, which was no doubt a helpful influence to the transaction of public business.'[29] Those who attended were generally greeted by silences from the president and were frequently frustrated to be so close to him but unable to discuss policy with him. Nor did the breakfasts assist his relationship with Congress, as will be seen.

The third arm of government in which the president's style of governing expressed itself was in his contacts with his personal confidants and office staff. Harding had his 'Ohio gang' and Coolidge had his Massachusetts confidants:

---

25 Johnson, 'John Calvin Coolidge', pp. 316, 317. Coolidge did not appoint a vice-president from August 1923 until he formed his own administration in March 1925 when he chose Charles G. Dawes. Some of these changes were imposed on Coolidge because he inherited the Teapot Dome oil-leasing affair. When it became politically expedient in that he was under pressure from the Senate and the public, he allowed both Daugherty and Denby to leave the cabinet. But it was Wallace who would cause Coolidge the greatest problems in terms of policy. The former championed the McHary–Haugen farm relief bill which sought government purchase of farm surpluses at set rates for resale in international markets. The bill epitomized government intervention in agriculture, which Coolidge, Hoover and Mellon utterly opposed. Coolidge kept Denby in office until the latter's death in 1924.   26 Coolidge, The autobiography, p. 204.   27 J. Hoff Wilson, Herbert Hoover: forgotten progressive (1975), p. 84.   28 Murray, The Harding era, p. 500.   29 Coolidge, The autobiography, pp. 209–10. On a social level, the Coolidges were most hospitable. They had 102 house guests in the White House during five years and seven months, compared to Taft who had thirty-two house guests in four years, Wilson who had twelve in eight years and Harding who only had five. R.H. Ferrell, 'Calvin Coolidge, the man and the president' in Haynes, Calvin Coolidge, p. 139.

Frank W. Stearns, the Amherst-educated businessman, William M. Butler, a textile manufacturer and another Amherst man, Dwight Morrow who was a banker in the J.P. Morgan company.

The relationship between the 'Massachusetts gang' and Coolidge differed from that between the 'Ohio gang' and Harding. Firstly, until Morrow's appointment, none of Coolidge's circle held public office and, therefore, could not dispense favours themselves even if they wanted to. Secondly, Coolidge was a self-contained man who consulted with his friends when he needed to, but otherwise held his own counsel. Even when Coolidge called Stearns into his office the two men might simply remain silent for anything up to an hour. Thirdly, Coolidge, the public servant, abhorred the patronage and cronyism associated with Harding and the 'Ohio gang' and would not have countenanced a continuation of it under his watch, although his favouring of Amherst men in his appointments was noticeable.[30] Despite this last factor, the new president would be in no way compromised by his circle of associates.

His choice of office staff was careful also. C. Bascom Slemp, a former representative for Virginia, was chosen as private secretary to replace George Christian, who departed to become Florence Harding's private secretary. Slemp was chosen partly because his political knowledge of Congress would be useful to the president in his dealings with that body, particularly if the latter went for re-election. His quiet personality also complimented Coolidge's.[31] Slemp was replaced in 1925 by Everett Sanders, a former congressman from Indiana, whose assistant was Edward T. Clark, another Amherst man.[32] Each appointment was significant and of some practical use to the president.[33]

The style of his governing and the composition of his circle of advisers suggested further changes in the style of presidency. Delegation was a key component of the *modus operandi*, but so also was presidential attention to detail and application of existing laws. He placed enormous faith in the quality of the men who formed his cabinet and in the co-operation of a Republican-dominated Congress. It remained to be seen if this faith would be repaid. He was a man prepared for the presidency in intellectual, political and administrative terms, whether or not he was suitable for the post.

30 The alcohol which fuelled many of the Harding parties in the White House was banned under Coolidge who scrupulously adhered to the prohibition. Sobel, *Coolidge*, p. 241.   31 Quoted in W. Allen White, *A puritan in Babylon: the story of Calvin Coolidge* (1938), p. 276. The White biography has been the subject of much discussion among historians not least because of criticism of his perpetuation of the Coolidge stereotype as silent, lazy, inactive, reactionary, devoted to big business and a misanthrope. See Stern, 'William Allen White', pp. 57–68.   32 Sobel, *Coolidge*, pp. 240–1; Ferrell, *The presidency*, p. 27. Dr Sawyer was retained as the White House physician. Library of Congress (hereafter LC), Manuscripts Division (hereafter MD), Edward T. Clarke Papers, 'Introduction'.   33 Also he continued Harding's practice of holding twice weekly press conferences and successfully handled the press who were not only respectful and courteous to him, as was the practice of the time, but appeared to have liked him also. Sobel, *Coolidge*, pp. 239–40.

Coolidge and foreign policy

Harding may have lacked Coolidge's intellect and had little facility for original thinking but he had far more experience in foreign policy, as was indicated previously. Coolidge had never travelled outside the United States and had little interest in doing so. In early March 1924, he told Isa Howard, wife of Esmé Howard, the British ambassador to the US, that 'he thought he would never visit Europe because America had everything he needed to learn.'[34] Even though he was widely read on government and governing and had books on US foreign policy in his library, as a politician he was primarily interested in domestic matters, believing that the key to US prosperity and progress lay mainly in the promotion of the national economy. This position was evident early in his gubernatorial years.

Once the US entered the war, he was fully behind the patriotic effort. The peacemaking posed him problems just as it did most other politicians. The League of Nations had become a divisive issue. Some inkling of Coolidge's position emerged on 24 February 1919. As governor of Massachusetts, he had to welcome Woodrow Wilson when he arrived in Boston from the Paris peace conference. Coolidge recalled 'I made a short address of welcome, pledging him my support in helping settle the remaining war problems.'[35] His words were interpreted by some as supporting the League of Nations but Coolidge refused to be drawn out any further. A reporter asked, 'Governor, what do you think of the League?' Coolidge replied: 'I am the governor of Massachusetts. The state of Massachusetts has no foreign relations. If ever I should hold an office calling for action or opinion on this subject. I shall put my mind on it and try and arrive at the soundest conclusions within my capacity.'[36] His elevation to national office provided the opportunity.[37]

Following his vice-presidential nomination by the Republican convention in 1920, he delivered a speech on 27 July, in which he described the League of Nations as 'subversive of the traditions and independence of America.' But, he continued, the Republican Party 'approves the principle of agreement among nations to preserve peace, and pledges itself to the making of such an agreement, preserving American independence and rights, as will meet every duty America owes to humanity.' Coolidge maintained this position throughout the election campaign.[38] The temporizing approach appealed to Borah and the irreconcilables as well as to Lodge and his reservationists. Not surprisingly, it was a situation which Coolidge did not rush to change.[39]

---

34 Quoted in B. McKercher, *Esmé Howard: a diplomatic biography* (1989), p. 277.   35 Coolidge, *The autobiography*, pp. 125–6. He then began a 'friendly relationship' with the Wilsons. Ibid.   36 Quoted in Sobel, *Coolidge*, pp. 148–9; ibid., p. 149.   37 Coolidge, *The autobiography*, p. 167.   38 Quoted in Sobel, *Coolidge*, p. 202; ibid., pp. 203, 214.   39 T.A. Smiddy, the Irish Free State representative in the US, believed in April 1923 that the Harding administration was 'seeking a diplomatic way of entering the League.' National Archives of Ireland (hereafter NAI), Department of Foreign Affairs (hereafter D/FA), 28/189, Smiddy to FitzGerald, 20 April 1923.

Almost immediately there was speculation that he knew little of foreign affairs. Hughes' decision to cancel all press conferences in the week following Harding's death led the Hearst-owned press to announce that it was, in Hughes' words, because 'I have been unable to ascertain definitely your [Coolidge's] views in relation to foreign affairs.' Naturally Hughes denied this 'as absolutely false' in a personal and confidential letter to Coolidge on 7 August.[40] On the other hand, William Phillips, who was acting secretary of State when Coolidge was catapulted into office on 3 August, recalled that on the following day Coolidge told him that the government was 'playing too close to the League and that an explosion in Congress might be the result.' Significantly, Coolidge did not mind a 'public explosion' directed against Congress, but he disliked the idea of a congressional explosion directed against the presidency.[41] With the exception of this exchange, his own views on the League of Nations remained hidden and he confirmed Harding's agenda at his first cabinet meeting on 14 August. Among the foreign policies which he fully supported were the collection of war debts, participation in the World Court, prevention of Soviet recognition, the improvement of relations with Latin and South America, further restriction of immigration and maintenance of the protective tariff system.[42]

Coolidge spent the period from August to the middle of November examining the detailed-workings of all government departments, because he believed it would help him to discuss the state of the union in his first message to Congress on 6 December, the first to be broadcast on radio. In it he elaborated further on foreign policy; 'For us peace reigns everywhere. We desire to perpetuate it always … The world has had enough of the curse of hatred and selfishness, of destruction and war. It has had enough of the wrong use of material power … The time has come for a more practical use of moral power.'[43] In specific terms, he added that US naval strength would be maintained at the Washington treaty limits.[44] Even though William Castle, chief of the west European division in the State Department, wrote in the following weeks, 'the President has little knowledge of foreign affairs', Coolidge's emphasis on peace and opposition to war appealed to the US public and would assist him in winning the 1924 election.[45] After his election victory the gap between his principles and his conduct of foreign policy became noticeable when the US intervened in China and Nicaragua in 1927. On these occasions, aggressive impulses combined with pressure from interest groups predominated in his foreign policy and he followed precedent, pursuing a version of nineteenth century 'gunboat diplomacy' in order to protect US citizens and property.[46]

40 Calvin Coolidge Papers (hereafter CCP), series 1, 19 Misc-20, June 30, 1924, roll 26, Hughes to Coolidge, 7 August 1923.   41 W. Phillips, *Ventures in diplomacy* (1952), p. 59.   42 CCP, series 1, 31A continued 38, roll 39, Wile, 'President Coolidge's first meeting'.   43 Quoted in A. DeConde, *Presidential machismo: executive authority, military intervention and foreign relations* (2000), p. 110.   44 Murray, *The Harding era*, p. 501.   45 Herbert Hoover Presidential Library, Iowa (hereafter HHPL), William R. Castle Papers (hereafters WRCP), WRC diary, 30 January 1923.   46 DeConde,

A further major theme in Coolidge's foreign policy was support for the expansion of US business abroad. He admitted that anything relating to the functions of the government interested him but its economic relations always had a 'peculiar fascination' for him.⁴⁷ He was a firm believer in the importance of domestic and foreign commerce to the promotion of America's national progress and wealth. This pro-business policy would come to characterize both the decade of the 1920s in US relations with the wider world and the Coolidge administration in general.⁴⁸ Given Coolidge's views and the presence of Mellon and Hoover in government, this was not surprising. Responsibility for implementing foreign economic policy lay mainly with Hoover, while it was Hughes and his State Department machinery who oversaw the diplomatic and consular aspects of foreign policy, at least until his resignation in 1925 when Frank B. Kellogg took over.

Coolidge adopted a strict interpretation of the constitutional boundaries of the president/secretary of State relationship:

> The Secretary of State is the agency through which the President exercises his constitutional authority to deal with foreign relations ... All the intercourse with foreign governments is carried on through the Secretary of State, and a national of a foreign country can not be received by the President unless the accredited diplomatic representative of his government has made an appointment for him through the State Department. All foreign approaches to the President are through this Department.⁴⁹

Coolidge's promotion caused little or no change in Hughes' ability to personally control the foreign policy machinery and policy including the practice of limiting the opportunities for non-accredited foreign persons to gain access to the president. Hughes, therefore, continued to personally implement the Harding policy agenda, as outlined by Coolidge in August and December 1923. Hughes did not personally know Coolidge prior to the latter's appointment as vice-president and later described him as the 'calm little Yankee.'⁵⁰ Coolidge's personality and his hands-off approach to governing suited Hughes, who believed that they 'got along admirably together'. Other factors that helped the relationship

Presidential machismo, p. 111.   **47** Coolidge, *The autobiography*, p. 181.   **48** The extent to which the owners of US wealth translated into national and international influence during the Republican period remains a matter for discussion between historians of US foreign relations in the 1920s. For further on the historiography of the debate see B. McKercher, 'Reaching for the brass ring: the recent historiography of interwar American foreign relations' in M.J. Hogan (ed.), *Paths to power: the historiography of American foreign relations to 1941* (2000), pp. 198–201. Among the first documents passed by Hughes to Coolidge was a letter from the US minister to Colombia, Samuel H. Piles, which stated that Senator William Lorimer was trying to obtain from the Colombian government a concession to build a railroad from Bogota to the Atlantic ocean. Lorimer requested Piles to inform the president of his intention and 'of the great possibilities in Colombia.' CCP, series 1, 19 Misc-20, June 30, 1924, roll 26, Hughes to Coolidge, 14 August 1923.   **49** Coolidge, *The autobiography*, p. 205.   **50** Quoted in M.J. Pusey, *Charles E. Hughes*, 2 vols (1963), ii, pp. 427, 426.

were, firstly Hughes' decision not to run for the presidency in 1924, which Chief Justice Taft informed Coolidge of soon after his return to Washington in August 1924, and secondly, Coolidge's early praise for Hughes as the 'greatest Secretary of State this country ever had.'[51] There are three areas to examine in the Coolidge/Hughes relationship: policy, appointments and reform.

Reform of, and efficiency in, government were Coolidge's cherished aims so Hughes' plans found ready support from the new president. Coolidge had endorsed the Foreign Service [Rogers] bill on 10 October 1923.[52] The legislation was enacted on 24 May 1924. It amalgamated the diplomatic and consular services into one single foreign service in which personnel could interchange between the two branches and which had a single salary scale to assist this interchangeability. It authorized the payment of allowances to representatives in foreign capitals 'to eliminate the possession of large private means as an essential qualification for appointment' and it created titles and grades for the whole service.[53] Efficiency records would be kept for all officers. The new structure meant that the opportunities for political interference at any stage of an appointment were greatly reduced. Increases in salary, retirement and disability pensions, representation allowances and home leave also added to the attractions of a foreign service career.[54] Some times these divisions were difficult to implement in reality as will be seen in chapter twelve. It was not until after the second world war that the division of work and the élite background of the diplomatic corps finally came to an end, although the élitist spirit among foreign service officials was perpetuated.[55] Nonetheless, the institution of the Rogers Act and application of the principle of professionalism was welcomed by the president, public and Congress alike. Moreover, the Rogers' Act came to be regarded as the 'great basic charter of the modern diplomatic service.'[56]

Two posts, those of minister and ambassador, were excluded from the classification system implemented under the Rogers legislation.[57] Consequently, these two highest positions remained subject to political influence. Coolidge believed

---

51 Quoted in Ibid., p. 564.   52 CCP, series 1, 19 Misc-20, June 30, 1924, roll 26, Hughes to Coolidge, 10 October 1923.   53 Ibid., Senate Committee on Foreign Relations Report (to accompany H.R. 13880), no. 1142, 13 February 1923.   54 J.E. Findling, *Dictionary of American diplomatic history* (1980), p. 414. The act was named for its congressional sponsor, Republican Representative John J. Rogers (Massachusetts) but Wilbur J. Carr, director of the Consular Service since 1909, helped draft it. H. DeSantis & W. Heinrichs, 'The Department of State and American Foreign Policy' in Z. Steiner (ed.), *Foreign ministries of the world* (1982), p. 589.   55 DeSantis & Heinrichs, 'The Department of State', pp. 580–1. Hoover also tried to improve the performance of foreign commercial attachés who offered extensive information on trade and statistics to facilitate the expansion of US business abroad.   56 Quoted in Pusey, *Charles E. Hughes*, ii, p. 420. There remained opposition in Congress among the isolationists to the US about the need to have ambassadors at all because communications had become so advanced. Hughes outlined his views on this in a paper to the US Chamber of Commerce on 18 May 1922. Ibid., p. 419.   57 DeSantis & Heinrichs, 'The Department of State', p. 580. However, foreign service officers could now be promoted to ministerial posts.

that 'one of the most perplexing and at the same time, most important functions of the president, is the making of appointments.'[58] He was soon immersed in the task. When he arrived back to Washington on 8 August, following Harding's funeral in Marion, Ohio, there was 'an unseemly scramble to get the new President's ear.'[59] Coolidge applied his guiding philosophy of consultation when making appointments. In some few cases, he acted alone. But 'usually' they were made with the advice and consent of either the relevant Republican senator if the appointment was at state level or the relevant departmental secretary if it was a national one.[60] Another factor informing his decision was to appoint 'men of knowledge and experience who have sufficient character to resist temptations. If that standard is maintained, we need not be concerned about their former activities ... It should be possible to choose a well-qualified person wherever he can be found.[61] Finally, Coolidge accepted that the existence of the Senate veto of nominations meant there was 'little danger' that a president would abuse his authority.[62] Coolidge maintained Harding's cabinet, many of his White House staff and all his appointments in the administration, boards and commissions, in his first term. His only significant diplomatic interventions occurred in 1923, when he replaced George Harvey with Frank B. Kellogg as ambassador to the Court of St James in London. Kellogg, who, having been defeated as a candidate for re-election to the Senate for Minnesota, had returned to his legal practice and was surprised by the offer.[63] In his second term, Coolidge replaced Charles Evans Hughes with Kellogg as secretary of State in 1925 which will be discussed later in the chapter.[64]

Hughes regarded Kellogg as a 'conscientious and hard-working' person and he had corresponded with the senator previously on foreign affairs matters.[65] The

---

58 Coolidge, *The autobiography*, p. 225. 59 Quoted in Pusey, *Charles E. Hughes*, ii, p. 564. 60 On 10 December 1923, Coolidge notified Republican senators that he intended to consult them about appointments in their own state because some had suggested that it 'might save embarrassment' if senators could be notified before such appointments were made. He agreed and instructed the heads of departments to act accordingly. CCP, series 1, 19 Misc-20, June 30, 1924, roll minute, 10 December 1923. Hughes clarified with Coolidge that the new policy applied only to 'routine appointments' and not consular officers and diplomatic secretaries whose appointment was made according to various executive orders. Coolidge noted 'your assumption is correct.' CCP, series 1, 19 Misc-20, June 30, 1924, roll 26, Hughes to Coolidge, 15 December 1923. 61 Coolidge, *The autobiography*, p. 225, 226, 227. 62 Ibid., p. 227. 63 G.H. Stuart, *The Department of State: a history of its organization, procedure and personnel* (1949), p. 276; Root quoted in Sobel, *Coolidge*, p. 340; L. Ethan Ellis, *Frank B. Kellogg and American foreign relations, 1925–1929* (1961), p. 7; HHPL, WRCP, box 8, countries correspondence file, England 1920 to December 1926, Castle to Sterling, 5 October 1923; D. Bryn-Jones, *Frank B. Kellogg: a biography* (1937), p. 131. 64 By mid-1923, Harvey was distrusted by some diplomats in Washington and in his own embassy and Robert Cecil who had responsibility for the League of Nations in the second Baldwin government described Harvey as 'tiresome.' HHPL, WRCP, box 8, countries correspondence file, England 1920 to December 1926, Boylston A Beal to Castle, 30 April 1923; D. Cameron Watt, *Succeeding John Bull: America in Britain's place 1900–1975: a study of the Anglo-American relationship and world policies in the context of British and American foreign policy making in the 20th century* (1984), p. 55, n.57. 65 LC, MD, Charles Evans Hughes Papers (hereafter

new ambassador was sixty-seven years of age when he arrived in London on 30 December 1923. His qualities of hard work, reliability and efficiency were needed in the embassy. On 7 April 1924 he wrote to Castle, 'we have a perfectly harmonious and happy family in Grovesnor Gardens and everybody is pulling together ... while I don't wish to say anything about my predecessor, I can't understand how he could run this office and not be here every day ... and I find the staff very pleased with this arrangement.' Frederick Sterling, now a counsellor in the London embassy agreed, 'things are going very cheerfully in the embassy.'[66] Apparently Kellogg's negative personality traits such as caution, naïveté, and a quick temper had not yet emerged.[67] More important was the comment of another diplomat, Frederick Dolbeare, who felt that 'the whole temper of the Foreign Office has changed since January first. This may be attributed to the obvious sincerity of our new chief, the good impression Sterling has made and the departure of the most noble but petulant Marquess [Curzon].'[68] Kellogg was indeed fortunate to arrive when Ramsay MacDonald, prime minister of the new Labour government that took office on 22 January 1924, also assumed the foreign secretary post. The additional staff which Harvey had demanded had also finally arrived. Butler Wright in the London embassy hoped that all would result in 'a better distribution of work and increase productivity.'[69]

Kellogg was a political appointment and had not been Coolidge's first or second choice for the post. He began with little experience of foreign policy and no familiarity with diplomacy but he had the president's imprimatur and much good will from all quarters. When his appointment as ambassador to London was noted in the British embassy's 1923 annual report the potted biography noted that he had 'lived most of his life in Minnesota' but had 'travelled widely'.[70] In other words, the British diplomats knew little about him and, therefore, were unable to make comments on his suitability for the London posting. It remained to be seen how he would handle the issues which dominated US relations with Britain at the end of 1923, namely war debts/reparations, restrictions on naval armaments, the extent of the US role in the organization of peace, the continuation of the Fordney–McCumber Tariff Act (1922), the enforcement of the Volstead Act on British ships in US waters and possible co-operation over the development of the

CEHP), containers 38–9, file Frank B Kellogg (ii), Hughes to Kellogg, 17 July 1922; Pusey, *Charles Evans Hughes*, ii, p. 613. 66 Ibid., Kellogg to Castle, 7 April 1924; ibid., Sterling to Castle, 30 April 1924. 67 L. Ethan Ellis, 'Frank B. Kellogg (1925–1929)' in N.A. Graebner (ed.), *An uncertain tradition: American secretaries of state in the twentieth century* (1961), p. 150. 68 HHPL, WRCP, box 3, countries correspondence file, England 1920 to December 1926, Frederick Dolbeare to Castle, 30 April 1924. 69 Ibid., Blair to Castle, 18 July 1923. Kellogg hoped that Post Wheeler stationed in London would be replaced however, the latter was well-connected. Immediate to Kellogg's appointment, he received letters from Senator W.B. McKinley and Judge George Sutherland to maintain the disruptive Wheeler. LC, MD, CEHP, containers 38–9, File Frank B. Kellogg (1), McKinley to Kellogg, 8 November 1923, Sutherland to Kellogg, 30 October 1923. 70 The National Archives, London (hereafter TNA), Foreign Office (hereafter FO) 371/9635, United States, Annual Report 1923, pp. 70, 105.

oil resources of Mesopotamia.[71] For the first time, a US ambassador would not be faced with the campaign for Irish independence but Kellogg remained responsible for the Ireland region and its diplomatic relationship with the US so long as the US government did not appoint a minister or ambassador to the Irish Free State.

In March 1925, Kellogg had been in London for just fifteen months when Coolidge recalled him to Washington to replace Hughes as secretary of State. The former believed that his 'success' at the Court of St James had contributed to the president's decision.[72] However, the Foreign Office, now under Austen Chamberlain, saw him as 'a somewhat tired man, who had lost his power of grip and decision.'[73] His successor, Alanson B. Houghton, was even less welcome.[74] He had been a political appointee of the Harding administration to the ambassadorial post in Weimar Germany in 1922, where he performed well, persuading the German leadership to accept the Dawes plan in 1924. In 1925, Castle picked up some rumours that he was becoming too 'pro-German', although he believed that Houghton 'never for one moment forgot that he was an American.' The accusation certainly did not prevent Coolidge transferring him to London in April 1925 as Kellogg's replacement.[75] His Republican credentials, proven diplomatic record and favourable personality made the move almost inevitable. Castle regarded him as one of Coolidge's 'loyal supporters and ... a splendid man', who was the 'man to be Secretary of State.'[76]

Houghton, although 'naïve' and 'trusting', was more even-tempered than the volatile Kellogg and by November 1925, Ray Atherton could report from the London embassy that Houghton 'daily increases his official prestige and personal popularity ... the embassy is very much on the map in London.'[77] Nevertheless, Houghton was constantly suspicious of British foreign policy motives, not least because his view of US–British relations encompassed the wider European context. In 1925, soon after his arrival, he complained to Castle about Britain's role in generating an 'anti-American feeling' in Europe and about the absence of 'gratitude' outside of Germany towards the US for lending money by the 'hundreds of millions.' He did not believe that Britain would ever attack the US, but thought it was 'setting out in a campaign ... in which she purposes to regain her old position ... powerful.'[78] He remained in London until 1928, by which time

71 CCP, series 1, 19 Misc-20, June 30, 1924, roll 26, Hughes to Coolidge, 18 August, 31 October 1923.   72 Bryn-Jones, *Frank B. Kellogg*, p. 162.   73 McKercher, *Esmé Howard*, p. 288.   74 Houghton was a large manufacturer who served two terms as a member of Congress representing New York. K. Bourne and D.C. Watt (general editors), *British documents on foreign affairs* (hereafter *BDFA*), part 11, series C, North America, 25 vols. (1986–95), xiv, The Republican Ascendancy, 1919–28, Annual Report for the United States for 1924, p. 126.   75 HHPL, WRCP, Box 3, file 25, Castle to Blair, 29 May 1925.   76 Ibid., file 26, Castle to Sterling, 23 March 1926.   77 Ibid., Castle to Sterling, 23 March 1926; ibid., Box 33, Castle, 'The tools of American diplomacy, p. 12; ibid., Box 3, file 26, Atherton to Castle, 9 November 1925.   78 Ibid., Box 3, Countries Correspondence file, England 1924 to January 1933, Houghton to Castle, 28 September 1925, 23 December 1925. Houghton's 'trusting strain' got him into trouble in 1926 when he gave a

US–British diplomatic relations had sunk to an all-time low on the naval disarmament issue and 'anglophobia' and 'anti-Americanism' pervaded US and British official circles respectively. This did not affect Coolidge's admiration for Houghton's 'discretion and ability.'[79]

With the exception of Kellogg's appointment as ambassador, Coolidge's imprint on the machinery and policy of US foreign relations was minimal during his first term. Hughes discouraged any possibility of the US recognizing the Soviet Union, so Coolidge followed the Harding and Wilson hard-line approach, while allowing US capitalists to trade with the USSR. When it came to organizing peace, Coolidge and Hughes shared a belief in the principle of co-operation between states, though not as it was embodied in the League of Nations and the World Court. Coolidge was also influenced by the public rejection of Wilsonian internationalism and by pressure from within his own party. Nevertheless, he appointed US representatives as 'observers' and as 'experts' to affiliated League organizations while calling for general conferences to be held on promoting further arms limitation and international law. Although the former was not to occur until 1927, he continued the Harding/Hughes path in December 1923, recommending to Congress US adherence to the World Court, accompanied by an anti-League of Nations reservation.[80]

Achieving stability and prosperity for the US and the world was related in the Coolidge/Hughes agenda to the settlement of war debts and reparations. Coolidge was determined that the debts should be paid, but throughout 1923 and 1924 Mellon negotiated with the individual debtor governments on interest rates and periods of repayment. It is unclear whether Coolidge ever actually said 'They hired the money, didn't they?' although his wife, Grace, said it sounded like her husband. While insisting on repayment, the Coolidge government restricted the entry of European goods into US markets by maintaining protectionism through the tariff legislation. Against the background of a decade of American prosperity Coolidge, Hughes and Kellogg had no interest in linking the issues of repayment and tariff reduction.[81]

The other route to US prosperity lay in finding a settlement for the reparations issue. Again Coolidge supported Hughes' policy of extracting as much

confidential briefing to US reporters on the situation in Europe. His frank views, previously expressed to Coolidge were reported in the *New York Tribune* and the *Philadelphia Public Ledger*. Ibid., Castle to Sterling, 23 March 1926.   **79** B.J.C. McKercher, *The second Baldwin government and the United States, 1924–1929: attitudes and diplomacy* (1984), p. 140; CCP, series 1, 64 continued to 69 July 10,1925, roll 53, Coolidge to Houghton, 31 October 1928. The refusal of the British to enforce US prohibition law was another cause of US–British friction. HHPL, WRCP, Box 3, Countries Correspondence file, England 1924 to August 1925, Castle to Beal, 21 June 1926.   **80** D.R. McCoy, *Calvin Coolidge: the quiet president* (1967), pp. 177–92. The revisionist version of Coolidge's foreign policy is examined in S.A. Schuker, 'American foreign policy: the European dimension, 1921–1929' in Haynes, *Calvin Coolidge*, pp. 297–304.   **81** McCoy, *Calvin Coolidge*, pp. 189–91; Schuker, 'American foreign policy', pp. 299–301.

as he could from the German government and, in October 1923 after the
French and Belgian occupation of the Ruhr due to German non-payment, the
latter proposed the establishment of an international commission of experts. In
December, Coolidge kept faith with his belief that US business leaders could
contribute to the solution by appointing to it the US financiers Charles G.
Dawes (later vice-president), Henry M. Robinson and Owen D. Young. They
had no official mandate but their appointment meant that Coolidge was not
open to public criticism of US interference in European affairs. Coolidge
remained outside the reparations negotiations that resulted in the Dawes plan
which was announced in April 1924.[82] During his first term, Hughes led the
way in implementing Harding's, and now Coolidge's, foreign policy although
the new president was able to act, if he presumed it necessary.

On 31 August 1923, in his first foreign policy act, Coolidge adopted Hughes'
recommendation and restored formal diplomatic relations with Mexico.[83] In a
speech to the National Republican Club on 12 February 1924, he justified the
decision and a subsequent one to allow the General Alvaro Obregon-led gov-
·ernment to purchase US weapons with US loans, to deal with its opponents;
'we recently reached the opinion that President Obregon has established a government which is stable and effective, and disposed to observe international
obligations. We, therefore, recognised it'. Recognition of Mexico did not lead
to a period of calm in Mexico's domestic or foreign policy but it offered an
early opportunity to identify Coolidge's criteria for recognition of a state. In
order of priority these were that firstly, a formal agreement on pre-existing
issues was reached between the two sides, secondly, US interests, specifically
business, had to be protected and finally, an apparently permanent, functioning government was in place.[84] Although his action has to be interpreted in the
light of the combination of specific strategic, geographical, economic and political conditions that pertained in Mexico and in the US in August 1923.
Nevertheless, it remained to be seen whether these criteria would be applied
to Ireland's application also. Gaining official US recognition for the new Free
State was a priority for the Irish government in summer 1923 but it had to deal
with an altered scenario in the US. The combination of Coolidge's guiding foreign policy principles, his view of US–British relations, his modus operandi in
governing and his relationship with Hughes, along with the role and influence
of State Department officials, Congress, public and private interest groups,
would all dictate whether that recognition would be granted and how other
Irish issues would be treated.

82 McCoy, *Calvin Coolidge*, pp. 190–2; Schuker, 'American foreign policy', pp. 301–2.   83 Warren
G. Harding Papers (hereafter WGHP), series 4, 1921–1923, Secretary of State, roll 144, presidential case file, file 20 secretary of state, folder 19 Charles E. Hughes, Hughes to Harding, 23 July
1923.   84 Quoted in Sobel, *Coolidge*, pp. 346–7; ibid., p. 347.

Coolidge, Ireland and foreign policy

Coolidge hated being labelled and, when asked to describe himself, usually he said he was a Republican and nothing else. He was raised in a Republican family, town, college and state and by August 1923, had lived under Republican presidents for thirty-five of his fifty-one years. As was the case with most aspects of his life, Coolidge was more than just a Republican. Throughout his political career, from 1897 to 1929, he attracted Democratic votes, including those of Irish-Americans. By 1919, in a period when the rising tide of immigration contributed to radical changes in US political life, not least in Massachusetts, Coolidge was the state's most popular leader.

He was born into a state, Vermont, that was quintessentially 'yankee', but it had not been untouched by immigration. From its founding in 1791, the Irish, Italians, Scots, Welsh, Jews and French-Canadians had played an active part in the development of the Green Mountain state. Work was available in textile and saw mills, quarries, loading and unloading ships and railroads in the rapidly industrializing state. The 1860 census noted that 4.3 per cent of Vermont's 315,098 inhabitants had been born in Ireland, a higher percentage than in either Maine or New Hampshire. The figure does not include the children born in Canada and the US to Irish parents or the descendants of earlier immigrants. Feeney suggests that the Irish-American population of Vermont could have been between 10 and 12 per cent of the total. Although most of the Irish congregated in the urban areas, where the demand for unskilled labour was high, some settled in rural areas to farm. J.W. Stickney, a friend of Coolidge's, noted of Plymouth Notch in 1887, 'The absence of railroads, and of a foreign population consequent upon railroad towns is escaped, and no real cause exists here for trouble.'[85] Plymouth Notch was a homogenous society in ethnic terms. However, in political terms there were developments afoot that would bring Coolidge into contact with Irish-America.

By the end of the nineteenth century, as was the case elsewhere in the US, the Democrats had mobilized the ethnic votes and had begun to wrest control of representative positions from the Republican establishment. In Vermont, this development was most evident in the larger urban areas around Burlington, Montpelier and Rutland, with individual Irish-American politicians such as Limerick-born Dr John Hanrahan, who was twice-elected president of Rutland village council and dominated the Democratic Party at state level in the 1880s and 1890s, coming to the fore while in 1903 James Edmund Burke began his Democratic control of the mayoralty of Burlington, which lasted until 1935.[86] Although it was not until 1954 that the Democrats gained controlled at state level, their increasing predominance at local level brought the politically active

85 V. Feeney, 'Vermont' in M. Glazier (ed.), *The encyclopedia of the Irish in America* (1999), pp. 924–7; quoted in Sobel, *Coolidge*, p. 21.   86 Feeney, 'Vermont', p. 927.

Republican Coolidge family into close contact with Democrats. Coolidge recalled that the 'spirited contests' between the Democrats and Republicans in Plymouth Notch were 'not along party lines' and that a Democrat served as 'moderator by unanimous choice.' This individual 'was a man of sound common sense and an excellent presiding officer, but without much book learning.'[87] The young Coolidge believed that it was important to have good government than a Republican one. Such views led him to view capable Democratic opponents in a different light to that which might have been expected.

In 1895, Coolidge came to live, work and establish his political base in Northampton in Massachusetts. It was a state where the effect of immigration on its political life was more immediate than it had been in Vermont. By 1900, more than sixty per cent of the Massachusetts population was of either first or second-generation immigrant parentage and in the eastern part of the state they formed a majority.[88] Consequently, Republican dominance in the east, particularly Boston, was being threatened more than the western part where Northampton was situated. Nonetheless, in 1895 the young Republican soon encountered a greater religious and ethnic mix in this sizeable town of 15,000 people than he had than Plymouth Notch.

It was at a personal level that one of Coolidge's most enduring links with Irish-America emerged. During his legal apprenticeship he worked hard, but also found time to renew his friendship with James Lucey, who was born in county Kerry, Ireland. Coolidge had first met him as a student at Amherst College. Lucey owned a shoe making shop situated not far from Coolidge's office. Coolidge often visited the shop to listen to Lucey and his friends talking. It was to Lucey that Coolidge sent his first letter from the White House. The president wrote, 'I want you to know if it were not for you I should not be here. And I want to tell you how much I love you.' According to White, who regarded the friendship as slightly illogical and as evidence of Coolidge's sentimentality, Coolidge learned much from Lucey about the art of politics and local politics. Through Lucey, Coolidge met men who he had no other chance to meet and learned about the techniques of 'personal, direct, vote-getting.'[89] Both were useful for a budding political career.

Once he set foot in the political waters as a member of his local Republican Ward Committee and then, in 1898, as a member of the city council, he garnered Irish-American votes. The factors which contributed to this success were that he had Lucey and his friends behind him and that he was not afraid to campaign in ward seven and other wards where the Irish lived, using Lucey's ways of getting those votes. He recalled, 'I called on many of the voters personally, sent out many letters, spoke at many ward rallies and kept my poise.' Nor was he averse to distributing drinks and cigars. As general counsel for Springfield

---

87 Coolidge, *The autobiography*, p. 22.   88 Sobel, *Coolidge*, p. 67.   89 Quoted in White, *A puritan*, pp. 248, 60.

Breweries company, which was controlled by a board dominated by Irish-American Democrats, his 'wet' credentials were established among the majority of bar-owners in Northampton, although personally he was a temperate drinker. He also sought out the leaders of organized labour and won their support and numbered Catholics and Protestants among his friends at a time when these religious differences mattered. Finally, his personal qualities as a hard worker with a simple lifestyle brought him respect.[90] Writing in 1929, the journalist Charles Thompson wrote about Coolidge:

> When he began to stir about in the politics of Northampton the bewildered Republicans in that city learned there was a body of voters there whom they came to classify as 'Coolidge Democrats'. He first went to the Legislature from a Democratic district, and as he spread out locally the Coolidge Democrats spread out too – spread out all over Northampton.[91]

In his first campaign for mayor in 1909, he recalled that 'most of my old Democratic friends voted for me.' He secured the presidency of the state senate with the support of twenty-one Republicans and ten Democrats. In his third campaign for the state lieutenant governor position, he came within 2,500 votes of carrying Democratic Boston and took the vote of two of the state's three cities in the second campaign for governor in 1919.[92] In other words, Coolidge had reached out to Democratic voters and leaders, to organized labour and to independents when it suited him. He admitted that, once in the state senate, he developed close relationships with his Democratic colleagues; 'The Boston Democrats came to be my friends and were of a great help to me in later times'.[93] One such friendship was with Jim Timilty.

Coolidge had served in the Massachusetts senate with Jim Timilty, a Democrat and labour leader of the Roxbury Crossing ward. As noted previously, Coolidge's voting record followed the party line yet he came to be seen as a progressive Republican.[94] Thus, there was much for Timilty and his colleagues to admire in Coolidge. While they came from different backgrounds they developed a friendship and respect for one another. Later, when Coolidge was governor of Boston and facing the threat of the police strike in early September 1919, Timilty visited Coolidge:

> I just went in to see my little pal and tell him not to worry over all this mush about a general strike. You know, I'm president of the largest labour organization in the state, the city and town labourers' organization, with

90 Coolidge, *The autobiography*, p. 100; R.C. Garvey, 'Coolidge and the Northampton Irish: a strange alliance', 71–2; M.S. Dukakis, 'From the legislature to the corner office: an assessment of Coolidge's performance as a Massachusetts political leader', 36–7; Sobel, *Coolidge*, pp. 47, 51, 52.   91 Quoted in Sobel, *Coolidge*, p. 52.   92 Coolidge, *The autobiography*, p. 100; Dukakis, 'From the legislature to the corner office', 37.   93 Coolidge, *The autobiography*, p. 103.   94 Quoted in Sobel, *Coolidge*, p. 62.

the largest membership of any union in Massachusetts. I just told Cal that 'we won't go out', and we have more votes in the central labour organization than any of the others. You see, Cal's my kind of guy, and he's right about those damned cops.[95]

Obviously Timilty had other reasons for not supporting the Boston police but, if the story is true, his relationship with Coolidge went beyond a working one. He was reported as often saying, 'Calvin Coolidge can have anything he wants from me.'[96] Subsequently, Coolidge was re-elected governor and believed that 'many of the wage earners both organized and unorganized, who knew I had treated them fairly, must have supported me, for I won by 125,101 votes. The people decided in favour of the integrity of their own government.'[97] Indeed it may have been a combination of Coolidge's integrity, commitment, astuteness and energy, along with his labour record, which made him one of the most popular and respected political figures in Massachusetts by 1921. Following his installation as president, John Devoy of the *Gaelic American*, like most other commentators, had little to say about Coolidge save that 'he is a man of great firmness, of character as he clearly showed when Governor of Massachusetts ... he comes of old puritan stock and has their stern and unbending character.'[98]

Another significant friendship that brought Irish-America into his world was with Cardinal William O'Connell, archbishop of Boston. O'Connell was elevated to cardinal in 1911 and set about reorganizing the finances and administration of an extensive, haphazardly run archdiocese. Even though he fostered a separate Catholic culture which was unwelcome to many Americanizers, he also helped to break down barriers to the full inclusion of Catholic Irish immigrants into US life.[99] The archbishop tended to distance himself from those politicians who were most like himself; Catholic, Irish and ambitious. He wanted to establish a separate power base beyond the Catholic community. Consequently, he deliberately cultivated and maintained close and friendly relations with many Protestant members of the city's establishment.[1] Nonetheless, as indicated in chapter three, O'Connell had spoken out in support of Irish independence in the years after 1916.[2] But this did not mean that he would bring Irish issues to Coolidge's atten-

95 Quoted in White, *A puritan*, pp. 157–8.   96 Quoted in Sobel, *Coolidge*, p. 137.   97 Coolidge, *The autobiography*, p. 134.   98 *Gaelic American*, 11 August 1923.   99 V.A. Lomparda, 'O'Connell, William Henry Cardinal (1859–1944)' in Glazier, *The encyclopedia*, pp. 714–15; T.H. O'Connor, *The Boston Irish: a political history* (1995), p. 197.   1 J.M. O'Toole, *Militant and triumphant: William Henry O'Connell and the Catholic Church in Boston, 1859–1944* (1992), pp. 124, 233–4. During O'Connell's time in Rome in the 1880s, he also developed friendships with 'non-Catholic' Americans including US ambassadors and their families. He was the first Catholic prelate to call on Esmé Howard, the British ambassador, after the latter was posted to Washington. Although there was no mention of religion, O'Connell described him as 'this noble Catholic Ambassador of Great Britain' and seemed impressed by Howard's wife, 'the Roman Princess Bandini ... whose family ... were among my dearest friends.' W. Cardinal O'Connell, *Recollections of seventy years* (1934), pp. 192, 194; TNA, FO371/ 9628, Howard to Foreign Secretary, 30 September 1924.   2 He received de

tion unless it suited his principal aim of embedding catholicism within US society. O'Connell recalled that 'from President McKinley to President Franklin Roosevelt, I ask[ed] no favours, but only wish[ed] to serve.'[3]

Yet, O'Connell's silence during the strike by the Boston police force in autumn 1919 may have impressed Coolidge in his role as governor of Massachusetts.[4] O'Connell was an early visitor to the White House on 24 September 1923 and corresponded with Coolidge during his presidency.[5] During one visit with Coolidge when he found the 'silence that was characteristic of him ... embarrassing', O'Connell told a story that made the president 'actually roar with laughter.' O'Connell recalled 'though I had known the President for many years in Boston and Washington, never until that moment had I seen him so utterly unself-conscious.'[6] Coolidge also remained friends with Monsignor James O'Connell, who was not related to the archbishop but corresponded with Coolidge from Rome and Venice between 1923 and 1925.[7] O'Connell's letters were warm and friendly in tone and provided the president with an insight into the troubled European world. These contacts were not without danger for the president since anti-Catholic prejudice and bigotry remained rampant throughout Republican circles. Indeed the Coolidge papers contain several letters accusing Grace Coolidge of being a 'Catholic' and another objecting to O'Connell lunching at the White House.[8] Coolidge, therefore, entered the White House as a Republican president with a significant set of personal and political ties with Irish-Americans in the Democratic, Catholic and labour ranks. Such connections did not imply a willingness to act on Irish-America's behalf but did suggest an understanding of the Irish-American community.

Coolidge's record on Irish-related issues up to 1921 gave little hope of any change in America's Irish policy to the leaders of the various Irish campaigns. Until this time Coolidge had not made any public statements about Irish affairs,

Valera, presided at a memorial mass for Terence McSwiney, addressed 12,000 Irish-Americans in New York in December 1918. But O'Connell was the ultimate diplomat and prior to the speech had informed the British ambassador that he wished 'no ill to England and he is forced to use vigorous language in order to retain control of the forces he is attempting to lead.' O'Toole, *Militant and triumphant*, p. 234.   3 O'Connell, *Recollections*, p. 228.   4 O'Toole, *Militant and triumphant*, p. 130.   5 LC, MD, The Papers of Calvin Coolidge Series 4 (hereafter CCP), container 288, box 289, appointment book, 24 September 1923. There is no correspondence from Coolidge in the O'Connell papers. However, prior to Coolidge's departure from office, he sent his usual Christmas greetings to which O'Connell replied saying 'without striving for any passing popularity you have quietly won the complete confidence of the whole nation.' Archdiocese of Boston Archives, William Henry O'Connell Papers, O'Connell to Coolidge, 25 December 1928.   6 O'Connell, *Recollections*, p. 360.   7 Monsignor O'Connell should not be confused with Archbishop O'Connell's nephew, also Monsignor James P.E. O'Connell who was excommunicated in November 1920 for having maintained a wife, Frankie Johnson Wort, and an exclusive family home in New York city for the previous seven and a half years. O'Toole, *Militant and triumphant*, pp. 176–94. The author is grateful to Robert Johnson-Lally, Archivist, Archdiocese of Boston for confirming this view.   8 CCP, roll 3, President Personal File (hereafter PPF) 751, Series of letters from O'Connell to Coolidge, 1923 to 1925; ibid., PPF 2, series of letters 'accuse' Grace Coolidge; ibid., roll 5, crank letter, undated.

had supported US entry into world war one on the allied side and, in 1919 at least, had seemed to be a supporter of Wilsonian internationalism. During the presidential campaign in 1920, he believed that it was not his place to raise issues or create policies.[9] At the same time, he had strong views on the impact of ethnic groups on US political culture:

> Our country is not racially homogenous ... the several nationalities represented here are loyal to the United States, yet when differences arise between European countries, each group is naturally in sympathy with the nation of its origin.

While personally devoid of bigotry and prejudice, he was an astute and practical politician as evidenced by the following two examples. He was critical of the excessive influence wielded by ethnic minorities in Congress, which meant that 'the senate is always attempting to interfere, too often in a partisan way, and many times in opposition to the President.' Looking back in 1929, he admitted this was one reason why he had opposed US entry into the League of Nations, because 'the votes of our delegates would all the time disturb our domestic tranquillity here.'[10] The lobbying activities of Irish-Americans offered Coolidge a prime example of such political manoeuvring.

His pragmatism also outweighed his philosophy in relation to immigration and the rise of nativism. Coolidge backed the continuing congressional movement to limit the inflow of peoples into the US by supporting the 1921 Immigration bill which instituted quotas. In his first state of the union address, in December 1923, Coolidge augmented the movement to limit immigration by saying, 'Those who do not want to be partakers of the American spirit ought not to settle in America ... America must be kept American.'[11] In 1924, he would be asked to sign another immigration act and to respond to the emergence at national level of the 'anti-negro and anti-Jew and anti-Catholic Ku Klux Klan.' Both developments greatly concerned Irish-America and the Irish Free State representatives.[12] Coolidge's record to date suggested that politics might win over principle but this remained to be seen.

Nonetheless, before he had become president in August 1923 there had been one occasion when Coolidge was identified in a positive fashion with an Irish cause, namely the fund-raising of the American Committee for Relief in Ireland, as indicated in chapter eight. This non-partisan cause appealed to his humanitarian nature as it did to that of many other Republicans, including President Harding and secretaries Hoover and Weeks. Following Harding's endorsement, Coolidge gave his support to the national fund-raising effort.[13] Between March

---

9 Coolidge, *The autobiography*, p. 151. 10 Ibid., pp. 150–1. 11 Quoted in McCoy, *Calvin Coolidge*, p. 200. 12 Quoted in Sobel, *Coolidge*, pp. 318, 319. 13 *Report of the Irish White Cross to 31 August 1922* (1922), p. 38.

1921 and August 1923, he made no other gestures towards Irish causes, nor did he meet with Irish or Irish-American representatives. In summer 1923, it was difficult to see how such representatives could gain access to the new president unless he wanted to meet them or Hughes supported the request.

There were two impressions abroad about Coolidge up to the time he became president. One view was that he was aloof and inaccessible to the public and to people he did not know and who could not be of benefit to the effectiveness of his government. On the other hand, he could be affable and friendly. During his presidency it was his 'policy to seek information and advice wherever I could find it.'[14] Among those to whom he turned for counsel was George Harvey and Samuel Gompers, both were already condemned by many republicans as 'pro-British', and the Republican radical Senator William Borah.[15] The advisers he turned to most frequently were his respective secretaries of State. Hughes' actions on disarmament and debt had already condemned him in the eyes of radical Irish-Americans as pro-British and unsympathetic to any Irish causes. Consequently, he was unlikely to be of little use in the promotion of Irish issues during the Coolidge tenure. Little was known about Kellogg but his tenure in London combined with a speech he delivered as secretary of State at the dedication of the Thomas MacDonagh memorial at Pittsburgh on 18 August 1926, in which he dwelt on the Anglo-Saxon origins of the US people, was enough to condemn him as an 'anglomaniac' in the eyes of John Devoy at least.[16] However, during Kellogg's tenure Coolidge took a more direct interest in foreign policy, closely supervising it and occasionally sending Frank Stearns to the State Department to elicit unofficial views.[17]

The firm grip which the State Department had over foreign policy and access to the president did not mean that the Irish-Americans would not seek out other channels of communication with the president. Few presidents could afford to cut themselves adrift from interest and lobbyist groups during their presidency. Business groups remained influential in the White House and senior congressional figures from within his own party and the opposition, along with his advisers, continued to communicate directly with Coolidge or through his White House staff. But diplomatic protocol could be invoked when the president wished to avoid meetings with undesirable groups or individuals.

*

Little was known about Coolidge when he was catapulted into the presidency in summer 1923. Against a background of prevailing disinterest in Irish affairs in

14 Coolidge, *The autobiography*, pp. 186–7.   15 Cordell Hull, chairman of the Democratic National Committee found Coolidge to be 'affable.' C. Hull, *The memoirs of Cordell Hull*, 2 vols (1948), i, p. 127.   16 *Gaelic American*, 25 August, 5 May 1927.   17 Schuker, 'American foreign policy', pp. 291–2. George Harvey remained close to Coolidge and the president received people on Harvey's recommendation. CCP, series 1, 31A continued 38, roll 39, Slemp to Harvey, 29 January 1925.

the White House and State Department, improving US–British relations, a divided and weakened republican Irish-American community and the presence of rival Irish representatives in the US, two issues – releases of US citizens imprisoned in Ireland and recognition of the new Irish Free State – provided the new administration with an opportunity to reveal its position on Irish matters.

CHAPTER ELEVEN

The Coolidge administration and Ireland: releases, recognition and representation, 1923–1926

Just as Coolidge's installation in the White House in August 1923 seemed to bring change and continuity for the US public, in the Irish Free State, William T. Cosgrave called a snap election for 27 August. The government did not make as many gains as expected, holding its vote at 39 cent which gave it an additional 5 seats. Sinn Féin won an unexpected 27.6 per cent of the national vote and had 44 seats.[1] Consul Hathaway described the latter result as a 'cause for anxious thought.'[2] Nevertheless, the results gave Cosgrave's party, Cumann na nGaedheal, a mandate to continue governing. Desmond FitzGerald remained minister for External Affairs with Joseph Walshe as his acting secretary. There was little change in the government's foreign policy, although some politicians asked whether Ireland needed one at all. Nonetheless such a policy existed, being based on two principles: firstly, the promotion of Ireland's independent status and secondly, the establishment of sovereignty. Anglo-Irish and Commonwealth relations remained a central theme but, from September 1923 onwards, membership of the League of Nations and the establishment of bilateral relations were regarded as avenues for the promotion of the Free State's separate and distinct image and its statehood. Free State foreign policy would be limited but definite, having an interest in ensuring a stable international climate, supporting the rule of law, trying to capitalize on its mother-country status and avoiding antagonizing the British authorities in order to obtain greater freedom of action as a dominion.[3]

Its US policy addressed those immediate and on-going issues which Timothy Smiddy, Free State representative in Washington, and Lindsay Crawford, Free State trade representative in New York, were working on. In August 1923, Smiddy outlined his agenda:

---

1 J.J. Lee, *Ireland, 1912–85: politics and society* (1989), p. 94. 2 National Archives and Records Administration, Maryland (hereafter NARA), Records of the Department of State relating to the internal affairs of Great Britain, 1910 to 1929, Record Group 59 (hereafter RG59), Microfilm (hereafter M), 580/220, 841d.00/617, Hathaway to Hughes, 6 September 1923. 3 G. Keown, 'Taking the world stage: creating an Irish foreign policy in the 1920s' in M. Kennedy & J. Morrison Skelly (eds), *Irish foreign policy 1919–1966: from independence to internationalism* (2000), pp. 25–31.

1. [Immigration] quota	Securing a separate category for the Saorstát.
2. Shipping	Preventing the taking over of the Moore-McCormack line by a British company which intends to call at western British ports only.
3. Shipping	Preventing the US shipping lines from abandoning the Cobh [Queenstown] call.
4. Dáil funds	Exercising sufficient influence to prevent state judges making political statements containing implications against the Saorstát government.
5. Publicity	Refuting Irregular propaganda.[4]

Not included in the list were gaining recognition for the Free State, the expansion of financial, trade and commercial links between the two countries and the gaining of US government support for Free State membership of the League of Nations, or, at the very least, not antagonizing anti-League elements inside and outside the US administration.[5]

On the US side, Irish affairs had a low, perhaps even a non-existent, profile in the Coolidge/Hughes foreign relations agenda in August 1923. Three Irish issues required the attention of lower-level officials in the State Department: the status of the Irish Free State mission, the unresolved recognition issue and the achievement of peaceful conditions in the new Free State. Chapter nine discussed the co-operative effort that was made by the three governments in late 1922 and 1923 to prevent arms and ammunitions from reaching the anti-treaty irregulars. By summer 1923, the focus of this work was on stopping the irregular leadership exploiting the arrest, imprisonment and execution of Irish Republican Army (IRA) prisoners by the Free State government to win Irish-American and American political and public support. It was vital that supporters of the Free State ensured that the US support base of the anti-treaty side did not expand.

Releasing IRA prisoners

Soon after Harding's death, Smiddy met with Castle in the State Department. Following the precedent set by Hughes in the Mary MacSwiney case, the meeting on 15 August 1923, represented the highest official level to which the Free State mission had access without the intervention of the British embassy. The following day Castle sent a note of the meeting to Hughes. He described Smiddy as

4 National Archives of Ireland (hereafter NAI), Department of Foreign Affairs (hereafter D/FA), Early Series (hereafter ES), 28/189(2), Smiddy to Dublin, August 1923.   5 On 6 September, Hathaway in Dublin, reported that following Cumann na nGaedheal's victory in the general election in August, a delegation left for Geneva to support the Irish application for admission to the League of Nations. NARA, RG59, M580/220, 841d.00/617, Hathaway to Hughes, 6 September 1923.

the 'so-called representative' and noted that he did not bring up any 'particular cases.'[6] In Smiddy's version of the meeting he asked Castle 'what steps, if any,' could be taken by the US government to prevent speeches being delivered and monies collected to purchase guns and ammunition to be used against the Free State government. The latter replied that his government 'was strongly hostile' to such activities, but that, unless the existence of a specific organization for such purposes could be proved, his government could not act. Smiddy was unhappy with this response which, he felt, amounted 'to no action.'[7] He did not pursue the matter with Castle and it was the American Association for the Recognition of the Irish Republic (AARIR) and Clan na Gael that campaigned for US government help to secure the release of republican prisoners from Free State prisons and put an end to the executions of IRA members.

The Irish civil war had ended on 30 April 1923 with the IRA ceasefire declaration. By the end of June 1923 a total of 927 people were dead, including 77 executed.[8] In early 1923, Smiddy and Crawford were deeply concerned about the effect of the government's handling of the irregular prisoners on the US public and on their agenda generally. Crawford forwarded requests from New York for clemency for the republican prisoners from Free State supporters to FitzGerald.[9] In late January, Smiddy asked FitzGerald to explain to US journalists in Dublin that when executions were carried out 'the statement "found in possession of arms"' should be prefaced by some 'such words as "treason to the Free State".' A few days later he warned that the executions of women would not be a 'good policy' because the US public 'would very much deplore it.'[10] But he felt that 'sympathetic prominence' was given to Cosgrave's ultimatum to the irregulars.[11] In September, Hathaway reported that approximately 11,000 prisoners, including Eamon de Valera, were in custody and that many had not been tried.[12] He explained de Valera's arrest in the following terms: 'It is easy to criticise the government ... but hard to know what other course they could have taken with a due regard to public safety.'[13] As soon as Irish-American republicans heard the news of de Valera's arrest, attempts were made to bring Irish affairs back to

6 Herbert Hoover Presidential Library, West Branch, Iowa (hereafter HHPL), William R. Castle Papers (hereafter WRCP), WRC diary, 15 August 1923.   7 NAI, D/FA, 29/189(2), Smiddy to FitzGerald, 16 August 1923.   8 J. Augusteijn, 'Irish Civil War' in S.J. Connolly (ed.), *The Oxford companion to Irish history* (1998), p. 265.   9 NAI, D/FA, ES, 29/190, Lindsay Crawford to FitzGerald, 18 March 1923; ibid., 189(4), Friends of Irish Free State, 18 March 1923.   10 Ibid., 29/189(4), Smiddy to FitzGerald, 23 January 1923; ibid., 29/190, Smiddy to FitzGerald, 18 January 1923.   11 Ibid., 29/190, Smiddy to FitzGerald, 19 February 1923.   12 NARA, RG59, M580/220, 841d.00/617, Hathaway to Hughes, 6 September 1923; T.P. Coogan, *De Valera: long fellow, long shadow* (1993), p. 356; M.V. Tarpey, *The role of Joseph McGarrity in the struggle for Irish independence* (1976), p. 213. The Free State government's treatment of IRA prisoners led to the resignation of George Gavan Duffy as minister for Foreign Affairs on 25 July 1922. University College Dublin Archives (hereafter UCDA), George Gavan Duffy Papers (hereafter GDP), P152/261, Duffy to Cosgrave, 16 July 1922.   13 NARA, RG59, M580/220, 841d.00/617, Hathaway to Hughes, 6 September 1923.

national prominence in the US. The campaign was orchestrated by the AARIR, the Irish Republican Defence Fund and Clan na Gael.

In April 1923, the AARIR numbered less than 70,000 members, but it had re-organized itself under the direction of John F. Finnerty and Donal O'Callaghan, remaining firmly behind de Valera. It mobilized its remaining branches to fund-raise, pass resolutions of sympathy and lobby politicians on behalf of the republican prisoners.[14] The third annual convention of the AARIR was held Boston on 22 July and among the attendance was de Valera's mother, Catherine Wheelright and, of course, the obligatory British agent.[15] The other Irish-American organization involved in the campaign was Clan na Gael. It also had suffered a loss in membership due to the 1921 Anglo-Irish treaty. However, Joseph McGarrity remained an influential figure at the centre of the reduced group and was able to raise $250,000 to aid de Valera's Sinn Féin party during the August 1923 elections and to lobby his political contacts for the release of the IRA prisoners.[16] By 17 August, AARIR branches in Massachusetts and New York had sent several letters to the White House requesting Coolidge's intervention. These were forwarded to Hughes without comment.[17]

Smiddy welcomed de Valera's arrest on 15 August and felt that the action answered a frequently asked question, 'Why is de Valera not captured?' Nevertheless the action did not lessen his concerns about the image the Free State government was presenting to American eyes.[18] Not surprisingly, the story of de Valera's arrest soon gained coverage in the Irish-American and US newspapers. The British consul in Boston sent copies of the *Irish World* and the Hearst-owned, nation-wide *Boston Globe* back to the Foreign Office in London. The latter newspaper reported that the Boston branch of the AARIR had sent $3,000, with an expression of their support, to de Valera.[19] The lobbying also reached Mrs Grace Coolidge. One letter she received was from Dorothy Godfrey, a US citizen who asked for an interview with the first lady 'for the sake of humanity.' Godfrey had received a first hand account of events in Ireland from a school-teacher, Miss Herbert, another American, who spent her holidays there 'and went all through the country to see things in their true light, and not as our bought press tells us.' Herbert reported:

14 F.M. Carroll, 'American Association for the Recognition of the Irish Republic (AARIR)' in M. Funchion (ed.), *Irish American voluntary organizations* (1983), pp. 11–12; Library of Congress (hereafter LC), Manuscripts Division (hereafter MD), Thomas J. Walsh Papers (hereafter TJWP), file American Committee for Relief in Ireland, Thomas Francis Meagher to Walsh, 30 June 1923, M.J. Hannan to Walsh, 14 November 1923.   15 NAI, Department of the Taoiseach (hereafter D/T), S series files (hereafter S), 3346, Gray to Henry Chilton, British embassy Washington, 24 July 1923, forwarded by Curzon to Healy, 14 August 1923.   16 Tarpey, *McGarrity*, pp. 211–13.   17 Calvin Coolidge Papers (hereafter CCP), series 1, 19 Misc-20, June 30, 1924, roll 26, Covering letter from Christian to Hughes, dated 15 August, 17 August.   18 Ibid., 29/190, Smiddy to FitzGerald, 21 February 1923; ibid., Smiddy to FitzGerald, 20 August 1923.   19 Ibid., D/T, S3346, Henry Chilton, British embassy Washington to Curzon, 17 August 1923, forwarded by Curzon to Healy, 1 September 1923.

so much sorrow there, that it is almost unbelievable ... Mr de Valera is
in some jail, no one knows where, his wife and seven children, the oldest
about 12 years is kept in suspense in Ireland, and his old mother is living
in Rochester, New York thinking of her first born son in jail, and no
knows what he is suffering, they may at any moment hang or shoot him
... If anything should happen to President de Valera, a great wrong will
be done to mankind, and no one knows where this will end for they have
born some heavy crosses, but this will be the torchlight throughout the
world. He must be avenged.[20]

Edward Clark, Coolidge's secretary, replied on 20 September and the answer
revealed more about Calvin Coolidge's view of his wife's duty and responsibility as first lady than of her views on Ireland:

You will understand that Mrs Coolidge, however interested she may be
in the various domestic and foreign problems which confront us, cannot
properly give what might be construed as a hearing upon a matter in which
she has not part, and which is solely within the jurisdiction of Congress
or the Executive Department. Such a decision does not in any way imply
a lack of sympathy or desire to give assistance when it is needed, but is
simply a rule which she, as well as others filling the same position, have
been forced to adopt.[21]

Grace Coolidge was never accused of exerting political influence on her husband.[22]
Politics and family were separate throughout his presidency and she was not part
of his 'political family.'[23] Nonetheless, it was this sort of AARIR-inspired petition
that circulated in September 1923 and tried to appeal to individual Americans'
humanitarian instinct as had been the case during the 1921 ACRI campaign.

In early October 1923, the AARIR campaign escalated, following receipt of
news that the prisoners in Ireland had gone on mass hunger strikes to obtain
political status and avoid being treated as ordinary criminals. US Consul Henry
Starrett, appointed to the Belfast office earlier in 1923, reported on 5 November,
that there were five hundred republicans in prisons in Belfast and Londonderry
and on the internment ship, *Agenta*, and that some had gone on hunger strike to
secure their release.[24] De Valera did not join them but rumours began to circulate in AARIR circles in the US that he might be executed. This news combined
to de Valera's continued detention and the hunger strikes, was sufficient to esca-
late fears. On 5 October, a Catholic priest, Michael Hannan, from Butte, cabled
Senator Thomas J. Walsh, his Democratic representative, to inform him there

20 CCP, roll 116, PPF, 308, Godfrey to Grace Coolidge, 14 September 1923.   21 Ibid., Clark to
Godfrey, 20 September 1923.   22 Quoted in B. Boyd Caroli, *First ladies* (1995), pp. 166–7.   23
W. Allen White, *A puritan in Babylon: the story of Calvin Coolidge* (1938), p. 256.   24 NARA,
RG59, M580/220, 841d.00/639, Starrett to Hughes, 5 November 1923.

was the prospect of a court martial trial for de Valera. He asked Walsh to meet Coolidge and ask him to intervene with the Free State government.[25] Five days later, the officers of the Phil Sheridan Club, the Thomas Francis Meagher branch of the Annaconda AARIR and the Annaconda branch of Cumann na nBan also telegraphed Walsh and appealed for him to do something on de Valera's behalf.[26]

Walsh received both telegrams just before he opened the Teapot dome hearings. He replied to Hannan on 5 October, 'I share the horror you feel at ... well-grounded fears at the execution of de Valera. Will act on your suggestions.'[27] Immediately after receiving Hannan's telegram he called on Coolidge and 'at his suggestion' on Hughes. On 10 October, he reported to Hannan on his meetings:

> Neither gave any assurance that any action would be taken, thought the President said, in what seemed a somewhat knowing way, that he did not believe there would be an execution. I endeavoured to impress both of them with my own intense feeling of horror at such a culmination to the unfortunate strife which has prevailed, and to leave them with the view that the American people would shudder at such barbarity.[28]

In another version of the meeting, he told the Annaconda group that he urged Coolidge and Hughes 'in the name of humanity' to make some representation to the Free State government of American 'horror' at the possibility of de Valera's execution.[29] This was not the first time that these civil war issues had been raised with Hughes.

Earlier in the year, Hughes had received telegrams from the constituents of Senator Medill McCormick (Illinois) and Congressman Frank Crowther (New York), protesting against republican executions in Ireland and treatment of US citizens there and requesting US government intervention in the Irish civil war. In a formal acknowledgement to McCormick, Hughes thanked the senator for forwarding the telegrams and, on 5 and 7 March 1923, described the events as 'alleged executions of "political prisoners" in Ireland.'[30] Hughes had not advised Harding to act on the matter on that occasion. In October 1923, when he was approached by Senator Walsh about de Valera's arrest and possible execution, he did not alter his position or advice to Coolidge. Later in the same month Hathaway informed Hughes that he had not acted on a telegram received from the Erskine Childers Club of Schenectady, New York, requesting him to ascer-

25 LC, MD, TJWP, M. Hannan to Walsh, 5 October 1923. 26 Ibid., James Hamill, John Murphy, Bessie Cafferty to Walsh, 10 October 1923. 27 Ibid., Walsh to Hannan, 5 October 1923. 28 Ibid., Walsh to Hannan, 10 October 1923. 29 Ibid., Walsh to Hamill, 10 October 1923. 30 NARA, RG59, M580/220, 841d.00/588, McCormick to Hughes, 26, 28 February 1923, Hughes to McCormick, 5, 7 March 1923, Crowther to Hughes, 19 April 1923, Hughes to Crowther, 26 April 1923. Hughes also received reports of republican agitation from consuls in Cape Town, South Africa and Melbourne, Australia, ibid., 841d.00/594, Charles J. Pisar to Hughes, 6 March 1923, ibid., 841d.00/609 and 841d.00/613, Ray Fox to Hughes, 7 June 1923, 23 July 1923.

tain 'the present conditions and whereabouts of Mr de Valera, and, if alive, to demand his release.' Hughes reassured his Dublin consul on 8 November:

> The Department approves your having taken no action in the matter. For your confidential information and for such discreet use as you may deem advisable in replying orally to requests of this nature, you are advised that, following established practice in cases of this character, the Department finds it is not in a position to make representations to the British government or to the government of the Irish Free State on behalf of an individual who is not a citizen of the United States.[31]

Hughes used the fact that de Valera was not a US citizen to avoid intervention. Coolidge and Hughes' decision to remain aloof from the Irish republican prisoners' affair did not prevent the AARIR from continuing its campaign during the rest of November.[32]

The New York branch organized a series of meetings to urge government intervention on humanitarian grounds. Resolutions were forwarded to other AARIR branches and sympathetic politicians for presentation in Congress and to Coolidge.[33] Hughes and Coolidge continued to receive appeals for intervention directly from Republican Party members and indirectly through Congressman Edward J. King and senators Borah, James W. Wadsworth, David I. Walsh and B.K. Wheeler. None merited more than the standard reply from Hughes and Coolidge's private secretary, Bascom C. Slemp.[34] Senator Walsh remained a target for the AARIR. He was invited to attend two AARIR-organized mass meetings on 4 and 18 November. Following the first of these Austin Ford, chairman of the New York AARIR branch, wrote to Walsh emphasizing the non-political and non-denominational nature of the campaign. He then went on to ask Walsh to call on Coolidge and present the resolution for official intervention.[35] However, Walsh felt that he

---

31 Ibid., M580/220, 841d.00/633, Hughes to Hathaway, 8 November 1923; ibid., 841d.00/617, Harvey to Hughes, 1 October 1923. Harvey warned Hughes about AARIR-organized protests to greet Lloyd George's upcoming visit which had an official imprimatur and included meetings with Coolidge. These demonstrations which embarrassed the US administration may not have helped to promote the republican cause with Hughes.   32 Mrs Adella Christy, president, Ladies' Auxiliary, Ancient Order of Hibernians also requested a meeting with Coolidge to discuss the plight of political prisoners in the Free State. CCP, series 1, 296 continued 319 17 June 1926, Christy to Coolidge, 24 November 1923.   33 LC, MD, TJWP, Austin Ford to Walsh, 31 October 1923, M.J. Hannan to Walsh, 14 November 1923.   34 NARA, RG59, M580/220, 841d.00/632, Rep. King to Coolidge, 27 October 1923, John J. Sullivan to Coolidge, 5 November 1923, Hughes to Sullivan, 13 November 1923, Wadsworth to Slemp, 7 November 1923, Ford to Wadsworth, 5 November 1923, Hughes to Wadsworth, 19 November 1923, Wheeler to Coolidge, 7 November 1923, Hughes to Wheeler, 19 November 1923, Borah to Coolidge 10 November 1923, Slemp to Borah, 10 November 1923, Ford to Walsh, 9 November 1923, Walsh to Coolidge 17 November 1923, Slemp to Walsh, 19 November 1923.   35 LC, MD, TJWP, Austin Ford to Walsh, 31 October 1923, M.J. Hannan to Walsh, 14 November 1923. Ford wrote 'humanity demands unconditional release immediately', while Hannan

had done enough on behalf of this Irish cause and, as the consummate politician, he simply suggested, on 13 November, that one of the New York senators should be asked to present the resolutions to Coolidge.[36] A few days later, Walsh clarified his position to Michael Hannan. He wrote that he had gladly asked Coolidge 'to forestall de Valera's execution ... as it would be a crime, crying to Heaven for vengeance, to take his life.' On the other hand, he believed that 'the established [IFS] government might be justified as a measure of safety in incarcerating him.'[37] Walsh did not attend any of the AARIR meetings in New York and believed that it would be futile again asking Coolidge and Hughes to change their minds.[38]

Another influential Republican politician to whom appeals were made was John T. Adams, chairman of the Republican National Committee. Joseph McGarrity, the Clan na Gael leader, met Adams on 31 October and asked him to intervene with the British government to secure the release of the prisoners. McGarrity emphasized the 'united front' within Irish-American circles demonstrated by the $250,000 collected for the dependents of the prisoners and, therefore, any action by Adams would not be interpreted as strengthening civil war divisions. Instead it would be regarded as a humanitarian gesture. Adams, like Coolidge and Hughes, was not convinced by the arguments and did not act.[39]

In the meantime, the State Department continued to receive political reports from US consuls in Ireland on the situation. On 17 November, Starrett reported that the IRA hunger strike in Northern Ireland prisons had been abandoned ten days previously and proffered the Unionist government's explanation that it was due to the prisoners reaching '"a limit of physical endurance".' The unionist bias in his explanation was not surprising as his informants were generally government supporters. Arthur Bliss Lane commented to Castle; 'a good report but I think unduly optimistic and a bit biased by his [Starrett] surroundings ... *vide* Hathaway's report sent you this morning.'[40]

Hathaway's report offered a more nuanced analysis of the prisoner issue. He said that the number of republicans on hunger strike had decreased to 296 and FitzGerald told him that the government did not have sufficient formal evidence to convict de Valera. He also reported the first death of a hunger striker, Denis Barry from Cork, saying that others were near death. More importantly, Hathaway now felt that

noted the meeting on 18 November was for the purpose of 'voicing ... sentiments from a purely humanitarian point of view.' Ibid.   36 Ibid., Walsh to Ford, 12 November 1923.   37 Ibid., Walsh to Hannan, 16 November 1923. The net result of his report on the Teapot dome scandal was to condemn the carelessness of Congress in 1920.   38 Ibid., Walsh to Hamill, 17 December 1923.   39 Tarpey, *McGarrity*, p. 213.   40 See NARA, RG59, M580/220, 841d.00/641, Starrett to Hughes, 20 November 1923 for evidence of his closeness to the Unionist Party and government; ibid., 841d.00/642, Starrett to Hughes, 17 November 1923. However, his dispatch dated 20 November merited praise from Phillips who wrote on 14 December, that it 'was read with interest' and was 'of value' to the Department particularly in relation to the Free State and preferential treatment. NARA, RG59, M580/220, 841d.00/641, Phillips to Starrett, 14 December 1923; ibid., ABS to Castle, undated probably mid-January 1924.

the position of the Irish government in the matter seems to be sound, yet it is a pity that they had not shown a little more breadth of sympathy with the state of mind of men who would carry their protest to this length, and doubly a pity that whether from failure of tact, or of sympathy, or of vision, they have failed to find means of putting an end to the situation before it reached the last extremity. Whether the government's position be hurt by the issue of the hunger strike or not, bitterness is added to the already lamentably great amount of bitterness standing in the way of harmonious development in Ireland.[41]

This astute opinion of the situation was read by Castle and it served to reinforce the non-intervention policy. The humanitarian argument that had initially swayed Senator Walsh and other politicians had been undermined, since de Valera's life was no longer in danger either from execution or hunger strike; the Sinn Féin leader did not take part in the latter action 'in the best interests of the cause.' Following the deaths of several hunger strikers, and with opposition mounting in Ireland and the US, Cardinal Michael Logue, archbishop of Armagh, intervened on 24 November to secure an end to the hunger strikes and the beginning of the prisoners' release.[42] However, this development did not stop republican Irish-America from demanding action by the Coolidge administration to secure the release of all the male and female prisoners, particularly as Congress reconvened on 3 December and 1924 was a presidential election year.[43]

In December, congressmen John F. Carew (New York), A. Piatt Andrew (Massachusetts), Scott Leavitt (Montana) and Senator David I. Walsh (Massachusetts) forwarded AARIR resolutions to Hughes. The State Department sent the stock reply and in the case of Carew the resolution was returned.[44] Neither was Hughes moved by a letter from J.J. Castellini of Cincinnati, a US citizen of Italian born parents who was married to an Irishwoman and was a firm de Valera supporter.[45] Castellini reminded Hughes that the 'pleas of the Cubans, the Armenians, the Russians, the Japanese, as well as those of former enemies, Germany and Austria met with satisfactory and praiseworthy response.' Hughes was not moved to change his mind.[46]

41 NARA, RG59, M580/220, 841d.00/640, Hathaway to Hughes, 21 November 1923. 42 Coogan, *De Valera*, p. 363. 43 NARA, RG59, M580/220, 841d.00/647, J.J. Castellini to Hughes, 14 December 1923. 44 Ibid., 841d.00/642, Hughes to Carew, 14 December 1923; ibid., 841d.00/648, Leavitt to Hughes, 17 December 1923; ibid., 841d.00/644, Andrew to Coolidge, 23 December 1923, Hughes to Andrew, 24 December 1923; ibid., 841d.00/645, Walsh to Hughes, 20 December 1923, Hughes to Walsh, 24 December 1923. 45 Castellini was an attorney who had attended the Irish Race Convention in the Mansion House in Dublin in 1922, was a member of the AARIR national committee. Smiddy described him as 'a full fledged so-called Irish republican.' NAI, D/EA, ES, 29/191, Smiddy to Walshe, 3 April 1924. 46 NARA, RG59, M580/220, 841d.00/647, Castellini to Hughes, 14 December 1923, Castle to Castellini, 25 December 1925. UCDA, Eamon de Valera Papers (EVP), P150/1101, *The Post and Times Star Cincinnati*, 3 May 1969.

The impact of this campaigning on the US public and policy in 1923 can be gauged from the reactions of the ever-vigilant British diplomats:

> Interest in the affairs of Ireland has undoubtedly decreased during the year. The [AARIR] and the Irish Republic Defence Committee continued, however, to hold meetings at various times and in various places, at some of which so-called emissaries of de Valera spoke and considerable sums of money are said to have been collected.
>
> The Friends of Irish Freedom, on the other hand, sent a telegram to Cardinal Logue at Armagh stating that 99 per cent of the American people endorsed the stand he had taken against anarchy and chaos under the "insane leadership of de Valera" and thus apparently declaring themselves in favour of the Free State.[47]

The AARIR branches members, particularly in New York and Boston, kept the prisoner issue, particularly de Valera's case, in the limelight throughout the first four months of 1924 and held British officials' attention. The Washington embassy, was so inundated with telegrams and letters from Irish republicans during February and March that Henry Chilton requested permission from the Foreign Office to ignore the communications and not even acknowledge them. The Free State government was consulted and agreed that Chilton's suggestion should be adopted.[48] The Dublin government added three requests; firstly, it asked to be given copies of communications which might emanate from 'sources of political or social importance' in the US for information purposes, secondly, such communication should be treated as confidential and thirdly, if an acknowledgement for any communication on the situation received in the Washington embassy were needed, it should come from the Free State and not the British government.[49] Ronald Campbell in the Foreign Office, who had spent five years in the US embassy from 1914 to 1919, and whose views on US foreign policy were well-respected by his colleagues, doubted if it was advisable 'to encourage in any way direct communication with Dublin, to the exclusion of the embassy at Washington, the F[oreign] O[ffice] and the C[ommonwealth]O[ffice]', nor did he feel that such correspondence should be treated as confidential. He had no difficulty with Dublin being part of the information loop about Irish republican activities in the US but would tolerate nothing that amounted to separate representation in Washington. The matter went to a higher level and both Colonial Secretary James H. Thomas and Ramsay MacDonald, who had added the post of foreign secretary to that of prime minister, supported his position.[50]

47 The National Archives, London (hereafter TNA), Foreign Office (hereafter FO), 371/9635, Annual Report, 1923, p. 17.   48 NAI, D/T, S3346, Healy to Curzon, 19 February 1924, Curzon to Healy, 1 March 1924.   49 TNA, FO371/9623, Healy to Thomas, 19 February 1924.   50 Ibid., Thomas to Eyre Crowe, 22 February 1924, R.I. Campbell, 25 February 1924, G.R. Warner, 29 February 1924.

In early April 1924, Esmé Howard reported that Irish republican activity on the release issue was escalating in the US. Senator William H. King, the isolationist Democrat from Utah, twice warned Howard that the Irish 'extremists were very active throughout the country' and in Congress.[51] Howard took the information seriously because King had told him that he favoured home rule for Ireland but had 'no sympathy with the republican movement.' In the Foreign Office Campbell minuted 'a recrudescence. They [irregulars] have been quiet for many months.'[52]

The frequency of reports on the agitation from Smiddy, the British embassy and legation officials increased during the month. Smiddy was in no doubt but that the appeals to Congress would be 'ineffective', not least because Coolidge and Hughes had rebuffed the earlier appeals and because the 'American people and press have long since ceased to be interested in de Valera and his propaganda.'[53] Nevertheless, on 14 April, Smiddy reported to Dublin that Congressman Fiorello H. La Guardia of New York had moved an AARIR resolution in the House of Representatives for Congress and Coolidge to appeal to the British government for the prisoners' release. Smiddy followed this bulletin with newspaper cuttings that detailed AARIR approaches to politicians and indicated that the main plank of the AARIR congressional campaign was that de Valera 'is an American citizen who does not owe allegiance to the Irish Free State because an actual republic does not exist.'[54] Soon he learnt that the AARIR had persuaded Charles Murphy, the Tammany Hall boss, to ask the New York Congressman John Boylan to petition Congress for de Valera's release. He feared that Murphy's involvement might adversely affect the forthcoming court case in New York on the ownership of the Dáil bond certificates.[55] Smiddy need not have worried about political factors influencing the legal procedure, as will be seen later. The comment, however, does reveal the extent of his concerns about the AARIR's influence within US labour and political circles in spring 1924, although he was relieved that Hughes decided not to meet de Valera's mother at this time.[56]

51 NAI, D/T, S3346, Howard to Ramsay MacDonald, 3 April 1924. Although de Valera was still in prison he was still devising plans to bring his US support base under tighter control and proposed a directorate to include Joseph McGarrity, John Finnerty, John Goff, Frank P. Walsh, Leo McSwiney, J.J. Castellini and a representative of the Ladies Auxiliary of the Ancient Order of Hibernians. UCDA, Kathleen O'Connell Papers, P155/12, series of letters, January to February 1924.   52 TNA, FO371/9623, Howard to MacDonald, 3 April 1924, RI Campbell, 16 April 1924. 53 NAI, D/FA, ES, 29/190, Smiddy to FitzGerald, 18 April 1924.   54 Ibid., Smiddy to FitzGerald, 18 April 1924. On 16 April the *Boston Globe* reported that the House Committee on Foreign Affairs gave a hearing to a resolution which instructed the State Department to use the 'good offices' of the government to secure de Valera's release.   55 NAI, D/T, S1369, Smiddy to FitzGerald, 14 April 1924.   56 NARA, RG59, M580/221, 841d.oo/682, Hughes note, 24 April 1924. Smiddy need not have worried about labour either. McKillen's work on the Chicago Federation of Labor, the most active of labour groups on Irish issues in the American Federation of Labor, reveals that during the Irish civil war it had lost support because many Irish-American workers viewed de Valera's position as synonymous with that of Lenin and the Bosheviks in that the Irish leader was also

Of particular interest in Howard's information on irregular activities to the Foreign Office and the Free State government were the occasions when politicians were involved. On 7 May 1924, Howard noted that a meeting three days earlier in Washington was attended by senators Lynn J. Frazier (North Dakota) and LaGuardia. At it LaGuardia had declared that the US government should intervene to get de Valera released. Howard also sent to the Foreign Office copies of an AARIR propaganda document 'of facts regarding' de Valera's imprisonment prepared for congressional politicians which he described as 'typical' of the propaganda being circulated.[57] Campbell reassured his colleagues in the Foreign Office that the propaganda was 'probably most unwelcome to Americans in general and to members of congress in particular', while William Tyrell, assistant under secretary of state in the Foreign Office, drew solace from the view that 'the Irish agitation … is a matter between the US and the Irish Free State – it is the latter and not us who are detaining de Valera.'[58]

The fact that 1924 was a presidential election year added significance to this revived republican activity. In May, despite his confidence, Campbell was worried that the republican propaganda was 'tuned with a view to the elections' in November and that it was worded 'to play on the susceptibilities' of the Irish voter. Similarly Tyrell did not trust the US Congress not to respond to the irregular agitation.[59] Later in the month Howard reported that La Guardia and Boylan had indeed introduced a resolution in the House of Representatives protesting against de Valera's imprisonment. Boylan called on Coolidge's government to demand de Valera's release because he was a US citizen and entitled to the protection of the US government. According to Howard, Boylan was frequently interrupted during this speech.[60] Even though the Irish question had been largely settled to the satisfaction of the Dublin and London governments, the potential of an Irish issue, this time de Valera's release, to rouse support in an election year among some sections of the US public and specifically among the Irish-American community and politicians, once again aroused discussion in the Foreign Office and the Washington embassy. Ultimately neither the US nor British governments asked the Cosgrave government to release the republican prisoners.

Ironically, the Free State government had become particularly sensitive to the consequences of negative publicity in the US. At a time when Smiddy was try-

trying to destroy an elected revolutionary government. E. McKillen, *Chicago labor and the quest for a democratic diplomacy 1914–1924* (1996), p. 183.   **57** NAI, D/T, S3346, Howard to MacDonald, 7 May 1924. The Free State also received reports of irregular propaganda activities in Paris and Brussels from the British ambassador to Belgium, George Grahame. NAI, D/FA, D Series (hereafter D), 3805, Grahame to MacDonald, 6 May 1923; TNA, FO371/9623, Howard to MacDonald, 7 May 1924.   **58** TNA, FO371/9623, Campbell, 20 May 1924, Tyrell, 21 May 1924.   **59** Ibid., Campbell, 20 May 1924, Tyrell, 21 May 1924, Howard to MacDonald, 19 May 1924. The ambassador also reported that Peter Golden had arrived in Boston to institute a campaign for the AARIR which would consist of public meetings to raise funds for the 'rebel elements in southern Ireland.' **60** NAI, D/T, S3346, Howard to MacDonald, 23 May 1924.

ing to establish the reputation of the Free State as a legitimate, stable state worthy of official recognition and to build economic contacts, such attention was unwanted. As had been the case in the past, Irish-American agitation always had the potential to force a reaction from Congress and the executive whatever about its efficacy. On this occasion, it added to the pressure on Cosgrave to move on the prisoner issue. His government began to release prisoners in December 1923, but a number of domestic forces coincided to accelerate the procedure also. Firstly, inside the Dáil the Labour Party raised the prisoner issue on a regular basis and secondly, the Northern government fearing a House of Commons debate on the continued detention of Cahir Healy, a nationalist member of parliament, began to reduce the terms of release for republican prisoners.[61] Unsurprisingly, de Valera accorded the US agitation some importance in his transfer to more comfortable conditions in April and eventual release on 16 July.[62]

It is of greater significance to this study that the Coolidge government had stood firm in the face of its first test from republican Irish-America and had maintained the Harding and Wilson policy of non-interference in Irish affairs. The republican prisoner episode revealed once again that even a divided Irish-America could attract extensive press and political coverage for its campaigns. However, the actual power of such publicity and sympathy was negated by the endorsement by the interested American public and the administration of the Free State government, which was regarded as the vehicle for progress in Ireland.

Coolidge's non-interventionist approach on the above issue was not surprising. During his first term as president he was reliant on and readily accepted Hughes' advice on foreign policy. He was not personally interested in this decidedly minor foreign policy issue and he had practical immunity from congressional attacks because of his popularity with the public. Ironically, by mid-1924, the president's difficulties with Congress were out in the open but Hughes wrote to Kellogg in London on 29 May 1924, 'the political situation here is most extraordinary. The president is stronger every day, despite the disregard by Congress of his recommendations. The Congress, on the other hand, grows in unpopularity.'[63] It seemed that Coolidge would not only win the Republican Party's presidential nomination convincingly but that he had a good chance of being elected in the November election. Thus, irregular Irish-America's use of Congress as a path to Coolidge was powerless to affect action in Ireland.[64] What about the other Irish issue before the Coolidge administration: recognition of the Free State and

61 NARA, RG59, M580/220, 841d.00/654, Starrett to Hughes, 28 January 1924; ibid., 841d.00/654, Starrett to Hughes, 14 February 1924. Healy was released on 11 February 1924.   62 Coogan, *De Valera*, pp. 363–5.   63 LC, MD, Charles Evans Hughes Papers (hereafter CEHP), file Frank B. Kellogg 1921–25, Hughes to Kellogg, 29 May 1924.   64 Longford and O'Neill suggested that it was a combination of pressure from within the Irish and US legislatures that brought about his release thereby over-estimating the influence of Irish-America in the latter. Earl of Longford &T.P. O'Neill, *Eamon de Valera* (1970), p. 230.   65 NARA, RG59, M580/225, 841d.01B11/15, Chilton to Castle, 16 February 1923; ibid., Chilton to Castle, 19 February 1923.

its representative in Washington. Would Coolidge endorse the legitimacy of the Irish administration, having ignored its enemies?

Recognition and representation

In August 1923, there was no formal application before the Coolidge administration for US recognition of the Free State and the appointment of a minister plenipotentiary. Yet, in February 1923, the British embassy was instructed by the Foreign Office to inform the State Department 'privately' that the Free State government had appointed Smiddy as its agent in the US. Smiddy's purpose, as Chilton, in the British embassy, informed Castle, was to study the methods of public administration and look after Free State financial interests in the US. Chilton emphasized that he claimed 'no diplomatic character.' On 19 February, Castle replied accepting the situation.[65] The consequences of his indeterminate status made Smiddy's work difficult. On at least two occasions he had to use the services of Ambassador Auckland Geddes to make contact with the State Department. In May, Geddes agreed that Brooks, a first secretary in the embassy, would be available to Smiddy to help with 'all matters of an Irish nature that need reference to the State Department.' The latter hoped this would 'simplify and expedite such transactions in the future.'[66] When Smiddy met Castle on 15 August, he took the opportunity to elaborate on the situation, pointing out

> that his government has unnecessarily adhered to what we regard as obsolete formalities in their transaction with the Government of the Irish Free State by communicating with them through the British embassy on matters where no international policy is involved. I mentioned that they acted unlike other governments in this respect.[67]

Before the meeting, Castle had discussed the matter with Wilbur Carr, head of the Consular bureau and soon to be promoted to assistant secretary of state. Both men agreed that the US government's informal relationship with the Free State was the same as that with Australia. Consequently, Castle told Smiddy that his department's 'taking things up' with the Foreign Office was 'merely a continuation of an early practice', and that it implied in no way any 'lack of courtesy' to the Free State.[68] Smiddy's record of the meeting noted that Castle 'seemed to assume that no difficulty' would be put in the way of the recognition by the US government of a 'High Commissioner of the Irish Free State.'[69] Despite his impatience on the issue, Smiddy had employed his diplomatic skills and not antago-

---

66 NAI, D/FA, ES, 29/190, Smiddy to FitzGerald, 5 February 1923; ibid., 29/189(7), Smiddy to FitzGerald, 12 May 1923.   67 Ibid., 29/189 (2), Smiddy to FitzGerald, 16 August 1923.   68 NARA, RG59, 580/220, 841d.00/615, Castle to Hughes, 15 August 1923.   69 NAI, D/FA, 29/189 (2), Smiddy to FitzGerald, 16 August 1923.

nized Castle.[70] Indeed, Castle found Smiddy to be 'an intelligent, straightforward fellow and I had an interesting talk with him.'[71] Hughes read Castle's note of the meeting but no action followed. Instead the Irish representative dedicated himself to lobbying other officials including, on 16 August, Addison Southard, head of the commercial department of the Consular Service. At the end of August 1923, Smiddy concluded confidently 'the interest of ... Southard in conjunction with the assurance of help promised by Mr Castle will, at least, facilitate the path towards recognition.'[72] He also met with congressional politicians when they returned to Washington before Congress reconvened in December 1923.

The matter was not again discussed in the State Department until December 1923, when a reply had to be drawn up to a letter received from a Harvard law student. The draft reply stated the government was not considering recognition of the Free State and it had not accredited representatives of the Free State. The State Department's legal advisers questioned these statements on several grounds; the US Senate had, on 6 June 1919, passed the resolution which asked the American Commission to Negotiate Peace at Versailles to secure a hearing for de Valera, Griffiths and Plunkett so that they could present the 'cause of Ireland', while eight resolutions introduced into the US Congress between 1919 and 1921 had called for US recognition of the Free State. Finally, the Free State government was endeavouring to have a diplomatic representative in the US, as was Canada, and there was a 'danger' that the Free State might send a representative 'duly accredited' so far as it was concerned.[73]

The main reason why a letter from a law student attracted such attention was not just its content but because State Department officials regarded Boston to be a 'centre of sympathy for the Free State.' Consequently, W.R. Vallance, in the solicitor's office, suggested the following reply:

the Irish Free State is considered as one of the component parts of the British empire. The British ambassador and his staff at this capital represent the British empire. The United States did not recognize the so-called 'Irish Republic' and did not receive any representative from it.[74]

Effectively, the US administration was saying that it regarded the issue as a British one and that any approach for recognition of the Free State would have to come through that channel. Between January and June 1924, the Dublin government pursued the matter with its British counterpart.

---

70 Smiddy's standing with Castle may have increased also because of his reply to Castle on another matter. De Valera as president of the Irish Republic, sent a letter of condolence to Florence Harding on the death of her husband. She asked Castle for advice who then asked Smiddy. The latter indicated that no action should be taken and no recognition given to the letter. NAI, D/FA, 29/189(2), Smiddy to FitzGerald, 16 August 1923.   71 HHPL, WRCP, WRC diary, 15 August 1923.   72 Ibid., 29/189 (2), Smiddy to FitzGerald, 17 August 1923.   73 NARA, RG59, M580/225, 841d.01/67, The Solicitor's office to Hyde, 27 December 1923.   74 Ibid.

The Executive Council (government) of the Free State decided to raise the issue with the British government informally and, on 17 October 1923, Eoin MacNeill, the minister for Education and Free State representative on the boundary commission, who was in London at the time, was instructed to do it.[75] However, there was a delay in a formal request being sent to London for two reasons. Firstly, the Ministers and Secretaries bill was presented to the Oireachtas in November. It outlined the powers, duties and functions of government departments. Clause I (II) referred specifically to the department of External Affairs and included a reference to the proposed appointment of a minister at Washington. The British government, through the then Colonial Secretary Devonshire, wrote to Tim Healy, Free State governor general, on 29 November, indicating that, should any question arise in future as to the diplomatic and consular representation of the interests of the Free State abroad otherwise than through the British system, the Foreign Secretary would have to be consulted as had been the case when Canada asked for separate representation in Washington.[76] On 17 December, the Free State government removed the references to the proposed US appointment from the bill and agreed to consult with the British authorities before making any foreign appointments.[77]

The second reason for the delay in making a formal request for representation in Washington to the British government arose from Desmond FitzGerald's negotiations with London over the introduction of a Free State passport. These talks had been ongoing since 2 March 1923 and in December were foundering, even though the Irish had accepted all but one of ten British suggestions made in the previous August. The British authorities wanted to define Irish citizens as 'British subjects', which neither FitzGerald nor his government could accept, particularly when the civil war was continuing. Devonshire was willing to compromise but Foreign Secretary Curzon insisted on a clear indication on the passport that the holder of a Free State passport was a British subject. In late December, the matter was still unresolved when Ramsay MacDonald's Labour Party assumed office. The Free State government decided to wait until the Labour government was installed before pressing the passport and recognition issues. On 21 December, FitzGerald told his secretary Joseph Walshe, 'With regard to Smiddy, it seems better to wait before taking action in this matter until there is a new government here.'[78] The first signals from the London govern-

75 NAI, D/T, S1983A, Diarmaid O'Hegarty [secretary to Executive Council] to Eoin MacNeill, 19 October 1923.   76 NAI, D/T, S1983A, Devonshire to Healy, 29 November 1923.   77 Ibid., Healy to Devonshire, 21 December 1923; ibid., Cabinet Minute, C.2/23, 17 December 1923.   78 This account of the passport issue is based on J.P. O'Grady, 'The Irish Free State passport and the question of citizenship, 1921–4', 396–400; R. Fanning et al. (eds), Documents on Irish foreign policy, 3 vols (1998–) (hereafter DIFP), iii, NAI, D/T, S1971, enclosure, FitzGerald to Walshe, 21 December, 1923; UCDA, Ernest Blythe Papers, P24/128(3), Thomas to Healy, 13 May 1924. The IFS began to issue passports on 3 April 1924 without the words 'British subjects', even though British officials would not recognize them.

ment on the passports issue were not hopeful, as MacDonald accepted a Foreign Office suggestion that the words 'British subject by birth' had to be retained on Free State passports in order to adhere to the Anglo-Irish treaty and maintain imperial unity. FitzGerald also learned that at a meeting with the new under secretary of state for foreign affairs, Arthur Ponsonby, on 14 February 1924, that the recognition question would not arise until Canada's position was agreed. FitzGerald had raised the issue because of a letter received from Smiddy in Washington.[79]

By February 1924, the latter had become exasperated about the recognition situation.[80] The existing arrangement was no longer acceptable and he wanted relations put on a formal basis. He acknowledged that, while the embassy officials had acted in all the cases he brought to them, US government officials had not. He noted that whatever help he got from the British and US officials 'was purely by act of grace' and State Department officials would not act without a formal request from the British embassy first. So he felt:

> It will be undignified, without official credentials, to attempt any longer to induce the government departments of the US *to take action* in important matters that concern the Irish Free State ... my relations to the government departments of the USA and to the British embassy is anomalous and somewhat invidious whenever *action* on behalf of the Irish Free State is to be initiated by me here.[81]

He recommended that either the Foreign Office should instruct the British embassy in Washington to take action on his direction in matters that affected only the Free State or that he be accredited as the representative of the Free State by the US president. Naturally he favoured the latter because it would facilitate

> all the relations of the Free State with the USA government, and it will indicate in a striking manner to the Irish-Americans that the Irish Free State is a self governing, independent nation, and will tend in an effectual manner to counteract the Irregular campaign here and illustrate the futility of the American people to subscribe moneys for the establishment of an idea which is practically achieved.[82]

In early February 1924, Smiddy believed that the 'ground [was] prepared' in Washington for an approach by the British government to the US government on the representation issue. Another reason for his optimism was that Hughes had recently suggested that the Free State might warrant a separate immigration quota, a suggestion which the Irish envoy interpreted as an acknowledgement of

---

79 TNA, Colonial Office (hereafter CO), 739/27, minute of meeting, 14 February 1924; O'Grady, 'The Irish Free State passport and the question of citizenship, 1921–4', 400. 80 NAI, D/FA, ES, 29/191, Smiddy to FitzGerald, 11 February 1924. 81 Ibid. 82 Ibid.

Free State independence. He ended his letter to FitzGerald with the question 'Is the British Foreign Office ready to present it?'[83] It was an apposite comment on the British position as the Free State representation and recognition issue would create disputes both between the Foreign and Colonial offices, between the Foreign Office and the dominions and among the dominions. Before the role of British officials is examined, FitzGerald's reaction to Smiddy's proposal must be noted as should that of the Coolidge administration to the idea.

By February 1924, the independent status of the department of External Affairs had been confirmed in the Ministers and Secretaries 1923 Act. In practice the resources of the department remained small and its standing with some members of the Free State administration, government and Dáil low. Kennedy has charted the closure of missions in Rome and Berlin in 1923 and 1924 and the reduction of the Paris mission to a consular role, while there was a constant threat to merge External Affairs with the department of the President. This cost-cutting was supported by some officials and politicians who viewed External Affairs as an extravagance. Hathaway reported later that this criticism was partly due to 'personal dissatisfaction' with Minister FitzGerald and to a 'feeling' that the latter had not made the most of his opportunities.[84] Yet, against this background, FitzGerald and Walshe had orchestrated new initiatives such as Free State membership of the League of Nations in September 1923, Irish contributions to committees and debates during the 1923 League of Nations Assembly and attendance at the imperial conference in October 1923, along with handling matters arising from ongoing bilateral relations.[85] Establishing the independence and sovereignty of the Free State was proceeding apace and, when taken with Smiddy's urgent request in February 1924, emphasized the need for action on the US issue.

In the week after he had received Smiddy's letter, FitzGerald discussed the matter with officials in the Colonial and Foreign offices in London but was given little hope. Upon his return to Dublin, he told Hathaway, on 19 February 1924, that 'the appointment was agreed to informally' and would be soon followed up with a formal request to London. Hathaway immediately wrote a personal letter to Castle in the State Department to inform him of the move and to state that, while FitzGerald recognized that difficulties might arise in the form of procedure, he was confident that 'the matter would go through promptly.'[86] At its meeting, on 1 March, the Free State government approved the appointment of an Irish minister plenipotentiary and envoy extraordinary to the US and on 3 March a formal request was transmitted by Governor General Healy to Colonial Secretary Thomas.[87] In the letter Healy stated that his government was, firstly,

83 Ibid.; NARA, RG59, M580/225, Phillips to Chapple, 26 January 1924.   84 M. Kennedy, 'Introduction' in *DIFP*, ii, p. xiv; NARA, RG59, M580/221, 841d.00/769, Hathaway to Secretary of State, 14 May 1925.   85 Kennedy, 'Introduction', pp. xi–xv and see *DIFP*, ii, for further on all these activities; M. Kennedy, *Ireland and the League of Nations, 1919–1946:international relations, diplomacy and politics* (1996), p. 43.   86 HHPL, WRCP, Box 3, England, 1920–25, Castle to Sterling, 12 March 1924.   87 NAI, Extract from minutes of a meeting of the Executive Council, C.2/57, 1

convinced of 'the urgent necessity' of appointing an Irish minister in the US for financial and commercial reasons and because of 'the pressing problems' of Irish emigration to the US. Secondly, the government considered Smiddy to be a 'suitable person' to assume the position and thirdly, it would be 'glad' if the British government could immediately ask the US government whether Smiddy would be *'persona grata'* to Coolidge and Hughes.[88] It soon became clear that the procedure might not be straightforward.

Upon receipt of Hathaway's news, Castle wrote a personal note, on 12 March, to Frederick Sterling in the London embassy because 'this information may be of more than passing interest to you.' Castle admitted that apart from Hathaway's note, 'the only information we have had, however, regarding a minister from the Free State being accredited is what we have read in the press reports from London.' Clearly, the matter was not a live one for the State Department. Castle outlined Smiddy's position; '[he] carries on, with the approval of the British embassy, certain technical matters connected with Free State affairs.'[89] Sterling was equally taken unawares and was 'very glad to get the tip.' When the opportunity arose on 25 March, Sterling raised the matter 'very discreetly' with G.R. Warner, the acting head of the American department in the Foreign Office. Sterling found Warner 'rather reticent' on the matter. In substance, the British official said that there had been some talk of the Free State appointing a minister to the US but it was still 'all in the air and nothing definite had been decided.' Warner equated the position to that of Canada, which had been in discussion for 'several years' and he also intimated that

> it was a very embarrassing question to the British government (and thought it would be such, as well, to the United States government) on account of difficulties which would be created by the situation; for example, the difficulty of determining the particular subjects which should be taken up with the Irish minister.[90]

Sterling informed Castle that 'while I did not learn much I shall keep the matter in mind, and I thank you for calling my attention to it.'[91] Warner's reticence on the subject was re-confirmed to Sterling at a further meeting on 14 April.[92]

There are two issues to be noted here: firstly, Warner's decided negativity on the question of independent status for the Free State in Washington and secondly, the extent to which Castle and Sterling were caught unawares by Hathaway's news despite Smiddy's opinion.

Regarding the British position, in early 1924 there was some disquiet within the Foreign Office about two issues. These were the dominions' role and rights

March 1924.   **88** TNA, FO371/9627, Healy to Thomas, 3 March 1924.   **89** HHPL, WRCP, Box 3, England, 1920–25, Castle to Sterling, 12 March 1924.   **90** Ibid., Sterling to Castle, 26 March 1924.   **91** Ibid., Sterling to Castle, 26 March 1924.   **92** TNA, FO371/9627, G. Warner, 14 April 1924.

in foreign affairs, including the issue of separate diplomatic representation, and the status of a dominions' representative *vis à vis* the resident British representative. During winter 1923 and spring 1924, the Free State government had extended its diplomatic independence by joining the League of Nations, proposing to have passports without a reference to the British empire, moving towards registering the Anglo-Irish treaty (1921) with the League of Nations and, in February 1924, requesting separate representation in Washington. Foreign Office officials were spared having to act on the latter at that time because, as Warner told Sterling, no agreement had been reached on the Canadian government's representation in Washington. However, on 13 March, Warner noted that the Canadian government had not 'dropped' its request and was considering the appointment of Arthur Currie as its minister to the US. However, Warner was relieved that it was no longer proposed that the Canadian minister 'should take charge of the embassy in the ambassador's absence.'[93] This Canadian move, combined with a letter sent by C.T. Davis in the Colonial Office to Eyre Crowe in the Foreign Office, on 11 March 1924, forced officials in the Foreign Office to move on the Free State request.[94]

Davis was directed by Colonial Secretary Thomas to pass on the Free State government's correspondence to Ramsay MacDonald. Davis explained to Crowe and MacDonald that Thomas had accepted that articles one, two and three of the 1921 Anglo-Irish treaty placed the Free State in the same constitutional relationship with the British government as Canada and that, because it had been agreed to give Canada separate representation in Washington, he felt the government was bound to give similar assistance to any dominion government which wished to appoint a diplomatic representative of its own at Washington. Thomas disagreed with the Foreign Office position on the issue and believed there 'were no grounds', including waiting until the Canadian government decided whether or not to make its appointment, on which the government 'could justify postponing action' on the Free State request. He suggested that all the dominion governments be informed of the Irish proposal and of the government's position on the matter. Thomas recommended the immediate appointment of a Free State minister in Washington. On the matter of precedence, he expected the Free State government to accept that its representative would be ranked with other dominions' representatives in accordance with length of appointment and after the British ambassador. Thomas wanted an immediate reply as he was meeting President Cosgrave in a few days.[95]

It was clear that Thomas had taken a direct interest in the Irish request. He had replaced Devonshire as colonial secretary and Kevin O'Shiel regarded him as a 'moderate labour man' who had not been 'conspicuously friendly to us' in the past.[96] However, in early 1924 Thomas was sympathetic towards the plight

93 Ibid., G Warner, 13 March 1924.   94 Ibid., Davis to Warner, 11 March 1924.   95 Ibid.   96 *DIFP*, ii, NAI, D/T, S1801D, Kevin O'Shiel, 28 January 1924.

of the Free State government due to the threats facing it, specifically the army mutiny in March 1924 and the severe criticism it was receiving in the Dáil over its failure to confirm its independence.[97] At the end of March, the Colonial Office had offered a solution on the passport issue which would, in the words of Frederick Adam in the Foreign Office, effectively give the Free State authorities 'a free hand ... to do what they liked.'[98] Thomas encountered even stronger opposition from the Foreign Office on the representation matter.

Warner accepted that the Free State government desired the appointment of a minister because it 'would render it easier to deal with the Sinn Feiners in the US.' He believed the immigration question had 'also got a good deal to do with' the Irish request and he pointed out that 'any advantage which the Irish Free State may obtain as regards their quota will almost certainly be at the expense of the United Kingdom.' His other objective was that if the Free State appointed a minister, Canada and the other dominions would follow and 'difficult questions of procedure will arise, both as between the United Kingdom and the Dominions and as between the latter.' Nevertheless, he believed that the government had little room for manoeuvre on the issue because of the Canadian precedent. Consequently, he provided a stalling tactic by recommending that the dominions be consulted before any decision was taken. He was insistent also that there would not 'appear to be any question of an Irish minister taking charge of the embassy.'[99] His colleague, Adam, believed that Thomas' letter 'goes too far.' He suggested that the Free State representative need only be a 'trade representative' and that the Free State request to appoint an envoy extraordinary and minister plenipotentiary should 'be resisted.' Moreover, if the Free State appointment was made, he recommended that the counsellor at the British embassy in Washington should be given the rank of minister plenipotentiary so as to outrank the Dominions' representatives in the absence of the ambassador and that office accommodation entirely separate from the embassy staff would be needed. Adam concluded his note by reminding his colleagues that the Free State representative would be 'precluded' from negotiating or signing treaties with the US government without consulting the governments of the other parts of the empire.[1] In other words, while he accepted the principle of separate representation for the Free State, he was determined to ensure that it would be at the lowest level, have the least amount of authority and have no chance of being equated with the top ranking British officials in the embassy.

Among the more senior Foreign Office officials who also commented on 14 March was William Tyrell who 'could foresee nothing but confusion and fric-

---

97 K. Middlemass (ed.), *Thomas Jones: Whitehall diary, volume 1, 1916–25*, 3 vols (1969), i, 19 March 1924, p. 271.   **98** O'Grady, 'The Irish Free State passport and the question of citizenship, 1921–4', 402. On the same day, the Colonial Secretary asked Thomas Jones to act as an intermediary between himself and Cosgrave, the latter crossed to Ireland to try to persuade Cosgrave to resume negotiations on the boundary question. Middlemas, *Thomas Jones*, i, 27 March 1924, p. 274.   **99** TNA, FO371/9627, Warner, 13 March 1924.   **1** Ibid., Adams, 14 March 1924.

tion if Irish and Canadian ministers at Washington get mixed up with the British ambassador. Do not let us divorce power from responsibility.'[2] Eyre Crowe 'strongly' supported this view. He believed that independent dominion representation was a 'long step towards separation' of the empire. He wanted the arrangements to be 'clear and logical, and let us retain our own freedom, so that H[is] M[ajesty's] ambassador shall have no responsibility whatever for what the Dominions' representatives do.' It would be the British counsellor in the Washington embassy who should have precedence when in charge of the embassy during the ambassador's absence. He compared the whole arrangement with the former separate diplomatic representation of Bavaria in Paris, which was 'altogether detached and independent' from the Imperial German embassy, there. Using this precedent was telling because as Crowe concluded, 'in the end it became an empty farce, because no action by the Bavarian legation unsupported by the weight of the German ambassador's authority, was found to be effective.'[3]

MacDonald saw no alternative but to propose the appointment even though it would be a 'dangerous and difficult path' with the possibility of the Free State gaining on the immigration quota issue at Britain's expense. He accepted that the appointment could not be at the level of 'envoy extraordinary', the Free State minister had to be 'entirely independent' residing outside the embassy and the British ambassador would have no responsibility for the actions of the minister. But he did agree that the respective dominion governments be contacted for their opinions.[4] C.W. Dixon, in the Colonial Office, tried to counteract the latter move and rejected any suggestion that the dominions should be encouraged 'to object.' Also he opposed that the Free State minister would be 'entirely independent' of the embassy which he felt was 'quite contrary' to the proposed Canadian arrangement.[5] Lionel Curtis, the Colonial Office adviser on Irish affairs, requested a meeting with Warner of the American department.

They met on 9 April and Curtis wanted the Foreign Office to drop its insistence on the independence of the Free State minister in Washington which only served 'to drive the Free State out of the empire.' Warner stated that this would have to be referred to MacDonald as prime minister and reported to his superiors that the matter was one of 'extreme urgency' for the Colonial Office because of the instability in the Free State, which suggested that the 'difference of opinion' between the two departments on the relationship of the Free State minister to the British embassy might be settled at a later stage.[6] Adam and Crowe did not agree. They were annoyed that Curtis was using the threat to the stability of the Free State government to put pressure on the Foreign Office to extract a quick decision.[7]

The Foreign Office position hardened and was synopsized by Adam as follows:

2 Ibid., Tyrell, 14 March 1924.   3 Ibid., Crowe, 14 March 1924.   4 Ibid., Warner to Davis, 20 March 1924; TNA, CO739/27, Warner to Davis, 20 March 1924.   5 TNA, CO739/27, CWD, 21 March 1924.   6 Ibid., FO371/9627, Warner, 9 April 1924.   7 Ibid., Adams, 9 April 1924.

> This experiment, to which we are unfortunately committed seems about to be put to the test; it is foredoomed to failure. The US government will turn to the central authority of the empire in every case in which they think that the IFS government is unable or unwilling to satisfy their requests.[8]

Thus, not only did the Foreign Office not support the appointment but, if it had to accept it, it wanted complete separation between the Free State and British diplomatic representatives in Washington. Adhering to this position became difficult in mid-April when the pressure began to mount on the British government to fulfil its promise to the Free State leaders.

In mid-April, a number of press reports in British and US newspapers announced Smiddy's forthcoming appointment as the Free State minister at Washington.[9] A further report in *The Times* on 8 May, prompted Lord Selbourne, a friend of southern Irish unionists, to ask the government firstly, if it was correct that a Free State minister was to be appointed to Washington and whether the government had objected, secondly, under what clause of the Anglo-Irish treaty was the appointment to be made and, thirdly, what steps did the government propose to take 'to harmonise the representatives of the British ambassador and of the IFS minister in respect of matters which concern both GB and Ireland or the whole British empire.' Tyrell saw the hand of the Colonial Office at work and believed that the question could have been withdrawn if the Colonial Office 'really wished to do so' and he admitted that the latter part was 'most likely to be embarrassing' to his office.[10] Another source of pressure on the Foreign Office came from Ambassador Howard in Washington, who asked it for direction in the light of US press reports and queries from journalists about the imminence of the Free State appointment.[11] The disagreement between officials in the Foreign and Colonial offices on the status and authority of the Free State and British representatives in Washington had now become the main reason for the delay in responding to the Cosgrave government on the matter, although it was not unwelcome to the Foreign Office.

At this time Foreign Office officials found a further excuse to move slowly when reports from Washington suggested that the State Department might not welcome the appointment either. Warner deduced from *The Times* article on 14 April that the appointment of a Free State minister 'would not be acceptable [to the State Department] unless the British government deemed it advisable.'[12] Three days later, the Foreign Office received one of its regular reports from Robert Wilberforce, director of the British Library of Information at New York city. the propaganda arm of the British government in the US.[13] Wilberforce had learnt that the Coolidge

8 Ibid., Adams, 9 May 1924.   9 Ibid., *Washington Post*, 11 April, *Times*, 14 April, *Observer*, 14 April, R.I. Campbell undated.   10 *Oxford Dictionary of National Biography*, 60 vols (2004), xlii, pp. 549–51; TNA, FO371/9627, Tyrell, 16 May 1924.   11 Ibid., Howard to Foreign Secretary, 16 April 1924.   12 Ibid., Warner, 14 April 1924.   13 B.J.C. McKercher, 'The British diplomatic serv-

administration 'is not at all anxious to be saddled' with a Free State representative but would be unable to refuse one if he were because of the 'Irish vote.' He supported the Foreign Office position by indicating that any US administration, either Republican or Democrat, would want to receive explicit information on the status of the Free State representative in Washington and 'how far dealings with him may be considered to be the same as dealings with any other diplomatic representative.' In other words, the State Department would want the details of the arrangements to be clarified prior to the appointment being made.[14] It was the clarification of 'rank and relative importance' that was useful to William Tyrell in his attempt to delay the Free State appointment. Two days later, he replied to Howard that, in view of the Canadian precedent, it was not possible for the government to object to the Free State appointment in Washington. However, he viewed

> the appointment of Dominion ministers at Washington with some apprehension and it is possible though perhaps not probable that the US government may spontaneously raise objections when they realise the complications involved. You should be careful not to say anything which could be taken as indicating that His Majesty's Government welcomes such appointments.
>
> For the present, the best course would be for you to excuse yourself from discussing the question of the appointment of an Irish Free State Minister on the ground that you have no instructions.[15]

Tyrell did not want Howard to communicate any enthusiasm for the Free State appointment to the State Department and, if it was not made, it might be possible to place the blame on the Coolidge administration. Unfortunately for Tyrell, Wilberforce's intelligence was counteracted by another newspaper report. Howard informed London that the Washington correspondent of the *New York Times* stated that the US government's attitude to the Free State appointment was one of 'courteous receptivity' but that the 'initiative must be taken by His Majesty's government.'[16] The only remaining hope for the Foreign Office opponents of the appointment now lay in the conditions that had been attached to the British response to the Free State government.

When, on 24 April, Thomas finally replied to the Free State government he said that in view of the constitutional precedent established in the Canadian case,

ice in the United States and the Chamberlain Foreign Office's perceptions of domestic America, 1924–27: images, reality and diplomacy' in B.J.C. McKercher & D.J. Moss (eds), *Shadow and substance in British foreign policy, 1895–1939: memorial essays honouring C.J. Lowe* (1984), p. 224; B.J.C. McKercher, *The second Baldwin government and the United States, 1924–29: attitudes and diplomacy* (1984), p. 33. **14** TNA, FO371/9627, Wilberforce to News Department, FO, 17 April 1924. **15** Ibid., Tyrell to Howard, 19 April 1924. **16** Ibid., Howard to Foreign Secretary, 2 May 1924. On 22 February 1924, the Washington correspondent of the *New York World* reported that the US administration would accept any representative from the Free State, if it was approved by the British government. *New York World*, 22 February 1924.

the British government was ready to approach the US administration about the appointment of a minister plenipotentiary at Washington. However, while the British government accepted the proposal in principle this was subject to both consultation with the dominion governments and guarantees from the Dublin government about the diplomatic unity of the empire and the status of the Free State representative.[17] There was no mention of the conflict between the Colonial and Foreign offices because Thomas intended that a Free State commitment to adhere to the principle of diplomatic unity would be sufficient to resolve the issue.[18]

Although the dominion governments did not have the right to veto the proposal, a circular telegram had been sent two days previously to the governors general of Canada, Australia, New Zealand and the Union of South Africa. Thomas emphasized that he did not believe the proposed arrangement would denote any 'departure from the principle of diplomatic unity of the empire' and that the resolution adopted at the 1923 imperial conference regarding the right of the empire to act en bloc when negotiating and signing treaties would be unaffected and would include the Free State.[19] The governments of the Union of South Africa and Canada responded within six days of being contacted by London and both approved the action. However, on 9 May the Australian government suggested that the question was not urgent and should be discussed at the next imperial conference.[20] William Ferguson Massey, the New Zealand prime minister, understood the need for special Canadian representation at Washington but he was 'strongly of the opinion that if the present proposal is given effect, the first step towards disruption of the Empire will have been taken.' He believed that 'union can only be maintained by a single representative of the Crown in every foreign capital.' Massey, therefore, was 'unable to support the proposal.'[21] Neither position was surprising as both premiers had expressed strong opposition to the Canadian precedent at the 1923 imperial conference.[22]

The response from the Free State government on 16 May did not provide the Foreign Office with a reason to delay. There was a tacit acquiescence that the Irish minister would not be accredited as 'Envoy Extraordinary' and, therefore, he would not exercise authority over the British embassy in Washington in the absence of the ambassador.[23] Between 16 May and 18 June, the Free State government received no further communication on the matter. Joseph Walshe blamed the Foreign Office and believed that the Free State had 'no friends there.'[24]

17 NAI, D/T, S2366, External Affairs, 4 July 1946.   18 TNA, FO371/9627, 'Separate diplomatic representation at Washington of the Irish Free State', 27 May 1924.   19 NAI, D/T, S1983A, Thomas circular telegram, 22 April 1924. See *DIFP*, ii, UCDA, P4/898, Edward J. Phelan to Hugh Kennedy, 26 October 1923 for exposition of the position on ratification.   20 NAI, D/T, S1983A, Healy to Thomas, 9 May 1924.   21 Ibid., Jellicoe to Thomas, 3 May 1924.   22 *DIFP*, ii, NAI D/FA, D3601, Extract from a memorandum prepared by Joseph Walshe for the imperial conference on the Free State's position regarding the signature of treaties by Dominions, undated probably autumn 1923.   23 NAI, D/T, S1983A, Healy to Thomas, 16 May 1924.   24 NAI, D/FA, Letter Books, London 1924, Walshe to MacNeill, 27 May 1924.

With both the Foreign and Colonial offices still at loggerheads, the initiative to resolve the impasse came from Secretary Thomas, who suggested on 24 May that, firstly, a further communication be sent to the US, Australian, New Zealand and Free State governments and, secondly, a meeting be held between himself, MacDonald and the respective permanent under secretaries to discuss the matter.[25] Within the Foreign Office, Campbell felt that 'the Colonial Office are going too fast ... The matter appears too grave, in view of the differences of opinion revealed, to be dealt with in a hurry.' He wanted Australian and New Zealand 'fears' about the danger to imperial unity allayed before going any further.[26] His colleague Robert Vansittart agreed.[27] On 28 May, Ramsay MacDonald accepted Thomas' invitation to meet but stated that, in view of the 'present divergence between the two departments, and amongst the governments of the empire, on important points', he opposed any further communications on the matter to be sent to any of the governments involved.[28]

The meeting did not take place until 19 June, by which time it was imperative to resolve the difficulties because FitzGerald had again announced Smiddy's imminent appointment in the Dáil and Selbourne's question was due for answer in the House of Lords on 25 June.[29] At the key meeting on 19 June, attended by MacDonald, Crowe and Cecil Hurst (legal adviser) from the Foreign Office and Thomas, Davis and Curtis from the Colonial Office, the prime minister confirmed that there could be 'no question' of the government 'going back upon the undertakings' embodied in the Anglo-Irish treaty and the despatch of 24 April. Finally, the principle of a separate representative was settled and a formula was written out to deal with the 'details.'[30] It was agreed that

> *a.* Matters exclusively affecting Irish affairs would be under the control of the Irish minister.
>
> *b.* The question of whether a matter related exclusively to Ireland or not was not to be decided by the Irish minister alone, but to be decided in consultation with the Ambassador; if they were unable to come to an agreement, the point must be decided in London after consultation between the two governments concerned.
>
> *c.* There must be no attempt by the Irish minister to deal with imperial affairs or with affairs concerning some Dominions other than Ireland; on these matters the Ambassador would take the necessary action under instruction from London.
>
> *d.* The Irish minister would be entitled to the benefit of the help and advice of the Ambassador and of the staff but the Ambassador would not

25 Ibid., Davis, 24 May 1924.   26 Ibid., Campbell, 26 May 1924.   27 Ibid., Vansittart, 26 May 1924.   28 Ibid., Vansittart to C.T. Davis, 28 May 1924.   29 *Parliamentary Debates Dáil Eireann* (hereafter *PDDE*), 6, 13 June 1924, col. 2317; *DIFP*, ii, NAI, D/T, S1801H, Cosgrave to MacDonald, 4 June 1924, O'Higgins to Cosgrave, 10 June 1924, Cosgrave to MacDonald, 17 June 1924.   30 TNA, FO371/9627, Minutes of meeting, 19 June 1924.

be in any way responsible for what was done by the Irish minister, nor would the Irish minister be in any way under the control of the Ambassador ... If the Irish minister played the game, he might be quite certain of receiving all the help the Ambassador could give.

    e. Matters exclusively affecting Ireland being in the hands of the Irish minister, and matters affecting the empire as a whole or other Dominions being in the hands of the Ambassador would not exclude the ministers asking for the Ambassador's help in particular cases, and *vice versa*.[31]

Clearly Ramsay MacDonald backed Thomas over his Foreign Office officials.[32] The latter lost out on the 'practical points' also. Not only did MacDonald favour an on-going relationship between the two representatives in Washington but the extent of this help and advice was not outlined. Instead it was agreed that it would depend on the 'personal relations' between the two men and upon their 'personal characteristics.' Moreover, the only sop given to his officials was a delineation of areas of responsibility for the Free State minister which his government would be asked to accept.[33]

    At the same meeting, MacDonald also agreed that the Australian and New Zealand governments would be informed that the action could not be delayed.[34] Finally, he decided that a face-to-face meeting was needed between the Irish and British sides to finalize the matter.[35] Indeed he had already agreed this with Thomas, who had written a letter of apology to William Cosgrave on 18 June.[36] The Colonial Secretary's embarrassment about the lack of contact between the two governments led him to explain that the Foreign Office needed some 'practical points' clarified and that he had been ill. In these circumstances he believed 'a few hours talk may save weeks of correspondence.'[37] Hereafter, matters moved swiftly.

    A conference to settle 'important matters of detail' took place in London on Saturday 21 June and Monday 23 June. Significantly, five Colonial Office officials attended but only Hurst from the Foreign Office. On the Irish side, FitzGerald was accompanied by Seán Murphy, administrative officer. The Irish representatives accepted all the principles set out above and it was agreed that, in order to avoid any possibility of the Irish minister in Washington dealing with matters of concern to other parts of the empire, the minister should keep in close touch with the British ambassador. But he would not be in any way subject to

31 Ibid., Hurst, 'Irish Representation at Washington', 22 June 1924.   32 Foreign Office objections now included the argument that if the irregular campaign in the US 'was to become intense', the Free State representative might 'provide too easy a target' or become involved in 'political intrigue' and damage the Free State government. TNA, FO371/9623, Campbell, 5 June 1924.   33 TNA, FO371/9627, Hurst, 'Irish Representation at Washington', 22 June 1924.   34 NAI, D/T, S1983A, Thomas to Jellicoe, 19 June 1924.   35 TNA, FO371/9627, Minutes of meeting, 19 June 1924.   36 Ibid., Davis to Crowe, 18 June 1924. The letter to Cosgrave was despatched 'after personal consultation with P[rime] M[inister].' Ibid.   37 NAI, D/T, S1983A, Thomas to Cosgrave, letter and telegram, 18 June 1924.

the ambassador's control. Both sides agreed that their respective instructions to their Washington representatives would be exchanged for purposes of information. FitzGerald secured the omission from the Irish representative's credentials of the words 'attach him to our embassy' as well as the omission of the countersignature of the British foreign secretary. Not surprisingly, he failed to have the words 'the United Kingdom of Great Britain and Ireland' omitted from the king's title since any change of titles would have required an act of parliament and consultation with the dominions. FitzGerald stated that, with regard to the method of raising the matter with the US government, his government 'would prefer that a formal communication should be made to the US government without any preliminary informal enquiry.'[38]

Finally, FitzGerald agreed that the British side could not ensure that the US government would accept the proposal, despite Smiddy's assurances to the contrary, but he was anxious that if the Americans declined it should be made clear that it was from the US side that the refusal had come and not from the 'unwillingness' of the British government.[39] Hurst agreed because of the effect this might have on the 'internal politics' of the Free State, particularly the 'stability of Mr Cosgrave's government', which had now become important to the Foreign Office despite Tyrell's earlier stance. In private afterwards, Hurst wanted the matter clarified also because he believed that it was 'quite probable' that the Coolidge administration would 'dislike' the new proposal and that, while they might be 'afraid to decline altogether', because of the Irish vote and the approaching presidential election, 'they will endeavour to evade it and throw the blame on to His Majesty's government.'[40] Ramsay MacDonald read the minutes of the conference and 'entirely' approved.[41] On 24 June, the Free State government agreed to appoint Smiddy as minister plenipotentiary to the US.[42]

---

38 Ibid., Notes of conversation at the Colonial Office, 21, 23 June 1924. FitzGerald told Hathaway, that in order to get immediate action, he told British officials that he could not put the Lausanne treaty before the Dáil 'without satisfactory answers' on the Washington post and passports issue. The Lausanne treaty ended the state of war between the British Commonwealth and the Turkish people but the Free State government was not involved in the negotiations or was a signatory of it. The Executive Council finally agreed to present the treaty to the Dáil on 10 June provided the two questions were settled. However, it was not until the British agreed to the Washington minister that FitzGerald placed the ratification before the Dáil on 1 July. Although the difficulties arising from the refusal by British consuls in the US to recognize Irish visas was not resolved between the two countries, there was an informal agreement that from 13 July 1924, the Free State passport agent in New York would issue visas for direct travel to the Free State and the British consuls issue a supplementary one for onward travel to Britain, free of charge. The arrangement would operate in the reverse also. NARA, RG59, 580/221, 841d.00/705, Hathaway to Secretary of State, 17 June 1924; DIFP, ii, NAI, D/T, S3176, Extract from minutes of a meeting of the Executive Council (C.2/104), 10 June 1924; NARA, RG59, 580/221, 841d.00/707, Hathaway to Secretary of State, 26 June 1924.   39 NAI, D/T, S1983A, Notes of conversation at the Colonial Office, 21, 23 June 1924.   40 TNA, FO371/9627, Hurst, 'Irish Representation at Washington', 22 June 1924.   41 Ibid., Crowe, 21 June 1924.   42 NAI, D/T, S1983A, Executive Council, C..2/110, 24 June 1924.

The stage now switched to Washington, where the attitudes of Esmé Howard, Charles Evans Hughes and Calvin Coolidge towards Free State recognition and representation became important. Howard's diplomatic experience, understanding of US foreign policy and concept of Anglo-American relations made him stand out from his predecessors over the previous ten years He had arrived from his Madrid ambassadorship to Washington in March 1924 to replace Auckland Geddes, a political appointment. Howard faced a daunting task because British representation in the capital city had lacked dynamism and purpose of action for almost a decade.[43]

Geddes' weaknesses were plain for all to see. He suffered from an impolitic nature, bad public relations and advancing blindness. He spent most of the last year of his tenure seeking a cure for his blindness at clinics outside the US. By contrast Howard's experience, beginning with an appointment in Ireland in 1885 as assistant private secretary to the viceroy was extensive. He was chosen because he was a 'proven diplomat with sound analytical skills and a calm approach to problems.'[44] Howard was also advantaged in his new appointment because he was knowledgeable about the mechanics of the US political system and had Republican and Democratic friends and contacts. Nor did the complexity of US foreign policy faze him. He sympathized with policy-makers who had to balance protecting US interests and appeasing 'powerful domestic groups like traders, manufacturers, and Irish-, German-, and other hyphenated Americans.' On Anglo–American relations, he was an 'Atlanticist' who believed that Britain's primary relationships should be with the US and the rest of the empire rather than with Europe. Indeed, he viewed the Anglo–Canadian relationship as an integral part of the Anglo–American link. More importantly, he treated US relations with all of the independent dominions, 'especially the Irish Free State', as 'components of the general imperial relationship with Washington.' He had learnt much from his Dublin posting in the 1880s, 'I left Ireland ... a convinced believer in the necessity, if we are ever to have peace, of giving local autonomy to Ireland, which then went under the rather elastic name of Home Rule.' Unlike Geddes he believed that the empire was not a 'static entity' and that dominions could have their own distinct foreign-policy interests.[45]

In May and early June 1924, he took two opportunities to demonstrate this position. He did not object when Charles Murphy, the postmaster general of Canada, bypassed the British embassy and directly arranged an interview with Coolidge and secondly, he absented himself from a treaty-signing occasion between Ernest Lapointe, Canadian minister for Justice, and Hughes.[46] Smiddy concluded that on these 'small' affairs Howard's behaviour had pleased the State

43 B.J.C. McKercher, *Esmé Howard: a diplomatic biography* (1989), p. 272.   44 Howard also held positions in Crete, Washington, Budapest, Berne, Stockholm, Paris and Madrid. Ibid.   45 McKercher, *Esmé Howard*, pp. 324–5, 10. Howard's support for Irish home rule placed him on the side of the Liberal Party and he unsuccessfully contested a seat in the 1892 general election. Ibid., p. 18.   46 NAI, D/FA, 29/191, Smiddy to FitzGerald, 7 June 1924.

Department and Canada.[47] Thus, when it came to the matter of a separate representative for the Free State, Howard did not oppose it or attempt to delay it. Other reasons for his support related to his abhorrence of the irregulars, particularly de Valera, whom Howard's biographer described as 'treacherous and unscrupulous' and his wish to stabilize the Free State.[48] Howard had no qualms about Smiddy being appointed; 'as soon as I saw Professor Smiddy I realised that we should be able to understand each other.'[49]

The Foreign Office cabled Howard at 9.45 pm on 23 June, instructing him to ask the US government to appoint a Free State minister plenipotentiary at Washington. At the time Howard was attending the Democratic Party national convention in New York and, once informed of the telegram, he left immediately for Washington to present it personally to Hughes. The matter of informing the State Department had now become urgent for the British government, which faced the embarrassment of Lord Arnold, the government spokesman in the House of Lords, announcing the decision in his answer to Selbourne's question on 25 June, without the US government having been informed. The formal document for the US government, setting out the basis and parameters of the appointment, had not arrived in the Washington embassy on the morning of 25 June and Howard was forced to inform Hughes by telephone of the request and that the official document was on its way.[50] During a scheduled meeting with Hughes on the following day, which covered refugees in Greece and British interests in Mexico, Howard handed a note to the former stating that his government deemed it desirable that those matters which related exclusively to the Free State should be handled in Washington by a 'minister plenipotentiary accredited to the US government.' Matters which were of imperial concern or which affected other dominions as well as the Free State would continue to be handled by the British embassy. Hughes told Howard that the government was in 'cordial agreement' with the request and his government would be 'glad' to receive the minister plenipotentiary. The State Department record of the meeting states that when Howard raised the question of what matters might be within the competence of the Irish legation and what within that of the British embassy, Hughes 'supposed that if any such questions arose it could easily be settled informally.'[51] Howard stated that 'these could only be settled as they arose.'[52] He also pointed out that the proposal was to accredit a minister plenipotentiary and not an envoy extraordinary so that his rank would be below that of the envoy.[53]

Obviously, the request was not unexpected. Hughes and Castle discussed it on the morning of Hughes' meeting with Howard on 26 June and it was clear

47 Ibid.   48 McKercher, *Esmé Howard*, p. 360.   49 Lord Howard of Penrith, *Theatre of life: life seen from the stalls, 1905–36*, 2 vols (1935), ii, p. 515.   50 NAI, D/T, S1983A, Howard to Foreign Office, 26 June 1924.   51 LC, MD, CEHP, file Great Britain, William Phillips, Office of the Secretary, Memo. of interview with the British interview, 26 June 1924.   52 NAI, D/T, S1983A, Howard to Foreign Office, 26 June 1924.   53 LC, MD, CEHP, file Great Britain, William Phillips, Office of the Secretary, Memo. of interview with the British interview, 26 June 1924.

that recognition was a foregone conclusion and that the remaining matter was whether Smiddy was acceptable to them. Hughes 'wanted to know about Mr Smiddy, who is to be appointed Irish minister.' Castle told him about the 'little man' and said that 'we could not object if we wanted anyone from Ireland.' Thus, when Howard 'formally asked for Smiddy's recognition' and also 'that we take over British interests in Mexico. Both were agreed.'[54] On the same day, Hughes informed Coolidge that the US government 'would be glad' to receive a minister plenipotentiary of the Free State 'as suggested in the embassy's communication.' He reassured the president that the arrangements would not denote any departure from the principle of the diplomatic unity of the empire. Coolidge did not object and simply ticked Hughes' letter.[55] Hughes officially informed Howard on 28 June that Coolidge, 'always happy to meet the wish of His Majesty's government in every proper way, will be pleased to receive a duly accredited minister plenipotentiary of the Irish Free State on the footing you indicate.'[56] Also on 28 June, Thomas immediately informed Healy in Dublin that the US government would accept a Free State representative.[57]

Smiddy did not present his credentials to Coolidge until 7 October 1924 because, according to FitzGerald, even though the Free State government requested the British government on 3 July to ascertain if Smiddy would be acceptable to the US government, the British delayed until 8 August to officially forward Smiddy's name to the State Department for approval. Nor did Smiddy receive his credentials, signed by King George V, until 23 September.[58] The explanation for this lay with the Foreign Office once again.

The Foreign Office fought a rearguard action to have Henry Chilton, the counsellor at the British embassy in Washington, upgraded to the rank of envoy extraordinary and minister plenipotentiary in order to outrank Smiddy who would be at minister plenipotentiary level only. Tyrell hoped that whenever the question of precedence between these two representatives arose Chilton would 'have the "pass" over the Irishman' especially when Chilton was in charge of the embassy.[59] The State Department did not agree believing that the Foreign Office position 'does not appear wholly sound' and Joseph Grew quoted from the diplomatic rules used at the congresses held in 1815 in Vienna and 1818 in Aix La Chapelle.[60] Although the matter was not resolved once Howard received Smiddy's signed credentials, he delivered them to him on 23 September. They discussed

---

54 HHPL, WRCP, WRC diary, 26 June 1924, p. 203; LC, MD, CEHP, file Great Britain, William Phillips, Office of the Secretary, Memo. of interview with the British interview, 26 June 1924. NAI, D/EA, 29/190, J.S. Cullinan to Cosgrave, 21 August 1924.   55 CCP, roll 116, PPF, 308, Hughes to Coolidge, 26 June 1924.   56 NAI, D/T, S2366, Hughes to Howard, 28 June 1924, appendix 1, External Affairs, 4 July 1924.   57 Ibid., D/T, S1983A, Thomas to Healy, 26 June 1924.   58 Ibid., Healy to Thomas, 8 July 1924; UCDA, Desmond FitzGerald Papers (hereafter DFP), P80/424, FitzGerald to Senator N.A. Belcourt, 13 August 1924. FitzGerald repeated this criticism of the Foreign Office again in the Dáil on 12 August. *PDDE*, 8, 12 August 1924, 2403.   59 TNA, FO371/9628, Sterling to Grew, 3 July 1924.   60 Ibid., Grew to Sterling, 26 July 1924.

whether Howard would be present at the White House ceremony but the ambassador worried that his presence 'might be made the subject of attack among some of [Smiddy's] nationals.' So he left the decision entirely to the latter to decide whether he should attend on his own or be accompanied by Howard. Smiddy decided it would be better to 'go alone.'[61] Smiddy then formally asked Hughes to be presented to Coolidge and on 7 October, the event took place.[62]

Undoubtedly the Foreign Office's role had delayed the appointment but others believed that the fault lay on the US side, where the State Department had been influenced by an irregular-motivated smear campaign against Smiddy. J.S. Cullinan from Houston, Texas, an Irish-American supporter of the Free State and friend of Cosgrave's, Cullinan provided Cosgrave with a raft of statements from individuals both inside and outside the US administration who had met Smiddy. On 21 August, Cullinan summarized the criticisms levelled at Smiddy. The most important of these were an inappropriate association with his secretary.[63] The allegation was potentially personally and professionally damaging to Smiddy who was a married man with a family in Ireland. As the envoy designate, he could not afford to be the target of scandal and gossip. However, the accusation did not appear in any of the documents forwarded to Cosgrave except Cullinan's letter and report of 21 August, or in the press and may have emanated from one of Cullinan's source only. Despite this allegation Cullinan felt that Smiddy was suited to the huge task that lay ahead, but he suggested to Cosgrave firstly, that a new secretary be engaged 'preferably an American of such personality, social standing and diplomatic experience as would ensure capable management of the office', secondly, that an attorney be appointed to 'aid and guide your ambassador' and thirdly, that he would, if Cosgrave wanted, 'after conferring with dependable advisors, submit the names of persons thought to be qualified for either or both positions'.[64]

Until this time there had been no doubt but that Smiddy would take up the new position in Washington. However, upon receipt of the Cullinan report, Cosgrave contacted FitzGerald in Geneva who already knew about the accusations, which had 'given him a good deal of concern' and they occupied his 'mind so much.' Before leaving for Geneva he had spoken to Daniel Cohalan, then visiting

61 Howard, *Theatre of life*, ii, p. 515.   62 CCP, roll 116, PPF, 308, Hughes to Slemp, 1 October 1924, Slemp to Hughes, 2 October 1924. The Foreign Office pursued Chilton's upgrade into February 1925 when Smiddy learned that at state functions the Free State minister would take precedence over the minister plenipotentiary and envoy extraordinary resident in the British embassy, namely Chilton. NAI, D/FA, ES, 29/192, Smiddy to FitzGerald, 6 February 1925; NAI, D/EA, GR983, Smiddy to FitzGerald, 5 June 1924. The additional credentials 'envoy extraordinary' were added in February 1927. Smiddy presented his new letter of credence to Castle on 21 April 1927, the latter accepted that the change was 'because Mahoney had all the titles.' Both men agreed that, as it was 'merely a change of title' and that Smiddy would not ask to be presented to Coolidge again. *DIFP*, iii, NAI, D/T, Healy to Amery, 19 February 1927; HHPL, WRCP, WRC diary, 21 April 1927; CCP, roll 118, file 308, Butler to State Department, 25 January 1927; *The Times*, 18 June 1929.   63 NAI, D/EA, G11/24, Cullinan to Walsh, 21 August 1924.   64 Ibid., Cullinan to Walsh, 21 August 1924.

Dublin, about the matter. FitzGerald was convinced the allegations were part of the irregular campaign against Smiddy in the US and he was prepared to go there to counter it. Cohalan advised him not to go until November, after the presidential election had taken place, as his presence in the US might be given some 'political significance.' FitzGerald was guided by Cohalan.[65] Immediately FitzGerald returned to Dublin and on Saturday 20 September, he and Cosgrave decided that Smiddy should be asked to return to Ireland and a telegram and letter were sent to Smiddy on the same day. FitzGerald wrote to Smiddy as 'your friend D.F. and not from the minister.' But he emphasized that the visit must not be publicized and that, if it was, he must imply it was for personal business and not because of an order from FitzGerald. He continued, 'I do this because I have reason to believe that there are certain people over there working against you personally, and they might be glad to give the suggestion about … your being called back implies reprimand.' The reason the minister wanted Smiddy back was 'to put you *au fait* and on your guard' and discuss the whole matter of 'the personnel of your new office and a dozen other matters.'[66] Smiddy returned to Ireland.[67] Clearly FitzGerald and Cosgrave had heeded Cullinan's warnings, but not to the extent of preventing Smiddy from presenting his credentials to Coolidge on 7 October. He remained at his US posting until January 1929 and was then moved to the London post.[68]

The two-month delay in Smiddy's presentation of his credentials to Coolidge may be explained less by the irregular smear campaign against Smiddy's appropriateness or by any State Department's objections to him and more by deliberate stalling tactics from Foreign officials. However, it must also be noted that the Free State government was fortunate to have the recognition issue settled before the Conservative government under Bonar Law came into office on 5 November 1924. A central tenet of Conservative policy was the protection of the unity and sovereignty of the commonwealth and this was immediately displayed in its objection to the Free State registration of the Anglo-Irish treaty with the League of Nations.[69] Foreign Office officials' objection to the Washington

65 NAI, D/T, S1983B, FitzGerald to Cosgrave, 12 September 1924. 66 Ibid., D/FA, Minister's Office files (1924), FitzGerald to Smiddy, 30 September 1924. 67 Ibid., ES, 19/191, Smiddy to Walshe, 30 September 1924. 68 In January 1925, Hathaway reported on a meeting with Walshe and FitzGerald that covered Smiddy's withdrawal of his acceptance of an invitation from the Sulgrave Institute (a bastion of the English-speaking world) in Washington. He reported the two men to be 'considerably perturbed' at the action because of the lost opportunity for a speech to emphasize 'the independent position' attained by a dominion but also recognized the strength of Cohalan and Devoy's opposition. Starrett in Belfast noted that the decision was represented in the *Northern Whig* as appeasing these elements. Smiddy's subsequent explanation for his withdrawal did not satisfy FitzGerald who told Hathaway that the Irish minister 'had lost his head and that he would have to be recalled.' In March 1925, the government decided not to accede to Smiddy's request that his family join him and they did not do so until 1927. NARA, RG59, 580/221, 841d.00/748, Hathaway to Secretary of State, 29 January 1925; ibid., 841d.00/749, Starrett to Department of State, 31 January 1925; ibid., 841d.00/752, Hathaway to Secretary of State, 19 February 1925; NAI, D/T, S1983B, Meeting Executive Council, Cab.2/170, 2 March 1925. 69 Kennedy, *Ireland and the League of Nations*, pp.

appointment might have found greater support from their new political masters than they had done during Labour's tenure.

But why did the Coolidge administration agree to a Free State minister in Washington? The answer lies partly in the fact that the British government requested it but a second explanation is that between March and June 1924, Hughes had already accepted the status, legitimacy and territory of the Free State dominion, through his handling of, firstly, the re-organization of US consular districts in Ireland, secondly, the passage of the 1924 immigration legislation and thirdly, the voting procedure in the proposed world court. A fourth explanation lies in US domestic politics.

There was no US diplomat based in Ireland and US representation was at consular level under the control of the consul general and ambassador in London. However, the question arose as to whether the workload of the consuls, which was examined on average every three years, merited an upgrading of representation. Consul general at large Robert Frazer visited Dublin between 31 May and 6 June 1924 and, following his inspection, recorded that 'we shall probably always have to have an officer of high grade at Dublin, and no reason is known why his office should remain under the supervision of our consulate general at London rather than be an independent consulate general itself.'[70] He brought forward a further reason for upgrading the Dublin office, which Starrett in Belfast had earlier raised on 16 January 1924. Both men were concerned about the existing territorial arrangements and possible changes arising from the proposed boundary commission.

In early 1924, State Department officials considered the boundary question to be the most serious issue affecting Ireland as a whole at the time. Wilbur Carr instructed US consular officials in Ireland to report specifically on any developments regarding the boundary issue and this will be examined in chapter thirteen.[71] By this time, although Eoin MacNeill had been nominated by the Free State government to the boundary commission, neither the representative from Northern Ireland nor the chairman had been decided upon. Despite this lack of progress, Walshe in External Affairs, had acted on the implications of the existing situation. Earlier in 1923, he had asked Smiddy whether it was possible to ask the State Department to amend the Belfast and Dublin consular districts because the former covered the whole of Ulster, including counties Cavan, Donegal and Monaghan, along with Leitrim, that were now part of the Free State. Walshe wrote that the current arrangement whereby Free State citizens in these counties had to go to Belfast to get visas for their passports was causing 'inconvenience and annoyance.' He asked if an immediate modification of the consular districts could be arranged.[72] He also approached Hathaway about the 'urgent necessity of changing

66–71.   70 NARA, Inspection Reports on Foreign Service Posts, 1906–1939 (hereafter IRFSP), Dublin, Ireland, June 1924.   71 NARA, RG59, 580/220, 841d.00/610, Wilbur Carr to Henry Starrett, American consul, Belfast, 15 August 1923. Starrett had replaced William Kent in 1923 as consul; ibid., minute, ABL to Castle, undated, probably mid January 1924.   72 NAI, D/FA, Letter Books Washington 1923–4, Walshe to Smiddy, 2 January 1923.

the American consular areas of Belfast and Dublin so as to include in the latter that part of the province now lying outside the territory of the Belfast government.' Walshe accepted that any changes would be subject to the findings of the boundary commission. He expected the consular changes to take effect by the end of February 1923.[73] This did not happen as British Conservative ministers delayed it and, in January 1924, Starrett again recommended to the State Department a modification of the Belfast and Dublin consular districts because the existing arrangement was a 'source of trouble and embarrassment.'[74]

However, it was not until March 1924 that both Carr and Hughes agreed to the consular division changes in Ireland but asked Kellogg in London for his opinion because of the on-going boundary issues.[75] By mid-April, Kellogg had not replied and Arthur Bliss Lane recommended to Castle 'we might as well go ahead with the readjustment of the consular districts in Ireland'. Castle agreed.[76] A few days later, Kellogg's reply reached Washington. He felt that US any action on the issue might be interpreted as an indication of favouritism toward one or the other political factions in Ireland.[77] Lane agreed and suggested to Castle that the decision be deferred until after the US presidential elections in November; 'otherwise we might be accused of going after the Irish vote in this country.'[78] In July, Smiddy was informed informally by a State Department official that the changes had taken place. However, they did not come into force until January 1926 after the boundary commission had collapsed and the Free State, Northern Ireland and British governments had agreed to retain existing frontiers.[79] Nevertheless, by agreeing to shift the consular boundaries in March 1924 in order to deal with the territorial realities of the northern and southern states, the State Department accorded official recognition to the Free State and Northern Ireland and the partitioned island.

A second issue which similarly accorded recognition to the Free State before June 1924 was the question of US membership of the World Court. This was controversial in spring 1924 when, in order to deflect Democratic criticisms of Republican inertia on the topic, the Senate Foreign Relations Committee appointed

73 Ibid., Department of Justice, 1922–5, Walshe to McGilligan, 5 January 1923.   74 K. Middlemas, J. Barnes, *Baldwin: a biography* (1969), p. 207; quoted in NARA, IRFSP, Dublin, Ireland, June 1924.   75 NARA, RG, 59, M580/220, 841d.00/652, Phillips to Kellogg, 18 March 1924.   76 Ibid., Lane to Castle, 14 April 1924, quoted in section 57.   77 Quoted in NARA, RG84 Foreign Service Posts of the Department of State. Ireland, Dublin embassy, Security Segregated Records 1936–49. Box 15, file 710, Department of State, Division of Historical Policy Research. Research project no. 73, July 1948, p. 5. In February 1923, Howard informed Hughes that he had been asked to take up the question of establishing a US consulate in Londonderry, now part of Northern Ireland. Howard did not offer any supporting arguments and instead stressed that he was 'merely discharging his duty in mentioning the matter and that he did not know what business there was to justify a consulate.' LC, MD, CECP, Box, 157–8, file Great Britain, Geddes, 23 February 1923.   78 NARA, RG59, M580/221, Lane to Castle, 25 April 1924.   79 NAI, D/FA, Letter Book, Washington, 1925, Walshe to Smiddy, 2 May 1925; NARA, IRFSP, Dublin, Ireland, June 1924, handwritten note 'already done' ABL, 24 September 1924; NARA, RG84, Box15, file 710, United State policy on the Irish partition question, July 1948, p. 6.

a sub-committee to conduct hearings and report on US participation in the court. It was not necessary for the US to belong to the League of Nations in order to belong to the World Court, but opponents of US adherence to the court proposed a number of amendments to dilute its role therein. On 22 May 1924, Senator George Pepper had introduced a resolution to reduce the voting strength of the British dominions and Hughes had discussed this with Kellogg on 29 May. Hughes described Pepper's amendment as 'objectionable because this attempts to deprive the British dominions of a vote, as members of the larger group, in the election of judges.' He could not see why 'we should insist upon such a course.' Secondly, unlike Pepper, who he said was 'living in the past' he regarded the fact that the 'Irish Free State is now a member of the League of Nations and with the Dominions would have a right to vote for judges under the present statute' as a positive development It was clear to Hughes that, as the US and British empire, including the Free State, shared traditions of 'independence and impartiality' and if the 'voting rights of the British dominions as members of the larger group of fifty or more states is to be regarded as having any particularly significance, that significance should lead us to favour their inclusion rather than to oppose it.'[80] No action on the World Court question had been taken by the end of 1924 but Hughes accepted that the Free State should have separate dominion status within the empire and at the League of Nations and its attendant organizations.

Immigration was the third context where Hughes' view on the dominions' status was important for the Free State. By 1924 restricted immigration was no longer a matter of debate in Congress but a foregone conclusion. Instead of debating the principle of restriction the extreme and moderate restrictionists debated, among other issues, what census should be used as the basis for the quotas, and what size should they be? Consensus emerged around an idea proposed by Senator David A. Reed, chair of the Senate Immigration Committee, and John Trevor, a lobbyist for patriotic societies. They proposed that immigration quotas should be based on 'national origins' and, in Ngai's words, they tried 'to make race-based laws appear to be not racist.'[81] During the congressional debate on the legislation, it became a priority for the Free State government to get a separate quota and as large as possible.[82] Despite his unofficial status and counter lobbying by British diplomats, in early February Smiddy felt that winning a Free State quota was 'more feasible' than one for Ireland 'as a whole' for political reasons.[83] His analysis proved correct as Hughes had written to Congressman Albert Johnson, chairman of the House Committee on Immigration, with suggested amendments for his act, including the provision for separate quotas for the self-governing dominions within the British empire. Smiddy asked Daniel Cohalan to use his 'influence' with Johnson to accept

80 LC, MD, Charles Evans Hughes Papers, file Great Britain, Hughes to Kellogg, 29 May 1924.   81 M.M. Ngai, 'The architecture of race in American immigration law: a re-examination of the immigration act of 1924', 68, fn. 4.   82 NAI, D/FA, Letter Books, Department of the President, 1923–8, FitzGerald to Cosgrave, 1 February 1924.   83 Ibid., ES, 29/191, Smiddy to FitzGerald, 8 February 1924; ibid., Smiddy to Walshe, 28 February 1924; ibid., Smiddy to FitzGerald, 8 February 1924.

that particular amendment and told FitzGerald that if Hughes' amendment was accepted by the House committee 'all administrative difficulties will removed for a separate quota for the IFS.'[84] On 18 March, Smiddy cabled FitzGerald that the House had adopted the Hughes amendments.[85] Once the Johnson bill endorsed the principle of a separate quota for the Free State, the same principle was included in the Reed bill by 27 March, when the latter was reported to the Senate.[86]

The Johnson–Reed immigration bill finally became law on 26 May 1924 and set out an annual quota of 164,667 to apply until 1 July 1929. From then onwards, the national origins quota system would be applied, the total figure would be lowered to 150,000 and 1920 would become the base year.[87] The restrictionists' goal was achieved. Even though the legislation was now law and regulations had been published, the whole question of a separate quota for the Free State was re-opened at one of the Quota Board's sub-committee meetings in June. Smiddy learned unofficially that the statisticians in Commerce Department had identified three problems: a) 'administrative difficulties' in allocating a separate Free State quota, not just in the short term but from July 1929 onwards, b) fears that Northern Ireland immigrants might use the Free State quota when the British quota was full and c) the absence of a boundary settlement on the island. Smiddy's informants told him that the State Department supported the Free State case for a separate immigration quota because they believed 'it is more consonant with the terms of the [immigration] Act – Northern Ireland being a political part of Great Britain and not being a self-governing dominion.' But the Commerce officials were motivated by a desire 'to avoid the difficulties which would entail investigations of a most complex character.' In this disagreement between politics and practice, Smiddy feared that the latter was 'likely to prevail.'[88] He was wrong as the differences were settled in the Free State's favour. The Free State quota was increased by one thousand and the Great Britain and Northern Ireland quota reduced by one thousand.[89]

The temporary quota agreed on for the Free State was 28,567 and that for Great Britain and Northern Ireland was 34,007. The permanent quotas for these separate regions were announced during the first month of Herbert Hoover's presidency in March 1929. The Free State quota was reduced to 17,853 and that for the United Kingdom (and Northern Ireland) increased to 65,721.[90] Despite

84 American Irish Historical Society, New York, Daniel J. Cohalan Papers, Box 16, folder. Correspondence T.A. Smiddy, Smiddy, Smiddy to Cohalan, 14 February 1924; NAI, D/FA, ES, 29/191, Smiddy to FitzGerald, 14 February 1924.   85 NAI, D/FA, ES, 29/191, Smiddy to FitzGerald, 18 March 1924.   86 Ibid., Smiddy to Walshe, 28 March 1924.   87 The Visa office estimated the number of persons who would probably wish to go to the US, if parents, wives and minor children of aliens resident in the US were given non-quota status; Italy had the highest numbers at 350,000. LC, WCP, Box 15, Department of State, Visa Office, undated.   88 NAI, D/FA, ES, 29/191, Smiddy to Walshe, 17 June 1924.   89 Ibid., Smiddy to Walshe, 1 July 1924.   90 Ibid., p. 21; Ngai, 'The architecture of race', 67. Official US recognition of the Free State also was evident in November 1922 when the government agreed to a British government request to send deportees of Irish origin directly to the Free State and Britain. BDFA, xiv, Annual Report for 1922, p. 83.

the later reduction in the Free State quota, the Dublin government had managed before June 1924 to have its dominion status within the empire recognized by the award of a separate quota.[91] It certainly benefited from Hughes' desire to recognize the self-governing dominions.[92]

The final reason for Coolidge's decision to agree to a Free State minister lay in the fact that 1924 was a presidential election year when securing votes mattered. In the 1924 campaign, the Republican nomination process and platform was straight forward enough. Two days after Coolidge addressed Congress, on 6 December 1923, he announced his candidacy for the republican presidential nomination and this was delivered to him on 12 June 1924, with Charles G. Dawes, a brigadier general during world war one, being his vice-presidential candidate. The 1924 Republican platform endorsed tax reductions, the retrieval of foreign loans, the expansion of foreign markets and stronger enforcement of prohibition while it opposed farm relief. Bowing to the left of the party and the presence of Robert La Follette, representing the Progressive Party, it favoured a constitutional amendment banning child labour, federal laws confirming an eight-hour day and an end to lynching. In foreign affairs it opposed membership of the League of Nations but supported participation in the World Court.[93] There was no reference to Irish issues, despite the efforts of the AARIR to obtain support for its IRA prisoner cause.[94]

By way of contrast, the former US ambassador to Britain, John Davis was nominated as presidential candidate with Charles W. Bryan, governor of Nebraska, gaining the vice-presidential nomination at the end of a long Democratic convention in New York which lasted from 24 June to 10 July. The party's divisions emerged into the open with northerners who were mostly urban, Catholic or foreign born and opposed to prohibition and the Ku Klux Klan opposing southerners who were Protestant, rural, supported prohibition and either supported or feared the Klan. The divided Democrats found it difficult to agree a platform and it differed little from the Republican one. It favoured a graduated income tax, farm relief, multilateral disarmament and a referendum to decide on the US membership of the League of Nations.[95] An attempt by the AARIR to gain the inclusion of a resolution recognizing the 'Irish republic' failed.[96] Commenting on the latter point, Howard, who attended the convention, wrote 'both the Republican and Democratic conventions were remarkably free from attacks upon Great Britain. Practically nothing was heard of the great cause of

91 Daniels & Graham, *Debating American immigration*, p. 23; Ngai, 'The architecture of race', 67–70. The Free State quota increased slightly to 18,700 in 1952 which remained in place until 1965. J.J. Lee, 'Emigration: 1922–98' in M. Glazier (ed.), *The encyclopaedia of the Irish in America* (1999), pp. 263, 264; Government Publication Office, *Statistical abstract of the United States, 1951* (1951), table 106, p. 93.   92 Daniels & Graham, *Debating American immigration*, p. 20.   93 J.W. Johnson, 'John Calvin Coolidge, 1923–1929' in M.I. Urofsky (ed.), *The American presidents* (2000), pp. 318–9.   94 NAI, D/FA, ES, 29/191, Smiddy to Walshe, 3 April 1924.   95 Johnson, 'John Calvin Coolidge, 1923–1929', p. 318.   96 NAI, D/FA, 29/191, Smiddy to Walshe, 19 June 1924.

Irish freedom.' He did indicate, however, that Davis' nomination was 'too much for the Hearst press, who promptly accused him of being pro-British because he belonged to the English-Speaking Union and had been ambassador in London.'[97] Such associations led John Devoy to castigate Davis' selection and describe him as 'Britain's pawn' as well as the 'standard bearer of the Ku Klux Klan.'[98]

The election campaign was described by Johnson as 'one of the strangest in US history.'[99] Coolidge accepted the nomination on 12 August but left the campaigning to Dawes who travelled the country while the president conducted a 'front porch' campaign. When he spoke he rarely mentioned Davis and Bryan or the electoral issues. Instead he talked on general topics but he used the radio effectively.[1] He attributed his lack of campaigning in summer 1924 to the death of his son, John, on 7 July.[2] Since Coolidge was not electioneering, Dawes and the Republican Party manager, William Butler, concentrated most of their attack on La Follette whom they accused of being un-American and a front for communism, rather than on Davis and Bryan. The latter concentrated on Coolidge's links to big business and corruption issues but the approach had little appeal to voters who believed in Coolidge's honesty and probity.[3] However, no party could afford to alienate any voters, even those that seemed wedded to the Democratic Party.

As indicated previously, Coolidge had garnered a substantial Irish vote for himself from the earliest days of his political career, particularly during the gubernatorial elections for Boston. During the 1920 presidential election and subsequently, he had made clear his belief in 'Americanism' and his abhorrence for the ethnic activism that divided the US public. Nonetheless the results of the 1920 election suggested that on that occasion Irish-America, just like the rest of ethnic America, had defected from the Democrats to the Republicans to sweep Harding and Coolidge into office. Domestic issues predominated and once in the polling booth Irish-Americans voted as American workers, not as Irish republicans.[4] Once in office as vice-president and, subsequently, president, Coolidge's record on Irish issues was safe and unremarkable; he supported the American Committee for Relief in Ireland campaign on humanitarian grounds and endorsed Hughes' non-intervention with the Free State on behalf of the IRA prisoners. This latter position reflected that held by the majority of Catholic, nationalist Irish-Americans, who viewed the Anglo-Irish treaty of 1921 as ending the war with Britain and supported the Free State government as the way forward.

Against this background, Coolidge and Hughes' decision in late June to accept the British proposal for a Free State minister in Washington and receive his credentials on 7 October 1924 would not have alienated most Irish-Americans voters. The majority of Irish-Americans who had supported the 1921 treaty and the

---

97 *BDFA*, xiv, Annual Report for 1922, p. 311.   98 *Gaelic American*, 9 August, 11 October 1924. 99 Johnson, 'John Calvin Coolidge, 1923–1929', p. 318.   1 Sobel, *Coolidge*, p. 301.   2 Coolidge, *Autobiography*, p. 190.   3 A.S. Link, W.A. Link, W.B. Catton, *American epoch: a history of the United States since 1900. Volume 1: 1900–1945*, 2 vols (1987), i, p. 211.   4 L.J. McCaffrey, *The Irish diaspora in America* (1976), p. 145.

Free State regarded the separate appointment in summer 1924 as an endorsement of the Cosgrave government in Dublin.[5] Consequently, the irregular smear
campaign, public meetings and articles in *Sinn Féiner* and the *Irish World* opposing the appointment served to emphasize the irregular threat to the Free State
and importance of defeating it.[6] None of the major US newspapers surveyed
weekly by the Irish department of Publicity during summer and autumn 1924
linked the Free State appointment to the up-coming election.[7]

Howard's review of 1924 confirmed the 'disappearance of Irish agitation and the
general lack of interest in Irish affairs since the establishment of the Free State.'[8]
In late August 1924, Coolidge saw no political danger in meeting with and hosting
a lunch for Edward, prince of Wales, who was on an informal and private visit to
play polo in the US at the time. The president could have postponed the visit
because he was in mourning for his son, John, who had recently died.[9] However,
the visit had more serious implications for Davis who failed to get it postponed and
then absented himself in the west coast during the visit.[10] The aspect of the visit
that concerned Coolidge and his manager, William Butler, was the potential criticism from the Catholic Church.[11] Howard subsequently reported that the luncheon in the White House was 'a great success from every point of view.' More significantly, where ever he went the young, handsome prince was received
enthusiastically by large crowds, with the only negative publicity coming from the
New York American owned by Hearst.[12] Almost twelve months previously, in
October 1923, Lloyd George's visit had provoked, in Howard's words, 'ineffectual
attempts' at protest by Irish republicans: one year on these were not even present.[13]

Nonetheless, in September 1924 the Republican election manager, William
Butler, was worried about Coolidge's chances of victory, but this was due to La
Follette's progressive platform which appealed to farmers and workers alike.

---

5 Throughout the period, Hathaway informed the State Department of the Free State government's
determination 'to enforce the restoration of law and order.' He confirmed that despite the pressure
on the government due to the army mutiny and IRA prisoners issue, it was enforcing law and order,
implementing economic policies and had the support of a majority of the public. See NARA, RG59,
580/220, 841d.00/670, Hathaway to Hughes, 24 March 1924.   6 *Irish World*, 1 March 1924, *Sinn Féin*
11 September, 11 October 1924.   7 UCDA, DFP, P80/324, 1 January 1924 to 13 February 1925.   8
BDFA, xiv, Howard to Chamberlain, 8 June 1925 in Annual Report for 1924, p. 234.   9 *Manchester
Guardian*, 20 August 1924. Hughes had not felt pressure either to cancel a visit to Britain in July 1924.
10 TNA, FO371/9634, Howard to Crowe, 22 August 1924; ibid., R.I. Campbell, 25 August 1924.   11
The prince of Wales' fast behaviour attracted press attention, particularly negative criticism from within
Catholic circles in the US, where people were already critical of Coolidge's failure to denounce the Ku
Klux Klan. In late August, Davis had done so as had La Follette. This silence combined to entertaining the prince of Wales could have been construed as anti-catholic and resulted in the total disaffection of the Irish vote. Coolidge never repudiated the organization by name and indeed Hiram Evans
of the Klan pronounced Coolidge the 'safe' candidate. *Manchester Guardian*, 20 August 1924; David
Burner, 'Election of 1924' in A.M. Schlesinger et al *History of American presidential elections, 1789–1968,*
11 vols (2001), p. 2482.   12 TNA, FO371/9634, Howard, 17 September 1924.   13 Ibid., FO371/
9635, Howard to MacDonald, 20 June 1923, Annual Report for 1923, p. 15.

However, by October these concerns had disappeared because of improved economic conditions, particularly a rise in wheat prices. Despite his minimalist
approach Coolidge triumphed on 4 November 1924, winning 54 per cent of the
popular vote. Davis received a mere 29 per cent and La Follette a creditable 17
per cent. Coolidge had a landslide victory in the electoral college with 382 votes.
Davis won 136 and La Follette just 13.[14] Davis carried the southern states,
Oklahoma and the larger northern cities as expected (although Coolidge won
New York and Alfred Smith was elected Democratic governor of New York city).
La Follette won in his home state of Wisconsin and Coolidge took the western,
central and remaining eastern states.

The British ambassador described the result as a 'remarkable swing towards
conservativism on the part of the great mass of public opinion.'[15] On closer analysis it seems that in the ten larger industrial centres between Chicago and Boston
it was La Follette who won the working-class vote, much of which was immigrant. This is further supported by Burner's comparative study of congressional
and presidential voting patterns. He suggests that in New England and the north
Atlantic states La Follette drew most of his vote from the Democrats and specifically from urban workers. He considers that La Follette's radicalism caused his
vote to fluctuate between different ethnic groups. For example, in New York and
Chicago he did well with the German and Jewish immigrant vote but won a
smaller percentage from the 'more conservative Irish' there.[16] In the absence of
a study of the destination of Irish-American votes, it seems likely that the protest
vote which went to Harding and Coolidge in 1920 either did not vote at all (only
51 per cent of those eligible to vote did so) or were more likely to have voted
for La Follette or Coolidge rather than for Davis. Certainly an 'Irish' vote failed
to materialize and affect proceedings, whereas its reappearance for Alfred Smith
in his fight against Herbert Hoover was a recognizable feature of the 1928 presidential election. Either way Coolidge emerged victorious from a campaign that
he fought not on issues and personalities but on principles and achievements
against a background of increasing prosperity. Coolidge colonized the middle
ground in the political spectrum and did as little as possible during the campaign, which appealed to the disaffected Democrat as well as Republican voter.
Howard wrote 'the silent politician is a new figure in American politics, and he
unquestionably caught on.'[17] It was a successful strategy.

*

Smiddy became Free State minister plenipotentiary to the US on 7 October 1924
and was the first dominions' representative to attain that status from the US gov-

14 P. Thompson, *Cassell's dictionary of modern American history* (2000), p. 508.   15 *BDFA*, xiv, Howard
to Chamberlain, 8 June 1925 in Annual Report for 1924, p. 234.   16 Burner, 'Election of 1924', pp.
2488–9. The Ku Klux Klan had targeted the seat of Thomas J. Walshe of Montana.   17 *BDFA*, xiv,
Howard to Chamberlain, 8 June 1925 in Annual Report for 1924, p. 234.

ernment. The significance of this for the Free State was outlined by Walshe to Kevin O'Higgins, Free State vice-president and minister for Justice in late October 1924:

> Professor Smiddy's appointment as minister in Washington established direct contact between us and the USA and completely eliminates the Foreign Office from the whole field of our relations with that country. America is the only country with which our relations are entirely free and independent from any outside control ... the main accomplishment in our foreign relations is the establishment of a minister plenipotentiary in Washington.[18]

Two years later, Secretary Kellogg agreed with Hackworth's legal opinion that Free State status should be described as a '*de jure* government within the British empire' and that, where possible, it was best for the State Department to refrain from defining the status of the Free State because of the 'publicity' and it would 'offend the British.'[19]

Despite this confusion, the Free State had been the first dominion to have gained such representation. The path had been long and complicated but the willingness of the Free State government to push and cajole the British government, combined with Smiddy's doggedness, the support of MacDonald, Thomas and Howard in Washington, contributed to gaining Hughes and Coolidge's approval. Howard hailed the appointment as 'one great change in the structure of the British empire.'[20] Similarly, by the appointment, but also on the consular district issue, World Court representation and immigration quota, Coolidge and Hughes accepted the right of the dominions to equal, independent states within the commonwealth. Moreover they also regarded the appointment as a step in the consolidation of the Free State arising from the Anglo-Irish treaty.

The president accorded with Hughes' recommendation on the representation matter, which pleased the majority of Irish-Americans and interested Americans who supported the Free State government over their irregular opponents. Yet, most Americans of all political hues inside and outside Congress were more interested in every day issues relating to the economy and, if they thought of foreign policy at all, it was in the context of expanding opportunities for US business, financial and commercial sectors. Consequently, while the diplomatic channel between the US and Free State administrations was clarified in October 1924, it was the US consuls on the ground in the Free State who implemented US policy.

18 NAI, D/J, Letter Books, 1922–25, Walshe to Secretary, Department of Justice, 21 October 1924.
19 NARA, RG59, M580/225, 841d.01/80, Castle to Hackworth, 1 December 1926; ibid. Castle, 11 December 1926; Division of Western European affairs minute, 3 January 1927, Grew to Davis, Polk, Wardwell, Gardiner and Reed, 12 January 1927; ibid., 841d.01/80, Hackworth to Kellogg, 8 December 1926; ibid., Hackworth to Kellogg, 5 December 1926; ibid., minute, PBG, 27 November 1926; ibid., Castle to Hackworth, 11 December 1926; ibid. minute Castle, 20 December 1926; HHPL, WRCP,WRC diary, 14 December 1926; ibid., 10 January 1927. 20 Howard, *Theatre of life*, ii, p. 512.

CHAPTER TWELVE

The US foreign service in the Irish Free State: upgrading and work, August 1923–March 1929

The Coolidge government had firmly backed the William T. Cosgrave-led Cumann na nGaedheal administration and wished it to succeed against the threat posed by the Eamon de Valera-led Sinn Féin. At the same time as his Irish policy was unfolding at a diplomatic level in Washington, Dublin and London, United States consuls were working on the ground in the Irish Free State. Throughout the period under review information, opinions and views, provided by US consuls in Ireland, had informed the formulation of policy in Washington. These men also had other duties and responsibilities to perform.

The appointment of Timothy Smiddy as the Irish Free State minister to the United States was a momentous occasion in the life of the new state and the fledgling diplomatic service. Moreover, the US government was not to make the reciprocal appointment of Frederick Sterling as its minister to the Free State until 1927. The background to the up-grading of the Dublin office and to Sterling's appointment will be discussed here along with the re-organizing of the Cork consular district and the organization and nature of consular work in the Free State in the post-civil war period.

Up-grading the status of US representation

The division of Ireland and the introduction of the Foreign Service [Rogers] Act in May 1924 had immediate consequences for those consuls who represented US interests in the Free State and Northern Ireland at that time. Until then not only was US official representation in Ireland at consular level but the highest position was that of consul. The consul general, Robert Skinner, who was based in London, held the supervisory role over all US consular representatives located throughout the British islands, while the US ambassador was the highest ranking US representative. In the Free State there were two consuls, located in Dublin city and Cobh (formerly Queenstown) in county Cork, along with three vice consuls in the Dublin office and two consular agents located respectively in the cities of Limerick and Galway. However, changes were at once forthcoming in terms of the personnel and status of the US presence in Ireland.

Robert Frazer, consul general at large, visited the Dublin office between 31 May and 6 June 1924 and, while he opposed Charles Hathaway's request for an additional vice consul, he recommended in his report to Wilbur Carr, director of the Consular bureau in Washington, that the office be raised to the status of a consulate general:

> The Irish Free State is now as completely separate a political entity as Canada; our office at its capital is as important a one in itself as some of our existing consulates general; several important nations have established consulates general at it; and unquestionably the government would immensely appreciate our establishing an office of that grade in the Free State.

Frazer did not know any reason why the Dublin office should remain under the supervision of the consul general in London rather than be an independent consulate general.[1] The recommendation was passed to Herbert C. Hengstler in the consular bureau on 25 September.[2] Hengstler and Carr were certainly familiar with the immensity of the workload conducted by the London office. In an overview of the situation prepared some time in 1923, Carr had noted that that office was one of the largest in the consular service due to the commerce between Britain and the US, the large US community resident there, the seasonal tourist trade and the supervisory role it had over thirteen other offices located throughout Britain and Ireland.[3] Consequently, the removal of the Free State from London's jurisdiction would reduce the demands on the London office. Moreover, Frazer's report made it evident to Carr, and indeed to Secretary of State Hughes, that the Dublin office earned sufficient income to cover the increased salary required for a consul general. This can be seen in table 12.1.

The Dublin office had forwarded $51,527.89 to the State Department, which would more than cover the $5–6,000 per annum salary of an officer at consulate general level. This latter issue was important for the State Department and for the Coolidge administration generally, as the US Bureau of the Budget and Congress were 'economically minded' at the time. The State Department's appropriations came under closer scrutiny than those of other government agencies.[4] Writing to Coolidge in October 1924, Hughes supported the immediate upgrading for other reasons:

1 National Archives and Records Administration, Maryland (hereafter NARA), RG59, Inspection Reports on Foreign Service Posts (hereafter, IRFSP), Dublin, June 1924. Argentina, Belgium and Germany each had a consul general representing their interests in Dublin in 1924. 2 NARA, RG59, IRFSP Dublin, Ireland, HBD to Hengstler, 25 September 1924. 3 Library of Congress (hereafter LC), Manuscripts Division (hereafter MD), Wilbur Carr Papers (hereafter WCP), Box 16, Volume of work in diplomatic and consular offices abroad, undated, probably 1923. 4 G.H. Stuart, *The Department of State: a history of its organizations, procedure and personnel* (1949), p. 275. Dublin, Belfast and Cobh featured on the list of fifty offices collecting the largest fees in the fiscal year ended 30 June 1931; London was at the top of it collecting $202,767 and Lyons in France at the

Table 12.1
Financial statement of Dublin office, 1922–3
($ dollars)

	Receipts	Expenditure	
Invoices	911.50	Salary of principal officer	4,500.00
Bills of health	35.00	Remuneration of consular agent	169.99
Landing certificates	2.50	Salaries of other career consular officers	5,431.25
Visas	66,215.00	Compensation of vice consuls in charge	
Miscellaneous (fees)	1,572.00	Clerk hire	4,723.46
Excess collections on		Contingent expenses	3,088.74
account of currency	3,026.18		
Gains by exchange on drafts	.65	Contingent expenses at agencies	
Any other (American passports)	144.00	Postage and other expenses at agencies	11.99
Other	20.00	Miscellaneous	321.69
		Any other post allowance	600.00
		US Veteran's Bureau	650.22
		Entry of aliens	1,174.52
Sub-total	71,926.83	Sub-total	20,671.86
Seamen's wages	282.55	Seamen's wages	282.55
		Relief of seamen	91.65
Total receipts at vice			
consulates and agencies	364.57	Balance remitted [to Washington]	51,527.89
Total	72,573.95	Total	72,573.95

Source: NARA, RG59, IRFSP, Dublin, Ireland, June 1924, p. 41.

[I]n view of the fact that Professor Smiddy is presenting his credentials to you today as Minister plenipotentiary to represent the interests of the Irish Free State in the United States, it seems to me to be appropriate to elevate immediately the American consulate at Dublin to the grade of Consulate General, with supervisory jurisdiction over the other consular offices in the Irish Free State.[5]

Hughes indicated that the move would be 'appreciated' by the Cosgrave government.[6] Coolidge replied to Hughes on the same day and approved the elevation.[7] Two days later, US ambassador in London, Frank B. Kellogg, informed the Foreign Office of the upgrading but emphasized that the appointment 'will be a supervisory office for the Irish Free State.'[8] The consular office in Belfast

bottom with $16,255. The offices based in Ireland collected as follows, Dublin, $39,875, Belfast, $31,488 and Cobh, $21,644. LC, MD, WCP, Box 16, Volume of work in diplomatic and consular services abroad, p. 4.   5 LC, MD, MD, Calvin Coolidge Collection (hereafter CCC), presidential, personal file, roll 4, Hughes to Coolidge, 7 October 1924.   6 Ibid.   7 Ibid., Slemp to Hughes, 7 October 1924.   8 National Archives of Ireland (hereafter NAI), Department of Taoiseach (hereafter D/T), series S (hereafter S), S10977, Kellogg to MacDonald, 9 October 1924.

remained at consular level under Skinner's supervision from London. The Dublin upgrading made sense financially but also resulted from the altered political realities in the Free State, a spirit of reciprocity and recent performance reviews of US officers based in Ireland.

There does not appear to have been significant discussion within the State Department about the candidate for the upgraded Dublin posting. Generally, a consul general could be transferred from another posting or an officer could be promoted to the position from within the service. Two sources of information were available to Carr and Hughes about the quality of consular officers in the Free State in 1924. There was the report of the Foreign Service Personnel Board (FSPB), which Hughes had forwarded to Coolidge in June. The FSPB, chaired by Under Secretary of State Joseph Grew, recommended changes to be made to the foreign service personnel under the new Rogers legislation. Some officers were not only to be recommissioned without further examination but promotions made on 5 June 1924 were confirmed. Among other officials appointed to the level of consul general class four were Charles Hathaway in the Dublin office and, significantly, Henry Starrett in Belfast.[9] Following congressional confirmation, Coolidge approved the FSPB recommendations in late June.[10]

A second source of information on the internal candidates came from Frazer's reports on the Dublin office, which he had visited between 31 May and 6 June, and on the Belfast office, which he had also visited between 7 and 12 June. He rated Hathaway and his vice consuls, Harold Collins and Richard R. Wiley as 'very good', while Albion W. Johnson, honorary vice consul and clerk, was rated as 'poor.' Although Frazer opposed Hathaway's request for an additional vice consul, he was fulsome in his praise of the latter. He clarified that the Dublin posting was unusual within the consular service. Whereas consuls were generally regarded as 'watchful sentinels of American producers' who had little to do with politics, Hathaway had been 'given to understand' that in the absence of a US diplomatic representative in the Free State, 'political work' was one of his, if not his most important duty. Frazer confirmed that Hathaway, along with doing

---

9 Calvin Coolidge Papers Microfilm collection (hereafter CCP), series 1, 19 Misc-20, June 30, 1924, roll 26, Hughes to Coolidge, 29 June 1924, Carr to Clark, 30 June 1924. Robert Skinner, the consul general based in the London embassy, was the only consular officer at grade one class whose efficiency rating was 'excellent' and who was recommended for recommission as foreign service officer at class one. Skinner was one of the few consuls who welcomed the Rogers bill believing that it would give him the opportunity to apply for a 'proper legation'. Ibid.; W.H. Heinrichs Jr, *American ambassador: Joseph C. Grew and the development of the United States diplomatic tradition* (1966), p. 99. Among another category of officers was William Patton Kent who had been based in Belfast from 1920 to 1923, was sixty-five years of age or over and had rendered at least fifteen years of service and, therefore, could be considered to be retired. Following the Belfast assignment, Kent saw out his last year in the foreign service as consul in Hamilton, Bermuda. He retired in July 1924 at the age of sixty-seven years. Ibid.; *Register of the Department of State, January 1, 1930* (1930), p. 92; *Register of the Department of State, May 1, 1922* (1922), p. 142. 10 LC, MD, CCC, presidential, personal file, roll 4, Carr to Clark, 30 June 1924.

administrative and routine tasks, devoted most of his time to writing 'exhaustively and very ably' on political and economic matters and left most of the trade promotion work to vice consul Collins. Frazer concluded that Hathaway was a highly educated man who was better able for the political rather than the trade promotion work. The inspector reminded his superiors that Hathaway's efforts had been found 'pleasing to the [State] Department' and that he had received a number of commendations.[11] Hathaway was the obvious choice to become the first US consul general in Ireland with, as Coolidge put it, 'supervisory jurisdiction over the other consular offices in the Irish Free State.'[12] His appointment was well received by the Free State government, which pleased William Castle, director of the Western European Affairs Division, who visited Dublin in October 1924.[13]

What about Northern Ireland? The State Department avoided possible accusations of impartial treatment towards the new Northern Ireland state when Henry Starrett was also promoted to consul general level in June. Significantly, though, the Belfast office remained at consular level.[14] Frazer had been less enthusiastic about Starrett's promotion and the possible elevation of the Belfast office than he was about Hathaway and the Dublin office. There was no caveat attached to Frazer's description of the activities undertaken by the Belfast consular staff. The work was deemed to be administrative, economic and then political in nature. Starrett was described as 'active, energetic, highly intelligent, and an excellent writer.' His ability to handle economic questions was well known to the Department and his political reports from Belfast had 'also been very satisfactory.' Starrett had 'expressed rather a distaste for writing trade letters, and these have not been all that might have been desired.' Frazer's reply to the question 'what should be the grade and class of the principal officer?' was as follows:

> He should be an officer of the highest grade from which the Department will, under the Rogers Bill, customarily designate officers to serve as consuls. That is, this need not be a consulate-general, but should be of the higher class of Consulate.[15]

While Frazer fully endorsed Hathaway's performance and the elevation of the Dublin post, the case for Starrett and the Belfast office was less solid. However,

11 US Congress, House of Representatives, Committee on Foreign Affairs, Hearings on H.Res. 3404, *To provide for the salaries of a minister and consuls to the Republic of Ireland*, 66th Congress, 2nd Session, 1920, James K. McGuire, p. 156; NARA, RG59, IRFSP, Dublin, Ireland, Inspector's comments on Consul Charles Hathaway's report, 10 June 1924. King George signed the exequatur empowering Hathaway to act as consul general in Ireland on 15 December 1924. NAI, D/T, S10977, Amery to Healy, 8 January 1925.   12 LC, MD, MD, CCC, presidential, personal file, roll 4, Slemp to Hughes, 7 October 1924.   13 Herbert Hoover Presidential Library (hereafter HHPL), William R. Castle Papers (hereafter WRCP), WRC diary, 11 October 1924, p. 302.   14 CCP, series 1, 19 Misc-20, June 30, 1924, roll 26, Hughes to Coolidge, 29 June 1924.   15 NARA, RG59, IRFSP Belfast, Ireland, Inspector's comments on Consul Starrett's report, undated June 1924.

Frazer recognized that Starrett worked very hard and, when this was combined to his longevity of service, beginning in 1903, and with his friendship with Wilbur Carr, his promotion under the new legislation was inevitable.[16] By promoting Starrett the State Department was able to avoid any possible criticism of uneven treatment of the two new states in Ireland. Nonetheless, the issue of further upgrading the Dublin office from consular to full diplomatic status remained a live one for the State Department, Smiddy and sympathetic Irish-America politicians and journalists as it had been at the time of the debate on the Mason bill in 1919.[17] Coolidge himself signalled the way forward on the matter.

On 29 August 1924, a friend of Smiddy's, Ralph C. Mulligan, Washington correspondent of the *Boston Post*, attended one of the regular press conferences in the White House and asked Coolidge about US diplomatic representation in Dublin. Coolidge replied 'that an act of Congress would be necessary to enable him to send an American minister to Dublin' and provide an appropriation to cover the salary.[18] Mulligan believed that Coolidge's statement

> lent itself to the assumption that he would be favourable to the idea, if and when Congress gave him the authority. This seems to be a case, therefore, where the friends of Ireland in Congress have an opportunity to come forth and help.[19]

Representatives of the Irish-American community, both inside and outside Congress, maintained the pressure on the administration for the next elevation of the Irish posting. In January 1925, Congressman J.J. Boylan of New York moved in the House of Representatives to attach an amendment to the State

---

16 Ibid.; LC, MD, MD, WCP, Box 8, 1924, Starrett to Carr, 20 May 1924, Carr to Starrett, 5 June 1924. Starrett also spent the period from 11 October 1922 to 1 March 1923 in the State Department in Washington. The appointment of Russell M. Brooks to the Belfast office in 1925 was an unusually complicated process. Brooks had served previously in the US consular office in Newcastle-Upon-Tyne where he and Consul Slater were accused by owners of British shipping companies of diverting passengers from British to US shipping lines by making it difficult for passengers to get visas and by hinting at the inconvenience likely to be encountered in the US unless they travelled on a US line. In July 1922, the Foreign Office became involved when Lord Curzon requested Auckland Geddes in Washington to inform the State Department that the British government intended withdrawing Slater's recognition and Brooks' recognition. Hughes refused to do so because his investigations had not substantiated the allegations. Curzon followed through with his threat and the State Department closed the office. The matter dragged on and in December 1923, the State Department proposed that the two men would be reappointed to other parts of the empire namely Slater to Canada and Brooks to Belfast and a public statement of exoneration be issued by the British government. K. Bourne & D.C. Watt (general eds), *British documents on foreign affairs* (hereafter *BDFA*), part 11, series C, North America, 25 vols. (1986–95), xiv, The Republican Ascendancy, 1919–28 Enclosure in Annual Report for the United States for 1922, pp. 9–11; The National Archives, London (hereafter TNA), Foreign Office (hereafter FO) 371/9635, Annual Report 1923, pp. 11–12.   17 NAI, D/EA, ES, 29/191, Smiddy to Walsh, 11 August 1924.   18 Ibid., Mulligan to Smiddy, 30 August 1924.   19 Ibid., Crawford to Walsh, 3 September 1924.

Department's appropriation bill that would provide for $10,000 as a salary for the 'distinguished American who shall be honoured by being the first minister sent by these United States to the Irish Free State.' Boylan was blocked because the amendment had not been recommended by the Bureau of the Budget or the appointment suggested by the State Department.[20] His suggestion earned him strong criticism from Eamon de Valera's supporters who remained adamantly opposed to any action that confirmed the independent status of the Free State.[21] However, the matter was being considered in the State Department.

In October 1924, Castle had visited US offices in western Europe. One of his meetings in London was with Senator James Douglas, vice-president of the Irish Senate, who asked him about US diplomatic representation in the Free State. Castle was worried that it would mean 'great political pressure in favour of the appointment of an Irish-American.' He elaborated on this view later in the month when he travelled to Dublin and told Cosgrave that he had one serious objection to further upgrading the Irish posting, namely that the US president would be subjected to political pressure and might appoint an individual opposed to the interests of the Free State, thereby embarrassing both governments.[22] Castle rigidly stuck to this position, which he again repeated to Smiddy in Washington in February 1925. Indeed, one of the reasons why Castle supported the upgrading of the Dublin post to consulate general and the purchase of respectable accommodation for the office was to forestall Irish demands for a US diplomatic presence in Dublin.[23] The conservative, moderating Castle had adopted an incremental approach to the issue. Lobbying for foreign appointments was an integral part of the system of political patronage exercised by all presidents, including Coolidge. Nevertheless, it was true that State Department officials constantly worried about providing partisan interests with further openings to lobby the administration and there was opposition to upgrading the US presence in the Free State outside Congress, albeit at a low-level. Coolidge, however, did not have to make a political appointment to Dublin since a candidate could come from within the foreign service.

As was mentioned previously, the Canadian government had explored the possibility of having a representative in Washington during the world war and had paid close attention to Smiddy's appointment to Washington. In 1927, it appointed Vincent Massey as minister to Washington and the British government considered sending a high commissioner to Canada who would be independent of the governor general.[24]

20 *Congressional Record*, 66, 3, 68th congress, 2nd session, 22 January 1923. 21 R. Fanning et al. (eds), *Documents on Irish foreign policy, ii, 1923–26*, 3 vols (hereafter *DIFP*) (1998–), ii, NAI, D/FA, Minister's Office files (1925), Smiddy to FitzGerald, 10 February 1925. 22 HHPL, WRCP, WRC diary, 14 October 1924, p. 310; *DIFP*, ii, NAI, D/FA, Minister's Office File (1925), Smiddy to FitzGerald, 10 February 1925. 23 HHPL, WRCP, WRC diary, 14 October 1924, p. 310; *DIFP*, ii, NAI, D/FA, Minister's Office File (1925), Smiddy to FitzGerald, 10 February 1925. 24 B.J.C. McKercher, *The second Baldwin government and the United States, 1924–29: attitudes and diplomacy*

With the British government recognizing the independence of the dominions, at least in terms of representation, Massey's appointment to Washington and the possibility of additional British appointments to the Free State and Canada, the path was open to extend US relations with these countries.[25] On 15 November 1926, Canadian Prime Minister W.L. MacKenzie King had told US Ambassador Alanson Houghton in London that he believed 'it would be a wise move on our [US] part to send a minister to Canada in return for Canada's having sent a minister directly to us.'[26] Within three weeks, on 1 December 1926, Secretary of State Frank Kellogg informed Houghton that as the British government had permitted these appointments, the US government wished to appoint a minister to each of the countries. Houghton was instructed to confer with Foreign Secretary Austin Chamberlain to determine whether such appointments would be acceptable to the British government and if they were, 'to whom would the Minister be accredited and to whom would he present his credentials.' Chamberlain replied to Frederick Sterling, in the US embassy in London, that 'these appointments will be most agreeable' and in these post-treaty days the appropriate procedure would be that they should be addressed to 'His Majesty the King' and presented to the governor general of the Free State and Canada as his majesty's representatives respectively.[27] Ironically Sterling would be appointed as the first US minister to the Free State. Coolidge also linked both ministerial posts and on 27 January annotated a memorandum to ask Kellogg if there was 'anything to report regarding our ministers to the Irish Free State and the Dominion of Canada.' Some time during the following two days Kellogg reported personally to Coolidge that the matter had been settled.[28] There was a wider context to these appointments.

In addition to their serving to cement US-Canadian and US–Free State relations, the appointments would ease some internal difficulties within the State Department. Kellogg had replaced Hughes as secretary of State in January 1925. Many observers had expected that the post would go to Herbert Hoover, secretary of Commerce, but Coolidge had appointed Kellogg. Castle, who worked with both men, believed that Hughes 'was extraordinarily able to take care of himself. No bores or fanatics stayed long in his office, and ... he was able to get rid of them without making enemies.' On the other hand, Kellogg 'struck a happy medium ... but he hated fools and, if he was tired, often irritated his callers.'[29]

(1984), pp. 168, 169.   25 In December 1926, Kellogg seems to have believed that the British government was about to appoint a minister to the Free State and to Canada. The latter appointment came about in December 1928 but the former occurred in 1931. Although in October 1926, Walshe and James McNeill, the Irish high commissioner in London, discussed the possibility of a British high commissioner being appointed to Dublin. See *Papers relating to the Foreign Relations of the United States* (hereafter *FRUS*), 1927, 3 vols (1942), i, Kellogg to Houghton, 1 December 1926; *DIFP*, iii, NAI, D/FA, unregistered papers, notes, October 1926.   26 HHPL, WRCP, Box 3, file 30, Houghton to Castle, 16 November 1926.   27 *FRUS*, 1927, i, Kellogg to Houghton, 1 December 1926; ibid., Chamberlain to Sterling, 6 January 1927.   28 CCP, Roll 118, file 308, State Department, 27, 29 January 1927.   29 HHPL, WRCP, Box 33, Castle, 'The tools of American diplomacy', p.

Among the issues Kellogg had to deal with was how to progress the reform of the foreign service, particularly the process of amalgamating the diplomatic and consular services and promotions of officers below the level of minister. It was the responsibility of the FSPB to make recommendations to Kellogg, who then presented them to the president. Grew favoured the appointment of professional diplomats over that of consular officers and political appointees. He was soon dissatisfied with Kellogg's slowness in making appointments, particularly when it came to promoting career diplomats. However, in September 1925 the situation was relieved by the availability of four additional posts: one at ambassadorial level in Argentina and three at ministerial level in Canada, the Irish Free State and Hungary.[30] The upgrading of the Free State posting, therefore, eased a difficult situation for Kellogg and Grew, who could now elevate another careerist.

The were many reasons why Hathaway might have expected to have been promoted from consul general to minister in the Free State: among them were his long tenure in Ireland, wide experience of the posting and the many commendations for the quality of his political reporting. Indeed Hathaway was asked by the State Department to continue his political reporting even after it was decided that Frederick Sterling would become minister of the Dublin legation because of staff 'inexperience in a complicated domestic situation.'[31] In addition to Hathaway having been regularly commended by the State Department for his political reporting, Sterling praised the quality of his work:

> During his assignment at Dublin he made a careful and thorough study of the constitution of the Free State, of the various Anglo-Irish agreements, of the laws of the land and its history; he was in touch with many officials of the government, with representatives in the Dáil and the Senate, and with private individuals of various shades of opinion. He was generally liked and respected.
>
> All this was reflected in his political reporting. His statements could be relied upon, and his analyses of the ever changing situations were exact, informative and often prophetic. He was thorough and conscientious.[32]

Despite his suitability, there were obstacles. Not only was Grew opposed to consular officers being promoted to diplomatic posts but Sterling was well-connected within State Department circles and also had experience of Irish affairs. He came from the

12.   30 Heinrichs, *American ambassador*, pp. 118–19.   31 NARA, Records of the Department of State relating to the internal affairs of Great Britain, 1910 to 1929, Record Group (hereafter RG), 59, M580/223, 841d.00/939, Sterling to Secretary of State, 24 February 1928; HHPL, WRCP, Box 8, File: Ireland, 1924–31, Sterling to Castle, 4 August 1927; NARA, RG59, M580/223, 841d.00/939, 841d.00/952, Sterling to Secretary of State, 28 April 1929. In April 1929, Sterling explained that there was no need to regularly report on political matters or indeed to offer a perspective from the Cobh office, because of the 'size' of the Free State and the fact that 'practically all political matters' were centred on Dublin. Ibid.,   32 NARA, RG59, M580/223, 841d.00/939, Sterling to Secretary of State, 24 February 1928.

diplomatic side of the State Department and indeed from an even more-monied background than Hathaway. The new Free State minister was born in St Louis in 1876 and educated in Switzerland and at Harvard University, where he obtained a law degree. He entered the diplomatic service after examination in January 1911. From then on he made his way up the promotions ladder and, following the reorganization of the State Department in 1909 when geographic divisions replaced the old diplomatic and consular bureaus, he was detailed home to the position of acting chief of the division of Western European Affairs in 1916. This latter position was significant as it was only foreign service officers with expertise and experience who were accorded these headquarters' postings, which were regarded as the 'key echelon in [the] management of ordinary relations with other nations' and gave these geographical divisions a large voice in both policy formulation and management.[33]

Sterling returned to the field in January 1918 with a posting to Paris, which was followed by promotion to secretary class two. His career continued to move upward with assignments to Lima and London. As counsellor in London from 1923 to 1927 he had served under Kellogg, who still referred to him as 'Fred' yet called his under secretary 'Mr Grew' and still regarded Sterling as a 'friend.' His immediate superior, Houghton, described him as 'the best in the world', while his colleagues in London and the State Department praised his work and abilities.[34] It was Kellogg's patronage that was most significant. On 29 November 1926, Grew presented Kellogg with the FSPB's recommendations for nine postings along with his own selection of names. According to Grew, all the board's candidates except for one Frederick Sterling, were unknown to Kellogg, the list did not include the name of any consul and all had established diplomatic reputations and powerful political backing. Kellogg rejected all the names except for that of his former counsellor in the London embassy. He formally presented the candidates to Coolidge on 28 January and again on 12 February who approved them.[35] The *Washington Post* understood that it was partly because of the 'divided

---

33 H. de Santis & W. Heinrichs, 'United States of America. The Department of State and American foreign policy' in Z. Steiner (ed.), *Foreign ministries of the world* (1982), p. 580. He was appointed in March 1911 as third secretary of the US embassy in Petrograd, then he was detailed to observe elections for the Constituent Assembly of Santo Domingo, he was in Peking and Petrograd again. In 1916, he married Dorothy William McCombs who was a member of a prominent Washington family. HHPL, Castle, 'Harvard men in the Foreign Service of the United States' in *Harvard Graduate*, 11 November 1929. *New York Times*, 15 September 1925.   34 HHPL, WRCP, Box 3, file 26, Houghton to Castle, 23 November 1925; Heinrichs, *American ambassador*, p. 110; HHPL, FBKP, roll 33, Sterling to Kellogg, 22 July 1928; HHPL, WRCP, Box 3, file England, 1920–25, Blair to Castle, 18 July 1923, 25 August 1923, Castle to Kellogg, 12 June 1924.   35 At the meeting on 28 January and another on 12 February, Coolidge agreed to the following promotions: Robert Woods Bliss (ambassador to Argentina), Leland Harrison (minister to Sweden), J. Butler Wright (minister to Hungary), William Phillips (minister to Canada), Hugh Gibson (ambassador to Belgium), Hugh Wilson (minister to Switzerland), Frederick Sterling (minister to the Irish Free State), Francis White and William Castle as assistant secretaries of State. See Heinrichs, *American ambassador*, p. 119; HHPL, WRCP, Castle diary, 28 January 1927, 12 February 1927.

opinion among the Irish people' that Coolidge had chosen Sterling, a 'service man' for this difficult post.[36]

There were other reasons why Sterling's selection attracted further press and congressional attention. Throughout 1927, Congress kept a close eye on all foreign service appointments and promotions, particularly if, according to one politician, they smacked of 'too much exclusive social politics'.[37] In December, the Senate launched an investigation into firstly, 'favouritism' in promotions of diplomats and, secondly, whether the diplomats on the FSPB had procured 'choice' foreign appointments for themselves. Among those named in a *New York Times* report was Frederick Sterling, who was not a member of the board that nominated him but did sit on it when he was on leave of absence in December 1926.[38] Even though the board only made recommendations and it was Coolidge and Kellogg who decided the appointments, the charges could be upheld as there was no consul among the nine selected, three of the ministers were members of the board, five were graduates of Harvard, two of Yale and one of Princeton universities, all had private incomes and most were close friends. None of the appointments was reversed. But three consul generals were promoted to minister in 1927 and in 1928 an amendment to the Foreign Service Act was introduced to remove serving diplomats from the FSPB to prevent 'favouritism' in appointments, transfers and promotions.[39] This amendment was passed in 1931.

Sterling survived the congressional attention and the change of government in 1929. Fortunately for him President Herbert Hoover and his new secretary of State, Henry Stimson, favoured having career men in diplomatic positions and were influenced by Castle's arguments for retaining Sterling in Dublin. In January 1929, Castle reassured Sterling that 'quite naturally the Department would do all it could to have you stay in Dublin' but he did not know if Hoover would heed departmental advice on appointments. By August, he confirmed that he had talked with Hoover and Stimson and 'made them feel that you ought to be kept in Dublin, both because you are liked and are doing a good job and because if the post were vacant the line of unsuitable political aspirants would be a very appalling thing.' Hoover had already made out a list of men 'who were to be retained for the good of the service' and Sterling's name was on it. He remained *in situ* in Dublin until 1934.[40] Thus, with Sterling's appointment the US government maintained a consulate general and a legation in Dublin. Sterling arrived in Ireland on

36 *Washington Post*, 3 February 1927.   37 Heinrichs, *American ambassador*, p. 122. The gap in status between the diplomatic and consular postings was significant to US diplomat Percy Blair based in the London who wanted to stay there rather than move to Geneva because that was a consular post and he knew it would be difficult to return to the diplomatic branch. See HHPL, WRCP, Box 3, file 28, Blair to Castle, 11 October 1926.   38 Heinrichs, *American ambassador*, pp. 122–3. *New York Times*, 31 January 1928.   39 LC, MD, WCP, Box 9, Kellogg reply to congressional committee, 21 June 1927. Among those promoted was Robert Skinner, consul general in London who had complained to Kellogg about the lack of integration and disproportionate promotion of diplomats over consuls; see Heinrichs, *American ambassador*, pp. 120, 122, 117.   40 *Washington Post*, 17 February 1929; HHPL, WRCP, Box 8, File: Ireland, 1924–31, Castle to Sterling, 9 January 1929, 12 August 1929.

25 July 1927 and presented his credentials to Governor General Healy, representing King George.[41] Many forces coalesced in his selection as the first US minister to the Free State. His appointment must be seen in the contexts of continuous congressional pressure to upgrade the Dublin post, the expansion of US representation in the empire and the reform of the service. Coolidge heeded State Department advice and did not make a political appointment. Sterling had diplomatic experience, a calm personality and knowledge of Irish affairs, all of which made him the ideal choice as the first US minister to the Free State.

The Cosgrave government was officially informed on 28 December 1926 by Leopold Amery, Dominions' Secretary, of Coolidge's intention to appoint US ministers to Dublin and Ottawa.[42] Three days later, the appointment was received 'with much satisfaction' and was found to be most 'agreeable' to the Cosgrave government. The Free State government also agreed with Amery's proposals that the credentials of the minister would be addressed to King George and presented to Healy.[43] Acting secretary in External Affairs, Joseph Walshe officially communicated Sterling's name to Cograve who endorsed the appointment on 1 February 1927.[44] Meanwhile, in Washington, Smiddy was officially told about Kellogg's choice of Sterling on 2 February and that the appointment would have the addendum 'envoy extraordinary.' Smiddy considered Sterling to be an 'excellent choice' and, later on, he reported home:

> He is reserved, unostentatious and a gentleman. As you are aware, he is a diplomat of career and brings to his post varied and valuable experience. I think there is little danger of his ever creating any embarrassment either for his government or for ours, which one holding such a position might easily do … he goes to the Irish Free State with a sympathetic attitude, and is anxious to learn something of her history, aspirations and problems, and to aid in enhancing the prestige of the Irish Free State in this country. His appointment has already increased the interest of the so-called 'Hundred per cent American' in the Irish Free State, especially those of the same class as himself. I feel quite certain that he will appeal very much to you personally.[45]

Smiddy believed that the appointment would accentuate 'our international status' and expand economic links.[46] Approving the upgrade and Sterling's appointment provoked no opposition from within the Cosgrave administration.[47]

---

41 *Washington Post*, 26, 31 July 1927.   42 NAI, D/EA, 18/3, Amery to Healy, 28 December 1926. 43 Ibid., Healy to Amery, 31 December 1926; ibid., Montgomery to Sterling, 6 January 1927.   44 Ibid., McDunphy to Walshe, 1 February 1927.   45 Ibid., Secretary to Private Secretary, President, Vice-President, Defence, Finance, Education, Industry and Commerce, Attorney General, 2 February 1927; *DIFP*, iii, NAI, D/FA, 321/1/1929, Smiddy to FitzGerald, 5 April 1927.   46 NAI, D/EA, 18/3, Secretary to Private Secretary, President, Vice-President, Defence, Finance, Education, Industry and Commerce, Attorney General, 2 February 1927; *DIFP*, iii, NAI, D/FA, 321/1/1929, Smiddy to FitzGerald, 5 April 1927.   47 Others were less pleased with the choice of Sterling, not surpris-

Hathaway was surprised that by late February 1927, no Free State newspaper had devoted an editorial to the significance of the appointment, whereas the *Belfast Newsletter*, on 19 February, had devoted a column titled 'Imperial Evolution' to it.[48] The *Irish Times* and the *Irish Independent* announced the probable decision on 3 and 4 February without comment, while the *Cork Examiner*, on 5 February, had a short editorial stating that the step followed from recent confirmation of the Free State status as an independent state at the 1926 imperial conference.[49]

However, when Sterling eventually arrived in Dublin in July 1927, his reception was different. Subsequently, he privately reported to Castle:

[A]side from the pomp and ceremony, the efficiency and dignity with which I was received, there was a great public interest coupled with an atmosphere of cordiality, which was beyond my expectations. This, of course, had been worked up by the government and quite properly so; for I came at an opportune moment to divert the public mind from the tragedy of horror of the murder of [Kevin] O'Higgins, and secondly, it was evidence of the present status of the Free State, which they like to think is practically complete independence.[50]

Hathaway reported that Sterling's arrival was regarded as a 'significant event' and that there was no adverse criticism, even from the de Valera side. Indeed he believed that the appointment was welcomed not just because of Irish–US friendship but because it again implied formal international recognition of the status of the Free State.[51] Similarly Lieutenant John C. MacArthur, US assistant military attaché based in the office of the Military Attaché in the US embassy in London, who visited Ireland in early 1928 reported that 'they feel greatly honoured in having a diplomatic representative from our government of the rank of minister.'[52]

ingly, the republican *Gaelic American* was dissatisfied because an Irish-American specifically a de Valera supporter, did not get the post and it blamed Smiddy for this. See *DIFP*, iii, NAI, D/FA, 321/1/1929, Smiddy to FitzGerald, 5 April 1927.   48 NARA, RG59, M580/223, 841d.00/898, Hathaway to Secretary of State, 21 February 1927.   49 Ibid., 841d.00/895, Hathaway to Secretary of State, 7 February 1927. *Cork Examiner*, 5 February 1927. Edward J. Phelan chief of the diplomatic division of the International Labour Organization, viewed the Sterling appointment as one of the 'results' of the 1926 imperial conference believing 'it completes the Smiddy appointment, which was an anomaly so long as the US did not reciprocate.' See *DIFP*, iii, UCDA, P80/557, Phelan to FitzGerald, 18 February 1927.   50 HHPL, WRCP, Box 8, File: Ireland, 1924–31, Sterling to Castle, 4 August 1927.   51 NARA, RG59, M580/223, 841d.00/922, Hathaway to Secretary of State, 30 July 1927.   52 Ibid., M580/240, 841d.20/1, 'The Irish Free State (Military)', 28 April 1928 in Sterling to Secretary of State, 11 May 1928. In September 1927, Smiddy asked Cosgrave to appoint a military attaché to the Washington legation to avail of US army experience in every phase of military affairs. In the following year, the Cosgrave government delayed pursuing a British suggestion that the British military attaché in the Washington embassy should act on behalf of the Free State legation as he did for the Canadian legation. See *DIFP*, p. 155, NAI, D/FA, EA, 1/26, Smiddy to Cosgrave, 22 September 1927; TNA, Dominions Office (hereafter DO), 35/51, Walshe to Harding, 26 November 1928.

Another reason why Sterling's appointment was welcomed by the Cosgrave government was that it acted as a stimulus to increase US representation in the Free State in other areas of foreign relations. MacArthur passed on to his superiors in London and Washington the Free State government's suggestion that it would be pleased to have a US military attaché regularly accredited to them and he said that some army officers wanted to have a US officer as an army instructor. Sterling agreed to take up the ideas with MacArthur's superior in London, Colonel John R. Thomas. On the economic front, Smiddy learnt that Julius Klein, director of the Bureau of Foreign and Domestic Commerce, obtained approval from Congress to appoint Hugh Butler, the commercial attaché in the London embassy, to the Free State. Smiddy had hoped for a separate appointment but made the best of it by noting that Butler was of Irish-American ancestry although an 'enthusiastic' Christian Scientist by religion.[53] Butler was in Ireland within a few weeks and began to make a general economic survey of the Free State which will be examined in chapter thirteen. An *Irish Independent* journalist concluded that Butler's appointment 'adds another link to the chains that bind the great republic to this country and it will help to develop and to foster trade between the two countries.'[54]

The physical conditions in which US consuls and diplomats in the Free State worked varied from office to office. By 1924, the consular office in Belfast was located in a modern office building in 2 Wellington Place, opposite the City Hall.[55] The situation was different in Dublin, where the office at 14 and 15 Lower O'Connell Street, was described by Frazer as 'a cheap, jerry-built looking building', approached through an 'unattractive entrance up a dark and narrow flight of stairs.' It was 'discreditable to the extreme.' Underneath the office were a barber's shop and a cheap eating-house. Although more space had been obtained in a recent move, the rooms were 'small, unattractive, inconveniently arranged and overcrowded.' Hathaway had previously suggested to the State Department, following the destruction of the Custom House, General Post Office, Four Courts and many of the streets near the consulate, that 'larger and better premises' should be obtained. He hoped that when the lease on the O'Connell Street premises expired on 31 December 1923, the office would move to the south side of the city, where rents were cheaper. This did not happen and in June 1924, he was worried that the locality did not favour visa work and that the floor was not strong enough to hold a recently obtained new filing cabinet. Both officials felt that the US government was not getting value for the rent being paid and Frazer encouraged Hathaway to continue looking for more suitable quarters. Once Wilbur Carr had read the report he agreed but reminded the new consul gen-

53 *DIFP*, iii, NAI, D/FA, 321/1/1929, Smiddy to FitzGerald, 5 April 1927. *Irish Trade Journal*, May 1928, p. 93. Carr in the State Department insisted that Butler would not be permitted to inspect or examine any of Hathaway's political reports. NARA, RG59, 580.241, 841d.50/8, Castle to Carr, 6 May 1927.   54 *Irish Independent*, 23 January 1928. Wainright Abbot was appointed as Sterling's secretary.   55 NARA, RG59, IRFSP Belfast, Ireland, pp. 11, 15.

eral that no contract for the rental of new quarters should be entered into without departmental approval, although Hathaway was permitted to requisition a new coat of arms to replace the existing 'faded and discoloured' one.[56]

During summer 1924, Hathaway succeeded in renting two floors in another building at 34 Lower Abbey Street, which he described as 'satisfactory in all respects.'[57] But when William Castle visited in October, he depicted the new quarters as 'atrocious, small, dark, ill-ventilated, really shameful.' Castle also felt that decent accommodation should be sought, because this would indicate to the Free State government the level of importance accorded by the US government to its local representation.[58] When Louis G. Dreyfus inspected the offices in July 1926 he found the central locations to be 'excellent' but 'the quarters are almost the worst' he had ever seen. On 1 October, the consulate moved again to separate three-story buildings at 15 Merrion Square North, in the south of the city on the outskirts of the business section. Dreyfus had mixed views about the new location, firstly, because it was not close to the business centre and secondly, mindful as ever of the need for economy, because it would be 'very spacious … possibly too large.' Clearly, there was space to accommodate the new legation staff along with the consular staff, but it was not to be.[59]

Sterling's appointment as minister meant that his staff and personal accommodation now became a matter of significance to the State Department. US governments were slow to purchase residences and offices abroad. But another part of the Rogers' legislative measures aimed to reduce the personal financial burden on heads of embassies and missions and to physically unite the diplomatic and consular establishments, which necessitated purchasing properties.[60] Houghton moved into the first US government-owned residence in London, located at Hyde Park, in 1926, while Sterling had rented 31 Belgrave Square in London. Once he had been appointed to Dublin he asked Smiddy if it would be possible to 'procure one of the vice-regal lodges if such are available' for the legation office and his personal accommodation.[61] Following negotiations with the government,

56 Ibid., Dublin, Ireland, June 1924, pp. 11–12, pp. 15–17; ibid., Carr to Hathaway, 29 September 1924; ibid., RG59, M580/219, 841d.00/531, Hathaway to Secretary of State, 10 July 1922.   57 Ibid., IRFSP, Dublin, Ireland, June 1924, pp. 11–12, pp. 15–17; ibid., Carr to Hathaway, 29 September 1924.   58 HHPL, WRCP, WRC diary, 14 October 1924, p. 310;   59 NARA, RG59, IRFSP Dublin, Ireland, July 1926, pp. 15–16.   60 LC, MD, WCP, Box 9, Kellogg reply to Congressional Committee, 21 June 1927, p. 19. Accommodation for the Free State legation in Washington consisted of a leased two floors of a 'well-appointed' house at 1800 Connecticut Avenue, William Macaulay occupied the flat in the top floor on a separate letting from the landlord. Smiddy was paid a rent allowance and lived in a hotel apartment. In December 1928, Walshe believed these arrangements to be satisfactory unless the government decided to buy a residential house to accommodate the offices and the minister plenipotentiary and his family. In New York, three rooms were leased at number one Broadway, but Walshe felt that a small house should be obtained to give a 'more individual character' to the IFS presence there. NAI, D/T, S1879a, Walshe, 6 December 1928.   61 LC, MD, WCP, Box 16, Manuscript 'Uncle Sam's diplomatic agents', p. 6; DIFP, iii, NAI, D/FA, 321/1/1929, Smiddy to FitzGerald, 5 April 1927.

he was given permission, in April 1927, to rent temporarily a lodge formerly owned by the British under secretary for Ireland in the Phoenix Park in Dublin on a three month basis, in order to allow him find a 'suitable residence.' However, in October the government agreed to rent him the former residence of the British chief secretary of Ireland, which was also located in the park.[62] The building was described by Sterling as a 'spacious and attractive property' and by a US visitor as the 'most beautiful of all American legations.'[63] Castle felt that 'the situation is ideal and evidently also the Irish feel that it was a great compliment to let you have it.'[64] Despite suggestions from Consul General Henry Balch in 1934 and 1938 that the legation staff should be 'amalgamated' with the consulate general office in Merrion Square, this did not happen.[65]

Frazer also visited the Cobh consular office in 1924 where he found similar conditions to those in Dublin. The US office was well located at number one Casement (Scott's) Square in a building on the main street, it was adjacent to the port and the rent was low. According to Frazer, its internal and external appearance was 'discreditable.' It was situated over a bar and occupied 'a shabby, ill-arranged, poverty-stricken looking building.' The offices were on three different floors and during the visa season were too crowded. Frazer also worried that, unlike the situation in the Belfast office, where there was an elevator, much time was lost in climbing and descending the three flights of 'rather narrow, steep stairs' between the different rooms. It was 'inconvenient in the extreme to work in' and he recommended a move 'at the first opportunity.' Nor did the appearance and location of the office compare favourably with that of other countries' consular offices. This also applied to the Dublin office.[66] The office remained in Cobh until December 1932 when it was relocated to 41 South Mall in Cork city, which was considered by US Consul Leslie E. Woods to be 'central and convenient to the public ... is within easy reach of the railway stations and hotels.' The visa office at Cobh was then closed and all immigration visa work consolidated in the Dublin office.[67] The decision also reflected the growing importance of Cork city as a commercial centre.

The State Department also maintained consular agents in Galway and Limerick, and these were visited by Frazer in May 1924. He spent one day, 28 May, with the Scottish-born Robert A. Tennant at the Galway office in New Dock. He described the location as 'satisfactory', since it was situated on the quays immediately adjacent to the Custom House. The agency and Tennant's private business occupied a 'small, neat, entire building, very conveniently situ-

62 NAI, S4070, O'Hegarty, secretary, Executive Council to Walshe, 14 April 1927; ibid., C.3/23, 7 October 1927.   63 NARA, RG59, M580/223, 841d.00/965, Sterling to Secretary of State, 6 December 1929; I.A. Marcosson, *Reborn Ireland* (1928), p. 8.   64 HHPL, WRCP, Box 8, File: Ireland, 1924–31, Castle to Sterling, 19 August 1927. Castle also hoped that it had enough bathrooms 'so that you can rest comfortably.' Ibid.   65 NARA, RG59, IRFSP Dublin, Ireland, April 1934, p. 4; ibid., July 1938, p. 7.   66 Ibid., Cobh, Ireland, May 1924, pp. 11–12.   67 Ibid., IRFSP, Cork, Ireland, March 1934, p. 2; ibid., Dublin, April 1934, p. 3.

ated for shipping work, on the one hand, and also very near to the business centre of the town.' As for the appearance, he found it 'as judged by local standards [to be] satisfactory.' It was of equal importance that the location and appearance of the Galway office should compare favourably with that of other countries.'[68] Tenant was to remain as US consular agent until 1945, when he was seventy-eight years of age.

Two days before his visit to Galway on 28 May 1924, Frazer spent the night in Limerick. There the office run by consular agent John A. Dinan was located in Bedford Row, which was 'very satisfactory' because it was on a 'good street, a short block away from Limerick's main central thoroughfare.' As was the case in Galway, the agency was conducted in Dinan's business offices, which occupied one corner of his large hardware establishment and agricultural machinery showrooms. Visitors to the agency had to walk through the shop in order to reach it. The building on the whole was modern and 'very creditable' for the purpose that it served. It compared favourably with other countries' offices. The only complaint that Frazer expressed was that he found consular papers and effects 'carelessly intermingled with the effects of Mr Dinan's private business' and he recommended that a small room be set aside exclusively for the conduct of consular business and the storage of consular effects.[69] Dinan was consular agent until 1928 and was not replaced. The importance of the Limerick region was to increase again following the establishment in 1939 of regular transatlantic flying boat services in and out of Foynes on the river Shannon in county Limerick. The outbreak of world war two and US involvement therein led to the establishment in 1943 of a vice consulate in Foynes.

The working environment for career consular officials in the Dublin and Cobh offices was inadequate when judged on the basis of the US government's own standards along with those of other countries' representatives. At the same time, the offices of the staff in Belfast and consular agents in Limerick and Galway were more than satisfactory while Sterling and his staff were ensconced in the Phoenix Park.[70] What was the type and nature of the work carried out by the US representatives in the Free State during the period 1923 to 1929?

Routine bureaucracy: assisting US citizens, residents, workers and tourists

The length of the working day was prescribed by the State Department. All consular personnel were expected to work each weekday from 9.00 a.m. to 4.00 p.m.

---

68 Ibid., Galway, May 1924, pp. 11, 15.   69 Ibid., Limerick, May 1924, pp. 11, 15.   70 As with most foreign postings, to survive the rigours, items were needed from home and records reveal that consuls and later diplomats requested External Affairs to apply to the Customs and Excise office for the usual abrogation of customs duty on wines, whiskey, champagnes, beer, gin, cheese, sugar, preserves, cigarettes, clothing, wireless, domestic delft ware. Ibid., D/EA, Letter Books, various, Foreign Ministers in Saorstát, 1921 and 1921.

and from 9.00 a.m. to 1.00 a.m. on Saturdays. Any variations from these hours which had not been sanctioned by the State Department were noted and would lead to a reprimand from Wilbur Carr. Both Hathaway and Vice-Consul Wiley both had telephones in their residences and dealt with urgent inquiries outside office hours.[71] At the Cobh office, summer time was the busiest period for John Gamon, Loy W. Henderson and J.S. Richardson and six clerks due to increased sailings and they rarely left the office at this time of year before 7.00 p.m. Gamon and Richardson were generally at their desks on Saturday afternoons and for part of the day on Sundays.[72] The State Department also outlined the reasons for having a US presence in a district: 'trade facilitation (exports to the United States) ... protection of the public health ... protection of existing or potential American interests ... services to American vessels and seamen ... political observation or political reasons ... assistance it may render to American tourists and travellers.'[73]

A central function of all US consuls, therefore, was to render services to those US citizens who were resident or in transit as workers and tourists. The arrival and departure of US-registered vessels and US sailors had to be documented. Legation records indicated that between 1923–4 and 1925–6, the number of US vessels that docked in Dublin port declined from 44 to 24. Some of the 50 US crew who arrived in the earlier period caused problems for the consulate. 33 seamen were shipped home, 9 were discharged, 13 deserted and 3 were destitute, although none of the men in the last category required a complete outfit of clothes from the consulate. Others were among the 46 'protection cases' which required formal or informal intervention with Free State government officials, shopkeepers, hotel owners or ticket agencies. US officials intervened with owners of ships to collect $282.55 in wages due to seamen. In the later period, 10 men were shipped home, none deserted, 4 were discharged and 3 needed assistance but not a complete outfit. Others were among the 15 protection cases requiring consular intervention at local level.[74]

Nor was there a great deal of need for the Cobh office to provide assistance to US seamen who arrived in that port; in 1923–4, 59 US vessels with 13 US crew docked and in 1925–26, 57 ships with 13 US crew. During the same two-year period, the number of US seamen shipped back to the US remained at 5, while 2 were discharged in the earlier period and 6 later on. In 1923–4, 1 deserted and 2 were given assistance and none deserted while 4 received assistance in 1925–6. Although the staff did not have to deal with any extradition cases, they did handle 38 'protection cases.' Two years later, there were 8 such cases and Consul Ferris noted that, although there were disputes between masters and seamen, they were usually settled amicably without consular assistance.[75]

---

71 Ibid., pp. 11–44.   72 Ibid., Cobh, Ireland, May 1924, pp. 11–44.   73 NARA, RG59, IRFSP Dublin, Ireland, June 1924, p. 11, Ibid., Dublin, July 1926, p. 8.   74 Ibid., June 1924, Consolidated Summary of Business; ibid., July 1926, Consolidated Summary of Business.   75 Ibid., Cobh, Ireland, May 1924, pp. 11–44; ibid., July 1926, p. 37.

The consulate service also looked after the affairs of other US citizens resident in the Free State. In 1923–4, there were several hundred naturalized citizens living in the Dublin district but only 88 were registered with the consulate; this had increased to 173 two years later. In Cobh, 300 citizens lived in the local district with 128 registered with the consulate; this had increased to 184 by 1925–6.[76] The work arising from this category of citizen involved not just registering each individual but assisting at times of crisis and forwarding US government correspondence, including pension cheques from the US Veterans' Bureau.[77] The consulates were also required to forward medical reports on retired US soldiers who claimed pensions back to the Bureau. In 1923–4, the Dublin staff handled 85 Veterans' Bureau cases and passed on $650.22 directly to retired US servicemen resident in Ireland or to relatives of deceased servicemen. Two years later, 116 cases were dealt with and $921.16 disbursed. In Cobh there were 89 cases in 1923–4 and $282.34 was disbursed; this increased to 95 cases and $1,441.60 two years later.[78] The repatriation of the bodies of deceased US soldiers to the Free State became an urgent matter of correspondence between Hathaway, External Affairs and Justice officials in April 1924.[79]

Consular officers also handled land cases arising from various circumstances, such as those which arose upon the death of US residents in Ireland or when US citizens living in the US laid claim to an Irish inheritance following the death of a relative in Ireland. On 21 June 1924, Carr asked Hathaway to check out one case, following an appeal by Congressman Vestal of Indiana on behalf of a constituent, Mrs H.B. Lee. The latter's mother, Mrs Katherine F. Hetherton, formerly O'Connor, sailed to Ireland on 24 May, died on 5 June and was buried in the family graveyard at Dysart in county Clare. It transpired that the deceased had $400 in checks and cash with her. Both Vestal and Lee suspected that a crime had been committed and Hathaway was asked to investigate the facts and supply a report along with the name of a law firm to ensure that the deceased's estate was handled properly. His report was to be sent directly to Vestal in Indiana.[80]

Of greater significance to their work in this area was the introduction of the Irish Free State Land Purchase Bill into the Dáil on 28 May 1923. The purpose of the bill was to enable the government, through a commission, to acquire land

76 Ibid., Dublin, Ireland, June 1924, p. 33; ibid., July 1926, p. 33; ibid., Cobh, Ireland, May 1924, p. 34; ibid., August 1926, p. 33.   77 Ibid., Cobh, Ireland, May 1924, p. 12.   78 Ibid., Dublin, Ireland, June 1924, Consolidated Summary of Business, Financial Statement; ibid., July 1926, Consolidated Summary of Business, Financial Statement; ibid., Cobh, Ireland, May 1924, Consolidated Summary of Business, Financial Statement; ibid., Cobh, Ireland, August 1926, Consolidated Summary of Business, Financial Statement.   79 NAI, Department of Justice (hereafter D/J), letter books, 1922–5, Walshe to Kevin O'Higgins, 7 April 1924.   80 LC, MD, Manuscripts Division (hereafter MD), Leland Harrison Papers (hereafter LHP), Box 46, Harrison to Carr, 21 June 1924. The issue of the taxation of US citizens owning property in the IFS was raised by Smiddy with Walshe in August 1926 arising from the case of Howard Harrington who sold his property in county Kerry because he was taxed 'to the full extent' by the IFS revenue authorities. NAI, D/FA, 30/193, Smiddy to Walshe, 6 August 1926.

compulsorily from landlords for distribution to tenants and present holders of uneconomic tracts in the congested districts (the poorer areas along the west coast from Donegal to Cork along with Leitrim and Roscommon). The 1923 legislation was expected to affect 70,000 tenants and to cost $120 million.[81] Although the changes were directed at landlords, they also affected all landowners. Two cases were dealt with by Hathaway in 1924 and 1925.

In February 1924, Harrison Stewart, a US citizen living in Washington, bought property in county Cavan from Margaret Stewart, also a US citizen. He then learned from H.P. Kennedy Solicitors, based in Cavan, that the land came under the Land Purchase Act and his ownership would be for fifteen years only. This information led him to write to Secretary of State Hughes on 30 April to inform him

> my land is not for sale and I should like very much to have information through your department, if possible, on this subject as it looks to the writer as though his land is to be confiscated against his will and turned over to somebody as purchaser at a price to be fixed by some commission without reference to the writer, who is the owner.[82]

Hathaway was instructed to 'discreetly investigate' the matter and report back on the case and also on the effects of the land act on the purchase of land in Ireland by US citizens.[83] Hathaway contacted the Irish Land Commission who replied informally that there was no record of the transfer of land to Harrison from Margaret Stewart, who was still considered the owner of the lands. Hathaway concluded that confiscation applied without discrimination to all holders of land regardless of nationality. But he admitted that because land owners were compelled to receive the purchase price of their lands in Free State land bonds, the market price of which was not certain, this could be construed as a confiscation of property and, therefore, a foreign government on behalf of its nationals, could object. Hathaway felt this was a question for the State Department to decide upon. Hathaway appeared to have more sympathy for the plight of the landless tenant than for Stewart and advised against other US citizens from buying land in the Irish Free State, except for their personal occupancy and in such areas as the land legislation would permit them to hold.[84]

Clearly, Stewart had been taken unawares by the Free State government's land reform policies but another case came Hathaway's way the following year. Thomas Conroy, a US citizen living in Jamaica Plain, Massachusetts, owned lands in county Galway which his father had bought in 1888 and bequeathed him. On 1 September 1925, he was informed by his agent in Galway that the

81 NARA, RG59, M580/247, 841d.52, Collins to Department of State, 12 June 1923.   82 Ibid., 841d.52/3, Stewart to Hughes, 30 April 1924.   83 Ibid., M580/247, 841d.52/3, Grew to Hathaway, 2 May, 1924.   84 Ibid., 841d.52/4, Hathaway to Secretary of State, 28 June 1924.

Land Commission had given him one month's notice of its intention to purchase the land 'on account of the congestion in that district.' Conroy appealed to his congressman, George Tinkham, who asked the State Department to act on the matter as Conroy 'is an American citizen ... [and] he does not wish this land taken by the Land Commission.'[85] On 21 September, Hathaway was instructed by Secretary Kellogg to investigate immediately 'the status of the case, and whether, any steps, [were] possible to prevent seizure.'[86] Three days later, he replied that the Land Commission was prepared to extend the 1 November deadline to 15 November to allow Conroy to get legal advice and, if necessary, to meet with the commission. Conroy would have to present his objections to the seizure and show that his land was not necessary for the relief of congestion. If he could do this, the Land Commission would not proceed any further but if he could not or if he failed to make contact before 15 November, the Commission would take over the land and fix a value for it. Hathaway warned that the Commission 'proceeds somewhat remorselessly to carry out the arduous duties imposed upon it by the Irish Land act.' He believed that Conroy's interests would be best served by coming to an amicable agreement with the Commission as fast as possible. Unless Conroy had 'very strong reasons', he advised 'it is probably useless for him to oppose their intentions.'[87]

Conroy did not take the advice and set sail for Ireland on 26 September, but not before he had made more representations to Kellogg through Senator Gaspar G. Bacon of the Massachusetts senate, 'to protect Mr Conroy's rights.'[88] Hathaway's role in the case was finished. The US government did not act on the matter perhaps because as Edwin King, US vice consul in Dublin, reported in 1929, the scheme would 'make for social and economic prosperity and political stability.'[89]

The demand for routine consular services in the Free State was inevitably extensive, particularly in the Dublin consulate. The establishment of the legation in 1927 did not affect this work nor the consulates' immigration and economic activity. It was in the implementation of US policy in these latter areas where ordinary US and Irish citizens came into contact with the US government.

Immigration work

By far the most important reason for maintaining the US consular offices in the Free State was related to the process of immigration – either providing emergency passports to US citizens or dealing with applications from non-US citizens for visas to enter the US.[90] In relation to the former, neither the Dublin

85 Ibid., 841d.52/6, Tinkham to Kellogg, 7 September 1925.   86 Ibid., Kellogg to Hathaway, 21 September 1925.   87 Ibid., Hathaway to Kellogg, 24 September 1925.   88 Ibid., 841d.52/8, Hathaway to Kellogg, 28 September 1925; ibid., 841d.52/9, Bacon to Kellogg, 21 September 1925. 89 Ibid., 841d.52/14, King to Secretary of State, 10 July 1929.   90 In 1921, the State Department

nor Cobh consulates offices were authorized to issue permanent passports to US citizens, but they could issue emergency passports and process applications which would be forwarded to the State Department in Washington later. In the year ended 30 June 1923, no emergency passport was issued by either the Dublin or the Cobh office. The Dublin consulate received 18 applications for passports and seven were received in Cobh. Two years later, the Dublin office processed 27 applications for passports, issued no emergency passports, amended 6 passports and extended 186 passports. In Cobh, officers processed 13 applications for passports, issued no emergency passports, amended one and extended 121.[91] The numbers were small and reflect the small size of the US community resident in the IFS during the 1920s. Between 1917 and 1926, both the Cobh and Dublin consular officials registered 357 US citizens and acknowledged that there were several hundred unregistered resident in the Dublin district and approximately 300 in the Cobh district. This was an under-representation of the size of the US community. The 1926 census indicated that 8,932 persons were classified as US born. Although this figure does not indicate the exact number of US citizens living in the Free State or the number of US citizens in transit for business, personal or tourist reasons, it does suggest that most US citizens resident in the Free State had little, if any, contact with the consular officers.[92]

Other passport cases brought the US consular staff into contact with the department of Justice and the Free State police. Firstly, there were deportations of US citizens. One such case was that of Michael Cowley, a US citizen who was in Mountjoy prison in July 1927. Hathaway was informed of the facts by Henry O'Friel, secretary of the department of Justice, and was asked to grant Cowley passport facilities in order that the desired deportation could take place.[93] A further category involved individuals who had been in a Free State prison for 'ordinary criminal offences' who applied to a local police station for a Free State passport with the intention of immigrating to the US. In summer 1924, Hathaway, Walshe and O'Friel agreed that police reports would be forwarded to the US consul general in London. A third category emerged from complaints

issued new instructions to consular officers announcing that Americans entering the US were no longer required to submit travel documents. But intending travellers to the US would be obliged to convince US immigration officers of their US citizenship. Kent was pleased with the change as it would deter 'undesirable citizens' who were naturalized but had lived in Ireland for a long period, from entering the US. He was convinced that this category of traveller in his Belfast district 'are active participators in crime ... and are fomenters of rebellion in other cases'. He had no difficulty with 'native born' American citizens returning home without passports. NARA, RG59, M580/218, 841d.00/348, Events of Importance period 13 April to 20 April 1921, American Consulate, Belfast to Secretary of State, 20 April 1921.   91 NARA, RG59, IRFSP Dublin, Ireland, June 1924, Consolidated Summary of Business, Financial Statement; ibid., July 1926, Consolidated Summary of Business, Financial Statement; ibid., Cobh, Ireland, May 1924, Consolidated Summary of Business, Financial Statement; ibid., Cobh, Ireland, August 1926, Consolidated Summary of Business, Financial Statement.   92 *Census of Population, 1926, iii, birthplaces* (1929), table 1a, p. 141.   93 NAI, D/J, letter books, 1922–5, Walshe to H.J. Friel, Secretary, 22 July 1927.

which Hathaway made to Walshe about interference with US passports by Free State police. In August 1924 Walshe informed Eoin O'Duffy, the police commissioner, that US passports were altered by police in William Street station in Limerick city, thus rendering them invalid. In the following month, two US passports, issued to Mollie Herbert and Julie Herbert of Limerick, were changed again in the same police station. When, on 22 September, this was discovered by the US consul at Cobh, the passports were rejected as invalid and new ones had to be issued. A similar rejection occurred in the case of a US passport issued to Miss L. McKinney owing to an endorsement made on it by Chief Superintendent H.J. Keegan in Letterkenny station in county Donegal.[94]

Undoubtedly the bulk of consular immigration work arose from applications by Free State citizens for visas who wished to immigrate to the US. Before examining the role of consular officers in administering the immigration system for such citizens to the US, it is worth reflecting on the reasons for the increase in applications between 1924 and 1931. The establishment of the Free State in 1922 might have been expected to signal the end of emigration, which Sinn Féin leaders denounced, to use Lee's words, as the 'single most serious obstacle to the prospects of social regeneration in Ireland.'[95]

Table 12.2

Immigrants admitted into the United States from Ireland, 1901–30

Year	32 counties
1901–10 (total)	339,065
1911–20 (total)	146,181
1920–4 (total)	81,456
	Irish Free State
1925	27,112
1926	27,590
1931	801
1921–30 (total)	220,591

Source: US Bureau of Statistics, *Statistical Abstract of the United States, 1926* (1927), table 96; ibid., *1937* (1938), tables 98, 99; ibid., *Statistical Abstract of the United States, 1951* (1951), table 107; Lee, 'Emigration: 1922–1998', pp. 264–5.

Table 12.2 reveals that in the pre-war period, emigration to the US from the thirty-two counties averaged approximately 35,000 per annum. The twenty-six counties of the future Free State accounted for in excess of 20,000 of this total. The numbers departing during the war years declined rapidly and in 1918 only

94 Ibid., Walshe to Friel, 7 May, 7 July, 22 August, 26 September 1924.   95 J.J. Lee, 'Emigration: 1922–98' in M. Glazier (ed.), *The encyclopaedia of the Irish in America* (1999), p. 263.

136 emigrants departed for the US. However, the recovery was underway by 1920, when more than 15,531 left Ireland to settle permanently elsewhere. Of these, over 12,000 went to the United States compared with 2,975 in 1919. In April 1921, emigrant figures recorded at US consulates in Ireland for the first quarter were double those of the same period in 1920. In 1925, when US authorities began to record separate data for the Free State, in excess of 27,000 emigrated and, despite the deteriorating economic conditions in the US, over 14,000 emigrated in 1930, but the level collapsed in 1931 when 801 emigrated. From then until 1946 the number never exceeded 1,000.[96] Thus, as table 12.2 indicates, during the 1920s the 'curse of emigration' continued, largely because the leaders of the new state had few economic solutions to the problem of unemployment.[97]

For others who departed in the early 1920s, the US offered political asylum as had been the case so often in past leading the department of Home Affairs of the First Dáil to restrict emigration during the Anglo-Irish war of independence. Throughout the Irish civil war approximately 10,000 anti-treaty Irish Republican Army fighters were imprisoned. Following the victory of their opponents, many believed they had little chance of employment in the new Irish Free State, particularly in state-funded work on the roads and railways. Jeremiah Murphy, the IRA fighter, in his memoir of Kerry, noted 'there was a lot of resentment among ex-IRA men ... There was a lot of talk about emigration.' Although he found work as a taxi driver in Killarney, by 1925 he yearned for the 'gaiety of the past' and decided to leave for the US.[98] For those who left either voluntarily or involuntarily, the United States still offered refuge.

So, at least in the period 1922 to 1929, it appears that the combination of a lack of employment in Ireland, the lure of work and the presence of friends and family due to chain emigration, combined to ensure that emigration to the US would continue. For these emigrants, whether prompted to leave by desire, duty, economic or political necessity, the US was still perceived as a land of freedom and a place of wealth. In other words, the perception of the US as a land of opportunity appears to have been as influential in the early twentieth century as it was by the end of the previous one.[99] Once the decision to emigrate was made, the intending emigrant had to consult the US consular officials based in Dublin and Cobh to apply for a visa.

By the early 1920s, administering US immigration legislation had become laborious for the consular service, not least because of the enactment of the 1924 Immigration Act. Chapter eleven indicated that this latest act was a 'permanent restrictive' immigration law and eight categories of people were barred from enter-

96 NARA, RG59, M580/218, 841d.00/351, Dumont to Secretary of State, 23 April 1921; NARA, RG59, M580/219, 841d.00/425, American Consulate Belfast to Secretary of State, 24 August 1921. This interpretation of the statistical data is based on Lee, 'Emigration: 1922–98', p. 263.   97 Lee, 'Emigration: 1922–98', p. 263.   98 J. Murphy, *When youth was mine: a memoir of Kerry, 1902–25* (1998), pp. 280, 300, 301.   99 For further on this see B. Whelan, '"What does America mean to you?": an oral history project, 1922–60', 84–104.

ing the US: contract labourers, Asians (except Japanese and Filipinos), criminals, persons who failed to meet certain moral standards, had certain diseases, were likely to become a public charge, were illiterate and were radicals.[1] In addition, section two of the 1924 law established for the first time a 'consular control system' that made consular officers responsible for the refusal of visas to immigrants who failed to comply with the provisions of the act or whom officers knew or believed to be inadmissible to the US under the legislation. The effect of these changes placed on the consuls the onus of, firstly, restricting immigration to the numerical limitations provided by law, and, secondly, withholding immigration visas from aliens believed to be ineligible for admission to the US.[2] Between May 1924 and July 1929, the consular officials in the Free State operated the temporary quota of 28,567 and subsequently a permanent quota of 17,853 that gave them, as Smiddy noted, 'extraordinary powers.'[3]

Section twenty-three of the 1924 act placed upon the individual 'alien' the burden of establishing his or her admissibility to the United States. The consular officer first had to record the request for a visa, and an appointment would then be made for the intending immigrant to be interviewed and examined by the consular officials. Failure to attend the interview could result in not getting another one until the next year, at least until 1931, when the quota was undersubscribed. The importance of the appointment is illustrated in the letter sent by Walshe to Garda Commissioner Eoin O'Duffy on 1 January 1926, which stated that on 5 November 1925, an application for a Free State passport was made by Patrick Briody of Kilbride, county Cavan to a Garda station in Cavan town. The application form was not received at the Passport Office in Dublin until 2 December. The delay caused Briody to miss his visa appointment at the US consulate and he lost his place in the quota. Apparently he was not alone; Walshe indicated that there were others cases where undue delay on the part of the police in forwarding the application for passports to the Passport Office caused 'considerable inconvenience to applicants' who intended to travel to the US.[4] One reason for the delay on the police side, was that the application process for a Free State passport was complex. The essential information required for a passport was place and date of birth, national status, destination, married woman's names, husband's age, a married man needed a signed statement from his wife that she would be supported during his absence, females under eighteen years of age had to outline the reason for the journey and parental consent, a photograph, signature and a birth certificate.[5]

In the new reality of the post-quota world, it was vital to have the correct documents and attend the visa meeting. Once the date was set a US official had

1 R. Daniels & O.L. Graham, *Debating American immigration, 1882–present* (2001), pp. 20, 18. 2 NARA, RG59, IRFSP Dublin, Ireland, July 1926, Drayfus to Hathaway, 22 July 1926. 3 NAI, D/FA, ES, 29/191, Smiddy to Walshe, 28 March 1924. 4 NAI, D/J, Letter books, 1922–25, Walshe to O'Duffy, Commissioner, Garda Siochána, 1 January 1926. 5 Ibid., Walshe to O'Friel, Secretary, D/J, 4 July 1924, 22 July 1923.

to personally examine the alien and carefully consider all the facts of the applicant's case. If the alien had not satisfactorily established that he or she was not excludable from the US under any of the provisions of the immigration laws, then the consular official had no other choice but to withhold the visa. The introduction of this step in the process was regarded by the State Department as having the 'great advantage of preventing unnecessary hardship and inconvenience' if the inadmissible alien was permitted to proceed to a port of entry in the US.[6] For the consular officer, it was time-consuming and after the act had been in place for one year, a plan was devised by the State Department, with the co-operation of the departments of the Treasury and Labour and the US Public Health Service, for the assignment of medical officers and immigration inspectors as technical advisers in certain consulates. They aimed to ensure that a thorough examination took place prior to departure which would reduce the numbers denied admission at the US port for physical or other reasons, help to fill the national quotas and lighten the financial burden on the shipping lines.[7] Fifty per cent of emigrants with passages were rejected at US ports of entry in the days after the examination was imposed.[8]

Although a medical officer was already in place in Cobh to issue 'clean' certificates to emigrants before they joined the liner, Assistant Secretary Grew assured Smiddy in June 1925 that the additional appointments would be made in consultation with the Free State government. Later in the month, Smiddy reported home that three US officials had departed for Cobh and London to explore the situation on the ground in both countries. He had not been consulted prior to their sailing for Ireland and, after consulting with British Ambassador Esmé Howard, both recommended that a written undertaking should be obtained that any medical examination held before embarkation would be 'final' and it was not open to the US immigration authorities on the US side to enquire further into the immigrant's health, 'save in very exceptional circumstances, such as the actual acquisition of diseases on board ship.'[9]

By the end of 1926, inspectors of the Bureau of Immigration, acting as technical advisers, had been assigned to consular offices in the Free State, Britain and Northern Ireland, Belgium, Netherlands, Germany, Norway, Denmark, Sweden, Poland, Italy, Czechoslovakia and Austria. Both the Cobh and Dublin offices had US Public Health Service surgeons and technical advisers to help the consular officers in the thorough examination of each applicant for an immigration visa. The advisers ensured that all the exclusionary categories were applied

6 HHPL, Commerce files, Ireland, Department of State, *The immigration work of the Department of State and its consular officers. Revised to July 1, 1932* (1932), p. 2.   7 Not filling a quota could attract unwanted attention. Ray Atherton sent a newspaper article from the London *Times* to the State Department which stated that the Free State quota for 1925 would be unfilled while there were long waiting lists for the Northern Ireland quota. NARA, RG59, 841d.56/8, Atherton to Secretary of State, 8 January 1926.   8 *Irish Times*, 6 December 1922.   9 NARA, RG59, 580.222, 841d.00/775, Castle to Grew, 3 June 1925; NAI, D/FA, Box 29, file 192, Smiddy to Walshe, 8 June 1925.

to each case and the medical officer conducted the mandatory medical examination. The intending immigrant experienced the impact of the new procedures immediately. When Jeremiah Murphy was called for an interview in the Cobh consulate in February 1925, he was granted a visa subject to passing the medical examination which he did. Subsequently, he sailed on the SS *President Harding* from Cobh in May. When he arrived in the port, he underwent a further examination, just as Smiddy and Howard predicted. He wrote home:

> Of course the morning brought this general run of examination. It was very tight indeed. Everything was examined in the line of clothes and body under a powerful electric light. He (the examiner) was no blind fellow indeed. I got a red label which indicated I had satisfied the inspector. Others got yellow labels so they had to be disinfected, fumigated and bathed in hot sea baths.[10]

Murphy arrived safely at Ellis Island, New York, where he was once again 'closely examined in reading, writing, heart, lungs, eyesight and general.' He proudly recalled that he 'landed a free man on the Battery Pier, New York.'[11]

By July 1925, as a result of the increased staff in seven US consulates in the Free State and Britain, the number of rejections on arrival in US ports had been reduced to a minimum and the number of refusals to issue visas on legal grounds had increased. The State Department noted there was 'no adverse comment' on the new arrangements in either the Irish or British press. This was understood to mean that a definite statement on inadmissibility to the US prior to departure was 'welcomed by the people most concerned.'[12] Table 12.3, covering the years 1927 and 1928, offers a closer view of the visa work of the officers and a wider perspective on the examination process undertaken by other intending immigrants.

Table 12.3 illustrates that of the eleven European countries that had been allocated technical advisers by 1927, the Irish Free State had the highest percentage of visa refusals with 10.6 per cent, followed by Poland and Czechoslovakia. Refusals in the Netherlands and Germany were slightly above the average of 7.2 per cent. The Scandinavian counties were all below the average while Denmark had the lowest of all the countries with 3.2 per cent.

There were three principal categories for refusal; medical, contributory and immigration. Table 12.4 outlines the principal causes for refusal by the US consular officials and technical advisers in the port of departure, in the same period.

Over half the refusals in the Scandinavian countries, Germany, Britain and the Free State were on medical grounds. Sweden had the largest proportion. Italy, Belgium and Poland had the smallest proportions of refusals for medical reasons. Occasionally, the medical examiners would diagnose incorrectly. During summer

---

10 Murphy, *When youth was mine*, pp. 300, 323.   11 Ibid., pp. 323–4.   12 HHPL, WRCP, Box 44, *The American Foreign Service Journal*, 30 July 1925, p. 61.

Table 12.3
Results of the intensive examination abroad of intending immigrants, fiscal year ended 30 June 1928

Country	Period covered by report	Number of immigrant applicants examined	Number refused	Per cent refused	Number refused on basis of surgeon's findings	Per cent of total refusals	Number refused on basis of Immigration Inspector's advice	Per cent of total refusals	Number applicants deferred for further evidence for treatment medical migration	Number of immigrant visas granted
Belgium	1 July 1927 to 30 June 1928	1,070	70	6.5	22	31	48	69	7/72	1,000
Czech.	16 Aug. 1927 to 30 June 1928	3,652	351	9.6	134	38	217	62	70/240	3,301
Denmark	1 July 1927 to 30 June 1928	3,364	110	3.2	59	53	51	47	131/106	3,254
Germany	Do	52,217	3,857	7.3	2,323	60	1,534	40	1,441/7,401	48,360
Great Britain and N. Ireland	Do	28,187	1,436	5.0	780	55	647	45	113/454	26,751
Irish Free State	Do	28,495	3,031	10.6	2,063	68	968	32	23/47	25,464
Italy	15 Aug. 1927 to 30 June 1928	11,294	548	4.8	166	30	382	70	22/1,640	10,746
Netherlands	1 July 1927 to 30 June 1928	2,380	185	7.7	78	42	107	58	51/246	2,195
Norway	Do	7,132	445	6.2	293	66	152	34	265/224	6,687
Poland	Do	10,066	1,013	10.0	359	35	654	65	1,032/1,449	9,053
Sweden	Do	10,576	496	4.6	398	80	98	20	770/239	10,080
Total		158,433	11,542	7.2	6,684	58	4,858	42	3,925/6,458	146,891

Source: Department of State, *The immigration work of the Department of State and its consular officers* (1929), table 2, pp. 5–6.

Table 12.4
Principal causes for visa refusal, 1927–8

Country

Belgium	Medical-mandatory: trachoma, tuberculosis.
	Immigration: illiteracy, L.P.C., A.C.L., moral turpitude, not entitled to section 3.2 visas, other causes.
Czech.	Medical-mandatory: mental defectives, trachoma, tuberculosis
	Contributory: heart disease, defective vision, varicocele, hernia
	Immigration: illiterates, L.P.C., A.C.L.
Denmark	Medical-mandatory: mental defectives, tuberculosis, loathsome contagious diseases, sclerosis
	Contributory: heart disease, defective vision, varicocele, eczema
	Immigration: L.P.C., A.C.L, criminal, moral turpitude, illiteracy.
Germany	Medical-mandatory: mental defectives, tuberculosis, loathsome contagious diseases
	Contributory: heart disease, defective vision, varicocele, hernia
	Immigration: L.P.C., A.C.L., illiterates, criminals.
Great Britain and N. Ireland	Medical-mandatory: tuberculosis, trachoma, mental defectives, loathsome contagious diseases
	Contributory: heart diseases, defective vision, varicocele, hernia
	Immigration: L.P.C., A.C.L.
Irish Free State	Medical-mandatory: mental disease, tuberculosis, trachoma, ringworm
	Contributory: heart disease, defective vision, physical defects, varicocele
	Immigration: illiteracy, L.P.C., A.C.L.
Italy	Medical-mandatory: trachoma, tuberculosis, mental defectives
	Immigration: A.C.L., illiteracy, moral turpitude, illegal entry.
Netherlands	Medical-mandatory: tuberculosis, mental defectives
	Contributory: heart disease, hernia, physical defectives
	Immigration: L.P.C., A.C.L.
Norway	Medical-mandatory: tuberculosis, loathsome contagious disease
	Contributory: physical defectives
	Immigration: L.P.C., assisted alien.
Poland	Medical-mandatory: mental defectives, trachoma, tuberculosis, ringworm
	Contributory: heart disease, varicocele, sclerosis, ankylosis
	Immigration: illiteracy, L.P.C., not entitled to status, A.C.L.
Sweden	Medical-mandatory: tuberculosis, nephritis, loathsome disease
	Contributory: heart disease, defective vision, defective teeth
	Immigration: assisted, L.P.C., A.C.L.

Notes:
L.P.C. likely to become a public charge. A.C.L. aliens under contract for labour or services of any kind. Section 3.2 of the act covered aliens visiting the US temporarily as a tourist, for business or pleasure. Source: Department of State, *The immigration work*, table 2, pp. 5–6; 'Immigration act of 1924', 86th Congress, 1st session, ch 185, 190. 26 May 1924.

1929, Mrs Duffy applied for a visa to travel with her three children to the US to join her husband, Walter, who had been in the US for over eighteen months. He had an address in Bridgeport, Connecticut, and was employed in skilled work. The children passed the medical examination but Mrs Duffy was rejected on the grounds that she had a slight defect in her right lung. She appealed to her local politician, P. Ua Dubhghaill, whom she knew personally, and he submitted to the department of External Affairs a statement signed on 12 September 1929, by Dr M. McKenny, assistant physician in Dr Steevens' Hospital, to the effect that he could find no trace of active tuberculosis in her lungs, she had not been ill and enjoyed remarkably good health. In view of this information and the hardship which the refusal of the visa would bring to the family, Minister McGilligan intervened and asked Cornelius Ferris, consul general in Dublin, if he would reconsider the case.[13]

Visa applications were also rejected for bureaucratic reasons. Article seven (a) of the 1924 act required that the application be accompanied by two copies of the applicants' 'dossier', along with prison and military records, two certified copies of a birth certificate and two copies of all available public records. It was not until 1 July 1924 that the US consuls in the Free State received instructions about the manner in which the article was to be interpreted.[14] It was soon usual practice for consular officials to require a passport and birth certificate from Free State citizens and the other documents, if available. During 1925, Ferris refused visas to Free State citizens because of discrepancies between information on passports and that on the holders' birth certificate. The occurrence of a number of such cases led to an agreement between the departments of External Affairs and Justice in September 1925 that the Free State immigration officer stationed at Cobh would be authorized to make minor alterations on passports if the applicant produced satisfactory evidence in support of such alterations. This would only be done in cases where the forwarding of the passport to the Passport Office in Dublin would be likely to cause the holder to miss their sailing to the US.[15]

Another of the criteria for entry to the US, if not the most important one, rested on section three of the 1917 Immigration Act, which excluded from the US 'persons likely to become a public charge': this clause continued into the 1924 act. The principle underpinning this provision was that in normal economic times the immigrant who was able-bodied, intended to work and had sufficient resources to support him or herself and their respective dependents until they arrived at the intended destination and could be expected to get work, would be admitted without any particular stress being placed upon the question of whether he or she had other assurances of support. Evidence of this flexibility emerged from the Duffy case, noted previously, and from the Monaghan case. In early 1931, Mrs

13 NAI, D/EA, Letter books, foreign consuls in Saorstát, 1929–32 and 1933–34, Murphy to Ferris, 5 December 1929. Ferris' reply is not present in the records.   14 Quoted in FitzGerald reply to Cooper, Parliamentary Debates Dáil Éireann (hereafter *PDDE*), 8, 2 July 1924, 208.   15 NAI, D/J, Letter books, 1922–25, Walshe to H.J, Friel, Secretary, D/J, 16 September 1925.

Monaghan's application for a visa was refused on two grounds; illiteracy and pub-lic charge. Her case was taken up by her political representative, Michael Óg MacPhaidin, who contacted President Cosgrave. Following this intervention, the consul general decided that both objections could be waived if her relatives in the US contacted the Commissioner for Immigration in Washington and entered into a bond to guarantee her maintenance if she was allowed to enter the US. If satis-factory sureties were provided, it was possible for the bond to be accepted and the US consulate in Dublin would be duly notified that the visa could be granted.[16]

However, interpretations of the underlying principle changed in abnormal times of widespread unemployment in the US, when there was greater likelihood that an immigrant might become a public charge if permitted to enter the US. Consequently, in September 1930 consular officers were told to pay particular care in examining intending immigrants to determine whether an alien would be likely to become a public charge.[17] This instruction combined with the reduced appeal of the US to the intending immigrant to effect a significant drop in demand for visas, as table 12.5 indicates.

Table 12.5
Number of visas issued for the Irish Free State under 1924 Immigration Act, 1925–32

Year (fiscal year ended 30 June)	Quota	Quota visas issued
1925	28,567	28,567
1926	28,567	28,276
1927	28,567	28,567
1928	28,567	28,567
1929	28,567	22,096
1930	17,853	17,853
1931	17,853	5,561
1932	17,853	335

Source: Department of State, *The immigration work of the Department of State and its consular offi-cers* (1932), tables 4, 5, 6, 7, 8, 9, 10, pp. 9–24.

In the context of the Free State, the State Department's primary aim of filling the quota was met, at least in the period 1925 to 1929. Patrick MacDonagh, the

16 Ibid., D/FA, Letter books, President etc., 1922–8, Murphy to Luccan, 20 June 1931. The papers do not indicate if Mrs Monaghan was granted a visa. Visas were issued to the Tipperary hurling team in May 1926 but Ferris warned the State Department to closely watch the group in the US which might be used to promote republicanism. NARA, RG59, 580.222, 841d.00/851, Ferris to Secretary of State, 11 May 1926. 17 Department of State, *The immigration work*, p. 3.

agent at Ellis Island for the Irish Emigrant Society, confirmed to the society that the quota was filled in May, September and November 1927 but he also said that while the majority of Irish emigrants entering the US had landed without difficulty, 51 people had been held at Ellis Island in May and 42 in September and November for special inquiry on the grounds of physical defect, lack of visas, being under sixteen years of age, being liable to become a public charge, or being unable to meet the requirements in reading and writing. These people had slipped through the consular net in the Free State but were detected on the US side.[18]

The consuls' visa work was further complicated by the large number of exceptions included in the 1924 legislation. They also had to decide whether individual applicants came within certain categories so as to allow preferred status within the quota to be applied or to accord non-quota status or issue a non-immigrant visa. Consular offices in the Free State issued between approximately 800 and 2,300 visas in these latter categories over the period from 1925 to 1932.[19]

The visa work also brought in substantial revenue from the Free State consulates for the US government. The 1924 legislation had included a provision that a visa would cost $9 while the head tax was $8, so fees of at least $17 for each individual visa issued were collected in the office. In 1924, the Dublin office collected $66,215 in fees and the Cobh office $53,221. Two years later, the totals were $148,937 for Dublin and $95,486 for Cobh: that comprised over half of the total income collected by the respective offices.[20] Fees were also collected from shipping companies whose ships crossed the Atlantic Ocean carrying passengers for the US. Companies such as the White Star Line and Cunard, among others, still employed agents throughout the country to sell transatlantic fares. The introduction of the quota and the examining role of the consular officials made it more

---

18 New York Public Library (hereafter NYPL), Emigrant Savings Bank Records, reel 59, Report of Agent at Ellis Island for May, September, November 1927.   19 Department of State, *The immigration work*, tables 4, 5, 6, 7, 8, 9, 10, pp. 9–24. NARA, RG59, IRFSP Dublin, Ireland, July 1926, Consolidated Summary of Business. Other categories of non-immigrants excluded from entry were those who appeared to be dangerous or undesirable for political reasons. This does not seem to have been applied to the Free State during the 1920s although there was an Irish dimension to the exclusion of Shapurji Sakatvala, a communist member of the British parliament and part of the British delegation to the Inter-parliamentary Union Congress to be held in Washington in autumn 1925. Among the inflammatory speeches forwarded by Sterling in the London embassy to Washington as supporting evidence for the ban was a letter he sent to the Irish Self-determination League in which he stated 'the British empire is made up of the aristocratic and cunning dirty dogs of Britain who will assail anyone's country at any time.' The Sakatvala case was one of many 'unpleasant controversies' foreseen in 1924 by State Department officials following the introduction of the immigration legislation. LC, WCP, Box 15, Sterling to Secretary of State, 21 September 1925; HHPL, LHP, Box 46, June–July 1924, 17 July 1924.   20 NARA, RG59, IRFSP Dublin, Ireland, June 1924, Consolidated Summary of Business, Cobh, Ireland; ibid., May 1924, Consolidated Summary of Business; Dublin, Ireland; ibid., July 1926, Consolidated Summary of Business, Remarks, p. 8; ibid., Cobh, Ireland, August 1926, Consolidated Summary of Business. One of the other aspects of visa work was to record whether visas were issued to Chinese citizens, there were no applications to any of the US consulates in the Free State in 1924 or 1926. Ibid.

difficult for the companies to guarantee entry to the US to the potential immigrant. The situation was open to abuse.

On 12 November 1924, five steamship agents were convicted in the Dublin police court of bribing two visa clerks who worked in the US consular office in Dublin. The agents had paid a fee to the clerks to bypass the usual procedures and make visa appointments for their clients and, thereby, to falsify official documents. Throughout the court proceedings Hathaway kept his superiors in the State Department informed, but the instructions he received changed over time. Initially Hughes wanted to avoid publicity and there was discussion in the State Department as to whether the clerks should be prosecuted. William Castle, who had visited Dublin a few weeks earlier, felt that there 'should be publicity over the fact that the United States government will stand no nonsense' either from its officials or from US shipping companies. He hoped that Hughes would agree to prosecute 'vigorously'. It seemed to him 'essential that we show these people that whatever their standards of morality may be we do not stand for that sort of graft, or any graft.'[21] By the time of the agents' trial, this view had been endorsed by Hughes, who had instructed Hathaway to follow up on all the prosecutions and to assure the Garda Siochána and attorney general of his 'hearty co-operation.' Hathaway expected the Free State government to revoke the licenses of the agents. The clerks were convicted of accepting bribes and were each fined £25 and costs. The agents' conviction had been secured because the clerks had agreed to turn state's evidence in order to secure the prosecution of the agents, who were fined between £5 and £75. They avoided a more serious charge of conspiracy and a circuit court trial. Although Hathaway believed the punishments to be light, he was pleased to have got 'the actual convictions on record.'[22] There may be two reasons for the hardening in the State Department's position; firstly, it illustrated the seriousness with which the enforcement of the immigration laws was now taken in these post-quota times and, secondly, Castle suggested that there was no desire to have a repetition of the Newcastle-upon-Tyne case, because this time 'we shall be in the wrong.'[23]

By 1928, the consular officials in the Free State had acquired a reputation for the strict enforcement of the regulations. In October, President Cosgrave's secretary, Paul Banim asked Minister McGilligan to intervene with US officials following the refusal of a visa to Fr Hubert Quinn OFM. The minister could not do so because, as Walshe explained, the US authorities 'have very strict regulations in connection with these matters, and it is extremely embarrassing that they should be asked by the government to break the rules and instructions of their own government.' He conceded that the US consul could exercise a degree of latitude, as had happened in the Duffy and Monaghan cases, but McGilligan concluded 'for

21 HHPL, WRCP, WRC diary, 11 October 1924, p. 300.   22 Ibid., Box 8, Ireland, 1924–41, Hathaway to Castle, 13 November 1924.   23 Ibid., WRC diary, 14 October 1924, p. 310. See p. 474, fn. 16 above for further on the Newcastle-upon-Tyne case.

a considerable time, however, it has been made a rule in this office that no requests of this kind should be made to the American consul.' Moreover he wanted all ministers and deputies to be informed that 'intervention in such cases cannot be made.'[24] Despite this request, in the following years McGilligan used his prerogative as minister to intervene in cases where visas were refused. The circumstances were mainly those where full information had not been provided to the US consular office; an additional hearing was requested to supply it but there was no presumption on the minister's part that the appeal would be successful.[25]

A further set of unusual circumstances which led to ministerial intervention emerged from two cases in 1925 and 1929, when two single women, Kathleen O'Reilly and Kathleen Brady, became pregnant by Herbert Steward and Thomas Ledwith respectively who were issued with US visas and later departed for the US. Both women gave birth and made statutory declarations to the effect that they had been seduced with promises of marriage. On both occasions, the local Catholic parish priest informed the department of External Affairs of the details and ministers FitzGerald and McGilligan respectively asked US consular officials in Dublin to intervene. Both men were held up on arrival at Elllis Island and later deported back to Ireland.[26]

Thus, the 1924 legislation enshrined a permanent change to US immigration policy and finally ended free immigration. The 1924 legislation remained in place until 1952, when the Harry S. Truman administration introduced a new statute. Throughout this period the US consular service implemented the act and in subsequent years all inspections of consular offices included an assessment of how the act was being administered. In 1926, the Dublin and Cobh offices were two of the largest US visa offices in the world.[27] Given that the bulk of the work related to the quota category, Consul General at Large Dreyfus was satisfied enough to rate the performance of the twelve visa clerks comprising the Dublin visa section between 'good' and 'excellent' and the thirteen in Cobh rated between 'fair' and 'excellent.'[28]

Not only was the consular service in the Free State efficient in carrying out the bureaucracy attendant to the visa work but their adherence to the immigration rules and regulations ensured that there were relatively few interventions by the Free State administration. However, in the eyes of many congressional politicians and consuls themselves, the main consular focus should be on trade pro-

24 NAI, D/FA, Letter books, President etc., 1922–28, Walshe to Banim, 5 October 1928.   25 There was the case of Michael Lord which President Cosgrave brought to McGilligan's attention in October 1929 and that of Mr and Mrs Batmazian who owned Hadji Bey et Cie company in Cork who were eventually granted a temporary visa to visit a daughter in the US. NAI, D/FA, Letter books, Foreign Consuls in Saorstat, 1929–32, Fahy to Ferris, 10 October 1929; ibid., Fahy to Boucher, 28 May 1929, 14 June 1929, 1 January 1929.   26 Ibid., Letter books, Foreign Consuls in Saorstat, 1929–32, Walshe to Ferris, 26 March 1929.   27 NARA, RG59, IRFSP Dublin, Ireland, July 1926, Dreyfus to Hathaway, 22 July 1926; ibid., IFRSP, Cobh, Ireland, August 1926, Dreyfus to Ferris, 8 August 1926.   28 NARA, RG59, IRFSP Dublin, Ireland, July 1926, p. 6; ibid., Dreyfus

motion rather than on handling recurrent administration matters and passport and visa applications. Indeed Dreyfus insisted that consular officials 'should endeavour to become experts in all' aspects of the job. The ideal situation was reached 'when all duties are performed in a consular office, we have a properly balanced and efficiently administered unit in the service. That is what the Department is striving for.'[29] The performance of the consular officers on this front will be examined next.

Economic work

By late 1923, Hathaway, Collins and Gamon were confirmed in their support for the Cosgrave government. They accepted that political independence would be matched by a policy of economic independence and self-sufficiency. Consequently, Free State economic policy had to be viewed in this context.[30] They were also realistic in their assessment of the barriers that lay in the way of economic recovery and the maturing of the US–Free State economic relationship. They accepted that most of the members of the new government were inexperienced both from a political and economic perspective, that the Free State was underdeveloped economically and that both industry and agriculture were in a depressed state.[31] Hathaway believed that the economic future of the Free State had to be built on an agricultural rather than an industrial basis. Not all members of the Free State government would have agreed with him. The comment represented further evidence of the permanency of the border and the loss of the most industrially advanced part of the island to the Northern Ireland state. On the fiscal front Hathaway described the situation as follows:

> The country had left the civil war only about six months behind and was still holding a large number of prisoners at great expense to the treasury, was still labouring under very burdensome army charges, but was beginning to feel a renewal of general confidence in the ability of the government to maintain order and to pay its bills; it had gone through a general election, and was on the point of launching its first government loan.[32]

He accepted, as did many other commentators, that this 'savage effort to pay as you go', which meant high taxation and low public expenditure, was 'a sound policy' so long as high taxation did not depress business activity.[33] Nor was he

to Hathaway, 22 July 1926; ibid., Cobh, Ireland, August 1926, p. 6; ibid., Dreyfus to Ferris, 8 August 1926. **29** Ibid., Dublin, Ireland, July 1926, p. 6; ibid., Dreyfus to Hathaway, 23 July 1926. **30** Ibid., RG59, M580/221, 841d.00/764, Hathaway to Secretary of State, 23 April 1925. **31** Ibid., M580/244, 841d.60/1, Hathaway to Department of State, 29 December 1923. **32** Ibid., 841d.51/61, Hathaway to Department of State, 20 March 1926. **33** Ibid., M580/244, 841d.51/61, Hathaway to Department of State, 20 March 1926.

blind to other factors hampering the economic position of the Free State in late 1923: the cost of caring for republican prisoners, the general labour unrest, the financial liability under article five of the 1921 treaty for a share of the British national debt, the 23 per cent electoral support enjoyed by the candidates 'pledged to subvert the existing form of government' and, finally, the unsettled boundary question. Hathaway felt that a combination of these factors led to continuous instability and affected public confidence.[34]

US trading links remained underdeveloped; US imports into the Free State in 1924 totalled $15,250,000, less than 5 per cent of total imports.[35] This was at a time when US economic horizons were expanding continuously: in 1910–14 total US exports had been valued $2.16 billion and this figure had risen to $4.16 billion in 1923.[36] The principal items imported from the US to the IFS were wheat, flour, maize, hops, barley, rye, linseed, corn, cotton seed oil, oatmeal, sugar, tobacco, machinery, motor cars, timber, tools and hardware, boots and shoes, tyres, brushes, brooms, dried fruits, hosiery and underwear. Hathaway provided a list of additional imports such as bacon, electrical goods, household hardware, medicines, car accessories, musical instruments (particularly phonographs), dental supplies, motor cycles, typewriters, packaged groceries and fresh fruits which were indirectly imported through British wholesalers.[37] The predominance of indirect trade was made evident in the low representation of US firms in the Free State.

In 1924, most of the US companies that had trade interests with the Free State supervised the work through branch offices maintained in Britain. Only 8 US manufacturers maintained branch offices in the Dublin district for the sale of their products and all but 1 of these was a subsidiary to a London-based main office. At least forty-two agents for US firms were located in the district and none was a US national.[38] In the Cobh district in 1924, the largest factory in the district was that owned by the American, Henry Ford. Hathaway knew of no instance where US importers or exporters maintained a main or branch office in the Dublin district. Most of the larger business houses had limited agencies or sub-agencies for one or more lines of US products. He knew of only two US citizens who acted as agents for US firms. Both of them handled their agencies in connection with other business. There were not enough US business interests in either the Dublin or Cobh district to warrant the organization of an American Chamber of Commerce.[39]

---

34 Ibid., IRFSP, Dublin, Hathaway, 28 May 1924.   35 Ibid., RG59, M580/244, 841d.51/61, Trade information sheet, American Consular District of Dublin, Irish Free State, revised 1 August 1925. 36 H.C. Campbell, 'European rehabilitation and American trade' in US Department of Commerce, *Commerce Reports*, 33 (18 August 1924), p. 402, table two.   37 NARA, RG59, IRFSP Cobh, Ireland, May 1924, Gamon, Trade promotion work at Cobh (Queenstown) Ireland, 15 May 1924; ibid., Dublin, Ireland, May 1924, Hathaway, Trade promotion work at Dublin, 28 May 1924.   38 Ibid., M580/244, 841d.51/61, Trade information sheet, American Consular District of Dublin, Irish Free State, revised 1 August 1925.   39 Ibid., IRFSP, Cobh, Ireland, May 1924, p. 30.

Vice Consul Harold Collins who supervised the commercial work of the Dublin office in 1924, spent virtually all his time on commercial work which included all phases of trade promotion and protection. As a result of this targeted work, the volume of replies to trade inquiries had increased and by mid-1924, it consumed 30 per cent of his time. Three-quarters of US commercial visitors who visited the consulate had definite trade objectives. In 1923, there had been 19 in total and 6 by early June 1924. The type of assistance which consulate staff rendered consisted of putting US visitors in touch with local firms and government officials and giving them helpful economic and trade information. Representatives of British branches of US firms also visited the Dublin district but did not generally call at the consulate as they were familiar with the territory and required little or no assistance.[40]

During 1923, the Dublin office had received 113 trade inquiries from the US, had pursued 22 trade opportunities and had interviewed 23 representatives of US business houses in connection with the extension of trade. Collins had made systematic efforts to expand the trading relationship by advertising, finding openings for US products and the judicious use of the World Trade Directory published by the US Department of Commerce and Trade Opportunity forms to bring business men in the Dublin district into direct touch with the consulate. He also forwarded to Washington more than fifty reports outlining specific opportunities for the expansion of US trade, commercial and financial products and services with the Free State in areas as diverse as US taxicabs and taximeters and windmills to roofing materials, tyres and batteries.[41]

In the same period, Gamon spent 30 per cent of his time in Cobh on commercial work and Loy Henderson approximately 35 per cent. They had replied to 97 trade inquiries from the US, followed up just 9 trade opportunities, become friendly with leading business men in the district and interviewed 7 representatives of US business houses in connection with the extension of trade.[42] In order to make the commercial information collected since 1922 permanent and accessible, a filing system had been instituted in the Cobh office. The availability of such information had become essential in 1924 because, according to Gamon, there were no 'trustworthy' trade magazines devoted to Free State commerce. During the previous two years he had invited the leading merchants of the district to register in the World Trade Directory and subsequently he submitted

---

40 Ibid., RG59, M580/244, 841d.51/61, Trade information sheet, American Consular District of Dublin, Irish Free State, revised 1 August 1925. In 1923–4, just a few cases of 'select hams' were exported directly from Limerick to the US along with a small shipment of skins. No US vessels called at or departed from Galway port in the same period. Ibid., Limerick, Ireland, May 1924, pp. 29–42; LC, MD, WC, Box 17, Fees collected at consular agencies for the fiscal year ended 30 June 1931.   41 Ibid., IRFSP, Dublin, Ireland, June 1924, p. 44. In 1926, during the coal strike in Britain, the Dublin office received several inquiries about US coal. Ibid., RG59, M580/222, 841d.00/852, Hathaway to Secretary of State, 20 May 1926.   42 NARA, RG59, IRFSP Cobh, Ireland, May 1924, Summary of business.

129 reports on the leading commercial houses in the district to the directory. The staff had compiled 33 voluntary trade reports and had forwarded 25 others requested by the State Department. Despite this systematic work, no US salesman or businessman visited the consulate in 1923 and not more than ten or fifteen US buyers or sellers had visited the district; those who did usually lacked the time to travel from Cork city to Cobh. Instead the consuls travelled the twelve miles to Cork city to meet five salesmen representing US companies. There is no record of any official contact between Gamon and the Ford company.[43]

By way of comparison, in Belfast, which was, in Frazer's words, 'by far the most important commercial and industrial city in all Ireland', hundreds of US linen buyers visited the city every year, although only four or five called at the consulate. Henry Starrett admitted, in his 1923 review of trade promotion, that this commerce continued independently of his office but he requested additional staff in order to fully exploit numerous other trading opportunities in the Belfast district for US firms.[44]

Further evidence of the small size of US trade with the IFS is found in the few complaints handled by the two IFS consulates. In 1923, officials handled just four complaints from Irish merchants against US firms, three of which were taken up directly with the interested parties in the US through the State Department. The fourth went to litigation. Only two complaints were made by US firms against Irish companies. Gamon admitted that they were few in number but felt that consular intervention had strengthened the feeling among businessmen in the Cobh district that the US government 'is interested in their receiving fair treatment in their transactions with the US.'[45] It would need more than good will to expand direct trade.

Both Hathaway and Collins each raised more significant difficulties relating to the economic structure of the Free State that would need to be overcome to facilitate the wider expansion of direct trade; firstly, practically all foreign business was conducted through Britain and notwithstanding the establishment of the Free State, the bulk of the import and export business took place through the medium of 'British agents and jobbers.' In 1924, the amount of foreign goods imported into Britain and re-exported to the Free State was £11,216,000, of which the US officials calculated more than half represented US products. Both men felt that there was a strong probability that their own and the Free State government's efforts to bring Irish importers into direct contact with foreign distributors would increase the volume of direct trade. They also believed that, as the economic entity of the Free State became more clearly defined and a national mechanism for direct trading was built up, progress would be forthcoming.

---

43 Ibid., Gamon, Trade promotion work at Cobh (Queenstown) Ireland, 15 May 1924.   44 Ibid., Belfast, Ireland, June 1924, p. 12, Annual Declared-Export Return to 31 December 1923, Trade promotion work at Belfast, 19 May 1924.   45 Ibid., Cobh, Ireland, May 1924, Gamon, Trade promotion work at Cobh (Queenstown) Ireland, 15 May 1924.

Indeed Gamon noted a 'marked tendency' towards direct trade which had developed in the two-year period since he arrived in February 1922.[46] Both consuls saw many openings for US imports; the primary ones were motion pictures, cigarettes and tobacco building supplies, timber, fertilizers, millinery, sporting goods, canned foods, machinery and equipment (agricultural, industrial, domestic, luxury), radio, vehicles (buses, trams, omnibuses, railway carriages). In 1924, the Bureau of Commerce inquired about openings for the sale of all types of US electrical equipment in the light of the development of hydro-electrical works on the River Shannon in 1925.[47]

Similarly, the threat of competition to US-produced goods from either foreign or domestic-produced items was regarded as one that could be overcome in the future. The Free State market was regarded as 'highly competitive', with Britain and Germany being the main opponents. The former enjoyed the advantage of being strongly entrenched in the market, favourably situated geographically and having a monetary system identical with that of the Free State. Domestic production was not regarded as a substantial threat because the Free State was 'industrially undeveloped' and relied heavily on imports of manufactured articles for consumption purposes and on large quantities of unmanufactured food-stuffs. In only a few lines, specifically woollen goods, confectionery, flour and boot polishes and cars, did domestic production prevent or interfere with the importation of US goods.[48]

A further advantage enjoyed by British and dominions' suppliers in the Free State markets was preferential customs treatment, which meant that their products were dutiable at the imperial preferential rate of 33.3 per cent. Although both consuls had reported to Washington that the Cosgrave government favoured a policy of 'free trade', customs tariffs on some locally manufactured and luxury goods were introduced in the 1923 budget for 'protective' and 'revenue' purposes. The consuls had also passed on to the State Department the Free State government's announcement that other manufacturing projects would be protected if the experiment proved satisfactory.[49] They were hopeful that the 'free trade' versus 'protectionism' debate would not lead to a victory for the proponents of the latter. Throughout the 1920s, the pressure for tariffs continued to mount, particularly after the entry of Fianna Fáil into the Dáil in August 1927, but it was not until November 1931 that the Cosgrave government relented and introduced the

46 Ibid., Bureau of Foreign and Domestic Commerce, 'The Irish Free State. An economic survey', no. 62; ibid., Dublin, Ireland, May 1924, Hathaway, Trade promotion work at Dublin, 28 May 1924. 47 Ibid., RG59, M580/249, 841d60 and 78, Carr to Hathaway, 15 November 1923, 3 August 1925. 48 Ibid., IRFSP, Cobh, Ireland, May 1924, Gamon, Trade promotion work at Cobh (Queenstown) Ireland, 15 May 1924; ibid., Dublin, Ireland, May 1924, Hathaway, Trade promotion work at Dublin, 28 May 1924.   49 Ibid., Cobh, Ireland, May 1924, Gamon, Trade promotion work at Cobh (Queenstown) Ireland, 15 May 1924; ibid., Dublin, Ireland, May 1924, Hathaway, Trade promotion work at Dublin, 28 May 1924. On 29 December 1923, Hathaway, in his report on the Fiscal Inquiry Committee noted that the IFS government 'definitely rejects protection as a fiscal policy. Only one industry is slated for protection.' NARA, RG59, M580/244, 841d.60, Hathaway, 29 December 1923.

Customs Duties Act.[50] Although the discrimination suffered by US exporters in the Free State markets was unacceptable to US authorities, it had to be understood in the wider context of Free State exporters facing the difficulties in accessing US markets caused by the existence of the Fordney–McCumber Act, introduced in 1922. This, according to J.J. McElligott, assistant secretary in the Irish department of Finance, had raised tariff walls around US producers and raised prices. The Free State government attempted to negotiate exemptions through bilateral commerce treaties which will be examined later.[51]

Hathaway and Collins did act on one potentially damaging issue. Both agreed that there was 'no prejudice' in their respective districts against US-made goods. On the contrary, they believed that such goods had a reputation for 'quality, attractive appearance and uniformity,' although Hathaway admitted that Irish buyers were 'very bad shoppers prone to take what is offered without further inquiry.' They reported complaints from the local business community in both districts that some US exporters did not live up to their agreements in regard to deliveries of merchandise, 'careless' business methods and inflexible credit terms. Some US exporters did not match British credit terms and preferred to do business on a larger scale than was possible in the Free State.[52]

The entrenched position attained by British manufacturers in the Free State market was also mirrored in the banking field. The ten leading banks were subsidiaries of British banks and Hathaway believed, therefore, that none would assist 'to the fullest extent' the development of US trade in the Dublin district. This had led his predecessor, Dumont, to suggest in May 1920, that a US bank be established in Ireland. Gamon confirmed this situation but presumed that the banking service was acceptable because he had not received any complaints from US businessmen. By 1924 both consuls believed that the current volume of direct trade did not warrant the establishment of a US bank in the Free State, although Hathaway acknowledged that having a US bank, with the 'prestige and financial assistance which it could lend', would be a valuable aid in building up US trade in the developing Free State.[53]

The final condition considered important to the development of direct trade was transportation. Not surprisingly, passenger transportation between Cobh and the US was considered sufficient and the service was satisfactory. In 1928, there were further improvements in the passenger connections. For example, on 27 August two US passengers had landed in Cobh from the Cunard liner, *Scythia*

50 Ibid., M580/223, 841d.00/935, Sterling to Secretary of State, 2 November 1927; R. Fanning, *The Irish Department of Finance* (1978), pp. 205–06. 51 McElligott quoted in Fanning, *The Irish Department of Finance*, p. 205. 52 NARA, RG59, IRFSP Cobh, Ireland, May 1924, Gamon, Trade promotion work at Cobh (Queenstown) Ireland, 15 May 1924; ibid., RG59, M580/223, 841d.00/867, Hathaway to Secretary of State, 19 August 1926; ibid., IRFSP, Dublin, Ireland, May 1924, Hathaway, Trade promotion work at Dublin, 28 May 1924. 53 Ibid., Dublin, Ireland, May 1924, Hathaway, Trade promotion work at Dublin, 28 May 1924; ibid., Cobh, Ireland, May 1924, Gamon, Trade promotion work at Cobh (Queenstown) Ireland, 15 May 1924.

and, within a few hours, had boarded the Imperial Airways seaplane, *Calcutta*, to fly to Cherbourg in France.[54] But there were problems with freight transportation. The Moore and McCormack company, which operated US Shipping Board vessels between the US and Free State ports, announced a new bi-weekly schedule but this was not maintained. Furthermore there was no regular service between the gulf ports of the US and the ports in the Cobh district, even though there was a demand for one. The bulk of US merchandise to the Free State was shipped through British ports, particularly Liverpool. The cross-channel steamships companies, controlled by both Irish and British interests, were opposed to direct shipment between the US and Free State.

There was some improvement in this situation in 1928. In February, the Cork Harbour Board was considering a measure to facilitate direct trade between the US, Cobh and Cork city. On 11 April, the board permitted transatlantic passenger vessels travelling between New York and Cobh to load or discharge at the latter port up to ten tons of cargo without becoming liable for the payment of tonnage dues as cargo vessels. This arrangement was intended to last for six months but was extended for a further year on 3 October when the tonnage limit was increased to twenty-five tons. Both extensions would assist the Ford motor company in Cork city, which could now avoid the additional expense and time of shipping machinery and parts from New York to Liverpool and then to Cobh, as well as in the reverse direction. There was strong opposition to the arrangement from the owners of the cross-channel shipping interests. When Hugh Butler, the US commercial attaché, praised the new measure during a talk at the Rotary club in Cork on 24 April, he was attacked by R.W. Sinnott, the president of the club, who was also owner of the Cork Steampacket company and was closely aligned with the British interests who controlled cross-channel transportation. But the Cork Harbour Board ignored these vested interests. Both Consul Hiram Boucher and Butler believed that the 'door is now open' for US exporters to ship merchandise of any kind from New York to Cobh on the passenger liners that sailed every few days for the Irish port. Irish exporters could also take advantage and Boucher reported an interest from exporters of butter, eggs and other dairy produce and from importers of US fruit. He hoped US exporters would take full advantage of this opening and develop direct trade in both directions.[55]

---

54 Ibid., RG59, M580/249, 841d.7961-5/1, Boucher to Secretary of State, 28 August 1928. The Free State government was alive also to US, British and French governmental interest in developing the Free State as a trans-Atlantic aerial base and to ensuring that it benefited from the 'position of unique value.' In 1929, the Free State government agreed to sign an air agreement with the US to regulate civil aircraft particularly the right of US airplanes to fly over Free State territory. NAI, D/FA, 8/28, Imperial Conference 1926. Questions of air policy for discussion; NARA, RG59, 580.249, 841d.7961-5/1, Boucher to Secretary of State, 28 August 1928.   55 NARA, RG59, M580/249, 841d.843/6, Boucher to Secretary of State, 3 February 1928; ibid., 841d.843/5, Boucher to Secretary of State, 3 May 1928; ibid., 841d.841/1, Boucher to Secretary of State, 6 October 1928; ibid., 841d.843/7, Boucher to Secretary of State, 6 October 1928. Boucher saw a profitable opening for the US Shipping Board here also and suggested that it should investigate the possibility of

The difficulties in the Dublin district were the reverse, with no direct passenger service and direct freight facilities which were described in May 1924 as 'adequate but slow.' The possibility of the German-owned Lloyd Steamship company bringing passenger ships from New York to Galway was noted with interest by Hathaway in January 1927.[56] The idea was promoted by Patrick McGilligan, minister for Industry and Commerce, during a trip to the US in September and October 1925 and in correspondence with Secretary Hoover. McGilligan invited the US administration and shipping interests to examine the possibility of using a deepwater Irish port as a passenger terminal and distribution centre for US companies in Europe. But these approaches came to nothing, despite the offer by Hoover and E.S. Gregg, chief of the Transportation Division in the Bureau of Foreign and Domestic Commerce, to raise it with American shipping companies.[57] Meanwhile the US representatives on the ground in the Free State struggled to improve trading links under the existing conditions.

In May 1924, Frazer had praised Collins' trade promotion work in the Dublin district and he believed that little more could be 'asked or expected' of the staff.[58]

carrying some of the Ford merchandise in its ships.   56 Ibid., IRFSP, Dublin, Ireland, May 1924, Hathaway, Trade promotion work at Dublin, 28 May 1924; ibid., Cobh, Ireland, May 1924, Gamon, Trade promotion work at Cobh (Queenstown) Ireland, 15 May 1924; ibid., M580/249, 841d.77/4, Hathaway to Secretary of State, 15 March 1925; ibid., M580/223, 841d.00/891, Hathaway to Secretary of State, 10 January 1927.   57 Regarding internal transportation, Hathaway informed Washington after the amalgamation of the Irish railway system on 1 January 1925, 'it is hard to think that any changes present or potential, will make it materially more easy to sell goods or buy goods in the interior of Ireland.' Ibid., IRFSP, Dublin, Ireland, May 1924, Hathaway, Trade promotion work at Dublin, 28 May 1924; ibid., Cobh, Ireland, May 1924, Gamon, Trade promotion work at Cobh (Queenstown) Ireland, 15 May 1924; ibid., M580/249, 841d.77/4, Hathaway to Secretary of State, 15 March 1925; HHPL, Commerce Collection, Box 375, Ireland 1922–26, McGilligan to Hoover, 24 November 1925; ibid., Gregg to Stokes, Office of the Secretary, Department of Commerce, 16 October 1925, Hoover to McGilligan, 22 October 1925; ibid., Gregg to Stokes, 11 December 1925, Hoover to McGilligan, 16 December 1925. In December 1926, Hathaway reported on plans mooted by the British air service for the establishment of a transatlantic air service by airship which would land in the Free State and distribute its cargo to other parts of Europe by airplane. Three years later, Sterling reported on an 'experiment' where a plane would collect mail from a transatlantic liner from New York at Galway, fly to England, pick up English mail and return to Galway. The purpose was to demonstrate the greater speed whereby US mails can be received in England and replies returned than by the 'all ship' route. NARA, RG59, M580/222, 841d.00/824. Hathaway to Secretary of State, 31 December 1925; ibid., M580/223, 841d.00/85, Sterling to Secretary of State, 21 August 1929.   58 Ibid., IRFSP, Dublin, Ireland, June 1924, p. 44. Not surprisingly the role of Colonel James Fitzmaurice, the officer commanding the Free State air corps, in piloting the Junkers aircraft, the *Bremen*, on the first east-west transatlantic flight in May 1928 emphasized the strategic location of the Free State between the US and Europe. During a reception for Fitzmaurice and his co-pilot Captain Herman Köhl, Coolidge told Ftizmaurice, 'It seems to me Ireland is a logical point of departure and arrival for aviation between Europe and the USA.' Fitzmaurice repeated his views in a speech delivered the following day to the Society of the Friendly Sons of St Patrick in the Hotel Astor. *DIFP*, iii, NAI, D/T, S5659, Smiddy to Cosgrave, 6 May 1928; American Irish Historical Society, New York, The Society of the Friendly Sons of St Patrick Papers, Yearbooks, 1028, pp. 106–7.

He felt that trade promotion in Cobh had been hampered by the recent 'civil disorders', the under-staffing of the office and the large amounts of visa work the officials performed. During the summer months in 1923, Gamon and Richardson worked seven days each week. Frazer concluded that 'all things considered', Gamon had done 'very creditable' trade promotion.[59]

Two years later, in 1926, Louis G. Dreyfus visited both offices and, notwithstanding the considerable amount of visa work in both, felt that an adequate volume of commercial work had not been conducted by the Dublin staff, while Gamon's departure from the Cobh office had weakened the commercial work there. There were delays in submitting reports from Dublin and only 313 World Trade Directory reports had been completed, which was 'less' than at most of the other offices in cities of the same size. For example, the work conducted by Russell Brooks in Belfast was 'much superior' to Collins' in Dublin in every branch of commercial duties. He felt that there was a lack of 'push' at the Dublin office that he blamed this partly on Collins, whom he rated as 'high average', and partly on Hathaway's disinterest in the commercial work.[60] Hathaway and Cornelius Ferris, the new consul in Cobh, still blamed structural weaknesses in the Free State economy and believed US exporters to be 'inflexible, unaccommodating and difficult to do business with.'[61] Despite these problems, US imports into the Free State had increased from 5 per cent of the total in 1924 to 8 per cent in 1926. The latter was described by Butler as 'unusually high' and he offered 'industrial disturbance' in Britain as the reason why there was now more direct importing from the US into the Free State. However, the percentage did not provide an accurate picture of US trade with the Free State because it did not include the goods re-imported through Britain, valued at £10,408,000 in 1926, half of which may have been US products.[62] Three years later, in 1929, the US share of Free State markets had not moved beyond 8 per cent.[63]

59 NARA, RG59, IRFSP Cobh, Ireland, Inspector's comments on Consul Gamon's report, 31 May 1924. 60 Ibid., Dublin, Ireland, Note by Louis G. Dreyfus, 24 July 1926; ibid., Cobh, Ireland, August 1926, Dreyfus, 10 August 1926; ibid., Dreyfus to Hathaway, 23 July 1926. 61 Ibid., Dublin, Ireland, July 1926, Hathaway, Trade promotion work at Dublin, 8 July 1926; ibid., Cobh, Ireland, August 1926, Ferris, Trade promotion work at Cobh, 22 July 1926. One example of this was evident in 1927 when US exporters of potatoes and plant products failed to abide by Free State regulations and obtain a permit and a license to accompany the shipment. After the Dublin postal authorities detained seven parcels of seed potatoes from the US for contravening the 1920 Potatoes Importation Order, it became a matter of correspondence between Smiddy, the departments of State and Agriculture. This issue was aggravated because of the embargo imposed on the importation of US and Canadian potatoes by the Free State on 1 November 1924, Britain on 23 December 1924 and Northern Ireland on 3 January to prevent the spread of Colorado beetle diseases. Potatoes came under attack again in 1929 but this time US farmers proposed to Congress 'an added tariff on Irish potatoes.' NARA, RG59, M580/248, 841d.612/1/2/3, Minister for Lands and Agriculture to Walshe, 3 May 1927, US Department of Agriculture to State Department, 6 June 1927, Castle to Smiddy, 20 July 1927; FRUS, 1925, xi, Hughes to Kellogg, 29 December 1924, 3, 5 January 1925, Hathaway to Hughes, 9 January 1925; Congressional Record—House, 71st Congress, 1st session, Nelson, 16 May 1929, 1434. 62 'Foreign views of Irish trade', 93. 63 K.A. Kennedy et al., The

The opportunities uncovered for US producers and manufacturers in the Free State were matched by those for investors. In 1921, Dumont had suggested that Irish capitalists were 'essentially conservative', preferring 'to leave their money at interest.'[64] The situation had not changed by 1923–4 at which time, as Fanning has pointed out, a strained relationship existed between the banks and the department of Finance on the matter of borrowing. In this clash of orthodoxies, the latter came around to favouring a public issue to fund its capital commitments. British Treasury officials discussed the possibility of the Free State government turning to the US to borrow money and they supported such a move. In 1923, the Free State government set about raising capital from its own citizens through the first National Loan. Although the bonds were issued in pounds sterling, they were in part underwritten by the Guaranty Trust Company of New York. The bank sought the advice of the secretary of State on 24 November 1923 who did not object.[65] By 7 December 1923 it had been over-subscribed by approximately £200,000, which became apparent when it was first quoted on the Dublin stock exchange on 7 January 1924.[66] The influential *Washington Post* noted, on 10 January 1924, 'the Irish Free State has just given evidence of its own stability and the confidence it inspires in its citizens by the success of its first public loan.'[67] It boded well for future flotations in the US money markets.

Against this background of conservatism, consular reports in 1924 revealed the many openings that were seen to exist for US capital; the development of the railway, shipping, canals and inland waterways and road systems, hydro-electricity, beet and the fishing industry. Many of these reports were unsolicited but others resulted from requests from US officials. One of the largest projects that might have been expected to attract US capital was the 'grandiose' Shannon hydroelectric scheme.[68] From the time when the building of the hydroelectric station was first mooted in 1923, the consular service kept the State Department informed about the preparations. By 5 May 1925, the Dublin office had sent six reports to Washington on the project.[69] No US, or indeed British, firm took up the opportunity.

It was soon clear from the on-going government discussions that the German firm, Siemens–Schuckertwerke was favoured for the construction of the station.

economic development of Ireland in the twentieth century (1988), p. 183.   64 NARA, RG, 59, 580.248, 841d.51/628/3, Dumont to Secretary of State, 21 June 1921.   65 The role of the Guaranty Trust company is based on F.M. Carroll, *Money for Ireland: finance, diplomacy, politics and the First Dáil Éireann loans, 1919–1936* (2002), p. 78, fn., 1. Michael Collins had worked in the London branch of the Guaranty Trust Company of New York.   66 Fanning, *The Irish Department of Finance*, pp. 88–98. In March 1925, Hathaway reported 'tension' between the government and the banks and later in April he reported 'the banks will look to London and feel themselves part of the British financial mechanism.' NARA, RG59, M580/221, 841d.00/762, Hathaway to Secretary of State, 9 April 1925; 841d.00/763, Hathaway to Secretary of State, 16 April 1925.   67 *Washington Post*, 10 January 1924.   68 NARA, RG59, M580/221, 841d.00/760, Hathaway to Secretary of State, 2 April 1925.   69 Ibid., M580/248, 841d.51/6463, 13 March, 2 December, 23 December 1924, 24 February, 20 March, 8 April, 5 May 1925, annual report, 12 August 1925.

This was confirmed in the Dáil debate on 2 April when it was made clear that the required £5,200,000 would be state funded and that competitive bids for engineering and supplies would not be invited.[70] Both Thomas McLaughlin, first director of the Electricity Supply Board (ESB), and Minister McGilligan, who conceptualized and organized the project, were impressed by the Siemens approach from the start. The firms' officials believed in its feasibility and produced concrete proposals.[71] Cosgrave confirmed, in early April 1924, 'no firm other than Messrs Siemens has sought an opportunity to put forward proposals relating to the Shannon, and consequently no other firm has been given that opportunity.'[72]

It was not until the white paper had been produced that Smiddy in Washington expressed his surprise to Minister FitzGerald, that US companies such as General Electric, Westinghouse or Stone and Webster had not become involved. This query directly arose out of a letter he received in May from Edward N. Hurley, a wealthy Chicago-based, Irish-American and former chairman of the US Shipping Board, who suggested that the Free State government contact 'the leading electrical firm in the world', the General Electric company. After all, Hurley wrote, why give the contract to a German firm when the US 'was by far the most advanced nation of the world in the field of hydropower utilisation and electricity generation.'[73] McGilligan clearly outlined the government's position in his reply to FitzGerald on 16 June 1925:

> The German firm is now about to reap the reward of its enterprise, its scientific methods of investigation, its engineering repute and its tenacity in face of an unenthusiastic reception by the Irish government ... But it is clear that our natural leaning towards America cannot bring us to the point of letting that country in to exploit other people's discoveries. We must reward diligence and enterprise no matter from what source they come.[74]

For McGilligan, US interest in the project had come too late and might increase the costs. Hathaway agreed with McGilligan, but was in no doubt an opportunity had been lost; 'that the Siemens–Schuckertwerke obtained the Shannon contract is to be attributed solely to the fact that Siemens' engineers and financiers preceded Siemens' salesmen in the field.' The Dublin consul felt that US interests had been 'conspicuously deficient' in this sort of trade promotion.[75]

Nor did Collins expect any other opportunities for US firms to arise out of the project, since the proposed legislation 'appears definitely to exclude American contractors and manufacturers from worth-while participation in contracts aris-

70 PDDE, 6, 2 April 1924, 2730.   71 L. Schoen, 'The Irish Free State and the electricity industry, 1922–27' in A. Bielenberg (ed.), The Shannon Scheme and the electrification of the Irish Free State: an inspirational milestone (2002), pp. 28–37. During his research, McLaughlin had studied similar schemes in Europe, the US and Canada.   72 PDDE, 6, 2 April 1924, 2730.   73 Quoted in Schoen, 'The Irish Free State', p. 37.   74 Quoted in Ibid., p. 36.   75 NARA, RG59, IRFSP Dublin, Ireland, July 1924, Hathaway, Trade promotion work at Dublin, 8 July 1926.

ing out of the Shannon development.'[76] During his visit to the US in late 1925, McGilligan met with representatives of the US electricity industry to discuss the possibility of US companies relieving the burden on the Irish government by distributing the electricity that would be generated. McGilligan discovered that supplying and distributing electricity in the Free State would not be sufficiently profitable for any private firm. But no US form expressed sufficient interest in the project. In late 1926, the government decided to establish the ESB, a state-sponsored body, to control all aspects of production, transmission and distribution.[77] The remaining openings for US involvement, therefore, lay in supplying electrical goods and equipment to domestic and commercial consumers. Hathaway had already informally asked FitzGerald in External Affairs, to ensure that universal standards were used 'in the interest of fairness to electrical apparatus manufacturers other than German.'[78]

Although this opening was missed, others were pursued. In June 1921, Dumont had pointed out that 'fishing along the Irish coast, particularly the sheltered parts washed by the Atlantic, is excellent' and that it offered 'great opportunities' for US concerns with capital to modernize the industry. Despite falling yields, indebtedness, lack of investment and transportation problems, he felt that the presence of good fish stocks, plentiful Irish labour, an existing US market and US ships returning home with light or no loads could be turned into 'large profits.'[79] The following years of disturbance depressed the industry but by 1924 Hathaway was able to report on the organization and plans of the Irish-American Fisheries Company Limited. It intended to establish canning factories in the Free State. Unfortunately, the venture came to nothing because the US promoter, F.C. Eggina, was arrested in Dublin the previous October for failing to register as an alien and for fraud.[80] Three years later, Ferris in Cobh reported the same opportunities but this failed to elicit any response from a US investor.[81]

The process went further on the issue of mineral development. While each consul had to report on the presence of mineral deposits and industries in their district, the installation of Herbert Hoover, with his mining background, as secretary of Commerce added a further impetus to consular activity in the area. Hathaway was reprimanded in 1925 for failing to send in a report on mineral production statistics in the Free State, even though none existed for the period 1922 to 1925.[82] In the following April, he passed on to Washington a press report on

76 Ibid., RG59, M580/248, 841d.51/6463/9, Collins to Secretary of State, 8 April 1925. 77 Schoen, 'The Irish Free State', pp. 42–4. 78 NARA, RG59, M580/248, 841d.51/6463/9, Collins to Secretary of State, 8 April 1925. McLaughlin went to the US in 1928 to get information on marketing the uses of electricity to the public and a public relations department was established on 1 July 1928. But it was Siemens that was ready to capitalize on any new markets by opening a subsidiary for electrical products in Dublin at the beginning of 1925. Schoen, 'The Irish Free State', pp. 46, 47. 79 NARA, RG59, M580/248, 841d.51/628/3, Dumont to Secretary of State, 21 June 1921. 80 Ibid., 841d.51/628/6, Hathaway to Secretary of State, 24 December 1924. 81 Ibid., 841d.51/628/8, Ferris to Secretary of State, 7 March 1927. 82 Ibid., 841d.51/63/12, Hathaway

the discovery of phosphate rock deposits in county Clare and he contacted the owner and the relevant Free State department for further information. When a report appeared in the July edition of the *Chemical Trade Journal and Chemical Engineer*, Louis Domeratzky, the liaison officer between the Commerce Department and the State Department, asked for a full report on phosphate rock deposits, and particularly on efforts to develop and utilize such deposits. In his reply of 8 September, Consul Collins confirmed that it was a 'valuable' deposit and he was trying to meet with Michael Comyn, the owner, to discuss his intentions and the possibilities which might arise for US participation in development work. The latter was confirmed in a telegram sent by Hathaway on 17 September, which stated 'owner interested to have American capitalists and technicians survey and develop property' although Comyn had received an offer from a British group.[83]

The urgency implied in the telegram did not lead to immediate action in the Commerce Department. Copies of Collins' report were sent to the Phosphate Export Association and the Manufacturing Chemists' Association while a shortened version went to the leading US chemical companies. The Phosphate Export Association decided to have its London representative investigate the matter.[84] It is not clear what happened subsequently, but the episode demonstrates the limitations in the role of US consular officials who could only act under instructions and were simply conduits of information between the Free State and the State Department. Decisions on following up recommendations lay with officials in Washington, their networks of communication and their contacts with the private sector.

The bulk of the consular officials' economic work focused on expanding the US–Free State relationship, but attention was paid also to the reverse tide. Although this was not a priority, the growing US economy and population also needed the importation of foreign goods, despite the predominance of protectionism. In the period 1910–14, European countries provided 49.6 per cent of US imports. This declined to 30.5 per cent in 1923. The drop in the volume of European goods was mirrored by an increase in Asian imports. Despite the reduced reliance of the US on European imports and the existence of a balance of trade with Europe that favoured the US, the Commerce Department in August 1924 ostensibly supported the return of 'economic and financial stability for Europe' and expected 'keener competition' following the Hughes–Hoover line.[85]

to Secretary of State, 15 June 1927.   83 Ibid., 841d.51/6377, Domeratzky to Carr, 9 July 1926, Grew to Hathaway, 20 July 1926; ibid., 841d.51/6377/1, Hathaway to Secretary of State, 17 September 1926; ibid., 841d.51/6377/2, Collins to Secretary of State, 8 September 1926.   84 Ibid., 841d.51/6377/3, Domeratsky to Carr, 4 October 1926, Kellogg to Hathaway, 9 October 1926. In 1925, Hathaway's report on the beet industry and the proposed involvement by Belgian interests provoked Thomas Marvin of the US Tariff Commission to write to Coolidge about the effect on US imports. CCP, series 1, 296 continued 319 17 June 1926, roll 116, Marvin to Coolidge, 30 April 1925.   85 W. LaFeber, *The American age: United States foreign policy at home and abroad since 1750*, 2 vols (1989), ii, p. 343.

In 1922, European countries provided the US with 40.3 per cent of its manufactures, 26.4 per cent of its semi-manufactures, 21.7 per cent of its crude materials for use in manufacturing and 10.5 per cent of its foodstuffs.[86] Against this background, the consular service had an important role to play and once again there was room for growth of the Free State–US trading relationship.

In 1924–5, the value of direct exports to the US from the Free State was $958,900, less than 0.25 per cent of total trade. Of this $863,866 was declared at the Dublin consulate and the remainder at Cobh. Exports from the Belfast district in 1923 were worth over $28 million, comprised largely of textiles.[87] In 1924, 95 per cent of the exports from Cobh went to Britain and the dominions.[88] The principal exports from the Free State to the US were livestock, poultry, eggs, butter, margarine, bacon, hams, fish, beer, ale, stout, whiskey, charged water, woollen goods, poplin and laces. Also exported from Dublin in 1924 were antiques and waste paper, while Cobh shipped mackerel and horses.[89] At the ports of departure, the consuls had a bureaucratic role in inspecting ships and cargoes to ensure that US customs regulations were complied with, collecting fees and recording exports. They also provided information on US markets. The staff in Dublin assisted three Irish businessmen who visited the US in 1923 with the aim of finding markets for their products. Each was given full information on US business conditions and regulations, although one of them complained subsequently about the lack of attention he received from officials in the Commerce Department and the American Chamber of Commerce.[90]

However, the majoriy of the work promoting direct Free State–US trade was conducted by the Cosgrave government and its representatives in the US who had significant economic expertise as Smiddy had been a professor of economics prior to his US appointment while Lindsay Crawford, who was appointed as trade representative in New York between 1922 and 1929, was directly responsible to the minister for Industry and Commerce.[91] By 1925, E.J. Riordan, sec-

86 Campbell, 'European rehabilitation and American trade', pp. 402–4.   87 NARA, RG, 59, 580.244, 841d.51/61, Trade information sheet, American Consular District of Dublin, Irish Free State, revised 1 August 1925; ibid., American consular district, Cobh, Irish Free State, revised September 1925. NARA, Belfast, June 1924, Annual Declared Export Return.   88 NARA, RG59, IRFSP Cobh, 1924, Gamon, Trade promotion work at Cobh (Queenstown) Ireland, 15 May 1924.   89 Ibid., RG59, M580/244, 841d.51/61, Trade information sheet, American Consular District of Dublin, Irish Free State, revised 1 August 1925; ibid., American consular district, Cobh, Irish Free State, revised September 1925.   90 Ibid., IRFSP, Dublin, Ireland, June 1924, p. 44.   91 NAI, D/FA, ES, Box 31, file 202, Crawford, 1923, p. 21. Throughout the 1920s, Smiddy was still dealing with the challenge of republican activists in the US, Seán T. O'Kelly was the republican envoy in New York and Mary MacSwiney embarked on a six month tour from January to June 1925. But the strength of the movement was weak. Joe Begley working out of the office of the Republican envoy reported to her on 23 July 1925, 'total membership [of AARIR] is 10,000 … money is very slow and the demands from home are insistent as usual.' A few months later, she confirmed to de Valera 'on the whole I am very disappointed' although she attracted some press attention because of her possible illegal entry into the US. Hathaway noted that a section in the republican organ, *Sinn*

retary in Industry and Commerce, was satisfied that Crawford had achieved a 'considerable' amount of commercial work. The latter had resolved a number of disputes between Irish exporters and US importers concerning payment of accounts, particularly where fish exports were concerned. He had also helped with the establishment of the Irish Fish Exchange and the development of US openings for Free State-produced bacon, oatmeal, woollens, hosiery, lace and poplin. With regard to the latter he had to involve himself in preventing US firms from 'mis-describing and mis-branding foreign goods as "Irish".' He brought a number of cases to the attention of the Federal Trade Commission in Washington and, in the case of poplin, got a favourable decision, while the other two had not been resolved by April 1925. The final aspect of Crawford's work was bureaucratic as was the case with his US counterparts in the Irish Free State.[92] He gathered information on the activities and commercial reputations of 330 US firms that were likely to be interested in importing Free State products. Other subjects that were investigated were tourist development, industrial assurance, trademarks, merchandise marks, exhibitions and customs regulations.[93] But it was US protectionism that posed the greatest obstacle to the expansion of Free State trade to the US.

Reports by Crawford, Smiddy and Senator James Douglas, a businessman and leader of the Free State Senate, confirmed that the Coolidge government would not consider a reciprocal commercial treaty with the Free State.[94] Throughout the 1920s, the Cosgrave government received representations from companies manufacturing goods such as shirts, woollens, linens, hosiery, poplin,

Féiner, lauded the 'presumed inability of the State Department to take any action with respect to her ... without raising a storm of Irish-American opinion greater than the Department is presumed to be able to endure.' The piece was noted in the State Department. By late March, Hathaway felt that the level of publicity in Dublin merited a public statement of 'fact' from the State Department. But Castle discussed the matter with Smiddy who reported that his department 'wanted to stay out of that row as much as possible since it was up to the Department of Labour to find out how she got here.' University College Dublin Archives (hereafter UCDA), Mary MacSwiney Papers (hereafter MMP), P482/120(12)/1, O'Kelly to McSwiney, 23 April 1925; ibid., McSwiney to de Valera, P482/120(42), 27 June 1925; NARA, RG59,M580/221, 841d.00/753, Hathaway to Secretary of State, 5 March 1925; ibid., 841d.00/757, Hathaway to Secretary of State, 19 March 1925; ibid., M580/222, 841d.00/775, Castle to Grew, 3 June 1925.   92 *DIFP*, iii, NAI, D/FA, Gr509a, E.J. Riordan to Walshe, 30 April 1925, enclosure. Any transgressions from US import regulations were handled by Smiddy and his colleagues. See NAI, D/FA, 30/193, for a case involving meat imports in May 1926.   93 *DIFP*, iii, NAI, D/FA, Gr509a, E.J. Riordan to Walshe, 30 April 1925, enclosure.   94 UCDA, Desmond FitzGerald Papers, P80/422(1), Smiddy to FitzGerald, 22 December 1923; ibid., P80/406(1), Douglas to FitzGerald, 16 October 1924. James Douglas met with Reeves the general manager of the US National Automobile Chamber of Commerce in September 1924 and suggested the possibility of reducing the tariff on American automobiles in return for which, as a *quid pro quo*, the US government would grant a reduction in tariff on Irish linen. When Pyke Johnson, the Washington representative of the organization, raised this with the State Department but was told that 'it was contrary to our policy to discriminate ourselves which would result from the granting of a special privilege' as suggested by Douglas for Irish linen. HHPL, LHP, Box 46, August–September 1924, 10 September 1924.

lace, bacon, butter, biscuits and pickled mackerel, saying that they could carry on export trade with the US, if only the tariffs on their goods were not so high. Similar views appeared in the newspapers from time to time.[95] The absence of a commercial treaty also gave government critics an opportunity for attack. The *Irish Man* paper of the labour movement noted that 'if a trade agreement were in operation giving a reduction on the duty on American motor cars and other manufactures, not only would our own woollen industry benefit, but Belfast would have a practical object lesson in the value of being inside the Irish fiscal system.'[96] The Free State government failed to negotiate a treaty to reduce the 'onerous duties' on Free State imports into the US during its tenure because firstly, US policy aimed to avoid any changes on a reciprocity basis and secondly, the Free State could offer no concession which would prove an adequate compensation to the US government for any given tariff reduction it would make.[97]

The impact of this situation was clearly set out by Smiddy on 5 April 1927:

> In consequence of high tariffs in this country against those articles which, with the development of modern efficiency on our part, we might export, I see at present little prospect of any substantial increase in our exports to the USA.[98]

During the 1930s, no fewer than ten approaches were made by Irish administrations to the US government, until discussions about a trade agreement finally began in January 1938, only to be abandoned due to the outbreak of war.[99] Nor were those congressional politicians who were usually well disposed towards the Free State, sympathetic towards any changes in the tariff system that would affect their own constituencies. For example, none of the New England senators could recommend reduction in the tariff on wool in early 1927 because of the impor-

---

95 NAI, D/EA, 7/73, Memorandum, undated, probably1929. 96 The *Irish Man*, 14 May 1927. 97 *DIFP*, iii, p.285, NAI, D/FA, 7/73, MacWhite to Henry L Stimson, 10 May 1929; NAI, D/EA, 7/73, Memorandum, undated, 1928 or 1929. MacWhite replaced Smiddy as minister to the US in 1928 and Stimson replaced Kellogg as secretary of State in 1929. 98 *DIFP*, iii, p.104, NAI, D/FA, EA 231/1/1929, Smiddy to FitzGerald, 5 April 1927. 99 The Free State delegation to the World Economic Conference held in Geneva in May 1927, at which the US was represented, proposed an amendment in the commerce sub-committee 'to call a halt to the excessive increase in tariffs' but withdrew it in the fact of US and French opposition. NAI, D/FA, LN 30(b), Report of the IFS delegation, May 1927. In December 1929, both Cosgrave and McGilligan were concerned about the Hawley–Smoot Tariff act then in Congress which might affect import into the US of tractors manufactured by the Ford company in Cork. Macaulay worked hard to explain to Congress members the 'great injury' which closure or reduction of the industry would have on Cork. But he reported in April 1930 that the IFS tractor industry had 'little to fear' from the final form of the bill. The tariff on woollens and lace was increased. The motor industry remained safe because of the pressure brought to bear and the French government threatened to impose an import tax on US vehicles. Macaulay maintained that the Free State administration was weakened in relation to tariffs because of its inability to bargain or pass retaliatory measures. NAI, EA, 231/1/1929, Macaulay to Cosgrave, 22 November 1929; ibid., Macaulay to Walshe, 6 December 1929, 21 April 1930.

tance of the woollen industry in the economic life of the state. Indeed protectionism intensified in 1930 leading towards the passage of the Hawley–Smoot
tariff act in June 1930.[1] Free State trade with the US totalled 2 per cent of total
trade in 1929 and fell to 1 per cent in 1938.[2]

Capitalizing on the extensive Irish-American tourist market was a constant
theme in the correspondence from the Free State administration in Dublin to
Smiddy. The first 'personally conducted tour to Ireland arranged by any shipping company' took place in early summer 1922, when the Cunard line brought
450 tourists from Boston to Cobh. But the civil war postponed the Tailteann
Games from summer 1922 to 1924 because of US fears for the safety of their
team. The ending of the upheaval signalled the expansion in tourism numbers
from the US. In January 1925, with government encouragement, the Irish
Tourist Association was established to amalgamate the regional tourist associations into a national tourist body.[3] The following month Smiddy was asked to
establish an information bureau in the New York office, but he would not undertake this without additional staff. His response in March also pointed out the
dangers in compiling a list of tourist and steamship agencies' office where the
intending tourist could purchase tickets. He felt such an action might lead to
'charges of discrimination and favouritism' and lead to a situation similar to that
which closed the US consulate in Newcastle-upon-Tyne in England, referred
to previously.[4]

---

1 NAI, D/EA, 7/73, MacWhite to Walshe, 13 February 1930. The legislation raised import duties
on a range of farm products and manufactured goods to an average level of forty two per cent.
Congress approved it in June in an attempt to help constituents affected by the depression. The
effect of this legislation on the Free State economy will be examined fully in a future work. 2
Kennedy et al, *The economic development*, p. 183; *DIFP*, iii, NAI, D/FA, 7/73, Macaulay to Walshe,
11 June 1929; ibid., EA, 231/1/1929, Smiddy to FitzGerald, 5 April 1927; ibid., NAI, D/FA, 7/73,
Macaulay to Walshe, 11 June 1929. 3 *Irish Times*, 9 June, 17 July, 17 October 1922; J. Deegan &
D.A Dineen, *Tourism policy and performance: the Irish experience* (1997), p. 10. 4 NAI, D/FA, Box
29/192, Smiddy to Walshe, 12 March 1925. In 1925, there were three officers, a secretary and a
messenger in the New York office and in Washington, there was Smiddy, an acting secretary and
a stenographer. Smiddy constantly struggled with insufficient funds for entertaining, travel and the
salary levels. Moreover, taking on additional work in the New York office might have added to the
existing friction between Crawford, the Trade Representative and the Passport Control Officer,
Matthew Murphy. In October 1926, William Macaulay became so frustrated at not being officially
appointed as first secretary in the Washington legation or receiving appropriate remuneration, that
he offered his resignation. Smiddy had not helped Macaulay's cause by telling Kellogg that Macaulay
was the first secretary without having received consent or approval from FitzGerald. By late 1926,
there was no consulate staff located in the US still. The following year Smiddy requested the
appointment of a military attaché to the Washington legation. It was not until 1929 that McGilligan
considered the elevation of Macaulay's position in Washington, the creation of a consulate in New
York and a passport control office in Boston. NAI, D/FA, Box 29/192, Smiddy to Walshe, 12 June
1925; *DIFP*, iii, NAI, D/FA, Box 30, file 193, Smiddy to FitzGerald, 1 October 1926; ibid., NAI,
D/T, S5337, Walshe, December 1926; ibid., NAI, D/FA, 1/26, Smiddy to Cosgrave, 22 September
1927; NAI, D/EA, ES 330/193, Macaulay to Walshe, 18 September 1926; UCDA, McGP,
P80/416(1), McGilligan to Murphy, 16 August 1924.

However, in July 1925, Crawford drew up a memorandum on the topic which demonstrated that tourist traffic to the Free State had showed a 'marked increase' over the past year, regardless of official encouragement. He estimated that the number of Americans and Canadians visiting would be at least 10,000 which could result in an influx of $3 million in foreign capital. However, he felt that this 'valuable asset' had to be safeguarded and expanded properly.[5] Although the tourist trade was hampered by inadequate state support and lack of planning, Crawford's prediction appeared to be borne out. US Commerce Department officials told Michael MacWhite, Smiddy's successor, that US tourists to the Free State in 1927 spent $8 million and MacWhite expected the sum to reach $15 million in 1929.[6] This latter figure had not been reached in 1950.[7] It was to be a slow growth.

Smiddy also busied himself implementing the government's strategy to entice US capital to follow the lead given by the Ford motor company into the Free State. He handled individual requests from Irish-Americans committed to developing Irish resources such as Howard Harrington's idea of developing a 'free port' and large hotels along the main tourist routes in the Free State.[8] Another came from 'some promoters and financiers' who contacted Smiddy to get information on the Shannon scheme with a view to approaching the Westinghouse company about the 'construction and financial side.' Smiddy learned that they had 'good connections' and cabled Walshe on 3 April 1925, but the government had already decided on the German company.[9]

The Irish diplomat often gave US businessmen visiting the Free State letters of introduction to President Cosgrave, as did Free State supporters in the US such as Daniel Cohalan. Among them was one issued in February 1924 to James McGurrin of New York city, who was managing director of the Irish Enterprises Corporation. McGurrin aimed to return to Ireland in order to expand his circle of Irish exporters of woollens and other materials. Another was given to J.W.

5 *DIFP*, iii, NAI, D/FA, GR459/9, Crawford to Smiddy, 16 July 1925. Visiting relatives was one reason for such short-term visits and others related to attendance at specific events such as the Tailtean games in 1924 and 1928 and of course the Eucharistic congress in 1932. Smiddy also discussed the development of tourism between the US, Free State and Britain with British embassy officials in 1927. NAI, D/T, S5472, Smiddy to Walshe, 11 June 1929. 6 *DIFP*, iii, NAI, D/FA, GR459/17, MacWhite to Walshe, 3 July 1929, 5, 17 October 1929. The directors of the National City Bank and a Delaware-based group led by Richard Beamish of the *Philadelphia Enquirer*, wanted to fund the construction of two or more hotels in the Free State because of increasing interest of US tourists in Ireland and lack of suitable accommodation. Ibid. 7 B. Whelan, *Ireland and the Marshall Plan*, 1947–57 (2000), p. 340. One example of the obstacles placed in the way of developing a tourist industry was the refusal by the department of Finance in 1929 to grant a reduction in the price of visas for US group tours. Eventually Finance agreed because the British had given the concession in 1927 but certain conditions were imposed. See NAI, D/FA, 102/75. 8 *DIFP*, iii, NAI, D/FA, GR246, Smiddy to FitzGerald, 2 January 1925. For further on investment see M.E. Daly, 'The economic impact of the United States on Ireland, 1922–1980' (unpublished), pp. 2–6. 9 NAI, D/FA, 29/192, Smiddy to Walshe, 3 April 1925. US expertise was also sought for the Commission on Banking and to assist with the organization of Irish railways.

Perry of Kansas city, Missouri who visited Ireland in March 1926 'to look over the economic field.'[10] However, by 1931 the practice of Free State representatives giving letters of recommendation, including the request 'to give all facilities' to intending visitors, was refined. According to Walshe, 'Americans don't know what the expression means, except that it makes them regard the Department as a Tourist Agency.'[11]

Smiddy's contacts also led him into banking circles. In January 1925, he met with Mr Lamont, a senior partner in the J.P. Morgan banking company, who told him that Free State credit 'stands high' in New York, even though reports of famine in the west of Ireland appeared in US newspapers and had been confirmed to the State Department by Hathaway.[12] Senator Douglas was in the US at the time and stressed that the reports 'will do great damage to our credit in every way unless it is immediately countered.' Cosgrave acted quickly. Hathaway reported to Washington on 29 January 1925, 'the government does not appear to expect anything that could be called famine', nor would it be calling for 'extraordinary relief appeals' in the US as it had in the past. Instead Hathaway identified the 'three radical political developments' which were hampering the 'government's credit' position; the 'uncertainty' surrounding de Valera's intentions, the boundary commission and the implications of the Free State government's responsibility for British debt as designated under the 1921 treaty.[13] It remained to be whether these difficulties would affect negotiations between officials in the National City Bank of New York and the Irish department of Finance about future loans.[14]

In 1927, the Cosgrave administration decided to launch the second national loan to raise $25 million for capital projects, including the Shannon scheme. The National City Bank handled the sale of $15 million worth of the bonds in the US.[15] The bank's directors contacted the State Department to ask for its views. The relationship between US bankers and the Harding and Coolidge administrations has been well documented elsewhere, particularly that between J.P. Morgan, Hughes and Hoover.[16] It continued into the Kellogg tenure. In March 1925, Leland Harrison made it clear to Kellogg that J.P. Morgan had agreed with

10 AIHS, Daniel F. Cohalan Papers (hereafter DCP), Box 18, folder 1, Cohalan to Cosgrave, 13 February 1924, 11 March 1926. 11 DIFP, iii, NAI, D/FA, 19/2, Walshe to MacWhite, 20 July 1931. 12 Ibid., NAI, D/FA, GR246, Smiddy to FitzGerald, 2 January 1925. For further on investment see Daly, 'The economic impact of the United States on Ireland, 1922–1980', pp. 2–6. In response to the famine reports the Irish Workers and Famine Relief Committee was established on 6 March 1925 in Chicago, by William F. Dunne, Joseph Manley and Thomas J. O'Flaherty. NYPL, Frank P. Walsh Papers (hereafter FWP), Box 27, Irish correspondence, 1925–6, O'Flaherty to Walsh, 6 March 1925. 13 NARA, RG59, 580.221, 841d.00/748, Hathaway to Secretary of State, 29 January 1925; Daly, 'The economic impact of the United States on Ireland, 1922–1980', p. 3; NARA, RG59, M580/221, 841d00/748, Hathaway to Secretary of State, 29 January 1925. 14 Irish Times, 21 August 1926. 15 NAI, D/FA, Letter Books, Washington (3), 1927, Blythe to Smiddy, 13 December 1927. 16 C.P. Parrini, Heir to empire: United States economic diplomacy, 1916–1923 (1969); LaFeber, The American age, pp. 343–7.

President Harding, on 6 June 1921, that the bank would 'keep the State Department informed of any and all negotiations for loans to foreign governments which may be undertaken by them.' The Department's announcement on the matter on 3 March 1922 included 'the public flotation of issues of foreign bonds in the American market.'[17] Accordingly, by May 1925 the Belgian, Czechoslovakian, French, Italian, Rumanian and Yugoslavian governments had applied for loans from the following American banking companies; J.P. Morgan, Dillon Read, Kuhn Loeb and Blair. In each case, the 'view' of the secretary of State was sought and he consulted with the secretaries of Commerce, and Treasury and with the president. Objections were raised to providing finance to Belgium, Czechoslovakia, France, Rumania and Yugoslavia. Consequently, the respective bankers were informed that an 'American loan would not be viewed with favour' unless certain conditions were met. In the Italian case, Andrew Mellon was already negotiating with the Italian ambassador on debt repayment and it was decided that 'raising objections' might, in the circumstances, 'tend to prejudice rather than to help the negotiations.'[18]

This was the context of the flotation by the Cosgrave government of the second national loan in 1927. On 2 December, Castle replied to the National City Bank that 'the Department of State offers no objection to this financing.' A cautionary note was included; 'the Department of State does not pass upon the merits of foreign loans as business propositions nor assume any responsibility in connection with such transaction, also ... no reference to the attitude of this government should be made in any prospectus.'[19] Nevertheless, Castle's action was significant for three reasons. Firstly, it gave the administration's imprimatur to the floating of a loan on Wall Street for the Free State. Secondly, it highlighted the State Department's confidence in the fiscal, economic and political state of the new state, even though Hathaway's information and Smiddy had been told by prominent New York bankers in October that the Cosgrave government's credit with Wall Street financiers had been adversely affected by the increase in de Valera's support in the recent election.[20] Finally, the on-going controversy surrounding the repayment of the first Dáil Eireann loan to US and Irish bondholders might have given it a reason to oppose, signal caution or just ignore the bank's request.

Bond certificates had been issued in the US beginning in 1920 to raise money for the first Dáil and bring about a free and independent republic of Ireland. In

17 HHPL, LHP, Box 46, May–June 1925, Harrison to Kellogg, 12 March 1925.   18 Ibid., State Department, 28 May 1925.   19 NARA, RG59, M580/246, 841d.51, Byrne to Secretary of State, 30 November 1927, Castle to National City Company, 2 December 1927. The government's fiscal position was further improved following the agreement reached on 3 December 1925 between the Free State, Britain and Northern Ireland which resolved outstanding political and fiscal difficulties and liabilities. Hathaway reported from Dublin on 20 March 1926, that the Free State emerged from the boundary crisis in a fundamentally favourable position in regard to national debt. Ibid., Hathaway to Secretary of State, 20 March 1926.   20 DIFP, iii, NAI, D/FA, EA, 231/1/29, Smiddy to McGilligan, 20 October 1927.

excess of $5.7 million had been raised in the US, of which $4 million was sent to Ireland and the reminder kept in banks in New York city in the name of the trustees. However, the establishment of the Free State led to the new government and its republican opponents making rival claims over control of the unspent funds in both the US and Free State. Frank P. Walsh summarized the republican position in January 1924, saying the bonds were raised for 'the Republic of Ireland … it would be a perversion of the intention of the great mass of the subscribers to permit the IFS, so called, to receive any part of the money.'[21] This was settled by court cases in Ireland and the US and pressure on the State Department by groups and politicians including senators Borah (Montana), Butler (Massachusetts) and Wandsworth (New York), representing both sides. In 1927, most of Irish bond holder were paid.[22] The last payment from the US monies to US bondholders was made on 24 February 1933 and those from the Irish state by mid-1936. Ironically, the latter was overseen by Eamon de Valera's government which had taken office in 1932.

It was against this background of controversy and pressure, that the State Department posed no objection to the floating of the Free State second loan on the New York bond markets on 3 December 1927 and over-ruled demands from Frank P. Walsh and John T. Ryan, de Valera's representatives in the bonds issue, to 'suspend' the flotation.[23] Throughout his negotiations on the bonds matter with Smiddy and in correspondence with Hathaway and latterly with Frederick Sterling, Castle emphasized his support for the Free State and viewed de Valera's supporters with suspicion.[24] Indeed during Cosgrave's first official visit to the US in January 1928, Castle commented on Cosgrave's 'exaggerated honesty' following a discussion on the bonds matter.[25] Three months later, Sterling informed the State Department that, given the recent successful flotation of the Dublin corporation loan, 'there need be no hesitation in placing part of the issue outside of the country.'[26]

21 See Carroll, *Money for Ireland* for a detailed study of the topic; NYPL, FWP, Box 27, Correspondence with subscribers to Irish bonds, 1924, Walsh to James J Morrissey, 26 January 1924.   22 Carroll, *Money for Ireland*, pp. 41–4; NARA, RG59, M580/246, 841d.51/158, Walsh to Castle, 28 May 1928; ibid., 580/246, 841d.51/113, Kellogg to Hackworth. on conversation with Wadsworth, 3 August 1926; ibid., 841d.51/93, Castle to Richardson, 1 September 1926; *FRUS*, iii, Castle to Borah, 11 February 1928; HHPL, WRCP, Castle diary, 21 May 1926; *FRUS*, iii, Castle to Borah, 11 February 1923.   23 NARA, RG59, 580.245, 841d.51/128, Hackworth to Walsh and Ryan, 10 December 1927. The matter was complicated also by the amount of work involved in verifying the claims alone. Over 300,000 people purchased Irish Republican Bonds details of which were recorded in over forty ledgers and over 309,000 certificates were issued. Some subscribers did not regard their subscriptions as an investment but merely as a donation towards a good cause and in many instances receipts were not kept. NYPL, Luke O'Connor Papers, Box 1, O'Connor to Matthew G Healy, 8 November 1929.   24 Carroll, *Money for Ireland*, p. 70. For analysis of the activities between the 1927 judgement and last repayment in 1933 see Carroll, *Money for Ireland*, pp. 71–91.   25 Castle discussed the bonds issue with Cosgrave on 26 January 1928 when the latter once again emphasized that his administration would repay the bondholders. NARA, RG59, M580/246, 841d.51/140, Castle to Hackworth, 27 January 1928.   26 Ibid., 841d.51-/60, Sterling

Castle regarded the bonds issue as 'a very disagreeable mess for us'; ultimately the State Department's involvement in the issue never went beyond an unofficial and advisory capacity and it resisted becoming a 'collection agency' for US subscribers.[27] This reflected the Coolidge administration's policy of non-interference in Irish affairs and also, in the mid-1920s, the US banking system. Both policies assisted the Free State fiscal strategy in the US; the Irish government was not forced to repay the bondholders and was permitted to launch the second loan in December 1927. It was over subscribed within two hours of being floated. Nevertheless, in the mid-1920s a further example of US direct investment in the Free State revealed the dangers of investing in the new state.

The Industrial Trust Company (ITC) was established in 1925 to provide long term finance for Irish industry and $49,490 of its capital was subscribed in the US. Hathaway described it 'as the first Irish enterprise in which American money has actually been invested.' Among the US subscribers were prominent Irish-Americans James A. Farrell, Nicolas F. Brady and Morgan J. O'Brien. The Dublin consul described the reaction in Dublin to the US involvement:

> Their action appears to be taken by the Irish government as an earnest sign of future financial support on a business basis. According to Dublin belief, it has always been easy to get in the United States subscriptions for Irish benevolent purposes, but it has always been difficult to convince American Irishmen that it was *safe to invest* money in Ireland. Considerable encouragement is now felt in that the men referred to and their associates had actually been induced to feel sufficient confidence to make an investment.[28]

By 1929, this venture had turned sour for the US investors. James J. Phelan, the Irish-American millionaire, wrote to Ernest Blythe, minister for Finance, on 18 June 1929, complaining that:

> The condition of the bank, indicated by the statements submitted, savours much of speculation, rather than the purpose for which at least we in America understood the bank was being formed at the time of its organization, namely to aid in the industrial development of the Irish Free State.[29]

Two months later he expressed to MacWhite his 'dissatisfaction with the way' the ITT was being managed. Instead of doing business in accordance with the

---

to Secretary of State, 1 April 1928. Smiddy had also secured the support of Vice-President Charles Dawes who told him how impressed he was with the 'ability of the Cosgrave government to govern and rehabilitate the country economically.' *DIFP*, iii, NAI, DFA, EA, 231/1/1929, Smiddy to Cosgrave, 21 July 1927.   **27** HHPL, WRCP, Castle diary, 6 January 1928; The phrase 'collection agency' was used by Hackworth during a meeting attended by himself, Castle, Walsh, Ryan, NARA, RG59, 580.246, 841d.51/143, memo., 8 February 1928.   **28** NARA, RG59, M580/222, 841d.00/829, Hathaway to Secretary of State, 21 January 1926.   **29** UCDA, Ernest Blythe Papers, P24/475, Phelan to Blythe, 18 June 1929.

character of the Trust, he felt that Senator Douglas, chairman, and Lionel Smith-Gordon had undertaken risks of a 'speculative nature.' Phelan, who was already displeased that Cosgrave had not visited Boston during his tour in January 1928, did not believe that there were any Irish-Americans who would invest money in the Free State 'on the expectation of getting a lower rate of interest than they would else where.' He could understand a wealthy man contributing a 'definite sum to an Irish enterprise for national or sentimental reasons, but to ask him to forego a part of the interest would be too severe a trial to his business instincts.'[30]

Daly's analysis of the ITT's records proved that his suspicions were correct, with 87 per cent of its investments being in British or foreign securities and only 13 per cent in Irish securities. Consequently, the 1929 stock market collapse led to the company becoming insolvent and it was wound up in 1933.[31] The initial optimism that surrounded this government-backed project and the launch of the second national loan failed to result in significant US investment in the Free State.

*

By 1928, despite official and private efforts on both sides of the Atlantic Ocean, the Ford company remained the most prominent example of US investment in the Free State. There was also a change of climate within the Free State administration. Attitudes towards foreign investment among officials and ministers became 'more hostile' towards the end of the decade. The stock market crash in 1929 combined with the British government's decision to remove sterling from the gold standard in 1931 to deter future government flotations on Wall Street.[32]

In late 1926, Harold Collins provided an overview of the harsh realities facing the Free State:

> The Free State has achieved political stability. A firmly seated national government functions from Dublin; the country is well-policed by an efficient constabulary; order prevails; life and property are safe, and no thinking person expects a recrudescence of militant republicanism. Economic stability is on the way, but remains to be achieved. Foreign trade results in a heavy actual adverse balance; productive efficiency in agriculture, the key industry, is low; transport is costly; prices are high; taxes are at an inconvenient level; there is embarrassing unemployment; business is dull; and private enterprise is almost everywhere lacking.[33]

30 NAI, D/T, S2263, MacWhite to Walshe, 26 August 1929.   31 M.E. Daly, *Industrial development and Irish national identity, 1922–39* (1992), p. 52.   32 Daly, 'The economic impact of the United States on Ireland, 1922–1980', pp. 6–7. One other channel through which US capital flowed into the Free State was emigrants' remittances. In 1926–7, emigrants remittances from the US less passage and travelling money, was approximately £2.2 million. *PDDE*, 23, 18 April 1928, 14.   33 NARA, RG59, M580/223, 840d.00/869, Hathaway to Secretary of State, 2 September 1926.

He explained that a combination of factors had produced this situation; the impact of world conditions, internal disorder and 'not the best human material' to achieve prosperity.[34] A few months earlier, Hathaway had tried to explain the human factor by suggesting that 'it comes hard to those who thought that the driving out of the English ended all trouble and ushered in an era of plenty, but it has come, and the realization is becoming an effective force in the country. There is reason to hope that over a period of years it will effect a considerable transformation of conditions.'[35] Both men felt the government had the policies for economic progress; stabilizing public finances, increasing agricultural production and stimulating manufacturing. Progress would not be rapid but Collins predicted that the prospects of achieving a 'stable and efficient national economy ... are good.'[36]

But there were other reasons for believing that the economic relationship between the US and the Free State might expand; firstly, throughout both of Coolidge's administrations, economic advancement remained central to US foreign policy priorities, secondly, there existed within the US a pre-existing level of interest in the nascent Irish economy as indicated in the previous chapter and finally, the Free State government was open to expanding economic links with the US. Julius Klein of the Bureau of Foreign and Domestic Commerce believed that 1927 marked a new stage in the US and Free State economic relationship. US interest in the Free State economy would increase due to the successful flotation of the Free State loan on the New York market in December 1927 and the recent appointment of a US minister in Dublin. Furthermore, Klein believed that these US actions confirmed the administration's confidence in the economic and political future of the Free State as did reciprocal visits by Cosgrave and Kellogg to the US and Irish Free State respectively.[37] Few could foresee the economic recession that would set in internationally after the Wall Street crash in October 1929.

34 Ibid.   35 Ibid., M580/222, 840d.00/827, Hathaway to Secretary of State, 7 January 1926.   36 Ibid., M580/223, 840d.00/869, Hathaway to Secretary of State, 2 September 1926.   37 'Foreign views of Irish trade', 93.

CHAPTER THIRTEEN

The US foreign service in the Irish Free State: political reporting and promoting US foreign policy, August 1923–March 1929

Charles Hathaway preferred the political to the economic side of his work at the Dublin consulate. There were two aspects to his political work; reporting on internal developments in the IFS and implementing US foreign policy objectives. In the former role he worried about the stability of the Irish Free State government. His views on the threats and challenges to the administration, particularly from Eamon de Valera and his Sinn Féin party, on the boundary question and on left-wing forces offer another perspective on this period of state formation. Hathaway's suspicion and wariness about de Valera and his colleagues mirrored those of his superiors in the State Department and White House. Consequently, when the anti-treatyites entered the Dáil in 1927 as Fianna Fáil, US officials had to re-assess their position and face the reality of a de Valera-led government in the Free State.

In its second term, Coolidge's foreign policy wavered between participation in and isolation from international affairs, while the Free State government regarded engagement with the wider world as a priority. Consequently, entry to the League of Nations and participation in the imperial conferences clarified the international status of the Free State but also provided the State Department, through Hathaway and Frederick Sterling, with another source of information on these international organizations. Other themes in US foreign policy were disarmament and the outlawing of war, and the Coolidge administration established international frameworks to realize these aims. Thus, the response of the Free State government to the Geneva conference and the Kellogg–Briand pact was important to the US government and brought the Free State for the first time into the realm of US foreign policy as an independent state. Other opportunities to regularize the US and Free State diplomatic relationship emerged out of reciprocal state visits.

Consular commentary on domestic politics

The sources of Hathaway's political reports were his frequent meetings with the Minister Desmond FitzGerald and Secretary Joseph Walshe in the department of External Affairs, occasional meeting with the minister for Defence, Richard Mulcahy, 'one of the most thoughtful political personalities', President Cosgrave, his circle of friends and the newspapers. Hathaway had little praise for the quality of Irish newspapers which he believed reflected London opinions only.[1] Regarding domestic politics, the central theme of his consular reports was the challenges posed to the stability and permanence of the Free State administration. Seven weeks after the outbreak of the March 1924 army mutiny, he was relieved to report that there was no further disorder and the government was in a stronger position than prior to it.[2] Nevertheless, the cabinet faction fighting revealed by the mutiny lingered into 1925, when Hathaway reported that it would require Cosgrave's 'considerable political strength' to 'disarm' the opposition led by Kevin O'Higgins, vice-president and minister for Justice.[3]

In the interim, Hathaway worried about another threat to the Free State government; the impact of the boundary issue for the government, which was 'for them in the nature of high explosive.' As explained in chapter eleven, in 1924 the State Department considered the issue to be of paramount importance and vital in stabilizing the new state. In May, Hathaway felt that if there was any evidence of hesitation on the part of the British government to establish the boundary commission, the position of the Irish government would become precarious and it might even fall.[4] From London, US Ambassador Frank B. Kellogg proffered the Foreign Office view that a settlement was imminent. However, Kellogg did not support this view and neither did Arthur Bliss Lane in the State Department.[5] In May and August, Harry Starrett offered the unionist perspective and fuelled fears of another civil war, this time between the forces of the Northern Ireland state and those of the Free State, if the James Craig government was forced into the boundary commission.[6] By autumn 1924, Hathaway

---

1 National Archives and Records Administrations (hereafter NARA), Records of the Department of State relating to internal affairs of Great Britain, 1910–29 (hereafter RG59), M580/221, 841d.00/735, Hathaway to Secretary of State, 4 December 1924; ibid., M580/249, 841d.911/-, Hathaway to Secretary of State, 18 February 1927. There were no US correspondents stationed in Ireland since 1923 but in 1927 there were seven correspondents in Dublin who worked for US news agencies and papers; William H. Brayden (Associated Press, *Chicago Daily News*), George McDonagh (United Press and chief reporter for the *Irish Independent*), Hugh Curran (*Chicago Tribune* and chief reporter for the *Irish Times*), Patrick J. Hooper (*Philadelphia Public Ledger* and *New York Evening Post* and formerly of the *Freeman's Journal*), Sean Ó Cuiv (*New York Herald Tribune*), Arthur Webb (*Brooklyn Eagle* and chief sub-editor of the *Irish Times*), Patricia Hoey (the Hearst press and associated news agencies). All except Webb was Irish. NARA, RG59, M580/249, 841d.911/-, Hathaway to Secretary of State, 18 February 1927.   2 Ibid., M580/221, 841d.00/691, Hathaway to Secretary of State, 7 May 1924.   3 Ibid., 841d.00/746, Hathaway to Secretary of State, 15 January 1925.   4 Ibid., 841d.00/691, Hathaway to Secretary of State, 7 May 1924.   5 Ibid., 841d.00/676, Kellogg to Secretary of State, 11 April 1924.   6 Ibid., 841d.00/679, Starrett to Secretary of State, 6 May 1924; ibid., 841d.00/704, Starrett to Secretary of State, 16 June 1924; ibid., 841d.00/713, Starrett to Secretary of State, 28 August 1924. Starrett's view of the uncompromising attitude of the Craig government was matched by a similar view coming from within official circles in London in late 1925. Ray Atherton in the US embassy reported that a senior official in the Dominions Office who

believed that the uncertainties surrounding the commission were undermining economic stability.[7]

The commission was eventually established in late 1924. Soon enough Hathaway revised his fears largely due to a lowering of the government's expectation of its results and secondly, the government secured its position with election victories in seven of nine by-elections in March 1925.[8] Not only did he feel that the electoral results gave the government a 'new lease of life', restored public confidence in it and improved its credit state but he felt it unified the government to carry on. Despite the victories, however, he was not at all certain that it marked the end of Sinn Féin so long as 'more than one-third of the electorate … can be induced to vote for the destruction of the state and the rupture of relations with Great Britain.' A leak in the *Morning Post* on 7 November 1925, signalling that the boundary commission would make only minor transfers of territory to both the Free State and Northern Ireland, raised the tension again. Hathaway reported widespread outrage in nationalist circles, 'unrest' and 'anxiety' among government supporters and the resignation of the Free State representative on the commission, Eoin MacNeill, who was also minister for Education. But he predicted that there would not be a 'government crisis', largely because of the absence of an alternative administration emerging from either inside or outside the cabinet.[9] The view from the US embassy in London was less tempered. Initially Ray Atherton, first secretary, hoped that the boundary question would now be finally taken out of British politics.[10] Starrett reported that the people of Northern Ireland would be 'satisfied' with the proposed territorial arrangements.[11]

All three US officials accepted that the work of the boundary commission had come to an end. On 26 November, Hathaway reported a rumour that there was a possibility of 'trading' article twelve (boundary commission) for article five (the Free State share in the British war debt) in the Anglo-Irish treaty. This concession, he believed, would greatly ease the 'strain' on the government and ensure its 'survival.' He thought that stability in the Free State was vital not just for the Cosgrave government but also from an international standpoint. He pointed

---

was a staunch conservative, spoke 'disapprovingly of the very hard and unyielding attitude' of the Craig government on the boundary question. Ibid., M580/222, 841d.00/810, Atherton to Secretary of State, 18 November 1925.   **7** Ibid., M580/221, 841d.00/718, Hathaway to Secretary of State, 30 September 1924. Hathaway was commended for the quality of this report which was noted in his record; ibid., Bliss to Grew, undated, Carr to Hathaway, 4 November 1924; ibid., 841d.00/720, Hathaway to Secretary of State, 9 October 1924.   **8** Ibid., M580/221, 841d.00/733, Hathaway to Secretary of State, 4 December 1924; ibid., 841d.00/757, Hathaway to Secretary of State, 19 March 1925.   **9** Ibid., 841d.00/757, Hathaway to Secretary of State, 19 March 1925; ibid., 841d.00/758, Hathaway to Secretary of State, 25 March 1925; ibid., M580/222, 841d.00/808, Hathaway to Secretary of State, 19 November 1925; ibid., M580/222, 841d.00/812, Hathaway to Secretary of State, 26 November 1925. See J.M. Regan, *The Irish Counter-Revolution, 1921–36* (1999), pp. 258–9.   **10** NARA, RG59, M580/1, entry '13 November 1925'; ibid., M580/222, 841d.00/813, Atherton to Secretary of State, 24 November 1925.   **11** Ibid., M580/222, 841d.00/809, Starrett to Secretary of State, 16 November 1925.

out to the State Department on 3 December, in a twenty-two page analysis of the 'grave' situation, that: 'If an acceptable adjustment is not found, the Irish question will be likely to spring into new life and again embitter the foreign relations of Great Britain and in particular those with the United States.'[12]

Five days later, Atherton reported that Cosgrave, Craig and their respective cabinet colleagues had met with Prime Minister Stanley Baldwin and Dominions Secretary Leopold Amery, but he did not indicate how the British government intended to deal with the Irish situation. However, he noted that Baldwin, who always favoured a 'compromise between extremes', would adopt the policy of 'bargaining with the debt as the easiest way out of the present trouble.'[13] A tripartite agreement between the governments of Britain, Northern Ireland and the Irish Free State was signed in London on 3 December 1925. The powers of the boundary commission under article twelve were revoked and the Free State relieved from any liability for British public debt and war pensions arising from article five. The status quo in Ireland was maintained. Hathaway reported majority support for the agreement from within Cosgrave's party. But he identified the Irish Labour Party as being opposed to the agreement and the de Valera side as in 'mentally riotous dissent.'[14]

With the government securing Dáil approval for the agreement on 15 December and 'all Ireland turning its attention to plum pudding', the position of Sinn Féin had become 'more of a concern' for the US consul. Hathaway admitted to the State Department that he had provided few Sinn Féin statements because of their 'frequent futility and [their] entire neglect of the facts and apparent unwillingness to deal with facts.'[15] But this did not equate with ignoring events in republican circles. In July 1925, he reported that discussion was 'rife' about the ending of the abstentionist policy and seemed to draw comfort from the idea that in such circumstances de Valera would have to retire into private life to make such a *volte face* endurable.'[16] Yet, he was sufficiently astute to see the logic in information received from 'responsible' government minister, who told him that there was support in the government for de Valera's republicans to enter the Dáil because 'it would be the best guarantee of enduring peace in the Free State.'[17] Before there were any developments within Sinn Féin circles,

12 Ibid., 841d.oo/812, Hathaway to Secretary of State, 26 November 1925; ibid., 841d.oo/817, Hathaway to Secretary of State, 3 December 1925.   13 Ibid., 841d.oo/814, Atherton to Secretary of State, 1 December 1925.   14 Ibid., 841d.oo/818, Hathaway to Secretary of State, 7 December 1925; R. Fanning et al. (eds), *Documents on Irish foreign policy, ii, 1923–26*, 3 vols (hereafter *DIFP*) (1998–), iii, NAI, D/T, S4720A, Agreement amending and supplementing the articles of agreement for a Treaty between Great Britain and Ireland, 3 December 1925, p. 533.   15 NARA, RG59, M580/222, 841d.oo/824, Hathaway to Secretary of State, 31 December 1925; ibid., M580/221, 841d.oo/741, Hathaway to Secretary of State, 31 December 1924.   16 Ibid., M580/222, 841d.oo/785, Hathaway to Secretary of State, 16 July 1925; ibid., 841d.oo/783, Hathaway to Secretary of State, 23 July 1925.   17 Ibid., M580/222, 841d.oo/789, Hathaway to Secretary of State, 13 August 1925.

a new party, Clann Éireann, was established. Even though its members had split from the government party, Hathaway reported that it was made up of 'disappointed, nationalistic, millenarians' who would only succeed with Sinn Féin support.[18] It was short-lived, but the re-shaping of republicanism in May 1926, when de Valera established Fianna Fáil brought the end of abstentionism closer.

Hathaway was temporarily replaced in Dublin by John Corrigan in April 1926 and the latter was less worried about the emergence of the new party, with its aim of entry into parliamentary politics following the abolition of the oath of allegiance to the British monarchy. Instead he preferred to view it as evidence of a weakening of the republicans and a boon to the Free State and US governments respectively. It was a theme that Hathaway pursued. Later in the month, he predicted 'the complete break-up' of the republican movement, not only because of the split but also due to declining support from its US supporters who were 'greatly embarrassed' by the internal divisions.[19] Not only was the de Valera-created American Association for the Recognition of the Irish Republic weaker than at any other time but Clan na Gael was intensely suspicious of the recent developments in republican circles. Eventually, on 15 June, it announced that it would support the Irish Republican Army and not Fianna Fáil.[20] Divisions within republicanism on both sides of the Atlantic were now out in the open. Yet, de Valera's tour of the US between February and May 1927 netted, not less than £20,000 according to Hathaway, and by other accounts much more, to fund the new party and a new newspaper, *The Nation*. These US funds, Hathaway believed, were vital to the future electoral success of de Valera and Fianna Fáil.[21]

De Valera arrived back to Cobh to face into a general election on 9 June 1927. Prior to this, Hathaway had reported the unlikelihood of any party gaining a 'working majority.' He felt that the fact that the government was 'intent on paying its bills, collect[ing] its taxes remorselessly ... and habitual[ly] preaching ... self-reliance to a mass of unselfreliant followers who seek free *panem et circenses*' would weaken its electoral position. But he expected the government's 56 seats to hold and over half of the 47 non-sitting republican seats to be lost to 'farmers, labour men, independents and Redmondites.'[22] Towards the end of the campaign he felt the combination of government ministers' speeches remaining 'intelligible' and a popular budget might return Cumann na nGaedheal to power. Nonetheless, he recognized that de Valera's Fianna Fáil had the only other chance of forming a single party government. Such a possibility forced him to rethink the republicans' ability to govern. A republican victory, he felt, would bring 'no considerable change except

18 Ibid., 841d.00/830, Hathaway to Secretary of State, 28 January 1926.   19 Ibid., 841d.00/845, Corrigan to Secretary of State, 15 April 1926; ibid., 841d.00/847, Hathaway to Secretary of State, 3 May 1926.   20 T.P. Coogan, *De Valera: long fellow, long shadow* (1993), p. 385.   21 NARA, RG59, M580/223, 841d.00/903, Hathaway to Secretary of State, 24 March 1927; ibid., 841d.00/913, Hathaway to Secretary of State, 16 June 1927. The amount contributed from the US and Australia was £29,782. Ibid., 841d.00/937, Sterling to Secretary of State, 1 December 1927.   22 Ibid., M580/223, 841d.00/899, Hathaway to Secretary of State, 28 February 1927.

... as arises out of individual competence', if it did not provoke 'friction' with Britain. In other words, he now believed that a de Valera victory would not desta-bilize the Free State or reverse economic and social policy, which was a possibil-ity if the Labour Party took office.[23] Although Hathaway admired the Labour leader, Thomas Johnson, and Labour's performance as the main parliamentary opposition, its left-wing ideology and links to communism made it less desirable as a government than de Valera's republican Fianna Fáil.

Hathaway telegraphed the State Department on 16 June and followed up on the same day with a detailed report revealing that the government party had won 47 seats, just 3 more than Fianna Fáil. De Valera's party, helped greatly by US money, came out of the election as victors and the government was left in a minority position in the new Dáil. Hathaway indicated that if Cosgrave was to form the next government on 23 June, when the new Dáil met, he would have to form alliances with either the farmers or independents. He believed that Johnson's party could not enter an alliance with either Cosgrave or de Valera without 'ruining itself in the eyes of its supporters', while de Valera, the other choice for prime minister, would have to dispense with the oath of allegiance to the British crown before he and his followers could partake in governing. On 17 June, the Fianna Fáil Party announced that its forty-four deputies would 'claim' their seats but would not take the oath and on the following day, that it 'was ready to form a government with the co-operation of all progressive non-impe-rialist persons.' For the first time the US consul had to consider seriously the possibility of de Valera holding office.[24] He felt that even if de Valera entered the Dáil and government, he now represented a 'milder type of republicanism' that did not want to 'precipitate conflict' with Britain. On the economic front, Fianna Fáil had a more detailed 'enunciation of protectionism' but there was no reason to anticipate that it would do anything 'essentially different' from its pred-ecessors. Indeed he favoured an alliance between the two parties that would make the Free State 'permanently successful.'[25] US administrators now had to think about the possibility of doing business with de Valera, hitherto their *bête noire*.

But this development was delayed because of the failure of Fianna Fáil deputies to take the oath on 23 June which Hathaway felt had been inevitable. De Valera had now become the kingmaker and the consul thought that if his fol-lowers chose 'to sulk in their tent', Cosgrave's minority government, including the 'powerful' Kevin O'Higgins as the new minister for External Affairs, might last for months or years. But the same day he reported rumours that some of de Valera's deputies wanted to enter the Dáil with or without the oath of allegiance.[26] His next communication informed the State Department of Kevin O'Higgins' murder on 10 July by the IRA which resulted in Secretary Kellogg forwarding

23 Ibid., 841d.00/903, Hathaway to Secretary of State, 24 March 1927.   24 Ibid., 841d.00/913, Hathaway to Secretary of State, 16 June 1927; quoted in D. Keogh, *Twentieth-century Ireland: nation and state* (1994), p. 45.   25 NARA, RG59, M580/223, 841d.00/913, Hathaway to Secretary of State, 16 June 1927.   26 Ibid., 841d.00/914, Hathaway to Secretary of State, 27 June 1927.

a letter of condolence to Smiddy and Cosgrave.[27] William Castle, as head of the Western European division, shared Hathaway's regret at O'Higgins' death and noted in his diary, 'he was the strongest man in the Irish Free State and his death will be a loss comparable to that of Michael Collins a few years ago. I wonder will the Irish ever learn that government by political murder is not the most approved or most successful form.'[28]

Although Hathaway felt that the act was spontaneous and was not linked to de Valera's followers, he saw it as a shock to public confidence and a blow to the Cosgrave government.[29] De Valera's reaction that the murder 'was inexcusable from any standpoint' was also noted. The tense situation was elaborated on in more detail following Hathaway's attendance at O'Higgins' funeral on 13 July: 'the general effect of genuine national mourning was very evident ... there was also ... a gloomy foreboding that the murder ... might prove the first step in the recurrence of organized political crime.'[30] But Hathaway's intelligence about the desire of some 'Fianna Fáilers' to take the oath and enter the Dáil proved to be correct and was confirmed by Frederick Sterling on 12 August. The new US minister also reported a conversation he had had with Cosgrave, revealing the president's expectation of imminent resignation and the Labour Party's establishment of a government.[31]

Faced by the danger of another outbreak of civil violence and in an attempt to get Fianna Fáil into the Dáil, the Cosgrave government introduced the Electoral Amendment bill, the Constitutional Amendment bill and the Public Safety bill.[32] Hathaway, who was asked by the State Department and Sterling to stay on in the Dublin consulate due to the quality of his reporting, informed Washington that the Public Safety bill was motivated by the government's belief that 'under-ground conspiracy is afloat' and that the only course of action open to it was 'to take the sternest measures against every suspect and to suppress everything that appears to teach disrespect for organized government.'[33] The electoral legislation sought to legally abolish the continuation of abstentionism. The three pieces of legislation were passed through the Free State Senate on 10 August and events moved swiftly after that. Hathaway felt that the government's stern measures had been proved correct when the Fianna Fáil deputies took the oath and entered the Dáil on 11 August. But now it seemed that the Cosgrave government would finally fall as Fianna Fáil and Labour would have more votes together.[34]

The Labour-led coalition failed to oust the Cosgrave government by one vote on 16 August and Hathaway thought it would be 'good tactics' if Cosgrave called

27 Ibid., 841d.00/915, Hathaway to Secretary of State, 10 July 1927; ibid., 841d.00/915a, Kellogg to Cosgrave, 11 July 1927; ibid., Kellogg to Smiddy, 12 July 1927.   28 Herbert Hoover Presidential Library (hereafter HHPL), William R. Castle (hereafter WRCP), WRC diary, 12 July 1927.   29 NARA, RG59, M580/223, 841d.00/917, Hathaway to Secretary of State, 11 July 1927.   30 Ibid., 841d.00/918, Hathaway to Secretary of State, 14 July 1927.   31 Ibid., 841d.00/920, Sterling to Secretary of State, 12 August 1927.   32 Keogh, *Twentieth-century Ireland*, p. 47.   33 NARA, RG59, M580/223, 841d.00/922, Hathaway to Secretary of State, 30 July 1927.   34 Ibid., 841d.00/923, Hathaway to Secretary of State, 11 August 1927.

a general election. But Cosgrave told Sterling that he hoped to be able to carry on without a dissolution 'for some months' because he wanted Fianna Fáil to participate in Dáil business, which might help to break down personal bitterness and pave the way for a 'rapprochement' between the two major parties. Cosgrave's conciliatory approach strongly appealed to Sterling and Hathaway, who believed it was the only way to avoid 'perpetual danger' to the Free State.[35] But even if his party won two up-coming bye-elections, Cosgrave's electoral position would be delicate and this led him to change his mind. On 18 August, he told Sterling that he would call a general election soon for three reasons; firstly, he did not have a 'definite mandate', secondly, there was greater support for Cumann na nGaedheal due to O'Higgins' murder and de Valera's reversal of abstentionism and finally, the business classes preferred the stability of a single party government rather than a Labour/Fianna Fáil alliance. John A. Costello, Free State attorney general, also confirmed this position to Hathaway. Sterling commended Cosgrave's 'astuteness and alertness 'to resolve the situation definitely one way or the other.[36] Despite his short tenure in the Free State, Sterling admired Cosgrave just as Hathaway and Castle did. The latter had been recently appointed under secretary of state and was deeply interested in Free State politics, not just because it had been part of his bailiwick as head of the Western European division but also due to his visit to Ireland in 1924. He wrote to Sterling on 19 August, 'the near fall of the government the other day was intensely interesting and I doubt whether it can stand when the Dáil reconvenes ... I wish the present crowd could stay in office.'[37]

But in line with his change of opinion, Cosgrave dissolved the Dáil on 25 August and called a general election for 15 September, despite Cumann na gGaedheal's victory in two bye-elections in Dublin county and Dublin city south with an increased vote.[38] Both US representatives reported on the short election campaign and emphasized the government's achievements and the 'just and accurate' Cosgrave line that only his party had the political experience to govern the country.[39] The gamble paid off for Cosgrave who won 62 seats to Fianna Fáil's 52 and Labour's 13. Sterling met with Cosgrave on 22 September when the results were known. The president told him that he would stand for the presidency of the Free State again when the Dáil resumed on 11 October and that 'he hoped to carry on without a change' but he was willing to enter into a coalition with Fianna Fáil 'to preserve the peace, credit and stability' of the country.[40] Cosgrave was re-elected president on 11 October by a majority of six votes and no other candidate was put forward by the Labour Party or Fianna Fáil. Sterling predicted that

35 Ibid., 841d.00/925, Hathaway to Secretary of State, 18 August 1927.   36 Ibid., 841d.00/926, Sterling to Secretary of State, 22 August 1927.   37 HHPL, WRCP, Box 8, File: Ireland, 1924–31, Castle to Sterling, 19 August 1927.   38 NARA, RG59, M580/223, 841d.00/928, Sterling to Secretary of State, 1 September 1927.   39 Ibid., 841d.00/929, Hathaway to Secretary of State, 8 September 1927; ibid; 841d.00/931, Sterling to Secretary of State, 13 September 1927.   40 Ibid., 841d.00/930, Sterling to Secretary of State, 22 September 1927.

sooner or later … Fianna Fáil will gain the ascendancy – and possibly it would be in the best interests of the country in the long run should this party be given a chance to show their hand and [be] permitted to govern – but it is fair to assume that in the meanwhile they will gain much by legislative experience and their theories will be reduced to fact.[41]

Cumann na nGaedheal remained in office until March 1932 and the five years in opposition provided Fianna Fáil with time to serve out its apprenticeship in parliamentary politics and wait for an opportunity to pounce on the government. The road to the rehabilitation of de Valera and his followers, in US eyes at least, was well on its way by early 1928 when Wainright Abbott, the US chargé d'affaires in Dublin, felt that a criticism by Tim Healy, the departing governor general, of the 'pedigree … of a prominent member' of Fianna Fáil, was 'regrettable, undignified, uncalled for and unfounded.'[42] In the following month, Sterling welcomed the 'rare spectacle' and 'unheard of occurrence' which saw de Valera and Cosgrave voting in the same lobby on a division on the amendment to the Dentists' bill in the Dáil.[43]

During the period 1922 to 1927, there were many challenges to the survival of the Cosgrave government and Free State stability. According to Hathaway's analysis, the survival of both government and state were inter-linked and inter-dependent. Although he was not blind to the structural weaknesses in the political and economic systems created by the Cosgrave government, he fully supported Cosgrave and his administration's efforts to survive, build a state and create a national identity. Part of this support for Cosgrave was also motivated by hostility to de Valera and by an unwillingness to see him in office. Indeed it was not until early 1927 that references to de Valera's followers began to appear regularly and in a non-military context in his reports. By summer 1927 he was ready to see de Valera share power with Cosgrave. But this did not occur.

Both Hathaway and Sterling were relieved that Fianna Fáil would spend some time in opposition to learn the trade of governing. Both men were also realistic enough to accept that a change of administration was 'inevitable' and would represent another sign of stability, if it was a peaceful change of government. Ironically, one factor which contributed to the ending of Cosgrave's tenure in office and brought de Valera to power was the economic effect of the Wall Street crash, which affected Ireland from 1930 onwards and also brought the demise of Hoover's presidency.

Although Hathaway came from the consular side of the house, the level of detail and analysis that infused his political reporting indicated a deep interest in Free State political affairs and he had a keen sense of the limitation of US

41 Ibid., 841d.00/934, Sterling to Secretary of State, 13 October 1927.   42 Ibid., 841d.00/938, Sterling to Secretary of State, 30 January 1928.   43 Ibid., 841d.00/940, Sterling to Secretary of State, 27 February 1928.

influence in Free State affairs, especially when US representatives were from the consular rather than the diplomatic side of the foreign service.[44] It was unfortunate, therefore, that his successor, Frederick Sterling, was disenchanted with some aspects of the Dublin posting, at least in the early days. The US congressional appropriation for the legation only began to operate from 1 July 1927, which meant that there were no administrative staff or resources in place prior to Sterling's arrival in Dublin. Consequently, his initial enthusiasm for the posting, expressed to William Castle in the following words: 'Bill, as they say in Texas, "I'm sure goin' to like this little ole hole"' was soon dissipated.[45] He devoted much of his attention in this early period to staffing and administrative matters. His first political report was not forwarded to the State Department until October 1927 and they were infrequent afterwards, which merited him a reprimand from Carr.

Throughout 1928 and 1929, he lamented the absence of 'constructive' and 'productive' parliamentary politics, particularly in a legislative sense, although he enjoyed watching Cosgrave's government being tested by de Valera and his party both inside and outside the Dáil. While the government had a full legislative programme, he believed that the majority of it was 'of little interest to the outside world.'[46] He appeared to be even more disappointed with the level of political activity during the parliamentary recess in summer 1929 and complained to Washington on 21 August, 'there have been no political speeches, no new issues raised and hardly any comment of interest in the Press.'[47] After the Dail reconvened in October, he reported that the schedule of business would be a heavy one but that it did not hold 'promise to be of particular interest from a foreign view point.' All parliamentary issues were of a 'purely local nature and interest.' In early December, he confirmed that it had been 'an uninteresting session.'[48] Yet, he made the most of the posting and lobbied Castle to stay on in the Free State after the change of administration from Coolidge to Hoover in Washington in March 1929:

> Apart from my desire to stay on here and speaking personally ... there is one consideration in the selection of a minister here which is important. It is the necessity of maintaining a correct balance in a very partisan and

44 H. De Santis & W. Heinrichs, 'United States of America. The Department of State and American foreign policy' in Z. Steiner (ed.), *Foreign ministries of the world* (1982), p. 582.   45 HHPL, WRCP, Box 8, File: Ireland, 1924–31, Sterling to Castle, 4 August 1927.   46 NARA, RG59, M580/223, 841d.00/946, Sterling to Secretary of State, 28 June 1928; ibid., 841d.00/955, Sterling to Secretary of State, 29 May 1929; ibid., 841d.00/955, Sterling to Secretary of State, 29 May 1929; ibid., 841d.00/956, Sterling to Secretary of State, 13 June 1929; ibid., 841d.00/957, Sterling to Secretary of State, 3 July 1929; 841d.00/958, Sterling to Secretary of State, 18 July 1929.   47 Ibid., 841d.00/959, Sterling to Secretary of State, 21 August 1929.   48 Ibid., 841d.00/963, Sterling to Secretary of State, 31 October 1929; ibid., 841d.00/965, Sterling to Secretary of State, 6 December 1929.

bitter situation and having friendly relations with <u>all</u> parties; and this I think I am doing. There are most marvellous opportunities for putting one's foot in it.[49]

But by 1931 he agreed with Castle that 'there is mighty little of [real work] in Dublin, no matter how agreeable the post may be.'[50] He remained in Dublin until 1934 when he was transferred to Bulgaria.

Another aspect of consular reporting at this time that merits attention was the attention paid to the left wing of Irish politics and life. Throughout the 1920s this was a permanent feature of all US consular and diplomatic reporting because of the constant fear both inside and outside the US administration about the spread of 'bolshevism.'[51] Just as US Ambassador Houghton reported from London in late September 1925 on Ramsay MacDonald's efforts to exclude communists from the Labour Party, Hathaway reported on the Dáil performance of the Irish Labour Party under Johnson's leadership until 1927. As shown above, Hathaway came to value the presence of the Labour Party in national politics, particularly since it offered an opposition to the government.[52] He may also have appreciated that Johnson was a respected political figure who helped to consolidate the Free State as a 'conservative regime.'[53] Certainly Hathaway saw few signs of revolutionary potential within Johnson's party and neither did William Castle, who met the Labour leader in 1924 and thought him a 'delightful person to talk with.'[54] Nevertheless, Hathaway kept a close eye on the 'Russian influence' in the Free State, particularly during the general strike in Britain in early 1926. In May, he forwarded to Washington a report on the returned James Larkin's links with international communism written by the Garda Commissioner in Dublin city.[55]

Evidence of links between Irish and Russian communists had already reached the State Department in January 1925 through its representative in Riga, Latvia. US Consul F.W.B. Coleman forwarded a copy of instructions sent to communist agents working in the Free State. Despite the visit of Bob Steward, an English communist, to Ireland later in October, a police report concluded in 1926 that Steward was critical of Larkin, whose own 'influence in Irish labour circles is practically nil.' Hathaway discussed the Larkin report with Garda Commissioner Eoin O'Duffy, who agreed with his conclusions that Larkin's 'stock

49 HHPL, WRCP, Box 8, File: Ireland, 1924–31, Sterling to Castle, 26 August 1929.   50 Ibid., Castle to Sterling, 14 January 1929.   51 De Santis and Heinrichs, 'The Department of State and American foreign policy', p. 582.   52 HHPL, WRCP, Box 3, file 1, Houghton to Castle, 28 September 1925. Houghton feared that Britain was 'drifting towards radicalism of some sort.' Ibid. NARA, RG59, M580.242, 841d.504/4, Hathaway to Secretary of State, 30 July 1923; ibid., RG59, M580/224, 841d.00B/3, Hathaway to Secretary of State, 13 May 1926.   53 Lee, J.J., *Ireland 1912–1985: politics and society* (1989), p. 172.   54 HHPL, WRCP, Box 8, File: Ireland, 1924–31, Castle to Sterling, 19 August 1927.   55 NARA, RG59, M580/224, 841d.00B/3, Hathaway to Secretary of State, 13 May 1926; Lee, *Ireland*, p. 172.

is very low at present.' He concluded that Irish labour 'as a whole is weak, that it makes a noise far out of proportion to its strength, that only a section, almost negligible in numbers, is really communist in principle, that neither the whole nor any part of it is probably capable of any serious disturbing action.'[56] Furthermore, he re-assured Washington that the communist ideology held little appeal in a country 'in which the small peasant proprietor is in over-whelming majority and ... 90 per cent of the people are devout Roman Catholics.'[57]

Despite this, two years later, in 1928, Jack Kearney, on behalf of Larkin, attended the Sixth Congress of the Communist International and Sussdorf, the US representative, forwarded to Washington a report on proceedings. Kearney was reported as saying there was 'very little communist work in Ireland' and that in the event of a war between the US and Britain, '75 per cent of the Irish' would be on the former's side.[58] Although communism made little headway among the Free State public, US officials paid constant attention to any signs of it which reflected more the situation in the US than a real threat in the Free State. Excessive fears of 'Reds' and 'bolshevism' among the US public and administration were highlighted in the British embassy's 1927 annual report.[59] While traditional political and social values were regarded by consuls as barriers against the spread of communism in Ireland, the Cosgrave government's attempt to establish a distinct social and cultural personality for the new state was criticized.

Hathaway believed the 'whole programme of a Gaelic Ireland', including official promotion of the Irish language, was 'naturally repugnant to the Anglo-Irish' section of the population and divisive. And he used the symbolism of the painting over by Post and Telegraph officials of 'British red' post-boxes with a thin film of 'nationalist green' paint to illustrate his point.[60] Similarly Harold Collins, vice consul in Dublin, believed that the government's censorship legislation beginning with the Censorship of Films Act, 1923, pleased the 'Irish-Irelanders.'[61] Other symbols including the official use of the Sinn Féin tricolour as the Free State flag and the use of the 'Soldier's song' as the national anthem 'surprised, amused and offended' him and other observers. Hathaway understood the context to this policy but hoped that there would be a 'swing away from the idealistic, patriotic and moral fervour' associated with Sinn Féin to the 'everyday bread and butter matters of the hour.' He saw tolerance of political, cultural and

56 NARA, RG59, M580/222, 841d.00/785, Hathaway to Secretary of State, 16 July 1925; ibid., 841d.00/847, Hathaway to Secretary of State, 3 May 1926; ibid., M580/224, 841d.00B/-, Coleman to Secretary of State, 7 January 1925; ibid., 841d.00B/3, Hathaway to Secretary of State, 13 May 1926.   57 Ibid., M580/222, 841d.00/785, Hathaway to Secretary of State, 16 July 1925; ibid., 841d.00/847, Hathaway to Secretary of State, 3 May 1926.   58 Ibid., M580/224, 841d.00B/2, Document file note, 19 October 1928.   59 K. Bourne & D.C. Watt (general eds), *British documents on foreign affairs* (hereafter *BDFA*), part 11, series C, North America, 25 vols. (1986–95), xx, The Republican Ascendancy, 1919–28, Annual Report for the United States (hereafter Annual Report) for 1927, p. 276.   60 NARA, RG59, M580/223, 841d.00/864, Hathaway to Secretary of State, 29 July 1926; ibid., M580/222, 841d.00/798, Hathaway to Secretary of State, 24 September 1925.   61 Ibid., M580/241, 841d.4061/6, Collins to Department of State, 3 March 1926.

religious differences as the key to 'good relations' both within the Free State and with Northern Ireland and Britain.[62] Cosgrave's opposition to the introduction of divorce legislation was regarded as pandering to the majority position of the Roman Catholic population while ignoring the minority Protestant view. Also Hathaway believed it prevented any future rapprochement with the northern unionists, although he admitted in 1927 that 'one sees less and less of priests and bishops in political affairs.'[63] By the end of the decade, Sterling took much comfort from the visit of Princess Mary and her husband Viscount Lascelles in autumn 1928 and that of the Earl of Birkenhead early the following year. He believed that these contacts, combined with the absence of demonstrations and the fact that each felt that it was safe to visit, were 'a good augury of the progress which order and stability is making in this country.'[64]

Implementing US foreign policy

Hathaway's reporting on internal conditions in the Free State was strongly influenced by a concern for the survival of the Cosgrave government and its attempt to carve out a national identity. This latter theme was also evident in consular reporting on Free State foreign policy. As indicated previously, the Coolidge government pursued a foreign policy based on US freedom of action which resulted in non-involvement in international organizations, but in engagement in international affairs to protect and promote US interests. On the vexed question of US participation in the League of Nations, British Ambassador Howard reported that during 1924, 'the mass of US citizens are still definitely opposed to, and in constant fear of, "future commitments and entanglements", but they don't object to the government co-operating with the League to a certain extent in conferences for specific objects.'[65] The congressional decision on US participation in the Permanent Court of International Justice (World Court) at The Hague, was shelved for another year until December 1925. However, Howard reported that Coolidge and Hughes were open to participation in a conference on limitation of

62 Ibid., 841d.00/905, Hathaway to Secretary of State, 29 March 1927; ibid. 841d.00/824, Hathaway to Secretary of State, 31 December 1925; ibid., 841d.00/898, Hathaway to Secretary of State, 28 February 1927. Hathaway's report on 29 March received a ranking of 'excellent' from his superiors. Carr commended it for being 'well-arranged', showing 'an admirable understanding of the problems' and 'commendable familiarity with the sources of information.' Ibid., 841d.00/905, Carr to Hathaway, 28 April 1927.   63 Ibid., M580/221, 841d.00/751, Hathaway to Secretary of State, 12 February 1925. US Consul General Thomas Bowman reported from Belfast that the Craig government devoted much time to isolating itself from the Free State and in March 1927 he noted the various 'absurd' proposals to ensure that mail intended for the northern state from Britain was forwarded by 'an all red route' instead of through Dublin. Ibid., M580/223, 841d.00/900, Bowman to Secretary of State, 1 March 1927; ibid., 841d.00/905, Hathaway to Secretary of State, 29 March 1927.   64 Ibid., M580/224, 841d.00PR/7, Sterling to Secretary of State, 28 December 1924.   65 BDFA, xiv, Howard to Chamberlain, 8 June 1925 in Annual Report for 1924.

armaments on two conditions: firstly, this could not happen until the US navy reached the ratio allowed by the Washington conference naval treaty and had something to bargain with at such a conference and secondly, arms limitation must not involve commitments in European politics. Nevertheless, the US government was fully engaged with the international community on matters relating to repayment of debts, electrical communications and control of arms traffic.

On the other side of the Atlantic, Hathaway reported on Ireland's participation in the League of Nations and imperial conferences in 1923 and 1926.[66] His explanations for Free State engagement with international affairs suggested that these were not only its demonstration of independence as a dominion but were also linked with domestic affairs. During 1923 he provided the State Department with a series of reports on Irish attitudes toward foreign relations that emphasized the government's wish to pursue 'independent foreign relations.'[67] In April of that year, he explained that Desmond FitzGerald had told him that the 'natural psychological tendency of the Irish would be toward independent control of their foreign policy.' He identified other influential forces at work as well: public opinion and 'goadings' of Sinn Féin.[68] Consequently, he advised his superiors in Washington that Free State participation in the League of Nations and in the imperial conferences should be seen as manifestations of such domestic forces. It was an interpretation that persisted in his reporting in 1923. He believed that the Free State government's forthcoming programme at the League of Nations, if it was admitted, would be one of 'watchful waiting, avoiding the initiative but profiting to the utmost by every move of Canada in the direction of independent action.'[69] The Free State was admitted on 10 September 1923 and its involvement during the early period was characterized by the campaign to register the Anglo-Irish treaty which was successfully completed on 11 July 1924. Hathaway worried that the action 'lessened [the] prestige' of an already 'weak' government and helped 'anti-treaty elements.'[70] But it served many purposes for the Free State government also by a) confirming the treaty as an international document and the state as a legitimate entity separate from the Britain, b) revealing flexibility in the commonwealth structure and c) indicating its support for the League system. In other words, it fulfilled foreign and domestic aims.[71]

In the following year, Hathaway told the State Department in its foreign relations and assertion of an independent status, the Free State government had made

66 NARA, RG59, M580/221, 841d.00/720, Hathaway to Secretary of State, 9 October 1924; ibid., M580/222, 841d.00/798, Hathaway to Secretary of State, 24 September 1925.   67 Ibid., M580/225, 841d.01/62, Hathaway to Secretary of State, 21 March 1923; ibid., 841d.01/63, Hathaway to Secretary of State, 24 April 1923; ibid., 841d.01/64, Hathaway to Secretary of State, 11 July 1923; ibid., 841d.01/65, Hathaway to Secretary of State, 1 August 1923; ibid., 841d.01/66, Hathaway to Secretary of State, 16 August 1923.   68 Ibid., M580/225, 841d.01/63, Hathaway to Secretary of State, 24 April 1923.   69 Ibid., M580/225, 841d.01/66, Hathaway to Secretary of State, 16 August 1923.   70 Ibid., M580/221, 841d.00/739, Hathaway to Secretary of State, 18 December 1924.   71 See M. Kennedy, *Ireland and the League of Nations, 1919–1946. International relations: diplomacy and politics* (1996), pp. 55–8.

no advance since the achievement of an Irish minister at Washington. One explanation offered for this was a 'shifting of [public] interest from the abnormal to the normal', he also felt that FitzGerald was performing poorly as minister for External Affairs and that Free State ministers were more concerned with domestic affairs and were not 'internationally minded.'[72] The focus on domestic issues was not surprising, given the turbulence but Hathaway's critical report could be justified. Ireland's participation in the League of Nations, at least until after the seventh assembly in September 1926, was, in the consul's words, 'made to serve the national *amour proper*.'[73] FitzGerald told Hathaway, in August 1926, that the Free State delegation did not have anything 'active to present' to the September assembly. But following that gathering Ernest Blythe, minister for Finance and a member of the delegation, offered the following assessment:

> [D]uring the last two years Ireland had been absolutely negligible at the Assembly, neither saying nor doing anything whatsoever; except correcting a small British mistake. I am satisfied that we had better stay at home than play the role of last year and the year before. On the other hand, good results can be got from our playing an independent and active role.[74]

After the meeting, Blythe initiated a re-appraisal and re-direction of League policy. Subsequently, Free State representatives actively participated in assembly debates and committees resulting in the winning of a council seat in September 1930.[75]

Hathaway's other criticism of the Free State League of Nations policy was that he believed that the government would pull out of the organization, if it no longer served Free State interests. In making this judgement he ignored the fact that self-interest also underpinned US non-adherence to the League of Nations. Despite its inconsistent nature, the Free State involvement served US interests in that it provided the State Department with an Irish view of proceedings at assembly and committee meetings at which the US was not represented. After the September 1926 meeting, Hathaway gave Washington a detailed account of the conference based on his discussions with FitzGerald and Walshe.[76] Access to such information remained important for the US government as the self-imposed policy of exclusion from the League of Nations continued throughout the 1920s.

---

72 NARA, RG59, M580/221, 841d.00/758, Hathaway to Secretary of State, 25 March 1925; ibid., M580/222, 841d.00/7800, Hathaway to Secretary of State, 1 October 1925.   73 Ibid., 841d.00/772, Hathaway to Secretary of State, 28 May 1925.   74 Ibid., M580/223, 841d.00/868, Hathaway to Secretary of State, 26 August 1926; Quoted in Kennedy, *Ireland and the League of Nations*, p. 91. 75 See Kennedy, *Ireland and the League of Nations*, see chapters 3 and 4; G. Keown, 'Taking the world stage: creating an Irish foreign policy in the 1920s' in M. Kennedy & J. Morrison Skelly (eds), *Irish foreign policy 1919–1966: from independence to internationalism* (2000), p. 35.   76 NARA, RG59, M580/223, 841d.00/874, Hathaway to Secretary of State, 7 October 1926.   77 HHPL, Leland Harrison Papers (hereafter LHP), Box 46, August–October 1924, Harrison, 20 October 1924;

In June 1929, William Castle confirmed that '[we] do not send anyone to the regular meetings of the League itself.'[77]

On the imperial front, US interest focused on the expanding nature of the British imperial structure, particularly any moves that would distance Canada from the empire and bring it closer to the US.[78] In mid-1925, Castle believed that a break-up of the empire was inevitable but that they would come 'very gradually' and at Britain's behest.[79] This view seemed to be confirmed by Hathaway's views that the Free State government would pursue an 'aggressive policy' at the imperial conference in October 1926, in order to carve out further independence for the dominions. It was clear to him that a primary Free State aim was to achieve 'practical international independence for the dominions', but that the degree of its success would depend on the support received from South African Prime Minister Hertzog and Canadian Prime Minister Mackenzie King.[80] Although Walshe confirmed for Hathaway the absence of an agreed position between the Free State and Canada prior to the opening of the conference, Ambassador Houghton in London identified the common interests:

> There is still a lively desire on the part of the Dominions to co-operate with Britain and in this way to obtain military and naval protection and as much preference as possible in British markets. But each of the Dominions has also a very strong sense of its own importance and insists upon its own right to freedom of action ... Probably some attempt will be made to deprive Downing Street still further of interference with them.[81]

Similarly, Percy Blair, also in the London embassy, believed in early October that 'several of the Dominions are going to try to force' the autonomy issue.[82] Houghton felt that 'rows' were inevitable particularly, with Hertzog present, and that the Free State was 'not likely to remain wholly quiescent' because of Austen Chamberlain's objection to the Free State decision a few weeks earlier, in September, to stand for a seat on the League of Nations council.[83] This decision and the defeat of the Free State candidature added an edge to the Free State's separatist agenda in London which Hathaway had already sent to Washington. The Irish wanted the right of appeal to the Judicial Committee of the Privy Council, the right of dominions to fly their own flags and clarification of the role

ibid., LHP, Box 47, May–December 1926, Harrison to Cabinet, 10 December 1926; ibid., WRCP, Box 3, File 35, Castle to Kellogg, 4 June 1929.   78 B.J.C. McKercher, *The second Baldwin government and the United States, 1924–29: attitudes and diplomacy* (1984), pp. 167–9.   79 HHPL, WRCP, WRC diary, 7 July 1925.   80 *DIFP*, iii, NAI, D/T, S5337, Walshe, December 1926; NARA, RG59, M580/222, 841d.00/854, Hathaway to Secretary of State, 3 June 1926.   81 HHPL, WRCP, Box 3, file 29, Houghton to Castle, 21 October 1926.   82 Ibid., file 28, Blair to Castle, 5 October 1926.   83 Ibid., file 29, Houghton to Castle, 21 October 1926. For further on the seat controversy see Kennedy, *Ireland and the League of Nations*, pp. 82–91.

of governor general.[84] But Houghton doubted if the conference would result 'in any very definite achievements.'[85]

Following its opening, Hathaway detected a change in the level of participation by the Free State delegates in both the formal and social activities; they 'are taking their place in the empire much more frankly and openly than at the one two years ago' which had been held in the immediate aftermath of the civil war.[86] Certainly O'Higgins conducted himself as an international statesman and used the occasion to present his version of Arthur Griffith's dual monarchy proposal for Ireland and Britain. Cosgrave's contribution on the responsibility of the dominions to assist Britain in case of war was noted by Castle as facilitating agreement between the parties.[87] Even though the latter proposal failed, both Cosgrave and Hertzog contributed to the Baldwin government's concession that the dominions were autonomous entities within the British empire but with equal status and in no way subordinate to one another in any aspect of their domestic or external affairs.[88] Houghton did not see any thing radical here and he dismissed the conference's main 'accomplishment' because he took a wider view of the question, whereas Hathaway based in one of the dominions directly affected, offered a more nuanced viewpoint.[89] Not only did he recognize the significance of these gains in terms of Free State dominion status but he worried about the domestic consequences for the Cosgrave government. He believed that the outbreak of republican violence in mid–November 1926 resulted from Free State gains and subsequent Unionist 'rejoicing' at the 'good relations' between the Free State and Britain.[90]

Nevertheless, it took the US government some time to fully recognize the claim of the Free State leadership to independent control over its own foreign

84 NARA, RG59, M580/223, 841d.00/868, Hathaway to Secretary of State, 26 August 1926; ibid., M580/223, 841d.00/875, Hathaway to Secretary of State, 14 October 1926. Also he informed the State Department that this aggressive political agenda would not be matched by an economic one because imperial preference was not of 'practical concern' to the Cosgrave government and it had no interest in directing Irish emigrants to the dominions.   85 HHPL, WRCP, Box 3, file 29, Houghton to Castle, 21 October 1926.   86 NARA, RG59, M580/223, 841d.00/868, Hathaway to Secretary of State, 26 August 1926; ibid., M580/223, 841d.00/875, Hathaway to Secretary of State, 14 October 1926; ibid., 841d.00/878, Hathaway to Secretary of State, 1 November 1926.   87 Regan, *The Irish counter-revolution, 1921–1936*, pp. 266–68; HHPL, WRCP, WRC diary, 29 December 1926.   88 Quoted in McKercher, *The second Baldwin government and the United States*, p. 168; HHPL, WRCP, Box 3, file 30, Houghton to Castle, 4 December 1926.   89 HHPL, WRCP, Box 3, file 30, Houghton to Castle, 4 December 1926. Subsequently, Castle also received a report on the conference from the Australian Prime Minister Stanley M. Bruce who told him that 'the definition of the Empire status arrived at ... was nothing except a definition of what already exists.' Ibid., HHPL, WRCP, WRC diary, 29 December 1926.   90 NARA, RG59, M580/223, 841d.00/882, Hathaway to Secretary of State, 18 November 1926; ibid., 841d.00/883, Hathaway to Secretary of State, 24 November 1926. Hathaway's twenty-eight page report on the Dáil debate on the delegation's report on the imperial conference received a rating of 'excellent' from the State Department. Ibid., 841d.00/887, Carr to Hathaway, 17 January 1927. Although in the same month, two State Department minutes query the consul's categorising of his reports as 'strictly confidential', particularly as British official material was sent sometimes by the London embassy also.

affairs. For example, chapter twelve revealed that Kellogg and Grew had accepted Hackworth's legal opinion and the Foreign Office view that the Free State government had a '*de jure*' status within the empire. Castle saw this as a 'shining example of the State Department's unwillingness to tell the truth', while a junior official was in 'despair' because she believed the State Department 'never recognise anything as *de jure*'. Nevertheless, throughout the late 1920s the US government's relationship with the Free State was not the one it would have normally had with a separate international entity or with an independent international unit, even though it had accredited Smiddy as a minister plenipotentiary.[91]

State Department officials were never quite sure of the Free State's actual status given the existence of so many 'anomalies and anachronisms' in its exercise of external sovereignty as a dominion.[92] In March 1927, Castle asked Houghton to find out from the Foreign Office if Washington could deal directly with dominion governments when it came to appointing consuls. Houghton's advice that this suggestion might be 'resented' was heeded and the whole matter dropped.[93] However, the Free State government saw the appointment in early 1928 of Hathaway's replacement, Cornelius Ferris, as US consul general to Dublin as an opportunity to move forward on the consular issue at least.

In 1928, Houghton presented Ferris' commission to the British government through Foreign Secretary Austen Chamberlain, even though Sterling was in place as US minister in Dublin. According to Sterling, Patrick McGilligan, minister for External Affairs, seized upon the action as 'irregular' and expressed his 'surprise' to the British Foreign Office.[94] Irish opprobrium focused on London, where Edward Hardinge, under secretary in the Dominions Office, gloated that even after Sterling's appointment the US government preferred to 'have dealings through H[is] M[ajesty's] G[overnment] in Britain rather than direct with Dominions government.'[95] Certainly the State Department did not wish to offend the British but as Smiddy said, 'we are rightly or wrongly regarded an integral

91 NARA, RG59, M580/225, 841d.01/80, Hackworth to Kellogg, 8 December 1926; ibid., minute, PBG, 27 November 1926; ibid., Castle to Hackworth, 11 December 1926; ibid. minute Castle, 20 December 1926; ibid., Grew to Davis, Polk et al, 12 January 1927; HHPL, WRCP, WRC diary, 10 January 1927. 92 The other anomalies related to a) the claim of the British government to control legislation of other dominion legislatures, b) the assumption in international treaties and conventions that the signature of the British plenipotentiary appointed on the sole advice of the British government bound the dominions, c) the role of the governor general in the dominions, d) the British insistence that dominions' laws applied only to the territorial area, e) the exercise of legislative authority by the British parliament over that of the dominions, f) the alteration of royal titles to reflect the separation of the Free State and United Kingdom and g) the position regarding the dominion governments' right of appeal to the Judicial Committee of the Privy Council. *DIFP*, iii, UCDA, P35/184, Memorandum by the Irish Free State delegation to the 1926 Imperial Conference, 'Existing anomalies in the British Commonwealth of Nations, London, 2 November 1926. 93 HHPL, WRCP, Box 3, file 31, Houghton to Castle, 3 March 1927. 94 NARA, RG59, M580/225, 841d.01/88, Sterling to Secretary of State, 2 May 1928. 95 The National Archives, London (hereafter TNA), Dominions Office (hereafter DO), 35/51, DO minute, 17 February 1928.

part of the British Commonwealth of Nations.'[96] The issue arose again in the context of Free State involvement in the Treaty for the Renunciation of War and the Kellogg–Briand pact.

A more reassuring note was struck in Hathaway's reports on another aspect of US foreign policy when the Free State government was informally asked by the State Department for its attitude on US adherence to the Permanent Court of International Justice. The Free State government instructed Smiddy to convey its support for the application.[97] However, US supporters of the World Court never managed to get congressional approval for membership. Consequently, the US did not participate in the World Court until after 1945, when the United Nations charter made it an integral part of the United Nations Organization.[98]

Coolidge was more successful in other multilateral aspects of his foreign policy. His twin aims of preventing war and saving money by reducing expenditure on naval building, particularly cruisers, led him on, 10 February 1927, to convene a conference in Geneva between the principal naval powers as a follow-up to the Washington naval conference of 1924. Initially he did not envisage a full-scale conference but simply a gathering of the four principal naval powers, Britain, Japan, Italy and France, in Geneva. Nor did he expect these countries to disarm by reducing their naval capabilities but rather that they would limit construction within agreed maximum limits.[99] Even though the Free State did not have a navy,

---

96 The matter of British government control of the machinery that issued exequaturs, full powers and commissions for consuls was raised again at the 1930 imperial conference. *DIFP*, iii, NAI, D/FA, Unregistered papers, Preliminary note on the 1930 imperial conference by the Department of External Affairs, September 1930. Quoted in Keown, 'Creating an Irish foreign policy in the 1920s', p. 35; *DIFP*, iii, NAI, D/FA, EA, 231/1/1929, Smiddy to FitzGerald, 5 April 1927.   97 Ibid., M580/222, 841d.00/836, Hathaway to Secretary of State, 1 March 1926; NAI, D/EA, 227/81, Kiernan to FitzGerald, 26 June 1926.   98 J.E. Findling, *Dictionary of American diplomatic history* (1980), pp. 380–1. Free State newspaper criticism of US policy in Panama, Nicaragua and Mexico in January 1927 as 'undisguised imperialism' was dismissed by Hathaway as 'of too little significance.' Thomas Bowman's report from Belfast in February 1927, provided the opposition view from the Catholic *Irish News* that focused on the plight of the Mexican Catholics. On the one hand, there was the US government's threatened military intervention in Mexico to protect US oil interests, to end President Calles' attacks on Mexican Catholics and to thwart the spread of bolshevism. But on the other, it was hoped that there would not be US military intervention 'for the sake of Christianity or humanity.' While the criticism in the *Irish Truth* in March 1927 that the Monroe Doctrine had grown out of all recognition but was needed to thwart 'poaching strangers.' Neither viewpoint induced the Free State government to condemn the US government's policy in southern America. In 1928, following the appointment of Dwight Morrow and resolution of the situation through negotiation, the Free State government condemned religious persecution in Mexico. Hathaway detected also an anti-American strain in newspaper reports but he did not think it widespread and attributed it to 'lazy editorial writing.' NARA, RG59, M580/223, 841d.00/891, Hathaway to Secretary of State, 10 January 1927; ibid., 841d.00/902, Hathaway to Secretary of State, 14 March 1927; ibid., 841d.00/896, Bowman to Secretary of State, 1 February 1927; W.I. Cohen, 'America and the world in the 1920s' in J.E. Haynes (ed.), *Calvin Coolidge and the Coolidge era: essays on the history of the 1920s* (1998) pp. 235–6; NARA, RG59, M580/223, 841d.00/908, Hathaway to Secretary of State, 14 April 1927.   99 McKercher, *The second Baldwin government and the United States*, pp. 60–1.

Hathaway reported that Coolidge's disarmament moves received 'unusual publicity' in the Dublin newspaper but he felt that the coverage reflected British concerns more than Irish ones.[1] Three aspects to the announcement should have merited Irish interest, firstly, would the Free State government be invited to attend separately from the British government? Secondly, what effect, if any, would a possible reduction in British naval units have on Irish security? Thirdly, how would the conference affect the disarmament activities of the League of Nations?

In February 1927, the British government consulted with the dominions' governments prior to replying to Coolidge's proposal but Hathaway worried that the department of External Affairs had not heard anything yet.[2] On 28 February, the British government's official reply to Coolidge's proposals stated that the Free State had not replied to the British inquiry. Hathaway pursued the matter with Walshe and learnt that administrative blunders in London and Dublin and Walshe's illness delayed it reaching the cabinet table. By the time it did, the British reply to Washington had been sent. So on 7 March, Hathaway reported that the matter was not given further consideration but he went on to explain that FitzGerald was quite unable to see how naval reduction affected the Free State or why the British government had consulted with it. Nonetheless, FitzGerald reassured Hathaway that the Free State government 'would wish the proposals well' but 'practically ... it was a matter between the United States and Great Britain and not of serious concern to any of the Dominions.' FitzGerald indicated that his government was more concerned about the gap in communications between the US and Free State governments revealed by Coolidge's proposals than about their content.[3]

The Cosgrave government finally came around in late March to discussing its response to the Coolidge proposals at FitzGerald's instigation. He believed that Free State participation at the Geneva conference should be 'avoided altogether' or, if this was not possible, 'only representation as a distinct entity' should be accepted. The main reasons for this caution were firstly, that if the dominions continued to allow themselves to be consulted about the strength of the British navy, and take part in conferences for its reduction they could not so easily continue 'to disclaim all interest' when asked to pay for its upkeep and secondly, if the dominions' governments were 'once regarded as part-owners of the British fleet and the British army' they would not only, in FitzGerald's opinion, find it hard 'to act as independent nations for any purpose internationally' but they would lose their 'only influence in the League as small unarmed nations'.[4]

---

1 NARA, RG59, M580/223, 841d.00/897, Hathaway to Secretary of State, 14 February 1927. 2 Ibid., 841d.00/898, Hathaway to Secretary of State, 21 February 1927. 3 Ibid., 841d.00/901, Hathaway to Secretary of State, 7 March 1927. 4 NAI, D/T, S4714A, Walshe to O'Hegarty, 8 March 1927. The Free State government had already refused on 28 January 1926 a British invitation to join a subcommittee on disarmament because it would not serve any 'useful purpose.' NAI, D/T, S14714A, Ibid., Governor General to Amery, 28 January 1926.

FitzGerald viewed Coolidge's disarmament proposals purely in economic and constitutional terms and the implications of naval disarmament for Free State coastal defence were never raised, even though there were discussions on this between the Free State government and the Dominions' Office from late 1926 onwards.[5] Disarmament was welcomed for what it promised globally not for its domestic implications.

The Free State government agreed with FitzGerald and both options – abstention and separate Dominions' representation – were communicated to London on 28 March, along with a statement of 'complete agreement' with the principle of disarmament. If individual representation was not possible then the Free State government believed that the dominion governments should abstain from attending.[6]

The suggestion that all five dominion governments be represented at the conference was not unwelcome to the British, whose senior officials were already discussing the probability of the conference's failure and how to deflect blame from Britain. On 12 February 1927, Ronald Campbell in the League of Nations department in the Foreign Office, felt that the British position was more complex than that of the US. The British government accepted the US wish to achieve naval equality but it wanted the Americans to acknowledge that Britain needed a substantial cruiser fleet because of its 'special needs', namely its 'insular position, its global commitments, and its dependence on naval forces to protect sea-borne commerce and defend imperial lines of communication.' The US position was seen to be much simpler and was dictated by domestic political forces. Campbell wrote that Coolidge 'has much to gain from a naval conference, whatever the measure of its success'. McKercher states that ultimately the US leadership wanted naval parity with Britain so that in the event of another war it could enforce the freedom of the seas for US commerce.[7]

5 G.R. Sloan, *The geopolitics of Anglo-Irish relations in the twentieth century* (1997), p. 181. Under articles six and seven of the 1921 Anglo-Irish treaty, the defence by sea of Ireland and Britain were the legal responsibility of the British navy. This enabled the British government to retain possession of Queenstown, Lough Swilly and Berehaven, along with storage facilities at Haulbowline Island and Rathmullen. Article six also provided for a review of these arrangements to take place five years after 1921, with a view to the Free State government sharing in the responsibility for coastal defence. However, between 1926 and 1929, it proved impossible for both governments to agree to hold a formal conference about the handing over of the ports to the Free State, the technical arrangements for coastal defence or the attendant financial obligations. Instead contact occurred at an informal level. In March 1929, Smiddy the newly appointed Free State high commissioner in London, complained to McGilligan that he was not informed about some of it. See NAI, D/T, S4798, Proceedings of sub-committee to examine details of suggested mine-sweeping service, 26 April 1927; ibid., D/EA, OhÉigeartuigh to Whiskard, 8 February 1927; ibid., D/T, S20A, Smiddy to McGilligan, 5 March 1929.   6 NAI, D/T, S4714A, Governor General to Amery, 28 March 1927.
7 McKercher, *The second Baldwin government*, pp. 61, 64, 65. Since late 1924, the Foreign and Colonial offices and Ambassador Howard had discussed the quandary of dominions' representation at any future disarmament conference and eventually favoured the attendance of a British empire delegation along with separate dominion governments. *BDFA,*, ix, The Washington conference and its aftermath, 1921–5, 'Memorandum respecting the issue of invitations for the dominions to attend

The divergent position of the two sides did not suddenly emerge in Geneva. Ambassador Howard detailed the propaganda campaign against Britain waged by the 'American Great Navyites' in the US press after the 1924 Washington conference.[8] On the specific issue of cruisers, the differences emerged in early March 1927 during the preparations for the Geneva conference.[9] For the British side, therefore, the prospect of having five separate dominion delegations under the umbrella of the British commonwealth, with each supporting the British position, would give a reality to its 'special needs' argument. Howard was asked to raise the issue with the State Department and on 11 April, he indicated that the Geneva meeting would take the form of a 'regular conference.' FitzGerald wanted a separate invitation from the US government for the Free State government and both Smiddy and Howard were instructed to secure it.[10] The matter did not cause discussion in the State Department where Kellogg presumed that the dominions would be sending 'fully empowered representatives' to Geneva.[11] FitzGerald returned to the Free State government on 18 May for a decision on whether the Free State should be represented. He outlined the advantages of participation:

> [T]his conference is very important from the constitutional point of view ... For the first time – if they are held to their agreement – the British will sign an international instrument of a purely political character on a basis of complete equality with the Dominions. The technical side of the discussions cannot, in any case, be influenced by the presence of the Saorstát representative, but for the purpose of maintaining and advancing our constitutional position representation is, in the Minister's view, essential.[12]

He had not changed his views and the government agreed and appointed Ftizgerald and Costello to represent it in Geneva on 12 June.[13] Having demonstrated its independence within the commonwealth, the Free State, and indeed other dominions' governments, were then asked by the British government to agree a common position before the opening of the conference.[14] Again FitzGerald viewed this through the narrow lens of status. He advised acceptance of the technical proposals which accorded with the disarmament principle and, 'as we have no navy, we are not interested in the precise technical effects of their application.' But he insisted that this 'assent' on the general principles would have to

---

a disarmament conference', 10 October, 1925, pp. 314–15; ibid., 4 November 1925, pp. 315–17; ibid., Chamberlain to Howard, 25 November 1925, p. 319.   8 Howard, Lord, of Penrith, *Theatre of life: life seen from the stalls, 1905–36*, 2 vols (1935), ii, p. 531.   9 McKercher, *The second Baldwin government*, p. 67.   10 NAI, D/T, S4714B, Amery to Healy, 11 April 1927 (seen by Cosgrave on the same day); TNA, DO35/26, Healy to Armery, 21 April 1927l.   11 *DIFP*, iii, NAI, D/FA, LN 4/7, Walshe to Oskar D. Skelton, 11 May 1927.   12 NAI, D/T, S4714B, Walshe to O'Hegarty, 18 May 1927.   13 Ibid., Secretary, Executive Council to Walshe, 19 May 1927; ibid., FitzGerald to Amery, 19 May 1927; ibid., Cab. 3/1, 24 June 1927, item no. 1.   14 NAI, D/T, S4714B, Amery to Governor General, 2 June 1927.

be communicated to the conference by the Free State representatives and not by the British.[15] The theme continued in FitzGerald's instructions to Michael MacWhite, the Free State representative at the League of Nations, who attended the opening sessions. He was told that, as Irish interest was purely 'constitutional', he should not to make any technical suggestions or modifications, since they might be used in the future by the British authorities as an argument to secure a financial contribution from the Free State toward its coastal defence; he should 'act as a silent member' unless the constitutional position of the Dominions as separate units for the purposes of representation was at issue.[16]

The delegations, including naval experts, met in Geneva on 20 June 1927. The main point of difference between the British and US sides was that of tonnage ratios for cruisers. The British delegation insisted on the doctrine of 'absolute need', based on its defence needs, while the US adhered to the doctrine of 'relative need.' Both groups disagreed on the priority of discussing the number of cruisers or tonnage limits.[17] By 4 July, Kevin O'Higgins, who had replaced FitzGerald in the delegation, reported to Cosgrave that he intended leaving Geneva as there was nothing which called for his attention and the negotiations were likely to be protracted. If an agreement emerged he would return to sign on behalf of the Free State.[18] O'Higgins did not return to the Geneva conference due to his assassination. From Washington, William Castle viewed the enforced postponement of the plenary session as giving the delegates time to 'cool off and talk a little sense.'[19] The discussions became increasingly difficult and attitudes hardened; on 14 July, Castle recorded: 'the conference in Geneva is not going well. I am worried about it only because our navy now seems to be taking an attitude as intransigent as the British.'[20] The third and final plenary session was set for 4 August. Each of the delegations was permitted to make a final statement of its limitation policies.

15 Ibid., Walshe to O'Hegarty, 10 June 1927.   16 UCDA, Michael MacWhite papers (hereafter MMP), P194/241, Walshe to MacWhite, 17 June 1927. Walshe was unsure as to when FitzGerald and Costello would arrive in Geneva. Kevin O'Higgins replaced Desmond FitzGerald as minister for External Affairs on 23 June 1927 after the general election on 9 June 1927. According to Hathaway, this change resulted less from FitzGerald's performance and was more in line with the practice of other dominion governments to give External Affairs more prominence by attaching it to the 'most powerful figure' in the cabinet. O'Higgins and Costello eventually arrived in Geneva on 27 June, one week after the conference opened. O'Higgins was assassinated on 10 July 1927 and replaced by Cosgrave as acting minister until Patrick McGilligan's appointment. NARA, RG59, M580/223, 841d.00/914, Hathaway to Secretary of State, 27 June 1927.   17 B.J.C. McKercher, *Esmé Howard: a diplomatic biography* (1989), p. 307; NARA, RG59, M580/223, 841d.00/965, Sterling to Secretary of State, 6 December 1929. The French government refused to participate in the Geneva naval conference.   18 NAI, D/T, S4714B, O'Higgins to Cosgrave 4 July 1927.   19 The opening of the next plenary session was postponed due to O'Higgins' death. Castle believed that this was 'probably a fortunate thing since this plenary session might well have been the last.' He attended the requiem mass held for O'Higgins in Washington on 13 July which he described as a 'really beautiful mass.' HHPL, WRCP, WRC diary, 12, 14 July 1927.   20 HHPL, WRCP, WRC diary, 14 July 1927.

Walshe outlined the Free State position to Diarmuid O'Hegarty, secretary to the government, in late June: 'Provided the constitutional position of the Saorstát was rigidly respected and safeguarded the Saorstát government was ready to support the technical proposals of the British government for the limitation of naval armaments.'[21] There was no shift from this position throughout the summer and MacWhite supervised Free State interests in an almost irreproachable way. Three days before the final session, the dominions' delegates met in Geneva, where William Bridgeman, first lord of the Admiralty, who led the British delegation with Robert Cecil, emphasized the importance of the 'united front' and requested that either they speak individually at the final meeting or empower him to do so. MacWhite met with the other dominions' delegates and drafted a letter to Bridgeman that supported the latter suggestion. On the same day, before it was to be sent, MacWhite cabled Dublin for authorization.[22] He did not receive a reply until 2 August, by which time the letter had been sent to Bridgeman. Walshe's reply reiterated the Irish opposition to collective representation: 'our special interests at home and in the United States make it essential you should speak for Saorstát [Free State] ... Saorstát representative alone can speak for Saorstát'. He emphasized that O'Higgins had urged the Canadians and South Africans to adopt the same position. Irrespective of whether the other dominions agreed or not, MacWhite was instructed to inform the final plenary session that the Free State government regretted that an agreement was not possible and to express the hope that another opportunity would emerge to reach an agreement to limit and eventually fully disarm.[23]

The telegram arrived too late for MacWhite, who had to explain to his dominion colleagues and Bridgeman that he would be departing from the agreed position. Bridgeman initially adopted a tough stance, to the effect that he had a letter that would 'speak for us', but agreed to MacWhite speaking after him. The Irish representative was the only dominions' delegate to do so and his statement accorded with Walshe's instructions. MacWhite who was not always in good standing with Walshe, may have attempted to compensate for his mistake by commenting subsequently that his statement made a 'profound impression on the audience, not so much because of what it contained, but of what it implied and, particularly, because I stood apart from Great Britain and the Dominions.' He stated that the Swiss press noted his separate contribution and a comment from a Japanese jurist attending the conference to the effect that the conference has been a failure for all except the Irish who had used it 'to assert their international status, in which they have fully succeeded.' MacWhite did not refer to the failure of the conference, the unwillingness of the Americans and British to yield to the other and the damage inflicted on Anglo–American relations. But he believed that US–Irish relations emerged stronger from the conference because

21 NAI, D/T, S471B, Walshe to O'Hegarty, 30 June 1927.   22 DIFP, iii, pp. 144–6, NAI, D/FA, LN, 4/7, MacWhite to Walshe, 5 August 1927.   23 Ibid., Walshe to MacWhite, 2 August 1927.

the US delegation, led by Hugh Gibson, interpreted 'our attitude as being favourable to themselves.'[24]

Naval construction continued apace, although the 1930 London naval conference, at which the Free State was also represented, set tonnage limits on various classes of smaller ships but resulted in practically no naval arms reduction. Sterling reported to the State Department later in 1929 that the representation of the Free State at the London conference would be 'purely academic as it has no navy' and still relied on Britain undertaking the coastal defence of the Free State pending the formal review of the 1921 Anglo-Irish treaty.[25] Consequently, the Free State approach to this attempt at naval disarmament was more constitutional than security driven and continued the position it had held in Geneva in 1927. Within one year, Coolidge's foreign policy gave the Cosgrave government another opportunity to illustrate its independence.

The final major international policy initiative of the Coolidge government was the Kellogg–Briand pact also known as the Pact of Paris. Aristide Briand, the French prime minister, first raised the idea of outlawing war 'as an instrument of national policy' in April 1927. Initially he sought a bilateral Franco–American treaty and in June 1927 he transmitted to Kellogg the draft of a pact of perpetual friendship between France and the United States and a joint renunciation of war as an 'instrument of their national policy towards each other.' The 'outlawry movement', as an early Kellogg biographer described it, had been gathering force in the US since 1918, alongside the more prominent peace movement. The groups demanded that the Coolidge administration respond to Briand's proposal.[26] Other observers saw Kellogg's plan as a way of securing the 'peace vote' for the Republicans with the presidential conventions due.[27] There was much opposition. Bryn-Jones, writing in 1937, described the situation as follows:

> The government was somewhat apprehensive. There were some members of Congress who were opposed to the idea, others who regarded it as fantastic, while in many quarters there lingered a suspicion that this was an astute move on the part of France to involve the United States in the complications of European politics. Within the government, too, there was some tacit opposition to be overcome.[28]

By August 1927, the cautious attitude began to change in certain quarters. The failure at Geneva, following from the collapse of the Locarno treaties and the Geneva protocol, had a 'profound effect' on Kellogg. He came to view the problem of securing peace in a different light and he moved towards the idea of a multilateral treaty renouncing war. If agreement could be reached to outlaw war

24 Ibid., MacWhite to Walshe, 5 August 1927. 25 McKercher, *Esmé Howard*, p. 307; NARA, RG59, M580/223, 841d.00/965, Sterling to Secretary of State, 6 December 1929. 26 D. Bryn-Jones, *Frank B. Kellogg: a biography* (1937), p. 225. 27 *Gaelic American*, 16 June 1928. 28 Bryn-Jones, *Frank B. Kellogg*, p. 227.

then the way was opened for other agreements, including armaments.[29] Borah, the classic isolationist, believed that a multilateral treaty offered a more effective way to keep the peace than the League of Nations. By the end of 1927 Coolidge had come around to this idea, as had the US public, and Kellogg suggested to Briand that the pact be broadened in scope to include all nations.[30] After an exchange of letters with the French government, the US government sent a preliminary draft of a treaty to Britain, Germany, Italy and Japan on 13 April 1928. On the issue of dominions' representation, Kellogg adopted a different approach. He told Esmé Howard in Washington that he would not speak to the Canadian and Irish Free State ministers on the subject because he realized that this was a matter of 'imperial concern to be dealt with by the British embassy.'[31]

The Free State government was consulted by the Dominions Office on 12 May and Sterling reported that it 'voiced its whole-hearted approval, without reservation' of the proposed pact for the renunciation of war. He went further, saying that the 'press and the country as a whole are enthusiastic' in its favour.[32] The Dominions' Office wanted a swift reply from Dublin but the department of External Affairs consulted with the Canadian government, which approved the treaty but could not accept the invitation to sign until the dominion governments were issued a separate invitation. External Affairs Assistant Secretary Seán Murphy recommended to his minister that 'in view of the Canadian reply, I don't think we can do otherwise than support them in their demand for a separate invitation.' In turn, McGilligan recommended to the government that the Free State's reply should be 'along the same lines.'[33] In his reply to London on 14 May, McGilligan suggested that the Free State should appoint its own plenipotentiary rather than have the British government sign the treaty on its behalf and also intimated that they were prepared to make an immediate reply if the US government made a direct request for the Free State government's views. This led Sterling to telephone the State Department on 15 May to inform it that these suggestions were a 'political move only in an endeavour to extend the scope of their dominion status and are no real obstacle to their support.'[34] On 24 May, he clarified this, saying that should the US government 'see fit ... to negotiate directly with the Free State on the matter, it would greatly please the *amour-propre* of the country and receive even more enthusiastic support if it were possible.'[35]

29 Ibid., p. 211.   30 R. Sobel, *Coolidge: an American enigma* (1998), pp. 354–7; NAI, D/T, S5637, External Affairs, 10 May 1928.   31 Quoted in NAI, D/T, S5637, External Affairs, 10 May 1928. 32 NARA, RG59, M580/225, 841d.01/85, Sterling to Secretary of State, 15 May 1928; ibid., M580/223, 841d.00/942, Sterling to Secretary of State, 24 May 1928.   33 NAI, D/EA, 27/11, External Affairs, 13 May 1928; ibid., Secretary of State, Canada to Walshe, 12 May 1928; ibid., Murphy, 12 May 1928. McGilligan then informed Ottawa 'we have sent a reply in similar terms.' Ibid., External Affairs to External Affairs, Ottawa, 15 May 1928.   34 NARA, RG59, M580/225, 841d.01/85, Sterling to Secretary of State, 15 May 1928.   35 Ibid., 841d.00/942, Sterling to Secretary of State, 24 May 1928.

Despite the Free State government's blanket approval for the proposed pact, there was also a security dimension, which Sterling explained to the State Department in May:

> It is only natural that any pact which would result in lessening the chances of war should be welcomed in the Free State, which with its exposed geographic position and lack of adequate defence make it a vulnerable prey to the Great Powers; and added to this is the ever present fear that in the event of another Republican war, Great Britain in assuming the defence of Ireland would again secure a lasting foothold here.[36]

In attempting to provide a wider context to the Free State response, the US minister showed a strong understanding of delicate domestic issues. His view on Irish defence arrangements had been informed by a recent review of the Free State army completed on 28 April by Lieutenant Colonel John C. MacArthur, assistant military attaché, who was based in the US embassy in London. Not surprisingly he concluded, as did Sterling, that the army was in an 'emerging stage' with room for improvement in almost every aspect of its activities. He also accepted Minister for Defence FitzGerald's view that the Free State was defensively vulnerable to an attack from any hostile nation.[37] These concerns influenced Sterling's perception of the Free State position on the treaty but did not feature in the Free State correspondence on the matter.

On 16 May, two days after the Free State reply had been sent to London, Smiddy was instructed that 'if asked [by the State Department], we will be glad to participate' in the treaty.[38] The Cosgrave government had also decided that if a separate invitation was issued, it should be transmitted through the US minister in Dublin and not through the Dominions' Office.[39] Smiddy was not consulted by the State Department, which received a copy of the British reply on 19 May, in which it was stated that to assure imperial unity and as a precondition of the Baldwin government's participation, the dominions and Indian governments would have to be invited separately.[40] Kellogg accepted this suggestion because it would broaden further the base of support for the pact.[41] On 22 May, Sterling sent a note to McGilligan extending an invitation from his government to the Dublin government to become one of the original parties to the proposed treaty.[42] The other four dominions' governments were issued with similar invi-

36 Ibid., M580/223, 841d.00/942, Sterling to Secretary of State, 24 May 1928.   37 Ibid., M580/240, 841d.20/1, 'The Irish Free State (Military)', 28 April 1928 in Sterling to Secretary of State, 11 May 1928. MacArthur noted 'the American mission' group of six Irish officers who were graduates of the US Command and Staff School at Fort Leavenworth, the Infantry School at Fort Benning and the School of Fire at Fort Sill. Ibid.   38 NAI, D/EA, 27/11, Walshe to Smiddy, 16 May 1928.   39 Ibid., D/T, S5637, Extract from minutes of Cabinet meeting, Cab. 4/31, 17 May 1928.   40 McKercher, *The second Baldwin government and the United States*, p. 141.   41 HHPL, Frank B. Kellogg Papers (hereafter FBKP), roll 2, Kellogg to Sterling, 21 May 1928.   42 NAI,

tations on the same day, as were the governments in Czechoslovakia, Belgium and Poland. The Free State government considered the matter on 29 May and approved McGilligan's draft reply which was communicated to Sterling the following day.[43] Along with outlining the government's warm welcome for the treaty and praising the US government's role in advancing the maintenance of general peace, it noted that there was nothing in the treaty that was 'inconsistent with the covenant of the League of Nations.'[44] Nor did it refer to the British suggestion that the treaty should include a reservation 'to the effect that members of the Commonwealth retain liberty to come actively to the assistance of another member in the event of emergency.' The government considered that any references to the commonwealth were 'unnecessary and undesirable' and it did not reply to the British note until 12 July 1928.[45] Other British 'reservations' attracted the attention of Fianna Fáil leader, Eamon de Valera.

Sterling reported in early June that Chamberlain's reply to the US invitation had evoked 'dark suspicions' in de Valera's 'mind' which led him to put a 'potentially embarrassing question to the government.'[46] On 23 May, the opposition leader asked Cosgrave firstly, if his government had been invited to participate in the treaty, secondly, whether his government was aware of the terms of the British reply before it was sent and thirdly, what was its attitude to the reservations included in paragraph ten of the British reply. Chamberlain's reply to Kellogg had noted that that there were certain regions of the world in which the British government would not tolerate 'interference.'[47] Paragraph ten became known as the 'British Monroe Doctrine' and there was no doubt but that reference was to Egypt and the Suez canal.[48]

De Valera chose to interpret paragraph ten differently. During the adjournment debate on 31 May, he stated:

> The matter is a very big one for our country. These reservations imply a right on the part of the Britain to say that wherever British interests, wherever British imperialism is affected, wherever they have interests, that they shall have a right to use war, that this right should be recognised by us, and by every signatory to this proposed pact ... then it goes further and it is used as an excuse by imperialistic nations to go in and interfere with the domestic affairs of these countries ... I think that our country, which has suffered from such, ought, in the most definite and explicit manner possible, to indicate that it does not stand for anything of that particular kind.[49]

D/EA, 27/11, Sterling to McGilligan, 22 May 1928, text of note; HHPL, FBKP, roll 2, Kellogg to Smiddy, 22 May 1928.   43 NAI, D/T, S5637, Extract from cabinet minutes, Cab. 4/33, 29 May 1928; HHPL, FBKP, roll 2, McGilligan to Kellogg, 30 May 1928.   44 NAI, D/T, S5637, McGilligan to Sterling, 30 May 1928.   45 Ibid., S5637B, McGilligan to Amery, 12 July 1928.   46 NARA, RG59, M580/223, 841d.oo/943, Sterling to Secretary of State, 7 June 1928.   47 *Parliamentary Debates Dáil Éireann (PDDÉ)*, xxiii, 23 May 1928, 1797–1800.   48 McKercher, *The second Baldwin government and the United States*, p. 114.   49 *PDDÉ*, xxiii, 31 May 1928, 2485.

McGilligan replied to de Valera that the government was no more interested in the British reply than it was in the French or Italian replies and confirmed that the Free State government 'alone had authority to speak for itself.'[50] Sterling reported de Valera's objections as simply an attempt to embarrass the government. But he felt that McGilligan 'ably handled' the matter.[51] De Valera's criticism did not stand in the way of Free State support for the original treaty or the revised version that was circulated in late June. Kellogg explained the changes to Smiddy on 23 June and the Irish minister indicated that his government 'would be delighted' to sign it. Five days later, Sterling confirmed that this revised version, which now included the dominion governments as original signatories, had been received 'exceedingly well' by the Free State government and press. On 16 July, Sterling forwarded the Irish reply to Washington and on the same day Chamberlain handed Atherton, in the US embassy in London, copies of British, Australian, New Zealand, South African and Indian acceptances.[52] Four days later, in addition to Britain, India and all the dominions, Germany, Japan, and France had accepted the revised shorter treaty.[53] The outstanding matters centred on the signature and ratification of the pact, both of which were required for it to come into operation. Kellogg was willing to go to Paris to sign the treaty with the European foreign ministers. During the following weeks arrangements were put in place for the signing in the Quai d'Orsay in Paris on 27 August. But before that event, the Free State administration benefited from a further deterioration in Anglo–American relations and found itself in the middle of an international contretemps.[54]

The normal procedure for signing international agreements was for the minister for External Affairs to sign on behalf of the government. Kellogg expected other foreign ministers to attend and, accordingly, McGilligan's name had been sent on 31 July to the Dominions' Office in London with a request for the king to issue him with full powers to sign the pact in Paris on 27 August.[55] However, the matter was re-opened. Once Sterling heard the news that the pact was to be signed he cabled his congratulations to Kellogg on 22 July, and asked him to visit

50 Ibid., 2488–9.   **51** NARA, RG59, M580/223, 841d.00/943, Sterling to Secretary of State, 7 June 1928. Support for the treaty was sent on 29 May to the government by the Irish section of the International League for Peace and Freedom and by the Dublin Yearly Meeting of the Religious Society of Friends. NAI, D/FA, 27/11, Bennett and Flynn to Cosgrave, 29 May; ibid., Wigham to Cosgrave, 21 May 1928.   **52** HHPL, FBKP, roll 2, State Department minute, 23 June 1928; ibid., Sterling to Kellogg, 28 June 1928; ibid., State Department (revised treaty) to Dublin, 20 June 1928; ibid., State Department memo., 6 July 1928; ibid., NAI, D/EA, 27/11, McGilligan to Sterling, 14 July 1928; HHPL, FBKP, roll 2, Sterling to Kellogg, 16 July 1928; ibid., Atherton to Kellogg, 16 July 1928.   **53** See, L.E. Ellis, *Frank B. Kellogg and American foreign relations, 1925–1929* (1961), pp. 207–9. Kellogg did not want a treaty so burdened with reservations as to be useless. He kept the British and French satisfied by including a body of additional documentation with the treaty. Ibid., p. 207.   **54** For further see F.M. Carroll, 'Protocol and international politics, 1928: the Secretary of State goes to Ireland', 45–57.   **55** HHPL, FBKP, roll 33, Kellogg to Borah, 16 July 1926; NAI, D/FA, 27/11, McGilligan to Amery, 17 August 1928.

Ireland during his trip to Europe as it would be a 'great courtesy' to the Free State.[56] Sterling's suggestion carried some weight, as he had worked with Kellogg during his tenure as counsellor in the London embassy and remained close personal friends with the secretary and William Castle. Dorothy Sterling and Clara Kellogg were also close friends.[57]

The idea was not new and had received Coolidge's imprimatur. Smiddy had suggested a presidential visit as far back as 1924 but Cosgrave raised it with Kellogg and Coolidge during his official visit to the US between 19 January and 3 February 1928.[58] Sterling mentioned it again to Kellogg in late April 1928 but the secretary was too busy with the treaty negotiations.[59] He declined a further formal invitation from the Free State government, delivered by Smiddy on 6 July, on the grounds that he could not leave Washington during the course of the negotiations on the treaty.[60]

The subsequent resolution of these problems combined with Kellogg's willingness to sign the treaty in Paris and Coolidge's support for a return visit to the Free State, cleared the way for the first official visit to the Free State by a foreign statesman.[61] Kellogg asked Coolidge on 13 July if he could absent himself from Washington for three weeks to attend the ceremonies in Paris.[62] He then told Houghton, on 28 July, 'I ought to go to Ireland for a day or two ... I cannot well go to Ireland without also going to Great Britain.'[63] Subsequently, provisional arrangements were made for the Irish and English trips to take place between 27 August and 4 September and Kellogg wrote to his wife on 1 August

56 HHPL, FBKP, roll 33, Sterling to Kellogg, 22 July 1928.   57 See HHPL, WRCP, Box 8; Bryn-Jones, *Frank B. Kellogg*, p. 269; *New York Times*, 15 September 1925; NAI, D/T, S4529, Smiddy to McGilligan, 9 January 1928.   58 NAI, D/EA, 29/192, Smiddy to FitzGerald, 2 July 1924; *DIFP*, iii, NAI, DT, S4529, Extract from Cabinet minutes, 13 December 1927; Bryn-Jones, *Frank B. Kellogg*, p. 269.   59 HHPL, WRCP, Box 8, File: Ireland, 1924–31, Castle to Sterling, 26 May 1928; HHPL, FBKP, roll 32, Sterling to Kellogg, 26 April 1928, 2 June 1928; ibid., Kellogg to Cosgrave, 2 June 1928. Cosgrave's 'pilgrimage', as Wainright Abbott, the second secretary in Dublin, described it to Kellogg, incorporated visits to Chicago, Philadelphia, New York and Washington, where he met with Irish-American political and business groups and individuals. He was accompanied by O'Hegarty, Walshe, FitzGerald and also they made a short trip to Ottawa. He also visited the Ford plant in Detroit on 29 January and found time to attend a dinner hosted by Mrs Joseph Leiter, Sterling's sister-in-law. Cosgrave's speech at the Drake Hotel in Chicago was broadcast over national radio on 21 January. He received an honorary degree from the Catholic University of America in Washington where he had a formal lunch with Coolidge and his cabinet and later a private meeting with Coolidge. Castle organized these meetings and detailed two Irish-American secret service agents to Cosgrave during the visit. Cosgrave did not visit Boston because Smiddy feared a 'hostile reception' and it was opposed by officials in the State Department, the National City Bank in Boston and other 'reliable' authorities. In New York he met with the Bond Club of Wall Street that consisted of the 'men who direct the investments of Wall Street.' Ibid., 841d.00/938 Abbott to Secretary of State, 30 January 1928; *DIFP*, iii, NAI, DT, S4529, Smiddy to McGilligan, 9 January 1928; *DIFP*, iii, NAI, D/T, S4529, Smiddy to McGilligan, 9 January 1928.   60 HHPL, FBKP, roll 2, State Department memo., 6 July 1928.   61 Ibid., roll 33, Kellogg to Borah, 16 July 1928.   62 Bryn-Jones, *Frank B. Kellogg*, p. 269; Ellis, *Frank B. Kellogg*, p. 209.   63 HHPL, FBKP, roll 33, Kellogg to Houghton, 28 July 1928.

that the Navy Department had placed the USS *Detroit* at their disposal to fit in two days in each country.[64]

In early August, there were was a separate development that worsened Anglo–American relations and threatened Kellogg's trip to Europe. Following the failure of the Geneva conference, the League of Nations Preparatory Commission for the Disarmament Conference continued the naval disarmament discussions with a US participant. There was no progress as both the US and British representatives remained at loggerheads over the key issue of the number and size of cruisers. However, the British and the French governments resolved their differences on these same issues in early summer 1928. It was this agreement which an ill Austen Chamberlain inadvertently announced in the House of Commons on 30 July.[65] The details were not communicated to Kellogg until 31 July and on 2 August, he instructed Ray Atherton in London to get clarification of the announcement from the Foreign Office. On the following day, he wrote to Coolidge in Wisconsin asking permission to visit Ireland and take up the Navy Department's offer of the use of the *Detroit*. He wrote 'I do not know how you feel about it. In view of the number of Irish in this country, it might be a courteous thing to do.'[66] Coolidge replied on 6 August, 'Please use your own judgement as to going to Dublin and as to using a cruiser.'[67] Three days later, Kellogg confirmed to Sterling that he would visit Dublin and asked if Cosgrave would be in Paris to sign the treaty, saying that he would return via London 'as I am afraid my failure to do so would be noticed.'[68]

By this time, however, US reactions to Chamberlain's announcement were beginning to materialize. Ray Atherton left R.L. Craigie in the Foreign Office, in no doubt but that the secret agreement had come like a 'bombshell to Washington' and, indeed, to the US generally.[69] Not only were Kellogg and Coolidge unaware of the agreement, but it limited the categories of cruisers needed by the US along with signalling a new Anglo–French friendship. Coolidge was furious and telegrammed Kellogg on 3 August to do nothing about the naval agreement. He added 'I do not especially like the meeting that is to be held in Paris. While it is ostensibly to sign the treaty, I can not help wonder whether it may not be for some other purpose not yet disclosed.' William Castle was afraid that Coolidge would get so angry and order Kellogg not to go to Paris which would lead to Kellogg's resignation.[70]

Kellogg had dedicated much time and effort towards the fulfilment of the pact. Subsequently, it would become his most notable achievement for which he would receive the Nobel Peace Prize in 1929. Thus, it was not surprising that he was willing to resign rather than not sign it on 27 August. But Kellogg and

64 Ibid., Kellogg to Clara Kellogg, 1 August 1928.   65 McKercher, *The second Baldwin government*, pp. 150–1.   66 Ibid., p. 151; HHPL, FBKP, roll 2, Kellogg to Coolidge, 3 August 1928.   67 HHPL, FBKP, roll 2, Coolidge to Kellogg, 6 August 1928.   68 Ibid., Kellogg to Sterling, 9 August 1928.   69 McKercher, *The second Baldwin government*, p. 151.   70 D.R. McCoy, *Calvin Coolidge: the quiet president* (1967), p. 375.

Coolidge could show US annoyance in another way. By mid-August, they had been fully informed about all aspects of the Anglo–French agreement. Ronald Cushenden, who was now acting Foreign Secretary, tried to pacify the Americans and privately criticized Chamberlain's announcement of a definite agreement.[71] Coolidge would not be pacified. On 17 August, the British embassy cabled the Foreign Office to say that Kellogg would probably spend two days each in Britain and Ireland after the signing ceremony in Paris.[72] But on the same day, Kellogg wrote to Coolidge that if he wanted, Kellogg would not 'go anywhere.'[73] The trip to England was off but not that to Ireland.

The first report on the altered arrangements appeared in the *Washington Post* on 27 August under the heading 'Diplomatic incident'. Albert Fox wrote that Coolidge, knowing the effect the decision would have, directed Kellogg to cancel his trip to London because he was 'displeased' with the Franco–British compromise. Fox explained firstly, that a trip to Europe without a visit to London 'would inevitably be a subject of comment', secondly, that Kellogg's links to London provided 'an added reason' for going and thirdly, that Kellogg's diplomatic experience at the Court of St. James precluded the possibility that he underestimated the 'significance to be attached to his avoidance of London.'[74] Reports from Esmé Howard also confirmed that the Anglo–French compromise had caused 'serious irritation' in the US, with every newspaper charging Britain with collusion. The White House press corps pushed Coolidge to comment on the 'authoritative reports [that] have been extensively published to the effect that you look with disapproval upon the agreement.' Other journalists used the word 'annoyed' to describe Coolidge's demeanour. Kellogg explained to newspapermen when he arrived in Plymouth that he did not have sufficient time to visit England.[75] However, a more likely explanation was that the president was illustrating his dissatisfaction by refusing to allow Kellogg to visit London while allowing him to visit in the Free State and instructing him not to comment on any subject except the signing of the treaty.[76] But it was the Free State that would benefit from the diplomatic snub and the sharp deterioration in Anglo–American relations.

This was the context for Sterling's suggestion to Ernest Blythe, minister for Finance and vice-president of the government, that Cosgrave and not McGilligan should sign the pact in Paris and return to Dublin with Kellogg on board the USS *Detroit*.[77] Cosgrave agreed although Seán Murphy wanted the minister for External Affairs to sign 'our first international treaty.'[78] Meanwhile, a reception committee was swiftly put in place for Kellogg's visit.[79] Thus, in late summer 1928, the Free State was on the brink of signing its first international treaty and

71 McKercher, *The second Baldwin government*, p. 153.   72 Ibid., p. 152.   73 See Carroll, 'Protocol and international politics', 52.   74 *Washington Post*, 27 August 1928.   75 Bryn-Jones, *Frank B. Kellogg*, p. 269; *The Times*, 24 August 1928.   76 McCoy, *Calvin Coolidge*, p. 375; Ellis, *Frank B. Kellogg*, p. 211.   77 NAI, D/EA, 27/11, McGilligan to Cosgrave, 14 August 1928; ibid., Murphy to McGilligan, 15 August 1928.   78 Ibid., McGilligan to Cosgrave, 14 August 1928.   79 Ibid., Walshe to Dempsey, 21 August 1928.

hosting the first official visit of a foreign statesman, thereby marking a pinnacle in its external affairs agenda.

The Kellogg–Briand treaty was signed in Paris on 27 August with Kellogg and Cosgrave among the signatories. For both men it represented a foreign policy triumph and for Cosgrave, his return to Dublin aboard the USS *Detroit* on 30 August was an additional bonus. During the subsequent four days, Kellogg and his wife, Clara, were feted publicly and privately.[80] The *New York Times* and *Washington Post* covered the successful visit and *The Times* admitted that the visit was an 'advertisement in America for the Irish Free State's stability and progress.'[81] Kellogg appeared to be genuinely moved by his reception telling Cosgrave, 'I wish to thank you again for your splendid reception. As I said today, I knew I would get a warm reception in Ireland. Everybody does. What a wonderful reception we have received! I shall remember it as the heyday of my life and, as I look upon it, it will be one of its brightest memories.'[82] A few weeks after his return to the US, Kellogg spoke at length of his 'great time' in Dublin and the wonderful reception he received, a view he repeated again to Michael MacWhite in March 1929.[83]

Undoubtedly, the Coolidge administration had used Kellogg's visit to the Free State as a diplomatic weapon in its skirmish with the British government about naval disarmament.[84] Yet, this wider international context may distract from the significance of the visit for US and Free State diplomatic relations; firstly, Kellogg's visit was approved by Coolidge, who had previously welcomed Cosgrave to the US and secondly, the US government had extended invitations to all the

---

80 See Carroll, 'Protocol and international politics', 53–5; Bryn-Jones, *Frank B. Kellogg*, pp. 270–2.
81 *New York Times*, 31 August 1928; *Washington Post* on 31 August 1928 noted 'Kellogg welcome in Dublin is lavish … Crowds cheer American Secretary of State wherever he appears.' *The Times*, 31 August 1928.   82 Quoted in Bryn-Jones, *Frank B. Kellogg*, p. 272. Other significant visits that took place between the US and Free State was that of Mayor Walker of New York who spent two days in the Free State at the end of August 1927. He was received formally by representatives of Dublin city council, the government, Cosgrave and Healy. He received the freedom of Kilkenny city. Sterling organized the visit for Walker and his party who received 'courteous treatment' from the legation in Ireland. Cordell Hull, chairman of the Democratic National Committee and future secretary of state, visited in mid-1925. Ambassador Houghton intended visiting in December 1926 but fell ill and was unable to travel. NARA RG59, M580/223, 841d.00/927, Hathaway to Sec, 26 August 1927; HHPL, WRCP, Box 3, file 30, LC, WCP, Box 9, Record of conversation, 15 December 1927; Houghton to Castle, 4 December 1926.   83 *DIFP*, iii, NAI, S5727, Smiddy to McGilligan, 2 October 1928; ibid., NAI, D/T, S2263, MacWhite to Walshe, 29 March 1929.   84 Although Hoover's presidency is outside the scope of this work, he believed in naval disarmament which he worked towards. In 1929, he tried to lessen the tension with the British government by inviting Ramsay MacDonald to Virginia. They agreed to new rations for warships and decided to hold a naval conference in 1930. According to Howard, he was excluded from policy debates on disarmament in London during this time but he reported to R.L. Craigie rumours from supporters of the 'Big Navy' idea that the US government should demand a naval base in Ireland 'as compensation for any compromise with Britain.' W. LaFeber, *The American age: US foreign policy at home and abroad since 1896*, 2 vols. (1989), ii, p. 351; McKercher, *Esmé Howard*, p. 345.

dominions' governments for both the Geneva conference and the Kellogg pact. By autumn 1928 the soon-to-be-replaced Coolidge administration had clearly demonstrated its support for the Cosgrave administration and the Free State. US–Irish relations were at their highest point, in contrast with US–British diplomatic relations, which were at their lowest point. This situation was a real cause of concern for British diplomats who for once could not blame republican Irish-American anti-British propaganda.

For the Cosgrave administration, despite the lingering concerns about US perception of its status, it had not only signed a major international treaty as an independent self-governing dominion and insisted that British reservations did not apply to it but, through the Kellogg visit, its special relationship with the US was consolidated; a position that Hathaway and Sterling had worked towards throughout the 1920s. Cosgrave's visits to New York and Washington were described in the newspapers as one of the 'outstanding' events of the week in the life of those cities. The same applied to Kellogg's visit, except that, as Wainright Abbot noted, it represented also a 'milestone in the history of the Free State.'[85]

Coolidge and Ireland: an overview

The workload for US consular officials in the Free State was extensive and wide ranging, not only because of the changing political and economic conditions in

---

85 Quoted Carroll, 'Protocol and international politics', 56. On 15 January 1929, the US Senate ratified the treaty by 85 votes to 1 and Kellogg was anxious to have all the other signatory governments' ratifications prior to leaving office on 4 March. In January 1929, the State Department asked the Irish government to ratify the treaty 'at an early date' so that it might come into effect 'as soon as possible'. On the following day, William Macaulay, the Irish chargé d'affaires, delivered his government's agreement to do so as soon the Dáil reconvened on 20 February 1929. McGilligan assured Abbot in Dublin that the document of ratification would arrive in Washington by 1 March. In anticipation of this, the instrument of ratification was forwarded to London on 14 February and once the Óireachtas approval was secured on 22 February, Macaulay was instructed to deposit both with the State Department which he did on 26 February. Sterling was critical of Fianna Fáil attempts with 'puerile arguments' to derail passage of the legislation which he felt were motivated by anti-government and anti-British sentiments than anti-pact reasons. Kellogg cabled his 'sincere thanks and deep appreciation' for Irish assistance during the 'negotiations' and for 'prompt action' in ratifying. The pact finally became effective on 24 July 1929 after the Japanese government deposited its instrument of ratification with the US government, by then forty-six nations had ratified it. HHPL, FBKP, roll 2, State Department memo., 16 January 1929; ibid., Macaulay to Kellogg, 17 January 1929; ibid., Kellogg to Sterling, 18 January 1919; NAI, D/FA, 27/11, Walshe to McGilligan, 21 January 1929; HHPL, FBKP, roll 2, Abbott to Kellogg, 24 January 1919; ibid.; NAI, D/T, S5637, McGilligan to Amery, 14 February 1929; NAI, D/FA, 27/11, External Affairs to Washington, 22 February 1929; HHPL, FBKP, roll 2, Sterling to Kellogg, 22 February 1929; ibid., Macaulay to Kellogg, 23 February 1929; ibid., Sterling to Kellogg, 25 February 1929; ibid., Kellogg to Macaulay, 2 March 1929; NAI, D/FA, 27/11, Sterling to McGilligan, 4 March 1929; HHPL, FBKP, roll 2, Kellogg to Macaulay, 8 March 1929.

Ireland and internationally in the period but also because of the ongoing reform in the US foreign service itself. These men, who represented US interests in Ireland, tried to promote and protect those interests. But how successfully did they do it in the Free State? The primary US aim between 1923 and 1929, when Coolidge left office, was to ensure the stability of the Free State and its government, which in turn would reduce the influence of Irish-American republicans within official US circles. In political terms, the US administration and its representatives in the Free State were constantly supportive of Cosgrave and his government but suspicious of de Valera and his followers. First Hathaway and then Sterling pounced on almost every de Valera statement which implied support for the IRA or a constitutional or financial break from Britain. Both supported Cosgrave and his administration but from the time when de Valera and Fianna Fáil entered the Dáil in August 1927 they expected the administration to fall.[86] Sterling expected de Valera to take power but preferred Cosgrave. However, he consoled himself and officials in Washington with the opinion that there would be an orderly and peaceful transfer of power.[87]

This support for the Free State had resulted in other gains too for the Coolidge government. By the end of his tenure, republican Irish-America was at its weakest. In 1929, the Friends of Irish Freedom and AARIR had a regular annual membership of hundreds not thousands. Maud Gonne MacBride, representing the Women's Prisoners' Defence League and the AARIR, failed to get sufficient public support in the US for her campaign against the treatment and conditions of republican prisoners in Free State jails and Cosgrave's Coercion act, even though she had the support of the New York-based International Committee for Political Prisoners.[88] Both Smiddy and Howard observed in 1929 that the Irish question had disappeared as a factor in US national elections and

---

86 NARA, RG59, M580/223, 841d.oo/953, Sterling to Secretary of State, 18 April 1929.   87 Sterling agreed with the consensus of political opinion in Dublin that de Valera's arrest in Northern Ireland in February 1929 'was stupid' and he believed that the Fianna Fáil tactic of attacking the government's economic record at the time represented 'a step forward in Fianna Fáil's education and a healthier state of party mind.' The first reference to an official meeting between a US representative and de Valera came in December 1929 when Sterling met with him to discuss his upcoming visit to the US. NARA, RG59, M580/224, 841d.ooPR/9, Sterling to Secretary of State, 11 February 1929; ibid., M580/223, 841d.oo/865, Sterling to Secretary of State, 6 December 1929. 88 American Irish Historical Society (hereafter AIHS), Friends of Irish Freedom Papers (hereafter FOIFP), 1916–36, Box 2, folder 5, minute, undated. Both the Irish and US organizations sent a joint appeal to Kellogg also on 24 June 1928. It was not until December 1931 when a US citizen, John Mulgrew, was imprisoned and sentenced under the Public Safety Act for membership of a 'communist organisation', Saor Éire, that a letter to the State Department led to Henry Balch, the US consul in Dublin, being requested to investigate the case. NYPL, International Committee for Political Prisoners Papers (hereafter ICPP), roll 6, Maud Gonne MacBride to Richard Baldwin, 1 March 1928; ibid., Baldwin to MacBride, 20 June 1928; ibid., ICPP, Press Release, 24 June 1928; ibid., Baldwin to MacBride, 14 June 1929; ibid., Baldwin to MacBride, 6 January 1932; ibid., Baldwin to MacWhite, 6 January 1932; ibid., Hackworth to Baldwin, 19 January 1932; ibid., State Department to Baldwin, 14 January 1932.

largely disappeared in local elections. Thus, while ethnicity remained a badge of identification for voters and while at election time they, just like other ethnic groups, had to be courted by candidates, the majority of Irish-Americans were supporters of the Free State also. Indeed in late December 1927 the extent of US public and official support for the Free State was identified by Atherton, in the London embassy, as being a cause of 'irritation' amongst the 'educated' classes in England.[89] In economic terms, US commercial links with Ireland were weak despite the best efforts of the consular officials. But Sterling detected a gradual improvement in the 'well-being' of the country by July 1929.[90]

But where the stability of the Free State government was confirmed during the period was in the area of foreign policy. The chief goal of the Cosgrave government in 1922 was to establish the Free State as an entity independent of Britain, and by 1929 it had achieved significant international recognition of that position through membership of the League, the right to independent diplomatic representation abroad and a big constitutional advance at the Imperial Conference and the Kellogg visit. In three of these actions the Coolidge administration had played a part in emphasizing the separate autonomy of the Free State. Not only had the US led the way by recognizing the first Free State minister plenipotentiary to the US but it had reciprocated with the appointment of the first US minister to Dublin, had simultaneously upgraded the Free State representative to envoy status and had maintained a consul general in Dublin, while in the US Smiddy had been succeeded by Michael MacWhite as minister plenipotenitary and envoy extraordinary in January 1929.[91] The Washington post was now described by Walshe as the 'very best post in the gift of the Saorstát.'[92] Kellogg recommended MacWhite to Coolidge as Smiddy's replacement; 'there would seem to be no reason why the appointment of MacWhite ... should not be agreeable.' Coolidge agreed and the succession took place without further comment.[93] At MacWhite's presentation ceremony in the White

89 HHPL, FBKP, roll 2, Atherton to Kellogg, 13 December 1927; DIFP, iii, NAI, D/FA, 17/17, Smiddy to McGilligan, 5 January 1929. A further foreign policy area where the US and Free State policy 'were much the same' as MacWhite explained to Castle, was in relation to the USSR. The Irish minister described the situation in 1930 as follows; 'a certain amount of trade was carried on between the two countries, but there was no official diplomatic contact'. DIFP, iii, NAI, D/FA 19/2, MacWhite to Walshe, 19 December 1930.   90 NARA, RG59, M580/223, 841d.00/958, Sterling to Secretary of State, 18 July 1929.   91 Other countries followed. Sterling reported home in May 1929 that agreement had been reached with the German and French governments for the exchange of diplomatic representatives. Count Gerald O'Kelly and Professor Daniel A. Binchy became the first ministers to France and Germany respectively. Charles Bewley became the first Free State minister to the Vatican which Sterling felt was a 'fortunate' choice. In December 1929, he reported the appointment of Dr Paschal Robinson as the first papal nuncio to the Free State. The British government followed by appointing a trade commissioner and the Polish government established a consulate general. NARA, RG59, M580/223, 841d.00/954, Sterling to Secretary of State, 19 May 1929; ibid., 841d.00/956, Sterling to Secretary of State, 13 June 1929; ibid., 841d.00/965, Sterling to Secretary of State, 6 December 1929.   92 UCDA, MMP, P194/248, Walshe to MacWhite, 20 December 1928.   93 CCP, series 1, 296 continued

House on 14 March 1929, Coolidge recalled that Smiddy's tenure was 'most happily remembered' and that 'unusually friendly relations' existed between the two countries, exemplified by the welcome given to Cosgrave and Kellogg during their respective visits to the US and the Free State.[94]

In addition to acquiring diplomatic recognition, Ireland's role in the League of Nations and imperial conferences drew Hathaway and Sterling's attention. Certainly, the development of the imperial structure, specifically after the 1926 imperial conference, was a concern for US foreign policy-makers. On the one hand, US officials and politicians feared each dominion gaining control over its own foreign relations and seeking separate voting rights at international conferences because this would strengthen the hand of the British government. But on the other hand, the loosening of the formal ties between the Free State, Canada and Britain provided an opportunity for the expansion of US relations with the two dominions. Sterling offered a progress report in July 1929: 'The government's foreign policy seems sound.'[95] Thus, he gave a stamp of approval to Free State appeals to the privy council, the appointment of a delegation to the naval conference in London and the moves to gain a seat on the League of Nations council. Yet, he always suspected that the constant expansion of the Free State status internationally, specifically within the League of Nations and the imperial conferences, was intended by the Cumann na nGaedheal government primarily to pre-empt Fianna Fáil criticism and to prevent the latter from gaining political ascendancy over the government at home rather than reflecting a genuine interest in foreign relations.[96] Whatever the motivation, the Free State had made great strides towards legitimacy and independence.

Moreover, by 1929, when this study ends, relations between the US and the Free State had been normalized. It is apposite to conclude with two encounters between the Free State minister and the new US president, Herbert Hoover and secretary of State, Henry Stimson. On 15 March 1929, Castle presented MacWhite to Hoover, who talked about the number of Irishmen in the US and told MacWhite he would have to make a lot of speeches. When the minister replied that he was not accustomed to making speeches Hoover said that he never knew an Irishman who was 'at a loss for what to say.' Although Castle worried that Hoover did not 'obey' his State Department instructions and say little or nothing, it was obvious that Hoover's words and the friendly tone were genuine in intent.[97] Subsequently, MacWhite developed a friendly relationship with Castle and Stimson. Two years later not only was he able to secure a meeting on the same day that he called to the State Department but the secretary of

319 17 June 1926, Roll 116, file 308, Kellogg to Coolidge, 10 January 1929; ibid., Clark to Kellogg, 11 January 1929. 94 UCDA, MMP, P194/281, President Coolidge reply, 14 March 1929. 95 NARA, RG59, M580/223, 841d.oo/958, Sterling to Secretary of State, 18 July 1929. 96 Ibid., 841d.oo/962, Sterling to Secretary of State, 27 September 1929. 97 HHPL, WRCP, WRC diary, 15 March 1929.

State's parting comment was 'that there was no person who entered that room for whom there was a more cordial welcome than for the Representative of the Irish Free State.'[98] It had been a long road but US–Irish diplomatic relations were regular and normal.

98 NAI, D/T, S2263, MacWhite to Walshe, 29 March 1929; ibid., 19 December 1930; *DIFP*, iii, NAI, D/FA, 11/3, MacWhite to Walshe, 22 January 1931.

CHAPTER FOURTEEN

Conclusion

The coming of a new president and party to power always excites the hopes and expectations of their voters and interest groups, many assume that change is imminent. It was no different for Irish nationalist activists in the US and Ireland when Woodrow Wilson took office in 1913, Warren G. Harding in 1921 and Calvin Coolidge in 1924.

By the time Woodrow Wilson came into power, an emotional mood infused the question of Irish freedom and independence. Wilson was knowledgeable about Ireland, having read widely on British and Irish politics, he had visited the country and he was a member of Catholic Irish-America's political home, the Democratic Party. But he was also part of the establishment and opposed to privileging hyphenated groups. Nonetheless, hopes were high among Irish-Americans that, as a Democratic president, he would at least be sympathetic towards Ireland. When he assumed office, Wilson had not expected to dedicate his time to foreign affairs but the outbreak of world war one changed that. Students of counterfactual history would enjoy discussing the question how Woodrow Wilson might have treated the Irish question if world war one had not broken out? It is, however, more enlightening to examine real events. Wilson's Irish policy was formed in the same way as the rest of his foreign policy, primarily by his personal view of the matter and to a lesser extent by advice from advisers, confidants, State Department officials and British officials in Washington. In the context of Ireland, his contacts with Joseph Tumulty, Edward House, Horace Plunkett, Ray Stannard Baker, George Creel and senators Walsh and Phelan were influential, but ultimately it was his scholarly reading and personal belief in democracy and self-determination that led him to be sympathetic to the Irish cause. That perspective was always balanced by the exigencies of the US–British relationship.

As *de facto* secretary of State and president, his Irish policy fell into three phases. Between 1914 and 1917, he supported Irish home rule, which appealed to Irish America, but this support was balanced by his suspicion of extreme Irish-America's perceived disloyalty to US neutrality. From 1917 to 1919, when his administration was under pressure to act on the Irish question and in the national interest, he intervened to try and bring a resolution. Though the Irish Convention was not welcomed by republicans, it served Wilson's needs. Finally, during 1919–20, despite Irish-American war-time loyalty, he was firmly set on non-intervention in the Irish question. As far as he was concerned Ireland had nothing to do with the peace conference and resultant settlement. During his final months in office, when he was in a weakened condition physically and politically, and embittered about Irish-Americans' role in the Senate and electoral defeat of his peace settlement, he intervened personally on an Irish issue but only to ensure that no leniency was shown toward Donal O'Callaghan.

Harding had been voted into office by many previously Democratic Irish-American voters. Little was expected of him on Ireland. Nonetheless, his style of government and personality led to a surprising early move on humanitarian aid for Ireland in March 1921. However, once he and Secretary Hughes had felt the full force of reaction from the British embassy he reverted to non-intervention. From then onwards, Irish issues were handled mainly by Hughes and his officials and treated in the wider context of US foreign policy interests, particularly the effect on US–British relations of debts and disarmament. Indeed Irish and Irish-American republican pressure on Harding, particularly through Congress, greatly diminished following the signing of the Anglo-Irish treaty.

Instead with the establishment of the Irish Free State, US–Irish relations become more akin to a normal inter-state relationship where issues are raised by representatives of governments and dealt with by their respective officials. It took Timothy Smiddy two years to become an accredited minister to the US government, as an 'unofficial' envoy of the IFS, and with Ambassador Howard's support, US officials increasingly dealt directly with him rather than going through British embassy officials. During what was initially a trying time for Smiddy, he overcame the scepticism and ridicule of some US officials and British diplomats and the hostility of 'irregular' opponents of the 1921 treaty to help gain official recognition of and legitimacy for the IFS.

Consequently, the Coolidge tenure represents the first period in US–Irish relations when an element of normality characterized the relationship. US representation in Ireland was upgraded from consular to consul general to diplomatic status and adjusted to acknowledge the partitioned island. The concerns of these US officials based in the IFS, and of their IFS counterparts in the US, now encompassed the full gamut of regular diplomatic and consular concerns.

For Irish nationalists in Ireland and the US, the path from dependence to independence had been long and, as US consular officers in Ireland consistently reported, many would always believe that their pressure on Wilson, Harding and Coolidge to intervene with respective British governments had resulted in progress towards the settlement of the problems of Irish independence and recognition at various times. However, this study reveals that irrespective of the extent and nature of the Irish contacts of these presidents and of republican pressure through the public, sympathetic individuals and Congress, each was motivated by the totality of concerns relating to their own views and the role of cabinet, party, public and national interest.

Appendix 1

US ADMINISTRATIONS, 1913–29

Period	President	Party	Secretary of state	US ambassador to Britain
1913–17	W. Wilson	Democratic	W.J. Bryan, 1913–15	W. Hines Page, 1913–17
			R. Lansing, 1915–17	
1917–21	W. Wilson	Democratic	R. Lansing, 1917–20	W. Hines Page, 1917–18
			B. Colby, 1920–1	J.W. Davis 1918–21
1921–3	W.G. Harding	Republican	C. Evans Hughes, 1921–3	G. Harvey, 1921–3
1923–4	C. Coolidge	Republican	C. Evans Hughes, 1923–5	F.B. Kellogg, 1923–4
1924–9	C. Coolidge	Republican	C. Evans Hughes, 1924–5	F.B. Kellogg, 1923–4
			F.B. Kellogg, 1925–9	A.B. Houghton, 1925–9

BRITISH ADMINISTRATIONS, 1913–27

Period	Prime minister	Party	Foreign secretary	British ambassador to US
1908–16	H.H. Asquith	Liberal	E. Grey, 1905–16	J. Bryce, 1907–13
1916–18	D. Lloyd George	Coalition	A. Balfour, 1916–19	C. Spring Rice, 1913–18
1919–22	D. Lloyd George	Coalition	Marquess Curzon, 1919–22	Lord Reading, 1918–20
				A. Geddes, 1920–2
1922–4	A. Bonar Law	Conservative	Marquess Curzon, 1922–4	A. Geddes, 1922–4
1924	J.R. MacDonald	Labour	J.R. MacDonald, 1924	E. Howard, 1924
1924–9	S. Baldwin	Conservative	A. Chamberlain, 1924–9	E. Howard, 1924–30

US CONSULS IN IRELAND, 1913–27

Belfast
H. Sharp 1910–20
W.P. Kent, 1920–3
H.P. Starrett (consul general), 1924–6
T.D. Bowman (consul general), 1926–31

Cork (Queenstown/Cobh)
W. Frost, 1914–17
C. Hathaway, 1917–19
M. Mitchell, 1919–21
J. Gamon, 1921–6
(consul general), 1924–7
C.M. Ferris, 1926–8

Dublin
E.L. Adams, 1909–19
F.T. Dumont, 1919–21
C.A. Bay (acting consul), 1921–2
C. Hathaway, 1921–4,

F. Sterling was appointed US minister and envoy extraordinary to the Irish Free State in 1927
Note: There is no definitive list of officers or lengths of service. The above dates are either of appointment, transfer or resignation.

Bibliography

PRIMARY SOURCES

IRELAND

National Archives of Ireland, Dublin
Department of Foreign Affairs
  D Series files
  Early Series files
  Letter books
Department of the Taoiseach
  S Series files
Department of Justice
  Letter books

National Library of Ireland, Dublin
Bourke papers
Peter Golden papers
John Hearn papers
Patrick McCartan papers
Joseph McGarrity papers
Art O'Briain papers
Excerpts from diary of John J. O'Brien snr
Horace Plunkett papers
John Quinn papers
John Redmond papers

National University of Ireland, Dublin, School of History and Archives
Ernest Blythe papers
Eamon de Valera papers
Gavan Duffy papers
Desmond Fitzgerald papers
Mary MacSwiney papers
Michael MacWhite papers

UNITED KINGDOM

The National Archives, London
Record Class, FO371, General Records of the British Foreign Office
Record Class DO35, Dominions Office
Record Class CO739, Commonwealth Office
James Bryce papers
Edward Gray papers
William Wiseman papers

Imperial War Museum, London
Sir Henry Wilson diaries

British Library, London
Balfour papers
Cecil papers
Northcliffe papers
Wickham Steed papers

UNITED STATES

American Irish Historical Society, New York
Daniel F. Cohalan papers
Friends of Irish Freedom papers

Library of Congress, Washington DC
William E. Borah papers
Wilbur Carr papers
Edward T. Clarke papers
Calvin Coolidge papers
Charles Evans Hughes papers
La Follette Family collection, (Robert La Follette)
Robert Lansing papers
Joseph Tumulty papers
Thomas J. Walsh papers
Woodrow Wilson papers

National Archives and Records Administration of the United States, Washington DC
Record Group 59, Inspection Reports on Foreign Service Posts, Dublin, Queenstown (Cobh),
    Belfast, Galway, Limerick
RG59, Records of the Department of State relating to internal affairs of Great Britain, 1910–29
RG63, Committee on Public Information
RG65, Bureau of Investigation
RG84, Foreign service posts of the Department of State

Archdiocese of Boston Archives, Boston
William Henry O'Connell papers

New York Public Library
Emigrant Savings Bank papers
International Committee for Political Prisoners papers
Luke O'Connor papers
Frank P. Walsh papers

Calvin Coolidge Presidential Library and Museum, Northampton
Calvin Coolidge collection (microfilm)

Herbert Hoover Presidential Library, West Branch
William R. Castle papers
Leland Harrison papers

Lewis L. Strauss papers
Pre Presidential, Commerce Department papers

Yale University Library Manuscripts and Archives Collection
Colonel E.M. House papers
Frank L. Polk papers
William Wiseman papers

Presidential papers microfilm
Warren Harding papers
Calvin Coolidge papers

Newspapers and periodicals

Gaelic American	*Manchester Guardian*	*Sinn Féiner*
Irish Independent	*Nation*	*The New Republic*
Irish Man	*New York Herald*	*Thoms' directory*
Irish Times	*New York Times*	*Times*
Irish Trade Journal	*New York World*	*Washington Post*

CD ROM
Colonial Office Record Series vol. 1. Dublin Castle Special Branch Files CD903 (Eneclann, Dublin, 2006).

OFFICIAL PUBLICATIONS

Bourne, K. & D.C. Watt (eds), *British documents on foreign affairs*, 25 vols (Bethesda, MD, 1986–95).
Census of Population, 1926, iii, birthplaces (Dublin, 1929).
Census of Population of Ireland, 1961, vol. III, part II, Birthplaces (Dublin, 1965).
Fanning, R., M. Kennedy, D. Keogh and E. O'Halpin (eds), *Documents on Irish foreign policy*, 3 vols (Dublin, 1988–).
Government Publication Office, *Statistical Abstract of the United States 1926* (Washington, 1927).
—— *Statistical Abstract of the United States, 1951* (Washington, 1951).
'Official Documents. Enclosure 1, Notice concerning passports and registration in consulates', supplement, 8 February 1915, *American Journal of International Law*, 9 (1915), 390.
'Official Documents. Supplement, Bryan to the diplomatic and consular officers of the United States of America, 17 August 1914', *American Journal of International Law*, 9, (1915), 118–9.
'Official Documents. Enclosure 3, Notice to American citizens who contemplate visiting belligerent countries', 17 November 1914', *American Journal of International Law*, 9 (1915), 390–1.
'Official Documents. Enclosure 1, Rules governing the granting and issuing of passports in the United States', supplement, 12 January 1915, *American Journal of International Law*, 9 (1915) 386–9.
'Official Documents. Lansing to the embassies and legations in Europe, 12 September 1914', *The American Journal of International Law*, 9 (1915), 377–8.
Parliamentary Debates Dáil Eireann.
Report of the Commission on Emigration and other Population Problems (Dublin, 1956).

United States Bureau of the Census
—— *Statistical abstract of the United States, 1937* (Washington, 1938).
United States Congress, *Congressional Record*
—— 'Immigration act of 1924', 86th Congress, 1st session, ch 185, 190. 26 May 1924.
—— House of Representatives, Committee on Foreign Affairs, Hearings on H.Res. 3404, *To provide for the salaries of a minister and consuls to the Republic of Ireland*, 66th Congress, 2nd Session, 1920.
—— 'The cause of Ireland and its relations to the League of Nations. Statement by Hon. W. Bourke Cockran before the Committee on Foreign Relations of the United States Senate. 30 August 1919' (reprint, Washington, 1919).
United States Department of Commerce
—— H.C. Campbell, 'European rehabilitation and American trade' in US Department of Commerce, Commerce Reports, 33 (18 August 1924).
United States Department of State
—— *The immigration work of the Department of State and its consular officers. Revised to July 1, 1932* (Washington, 1932).
—— *Papers relating to the foreign relations of the United States*, 19 vols (Washington, 1920–36).
—— *Papers relating to the foreign relations of the United States*, 1914 supplement the world war (Washington, 1928).
—— *Papers relating to the foreign relations of the United States*, 1915 supplement the world war (Washington, 1928).
—— *Papers relating to the foreign relations of the United States*, 1916 supplement (Washington, 1929).
—— *Papers relating to the foreign relations of the United States*, 1917 supplement 2 the world war, 2 vols (Washington, 1932).
—— *Papers relating to the foreign relations of the United States: The Lansing Papers, 1914–20*, 2 vols (Washington, 1939–40).
—— *Papers relating to the foreign relations of the United States*, The Paris Peace Conference, 1919, 13 vols (1942–7).
—— *Papers relating to the Foreign Relations of the United State*, 1927, 3 vols (Washington, 1942).
—— *Register of the Department of State, January 1 1914* (Washington, 1914).
—— *Register of the Department of State, January 1, 1930* (Washington, 1930).
—— *Register of the Department of State, May 1, 1922* (Washington, 1922).

SECONDARY SOURCES

Adler, Selig, *The isolationist impulse: its twentieth-century reaction* (London, 1957).
Allen, H.C., *Great Britain and the United States: a history of Anglo-American relations, 1783–1952* (London, 1994).
Ambrosius, Lloyd E., *Woodrow Wilson and the American diplomatic tradition: the treaty fight in perspective* (New York, 1987).
——, *Wilsonian statecraft: theory and practice of liberal internationalism during World War I* (Wilmington, 1991).
——, *Wilsonianism: Woodrow Wilson and his legacy in American foreign relations* (New York, 2002).
American Commission on conditions in Ireland: interim report, The (Chicago, 1921).
Andreassi, Anthony D., 'Francis Clement Kelley, 1870–1948' in Glazier (ed.), *The encyclopedia* (1999), pp 497–8.
Anonymous, 'William J. Bryan' in Bemis (ed.), *The American secretaries of state and their diplomacy* (1929), pp 6–7.

Augusteijn, Joost, 'Irish (National) Volunteers' in S.J. Connolly, *The Oxford companion to Irish History* (Oxford, 1998), p. 270.

Bailey, Thomas, *Woodrow Wilson and the great betrayal* (New York, 1945).

Baker, Ray Stannard, *Woodrow Wilson: life and letters*, 8 vols. (New York, 1927, 1931–9).

——, *American chronicle: the autobiography of Ray Stannard Baker* (New York, 1945).

—— & William E. Dodd (eds), *The public papers of Woodrow Wilson: college and state, educational, literary and political papers (1875–1913)*, 1 (New York and London, 1925).

Bannister, Robert C., jnr, *Ray Stannard Baker: the mind and thought of a progressive* (New Haven, 1966).

Barnes, James, A., 'Phelan, James', in Glazier (ed.), *The encyclopedia* (1999), p. 768.

Bayor, Ronald H., & Timothy J. Meagher (eds), *The New York Irish* (Baltimore and London, 1996).

Beatty, Jack, *The rascal king: the life and times of James Michael Curley, 1874–1958* (Reading, 1992).

Bell, J. Bowyer, 'The Thompson submachine gun in Ireland, 1921', *Irish Sword*, 8:31 (1967), 99–100.

Bemis, Samuel Flagg (ed.), *The American secretaries of state and their diplomacy* (New York, 1929).

Blake, Robert, *The unknown prime minister: the life and times of Andrew Bonar Law, 1858–1923* (London, 1955).

Blessing, Patrick J., 'Irish' in Stephan Thernstrom (ed.), *The Harvard encyclopedia of American ethnic history* (Cambridge, 1980), pp 524–45.

Blum, John M., *Joe Tumulty and the Wilson era* (Boston, 1951).

Bolling Wilson, Edith, *My memoir* (Indianapolis, 1938).

Bowman, John, 'De Valera on Ulster, 1919–20: what he told America' in *Irish Studies in International Affairs*, 1:1 (1979), 3–18.

Brogan, Hugh, *The Penguin history of the United States of America* (London, 1985).

Brown, Mary Elizabeth, 'Hayes, Patrick Joseph Cardinal' in Glazier (ed.), *The encyclopedia* (1999), p. 380.

——, 'Farley, John Murphy Cardinal' in Glazier (ed.), *The encyclopedia* (1999), p. 311.

——, 'Hayes, Patrick Joseph' in Glazier (ed.), *The encyclopedia* (1999), p. 380.

Brown, T., *Irish-American nationalism, 1870–1890* (Philadelphia, 1966).

Bryan, William Jennings, & Mary Baird Bryan, *The memoirs of William Jennings Bryan* (Chicago, 1925).

Bryn-Jones, David, *Frank B Kellogg: a biography* (New York, 1937).

Buckley, John Patrick, *The New York Irish: their view of American foreign policy, 1914–1921* (New York, 1976).

Buckley, Thomas H., *The United States and the Washington Conference, 1921–1922* (Knoxville, 1970).

Burchell, R.A., 'Did the Irish and German voters desert the Democrats in 1920? A tentative statistical answer', *Journal of American Studies*, 6:2 (August 1972), 153–65.

Burner, David, *The politics of provincialism: the Democratic Party in transition, 1918–1932* (New York, 1970).

——, 'Election of 1924' in Schlesinger et al, *American presidential elections* (1971), iii, pp. 2459–90.

Calhoun, Frederick S., *Power and principle: armed intervention in Wilsonian foreign policy* (Kent, 1986).

Campbell, Thomas F., 'Ohio' in Glazier (ed.) *The encyclopedia* (1999), pp 730–1.

Caroli, Betty Boyd, *First ladies* (Oxford, 1995).

Carroll, Francis M., *American opinion and the Irish question 1910–23: a study in opinion and policy* (Dublin, 1978).

—— (ed.), *The American Commission on Irish Independence, 1919: the diary, correspondence and report* (Dublin, 1985).

——, *Money for Ireland: finance, diplomacy, politics and the First Dáil Éireann loans, 1919–1936* (Westport, 2002).

——, '"All Standards of Human Conduct": the American Commission on Conditions in Ireland, 1920–21', *Éire–Ireland*, 16: 4 (winter, 1981), 59–74.

——, 'The American Committee for Relief in Ireland, 1920–22', *Irish Historical Studies*, 23:89 (May 1982), 30–49.

——, 'The Friends of Irish Freedom' in Funchion (ed.), *Irish American Voluntary Organisations* (1983), pp 120–1.

——, 'Irish Progressive League' in Funchion (ed.), *Irish American Voluntary Organisations*, pp. 206–10.

——, 'The American Commission on Irish independence and the Paris peace conference of 1919', *Irish Studies in International Affairs*, 2:1 (1985), 103–19.

——, 'Protocol and international politics, 1928: the Secretary of State goes to Ireland', *Éire–Ireland*, 26:4 (1991), 45–57.

——, 'The Admiral Sims incident: Irish-Americans and social tensions in the 1920s', *Prologue: Quarterly of the National Archives*, 25:4 (winter, 1993), 335–47.

——, *The American presence in Ulster: a diplomatic history, 1796–1996* (Baltimore, 2005).

Challener, Richard, 'William Jennings Bryan' in Graebner (ed.), *American secretaries of state* (1961), pp 79–100.

Clements, Kendrick, A., *The presidency of Woodrow Wilson* (Kansas, 1992).

Cohen, W.I., 'America and the world in the 1920s' in Haynes (ed.), *Calvin Coolidge* (1998), pp 233–43.

Connolly, Philomena, 'Irish Citizens Army' in Connolly (ed.), *The Oxford companion* (1998), p. 265.

Connolly, S.J., *The Oxford companion to Irish history* (Oxford, 1998).

——, 'Howth gun-running' in Connolly (ed.), *The Oxford companion* (1998), p. 251.

——, 'Anglo-Irish War' in Connolly (ed.), *The Oxford companion* (1998), pp. 15–16.

Coogan, Tim Pat, *De Valera: long fellow, long shadow* (London, 1993).

Coolidge, Calvin, *The autobiography of Calvin Coolidge* (London, 1929).

Cooper, John Milton, Jnr, *The warrior and the priest: Woodrow Wilson and Theodore Roosevelt* (Cambridge, 1983).

——, 'Thomas Woodrow Wilson' in Urofsky (ed.), *The American presidents* (2000), pp. 288–304.

Costello, Francis, *The Irish revolution and its aftermath, 1916–1923. Years of revolt* (Dublin, 2003).

Creel, George, *The war, the world and Wilson* (New York, 1920).

——, *How we advertised America: the first telling of the amazing story of the Committee on Public Information that carried the gospel of Americanism to every corner of the globe* (New York, 1920).

——, *Rebel at large: recollections of fifty crowded years* (New York, 1947).

Crews, Clyde F., 'Ireland, John Richard', in Glazier (ed.), *The encyclopedia* (1999), p. 417.

Cronin, Seán, *The McGarrity papers: revelations of the Irish revolutionary movement in Ireland and America 1900–1940* (Tralee, 1971).

Cronon, E. David (ed.), *Josephus Daniels: the cabinet diaries of Josephus Daniels, 1913–1921* (Lincoln, 1963).

Cuddy, Joseph Edward, 'Irish-American propagandists and American neutrality, 1914–17' in Walsh (ed.) *The Irish* (1976), pp 252–75.

——, '"Are the Bolsheviks any worse than the Irish?": ethno-religious conflict in America during the 1920s', *Éire–Ireland*, 11:3 (fall, 1976), 13–32.

Cuneo, Sherman A., *From printer to president: the story of Warren G. Harding* (Philadelphia, 1922).

Daly Mary E., *Industrial development and Irish national identity, 1922–39* (Syracuse, 1992).

——, 'The economic impact of the United States on Ireland, 1922–1980' (unpublished).

Daniels, Josephus, *Josephus Daniels, the Wilson ear: years of war and after, 1917–1923* (Chapel Hill, 1946).

Daniels, Roger, & Otis L. Graham, *Debating American immigration, 1882–present* (Oxford, 2001).

Daugherty, Harry M., *The inside story of the Harding tragedy* (New York, 1932).

David, Edward (ed.), *Inside Asquith's cabinet: from the diaries of Charles Hobhouse* (London, 1977).

Davis, Julia, & Dolores A. Fleming (eds), *The ambassadorial diary of John W. Davis: the court of St James', 1918–21* (West Virginia, 1993).

Davis, Troy, 'Diplomacy as propaganda: the appointment of T. A. Smiddy as Irish Free State minister to the United States', *Éire-Ireland*, 31:3 & 4 (fall/winter 1996), 117–30.

Deasy, Joseph, *Fiery cross: the story of Jim Larkin Irish Labour History Society Studies in Irish Labour History*, 9 (2004).

Deegan, James, & Donal A. Dineen, *Tourism policy and performance: the Irish experience* (London, 1997).

Devoy, John, *Recollections of an Irish rebel* (Shannon, 1969).

Digby, Margaret, *Horace Plunkett: an Anglo-American Irishman* (Oxford, 1949).

Doorley, Michael, *Irish-American diaspora nationalism: the Friends of Irish freedom, 1916–35* (Dublin, 2005).

Downes, Randolph C., *The rise of Warren Gamaliel Harding, 1865–1920* (Ohio, 1970).

Downing, Rossa F., 'Men, women and memories' in Fitzgerald (ed.), *The voice of Ireland* (1923), pp. 215–23.

Doyle, David, 'The Irish and American labour, 1880–1920', *Saothar*, 1:1 (1975), 42–53.

——, 'Cohesion and diversity in the Irish diaspora', *Irish Historical Studies*, 31:123 (May, 1999), 411–34.

Doyle, Joe, 'Striking for Ireland on the New York docks' in Bayor & Meagher (eds), *The New York Irish* (1996), pp. 357–73.

Dudley Edwards, Owen, 'American aspects of the Rising' in O. Dudley Edwards & Fergus Pyle (eds), *1916, The Eastern Rising* (London, 1968).

Duff, John B., 'The Versailles Treaty and the Irish-Americans', *Journal of American History*, 55, (December 1968–9), 582–600.

Dugdale, Blanche E.C., *Arthur James Balfour: first earl of Balfour*, 2 vols (London, 1939).

Dukakis, Michael S., 'From the legislature to the corner office: an assessment of Coolidge's performance as a Massachusetts political leader', *The New England Journal of History*, 55:1, (fall 1998), 36–42.

Duroselle, Jean-Baptiste, *From Wilson to Roosevelt: foreign policy of the United States, 1913–1945* (New York, 1968).

Eaton, Herbert, *Presidential timber: a history of nominating conventions, 1868–1960* (London, 1964).

——, *A history of nominating conventions, 1868–1960* (London, 1964).

Egan, Maurice Francis, *Recollections of a happy life* (New York, 1924).

Egerton, George. W., 'Britain and the "Great Betrayal": Anglo-American relations and the struggle for United States ratification of the Treaty of Versailles, 1919–20', *Historical Journal*, 21:4 (1978), 885–911.

Ellis, L. Ethan, *Republican foreign policy, 1921–1933* (New Brunswick, 1961).

——, 'Frank B. Kellogg (1925–1929)' in Graebner (ed.), *American secretaries of state* (1961), pp. 149–67.

Erie, Steven P., *Rainbow's end: Irish-Americans and the dilemmas of urban machine politics, 1840–1985* (London, 1988).

Esposito, David M., *The legacy of Woodrow Wilson: American war aims in World War I* (Westport, 1996).

Fanning, Ronan, *The Irish Department of Finance* (Dublin, 1978).

——, 'The Anglo-American alliance and the Irish question in the twentieth century' in J. Devlin & H.B. Clark (eds), *European encounters: essays in memory of Albert Lovett* (Dublin, 2003), pp 185–221.

Feeney, Vincent, 'Vermont' in Glazier (ed.) *The encyclopedia* (1999), pp. 924–7.

Ferrell, Robert H., *The presidency of Calvin Coolidge* (Lawrence, 1998).

——, 'Calvin Coolidge, the man and the president' in Haynes (ed.), *Calvin Coolidge* (1998), pp. 132–48.

——, 'Calvin Coolidge: the man and the myth', *New England Journal of History*, 55:1 (fall, 1998), 11–12.

Findling, John E., *Dictionary of American diplomatic history* (Westport, 1980).

——, 'Tasker Howard Bliss' in Findling (ed.), *Dictionary of American diplomatic history* (1980), p. 64.

——, 'Hughes, Charles Evans' in Findling (ed.), *Dictionary of American diplomatic history* (1980), pp 230–1.

——, 'Bainbridge Colby' in Findling (ed.), *Dictionary of American diplomatic history* (1980), p. 113.

——, 'George Brinton McClellan Harvey' in *Dictionary of American diplomatic history* (1980), p. 211.

Fisher, H.A.L., *James Bryce: Viscount Bryce of Dechmont, OM* (London, 1927).

Fitzgerald William G. (ed.), *The voice of Ireland: a survey of the race and nation from all angles by the foremost leaders at home and abroad* (Dublin, 1923).

Fitzpatrick, David, *Harry Boland's Irish revolution* (Cork, 2003).

Fletcher Johnson, Willis, *George Harvey: a passionate patriot* (London, 1929).

Foley, Patrick, 'Donovan, William Joseph' in Glazier (ed.), *The encyclopedia* (1999), p. 222.

Fowler W.B., *British-American relations, 1917–1918: the role of William Wiseman* (Princeton, 1969).

Freud, Sigmund, & William C. Bullitt, *Thomas Woodrow Wilson: a psychological study* (London, 1966).

Funchion, Michael F., (ed.), *Irish American voluntary organizations* (Westport, 1983).

——, 'Clan na Gael' in M.F. Funchion (ed.), pp. 74–93.

Fyfe, Hamilton, *T.P. O'Connor* (London, 1934).

Gardner, Lloyd, *A covenant with power: America and world order from Wilson to Regan* (New York, 1984).

Garvey, Richard C., 'Coolidge and the Northampton Irish: a strange alliance', *The New England Journal of History*, 55:1 (fall 1998), 71–2.

Gaughan, J. Anthony, *Memoirs of Senator Joseph Connolly (1885–1961): a founder of modern Ireland* (Dublin, 1996).

Gerard, James W., *My four years in Germany* (London, 1917).

Gerson, Louis L., *The hyphenate in recent American politics and diplomacy* (Lawrence, 1964).

Gilbert, Martin, *Churchill: a life* (New York, 1991).

Glad, Betty, *Charles Evans Hughes and the illusions of innocence: a study in American Diplomacy* (Urbana and London, 1966).

Glazier, Michael (ed.), *The encyclopedia of the Irish in America* (Notre Dame, 1999).

Golway, Terry, *Irish rebel: John Devoy and America's fight for Ireland's freedom* (New York, 1998).

Graebner, Norman A. (ed.), *An uncertain tradition: American secretaries of state in the twentieth century* (New York, 1961).

Grant, Philip A., 'President Warren G. Harding and the British war debt question, 1921–3', *Presidential Studies Quarterly*, 25:3 (summer, 1995), 479–87.

Grayson, Cary T., *Woodrow Wilson: an intimate memoir* (2nd ed., Washington, 1977).

Greene, J.R., 'Calvin Coolidge and the vice-presidency: his introduction to Washington politics', *The New England Journal of History*, 55:1 (fall, 1998), 73–6.

Gregory, Ross, *Walter Hines Page: ambassador to the Court of St. James* (Kentucky, 1970).

Griffin, William D., *The book of Irish-Americans* (New York, 1990).

Gwynn, Stephen (ed.), *The letters and friendships of Sir Cecil Spring Rice a record* (London, 1929).

Hachey, T.E., 'The Irish question: the British foreign office and the American political conventions of 1920', *Éire-Ireland*, 3:3 (autumn, 1968), 92–106.

——, 'The British Foreign Office and new perspectives on the Irish issue in Anglo-American relations, 1919–21', *Éire-Ireland*, 7:2 (summer, 1972), 3–13.

Harrell, Joy, 'Doheny, Edward Laurence' in Galzier (ed.) *The encyclopedia* (1999), p. 216.

Hart, Peter, 'The Thompson submachine gun in Ireland revisited', *Irish Sword*, 14:77 (1995), 161–70.

Hartley, Stephen, *The Irish question as a problem in British foreign policy, 1914–18* (New York, 1987).

Haynes, George H., *The Senate of the United States: its history and practice*, 2 vols (New York, 1938–60).

Haynes, John Earl (ed.), *Calvin Coolidge and the Coolidge era: essays on the history of the 1920s* (Washington DC, 1998).

Hendrick, Burton J., *The life and letters of Walter H. Page*, 2 vols (London, 1930).

Heinrichs, Waldo H., *American ambassador: Joseph C. Grew and the development of the United States diplomatic tradition* (Boston, 1966).

Hoag, C. Leonard, *Preface to preparedness: the Washington Disarmament Conference and public opinion* (Washington, 1941).

Hoff Wilson, Joan, *Herbert Hoover: forgotten progressive* (Boston, 1975).

Hogan, Michael J. (ed.), *Paths to power: the historiography of American foreign relations to 1941* (Cambridge, 2000).

Hopkinson, Michael, 'President Woodrow Wilson and the Irish question', *Studia Hibernica*, 32 (1993), 89–111.

—— (ed.), *The last days of Dublin Castle: the diaries of Mark Sturgis* (Dublin, 1999).

——, *The Irish War of Independence* (Dublin, 2002).

Hoover, Herbert, *An American epic: famine in forty-five nations, the battle on the front line 1914–23*, 4 vols (Chicago, 1961).

Howard, Esmé, Baron, *Theatre of life: life seen from the stalls, 1905–36*, 2 vols (London, 1935).

Hughes, Charles E., *The pathway to peace* (New York, 1925).

——, 'Some aspects of the work of the State Department', *American Journal of International Law*, 16 (1922), 355–64.

——, 'Some observations on the conduct of our foreign relations', *American Journal of International Law*, 16 (1922), 365–74.

Hull, Cordell, *The memoirs of Cordell Hull*, 2 vols (London, 1948).

Immerman, Richard H., 'Psychology' in Michael J. Hogan & Thomas G. Paterson (eds), *Explaining the history of American foreign relations* (Cambridge, 1996), pp 156–7.

Inglis, Brian, *Roger Casement* (London, 1973).

'Ireland's Appeal to America 1917. Address presented to Congress. July 23rd. America's appeal to Ireland. 1775. Two historic documents' (Dublin, 1917).

Jackson, Alvin, ' Ulster Volunteer Force' in Connolly (ed.), *The Oxford companion* (1998), pp 563–4.

Jeffrey, Keith, 'Curragh Mutiny' in Connolly (ed.), *The Oxford companion* (1998), p. 131.

—— 'Wilson, Sir Henry' in Connolly (ed.), *The Oxford companion* (1998), p. 593.

Jeffreys-Jones, Rhodri, *Cloak and dollar: a history of American secret intelligence* (2nd ed., New Haven & London, 2002).

——, 'Massachusetts labour and the League of Nations controversy in 1919', *Irish Historical Studies*, xix, 76 (September, 1975), 396–416.

——, *American espionage: from Secret Service to CIA* (New York, 1977).

Jessup, Philip C., *Elihu Root*, i (New York, 1988).

Johnson, John W., 'John Calvin Coolidge, 1923–1929' in Urofsky (ed.), *The American presidents* (2000), p. 315.

Johnson, Paul, *A history of the American people* (London, 1997).

——, 'Calvin Coolidge and the last Arcadia', Haynes (ed.), *Calvin Coolidge* (1998), pp 1–13.

Kennan, George F., *American diplomacy 1900–1950* (Chicago, 1970).

Kennedy, Charles Stuart, *The American consul: a history of the United States consular service, 1776–1914* (Westport, 1999).

Kennedy, Kieran A., Thomas Giblin & Deirdre McHugh, *The economic development of Ireland in the twentieth century* (New York, 1988).

Kennedy, Michael, *Ireland and the League of Nations, 1919–1946: international relations, diplomacy and politics* (Dublin, 1996).

——, 'Civil servants cannot be politicians': the professionalisation of the Irish foreign service, 1919–22', *Irish Studies in International Affairs*, 8 (1997), 95–109.

Kennedy, Ross A., 'Woodrow Wilson, World War I, and an American conception of national security', *Diplomatic History*, 25:1 (winter, 2001), 1–31.

Kenny, K., *The American Irish: a history* (Harlow, 2000).

——, 'General introduction: new directions in Irish-American history' in Kenny (ed.), *New directions in Irish-American history* (Madison, 2003), pp 1–11.

Keogh, Dermot, *Twentieth-century Ireland: nation and state* (Dublin, 1994).

Keown, Gerard, 'Taking the world stage: creating an Irish foreign policy in the 1920s' in Michael Kennedy and Joseph Morrison Skelly (eds), *Irish Foreign Policy 1919–1966: from independence to internationalism* (Dublin, 2000), pp 25–31.

Knock, Thomas J., *To end all wars: Woodrow Wilson and the quest for a new world order* (New York, 1992).

Koenig, Louis W., *Bryan: a political biography of William Jennings Bryan* (New York, 1971).

Kraut, Alan M., *The huddled masses: the immigrant in American society, 1880–1921* (Wheeling, 1982).

LaFeber, Walter, *The American age: United States foreign policy at home and abroad since 1750* (London, 1989).

——, *The American age: US foreign policy at home and abroad since 1896*, 2 vols (1994).

Lansing, Robert, *The peace negotiations: a personal narrative* (Boston, 1921).

——, *War memoirs of Robert Lansing, secretary of state* (New York, 1935).

Lasswell, Harold D., *Propaganda technique in the world war* (New York, 1927).

Lavelle, Patricia, *James O'Mara: a staunch Sinn Féiner* (Dublin, 1961).

Lazo, Dimitri, D., 'Lansing, Wilson and the Jenkins incident', *Diplomatic History*, 22:2 (spring, 1998), 177–98.

Leary, William M., Jnr, 'Woodrow Wilson, Irish Americans and the election of 1916', *The Journal of American History*, 54:1 (June 1967–8), 57–72.

——, 'Election of 1916' in Schlesinger et al (eds), *History of American presidential elections* (1971), pp 2245–70.

Lee, J.J., *Ireland 1912–1985: politics and society* (Cambridge, 1989).

——, 'Emigration: 1922–1998' in Glazier (ed.), *The encyclopedia* (1999), pp 263–6.

——, 'The Irish diaspora in the nineteenth century' in L.M. Geary & M. Kelleher (eds) *Nineteenth century Ireland: a guide to recent research* (Dublin, 2005), pp 165–82.

Levin, N. Gordon, Jnr, *Woodrow Wilson and the world politics: America's response to war and revolution* (New York, 1968).

Levin, Phyllis Lee, *Edith and Woodrow: the Wilson White House* (New York, 2001).

Link, Arthur S. (ed.), *The papers of Woodrow Wilson*, 69 vols (Princeton, 1966–94).

——, *Woodrow Wilson*, 5 vols (Princeton, 1947–65).

——, *Wilson: the road to the White House* (Princeton, 1947).

——, *Wilson: the struggle for neutrality. 1914–1915* (Princeton, 1960).

——, *Wilson the diplomatist: a look at his major foreign policies* (Chicago, 1965).

——, William A. Link & William B. Catton, *American epoch: a history of the United States since 1900: vol. 1, 1900–1945*, 2 vols (New York, 1987).

Lloyd George, David, *Memoirs of the Paris Conference*, 2 vols (London, 1939).

Lomparda, Vincent A, 'O'Connell, William Henry Cardinal (1859–1944)' in Glazier (ed.), *The encyclopedia* (1999), pp 714–5.

Londraville, Janis and Richard (eds), *Too long a sacrifice: the letters of Maud Gonne and John Quinn* (London, 1999).

Longford, Earl of, & T.P. O'Neill, *Eamon de Valera* (London, 1970).

Loughlin, James, 'Irish Republican Brotherhood' in Connolly (ed.), *The Oxford companion* (1998), pp 272–3.

Lowitt, Richard, *George W. Norris: the persistence of a progressive, 1913–33* (London, 1971).

McAdoon, William G., *Crowded years: the reminiscences of William G. McAdoo* (London, 1931).

McCaffrey, Lawrence J., *The Irish diaspora in America* (Bloomington, 1976).

——, 'Catholicism, Irish-American' in Glazier (ed.), *The encyclopedia* (1999), p. 132.

McCartan, Patrick, *With de Valera in America* (New York, 1932).

McCarthy, Denis J., 'The British' in O'Grady (ed.), *The Immigrants' influence* (1967), pp 85–110.

McCoy, Donald R.,'Election of 1920' in Schlesinger et al (eds), *History of American presidential elections*, iii (1971), pp 2349–85.

——, *Calvin Coolidge: the quiet president* (New York, 1967).

Macready, Sir Nevil, *Annals of an active life*, 2 vols (London, 1924).

MacDonagh, Oliver, *Ireland* (New Jersey, 1968).

McDowell, R.B., *The Irish Convention, 1917–18* (London, 1970).

McGurrin, James, *Bourke Cockran: a free lance in American politics* (New York, 1948).

McIvor, Aidan, *A history of the Irish Naval Service* (Dublin, 1994).

McKercher, Brian J.C., *The second Baldwin government and the United States, 1924–29: attitudes and diplomacy* (Cambridge, 1984).

——, *Esme Howard: a diplomatic biography* (Cambridge, 1989).

——, 'Reaching for the brass ring: the recent historiography of interwar American foreign relations' in Hogan (ed.), *Paths to power* (2000), pp 198–201.

——, 'The British diplomatic service in the United States and the Chamberlain Foreign Office's perceptions of domestic America, 1924–27: images, reality and diplomacy' in B.J.C. McKercher & D.J. Moss (eds), *Shadow and substance in British foreign policy, 1895–1939: memorial essays honouring C.J. Lowe* (Alberta, 1984), pp. 221–47.

McKillen, E., *Chicago labor and the quest for a democratic diplomacy, 1914–24* (Ithaca, 1996).

MacLoughlin, Mariana, 'Nationalism and world war one' in Glazier (ed.), *The encyclopedia* (1999), pp 652–3.

Maher, J., *Harry Boland: a biography* (Cork and Dublin, 1998).

Mansergh, Nicholas, *The Irish question, 1840–1921 A commentary on Anglo-Irish relations and on social and political forces in Ireland in the age of reform and revolution* (London, 1975).

Marcosson, Isaac A., *Reborn Ireland* (New York, 1928).

Martin, Robert F., 'Warren Gamaliel Harding' in Urofsky (ed.), *The American presidents* (2000), pp 303–12.

Middlemass, Keith (ed.), *Thomas Jones: Whitehall diary*, 3 vols (London, 1969–71).

— & John Barnes, *Baldwin: a biography* (London, 1969).

Miller, Kirby, *Emigrants and exiles: Ireland and the Irish exodus to North America* (Oxford, 1985).

Mock, James R., & Cedric Larson, *Words that won the war: the story of the Committee on Public Information, 1917–1919* (Princeton, 1939).

Mooney Eichacker, Joanne, *Irish republican women in America: lecture tours, 1916 to 1925* (Dublin, 2003).

Moore, Edmund A., *A Catholic runs for president: the campaign of 1928* (New York, 1956).

Moran, Kenneth O., *Consensus and disunity: the Lloyd George coalition government 1918–22* (Oxford, 1979).

Moran, P.R. (ed.), *Warren G. Harding 1865–1923: chronology, documents, bibliographical aids* (New York, 1970).

Moss, Malcolm, (ed.), *H.L. Mencken: a carnival of Buncombe* (Baltimore, 1956).

Moynihan, James, H., *The life of Archbishop John Ireland* (New York, 1976).

Mulder, John M., *Woodrow Wilson: the years of preparedness* (Princeton, 1978).

Murphy, Jeremiah, *When youth was mine: a memoir of Kerry, 1902–25* (Dublin, 1998).

Murray, Robert K., *The Harding era: Warren G. Harding and his administration* (Minneapolis, 1969).

——, *The politics of normalcy: governmental theory and practice in the Harding-Coolidge era* (Toronto, 1973).

Nelson, Bruce, 'Irish Americans, Irish nationalism and the "social" question, 1916–1923', *Boundary 2: an international journal of literature and culture*, 31:1 (spring, 2004), 147–79.

Nevins, Allan, *Henry White: thirty years of American diplomacy* (New York and London, 1930).

Ngai, M.M., 'The architecture of race in American immigration law: a re-examination of the Immigration Law of 1924', *Journal of American History*, 86:1 (June, 1999), 67–92.

Nicolson, Harold, *King George the fifth: his life and reign* (London, 1952).

Noer, Thomas H., 'The American government and the Irish question during World War I', *South Atlantic Quarterly*, 72 (winter, 1973), 95–114.

O'Connell, William Cardinal, *Recollections of seventy years* (Boston and New York, 1934).

O'Connor, Emmet, *James Larkin* (Cork, 2002).

O'Connor, Harvey, *Mellon's millions, the biography of a fortune: the life and times of Andrew W. Mellon* (New York, 1933).

O Connor, Thomas H., *The Boston Irish: a political history* (Boston, 1995).

O'Doherty, Katherine, *Assignment America: Eamon de Valera's mission to the United States* (New York, 1957).

O'Grady, Joseph P., (ed.), *The immigrants' influence on Wilson's peace policies* (Kentucky, 1967).

——, *How the Irish became Americans* (New York, 1978).

——, 'The Irish Free State passport and the question of citizenship, 1921–4', *Irish Historical Studies*, 26:104 (November, 1989), 396–405.

O'Halpin, Eunan, *Defending Ireland: the Irish State and its enemies since 1922* (Oxford, 1999).

O'Reilly, Kenneth, *Hoover and the UnAmericans: the FBI, HUAC and the Red Menace* (Philadelphia, 1983).

O'Riordan, Manus, 'Larkin in America', *Saothar*, 4, (1978), 50–3.

O'Toole, G.J.A., *Honorable treachery: a history of US intelligence, espionage and covert action from the American revolution to the CIA* (New York, 1991).

O'Toole, James M., *Militant and triumphant: William Henry O'Connell and the Catholic Church in Boston, 1859–1944* (Notre Dame, 1992).

Oxford Dictionary of National Biography, 60 vols (Oxford, 2004).

Parrini, Carl P., *Heir to empire: United States economic diplomacy, 1916–1923* (Pittsburgh, 1969).

Parsons, Edward R., 'Some international implications of the 1918 Roosevelt-Lodge campaign against Wilson and a Democratic congress', *Presidential Studies Quarterly*, 29:1 (1989), 141–159.

Pershing John J., *My experiences in the world war* (New York, 1931).

Peterson, H.C., *Propaganda for war: the campaign against American neutrality, 1914–1* Norman, 1939).

—— & Gilbert C. Fite, *Opponents of war 1917–18* (Washington, 1958).

Phillips, William, *Ventures in diplomacy* (Boston, 1952).

Plischke, Elmer, *Diplomat in chief: the president at the summit* (New York, 1986).

Pratt Fairchild, Henry, *Immigration: a world movement and its American significance* (New York, 1925).

Pusey, Merlo J., *Charles Evans Hughes*, 2 vols (New York and London, 1963).

——, 'Charles Evans Hughes', *American Historical Review*, 62 (October 1956–July 1957), 417.

Reading, the marquess of, *Rufus Isaacs: First Marquess of Reading, 1914–35* (London, 1945).

Regan, John M., *The Irish Counter-Revolution: treatyite politics and settlement in independent Ireland, 1921–1936* (Dublin, 1999).

Reid, B.L., *The man from New York: John Quinn and his friends* (New York, 1968).

Report of the Irish White Cross to 31 August 1922 (Dublin, 1922).

Riddell, George, Baron, *Lord Riddell's war diary, 1914–18* (London, 1933).

Roskill, Stephen, *Naval policy between the wars, 1919–29*, 2 vols (London, 1968).

——, *Hankey, man of secrets, vol. 1, 1877–1918* (London, 1970).

Rowland, Thomas J., 'Strained neutrality: Irish-American Catholics, Woodrow Wilson and the *Lusitania*' in *Éire-Ireland*, 30:4 (winter, 1996), 58–76.

St John Gaffney, T., *Breaking the silence: England, Ireland, Wilson and the war* (New York, 1930).

Santis, Hugh De and Waldo Heinrichs, 'United States of America: the Department of State and American foreign policy' in Zara Steiner (ed.), *Foreign ministries of the world* (London, 1982), pp 576–602.

Schlesinger, Arthur M., Fred L. Israel, William P. Hansen, *History of American presidential elections, 1789–1968*, 11 vols (Philadelphia, 2001).

Schoen, Lothar, 'The Irish Free State and the electricity industry, 1922–27' in Andy Bielenberg (ed.), *The Shannon Scheme and the electrification of the Irish Free State: an inspirational milestone* (Dublin, 2002), pp 28–37.

Schwabe, Claus, *Woodrow Wilson, revolutionary Germany and peacemaking, 1918–19* (Chapel Hill, 1985).

Schwarz, Jordan A., *The speculator: Bernard M. Baruch in Washington, 1917–1965* (Chapel Hill, 1981).

Seymour, Charles (ed.), *The intimate papers of Colonel House*, 4 vols (London, 1926–8)).

Sheehy Skeffington, Hanna, *Impressions of Sinn Féin in America* (Dublin, 1919).

Sinclair, Andrew, *The available man: the life behind the masks of Warren Gamaliel Harding* (New York, 1965).

Sloan, G.R., *The geopolitics of Anglo-Irish relations in the twentieth century* (London, 1997).

Small, Melvin, *Democracy and diplomacy: the impact of domestic politics on US foreign policy, 1789–1994* (Baltimore, 1996).

Smith, Albert E., & Vincent de P. Fitzpatrick, *Cardinal Gibbons: churchman and citizen* (Baltimore, undated).

Smith, Tony, *America's mission: the United States and the worldwide struggle for democracy in the twentieth century* (Princeton, 1994).

Sobel, Robert, *Coolidge: an American enigma* (Washington, 1998).

Spalding, Thomas W., 'Gibbons, James Cardinal', in Glazier (ed.), *The encyclopedia* (1999), p. 361.

Splain, John J., '"Under which King?" The tragic-comedy of President de Valera's errors in the United States' in Fitzgerald (ed.), *The voice of Ireland* (1923), pp. 242–55.

——, 'The Irish movement in the United States since 1911' in Fitzgerald (ed.), *The voice of Ireland* (1923), pp. 225–36.

Startt, James D., 'American propaganda in Britain during world war one', *Prologue: Quarterly of the National Archives*, 28:1 (spring 1996), 17–35.

Steigerwald, David, 'The reclamation of Woodrow Wilson', *Diplomatic History*, 23:1 (winter, 1999), 79–101.

Stern, Sheldon M., 'William Allen White and the origins of the Coolidge stereotype', *The New England Journal of History*, 55:1 (fall, 1998), 57–68.

Stone, Ralph, *The irreconcilables: the fight against the League of Nations* (New York, 1970).

Stuart, Graham H., *The Department of State: a history of its organisations, procedure and personnel* (New York, 1949).

Sullivan, Margaret, 'Fighting for Irish Freedom: St Louis Irish-Americans, 1918–22' in Walsh (ed.), *The Irish: America's political class* (1976), pp. 184–206.

Tansill, Charles, *America and the fight, 1866–1922: an old story based upon new data* (New York, 1957).

Tarpey, Marie Veronica, *The role of Joseph McGarrity in the struggle for Irish independence* (New York, 1976).

Temperley, Howard, *Britain and America since Independence* (Hampshire, 2002).

Thayer, William Roscoe, (ed.), *The life and letters of John Hay*, 2 vols (Boston and New York, 1915).

Thompson, Peter, *Cassell's dictionary of modern American history* (London, 2000).

Trani, Eugene P., & David L. Wilson, *The presidency of Warren G. Harding* (Lawrence, 1977).

Tumulty, Joseph, *Woodrow Wilson as I know him* (London, 1922).

Ultan, Lloyd, *The presidents of the United States* (New York, 1989).

Urofsky, Melvin I. (ed.), *The American presidents* (New York, 2000).

Vansittart, Lord, *The mist procession: the autobiography of Lord Vansittart* (London, 1958).

Von Bernstorff, Johann, *My three years in America* (London, 1930).

Walsh, James P. (ed.), *The Irish: America's political class* (New York, 1976).

——, 'Woodrow Wilson historians vs. the Irish', *Éire-Ireland*, 11:2 (spring, 1967), 55–65.

Walshe, Cathal J. (ed.), *Notable US ambassadors since 1775: a biographical dictionary* (Westport, 1997).

Ward, Alan J., *Ireland and Anglo-American relations, 1899–1921* (London, 1969).

——, 'America and the Irish problem, 1899–1921', *Irish Historical Studies*, 16:61 (1968–9), 64–90.

Ward, Margaret, *Hanna Sheehy Skeffington: a life* (Cork, 1997).

Warman, Roberta Mary, *The Foreign Office, 1916–18: a study of its role and functions* (New York and London, 1986).

Watt, D Cameron, *Succeeding John Bull: America in Britain's place 1900–1975* (Cambridge, 1984).

West, Trevor, *Horace Plunkett: co-operation and politics, and Irish biography* (Gerrards Cross, 1986).

Whelan, Bernadette, *Ireland and the Marshall Plan*, 1947–57 (Dublin, 2000).

——, '"What does America mean to you?": an oral history project, 1922–60', *North Munster Antiquarian Journal*, 43 (2003), 84–104.

——, 'A family business? Irish women revolutionaries in the United States, 1916–21' (unpublished).

——, 'The consuls who helped sink a fleet: Union consuls in Ireland, intelligence and the American civil war' (unpublished).

White, William Allen, *A puritan in Babylon: the story of Calvin Coolidge* (New York, 1938), p. 276.

Widenor, W.C., *Henry Cabot Lodge and the search for an American foreign policy* (Baltimore, 1980).

Will, Allen Sinclair, *Life of Cardinal Gibbons, Archbishop of Baltimore*, 2 vols (New York, 1922).

Willert, Arthur, *Washington and other memories* (Boston, 1972).

Wilson, Trevor (ed.), *The political diaries of C.P. Scott, 1911–28* (Ithaca, 1970).

Wilson, The messages and papers of Woodrow, 2 vols. (New York, 1924).

Willson, Beckles, *Friendly relations: a narrative of Britain's ministers and ambassadors to America, 1790–1930* (London, 1934).

——, *America's ambassadors to England (1785–1928): a narrative of Anglo-American diplomatic relations* (London, 1928).

Young, Kenneth, *Arthur James Balfour: the happy life of the politician, prime minister, statesman and philosopher, 1848–1930* (London, 1963).

Zebel, Sydney H., *Balfour: a political biography* (Cambridge, 1973).

Index